CHINA BUSINESS

environment
momentum
strategies
prospects

Zhou Linong
Baptist University of Hong Kong

PEARSON

Prentice
Hall

Singapore   London   New York   Toronto   Sydney   Tokyo   Madrid
Mexico City   Munich   Paris   Capetown   Hong Kong   Montreal

Published by
Prentice Hall
Pearson Education South Asia Pte Ltd
23/25 First Lok Yang Road, Jurong
Singapore 629733

Pearson Education offices in Asia: *Bangkok, Beijing, Hong Kong, Jakarta, Kuala Lumpur, Manila, New Delhi, Seoul, Singapore, Taipei, Tokyo, Shanghai*

Printed in Singapore

5   4   3   2   1
08   07   06   05

ISBN 981-244-930-2

Contents

List of Figures and Tables

China business has become a subject that is widely taught and learned around the world during the last two decades. The growing weight of China's economy has attracted more attention from the outside world, and more business opportunities and signed deals draw increasing volume of foreign investment into this growth market. Whether this market is huge with potential or otherwise is now a topic repeatedly debated in Western business and academic circles.

Along with steady economic growth and unabated foreign investment inflows, large numbers of Western companies set up their business in mainland China, and thousands of foreign executives live and work there. In the two decades after China opened herself, a procession of business success and failure emerged as excellent cases for focused business study, and China business now has sufficient information to be examined more systematically.

Topical study of the Chinese economy and China business began from the early time of changes, and scholarly publications and guidebooks are aplenty. Despite this numeric achievement, there remains a paucity of textbook-style publications of comprehensive knowledge of China business. A few books which bear "China business" in their titles are either early works or collections of separate research. This study is yet another attempt to present a framework and certain overall summaries of China business for university students and enterprise managers alike. "Environment" covers essential knowledge and background information of this market, including cultural traditions, political systems and diversities. "Momentum" implies currents and vitality of changes in the economy, especially newly emerging trends since China's WTO accession. "Strategies" refers to various approaches to doing business by domestic Chinese and foreign companies and evaluation of their business performance. "Prospects" attempts to offer certain summaries of current trends and direction of future movements, which may benefit long term planning of business corporations. The aim is to provide essential information in most areas, in particular in FDI, and to place the learning of China business in perspective. Understanding the nature and gaining practical knowledge—these are the goals for putting this manuscript together as a systematic and consistent work.

In text contents, the Overview introduces the common views and perceptions regarding the cultural background of business operations in the China market.

Part I presents background information to date on Chinese characteristics and national conditions, and explores the essential factors in this economy.

Part II focuses on more recent trends of change, tracing reforms undertaken and major turns in economic development.

Part III lists key issues that will determine the future direction of the economy, and discusses in detail major initiatives to clear obstacles and handle scenarios of potential crises.

Part IV takes the standpoint of foreign investors and examines overall performance of multinationals and their process of entering the China market.

Part V provides summaries of major types of business strategies in international practice and those adopted by multinationals in the China market.

Part VI deals with several business cases in more detail and divides them into two categories: cases of domestic Chinese business and of foreign companies operating in China. The first category covers Chinese companies and their business practice and strategies, and the second category focuses on the well-known cases of foreign multinationals, making assessments of their successes and setbacks.

Part VII reviews and analyses past predictions and statements made by experts on economic reforms and growth of China, and on this basis attempts to draw certain preliminary conclusions on the future prospects of this economy, business environment, and of operations of foreign companies in this market.

An Overview

Observations or perceptions of other peoples are crucial in doing business with them. For modern-day enterprises, entering a new market poses serious questions to the top management, and the decisions made, to a large extent, depend on their understanding, or lack of it, of the overall business environment and related issues of that particular market.

Two opposite tendencies are prevalent in making such business decisions.

One is the **normative** tendency that focuses on the outward application of general rules and common practices in the social and business environments at home. For companies from outside of an economy, they usually first measure whether the established rules and ways in that economy are compatible with their own, and would happily proceed if conditions there are similar.[1] Multinational companies have great resources to make estimates and calculations about future business earnings if their expansion into another market is carried out according to plans. To many of them, this is just an extension of business scope, and following the familiar rules is a relatively simple step to take. This assumption implies that their past practice would ultimately offer them a path to new markets.

The other is **cultural- or area-specific tendency**, which often views working in another market as a formidable task, on top of usual handling of business operations. There are additional concerns to be addressed and more effort on coping with local, rather than international, issues. Behaviours and cultural traits are seen as the main barriers, being hard to explain, and emerging difficulties are beyond imagination. Such a tendency makes a company wary of unfamiliar environments and odd (to them) happenings. This tendency may direct a certain company to be more prepared, with sufficient local knowledge and patience to undertake market entry. However, it happens that they also bend to pressures from the environment, blame certain unfavourable local conditions, wrap up and leave.

Both of these two tendencies are common and interchangeable. A company with grand plans and ample experience may move into a new market in a rush, but after a few hassles and bumps, turn to pay more attention to local issues and adapt well. A company which overemphasised local barriers and inertia may discover ways to tackle the problems and find common grounds with local business partners. In these days of globalisation and fast communication, companies and peoples realise that the more you meet local demands, the more you are internationalised, or globally-oriented, to use the fashionable term. It is on the basis of this understanding that more and more local employees are placed at executive posts of branches and subsidiaries of multinational corporations. It seems that the best way to reconcile these two tendencies is to blend globalisation with localisation.

East Asia and China

China business shares themes and trends with other East Asian economies. In general, the similar path of economic development is the background for these economies to be studied as a group, and links can be established between the Chinese economy and economies of other East Asian countries.

Since the days of "economic miracles" of Japan and Asian tigers, doing business in the East has been an increasingly popular subject in research and in business circles. The catch-up in economic growth and market power in Asian economies presents a challenge for researchers to provide plausible explanations. Focuses are mostly on differences from, rather than similarities to, the West, and sometimes explanations of movements are based primarily on observations of exotic cultural traits. To demonstrate the stark contrast, great effort has been made to distinguish what are unique in the West and completely alien in the East, or vice versa. The term "European miracle" has been put out for a while as a counter argument for the more recent Asian phenomenon in economic development.[2] On the other hand, many in China see the revival of economic strength as a natural happening after centuries of earlier advancements and stagnation in modern times. The rise of China is but one of the events among the wider economic booms in East Asia, and this represents a new challenge to academic and business studies.

China

China is a unique case because she embodies a number of characteristics.

First, she is the origin of mainstream cultures in numerous East Asian economies, in particular newly industrialised economies (NIEs). Previous studies on those NIEs have touched upon the issue of their connections in varying degrees with China's heritage and economy and could lend references in many areas. It seems that cultural explanations for modern Asian development are ultimately tested here. A satisfactory generalisation of social and cultural forces for, say, Taiwan should also be applied to mainland China. This either simplifies or complicates the studies on Asian economies. Researchers face a trap in drawing conclusions on East Asian development. For instance, in past studies, many positive factors were listed for Japan's transformation and rise in modern history, but these factors are not sufficiently convincing when China is also examined. For certain identified characteristics such as collective actions, hierarchy and respect to the elders, and even stable employment in enterprise management, there is simply little difference between these two ancient societies. In spite of these, scholars tend to attribute success to certain prominent factors and fail to note there is another bigger case to prove.[3] The fact that China had exported great cultural influence in past centuries presents researchers with a more challenging task.

Second, China is a place with old traditions and radical socialism, both very strong and deep-rooted. Traditions give people the impression of conservative moods and preferences. On the other hand, previous waves of revolutions and upheavals in modern China brought out strong undercurrents of left-leaning, patriotic and aggressive manners. These two contradictions blurred people's views on the direction of the economy and have led to mixed perceptions. For certain particular movements or events, observers and pundits could make their comments on the basis of either cultural heritage or modern-day political brainwash. It is common for Western scholars with expansive knowledge of Chinese history to trace current events and movements back to traditional dynastic cycles and court intrigues.[4] It is therefore a more demanding task to explain, let alone predict, the ongoing changes in China's economy. The central point is how to judge what is and will be the mainstream in this mixture.

Third, China has gained growing economic power and demonstrated enormous market potential in recent years. She is no longer merely one of the oldest civilisations puffing under the weight of traditions, but a more dynamic and assertive player in international trade and the world economy. The sheer size of the economy creates a more favourable impression to investors the world over. With the uplifting in economic status and ranking, China has exerted greater influence on her economic and trade partners. Being a world power or not, business and general situation in China now radiate effects on many concerned parties. Growth projections by and large are not dismissing China's economy, and, especially in bad economic times, many look to China for an alternative to existing business choices. In spite of some optimistic assertions that the United States has been the "only possible exceptionalism to economic pattern of development",[5] its economy faltered in 2000, the beginning of a new millennium, plagued by burst bubbles, recession, corporate scandals, skyhigh twin deficits and feeble jobless recovery. This extraordinary event finally makes a big dent on the false perception that you only need to look West. All these draw more attention to the characteristics of China, and make doing business there, as well as analysing the society, a more fascinating and potentially more rewarding option.

Returns on Investment

To foreign investors, cultural traits may not mix well with their primary concerns of money flows and profits. It is common that multinationals and investing companies give fewer considerations of the side issues of coping with local native traditions. Unfortunately, these traditions often determine the end results of investment in that environment. When investors search average rates of returns around, they use loads of numbers for a comparison. For economies with varied forms of business environment, a rule of thumb is that the real rate of returns is the sum of normal rate minus local risks.

For example, an investment on company bond issues for a power plant normally yields 8% for ten years, and then due to conflicts with local authorities and partners, smoothing out difficulties unforeseeable at the beginning, new demands and requirements etc., the project is delayed, and finally the returns on investment is thinned out. The reduction in annual returns comes from the losses in work efficiency, additional payments and other frictions. The project may be operatable in the end, but the net returns to investors would be a few notches down after required adjustments. For this specific reason, foreign power or utility companies insisted on a higher rate of returns from the Chinese government for their investment projects in China.

Why Discuss Cultures in a Business Analysis?

One of the keys in solving problems in China business is in the interpretations of cultural diversities. This is a knotty issue to multinationals, since their operations have moved beyond national borders and intruded many markets of various societies. To understand culture and business environment in China requires a certain preliminary grasp on what you see in this complex. There are five factors worth considering.

Business Management is Done by People

People in various societies retain their behaviours in particular ways, and the cultural influence businesspeople are under is constant and lasting. Business doing adapts to the particular surroundings, patterns or norms. Even in the cases of cultural exchanges and immersions, the mainstream culture of one's own shows stronger signs of surviving in comparison with the other's. In a familiar business environment, cultural traits tend to be reinforced and strengthened, giving less room for modifications.

Changing Forms of Management Theories and Models

Production and trade in modern times evolved around people, and management theories and models changed forms more frequently in recent decades. In the end, these evolving theories and models tend to focus on the right target, the people in the market and organisations. There are now more inclinations to put people (consumers) at the centre stage of activity, rather than the manufacturers and their bulk. This trend is shown most clearly in the field of marketing, and is typified by Nokia's commercial catch phrase "connecting people", whose Chinese version literally declares "people as foundation", a century-old Confucian motto. As a rule, management studies now give more emphasis on people management, and on how to improve work conditions for employees and their morale, advocated by many that happy employees make happy companies and so happy end business results.

Take, for example, the matrix model used in many organisations. The matrix model has been applied in dealing with management in business corporations, especially in those multinationals that operate in numerous locations away from headquarters and national bases. To keep the right balance between central control and local flexibility for overseas branches, multinationals adopted the matrix model in early decades. This model relies on conventional layers of corporate management, giving greater authority to heads of local branches. In the meantime, other channels of control, along functional lines, were implemented, such as finance, technology, brand, planning, etc. A local branch reports to direct superiors of that particular region or country, but it also reports directly to heads of department at headquarters. The model complicated the procedures and created dual authorities for lower-level managers to bear. In decades before the 1990s, the matrix model was tested and then marginalised, mainly due to its complexity and lower efficiency. With the coming of age of the Internet and rapidly improved telecommunication, this model has regained its favour among multinationals and is widely adopted by company executives.

Through all of these changes and remodelling, the key question remains as how to best manage employees, giving them sufficient supervision while not putting more than necessary restrains on their work and creativity.

Revolutionary Changes in Modern and Contemporary History

World Trade and Market

With business activities spreading out more forcefully these days, it is thus possible that a production process can be supported by suppliers from other countries and consumers elsewhere. The mechanisms of the World Trade Organisation and fast-improving transportation give merchants and manufacturers more opportunities to deal with traders from other economies, leaving local and even national economies a reducing share in their total business activities. More secured environments and more profitable business operations have emerged to entice merchants in many countries to explore the wider networks and engage in trading with overseas partners. Dependence increases, and business appears more cost-effective.

Multinationals and Business Expansion

The emerging of multinationals marked a new era in business, and these gigantic organisations take care of their business across national borders. Their production and supply chains extend to vast territories, and handling these operations requires control and management of large, very different fields. To meet their overall corporate and profit targets, multinationals move into a non-stop process to seek new markets and opportunities elsewhere. It is an integral part of their business strategy to absorb any reasonably profitable business around the globe, regardless of the geographical varieties. As a result of this expansion mentality, multinationals are the first to encounter cultural differences and have to take up the challenges arising from new and unfamiliar conditions. They are the ones dealing with people, institutions and governments in totally different business environments, and whether the coping process is a satisfactory one determines the fate of their expansion and overseas investment. These put a great deal of pressure on business executives to acknowledge and master the art of cultural cohesion in trans-continental organisations. Businesspeople in such positions and multinationals in such a process are the first testers of cultural traits in another business environment, way ahead of scholars who summarised those traits later.

East Asian Economic Booms (1980s-1990s)

Processes of modern economic development show that it was mainly a European phenomenon. Even the rise of Japan in the latter half of the twentieth century did not change people's minds, since Japan had always been regarded as an exceptional case for Asia, and its rapid economic expansion is put into the category of Western economies. It was only when other East Asian economies and, in particular, the developed territories of mainland China, emerged that people realised there is another possibility of development in this part of the world. This new phenomenon is even more stunning, with several economies achieving continuous growth at high rates for considerable periods of time. Before the 1997 Asian financial crisis, NIEs displayed dynamics in all fronts, and after that quake, showed remarkable resilience and strong signs of recovery. All these pose new challenges to the conventional wisdom of European-centred thoughts on economic development and demonstrated a need to compare and learn. This phenomenon helped the spreading ideas of an Asian miracle.[6] Studies on Asian ways and cultures therefore flourished and moved from purely anthropological and cultural research to the impact and influence of such traits on business activities.

Greater China Phenomenon

A parallel line of this train of thoughts is the rise of Neo-Confucianism in recent decades. Great efforts have been made to re-evaluate this influential Chinese school of thought, Confucianism, in the process of economic growth and booms in East Asia, where many NIEs share this philosophy and statecraft. When mainland China began to show her enormous growth potential, the implications of Confucianism received more attention and credit. Many distinctive characteristics of Chinese societies are linked with early economic success, and some Chinese values are deemed crucial in business, similar to those of Protestant ethics highlighted by Max Weber.[7] Traditions are no longer seen as unwanted baggage for a society to be modernised. In the process of re-evaluation and debate, Confucianism is often portrayed as a key factor not to be missed. This perhaps overstates the case and attracts quite fierce rebuttals from critics and believers of Western superiority. In any case, the fact that the Greater China economies have performed reasonably well in recent decades gives certain credibility to the Confucianism claim and draws people's attention further to cultural issues and diversities.

The above are several factors which, when combined, lead to a need for examining cultural issues in business analysis of Chinese economy. There is a gap between the standard business practice in Western economies and the application of such practice in China business. Improving conditions in this market may narrow this gap, and better understanding of this market and culture will also do so.

Debate on Cultural Influence on Economic Development and Business

To avoid running the risk of overstatement, let us examine the debate on and examples of cultural influence on business and economic development.

Pro-argument

The contribution of certain cultural traits to East Asian economic growth has been probed and proved, an outstanding example being the profound influence of Confucianism on economic take-offs in the Greater China region. Herman Kahn's "Neo-Confucianism hypothesis is that the countries of East Asia have common cultural roots going far back into history and that under the world-market conditions of the past 30 years, this cultural inheritance has constituted a competitive advantage for successful business activity".[8] A group of such traits are clearly Chinese and will be discussed in later chapters. In general, proponents agree that these traits created economic stability and maximised returns on business activities.

Con-argument

Even at the height of Asian booms and cultural re-evaluation, there were sceptics and defenders of conventional wisdom. Professor Paul Krugman made the pointed observation in 1994 on the "Myth of Asia's Miracle".[9] According to him, East Asian economic booms are based on huge investment (foreign and domestic) and rapid expansion of production. He likened this way of growth to sausage making, implying an increase in size and number, with huge inputs supporting huge output, but little increase in efficiency and in Total Factor Productivity. Under such conditions, these economies would reach a limit and eventually slow down or halt under the weight of huge investment and debts. This new miracle has its own internal weakness and cannot last. The gap in productivity between Western and East Asian economies will by and large remain.

His view was not popular at the boom time of East Asia, but was later more or less vindicated by the Asian financial crisis in 1997 and the aftermath. Professor Krugman has since been invited back to Asia to offer more insights on future economic trends. The key is whether cultural uniqueness, which was brought out when causes for rapid East Asian economic growth needed to be reasonably explained, in fact matters, either in promoting or dismissing a new claim. Professor Krugman's observation does not give cultural uniqueness much thought and sticks with the common understanding of market and business in Western economies.

Cases of Cultural Differences in Business

Studies have been done on the actual effect of cultural differences in business. Professor Geert Hofstede conducted detailed surveys and comparisons on workers in different cultures and established certain models of behaviour patterns. "The naïve assumption that management is the same or is becoming the same around the world is not tenable in view of these demonstrated differences in national cultures." He also points to the influence of Confucianism in a Chinese business environment as the cause for certain types of business practice.[10] Such studies opened the door to cultural assumptions and provided useful empirical materials for further research, and for multinationals' field operations and human resource management as well.

In a recent case of cultural contrast and business essentials, Mr. Carlos Ghosn of Nissan, Japan provides an opposite example. Mr. Ghosn came to Japan in 1999 from Renault of France to manage the entire Nissan Motors, after the French car maker obtained majority shareholder status (37%) at Nissan. He managed the giant Japanese firm the French way and caused great stirs to Japanese business establishment and management traditions. The car maker turned the corner in less than two years and began to earn profits. Mr. Ghosn is now widely accepted by many Japanese business executives as the model manager. His famous remark is that "there is no such thing as a Japanese company, there are only good companies and bad companies". This very example of cultural mix gives weight to the idea that cultural diversities do not always determine the results of business decisions, and emphasis on cultural differences may be misplaced.

With the above brief introduction and explanation of both sides of cultural perceptions, we are ready to touch upon the major contents of China business. A key premise is the trends of change in China, which have eluded many observers, as would be shown later, and proved to be the only theme with certainty. Regarding the debate on cultural influence, it is essential not to lean heavily on any one of the two **tendencies** previously described, normative or cultural-or-area-specific. An understanding of particular cultural background gives people certain advantages in planning business strategies in the China market, while the ground swell of change in this economy in recent years have provided needed improvements and significantly lowered the entry bar.

Key Concepts

Two tendencies
European and East Asian economic "miracles"
China as a case with special characteristics
Returns on investment
Debate and views on cultural influence on economy and business

Discussion Questions

1. For an overall assessment of China business, how much of the emphasis would you place on cultural perceptions and diversities?
2. Between the normative and cultural-specific tendencies, what is the approach you would most likely adopt?
3. At the time of the Asian economic boom, what would have been your response to Professor Krugman's comments on sausage making?
4. Do you think that Mr. Ghosn's approaches would be successful in a major mainland Chinese corporation? And why?

Endnotes

1. For example, *The Economist* claims that the "giant sucking sound" of American factories disappearing into China is, in fact, mostly the continuing stampede of its firms into other rich countries' markets, due to their considerations other than cheap labour in China. "The Mystery of Manufacturing", *The Economist*, 25 September 2003.

2. Jones, Eric, *The European Miracle: Environments, Economies and Geopolitics in the History of Europe and Asia*, Cambridge, Cambridge University Press, 1981; *Coming Full Circle: an Economic History of the Pacific Rim*, Melbourne, Oxford University Press, 1993.

3. Cortazzi, Sir Hugh, *The Japanese Achievement*, London, Sidgwick & Jackson, 1990; Fairbank, J. K.and Reischauer, E.O., *East Asia: Traditions and Transformation*, Boston, Houghton Mifflin, 1989.

4. For example, Terrill, R., *The New Chinese Empire: and What It Means for the United States*, New York, Basic Books, 2003.

5. Jones, Eric, *The Records of Global Economic Development*, Northampton, MA., Edward Elgar, 2002.

6. Jones, Eric, *Coming Full Circle: an Economic History of the Pacific Rim*, Melbourne, Oxford University Press, 1993.

7. For example, Tu, Wei-ming (ed.), *Confucian Traditions in East Asian Modernity*, Cambridge, Mass., Harvard University Press, 1996; Yu, Tzong-shian and Joseph S. Lee (eds.), *Confucianism and Economic Development*, Taipei, Chung-hua Institution of Economic Research, 1995; and Weber, M., *Protestant Ethics and the Spirit of Capitalism*, New York, Charles Scribners, 1958.

8. For example, Adler, M.J., "Cultural Synergy: the Management of Cross-Cultural Organisations", in Burke, W. and Goodstein, L.D. (eds.), *Trends and Issues in Organisational Dynamics: Current Theory and Practice*, San Diego, California, University Associates, 1980, chapter 8; Hofstede, G., *Culture's Consequences: International Differences in Work-Related Values*, Beverly Hills, California, Sage, 1980; and Hofstede, G., "The Cultural Relativity of Organisational Practices and Theories", *Journal of International Business Studies*, Fall 1983, pp. 75–88.

9. Krugman, P., "The Myth of Asia's Miracle", *Foreign Affairs*, vol. 73, no. 6, 1994, pp. 62–78.

10. Hofstede, G. and Bond, M.H., "The Confucius Connection: from Cultural Roots to Economic Growth", *Organisational Dynamics*, 1988, no.16, pp. 4–21.

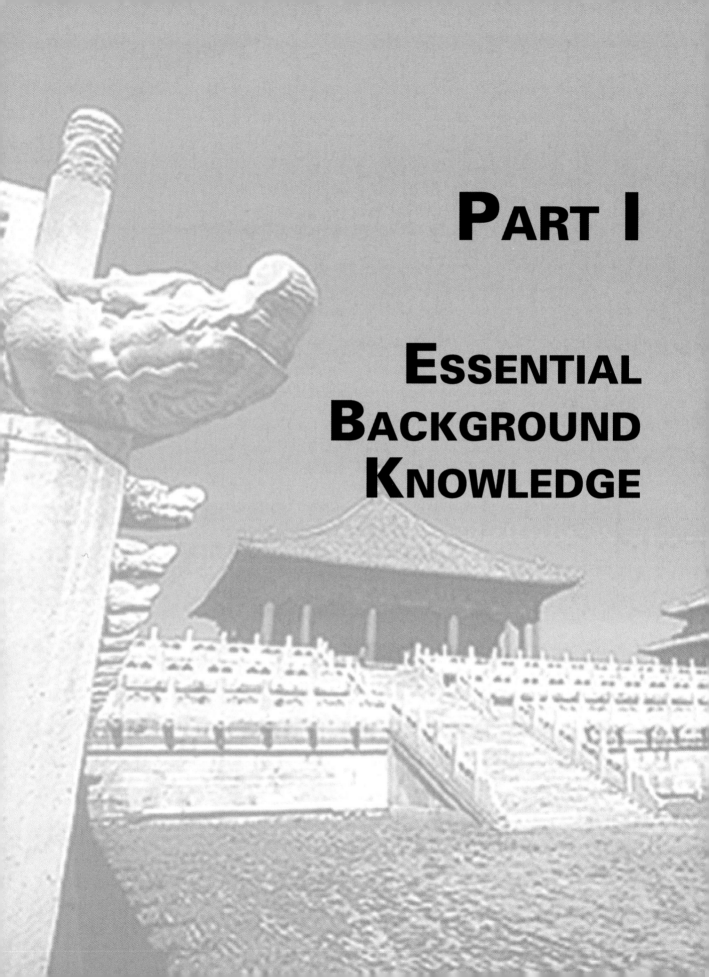

PART I

ESSENTIAL BACKGROUND KNOWLEDGE

1

Origins and Refinement of Chinese Culture

*C*omparatively speaking, Chinese culture is a more difficult topic for foreign learners than economic situations in China. There is so much to explain and digest, because of the long history of China, as indicated in the unbroken hereditary records of the Kong family from the time of the great philosopher Confucius. Any assumption regarding this culture would pale in front of its cultural complexity, and summaries are hardly sufficient to trace cultural roots and evolution. Despite this intimidating reality, this chapter will attempt to provide certain preliminary outlines of historical background and key components of Chinese culture as it is today. As particular cultural traits may make foreigners feel somewhat disorientated, a simpler version here would clarify and decipher, especially for the benefit of those whose main aims are business operations in the Chinese economy under this culture.

Various Definitions of Culture

A variety of definitions of culture are available, and most of them catch certain key elements. It is therefore sensible to make a summary of culture from different descriptions.

Culture is a complex whole, which includes knowledge, belief, art, law, morals, customs, and any capabilities and habits acquired by a man as a member of society. Culture is a way of life, with patterns of learned behaviour handed down from one generation to the next through the means of language and imitation. The meanings of culture are multiple. Culture can be seen as a social environment since that is the man-made part of the environment, in addition to natural resources and geographical features. Culture is an interactive and ongoing process, and shapes people's behaviour and perceptions of their own worlds and the world outside.

The influence of culture on behaviour can be shown generally in the political dimension and implications of a nation or a society. The shape and characteristics of these political entities reflect their cultural roots and backgrounds. At the historical stages of nation states in Western Europe, cultural uniqueness helped the formation of a nation away from another. In more recent times, the term "culture" is also added to other terms, thus there emerged organisational culture or corporate culture, where businesses or public organisations foster their own distinctive cultures, patterns of behaviour, management and leadership styles.

The different aspects of a culture are summarised in the following lists.

1. Essential components of culture
   - Positions and roles: there are distinctive positions and roles in a culture. A position or role at the cultural level may be a whole social class, such as scholar officials ("Literati") in ancient China, or proletariats in Marxist countries. The role of a particular position varies in different cultures.
   - Social structure: social structure refers to how social classes and social groups are related to one another, and how different positions within a social group are related to one another. It shows the pecking orders of social groups.
   - Values: these are guiding principles for life, judgements of relative importance and priority, reflecting learned and socially acquired needs, and general forms of social control.
   - Myths: these are stories and legends of early founders that convey the key values and ideals of a society. They help to explain the origins of a society, reveal a set of values for the society and provide models for personal conduct, in order to

inspire and bond the community. In regard to corporate culture, myths of company founders are enshrined in formal documents and training programmes.

- Rituals: they are expressive, symbolic activities and culturally sanctioned behaviours, and tend to be repeated over time. Ritual behaviour is dramatically scripted and acted out, and is performed with formality, seriousness and inner intensity. Rituals often evolve to behaviours and manners in everyday life.

2. Cultural processes

- Enculturation: this is the learning of one's own culture, acquisition and transmission from one generation to the next, a social process starting from infancy at home and being maintained by educational systems, resulting in a clear cultural identity.

- Acculturation: this is the learning of a new culture, a deliberate learning process, affected by motivation to learn and to enhance social competence.

3. Causes of cultural changes

- Military influences: conquest and invasion, which occurred in colonies, and military occupation; residents have to obey martial orders and accept new cultures.

- Administrative measures: government policies and new rules, such as the open door policy and the policy to enforce wide English education starting from primary level in China.

- Religious activities: influence of new religions, becoming either mainstream or sideline religions of the region. The influence of Buddhism in imperial China presents a pointed example.

- Business activities: trading and exchanges. Businessmen are often at the front line of cultural changes, since their business takes them closer and deeper into another culture, thus an understanding and even acculturation can happen. In imperial China, cultural influences from the West came through, first, the Silk Road, and then through sea trade. Muslims and Christians converted many native Chinese during these exchanges. In China business of today, foreign managers are the first to grasp *guanxi* and other common Chinese characteristics, and their ability to adapt proves amazing.

4. Strategies to cope with cultural invasion

- Individual mobility: abandoning one's original cultural identity and taking on another identity. These are more of individual choices for conceivable benefits.

- Social competition: resisting the foreign culture and minimising cultural shocks.

- Social creativity: re-defining elements of a comparison with foreign cultures and restoring the positive distinctiveness of one's cultural identity. This often includes re-interpretation of cultural symbols and makes them carry contemporary characteristics. For example, the abandoning of Confucianism under socialism in China was replaced with a revival of interest in Chinese traditions, and effort has been made to evaluate some of these traditions as factors to recent economic success.

- Languages: maintaining one's native language and safeguarding the dominant use of one's own language. Although it is less serious in mainland China than in Hong Kong, the Chinese language is under certain threats from the chipping in of English words.

Confucian Philosophy and Traditional Thoughts

The process of forming Chinese culture is shown in Figures 1.1 and 1.2. The key components of culture in modern China include Confucianism, Daoism, Buddhism, and socialism. The essential reading of Confucianism is *Lun Yu* (*the Analects of Confucius*); that for Daoism is *Dao De Jing* (*Way and its Power*). Buddhism has its own huge volumes of religious texts, while socialism in China followed the path directed in writings from Karl Marx to Mao Zedong.

Confucianism

This school of thought originated from Confucius' own writings and contributions from his disciples in the school. The emergence of this school coincided with the chaotic early periods of the Spring and Autumn and of the Warring States in Chinese history (722-221 B.C.). As new social orders challenged the old and regional powers battled each other, creative new thinking and ideas flourished. This was a time

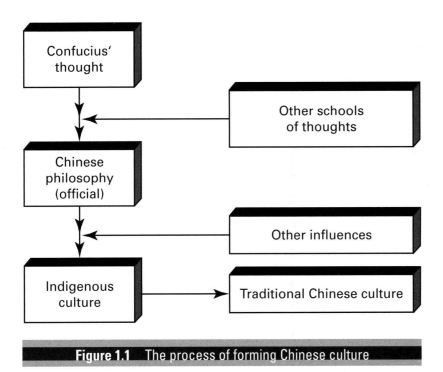

Figure 1.1   The process of forming Chinese culture

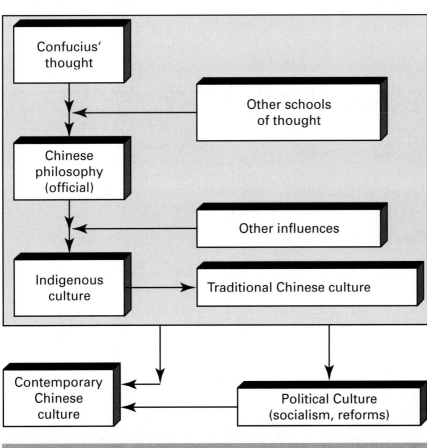

Figure 1.2   Cultural changes on the mainland

when learned scholars had a taste of the liberal pursuit of knowledge, similar to the time of the Greek civilisation. Confucianism was one of the influential schools of thought rising from the old teaching styles. Confucian scholars sharpened their teeth in constant debates with others on wide-ranging issues and topics in politics, philosophy, education, war strategies, primary industries and commerce. The first unified Chinese empire of Qin in 221 B.C. sealed the win of the Legalist school, not of Confucianism. The official status of Confucianism was established by imperial governments in much later times, and Confucius himself was enshrined as the philosopher of the state. It can be safely said that the guiding principles of Chinese states thereafter came from Confucianism.

The thriving of Confucianism depended on its ability to survive repeated challenges and crises, and on its agility to evolve itself. This is an issue of continuity and sustainability. Even when imperial authorities granted this school the high status of a state orthodoxy, Confucianism had to deal with threats and shocks, from religions and from the secular world. It achieved this through absorbing new elements from other schools of thought or religions, dropping obsolete elements, and developing new paradigms to keep up with the times. Some other thinking contributed to a fuller Confucianism, such as Buddhism and Daoism. Confucian scholars also added to or re-interpreted original Confucius' texts, in order to win in debate and to meet demands in a quite different world.

There are three key components in Confucianism: philosophy, political thoughts and education.

Confucian Philosophy

It is non-religious, human/society-based, and it focuses on natural courses of the universe and correlations.

As Confucius explained in *"the Analects"*, "Does Heaven speak? Yet the four seasons continue to change, and all things are born. Does Heaven speak?" He was also well known for not talking at all about unexplained strange occurrences and forces, as well as gods and immortals.

To Confucius, the natural course of the universe is cyclical, self-operating and permanent in motion, leading from one phase to the next phase. In his writing "*the Book of Change*", he described hexagrams in a course, "from one to two, to four, to eight", and these changes reach the climax (eight eight = 64) and turn to the opposite direction, and start a new cycle. The unique signs of hexagrams now appear on the national flag of South Korea, a country deeply influenced by ancient Chinese thinking and traditions.

From this rudimental philosophical thinking, it can be said that Confucianism is not a form of religion but thoughts on the society. He put forward the idea of the Mean (*zhong yong*). This refers to relations between the opposite sides, moderation, and a rejection of extremes and radicals. It can be applied to nature, humans and society. Confucius made "the Mean" the ultimate status of morality, unsurpassed in the sense of philosophy. The ideal for the social elite is to reach that point of "the Mean" but never overdo it. This implies a tendency in the social and political arena towards a well-kept status quo and equilibrium.

This ideal status is, of course, a **harmony**. It is based on trust and understanding, and it seeks compromise rather than confrontation. All exercises of a state rule aim at the goal of harmony in the society. Sacrifices are to be made for achieving this. Confucius promoted forgiveness and mutual understanding, as in his saying that "what you don't want done to yourself, don't do to others".

Confucian Political Thoughts

Dynastical empires in Chinese history drew heavily from Confucian political thoughts in their administration, though end results vary widely. Confucianism promoted a virtue-based rule, taking morality and benevolence as keys to good government.

The source of power is "mandate of heaven", for rulers to obtain authority over the whole country. It is vital for Westerners to understand that this "heaven" (*tian*) did not imply empowerment from the God. Based on the above-mentioned non-religious, natural course beliefs,

Confucianism had kept careful distance from any mentioning of the existence of an almighty God. "Heaven" is a term used to describe that unknown universe above, and does not refer to a particular god or being. On the contrary, the mandate of heaven needs to be obtained through exceptional effort. It had to be dependent on the virtues of rulers, making them work hard to earn it. From this belief, there was an implicit indication to followers of Confucianism that rulers could be rightfully removed, if they did not perform their duties and thus lost their mandate of heaven.

Trust and benevolence are seen as the keys in government. The first implies the keeping of words and promises, thus earning trust from others in return. The government is to keep its promises to the people. With ample food supply, large number of troops and people's confidence in a trustworthy government, the ruler can be assured of security of his mandate. In a harmonious relationship, the government could trust its populace and rule by benevolence. Confucius spent much time exploring the concept of an ideal person and concluded with a definition of a humane being. This is just another way to say that a person should be benevolent to other people and, as a ruler, to all his subjects. The ruler should do his duty, curb expenditures, and mobilise subjects for wars or public works during non-planting and non-harvesting seasons. If people have plenty of supplies, the ruler would not be poor either. The second Confucian sage after Confucius, Mencius, made a startling statement at that early time of history that "people are the most vital and precious, the state second, and the ruler last, in that order. Therefore, rulers who get approval from their people are to have the mandate of heaven." This is often claimed as an early call for political democracy, in a similar fashion to "of the people, by the people".

In response to social chaos and turmoil during the time of this school's emergence, Confucianism advocated tirelessly for social order and stability, and placed these two as top priorities in governance. There ought to be pecking orders from the ruler down to officials and to lower groups of subjects. The status of each social group is to be defined and maintained by rituals, showing respect to authority and to the state as a whole. From this ordered structure in government, it developed into a full set of relationships, later called five relationships (*wu lun*), between ruler/subject, father/son, husband/wife, elder/younger brothers and friends. The whole society is under the cover of these five relationships, and once people understand their social status, they would work to keep social order and stability. With the historical background of warring states and disintegration of kingdoms at the time of emergence of Confucianism, this emphasis on set relationships and stability is quite understandable.

Confucius paid much attention to nurture and train the "gentleman" or "great man" (*jun zi*), the person who was with sage qualities and to be a great ruler of vast territories. These qualities can be obtained through learning Confucianism. Social responsibility and the five cardinal virtues—humanity, righteousness, propriety, wisdom and faithfulness—were demanded of rulers and the social elite to be. They were to keep their life and practice up to these five virtues, so that the commoners, or people, would benefit from their rule over the society. Commoners are not supposed to have these virtues, and their fates leave them in another group as the ruled.

Confucian Education

Confucius himself was a dedicated teacher, with large numbers of students and disciples. If he achieved little in a political or military career, his teaching left a much more profound impact on Chinese history than he expected. Based on this experience, education is a key component of Confucianism, especially in the areas of nurturing and guiding the "gentleman" for the task of governing the populace.

A basic notion of Confucianism was that learning was for everyone. There would be no barriers and no difference for the nobility or for ordinary people. Confucius figured that people were closely similar in infant years; their differences in later life derive from their varying degrees of learning. He taught students of a variety of backgrounds, and he charged little as admission so that those students could continue to follow him. His motto was "teaching has no classification (of groups)." Being a member of the nobility did not guarantee a good learning and a chance to be a gentleman. In imperial states of later times, this principle of learning was faithfully followed, with quite widespread elementary learning and large numbers of government officials coming from backgrounds of poor families.

Confucian teaching focused on self-refinement and moral cultivation. Learning to be a gentleman was to be an embodiment of high morality and to take on great social responsibilities. Learning also covered civil duties and knowledge of state affairs. These prepared students to serve the rulers and the country. All of these are learning contents for people to become gentlemen, a member of the elite and in the ruling class (see Figure 1.3). A later interpretation of Confucian learning identified the major responsibilities of a gentleman as self-cultivation, running the family, administering the state, and making the Celestial Empire peaceful. Confucius had little to offer to students on subjects outside philosophy, politics and acceptable behaviours. He replied to enquiries by saying "if you want to learn farming or gardening, go to farmers and gardeners, I am no expert as they are."

The legacy of early Confucianism is summarised as follows:

❑ Evolutionary or conservative views were the mainstream, and moderation and compromise stand as better choices than radical moves. Although the ruled were justified in violently removing tyrants and those non-gentlemen, drastic changes to existing structures were not preferred. To a lesser extent, improvement or adjustment proves to be better than reform.

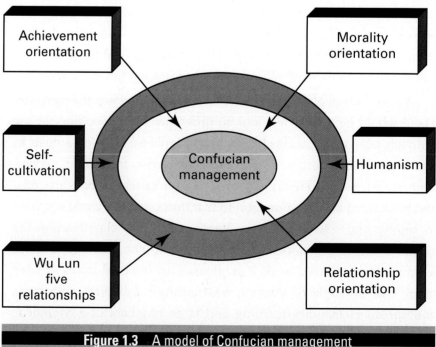

Figure 1.3   A model of Confucian management

❑ The society in the imperial era was not lacking social mobility and room for change. Confucian education ideas made it possible for ordinary people to learn knowledge, and through the imperial examination system, many low-class members could move up the ladder and enter officialdom. This mobility created a driving force for the society to keep strength in a time span of 2,000 years. There was also little restriction on people moving from one region to another, or from one line of business to another.

❑ The non-religious nature of Confucianism continued. The imperial state officially held no links with any religion, but relied on moral authority and cultivation to rule. The introduction of Buddhism to China cast great influence on rulers of a couple of dynasties and almost shook Confucianism off the reigning position. Confucianism, however, survived this religious onslaught and began a revival and then domination in state philosophy. A distinction between the two is that Confucianism appealed to the elite and officials, while Buddhism appealed mainly to commoners as a popular belief.

❑ Confucianism focuses on social relations and dealing with personal behaviours. It pays less attention to economic matters and practical issues. The ultimate knowledge is about how to rule the country as designed in Confucian doctrines. This neglect of practical knowledge perhaps cost China dearly in early modern times, in terms of few breakthroughs in technology and business practices.

❑ In the Confucian model, a centralised government is ideal for maintaining social order and stratifications. Power centralisation in the hands of the elite should not be replaced by a more decentralised structure. This tradition has lasted long and wide in people's beliefs.

❑ Following Confucius' own example, education of gentlemen became a top priority of the government. The unique Chinese imperial examination system was unparallelled in its complexity and perfection in the pre-modern world and produced large numbers of personnel for government posts. This system was borrowed heavily by the Europeans for their early forms of a civil servant system. This Chinese system continued to be improved amid various kinds of criticism. *Ancien régime* in China was well maintained over numerous crises by such a bureaucracy with unlimited supply of educated personnel. It had become a formidable state machine to draw intellectuals and talented youth into the bureaucracy. This tradition also influenced generations of Chinese, inspired by an entry into officialdom through the door of imperial examinations. Even after this century-old system was officially abolished by the Qing government in 1905, the traditional emphasis on education continued unabated, with Chinese families in mainland China and overseas mostly placing education of their children above many other goals in life.

These three key parts of Confucianism have their close inner connections. It is from a non-religious macro view of the universe that a consistent focus on people's behaviour and good government originated. It is also from a strong desire to improve governance that an emphasis on nurturing and educating gentlemen to be rulers was solidly formed upon. The core of Confucianism is the rule of benevolence, and a good government with balanced relations patterns and stability is the ultimate goal. Other issues, such as commerce, technology or liberal art, were thought to be sufficiently dealt with under this overall framework.

Daoism and Lao Zi

Daoism emerged with its legendary founder Lao Zi, and the sacred classic text of this school of thought is "*Dao De Jing*", meaning a book on the way and morality (or virtue). Lao Zi was active in a period of time similar to Confucius', but this classic text proves to be a collection of early pieces of thinking and later additions. Daoism gained its early fame and continued influence as a considerable competitor to the all-powerful Confucianism.

The essentials of Daoism as a school of thought excluded itself from being a religion. This school, however, did not avoid talking about unexplained natural phenomena and kept a reverent view of the universe. Perhaps with this curiosity and imagination the school later turned into a major popular religion in China, with numerous additions of rituals and preaching by creative leading Daoist clergies. The famous *Tai-ji* martial art, a Daoism invention, is perhaps well known to Western tourists and is a formidable match to the venerable Buddhist *Shao-lin* martial art.

"The Way" and "Qi"

The essence of Daoism is to see the world as a natural process, a view similar to Confucianism. The term *Dao* means the "way", depicting the way the universe moves. Another term is *qi,* literally "air" but is used here to imply material forces which could not be explained. Chinese scientists today describe this *qi* in terms of atoms or neutrons. This is perhaps not so far-fetched, since early Daoism had a brilliant vision to use *qi* as a general term for particles everywhere in the universe. Lao Zi observed that all the things in the universe originated from material beings, and these beings, in turn, originated from nothingness. It is from this Daoist term *qi* that a philosophical concept of positive and negative in all materials came about. A famous observation made by Daoism states that a foot-long stick can be halved and halved indefinitely, even as human eyes cannot see this halving process anymore. This gives a clear indication that the universe is formed by tiny particles of materials, and the movement of these particles created phenomena on this planet and in the whole universe. On this basis, early Daoism did not share the view that the world was created by a personified being, the God, and religious worshipping and preaching were extremely rare. It is the universe, with *qi* and nothingness, rather than the God, which works mysterious ways.

The second important figure in Daoism is Zhuang Zi, who embodied the high ideals of early Daoism. He was a freelancer, writing the most elegant and free-spirited poems and verses in Chinese history. His imagination and descriptions of nature were not matched by any in those early historical periods. His views were shaped by Daoism and "the way", thus there seemed no reason for a person to be bound by secular troubles and wounds. Zhuang Zi expressed his strong desire to run away from society and seek for an inaccessible haven. For both Lao Zi and Zhuang Zi, their strong belief in "the way" and the natural course of the universe made them feel incapable of doing anything, and they thus gave it up. Daoism kept away from politics and social movements in pre-modern China and had great influence over the populace, instead of over rulers and leaders.

The Yin and Yang

A prominent feature of Daoism is its concept of *yin* and *yang*, as the two opposite ends of *qi*. In fact, Daoism sees everything in the universe having a pair of opposite ends, such as in the example of male and female, so that the human race can survive. The interaction and rotation of these ends makes the world colourful yet stable. This perhaps is entering the field of modern physics. In the field of social sciences, this concept of *yin* and *yang* demonstrates contradictions, and a judgement on being right or wrong is required in these contradictions. People cannot eliminate these contradictions but they can make the two opposite ends work for their own good. A balance is essentially built on contradictions, and a masterful move by a great man can turn a nightmare into a triumph. A society is divided by a right wing and a left wing, and their effort may either destroy each other and the whole society or create acceptable balances. This idea of *yin* and *yang* is so fascinating that it cast great influence on many Chinese thinkers thereafter. The great Chinese revolutionary leader Mao Zedong wrote a masterpiece "On contradictions", which absorbed a great deal from the now standard Chinese wisdom of *yin* and *yang*.

Wu Wei

Another major contribution of Daoism to Chinese philosophy and thinking in general is the concept of "*wu wei*". It can be literally interpreted as non-action; the implication is with no action being taken, yet nothing is left undone. It originated from "the way", as seeing the universe work its own way, without interference or involvement from humans.

This classic philosophical idea has great impact on traditional administration and organisations in pre-modern times. *Wu wei* had been a guiding principle for rulers of Chinese empires. The common Chinese motto adds two more characters to the term, making it say "non-action, while administration is all done". A typical description is that "ruling a big country is like cooking a small fish; it is best if you don't stir or turn it over many times (making a mess). Using the way to rule the country, trouble-making immortals will disappear" (Lao Zi). Imperial governments routinely practised *wu wei* to deal with severe situations, chiefly in the ways of reducing tax and financial burdens on

Chinese peasants. This Daoist approach worked especially well during the founding era of a dynasty after a horrendous social upheaval, such as the transitional period between the Ming and Qing dynasties (the latter officially began in 1644). Successive energetic Manchu emperors tirelessly implemented measures to offer peasants breathing space and help a recovery in agriculture. The end result was a China as a recognised world power in the eighteenth century. The non-interfering nature of *wu wei* is, in some ways, similar to the Western term "*laissez-faire*" in early modern Europe. This approach may also provide certain incentives for forming a free market.

In government and in management, the Daoist concept *wu wei* advocates minimalism and much less unwanted interference, mostly from the government on business activities. For example, the government should consider reductions in taxes, regulations and restrictions or owning state-run monopolies, in order to allow more opportunities for market forces. *Wu wei* also opposes tight control in business operation and management and tends to allow more flexibility and initiatives from subordinates. In management style, *wu wei* encourages ruling by holding principles and offering guidance, instead of being buried in daily affairs. A leader who practises *wu wei* would make a clear distinction between top management and subordinates in terms of their responsibilities. Delegation of authority is a preferred way of operation. The concept of *wu wei* also requires leaders to make long-term plans, thinking of the benefits of the whole corporation, rather than finalising quick deals and getting short-term returns.

Legalism

A school of thought totally opposite to Confucianism and Daoism is Legalism. The Chinese character in this name is "*fa*", meaning laws. As a response to worsening social conditions and violent confrontations among regional powers, this school rejected the possibility that people naturally have good natures. They recognised that people need to be controlled by force, and the laws should be made very clear about the consequences if they were broken. This school expected to strengthen state power, halt disintegration and unify all territories. The approach to achieve this goal is through legalising everything. Strict laws would make people work hard, produce more and make soldiers fight gallantly, without deserters. Thus, Legalism took laws as the only means to salvage the human race and to create decent citizens and societies.

Legalism also invented the notion of equality. Laws are devised to supervise actions of all people. Under the state ruler, all officials and populace are subject to rewards and punishments stipulated in existing laws. No exception was to be given to anyone; noblemen and commoners face punishments in similar fashion. The state ruler can only grant occasional pardons to the convicted. This is perhaps not exactly the idea of equal legal rights in a modern society, but it is clear that this school of thought intended to solve problems in a strictly legal way, rather than the more benevolent ways of Confucianism. The school felt strongly about a unified state and uniform laws throughout the country. They longed for stability and power and were disgusted by internal wars and loss of social order.

One prominent figure of this school was Han Feizi, who in his writings devised ways to legalise this absolute power of state rulers and lifted rulers to the untouchable echelon of the society. Laws issued by rulers should be strictly applied to all subjects in the country, and any violation should be punished severely. This heralded the beginning of power centralisation in China. Members of Legalism very often served as advisers to powerful kings, and their proposals on rules and laws did leave big marks on administration in those territories. The outstanding example is Li Si, who served as prime minister of the Qin state. Under his stewardship, the ambitious Qin king finally unified all separate states by force and established the first empire in Chinese history in 221 B.C. This achievement more or less proves the effectiveness of Legalism in state administration and governance.

Legalism is often criticised for advocating a rule of harshness and cruelty. The two Han dynasties in following centuries reversed the course and honoured Confucianism as the official doctrine. In reality, Chinese empires ruled vast territories and population with both approaches: Confucianism to maintain social harmony and minimise revolts, and Legalism to regulate the society and suppress opposition. Legalism in name did not survive the upheavals after the downfall of the first Qin Empire. Its essence, however, lasted all the way throughout Chinese history, in routine administrative practice and in complicated state regulations. We can even see the Legalist elements in numerous "strike hard" campaigns in mainland China of recent times. Unlike

Confucianism, Legalism has no influence on overseas Chinese, since its principles are based purely on effectively ruling a state.

Buddhism

This Indian religion entered imperial China *en masse* during a period of extreme chaos and warring states in the fourth century A.D. As the absolute power of the central government deteriorated badly, the official Confucianism and unofficial Legalism doctrines lost credit, thus providing a fertile ground for a swift Buddhist expansion in China. Indian religious masters and Chinese monks made frequent cultural exchanges and visits, and they produced a large quantity of Buddhist religious texts and books in Chinese. The preaching of separation of soul and body and of a next life appealed strongly to many and drew large numbers of followers from royals to commoners. This religion reached its peak during the Tang Dynasty (623-907 A.D.), with imperial blessing and wide popular support. Its religious aloofness and concentration on self-motivated preaching mixed well with the escapist Daoism of China. The Indian religion became a native religion, with several influential sects founded and developed by leading Chinese monks. One of these sects called Zen spread to Japan and became influential ever since. This longing of the other world was seen by Confucian loyalists as tragically destroying state administration and benevolent rule. As the new Song dynasties emerged (960-1276 A.D.), Confucian scholars staged a revival of their preferred official doctrines, in the form of Neo-Confucianism. Buddhism lost its favourable position in the top layers of the society and became a popular belief among lower social groups. This is an early separation of religion and the state, Chinese style. Neo-Confucianism, however, drew various elements from Buddhism and made necessary additions to ancient Confucian concepts. This evolution of thought made Confucianism better adapted to changing situations and reinforced its official status. Since Buddhism is a religion, we can only provide a brief review here and will not start a religious study.

In summary, Confucianism and Legalism have little links with religions, in nature and in appearance. They both focus on the society and administration. In Chinese history, these two major schools of thought had earned their official status and demonstrated their practical influence on the society and people's behaviours. Daoism touched more upon philosophy and nature. Its escapist approach made it unsuccessful in gaining political influence. The less rigid nature of this school, especially *wu wei*, had great impact on behaviour patterns and Chinese traditions. It failed to become an official doctrine, but through religious transformations, it has immense influence on the secular populace. The localised religion Buddhism and the native religion of China, Daoism, represent many of the common secular beliefs in China.

Socialism

The emergence of socialism in China in modern times was a historical turn by chance. China began to be westernised since the Opium War with Britain that lasted from 1842 to 1844. China's effort to modernise was clearly shown in the self-strengthening movement of the 1860s onwards, during which the military, industry, commerce, education and the government itself underwent major changes, in order to copy the model of success of Western powers. China suffered badly in this process of transformation. First, Western powers, and later Japan, continued to make the rules to their advantage and grabbed astronomical figures of economic interests from China, in particular in the form of war indemnities. Second, the Paris Peace Conference, at the end of the First World War, granted enormous interests in Chinese territories to Japan, effectively making a war ally a colony of another ally. To many Chinese, including Chinese intellectuals, this was unjust and unfair treatment. They felt openly betrayed by this blatant display of Western power politics, in stark contrast to previous preachings of freedom and equal rights from the West. At this juncture, the success of the Bolshevik Revolution in Russia led to the downfall of the Tsar, and the Soviet-style socialism came to the attention of left-wing Chinese intellectuals. A new alternative was presented to them, who felt deeply disappointed at the outcomes of an application of Western ideas in China.

Socialism, as advocated by Karl Marx and implemented by the Soviets, was transferred to China with certain early success. One of the reasons was the tendency in China to emphasis equality and morality. The harmonious and benevolent rule favoured by Confucianism had led a number of emperors to exercise similar policies, and peasant rebellions commonly made calls for equal and fair shares of land ownership for all. The idea of equality had been deep-rooted. Combined with the Soviet socialism, the Communist Party of China found links with traditional Chinese ideals useful, and they appealed in their party campaigns directly to peasants and intellectuals. In a period of political disintegration and rampant official corruption, this socialist model appeared to breathe fresh air into politics, against stale patterns of imperial and capitalist exploitation of the populace.

The socialist model had other appeals to Chinese as well, namely stability and unity. These two ideas had been standard contents of Confucianism: stability for a benevolent rule, and unity for effective administration and guarded national interests. It was reasoned that China needed stability and central authority to be rid of Western imperial encroachment and widespread poverty, and that socialism and the Communist Party directed the path to reach this goal. Traditional Chinese conservatives in Confucianism had something in common here with certain elements of modern socialist ideals. These mixed understandings not only swept the Party to power in 1949 with relative ease, but also laid the foundation for a nationwide socialist system in following decades.

After the establishment of a socialist rule, the Chinese communists faced a dilemma in choice and unexpectedly moved towards a more ideological destination. The Chinese communists, especially Mao Zedong, borrowed heavily from Chinese culture and blended it with introduced socialist ideas. This marriage worked well in the pre-1949 years, but came to a point where, by socialist doctrines, traditional cultural baggage was to be abandoned completely. Confucianism, as the official ruling doctrine of the imperial era, had no place in a socialist country. For this ideological rationale, the Chinese communists had to stick to the Soviet line and waged numerous campaigns to eradicate past traditions. These were definitely unpopular and troubling even to top Chinese leaders, since they were originally the products of Chinese culture. The Cultural Revolution in 1966 gave the final blow to Confucianism and Chinese traditions linked with it. These political and ideological movements deprived Chinese people of their long-held beliefs, while the new socialism had only a short run of less than two generations. These are the reasons behind the reforms of the late 1970s, when China lost not only direction in economic development but also a core belief system of their own. Early cultural eradication and later money-chasing materialism during the reform years created a huge vacuum in Chinese thinking and guiding principles. It was not till the end of the 1990s that Chinese people realised that their cultural heritage, especially Confucianism, had been mistreated and needed to be revived.

A question is to be raised here: During the years of communists marching to their final victory, why did they choose the Soviets, not Americans, as their major sponsor for economic development? There were cordial relationships and exchanges between the headquarters of the Party and the US administration during and after the Anti-Japanese War of 1945. The United States had demonstrated their willingness and capacity to help during the war and early stages of the subsequent civil war. It could be that the socialist doctrines run against cooperation with capitalist countries. The communists in China, however, often acted differently from the Soviets, and the paramount leader Mao was a character who valued Chinese interests highly. The US administration was at the brink of recognising this communist government in 1949, but balked at this prospect due to domestic ideologies and international strategic considerations. Similarly, the Chinese communists turned to reject the US influence, as the latter backed the Nationalist government with its full might. At the strategic level, the Chinese communists were unable to step aside from the worldwide Soviet-US confrontation and thus chose to lean on to its northern neighbour. This choice came along with practical considerations of benefits and losses; the socialist system, regardless, was implemented in China in following decades after this taking of sides. Central planning, equal distribution and state-run social welfare were all taken as symbols of socialism and followed in principle, albeit with variations from, the more rigid Soviet practices.

Traditional Culture in Modern and Contemporary Times

Traditional Chinese cultures, in particular Confucianism, had been downgraded continuously since the early twentieth century. Political cultures have dominated people's minds and social movements. They are in two forms:

1. Anti-tradition (anti-Confucianism)
2. Socialism

The general anti-tradition trend turned Confucianism from an imperial orthodoxy to a political thought to be condemned. In comparison with newly introduced thoughts from the West, including socialism, Confucianism and other Chinese thinking seemed pale and clueless in answering critical questions and providing solutions to China's woes. Coupled with frustration towards the dying Qing state, this trend or public mood took traditions as one of the main causes for the backwardness of China. A blame game began by radical revolutionaries, prominent among them, Dr. Sun Yat-sen, the revered founder of the Republic of China after the downfall of imperial rule in 1911. It was for the populace to be rid of the bounds of traditions and wholeheartedly embrace Western things. A further severe blow came from the famous May-fourth New Culture movement. Its catch phrase is "smashing Confucian temples (idols)", and one of the achievements this movement made was to transform court mandarin language used by imperial officials into a standard language for all people in China to speak, thus simplifying the work of educating the populace. The written Chinese remained in the complicated form, until an even more radical type of simplified Chinese was sanctioned by the ruling Communist government after 1949.

The legacy of Chinese culture was eroded fast in this process of transplanting Western things for practical purposes. Past histories were publicly dismissed as without any true value in a new world. This trend was superseded by socialism, which takes Marxism doctrines as supreme thinking above any other, let alone the faded, useless Chinese native cultures. Radical ideas of constant changes and struggles made the primary Chinese traditions, such as stability, balance (the Mean) and family connections, irrelevant. Certain elements of Chinese culture, such as collectivism and social responsibility of the educated, were merged into socialist characteristics, in the forms of planned economy and Party leadership, and their origins in Chinese culture were turned over and banished. Other traditions were simply described as superstitious, for example *feng shui* and Buddhist rituals.

The final blow to traditional Chinese culture came with the Cultural Revolution (1966-1976). This political movement aiming at capitalist remnants made a near-total sweeping away of remaining cultural traditions during its course. Large-scale public campaigns against the "four olds" (jargons for things past) by Red Guards destroyed uncountable volumes of national treasures and art collections. The ideological purpose was to eliminate traditional cultural components from people's minds and to create new generations of Chinese of pure socialist ideals. Under strict Party and government control, this political movement seemed to work for a few years, and there was no public showing of beliefs other than socialism. The chaos created by this nationwide movement, however, eventually initiated counter undercurrents and broke the monopoly of the Party doctrines. The course was reversed swiftly at the end of this period, preceding the reforms, which inevitably caused a revival of traditional Chinese culture in many new forms.

The anti-tradition trend did not begin with the communists, but emerged as a response to the ineffectual actions against the intrusion of Western cultures at the end of the imperial era. Chinese traditions and culture had been blamed for many things unjust and undesirable. The more radical actions taken by the communists finally made an extinction of Chinese culture possible; they, however, initiated an end to all radical movements as well. In a more open and stable environment, virtues and true values of traditional Chinese culture have been re-discovered.

After decades of blame games and condemnation, Confucianism re-emerged as a credible and viable modern thinking for the Chinese. The coming to stage of Neo-Confucianism (different from the school of imperial age with the same name) followed the booms of East Asian economies since the 1980s. Confidence in traditional Chinese culture returned, as the so-called East Asian dragons are mostly influenced by Confucianism. Their economic success and nature of political stability represented verifiable evidences of the applicability of Confucian ideas.

With growing economic power and the Greater China phenomenon, covering Hong Kong, Singapore, Taiwan, later mainland China, and overseas Chinese, attempts had been made to justify traditional Confucian values in the modern world and re-establish a system for the right combination of both. Groups of scholars, prominent among them Professor Tu Wei-ming of the United States, re-examined Confucian texts and drew relevant clauses in reference to business and management thinking of modern times. This involves re-discovery and re-interpretation, and opinions, of course, differ. The Asian financial crisis has since put a damper on this enthusiastic new school of thought.

Overall, it has been a long process of evaluation of traditional Chinese culture, with early dismissal and condemnation, eradication, and a later revival of certain acceptable components. A more sensible evaluation is more likely after overbearing external influences have waned.

Chinese Thoughts on Organisations and Management

The running of a state bureaucracy requires certain skills which can be applied to running a business corporation. Ancient Chinese regimes and thinkers made many relevant observations and gained insights on administration and management. To them, management is essentially managing people, thus leadership qualities and nurturing of "gentlemen" should be top priorities among all administrative tasks. A discussion on traditional thoughts on such topics may help modern-day leaders and managers in their business operations. We are here taking some references from a number of early thinkers and summarising their views on administration.

The ultimate approach of administration is, of course, *wu wei*. This was first voiced by Lao Zi and later was agreed to by most Chinese philosophers. It is a macrocontrol mechanism, making less unwanted interferences and allowing the natural course to proceed. In particular, the government should exert less influence on business. There should be less control, in forms such as taxation, regulations, restrictions and state-run monopolies. Lao Zi further listed four levels of rulers. "The best ruler has his subjects unaware of his presence. The second best ruler makes subjects appraise him (willingly). The third best ruler makes subjects fear him. The worst ruler makes subjects disrespect him." Applying these classifications of leaders to a business organisation, you will get the point. These distinctions imply a preference towards minimal control over subordinates and more flexibility and initiatives from employees.

Another concept is in the saying "gentlemen do not carry out minor tasks." This implies a delegation of authority and shift of responsibility to persons in charge. A clear distinction is drawn between top management and subordinates in terms of their duties. It points particularly to top management about their major tasks in working out long-term plans. A leader with a tendency to be expert in a particular area or around a certain area may lose sight of future prospects. For rulers in the past, this saying provided a warning that their behaviours may cause harm to common people and they should focus on important policies across the country. To top management in modern organisations, this indicates that their priorities should be properly placed and they need to stay clear of the bounds or responsibilities of a middle-level manager.

On the matter of leadership, it is suggested that "gentlemen should treat relations with others sensibly, not agreeing with others against the principles." "Little men", on the other hand, "tend to join in small circles not based on agreed principles." This implies that leaders should not keep great distance from their subordinates. In the meantime, they should keep a clear head on principal matters and not let their close relationships with subordinates influence their major decisions. Leaders also exert positive influence over the whole organisation. Their exemplar behaviours would be watched closely and followed by their subordinates. This is described as "the wind of gentlemanly behaviour [that] blows over all grass leaning to one side." Proper conduct by leaders would lead to smooth operations even without them issuing any instructions.

Leaders should especially avoid the danger of abandoning principles and breaking one's own rules under temporary circumstances. Integrity and reputation are built up over the long run. Without them, failures are expected and nothing can be done. As a gesture of authority, leaders (gentlemen) should say less and take prompt actions. This is supposed to counter two kinds of styles. One is with plenty of talk, while doing very little. The other is with silence and slow response. The first style gives an impression of ineffectual empty talk, while the second style gives the impression of uncertainty in decision making, thus ruining subordinates' confidence in the leader. The above rule indicates an appropriate way of handling your employees and building up their respect for you. Centuries later, a senior banker of a major international bank in Hong Kong voiced agreement with this rule by saying that leaders should inspire employees by cutting short talks and acting promptly to achieve the set goals.

On dealing with internal and external relations, traditional Chinese thoughts again advocate "reaching the Mean as the ultimate goal". In regard to competition and rivalry, it is for leaders to "worry less about how others see you, make [an] effort to understand others". It is suggested by Lao Zi that "being wise is to understand others, being intelligent is to know oneself, being powerful is to overpower others, being strong is to exercise self-control." This applies to business relations, *guanxi*, and connections with partners and competitors. Leaders need to spend much of their time on dealing with these relations and exercise extreme control over strategies.

On this important point, **36 stratagems**, by Sun Zi, are often quoted in business guides as the essentials in survival of market competition. The strategies were first employed by this brilliant Chinese strategist in military science and for the purpose of battles. These include tactics of diversion, attacking, confusing, manoeuvring and trickery. To apply them to business may help achieve the goal of market dominance, but that could also lead to some totally opposite outcomes. If we put these strategies side by side with the Mean, we can see that the Mean is the essence of management in Chinese thinking and is placed as the ultimate art of effective administration. A far-sighted decision maker should be able to reduce tension and reach sensible conclusions amid all the fierce contests. The strategies, on the other hand, serve the purpose of tactical winnings and may help in claiming victories. In the business world, these would be an overdoing or overkill by the winning corporation and create tougher situations for future business. Market dominance or monopoly may generate negative effects on individual companies and on the economy as a whole. Examples of adopting these strategies to the full are Microsoft in the United States and Changhong Electronics in China. The latter attempted to dominate the TV market through hoarding tubes, but its failure to achieve that turned numerous fair competitors into fierce enemies in related industries.

On supervision of employees and organisations, traditional Chinese thought encouraged making one's own judgement and not being influenced or misled by outside opinions. It is suggested that "if the majority of the group hate or praise one particular person, it must be investigated", because the person in question has profoundly affected other people. This person may either be of a bad quality or of good leadership potential. It is said that "gentlemen don't select personnel only based on good words; they also accept all constructive advice and suggestions, even if these come from a person they don't like." To select potential leaders and right personnel, gentlemen must be modest and close to these candidates to earn their trust. Lao Zi advised that it is often the people with solid knowledge who don't speak, while those who want to show off make a great deal of speeches to hide their ignorance. Gentlemen (leaders) have to be conscious of this common human behaviour in their supervision of work.

These observations made by ancient Chinese thinkers are based on their experience, and they reveal certain inner working of organisations, be it a state department or a business corporation. These experiences are helpful for modern-day enterprises, especially in areas of leadership, personnel management and decision making.

Common Chinese Values

Chinese culture has passed through centuries of evolution, creating a combination of traditional philosophies and localised religions, and introduced socialism in contemporary China. Several key Chinese concepts exist and exert lasting influence on Chinese people on the mainland and overseas. These concepts include:

❏ **Achievement (social) orientation:** This is connected with the emphasis on education, and with social responsibilities and sense of mission of gentlemen (intellectuals, social elite, etc.).

❏ **Morality:** This is similar to the first orientation, in nature and in appearance. It is duty-based rather than rights-based, demanding high moral standards for top groups of the society.

❏ **Egalitarian commitment:** This is the consequence of socialist movements in China and teaching of doctrines. It also reflects the lingering effect of Confucianism on people's behaviours, pursuing a state of equal treatment and protection for the weak.

❏ **Harmony:** This is an intention and effort to maintain status quo and minimise conflicts. Solution to problems and restructuring should not damage the organisation as a whole.

❏ **Hierarchy:** This is solidly based on the traditional five relationships and on authority in administration during the imperial era. Bureaucratic norms in imperial and socialist periods have made ranks very important in government.

❏ **Loyalty:** This is not listed as one of Confucius' five cardinal virtues of leaders. Faithfulness may be a close concept, yet this was upgraded to a top value in rulers' choice. In business, the concept of loyalty later on contains a meaning similar to trust.

❑ **Modesty and implications**: In training gentlemen and choosing potential leaders, modesty was seen as a crucial characteristic. Traditional Daoist thinking warned people not to grow over-confident and over-estimate oneself. Many Chinese sayings express the same implication of modesty, such as that a person should be careful not to grow horns (threatening others), that water is the most hardened stuff though a liquid, and that an arrow shot from a bow cannot penetrate a piece of silk, due to it reaching the end of the shooting range.

❑ **Rituals:** These were designed by Confucian scholars in early history to preserve the dignity and enhance the authority of rulers and officials. To Confucius, every rite, gesture and way of display has its meaning, and sometimes it is worth fighting over the right rituals, because they represent the authority of a state or an organisation. The famous story of the first English official envoy to China, Lord Macartney, illustrates this point perfectly. The English noble was deeply troubled by the demand from Emperor Qianlong of kneeling and performing rituals accorded to a tributary state from afar. He was so relieved when the Emperor showed his benevolence by allowing him to perform rituals the English way. This was a rare exception in imperial China, where non-conformist conduct during official rituals could lead to dismissals and demotions. Western media today are fond of using the term "kowtowing" to express their displeasure over certain government concessions to the Chinese state, since they believe that the rituals of kneeling only satisfy the vanity of Chinese rulers. In business negotiations, Chinese officials and top managers tend to tightly observe recognised rituals and protocols. A mistake during these proceedings makes them feel a loss of face not only to the foreigners, but to their subordinates as well. Numerous anecdotal stories of negotiations with the Chinese depicted an unusual situation where a Chinese chairperson is, in fact, a junior officer and the shabby figure at the end of the line is the person really in charge. These stories give people an impression of Chinese negotiators skilfully playing the 36 stratagems with foreigners. According to the Chinese concept of rituals, however, this kind of practice is quite abnormal, and the respect for official ranks in China almost certainly excludes the likelihood of this behaviour.

❑ **Filial piety**: This came directly from the five relationships (*wu lun*) of early Confucianism and was reinforced by Neo-Confucianism as an officially sanctioned accord. The family head holds the control over the family, and children would obey directions and support parents financially in their old age. A breach of filial piety is a loss of morality, and imperial officials, even emperors, lost their positions if found guilty of this kind of wrongdoing. This cultural heritage differs sharply from the family customs of Western Europe. This sense of family obligations has been eroded markedly as a result of liberalisation and reforms, and younger generations of Chinese have the opportunity to choose a Western style of family life. Social conflicts and tension between the old and the new, of course, ensue.

❑ **Retribution**: The Chinese word is *bao*, a form of implicit social control over the populace. This concept derives from Buddhism, whose ideas of next life and samsara imply that the dead would be subject to final judgement and pay for the evils done in this life with suffering in the next life. As imperial and modern China were under secular state beliefs, the Chinese have less fear of the original sins central in Christianity. Retribution in Buddhism comes up as a compensation for the lack of religious feelings. This secular belief has its influence felt among many social groups, especially among overseas Chinese.

❑ **Accidental connections**: This is *yuan* in Chinese, which has much of the Daoist mystique. The natural course of the universe and material forces randomly make unexpected things happen, thus there are opportunities for people to grab. It can be applied to love affairs and marriages, with both parties drawn to each other by accident, or by *yuan*. It can be applied to official careers, where a promotion comes along with the chance to meet a senior official by *yuan*. It is more often in the business world of China today that the negotiating teams are said to have *yuan* to come together for a certain investment project. The Chinese side would first take this *yuan* as a courtesy and compliment to the foreign side. In business dealings, they do rely considerably on their sensing of *yuan* or lack of it, before building long-term relationships with a business partner. The well-known Chinese term *guanxi* leans heavily on this *yuan* at the introductory stage. The criteria of *yuan* include appearance, style, behaviours, conversation, sincerity, or something one cannot really put his finger on. Sometimes, it is accidental and is, in a sense, similar to the Western idea of first impression.

From the point of view of business dealings in connection with cultural background, a number of concepts with lasting influence on Chinese behaviours are discussed above. Their origins include major Chinese schools of thought, and the blend is quite thorough. Apart from the official Party doctrines, these values still command the strength to mould people's mindset in a subtle and comprehensive way. Foreigners could identify some of these in their contact with Chinese people and business partners. There are certainly other popular norms and specialised concepts, such as *feng shui*, which will not be discussed here. You may refer to specific titles to get references.

Key Concepts

Cultures
Confucianism
Daoism
The Mean
The mandate of heaven
"The way" and "qi"
Wu wei
Rituals
Yuan

Discussion Questions

1. What are the components of a culture, and how would cultural changes occur?
2. What components or concepts of Confucianism have links with modern-day Chinese society? Select one concept and search for its possible applications.
3. What components or concepts of Daoism have links with modern-day Chinese society? Select one concept and search for its possible applications.
4. Explain the compatibilities and contradictions between traditional Chinese thought and socialism. What reasons do you think there are for the eradication of traditions and China's own culture under socialism? And would Chinese culture survive and revive?

Related Readings

Cheng Li, *The World of Lao Zi, Truth and Nature: Dao De Jing*, with English translation of original text, Taipei, the World Book Company, Ltd., 2000.

Hofstede, Geert and Michael Harris Bond, "The Confucius Connection: from Cultural Roots to Economic Growth", *Organizational Dynamics*, 1988, no. 16, pp. 4–21

Hsu, I., *The Rise of Modern China*, New York, Oxford University Press, 1970.

Spence, Jonathan, *The Search for Modern China*, London, Hutchinson, 1990.

Tu, Wei-ming, *Confucian Traditions in East Asian Modernity: Moral Education and Economic Culture in Japan and the Four Mini-Dragons*, Cambridge, Cambridge University Press, 1996.

Commercial and Business Traditions

*T*his chapter will discuss commercial activities in traditional and modern China. It is a fact that China moved into the modern age long after many Western countries had done so, and China's culture and business traditions are questioned as hindering a modernisation process. Max Weber, familiar to many, had said that Protestant Christians contained that productive ethic of "work-and-save" that gave rise to modern capitalism. The lack of this business mindset in China is said to have delayed modernisation. From the previous chapter on ancient Chinese thought, especially on Confucianism, we see a persistent focus on the philosophical and political arena and an emphasis on government administration. Commercial and economic concerns seemed less prominent in pre-modern China. Thus, this chapter aims to discuss certain commercial activities and doing business in imperial and modern China while bearing this backdrop in mind.

Commerce in Traditional China

We understand that trade and commerce became more active from the time of the Warring States, partly because of the survival of early written records. An outstanding and comprehensive masterpiece by a Han scholar, *the Records of the Historian*, recorded many of the commercial activities from this period on to the Han Dynasty. As shown in the book, regional powers relied on trade for much needed natural resources and armouries, in a similar way to those feudal lords in the Middle Ages of Western Europe. Merchants and traders obtained favours from royals and rulers, and their flourishing business brought them enormous wealth, by the standards of that early time. Some of them even used this wealth to influence political power and support a particular kingdom against another. A smart merchant rose to the position of Prime Minister of the Qin state and died in a palace coup. This intruding of commercial interest into political affairs went against the thoughts of Legalism, which stressed that politics and state power should not be the domains for people pursuing material gains. Confucianism held the same belief.

Their calls were answered by later imperial authorities. Following the Confucianism doctrines, a set of social stratifications was formally installed. Four large social classes were identified.

The gentry class (*shi*) included learned Confucian scholars, bureaucrats and public servants, opinion leaders, educators, etc. In short, those with recognised education and close to the officialdom were in this class, and they were the interpreters and defenders of Chinese culture and values.

The farmer class (*nong*) included the main state revenue providers and potential gentry candidates. These were people in rural areas with land ownership, from landed gentry to small farmers. This class was the main source for state and local officials, after educated students had passed numerous imperial examinations. They were considered the backbone of an agrarian society.

The artisan class (*gong*) included tradesmen and handicraft workers. They were mostly small businesses with family-grown skills. As a minority group, they tended to form tight work-related circles and guilds to protect their interests. Famous examples were the silk and cotton weavers in southern Chinese cities, who rose against heavy charges laid by local authorities at the end of the Ming and Qing dynasties. Their revolts took place in similar fashion to the Boston Tea Party in 1773, during which American merchants revolted against British monopoly and taxation without representation. These groups followed the century-old practice involving a master teaching an apprentice, fine hand skills, and were conservative enough not to make inventions.

The merchant class (*shang*) included traders, dealers and merchandisers. They were widely considered as profit seekers and agents of social disturbances to an agrarian society. They were risk takers and rule breakers, seeking high profit margins to increase their wealth. They were both culture defenders if political orders remained intact (enjoying safe trade in a unified empire) and culture modifiers if social trends became unpredictable (seeking opportunities by opening to the West). Imperial governments laid certain severe restrictions on this class, forbidding them from entering imperial examinations and thus from receiving official authority. The members of this class were supposed to be in a non-official social classification, with the artisans. This rule turned benign towards early modern times, when the children of this class, if they worked hard to learn, were allowed to enter imperial examinations.

Restrictions on the merchant class came out of several concerns. The dominant Confucian thinking made the distinction between gentlemen and merchants. The former had their commitment to righteousness, and the latter to profits. In such a contrast, the rich merchants were naturally associated with a loss of righteousness, and as such, merchants could not be trusted to run state affairs. Another rationale was that the wealth in the hands of merchants could corrupt officials, turning away from Confucian morality. Furthermore, profit-chasing merchants, with their loan sharks and cheap land purchases, could force peasants off the land they tilled, making them vagrants. This sounded very serious to imperial authorities, who depended on land taxes as their main stable revenues. For these reasons, imperial governments continued the practice of restricting the growth of the merchant class. Ironically, under these policies, merchants were taxed much less than peasants, and the practice of laying charges on passing traders was often attacked in official reports and decrees. The merchant class fared better in this respect than the peasantry. This is perhaps a compensation for the loss of a strong political representation.

Despite official restrictions, trade and commerce were never in serious danger of being ruined or eliminated completely. Under a unified empire, commerce flourished as expected, trading wide-ranging products and resources across the country. Merchant families were the wealthiest in the areas they lived. In business practice, an early merchant became the idol of later generations. He coined the famous rules in commerce for basic business operations. He advised that one needs to watch closely the change of situation, take up what others drop off, and give away what others want to take. This reflects the general rule of supply and demand. As people give up on certain goods, prices will drop, making it a chance to buy them cheap. When people demand certain goods, prices will go up, and you need to provide them with full capacity to make big sales. This rule clearly has something to do with stock and foreign exchange trading. Another early business strategist advised on the time of investment, saying that people should invest in boats during a drought and in carts during a flood. This unusual advice indicates that you should notice the cycles in the economy and make preparations for sales of goods at a later stage. The principle illustrated in these two examples of traditional wisdom is that you can get business opportunities if you move in a direction that is opposite to others' and spot the right place and time to invest. This is, of course, easier said than done.

By the time of Song China (960-1165 A.D.), commercialisation in China had reached new heights. The government collected more state tax revenues from commerce than from agriculture. This is the first time such a thing had happened. Another first is the wide use of paper money by traders and the populace . The Song economy began a mini industrial revolution, with China's iron production per head at a level higher than that in Europe in 1700. Widespread commercial activities gave rise to paper money and credit in business.

It is the common observation among academics that these Song initiatives faded after the Mongol rule, and successive dynasties turned to an inward policy and a culturally conservative approach in state rule. Even with these constraints, commerce and trade in China moved forward, especially during the prolonged peace of the Qing Dynasty. By 1800, China remained a major world producer and exporter. Trade was relatively free and in China's favour. Britain took a mere 4.3% of the world's total output, while China took 33.3%. Large quantities of goods made in China were exported to Europe under fair trading conditions (no one forced the Europeans to buy), while Britain suffered a shortage of silver to pay for these imports. It was precisely because of this free trade between China and Britain that imperial China enjoyed a healthy long-run trade surplus. As a result of this trade, the British resorted to using opium as a key export item to China and brute force to solve its dire problem of a trade deficit.

The people engaging in commerce in this pre-modern society exhibited extraordinary agility and resilience. The merchant class, while politically downgraded, made it up with efficient business running and profit making to accumulate their wealth. Many of the businesses were conducted nationwide, including long-distance trade and money lending. The famous Shanxi and Anhui merchants used their enormous savings to enter numerous business lines and financed expansion to two dozen provinces. The control by these merchant families over a variety of businesses continued for nearly 500 years, crossing two long imperial dynasties, and their financial strength faded only after the intrusion of modern Western banks in the later half of the nineteenth century.

We can say with certainty that while commerce was by and large neglected in imperial China, this simply gave merchants a chance to accumulate their wealth and exert their influence on the economy in other ways.

Business and Industries in Modern China

China staggered in the first encounter with modern Western powers and was forced to open doors to foreign businesses and industries. Chinese domestic businesses now faced more formidable competitors from outside and had to make drastic changes to meet the challenges. Along with government-sponsored industrialisation and modernisation, private businesses in China took up the opportunities to transform themselves into modern businesses and get into new types of market competition.

Adaptations to Western Influences and Fundamental Changes

The cultural shocks left deep impressions. Many recognised the urgency to change. In regard to Confucianism and traditions, there were conservatives and moderates, and a new thinking focused on the relationship between substance and function, a popular concept at that time. The Chinese values and heritage, including Confucianism and the imperial state, were regarded as **substance**, which would be upheld firmly. Western technology and industries were seen as **functions**, which could be introduced and utilised fully for the renewal and stability of the empire. The intention was to improve, progress and modify, with the help of applicable Western practices. This was the rationale behind early reforms in the old structure.

On state policies, there came government drives to make needed cultural changes:

❏ In contrast to old social stratifications, commerce and business became more acceptable and respected in the society. The previous lower status accorded to merchants was raised to a higher level.

❏ Official career paths spanned from being qualified Confucian scholars to accomplished businessmen. This happened towards the end of the Qing Dynasty in the late 1890s.

❏ Western-style business became more fashionable, and job and business opportunities attracted more recruits crossing over from the more traditional careers.

❏ Industrial development and projects, in particular, were recognised as the crucial means to achieve national survival and development. Industries thus received relatively more attention and support from the imperial government.

The business world adapted swiftly to cultural clashes and modern hardware. With growing familiarity with things foreign, they began to take advantage by introducing modern technologies and creating new wealth.

The new forces and sources of income in the economy include:

❏ new players: foreign firms (trading, manufacturing, finance);

❏ new industries: mining, railways, weapons, machine tools, cement, banking, etc;

❏ new production methods in old industries: textiles, shipping, staple foods, paper, etc.

The first generation of Chinese entrepreneurs with traditional beliefs **and** knowledge of modern industries emerged in the late 1890s. They were eager learners of Western methods of production and management and held a strong will to compete in the market with domestic and foreign firms. They were also devoted to maintaining Chinese characteristics (forms and practice) in their businesses.

Many modern Chinese industries and companies concentrated in Shanghai, an international city with various foreign influences. They had first-hand experience in dealing with Western businesses. One group of people who had such experience were dealers working for foreign firms, called "compradors", the equivalent of heads of representative offices of foreign companies in China today. They were better English speakers than other Chinese and had some Western education. Some of these compradors left to form their own companies and continued to trade with foreign partners. Another group of people was the native Chinese merchants, who found new ways of making money and invested in new commercial or industrial projects. They shifted from old business sectors to new ones with expansion and competition in mind.

The Rong Family of Shanghai

The Rong family has been a leading family of industrialists for generations. Their main businesses were textiles and foods (flour), being the leader in both sectors (accounting for 30% and 25% of total national output respectively) in the 1930s. The first generation of industrialists left the countryside in Jiangsu Province in 1886 and set up a small moneylending firm. As that business accumulated sufficient funds, they moved into the industrial sector and set up one of the first Chinese-owned flour plants. It was a common practice at that time to hire foreign technicians and import equipment from Western countries for the plant. Due to competition, they also had to periodically upgrade to more advanced technology and equipment. When these businesses succeeded, they expanded into other sectors such as paper-making and banking. At the peak, the family owned more than 30 factories in many cities. They prevailed in constant competition with domestic, Western and Japanese companies.

The Rong family also initiated many reforms in floor management within the company. The widely adopted foreman system in early industrialisation was revamped at factories owned by the family. Apart from agreeing on the fringe benefits provided to workers, employers usually needed to deal with issues of industrial relations. Since the foremen in those days acted as leaders of small unions, controlling varying numbers of workers, it is important for the employer to handle these foremen firmly so that the power they held over the workers was considerably reduced. In addition, the Rong family introduced the popular Taylor's management system and accounting practice to its factories.

The Rong family flourished in domestic industries and represents the course of transformation of Chinese enterprises from traditional to modern business. The family's business was interrupted by the Great Depression and the Anti-Japanese War (most of its factories in Shanghai were flattened by Japanese bombers). By the time of the communist victory in 1949, family members had fled mainland China. One member of this family stayed behind and endured the following political movements as a representative of either a reformed capitalist or a counter-revolutionary. After the reforms began, he remained active in political circles and was named Vice President of China at one time. His own family members moved to Hong Kong to develop new businesses and have joined the ranks of Hong Kong's tycoons, owning several blue chip listed companies. The sense of doing commercial business remains in the family's blood.

Early Chinese Bankers

Old Chinese financial institutions were money shops and networks. They resisted the intrusion of modern foreign banks in China, but were eventually replaced by mainstream banking businesses. New types of Chinese banks emerged, with a new generation of bankers. A prominent example was a Shanghai banker who controlled at least three private banks: the Zhejiang Industrial Bank, the Bank of Salt Industry and Jin Cheng Bank. These banks were regarded as best-managed, private Chinese banks, leading in introducing savings accounts, assets portfolios and other management practices. They lent primarily to domestic industrial companies, for example funding a Chinese chemical company in competition with ICI. They were also the first to introduce services such as credit background (or record) checking for risk assessment, traveller's cheques, etc. in China.

These trials of modern businesses and industries opened new fields in the economy and boosted economic growth at certain periods. They accumulated some vital early experience in doing business. These businesses operated under extremely difficult circumstances, having endured tight government controls, political pressures and foreign invasion. As the new communist state was established, many of these capitalist groups spread out to other parts of the world and continued their operations. As a Western observer comments: "The Shanghai millionaires who fled to Hong Kong in 1949 were China's financial brains and managerial elite, bankers and industrialists with generations of family and clan experience in economics. ... They were the first Chinese to master Western banking and commercial practices. ... You could tell at a glance that the Shanghai Boys were not from Hong Kong. They looked like Boston bankers starting over in Atlanta. ... They were more cultivated, more efficient, more elegant than the (local) Cantonese. ...".

Mixed Practices of Traditional and Modern Management

The early generations of Chinese industrialists experimented what was later called cross-cultural management, being the ones bearing traditions and accepting modern capitalist values. Their astute business sense enabled them to absorb Western business essentials quickly and compete with foreign players at the same time. The term Chinese industrialists here does not include those who made their riches with the help of their political background and business monopolies. The wealthiest families in pre-1949 China came from politically powerful ones, with government authority and economic monopolies. Private enterprises, as described earlier, relied on their own shrewdness and business instinct to survive and develop. Their management thinking and practice also reflects their ability to change along with time and move forward.

The traditional concepts of ethics, trust and righteousness were readily applied by the manufacturer industrialists in the running of their factories in the early twentieth century. In short, industrialists tried to perform the traditional role of benevolent rulers in their new industrial establishments. Some of the thinking and practices include:

❑ To win trust from customers and suppliers: It is claimed that "industrialists should have the manners of Confucian scholars, in order to establish good reputation and lead in the business sector."

❑ To treat customers with care : "Treat customers fair; take no extra profits above reasonable levels."

❑ To establish product and company brand: "It is a common rule that the longer a company runs, the better its reputation, the bigger its business grows, and the more customers come."

❑ To apply the Confucian saying in doing business: "What you don't want done to yourself, don't do to others."

Family Values

Family values formed the backbone of a family business in this period. They are shown in the following five aspects:

1. Trust within circles

   Employment is provided on the basis of relationships of various kinds, mainly family, village, hometown, province, dialects, etc. Family trust protects their common interests and prevents loss of benefits to competitors.

2. Business as family

   Employers are the ones to provide benefits for their workers. It was advocated that workers should "love the factory as one's own home, work hard, [be] loyal" and to reciprocate when care is shown by the employers.

   Certain fringe benefits were provided to all the workers to promote a sense of shared goals. These benefits included providing facilities such as canteens, dormitories, clinics and schools, as well as organising festivals, providing jobs for employees' children, even assisting in funeral arrangements should an employee die, etc.

   Shanghai banks even began the experiment of offering company shares to all employees. This fits well with the traditional belief of family business and with employee motivation theories of modern times as well. An early form of pension scheme was also implemented, which retained 10% of employees' salary and to which the bank contributed 10%. The total of this accumulated sum would be paid to bank employees at the time of their retirement. This is certainly a worthy trial of superannuation schemes now common in developed economies, comprising compulsory and voluntary contributions. Both of these experiments in Chinese businesses illustrate the vision and pragmatism of early industrialists.

3. Trust and reputation in business

   The Yong On Group was a major chain of department stores and also had textile factories in Shanghai and Hong Kong. The Group was owned by a single family. The initial capital for the business came from many sources: borrowing from relatives and huge loans from banks (HSBC and Standard Chartered) that were guaranteed by local business leaders. This is a usual way of fund raising for family businesses. A large part of this funding was possible based on the business trust the family had earned from early operations, and endorsements from other businesspeople were invaluable for getting bank credit. Some of the money was borrowed from people who knew about this family only through word of mouth.

4. Face and social status

    These two ideas played a key role in doing business and the Jin Cheng Bank in Shanghai used them to its advantage. The bank devised ways to capitalise on people's subconscious concern about their social status and wanting to be treated differently from others. Big clients of the bank received special treatments, such as being welcomed by bank managers themselves, having their own room for doing transactions, and receiving other personalised services. Thus, clients would keep returning to enjoy these privileges.

5. Combining the advantages of both cultures

    Early Chinese industrialists found themselves doing business in an economy of mixed cultures, and they had the opportunity to compare both Chinese and Western ways of business and management. One of them made an observation: "I have compared especially European and American business management. While accepting their principles, I would not accept their methods wholesale. Each country has its own business and commercial background, its own social characteristics. People who excel in learning should grasp the essences, but not copy the forms and modes strictly."

The early Chinese industrialists opened a path for many Chinese family businesses in later periods. Old Chinese traditions still played a key role in their life and business, and surprisingly they did not impede their management and operations in general. With new business opportunities being created by industrial production and capital markets, these industrialists found there was new wealth to be made and gained huge profits in new lines of business. Even in the depressing state of political turmoil and war wreckage, these businesses struggled along and sustained their productive life.

Overseas Chinese Business Culture

Overseas Chinese refers to Chinese outside mainland China. A narrower application includes Hong Kong, Macau and Taiwan, while a wider definition includes those Chinese outside these three territories, in areas such as Singapore, other Southeast Asian countries and Chinese communities the world over. The majority of them work in small businesses or education, but a number of them have established huge businesses in various countries. Their business skills and management experience are well known. Under different business and legal environments, major overseas Chinese corporations have achieved business successes and thus sound financial status.

Case: Li Ka Shing and Hutchison

In 1978, bad management and low profits plagued Hutchison, the biggest, listed British company in Hong Kong, and the mammoth HSBC (the leading Hong Kong bank which had a considerable shareholding in Hutchison) was looking for candidates to take over the troubled company. Li Ka Shing, with his Cheung Kong Group, was selected. HSBC sold its shares in Hutchison to Li, and with Li's own purchase of more shares (for a total of 40%) from the market, he became the biggest shareholder of Hutchison, which made it possible for Li to put Hutchison under his own company's control. This is the first time a native Chinese business had acquired a famed British conglomerate in this British colony. The tide did change at last, making it possible to give favours to local Chinese businessmen, who for over a century had had to endure many implicit mistreatments in business and see precious business opportunities go to corporations owned by their British masters. With the rising power of mainland China and with the approaching of 1997, the British colonial authorities finally relented and began to let Hong Kong Chinese businesses have a bigger share of commercial gains. The scenario of HSBC allowing and financing a takeover of Hutchison by a local Chinese firm would have been unthinkable in earlier times. After this sensational takeover of a huge British company, Li successfully built up his reputation and established his business empire in Hong Kong. And business deals became much easier to do after this turning point. Soon enough, it was the British newspapers' turn to complain loudly that the Hong Kong economy was now in the hands of a small group of tycoons, this time not British, but local Chinese. By the early twenty-first century, the Li family is controlling two blue chip, heavyweight, listed companies, Hutchison and Cheung Kong, and numerous other listed and unlisted companies.

The Li magic is not confined to the enormous wealth he holds. His agility in adapting to new trends is also well known. Li's deal with European telecommunication giants makes a particular point. He sold his Orange shares and related 3G interests for a US$14.6 billion profit in 1999. At the height of the dot.com frenzy, Li also set up a new subsidiary company Tom.com. Although many dot.com companies collapsed when the bubble burst, Tom.com survived by making a critical transformation into a media business and expanding into the lucrative mainland China market.

The expansion of Li's business worldwide has created a huge stir as well as generated loathing from competitors and political opponents. Fear and paranoia about Li's business successes have led to misguided public perceptions. In the words of an American politician: A bid by Li's Hutchison on leases to the Panama Canal would make the US navy vulnerable to threats and blockades from the Chinese government, since Hutchison is an arm of the People's Liberation Army and the Chinese Communist Party will be working with the company to steal US intelligence at these ports.

As the richest man in Hong Kong, and perhaps in Asia, Li exemplifies traditional Chinese characteristics in many aspects. His lifestyle is simple and minimalist as he wears inexpensive wristwatches and plain suits. His funding for education and charity is well known, especially the huge donations which created a completely new university in Shantou (formerly Swatow). Following Confucian traditions whereby subjects are to be cared for by rulers, the employees of his companies receive good benefits, and loyalty is persistently fostered. When one of his sons sacked a considerable number of employees, due to the dot.com bubble burst and mismanagement, Li Junior was roundly criticised in the media for breaking the rules and acting unlike Li Senior, who always shows benevolence and concern to company workers.

Common Traits Among Overseas Chinese Businessmen

Maintaining traditional Chinese culture as the backbone: This is applied in business, social life and survival of their ethnic groups. The culture provides an adhesive for Chinese ethnic communities overseas, especially in societies where Chinese migrants as minority groups are under the rule of the majority ethnic group and are often deliberately marginalised. An example of this marginalisation is the official ban on using the Chinese language in public education of Chinese children in certain places. On these occasions, common Chinese cultural background provides needed support, and ethnic networks and connections serve as a guarantee of cooperation for reaching set business goals. As shown in the Li Kashing case, local Hong Kong businessmen offered invaluable help to Li's final bid for Hutchison, in terms of share transactions and moral support.

Family business is the main form of businesses, and this seldom changes to other forms, such as completely public companies or companies with external directors. The reliance on ethnic and community bonds in business operations is common, with businesses organising themselves into tight mutual aid associations. The authority of top management remains in the hands of family members. The nature of a family business does not change when part of the business is listed on the stock exchange. Both listed and non-listed companies come under the structure of this family business and under the management of the family head. Chinese family businesses control listed companies through majority shareholding. In those listed companies, the family business is responsible for company performance and returns to shareholders. The family business as a whole coordinates the operations of both listed and non-listed companies. Li Kashing and his sons control huge publicly listed Hong Kong companies and also manage many of their own non-listed companies.

Younger generations of Chinese obtained more extensive education in the West and gained a deeper understanding of Western business and management ethics. This provided them with a mix of Chinese and Western thinking, and added flexibility. Even within Chinese business, there is also the practice of adopting some Western methods and modifying Chinese traditions. In the case of Li Kashing, both of his top listed companies hire large numbers of professionals, and chief executives of these two companies often come from outside the family. In the media company his second son created, the current chief executive is a financial whiz originally from mainland China. All of these introductions of talents and Western management practices, however, do not change the Li family's ownership and control of the group company.

Issues Concerning Chinese Family Businesses

In regard to family businesses in China, it is worth noting the following points:

1. Most businesses in market economies around the world are in fact family businesses. This is simply due to the fact that as a small business with a single owner grows bigger, the control by this owner's family continues. There are indeed newly opened businesses being initiated by two or more partners, especially in professional fields, such as law firms or clinics, and during the dot.com period; yet large numbers of new businesses are opened by a single family.

2. Family businesses in general can last a long time, be flexible to changes and become well established. Large numbers of European companies are family businesses, such as those owned by the Prime Minister of Italy, Mr. Silvio Berlusconi, and they hold on to family traditions while retaining control. On the other side of the Atlantic, family business is common in the US, such as the Sears family and the Rockefeller family. It is in the public share offering process (being listed at the stock exchanges) and in introducing strategic partners that family businesses lose strict control over their companies and have the exterior appearance of a family-owned business toned down as well.

3. To help family businesses manage and expand their operations, they can turn to modern practices of recruitment and headhunting to find capable top executives to run their operations, domestic or global. Numerous motivation tools, such as salary packages with fringe benefits and stock options, are used to lure the needed talents. In this way, the family will not lose control over the company.

4. Under the Chinese culture, family business fits well with the Confucian ideal of the family being at the centre of the society and of all activities, and the cohesion from family ties within a company will provide stability to the business, especially during the initial years.

5. Chinese family businesses normally face problems on three fronts. The first are problems in the process of transition towards a situation in which firm family control remains while the business is open to market competition and successfully draws on outside talents. Second, there are problems in handling the growing size of their business. Small businesses are easier to handle and manage well with family help, while a larger company requires more personnel. This would require wider hiring range and searching for talents. There are also compatibility questions between the

capability of family members and the more challenging tasks ahead. These are closely linked with the first type of transition problem. Third, certain traditions may act as restraints on business expansion. For example, the Chinese idea of *yuan* may limit the range of businesses a company can do, since this tradition requires a satisfactory impression of the other company's boss before the talk of a partnership can even start. Therefore, business deals may be contained in a small circle. This has put great pressure on the head of the family to constantly make crucial judgements by himself.

Chinese Businesses on the Mainland

Since the beginning of the reforms, certain Chinese values have re-emerged on the mainland, under a changing environment and relaxed political situation.

1. Family values have become important again in business and life, and its existence significantly weakened collective thinking which dominated the previously socialist state.

2. People relations, in the forms of *guanxi* and connections, now play a key role in linking people and doing business, in a stark contrast to the previous period when relations were determined by revolutionary orientations. The five relationships in Confucianism continue to guide people.

3. Trust and local bonds are in fashion again, and business can be done smoothly between people with bonds or ties formed when they were classmates, in the military service, came from the same home region or village, etc.

4. Profit comes as a high priority in business, after a period of planned economy and production to meet quotas. Like merchants of old, personal wealth, savings and worship of good fortune return as common beliefs of Chinese businessmen on the mainland, perhaps even more so than before. Financial incentives, creativity and drive are more widely applied, forcing people to devise new ways to compete and increase their earnings.

5. *Feng shui* and other superstitions re-surfaced from past sweeping campaigns, and mainland Chinese businessmen started to warm up to these secular traditions in their business and life. It is for the

good of their business to have omens, and good signs, numbers, dates and formations all begin to indicate future prospects in some mysterious ways.

6. In Chinese personnel management, it is common that face saving, harmony and avoidance of overt conflicts play important roles in interpersonal relationships. Reciprocity (another version of *bao*) is the rule, under which employees are expected to be thankful for job opportunities and promotion, and their hard work is demanded in return. Employers and the top management also adopt an authoritarian style with employees.

7. In strategic business decisions, risk aversion and cautious moves are typical, and the emphasis is on consensus among peers. Reliance is put on intuition rather than on meticulous information collection and calculations.

As advocated by Neo-Confucianism from the 1970s, Chinese characteristics hold certain benefits for the economy and doing business. These are proved by recent success stories of a number of Chinese companies competing with foreign multinationals in domestic and overseas markets, in particular in the household appliances industry. The benefits are highlighted in a comparison with the performance of foreign multinationals, after taking into account Western culture and management style. Many believe that re-discovered cultural values hold some relevance even to doing business in the twenty-first century.

Related Chinese culture values include:

❑ Loyal to leaders/superiors: This loyalty in the imperial era was towards the rulers. In modern-day business, this may be seen as discipline required for team work. Loyalty enhances cohesion and respect towards the leader. In an age of free-flowing labour markets and sometimes high turnover rates, loyalty is a highly regarded quality of employees. As shown in some large Chinese companies, such as Haier, loyalty equals stability of the workforce and smooth running of business operations.

❑ Hardworking or industrious: This refers to the quality of labour. The industriousness has to be demonstrated at work, so that average productivity and quality control can reach desirable levels.

❑ Respect for officialdom: The old tradition made officialdom the only desirable career path. This tradition now can be transferred to a respect for education that produces high-calibre technocrats for economic management. The examples of Singapore and Taiwan are often cited as support for the relevance of this heritage.

❑ Adaptable to the environment: This point is particularly acute in the world today, where environmental protection underlies major government policies. The most relevant thinking comes from Daoism, which sees the universe as a self-propelled and natural course not to be disturbed or manipulated by humans. This is in stark contrast to the belief of invincibility of modern sciences to change the world at will. The concept of *wu wei* would be relevant to the current situation of waste and damage to the environment.

❑ Thrift: This Chinese tradition leads to high saving rates and the presence of sufficient private funds in the economy, benefiting the financing of major works and projects. This has been regarded as a major factor contributing to the steady growth of East Asian economies in past decades. The nature of these economies is vastly different from that of consumption-induced developed economies. A counter argument is that excessive savings result in less efficient investment and lower productivity. It is also suggested that economies under the influence of Chinese culture should consume more, in order to lift demand and increase GDP. Regardless, personal savings have helped finance many small Chinese businesses to start up their operations.

Socialist Culture in State Sectors

There are still state sectors and enterprises in this economy under the influence of a different culture, namely the socialist culture, rather than the traditional Chinese one. Their co-existence indicates certain compatibilities while revealing other differences.

Although state business and enterprises have grown more competitive and market savvy than a decade ago, they maintain certain values and practices of their own. Top among the characteristics prevalent under this political culture is public control of means of production (ownership). The State Assets Commission is in charge of this task and state enterprises bear the responsibility of keeping their assets intact. This requirement may have put constraints on them and caused them to miss some business opportunities.

They follow the egalitarian doctrine in socialism, and workers' pay and benefits are guaranteed. However, job security has been eroded rapidly, following several years of restructuring of state enterprises. Those left unemployed after the restructuring of state enterprises are still the focus of assistance from governments at all levels.

State enterprise employees, in general, hold a lethargic attitude towards innovation and rewards. Their work has been routinely assigned, and on the basis of equality they do not need to work any harder than the others. The system encourages a collective effort to reach certain targets, rather than individual initiative and extra effort. On the same basis, there is a common disdain of profits and wealth. This affects both employees and the management.

Some common characteristics in management:

❑ Chiefs of state enterprises on average earn much less than those in other types of businesses. Incentives prove insufficient to encourage better performance from them. Their main goal is to keep the status quo, rather than run a profitable corporation. Other priorities, such as securing a political career, promotion and secured retirement, occupy much of their time. This mentality derives from the appointment system of state enterprises, especially large ones.

❑ State enterprises commonly lack long-term planning and strategies. Their work is handed down from government bureaux in charge, and their own input is limited. For the same reason, they are unable to establish an effective and unique corporate culture for the enterprises under their charge.

❑ It is a typical practice under the appointment system that state enterprises depend heavily on the CEO's own capabilities. A company can thrive and be profitable under one energetic leader, but do badly under another. While large numbers of state enterprises suffer from losses and shrinking market shares, a number of state enterprises could be super competitive and market leaders. The difference lies in the capabilities of the leader of a particular company.

Private Businesses

Private business is in contrast to the state enterprises discussed above and collective businesses which represent collective interests of a particular group. Private business implies an individual's ownership and legal status in a business environment. Family business is also a non-state owned business and can be placed in the category of private business. It differs from business partnerships or shareholding companies and stresses on family ownership. A further discussion on business types in China is in Part II, Chapter 5.

Private and family businesses have gained strength in China since the 1990s. These are new forces in the economy and also the ones bearing marks of cultural heritage from the past. In the long run, private businesses will hold a majority share in the economy, and family businesses will be in the mainstream, similar to those overseas.

Case: The Hope Group

This involves a Liu family of four brothers from the inland province of Sichuan. Their Group company is the top private company in China (in market capitalisation), and *Forbes* magazine in 1995 ranked the brothers as the richest mainland Chinese. From a humble start in the feed industry, they are now the leader in that industry, with over 100 factories across the country, while their businesses have expanded into many other industries.

The Hope Group holds on to the traditional ways of doing business—keeping low profit margins. The feed industry is known for its low margin, and it is hard even to maintain it at a 5% level. Hope makes profits at such a level through cost-cutting, fund roll-over and quick asset accumulation. The Group company is still a first-generation family business, without the immediate worrying issue of transition and passing of authority on to a younger generation or to non-family business leaders.

Characteristics of the Liu family business:

- This is a typical Chinese family business, with little Western influence on management style or business operations. The direction of the company is decided by these four brothers
- A listed company of all the Liu family businesses, bearing the Hope name, is securely controlled by the family, with exclusive decision-making power and flexible investment strategies lying in the four brothers. While they bear their responsibilities to the shareholders of that listed company, they are free to pursue their other business goals in their own family companies.
- Professional managers are hired and allowed to run operations, but they do not share top authority and company assets. So far, non-family members have not gained inroads into the core leadership of the Group.

Liu Yongxing is the chairman of the Group company, at a nominally higher level than his brothers who take up chairmanships of their own separate companies. As such, he also serves as the chairman for the listed company within the structure of Hope Group. He discloses some of his views on life and business as follows:

- "Wealth does not bother me, I am now wearing a shirt of just 35 yuan."
- "I am going to leave just enough money to my children, to make them work harder."
- "To maintain a family business for many generations, company heads should keep learning and improving their own management skills."
- "If company heads are not able to do the job right, they need to hire the best from outside", but he did not elaborate if those from outside can control the company' assets.
- "A listed company bears a lot of responsibilities, and this is not a place to funnel money from small investors to our own companies (like some other listed companies did in China). That is against my **conscience** and basic values accepted by most people." He is referring to his role in that listed company as being different from that in his other sub-companies. Extra considerations are required in regard to the interest of shareholders of the listed company, unlike in his own family enterprises.

By and large, Hope Group is a family business similar to many Hong Kong companies. It is still a private owned business facing fewer constraints than many mainland state enterprises. It is a Chinese company with strong traditions and values, yet it is open to market challenges and opportunities.

A Summary on Chinese Culture and Business

1. Chinese culture is essentially not a closed one, its flexibility arising from its belief in the concept of harmony. It encourages absorbing desirable elements of other cultures, as in the case of native Chinese Buddhism.

2. In a market economy, companies under this culture are able to seek business opportunities quickly and compete effectively. This has been shown in examples of overseas Chinese businesses and some mainland Chinese companies.

3. Some characteristics of Chinese management styles are determined more by the external business environment and market conditions, rather than distinctive Chinese behaviours. An example is the

lethargic attitude towards innovation and rewards, which came about under the influence of a socialist egalitarian system, rather than being a phenomenon of extensive commercial activities under Confucian doctrines of the imperial era.

4. Past wisdoms on doing business and on managing organisations still hold relevance in China today, as running state affairs bears many similarities to running a commercial organisation.

5. The traditional emphasis of Chinese culture on people and relations could help solve internal conflicts and reduce tension in organisations. In this respect, the concepts of the "Mean", harmony and Buddhist mediation provide useful references.

6. The common practice in China since the 19th century has been to adopt Western management sciences in operations and to apply Chinese management philosophies in business running, that is, a managed combination of two approaches. The crucial difference is that Western management sciences focus on proper practice and exact mechanisms for a smooth operation. These are system- or procedure-related issues in micromanagement. Chinese management thinking, on the other hand, focuses on the entirety of an organisation, be it a state or a firm. This thinking takes the relations and balances as the most important consideration and strives to make fine tuning of the whole structure. It also emphasises the people factor, declaring managing people adequately as the ultimate goal in management. This thinking tends to lean towards macromanagement, holding *wu wei* as the desirable approach, preferring delegation, and dismissing a laborious leadership style and close supervision. The difference between the two approaches is that between the science and philosophy of management. Experiences of early modern Chinese industrialists have proved the possibility of merging these two kinds of thinking into a successful business operation.

7. In general, decision making in Chinese enterprises, state or private, typically means "the final say by a single person". This involves authority and an autocratic rule in organisations. There is less genuine trust in and delegation to managers at lower levels, and top executives hold absolute authority. Liu Chuanzhi, the successful business leader of Legend, the number one computer company in China, described how he ran the place with an iron fist. He admitted

that he is a strictly authoritarian manager. It was top-down all the way (in Legend). True to his words, Liu selected a younger manager Yang Yuanqing and named him his successor as chief executive of this gigantic company. Yang, thus, must satisfy Liu's own criteria in leadership qualities, management philosophies, shared goals, etc. For this top-down work and leadership style, top managers are often troubled by routine matters passed over by lower-level managers, who may harbour fears of making decisions or changes.

8. The majority of companies in mainland China may follow the examples of successful Hong Kong companies in management styles, while a number of leading state enterprises may follow the examples of foreign multinationals in operations. This is due to the general trend under which family businesses will become the main form of business. Established private businesses will eventually become family controlled businesses, and business founders choose to pass the overall ownership and authority to their family successors, even if they own a number of publicly listed companies. Hong Kong companies provide certain easy-to-copy models to mainland Chinese businesses. Large state enterprises are going to grow into world-class conglomerates, with market leading positions and supports of various kinds from the government. Some of the state-run corporations are already in the list of top 500 world companies, as estimated in assets and output, and their efficiency can improve along with vigorous applications of proven Western management practices.

Key Concepts

Social stratifications in pre-modern China

Substance and function

Family values and family business

Overseas Chinese

Neo-Confucianism

Socialist culture

Private business

Listed/public companies

Discussion **Questions**

1. How does one best relate Confucian ideas to business and management of modern-day corporations? Which of the traditional ideas of administration may be compatible with contemporary management concepts? On this point, present your views on the difference(s) between Western management sciences and Chinese management philosophy.
2. What are the reasons for eradicating Chinese traditions while implementing socialism on the mainland? Why did communist leaders also see traditional Chinese culture as an impediment to approaching a modern society?
3. Is the traditional concept of substance and function still applicable these days? What would be the substance and what would be the function in China today? What are the effective ways to make a new system work under certain cultural traditions?
4. Overseas Chinese business presents examples of a right mix of Chinese culture and Western technology and management. Debate on this observation.

Related **Readings**

Bergere, Marie-Claire, *The Golden Age of the Chinese Bourgeoisie: 1911-1937*, Cambridge, Cambridge University Press, 1989.

Brook, Timothy and Gregory Blue (eds.), *China and Historical Capitalism: Genealogies of Sinological Knowledge*, Cambridge, Cambridge University Press, 1999.

Haley, George Chin Tan and Usha Haley, *New Asian Emperors: The Overseas Chinese, Their Strategies and Competitive Advantages*, Oxford, Butterworth/Heinemann, 1998.

Hamilton, Gary (ed.), *Business Networks and Economic Development in East and Southeast Asia*, Hong Kong, Centre of Asian Studies, University of Hong Kong Press, 1991.

Hsu, I, *The Rise of Modern China*, New York, Oxford University Press, 6th ed. 1999.

Limlingan, V. S, *The Overseas Chinese in ASEAN: Business Strategies and Management practices*, Manila, Vita Development Corp., 1986.

Seagrave, Sterling, *Lords of the Rim: the Invisible Empire of the Overseas Chinese*, London, Corgi Books, 1997.

Spence, Jonathan, *The Search for Modern China*, London, Hutchinson, 1990.

Wang, Gungwu, *China and the Chinese Overseas*, Hong Kong, Commercial Press, 1991, in particular chapters 10 and 14.

Weinshall, Theodore D. (ed.), *Culture and Management: Selected Readings*, Harmondsworth, Penguin Books, 1977.

3

National Structures and Conditions

*T*his chapter is to examine the business environment in general terms, and China's national structures and economic conditions, including production and consumption. The aim is to present a macroview of the economy and megatrends of momentum. It is for individual companies to draw their own conclusions on investment in China, taking references from available headline figures.

Introduction to Business Environment

A business environment depends on various conditions in a particular economy and is closely linked with the state of ongoing operations of foreign enterprises. One key **objective** in studying a particular business environment is to be able to make the right judgements and decisions in investment and commercial operations. This is especially critical in this age of globalisation with corporations relentlessly trying to improve their efficiency on a global scale. Business people are usually familiar with the business environment at home. On entering overseas markets, however, this familiarity may give them a certain false sense of confidence and lead them to take for granted the ways of doing business in another economy. But they will need to go through a learning curve before they are able to fully appreciate the divergent nature of a relatively "alien" business environment and grow accustomed to handling situations well.

A study of a certain business environment has to be undertaken before any business planning is under way. This learning of an environment involves the basics, essentials and principles of doing business in that environment. The scope of such learning is wider than normal business analysis and often relates to non-economic factors and forces. The top priority is to identify rules, and if no clear rules exist in some circumstances, how that local economy is run and what approaches local businesses adopt. In this regard, business executives will have to face certain complex issues and gain an understanding of social mechanisms, in particular political forces that bear heavily on economic directions and business operations. While foreign multinationals have enormous resources for their entry into a new overseas market, their continued success there, however, may be constantly tested and failures are not rare. A key notion is that a successful business model at home may not be transplanted directly and smoothly to an overseas market.

Analysis of Business Environment

A comprehensive analysis of business environment serves to assess various business prospects for a corporation that wants to decide on its expansion strategy and market entry. These prospects will include:

1. Opportunities and risks

   It assesses in general terms whether market potential and business opportunities do exist in that market and will help the corporation to decide on the issue of entry. An analysis will seek information on trends of economic growth, political stability and directions, population and consumption, etc., from which to generate macro projections on business potential and expected returns. A growth market is always attractive to a corporation seeking expansion. For a balanced assessment, however, risks in making business deals over there must also be illustrated. This is not easy to do because either there are many unclear signals in a foreign market or those analyses undertaken are not able to detect and explain many uncertainties. There are no definitive analyses, and numbers sometimes do not present the full picture. There are bound to be contradictory optimistic and pessimistic estimates for making an entry decision. In short, analyses of opportunities and risks depend heavily on the degree of understanding of that business environment.

2. Economic efficiency

    This refers to efficiency in economic systems, in business transactions, and rate of returns on investment. It asks questions such as how efficiently the economy is run, what the costs of doing regular business are, how efficiently do government bureaux cope with procedures and administration governing business, and granting of permits and approvals, how freely capital and money flow in and out of the country, how much do tax regimes encourage people doing business, how transparent business information is, how speedy and clearly business disputes are settled at courts, etc. All these are undoubtedly major issues in an analysis of business environment, and they show the degree of market openness and the roles played by other systems, such as legal and policy making, in the economy.

3. Social efficiency

    This refers to common attitudes and behaviour patterns in a particular society, which may promote or discourage business activities. It covers social and cultural customs among different peoples and nations, and customs that have been built up and passed on for centuries. The enormous influence of these customs on a business environment are not to be lightly treated or dismissed, since some stubborn resistance from social customs have caused surprising outcomes for foreign companies operating in a different culture. A telling example is how the Indian holy worship of cows has ejected some American food giants—those relying on set menus using mostly beef—from that market.

    These differences in social customs existed even among Western economies. For example, Western European countries and the United States have different views on the purposes of doing business and on social welfare. The United States companies emphasise absolute efficiency and productivity, with their singular goal being to reach the number one spot in whatever business they are in. However, Western European countries take business gains as one way to lift their living standards, and social and personal welfare stand high on their agenda. They pay great attention to their social benefits, guaranteed state assistance and long holidays. Due to this general attitude, they maintain minimum wages, expect to receive company-paid holidays and overtime pay, and the governments and unions manage to prevent unreasonable and unfair dismissal of employees. As a result, Western European economies have had lower productivity levels and are less efficient in business than their US counterparts, but their satisfaction level and quality of life are high. This difference can be illustrated by Figure 3.1 showing a production possibilities frontier (**PPF**) curve. In economics principles, a PPF curve shows a position where an economy stands after balancing its total production capacity and the costs of reaching that level. Between maximum output and maximum leisure, Western Europe and the United States have chosen different approaches based on their own social customs and philosophies.

Another way to see the social efficiency issue is to compare cultural differences between societies, such as those between mainland China and Western countries. These refer to attitudes and social behaviour that are related to business activities and impact on social efficiency. For example, a mid-day nap was common for employees at government departments and enterprises

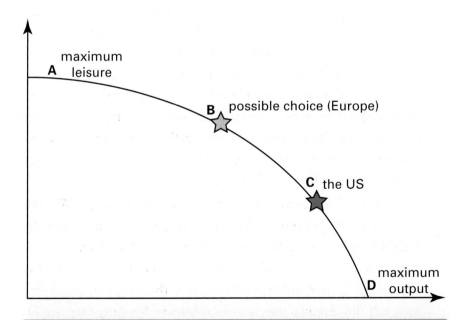

Figure 3.1   PPF: Trade-off between real GDP and leisure

in pre-reform China. This has been drastically changed during the reform years due to the push for modernisation and the desire to adopt Western-style management models quickly. A mid-day nap is now widely regarded as a waste of time and a sign of inefficiency. There are now, however, still some cases in Shenzhen and Guangdong province where certain Hong Kong companies allow employees to have a nap of one to two hours each day. The level of performance of employees after their nap is surprisingly high, and they are more energetic for the whole afternoon shift than if they were to forego their nap. A short workplace snooze is allowed by some American companies, based on the belief that a tired worker is an unproductive worker, while the custom of 'siesta' remains common in continental European countries. People practicing this hold the view that a mid-day nap reduces stress and tension, and improves overall productivity.

Major Aspects in an Analysis of a Business Environment

These six factors are usually considered in an analysis on business environment.

Demographics

This looks at the population which is further divided into segments such as urban/rural, age groups, sex, etc. The figures in a demographic study have two definite implications for business strategies: one is an indication of the target market (number of consumers, market potential, income-earning groups), and the other is that of labour (labour supply, wages and costs). A higher level of income for resident groups indicates more consumption and therefore sales potential, while this also points to dearer labour costs for employers. A higher percentage of urban residents would also indicate more sales opportunities and more effective intensive sales campaigns.

Political Aspects

This covers the nature of political entity (democratic, authoritarian, or dictatorial), political structures (centralisation, federation, autonomy or colonial), political stability (power transfer, leadership quality, national cohesion, popularity of policies, etc.), political balances (power balance among political parties or groups, civic groups, non-government forces and public opinion, which would express views on related issues and exert a certain pressure on the ruling government and its policies), and efficiency of state apparatus.

Legal Aspects

This is concerned with clearly defined legal structures and authorities, degree of independence of legal systems from state intervention, rule of law and its acceptance by the population, established laws regarding business and property ownerships, efficient and clean legal offices (courts and prosecutors), efficient execution by law enforcement offices (police bureaux), etc.

Social-cultural Aspects

This refers to common social customs and behaviours, attitudes towards savings and consumption, income, wealth and poverty, social welfare and equality, labour mobility, public education and literacy, religions, roles of public media, civic groups and special interest groups, citizens' participation, nationalism, etc.

Technological Aspects

This covers government policies on hi-tech industries, tertiary education, science and technology research, creativity and invention, patents and intellectual property rights, industrial bases, applied science in production and industries, skills and quality of the workforce, transfer of foreign technology, etc.

Environmental Aspects

This is concerned with natural resources and raw materials for industrial production, consumption requirements for essentials such as crude oil, minerals and water, exploration and conservation for sustainable development, import/export of major types of resources, pollution and waste management, recycling policies, etc. For companies that set up factories in other countries, there are perhaps particular concerns about environmental restrictions from the host country.

Impact of Business Environment

Changes in the business environment will have a considerable impact on all businesses within an economy. Changes of different natures will have varied levels of impact.

Affecting All Businesses

This happens when there are changes in national policies and laws, or when formal treaties are signed with multilateral organisations and with world bodies. A good example is China's entry to the WTO. People used to assess the impact of this entry on a few domestic industries, based on the items involved in China's commitments to the world trade body. They have since come to realise that the decision to join the WTO involves much more than initially expected, and this change has caused chain reactions to many industries. Eventually, this may fundamentally change the way of doing business in China.

Affecting Specific Industries

This happens when particular industrial policies and regulations are implemented, or when there are new rules set out by regulating authorities, increased market competition, newly emerged industries and products which offer new opportunities, shifting and changed consumption patterns, etc. For example, a new policy from the Ministry of Information Industries in Beijing on whether to charge two-way or one-way fees on mobile phone users directly affects the profit projections of several giant Chinese telecommunications companies and their overseas investors. Similarly, the arrival of short message service has been a much-needed boost to major Internet service providers in China, as it had come when these companies were on the brink of collapse due to the dot.com bubble burst.

Affecting Particular Companies

This relates to the micro economic area of business, and is closely linked with enterprise management, market competition in a particular region and different business strategies of individual companies. Even if domestic and foreign companies are operating in the same industry and same region, the outcomes can be quite different. It is crucial for business managers to recognise the changes in the environment and respond swiftly, grabbing emerging opportunities and avoiding incoming risks. A major change in the environment, such as China's WTO accession, may herald intensified market competition and demand drastic turns in business strategies. As shown in case studies and examples in this book, under similar business environments and government policies, individual companies could take widely different strategies and options in their operations and subsequently reach different end results of success or failure.

National Structures of China

Let us begin with a brief historical background of China's political system.

China has a long history that is similar to the Middle Ages of Europe. The imperial periods lasted over 2,000 years, and the modern history of China is marked by several key years.

❑ 1840: the first Opium War with Britain, which opened the country to Western influence;

❑ 1911: the Nationalist Revolution, which ended imperial dynasties and established the first Republic;

❑ 1949: the Communist Revolution, which saw the Communist Party gain ruling power and establishing the People's Republic;

❑ 1978: the beginning of reforms, which charted the course towards remarkable economic growth in China today.

Political Structures and Mechanisms

The administration of mainland China rests in the hands of the central government, whose organisations have been established and constantly retooled, and whose authority extended to the far corners of the country.

Administratively, China is divided into three categories, namely provinces, autonomous regions and municipalities. There are 22 provinces, five autonomous regions and four directly administered municipalities (namely Beijing, Tianjin, Shanghai and Chongqing), with over 2,500 counties and over 1 million villages. China has two special administrative regions (SARs), Hong Kong and Macau which were handed back by the United Kingdom and Portugal respectively. The region of Taiwan is another territory of China, its separation from the mainland being the result of civil wars of the late 1940s. The defeated Nationalist government ran Taiwan's affairs till a pro-independence political party took over in 2000. In international affairs, Taiwanese authorities held the seat of China at the United Nations until the mainland government (the People's Republic of China) took over the seat in 1972. The central government in Beijing has made numerous official proposals to reach eventual unification in future. It remains to be seen whether Taiwan will become another SAR of China or be swept away by local independence movements.

At the national level, the **three bodies** of modern politics perform separate functions. In most countries, these refer to the legislative, executive and judiciary bodies. The legislative body may be referred to as Parliament, Congress, Assembly, Council, etc. in different countries. This body comes to form through elections, selections or appointments, depending on the political systems. The executive body is what is usually referred to as the government and it runs the country. Its heads are elected or selected, while its apparatus are filled with unelected staff. The executive body represents the nation and is responsible for its national and foreign affairs. The judiciary body consists of courts, prosecutors and police departments. There are also clear separations in the roles played by these three organs of the judiciary body.

China's current political structures are similar in form, consisting of the three arms of the central government. Although there is a variety of interpretations of role separations among these three arms in a socialist China, there are noticeable boundaries between them, and each has its own functions (see Figure 3.2).

The Legislative Body—The National People's Congress

The National People's Congress (NPC) is the highest level legislative institution in China, with its clout increasing in recent decades.

The NPC convenes annual Congress meetings regularly in the early half of the year, with all representatives (delegates) attending to perform the required functions. Each annual meeting deals with a number of proposals, amendments and tasks, and the meeting normally lasts about two weeks.

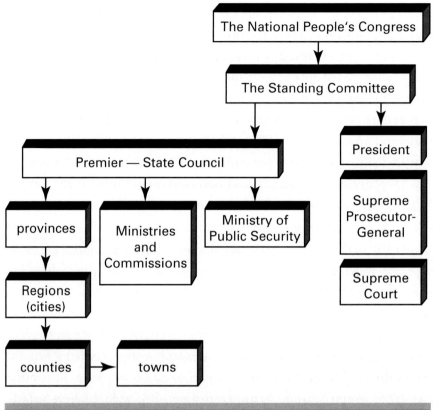

Figure 3.2   State legislative, executive and judiciary bodies

The major **functions** of the National People's Congress include the following:

❑   revise and amend the Constitution;
❑   pass laws;
❑   approve the appointment and dismissal of key government leaders, such as the President and Premier;
❑   approve national budgets and economic plans (such as five-year plans);
❑   rectify international treaties and declare wars.

The Constitution of China contains the foundation of legitimacy and guiding principles of the country. It is subject to revisions and amendments passed by the Congress, and there are four versions to date, namely 1954, 1975, 1978, and 1982 versions.

The 1954 version of the Constitution provides vital premises for the founding and running of the People's Republic and contains both socialist and moderate elements. The 1975 version reflects truthfully the impact of the Cultural Revolution and radical communist ideals, and it repudiated many moderate elements in the previous version. The 1978 version was rushed through to re-establish an accepted model of socialist nation without the radical elements prevalent in the 1975 version. The 1982 version reflects the ongoing comprehensive reforms and further eradicates radical communist ideas that contradict the guidelines of reforms towards modernisation. Thereafter, the Congress has yet to pass any new version of the Constitution, and changes have been made chiefly in the form of amendments and provisions to the 1982 version as situations evolve.

The representatives of the NPC are called delegates. They come from all districts and all walks of life. The basic yardstick is that each delegate comes from a district with a certain number of residents, similar to an electoral district in the West. District delegates first gather as a regional group before moving to Beijing for the meeting. Apart from this district selection, there are other categories of delegates that represent particular groups, such as the military, professional bodies, ethnic minorities and overseas Chinese. Those categories are similar to the professional sectors in the Legislative Council of Hong Kong. Currently there are about 3,000 national delegates of the Congress, with estimated ratios of one delegate for 240,000 urban residents and one for 960,000 rural residents.

The selection of delegates is a mixed process, with candidates selected on the basis of the population they represent or certain designated categories. Quotas for both district category and other categories are often set before the selection process begins. The whole selection process of National People's Congress starts from lower levels of administrative divisions every five years. The final lists of national delegates are decided by and gathered from each province. Provinces with larger populations provide more delegates. The places of delegates used to be filled by official appointments through this selection process. If the lower level authorities did not put someone's name on the ballot, that person would not have a chance to be norminated. These days, more district candidates incline towards an election approach rather than the conventional appointment approach, with candidates engaged in small-scale campaigns to win votes. The rationale behind this move is that it may enhance the candidates' credibility. A voting result is more convincing than an appointment by local authorities. This is more common in rural regions where leading members of the community hold great power and influence over villagers. As the practice of county-level elections is under way across the country, the numbers of Congress delegates who actively campaign for their tickets, sometimes against local authorities' will, is increasing. Some recent examples include the newly elected delegates for Beijing's Haidian district and that for Shenzhen in 2004. In the meantime, large numbers of delegates in designated categories still keep their reserved seats coming with their official positions or special interest sections in the government. These delegates are mostly appointed and go through a nominal process of selection, without having to run active campaigns. Hong Kong, Macau, Taiwan and overseas Chinese have their own groups of delegates to the Congress; many of them are old industrialists with a long time association with China and the government. The tenure for NPC delegates is five years. The year 2003 saw the most recent selection round for NPC delegates, and the Congress meeting held in April that year marked the start of a new five-year term of the Congress.

Every five years, the Congress delegates elect new members of the Standing Committee, which will carry out the tasks listed earlier as major functions of the Congress, after the meeting is completed. The current Committee members were elected in 2003, numbering 157. Unlike Parliaments in the West, delegates in China do not have their regularly scheduled annual seating time and they return to their normal duties once the annual meeting in Beijing is concluded. The designated parliamentary tasks are then left to the elected Standing Committee members. The Committee has no authority to make laws, only to examine amendments, which will be rectified by the Congress at the next session, and to pass regulations submitted by the executive arm of central government, namely the State Council. The Standing Committee also has the power to summon all members for an *ad hoc* meeting in case of an emergency. Separate sub-offices of the Standing committee are set up to deal with particular tasks and issues, such as the Foreign Affairs Office and the Legal Affairs Office. These sub-offices come under the Standing Committee and are not in a position to interfere with the functions of government branches under the State Council in similar areas of responsibility. For example, the Foreign Affairs Office has no authority to overturn a decision by the Ministry of Foreign Affairs.

There also exists a Political Consultative Council in the central government. This institution played a key role in the founding years of the People's Republic, when the People's Congress had not been formed and new laws and regulations needed to be quickly established. As the People's Congress became the official legislative body, the Council ceased to play that constitutional role from 1954 and turned into a consultative conference mainly for non-Communist Party figures. It had no authority to pass laws, only maintaining a national united front of non-Communist organisations and offering consultations to the ruling Communist Party.

The previously limited roles played by the People's Congress under a communist rule have been consistently expanded since the reforms, and the label of "rubber stamping Congress" has lost some of its implications. This comes from many factors, both internal and external. Reforms to local elections have made district delegates more of representatives of local interests, and laws and regulations passed through the Congress have come under closer scrutiny. Voting at Congress meetings has changed from raising hands to pressing buttons with the aid of computer programming. As such, opposition and dissent can be more easily expressed through vote casting, and "no" and "abstain" votes increase in regard to government budgets, work reports and proposals of new laws and amendments.

Under external forces, the government recognises the importance of legal procedures and issues. In the case of China's entry into the WTO, domestic laws will have to be compatible with international laws and practices, and so the work of the government must be standardised and more transparent. In this regard, the People's Congress will have a more significant role to play—to maintain balance, to make government actions legal, and to convince foreign investors that China is a rule-based nation.

Key reform policies have been initiated by the ruling Communist Party; however, major changes and new laws ultimately need approval from the Congress. Once an important change is made to law and the Constitution, there will no longer be wavering or backtracking. It becomes official. Hence, many business people in China watch very closely and anxiously when a piece of legislation is passed by the Congress. Repercussions are enormous. When an amendment granting private companies their legal status was written into the Constitution by the Congress in 1988, it led to phenomenal growth of private enterprises in the following years. Similarly, protection of personal earnings and human rights were added to the Constitution at the Congress meeting in early 2004. This marks a new thinking in the running of state affairs by the new leadership and offers much hope for millions of private entrepreneurs and middle-class members. From the perspective of doing business, the acts of the Congress have an extensive impact on all enterprises in the economy. On the other hand, the Congress also passes laws regarding various industries, such as company, banking and advertising laws, which regulate the respective industries and impact immeasurably on businesses within those sectors. Conversely, business sectors could now have more room to put forth their views to Congress delegates or, through business sector delegates, work to have a bill tabled and make amendments of their own, in regard to business. Two recent examples of such moves are Amway's effort to have a law passed to ensure that its direct sales business continues to flourish, and a proposal by a private Chinese company for a law to regulate octopus-like retail chains that threaten to make small businesses and shops in the cities go out of business.

The Executive Body—the President and the State Council

The **President** is nominated and approved by the National People's Congress and serves a five-year term as the head of the state. As in some Western countries such as France and the United States, the President of China occupies a position of supreme authority and great prestige, and is not just a figurehead. With a similar pole position in the ruling Communist Party, the President holds power to make long-term plans for the country. The President also names the Premier and directs tasks to the State Council for nationwide implementation, though he does not get involved in that process of implementation. The normal running of the central government and routine administrative tasks are handled by the State Council.

The **State Council** is the highest-level executive body of the government. It functions in a similar way to the cabinets of other governments, and focuses on managing the administration of the country with the authority defined by the Constitution. The State Council runs its business through two lines of control. One line is horizontal—to direct government offices at the top level, with numerous ministries and commissions under the State Council in charge of different types of state affairs. The other line is vertical—to direct and supervise provincial and local governments in their administration of territories. Legally, official government organisations include only those at the county level and above, though in reality those beneath this level, namely township and district offices, also have their chiefs widely regarded as government cadres.

The State Council has its decision making core at the top, consisting of the **Premier**, Vice Premiers and State Counsellors. The title of Premier indicates that the country of China is a centralist entity, and the Premier is working under the State President. In a federalist country, such as Australia, State Premiers represent their own state interests, while the Prime Minister represents the federal government and national interests. From a legal point of view, the State Council of China is not empowered to make laws, only to execute the laws passed by the National People's Congress. The Council, however, has the power to make regulations and extend their effects to the whole country in the name of the Council. These administrative regulations, in fact, have a more direct impact on local governments and on businesses as well. In response to ever changing conditions in the nation and the economy, the Council often drafts and issues many regulations to keep situations under control and maintain a steady progress. By the year 2000, there were 390 laws, 800 State Council administrative regulations and 8000 regional government regulations.

After years of reforms and with the WTO entry, the State Council faces fresh challenges to its long-time use of regulations as the number one tool in administration. Those administrative regulations will have to be compatible with laws, and the Constitution in particular, passed by the National People's Congress. A minor amendment to a law may lead to revisions in numerous government regulations, since the amendment overrides many past regulations that were in place. There are more and more incidents in which ordinary citizens sue governments for their negligence and violation of rights, shielding themselves with the Constitution and laws against certain draconian administrative regulations. In a recent case, people who were forced to leave their homes and have their houses demolished to make way for urban development projects filed law suits against municipal governments, claiming that their property rights enshrined in the Constitution should override government regulations authorising forceful removals. The central and local governments had headaches sorting out valid regulations from invalid ones. As a result of these legal actions, past regulations which authorised land reclamation in old-fashioned ways are gradually being phased out or annulled, giving way to regulations which redefine residents' right to land and properties. Real estate developers now face more restraints in carrying out their land development plans.

The internal regulations will also have to be compatible with the signed international treaties and with the rulings of international organisations, especially in areas of trade and opening of domestic markets. Failing to do this will give grounds to challenges from foreign governments and investors and lead to lengthy court battles and unfavourable arbitration by international organisations such as the WTO. All these make the State Council more restrained in issuing administrative regulations and more diligent in annulling the invalid ones.

A key task for the State Council is to maintain a healthy state of balance between the power of the central government and that of local governments. This is related to the degree of centralisation and central-local relations in a socialist country. Power concentration and decentralisation both occurred in pre-reform China, and the current leadership remains alert to this crucial issue. The provinces and directly administered municipalities represent local interests while serving under the central government. Their authority to issue local regulations often clash with national policies and regulations, and in so many cases their stand is opposite to that of the central government, resulting in tugs-of-war. Their intention is clearly to have a greater share of power, resources, preferences in development policies of the central government, etc. In the macroeconomic arena, actions taken by local governments often cause an overheating of the economy, through over-investment and spending against the advice from the central government. There are cases of discord between local and central governments, which will be discussed in later chapters.

The State Council normally treads the issue of central-local relations carefully and balances various local interests as even-handedly as possible. It acts as both arbiter and mediator in conflicts of interests. It is near impossible to return to the centralisation of the pre-reform era, so that this central-local relation needs delicate manoeuvring. The State

Council now consists of numerous heads of provincial governments, in order to manage this relation well. The central government has also vastly improved on its financial resources, through a more efficient tax collection and increasing foreign exchange reserves. A financially strong central government will have more clout to rein in local governments, and the authority of the State Council will be markedly reinforced.

The Judiciary Body

This consists of courts and prosecutors. Courts in China are called Peoples' Courts, ranging from the Supreme Court at the national level and Provincial High Court to Medium courts and District courts. The person in charge is called the President of the Supreme People's Court, but he is not necessarily a judge in the Supreme Court. There are over 220,000 court judges at different levels of the court system.

There is also the office of the Supreme People's Prosecurate at the national level. The chief prosecutor is called Prosecutor-General, and is in a position to file lawsuits and start investigations against individuals and organisations. Prosecutor offices at different levels are similar to those of the court system.

A special office of investigation, the National Office against Corruption and Bribery, was set up under the Prosecutor-General. Its establishment is in a similar vein to the Independent Commission against Corruption in Hong Kong, though its independence is less secured. The Office has its own branches throughout the country and is given the special task to investigate economic crimes and official corruption, away from common crimes. Since its regional offices are under the dual jurisdictions of provincial governments and the national office, investigations of local crimes are often hampered or blocked by local political figures and interest groups.

The various heads of the judiciary body are to report to each annual Congress session regarding their work progress. Increasingly, the general public is less satisfied due to rising criminal activities and worsening public security in recent years. Subsequently, Congress delegates voted down a number of times the reports submitted by the President of Courts and the Prosecutor-General on their work.

There is another government organ, the Ministry of Justice, in Beijing, whose head is in charge of legal matters. The Ministry handles affairs relating to prisons, lawyers, civil and criminal law suits, mediation, legislation, extradition, legal aid and studies and civil rights issues. It is the official representative of the nation on legal issues, within and without the country. As with the Ministry of Public Security, this Ministry is under the State Council and wears two hats, being part of the judiciary body as well as the executive body.

There are also lawyers within this judicial system. No distinction is made in China between lawyers and barristers, and legal cases can be dealt with by registered lawyers at and outside the court. Chinese legal systems and lawyers follow the traditions of continental laws, in contrast to the common law traditions in English-speaking countries and regions. The profession of law in China was released from suspension in the pre-reform years, and the Law on Lawyers in 1996 regulates their acts and behaviours. They have to pass national law examinations to be qualified as lawyers, and after receiving their certificates, are to be registered with an official legal association before engaging in practice. In theory, lawyers are independent from other organisations of the judiciary body, but in practice, law enforcement agencies do not always give lawyers full cooperation in legal cases and often view their defence of suspects as an impediment to justice. In the early years of reforms, lawyers were even detained by local police for defending suspects. These days, lawyers in China have entered the lives of many citizens, in criminal and business matters, and the social group of lawyers is commonly regarded as being of the middle class and earning high incomes. By September 2004, there were over 100,000 practising lawyers and over 11,000 law firms in business.

The police force of the nation is placed at different levels, from the Ministry of Public Security, provincial public security departments, district police bureaux and down to precinct police stations. The Ministry is to deal with public security and order, policing and crime prevention, while the relatively new Ministry of State Security deals with matters of national security and intelligence.

The Communist Party of China

As a socialist country, the Constitution holds that the Communist Party of China (CPC) is the country's ruling political party. Therefore, a study of China's political systems must include explanations of this supreme political power over the commonly recognised three bodies of modern politics. The Party was founded in 1921, with small groups of patriots longing for a new republic and independence from Western domination. The Party gained its legitimacy to rule chiefly through triumphant civil wars against the then ruling and corrupt Nationalist government and came to power in 1949. After going through several radical movements and considerable mismanagement of state affairs, the Party started wide-ranging reforms in 1978. Fifty years after its first claim to national power, the Party again hinges its legitimacy on popular support from the nation, through improving economic performance and providing social welfare.

Major Organs of the CPC

The structure of the CPC is similar to that of the national legislative and executive bodies.

1. The Central Committee consists of members who are selected at the Party Congress from party delegates in a way similar to what happens at the National People's Congress. The Party Congress convenes once in five years, and the selected Central Committee has a tenure of five years till the next Congress. It is for this committee to devise and approve major policies and personnel of the central leadership. The current Central Committee has 198 formal members and 150 alternate members.

2. The Politburo consists of members of the Central Committee of the Party and selects the General Secretary, who is officially the Party leader. It is the highest level decision-making body of the Party and thus the country. The Politburo has its formal and alternate members, the difference being in the right to vote on important issues.

3. The Secretariat of the Central Committee is the executive body that handles affairs after the Congress closes. It is the effectual power centre keeping the party machinery running, and sometimes has equal power to the Politburo, since the members of the latter are not all at the centre in times of emergency. The members of the Secretariat are also approved by the Central Committee by ballot at each Congress.

4. The Central Military Commission holds the sole authority to direct military affairs and manoeuvres. The Congress members cast their ballots to select the members and chairman of the commission. In theory, the Party General Secretary holds the conjunction post of the Chairman of the Military Commission. This, however, depends on the military credentials and influence of the Party General Secretary in office, and separation of the two posts has been the case in the past two decades. The military has a certain clout to allow an acceptable person to be their chairman, even if the person is no longer the Party's General Secretary. Since the end of September 2004, when Hu Jintao took over the Chairmanship from Jiang Zemin, the two top posts in the Party are now taken up by one person.

5. The Central Discipline and Inspection Commission deals with internal party disciplinary issues, targeting high-ranking party officials and local party bosses. Since party officials hold government posts, the Commission plays a key role in anti-corruption campaigns. It has the power to carry out its own investigations, supervise government actions and policies, and coordinate raids and arrests. The Commission focuses only on big cases, and if serious crimes are exposed, the Commission is allowed to discipline and fire party cadres and then pass them on to prosecutors for appropriate legal action to be meted out. The members of the Central Discipline and Inspection Commission also need appointment approvals at each Party Congress session.

6. The Central Advisory Commission was established in early reform years to vacate key posts to younger leaders so as to maintain party traditions and continuity. This Commission retained party and government elders; it thus functioned in a way similar to the Upper House of the British Parliament. Its main role was to be a stabiliser in political affairs, and commission members held enormous influence over incumbent party leaders, as a result of their past official careers and also with their former subordinates having risen through the ranks. Inevitably, this commission was abolished in 1992 by the Jiang Zemin leadership to minimise interference and to facilitate a smoother power transfer in future.

The Communist Party now has a membership of over 66 million and a network throughout the country and in most sectors. Party members are selected from all walks of life, pledging their loyalty and commitment to the Communist cause. The Party Constitution has been amended at the last Congress to allow non-working class people to be admitted as party members, including owners of private businesses. This change in party doctrines has been made to expand the bases and improve public acceptance of the ruling party, after long debates over the Party's future direction.

Party members are assigned as heads of administrative areas, overseeing local and regional government officials. They are still the majority group in the state administration and in official ranks. Along with recent drives to create a full-fledged public servant system in China, state organs have recruited large numbers of educated personnel who are not necessarily Communist Party members.

The Planned Economy in China (1953-1979)

Since the 1950s, China has adopted a planned economy, following the Soviet model. The major features of this system are the overwhelming shares the government (the state) holds in the economy and state control of economic activities, leaving market operations to a bare minimum. A planned (or command) economy is the embodiment of socialist doctrines. In general, socialist ideals include:

❑ public ownership of all assets;
❑ residents working for and making contributions to the society;
❑ equal distribution of public goods and wealth;
❑ collective responsibility and disregard of individual needs.

There are many forms of socialist practice in countries around the world. Besides former Eastern European countries under the Soviet influence, parts of the first three characteristics can be seen in some developed economies, such as western and northern European countries and Australia. Left-wing political parties there who recognise these social needs bear the names of Labour, Socialist or Democratic Socialist. The governments under these political parties have established comprehensive social welfare systems for all citizens and made full employment their top goal in office. They have even set up state-owned (public-owned) corporations so as to be able to exert varying degrees of control on the supply of public goods and facilities. In numerous cases during the past decades, when faced with severe financial and economic difficulties, these governments had carried out privatisation programmes to sell some public companies to raise funds, so that social welfare for all citizens could be maintained in principle. Their practice of socialist ideas is an example of the state functioning pro-actively in a market economy.

Socialist practices as seen in developed economies are vastly different from those seen in socialist Eastern European countries, and socialist experiments in the latter countries based on the implementation of all these four features have failed so far. The model of a planned economy once existed in real life and then proved its serious shortcomings. The state planning reflects the central feature of collectivism and a complete state rule in the economy.

Socialist practices in China are characterised by the following:

1. State ownership of property and labour

    The state became the sole owner of national resources and assets. It also employed all the workers in state-owned enterprises. This allowed the state to implement its far-reaching economic plans and to organise major projects using all resources available. The first rule of socialism was realised.

2. Elimination of private business and entrepreneurship

    Private business was excluded from the economy, initially through buy-outs and certain refund schemes in the early 1950s and later through nationwide bans. Other types of businesses in China's planned economy were extremely short of funding, resources and employees. The government in reality could not eliminate all private businesses, and in some cases, small businesses did exist in regions, especially in the years before the turbulent Cultural Revolution. This is perhaps a significant difference between the official Soviet model and the pragmatic practice in China. In the long run, however, these private and family businesses had no prospects to grow in size and to compete with state enterprises. The desires for and skills of doing business in the domestic market were thus soon lost.

3. Elimination of market and competition

    This refers to the situation where distribution and commerce all came under state planning, and market competition became nonexistent. Instead, competition for authority and resource allocations was common among local governments and among different government departments. Official procedures and red tape in the bureaucracy replaced the free forces of supply and demand in the market.

4. State control over production, distribution and public goods supply for residents

    Economic and production activities were planned and supervised by state bureaux, from the State Planning Commission at the top to lower levels of economic affairs offices. Natural resources and labour were routinely allocated for use to meet particular targets. On the other hand, full-scale social welfare formed the main obligation of the government. Most urban residents relied on state supplies under state planning, since most of them were employees of state enterprises or bureaux. They received regular payments and also rations for particular products. In short, this is a type of trade under the socialist system, where the public work for the state, and the state in turn provides all basic necessities.

5. The economy of shortages

    It is under such a distribution and supply system that an economy of shortages existed. People's living standards are determined and set by bureaucrats and party officials, according to their own plans. National and local demands for goods and services were calculated annually, and extra demand and varieties were not encouraged. With insufficient supply and artificial official estimates (of demand), general living standards remained low.

6. State bureaucracy and institutions

    Under a planned economy, the size of state bureaucracy kept growing so as to meet the needs of handling enormous amounts of planning tasks and for the survival of the bureaucracy itself. It is estimated that current employees and officials of Party and government departments number over 7 million, and formal employees in attached organisations such as education, health, science and culture number over 30 million. These groups of people are supported by government fund allocations in each national budget, and they include those people who are usually regarded as public servants in Western political systems. In a way not dissimilar to election promises in the West, ambitious political goals by the government often overshadowed realistic economic considerations. This characteristic is shown in the politicised campaigns of the Great Leap Forward, for China to increase industrial production rapidly in a short period of time in the late 1950s. Government bureaux could make up plans for big projects to be set up, the number of employees to be raised, but there was little consideration of final outcomes of costs and efficiency.

The consequence of implementing a planned economy was the formation of an inflexible economy accompanied by moderate economic growth. The economy of China was in a state of crisis in 1978 when the reforms began. This was due in part to the political turmoils of the Cultural Revolution, which caused widespread chaos in the central leadership and the state administration of the country. This too was due mainly to the nature of the planned economy. Under this system, the Chinese economy had experienced certain periods of considerable growth, especially industrial growth, which started from zero base. The overwhelming emphasis of the central planners was on heavy industries to build up a base for effective national defence, and this ambition was assisted by Russian aid in the form of 156 key projects in the 1950s. As a result, average industrial growth was, in fact, quite impressive. Gross agricultural and industrial outputs before 1978 grew at an average rate of 8.21%.

However, since the growth and particularly the consumption were planned, there was no real basis to expect incomes to increase steadily over the years. Under the government policy of low wages, low inflation and low spending except those on heavy industries, the average income that Chinese employees earned lagged more and more behind that of the employees in other countries. From the early 1950s to the end of the Cultural Revolution, employees in China were given few pay rises and received very low wages in comparison, and this caused widespread dissatisfaction, which led to great motivation to push for change once the dust of political campaigns had settled down.

There are still opposing views of whether better state planning without political radicalism could have achieved the desired results. It is clear, however, that a planned economy reduced the possibility of long-term steady growth due to the strict state planning and control on economic activities, wages, consumption and living standards. All these controls stifled efforts and creativity to produce more and better goods. A planned economy, even with Chinese characteristics, would inevitably give way to market mechanisms and competition.

Reforms from the late 1970s have dramatically changed the course of China's economic development and the socialist nature of the economy. Many key components of socialism and a planned economy have been modified, even abandoned. A market economy with a vibrant private business sector is on the rise. The change in this whole picture has been accompanied by remarkable economic growth. This fundamental turnaround will be discussed in later chapters.

National Conditions of China

For the economy as a whole, macroeconomic factors and figures draw most attention from both domestic residents and foreign investors. With these useful data, business prospects and market research can be established on some solid ground. For market potential, growth industries and inherent problems, such figures could project an overall picture of the economy and help businesses identify places for investments. In a precursory review, prospective investors can view general trends and moves, and get hints of what they imply. It is also possible that a long-term plan based on certain optimistic data could overcome any immediate worries about an alien culture and business environment.

Major Macroeconomic Indicators

The first things about an economy are its size and growth rates. These include the general capacity of production and consumption of the nation.

China has a population of 1.28 billion as at the end of 2002 and a national gross domestic product (GDP) in 2003 of approximately US$1.4 trillion, which is about 11.2 trillion yuan (the Chinese currency) at the current exchange rate. This places China at a high position in the world by total GDP. The GDP figure of an economy is often distorted by currency exchange rates and the prevalent living costs. To complete a piece of work, such as having a classroom desk built by a Chinese worker, the costs are much lower than using an American worker. The lower price of the final product subsequently leads the GDP value created by this work to be lower in China. To add up all work and factor in the effect of foreign exchange rates, the total GDP value is inevitably lower than that in a developed economy, though both peoples consume and enjoy similar products and services. If the purchasing power parity (PPP) criteria are applied, making the price of the same goods more or less a constant everywhere, China's total output value could be lifted, and its ranking moved up even higher.

Choosing between a GDP figure and an estimate under the PPP criteria depends on whether you see China as a developing or a developed economy, and this distinction was crucial and debatable during China's WTO negotiations. It also has an effect on people's perception of the China market and how strong or weak the purchasing power is for new and foreign goods. A point for market research is that while income levels are relatively low, spending on many essentials in life is also low, so that extra savings could be utilised to make other desired purchases of non-essentials.

In 2003, the government collected 2 trillion yuan worth of taxes, 1.41 trillion yuan for state tax and 630 billion yuan for local taxes. These figures do not include import tariffs and agricultural taxes. After the crucial fiscal and tax reforms in 1994, the central government is now in a much stronger position financially to direct local affairs and redress imbalances caused by regional disparities. Similarly, centrifugal forces from certain economically powerful provinces have been more effectively handled. This turnaround from a trend of decentralisation a decade ago has significant influences over the future of China's economic transition, adding financial resources on top of military and administrative forces for the central government to hold the country together and thus providing required security for the transition. A well-balanced financial structure could further push the country towards an acceptable and more democratic federal-state power share in the future, which has long existed in countries like the United States and Australia.

China has over US$500 billion in national foreign exchange reserves by 2004, and the total foreign debts amounted to US$193.6 billion at the end of 2003. Among them, 60% are medium- and long-term debts, many from favourable development loans offered by foreign governments. As such, the debt liability is manageable, and China is not likely to let its financial situation deteriorate into a crisis similar to that which occurred in East and Southeast Asia in 1997. For domestic debts, the central government has accumulated a total of 2.5 trillion yuan, approximately 25% of the total GDP. Again, domestic debts are often in the form of government bonds, totalling 800 billion yuan approximately, which support key infrastructure projects and industrial bases. These long-term bonds pose a relatively light burden on the government and will bring returns in future. There is also a large chunk of debts which are, in fact, bad bank loans to state enterprises, and these will ultimately be taken over by the central government for final disposal. A further discussion on this point can be found in Part II, Chapter 5. With the government in control of money supply (to print money) and massive national personal savings, domestic debts are pressing but not unmanageable. A government without immediate credit risks implies stability of the current economic systems and gives a certain assurance for investment.

The total of national personal bank deposits was over 10 trillion yuan in early 2003 and near 12 trillion yuan in early 2004. Personal savings have demonstrated a surprising disregard for very low interest rates that the government imposed on deposits and have moved along a continuous upward line. Many explanations could be offered on why this is the case, especially in regard to financial and enterprise reforms. It can be argued that investment options are not many, so people keep to their traditional ways of deposits and savings. It is also due to the transitional process, under which structural change and employment reforms highlight the vulnerability of many groups of residents in the economy. Savings are imperative for them to use as insurance against unexpected events. From the economics point of view, these huge savings can be more efficiently utilised and are closely linked with the patterns of investment and business returns.

In 2003, the national total of retail sales was 4.6 trillion yuan. This is a relevant figure to many market researchers and retailers, and the trends and fluctuations in national sales volumes need to be carefully monitored.

By the end of 2002, China had 660 cities, with an urban population of 353.4 million, among them 220.6 million non-rural residents, with the rest being rural residents living in cities. In the 25 years between 1978 and 2003, 150 million rural residents have moved into cities to work and settle down. The people who could be placed in the middle class number around 130 million. In the meantime, people over the age of 60 also number around 130 million. These figures point to a steady expansion of urban territories and thus more retail demand from urban residents, especially from people within higher income brackets. The general trends of transformation could also indicate some new business areas which cater specifically for older residents.

In 2003, revenues for restaurant businesses were 600 billion yuan. Fixed line telephone users number over 300 million, the highest in the world, and, after years of unrelenting promotion and falling prices, the number of mobile phone users reached 315 million by August 2004. In 2003 alone, 75 million mobile phone sets were sold to Chinese customers. These are the main reasons for several heavyweight manufacturers outside this industry to rush in and launch their own mobile phone brands to the market. Registered Internet users have surpassed 60 million, putting China in second place in the world.

In 2002, China had 14.62 million students studying for various tertiary degrees and half a million students pursuing post-graduate degrees. With a four-year long college education, rather than three years in many developed economies, China has a total of 19 million college students studying at tertiary level in 2003. Every year, 325,000 engineering students graduate. These are perhaps related to human resource issues and talent pools, which are essential for any company wishing to run a business in China.

On the production and output side, China has a total of 123 million hectares of arable land and produced a total of 440 million tons of grain crops in 2003. The primary industries' output have shrunk as a proportion of the national economy, but China has yet to completely solve the problem of feeding the population sufficiently. Agriculture is still a weak sector tying up large numbers of labourers. Wide areas in the western regions need enormous spending and effort before they can be transformed into fertile arable land.

China produced 222 million metric tons of raw steel in 2003 and consumed 240 million tons. China also imported about 150 million tons of iron ore for steel production. These gigantic orders are certainly music to the ears of resources exporters in a number of economies, such as Australia. Not surprisingly, an official announcement in early 2004 that the Chinese government had acted to curtail project investments and put the brakes on an overheated economy sent metal and mineral markets around the world spiralling down, and the Australian dollar instantly lost some value on foreign exchange markets. Those macroeconomic measures were aimed centrally at irrational and duplicated investments in certain sectors; however, existing production capacity will have a hard time to match mineral and metal consumption in China in the following decades.

China became a net crude oil importer again in 1993, and imported 70 million tons of oil in 2002 and 90 million tons in 2003, costing a total of US$25.67 billion. Domestic oil consumption reached 220 million tons in 2002, and domestic oil output was at 160 million tons. This gap is getting wider, with China's limited oil reserves and refinery facilities. It was estimated that China needs to import over 100 million tons of crude oil in 2004-2005, or 11 million barrels a day. Apart from the sensitive issue of national security, a shortage of oil supply could adversely affect many manufacturing industries and harm investment returns by interrupting otherwise smooth-running business operations and causing unexpected losses.

In 2003, power plants in China generated a total electricity output of 1.9 trillion kW. Despite this, there have been serious power shortages in many regions, especially in the more industrialised coastal regions and big urban centres. To counter this, local and municipal governments adopted stringent power control measures, and temporary suspensions of power supply became common. This has caused many factories to face the risks of work stoppage and delayed goods delivery. Uncertainty in production and supply chain management increased. This energy shortage derives partly from misjudgement in government planning of the late 1990s, when a future jump in energy consumption was not foreseen and building of new power plants were put on the back burners. The shortage can only be mitigated till 2007 when many new power plants will be near completion.

Production insufficiency in the above resource sectors puts great pressure on the national economy, and demands for these products are very inelastic as the people aim to achieve higher living standards. China needs huge quantities of energy to sustain a fair pace of industrial development and modernisation. Energy and manufacturing sectors could be the boom business areas, since demand clearly outstrips supply.

By August 2004, freeways in China reached 30,000 km, second only to the United States in length. This is a significant jump from zero kilometres in 1988. The building of freeways began from southern China, where Hong Kong companies showcased to Chinese road engineers how to build high-grade freeways and manage them profitably. Since then, this building process was in frenzy, reaching the current level of network density. Freeways are now a viable alternative to traditional means of freight and passenger transport through trunk roads or railroads and have increased people's mobility dramatically. To businesses, the existence of freeways facilitates the smooth and timely logistical and supply chain operations. It has also given a huge boost to China's motor car industry and given rise to many middle-class families with cars.

In 2003, a total of 4.44 million automobiles were built in China, among them nearly 2 million family cars being sold. China now has 4 million cars in government and public organisations, and privately owned cars number over 10 million, up from 1 million in 1992. These figures have well surpassed previous projections made by official and foreign institutes. Foreign car manufacturers who persevered and stayed on in the China market reaped huge benefits in 2003, among them Volkswagen, PSA (Peugeot Société Anonyme) and Honda. Those who were influenced years ago by pessimistic assessments on market potential have passed most opportunities over and now are scrambling to set up a foothold through mergers or joint ventures. Domestic manufacturers also participate in this fierce competition to expand their capacities and market shares where possible. The car industry in China is a story of complex momentum, causing immeasurable pains to certain foreign multinationals, while having now reached a stage of clear market potential and a matured industry with stable consumer bases and profits. This is a well-researched and tested case for marketing and investment studies.

Summary

Macroeconomic data are essential to studies of general market conditions in a business environment under consideration. These data give an overall view of an economy and help prospective investors to form an impression of the prevailing economic systems. For the China market, an understanding of national conditions needs to be gained even before any planning starts. The above headline figures of the Chinese economy serve two purposes. One is to outline basic trends and potential. From there, analysts draw the big picture and make estimates of gross outputs and market sizes. Optimistic economic forecasts often lead to waves of investment in order to gain future profits.

The other purpose is to indicate spots of troubles and limits in future growth, so as to be prepared for any shocks of slowdowns or setbacks. After two decades of reforms, economic fluctuations and cycles are now commonplace in China compared to the pre-reform era, as there is less strict central planning and businesses are more directly influenced by often unpredictable market forces. There have been numerous examples of investors getting 'burned' by entering the market at the stage of economic contraction. China's integration into the world market further heightened the risks inherent in its exposure to international economic uncertainties. One example of this exposure is the sporadic external pressure exerted on China's foreign exchange rates and trade barriers.

From growth and output data, another concern is over China's sustainable economic development. The faster the pace of growth goes, the more urgent the demand for resources and energy. Natural limits in resources supply to meet domestic consumption do exist, and they appear unsurmountable in many categories, especially involving large-scale purchasing on the international markets and importing. It seems that the transformation of the nation into a developed economy comes with huge costs. For individual companies, their operations in China may face severe energy shortage and subsequent shutdown at times.

In addition to these economic considerations, an understanding of the extent of political and cultural influence on the business environment in China is crucial. Normal business practices may encounter obstacles due to the staying power of socialist ideology, cultural traditions, bureaucratic red tape and local protection. Companies then must modify their ways of doing business to cope with domestic conditions and evolving government policies. Failing to note these influences may cause irreparable damage to their operations. Whether foreign investors find China a difficult or good place to do business often depends on their willingness and insistence to deal with these non-economic difficulties with an open mind and creativity.

From the above discussion and data presented, one can make a generalised observation that there are both real market potential and risks in the economy, and for any investment plans, these macroeconomic data should be factored in to draw plausible conclusions. It is apparent that the unique business environment and common economic cycles are now unescapable facts in China.

Key Concepts

Economic and social efficiencies (PPF curves)

Major factors in business analyses

Legislative, executive and judiciary bodies in China

Socialist practice and planned economy

National conditions and overall economic performance

Discussion Questions

1. What are the major differences between the legislative, executive and judiciary systems of China and models of the West? What will be the aspects that can be identified for improvement if you are put in a position to modify the current legislative systems?

2. How do China's political structures and administration influence the real-life business and the economy as a whole? Give examples of political changes and their repercussions on the business environment.

3. What are your views on the direction of central-local relations and relevant implications on an analysis of the China market?

4. What is your assessment of the socialist ideals and their practice in a planned economy, and what are the major differences between this economy and a market economy?

5. What do you see in those macroeconomic data and what are your overall views of economic trends, potential, and development bottlenecks in China? Give examples, wherever possible, on particular sectors and industries.

Related Readings

"Chasing the leader: are Europeans really so much worse off than Americans?" *The Economist*, 6 February 2003

Gilley, Bruce, "Provincial Disintegration", *Far Eastern Economic Review*, 22 September 2001

Harding, Harry, *China's Second Revolution: Reform after Mao*, Sydney, Allen & Unwin, 1987.

Lieberthal, Kenneth and Michael Oksenberg, *Policy making in China: Leaders, Structures and Processes*, Princeton, New Jersey, Princeton University Press, 1991.

MacFarquhar, Roderick (ed.), *The Politics of China: 1949-1989*, Cambridge, Cambridge University Press, 1993.

For up-to-date figures in regard to national conditions, these are not available even in the latest publications. Do check China Statistics Year Books in recent years and business reports in relevant journals, as listed in the Bibliography.

PART II

REFORMS AND PROGRESS

Internal Reform, Opening and Breakthrough

*T*his chapter will trace the course of reforms and opening, examine key junctures and approaches, and focus on major outcomes of painstaking restructuring.

Reforms in China have proceeded over a quarter of a century. The China at the time of early reforms was vastly different from the China we see today, and sharp contrasts between a socialist country and a growth market imply that dramatic changes have occurred in this country. It is quite hard for people to imagine the hurdles and obstacles along the path. As a shining example of a transitional economy, among many other developing and former socialist Eastern European countries, China has demonstrated a great deal of patience and perseverance in restructuring the economy and the society. The course of reforms passed numerous difficult phases, and the leadership displayed their reluctance and then willingness for reforms.

A Gradualist Approach

This is based on a few understandings. The strong belief at early stages that reforms should only make needed improvements prevented occurrences of sudden changes and shocks. After the turmoil of the Cultural Revolution, the issue of stability became paramount for all members of the leadership, whatever their political inclinations. Chaotic situations following free market frenzy sweeping Russia and Eastern European countries proved not desirable to the Chinese government. The leadership had little knowledge of market economic operations, and the acquaintance with Western systems had to be built from ground up, through interactions with foreign governments and investors. They also had concerns of the applicability and effects of transplanting Western models into China. On this point, they may be correct, considering the aftermath of **shock therapy** in Russia. That therapy was taken straight out of economics textbooks in the US and was recommended fervently by American academics, acting as advisers to the Russian government. The therapy included plans for fast track privatisation and hasty adoption of parliamentary democracy. To counter the advance of such shock therapy, the Chinese leadership proclaimed and faithfully followed a gradualist approach in their reforms. This approach is typified in Deng's famous saying of "groping stones while crossing river".

Stages and Breakthroughs

The course of China's internal reforms can be summarised in the following phases:

- ❏ 1978-1984: Reforms concentrated in rural agricultural areas.
- ❏ 1985-1988: Reforms extended into urban centres.
- ❏ 1989-1991: Economic austerity and readjustments dominated the scene.
- ❏ 1992 onwards: Wide-ranging reforms resumed, steady economic growth and real development ensued.
- ❏ 2001: China's WTO accession signaled China's effort to join in international systems and play according to the rules of the world.

Economic Reforms

The general goals of four modernisations were formally confirmed at an early stage of reforms. These include modernisations in agriculture, industry, science and technology, and national defence. In following years, the central leadership has turned their attention from these technical targets to fundamental structural changes and social transformation. It is a quantum leap from quantity to quality of development, and it is also inevitable that the leadership has to follow the general trend and make required adjustments even if they considered some moves as against their original wishes.

Land Reforms and Agricultural Household Responsibility System

China formerly adopted a commune system, which made collective production and living all in one. Public ownership and assets were protected, and rural population retained bare necessities for their families. Under reforms, the government began to heed the needs of peasants and allowed flexible measures being taken in regions. Local authorities started initiatives, making peasants pay their dues to the government and then keep surplus for their families. This experiment became accepted in many regions and encouraged peasants to work harder on their land. The central government finally gave a go ahead of this new scheme.

The centrepiece of this reform is the **household production responsibility system**, under which individual farmers were granted the right of land use and could make their own production decisions. They began to enjoy the returns after paying state taxes and local government charges. The higher the outputs from land, the bigger the profit margins for their labour and resources inputs. Since land ownership is officially in the hand of the state, farmers under this system initially obtained the right to farm for 15 years. From 1993, land use by farmers was extended for another 30 years, in order to give them longer-term assurance and protection.

With ideological barriers and socialist taboos in place, this transformation of a collective countryside into a land of individual farmers caused fierce open debates and infighting in the Party leadership. Regional authorities adopted their own different approaches, some of them pushing for changes, some watching cautiously on the sideline and others holding ground firmly. A number of provincial governments encouraged early experiment of responsibility systems and recommended strongly to the central leadership for a nationwide implementation. By early 1982, the number one directive issued by the Party's central bureau provided a conclusive statement, which confirmed the adoption of the new household responsibility system throughout the country. By 1983, the numbers of rural brigades with household responsibility system reached a 97% share of the total.

The previous rural institutions of people's commune continued to exist, despite this change to individual farmers in the countryside. They had certain administrative roles to play, apart from organising rural production. The government further eroded this authority by officially turning district and township committees to be the only local administrative units of the government. People's communes finally lost their meaning of existence and ceased to operate by the end of 1985. The symbol and substance of collective rural organisations in China disappeared forever.

The government facilitated the revival of agricultural development by making remedies to past price controls. Under central planning, agricultural products used to be sold to government collectors at artificially set low prices, and such sales hardly increased peasants' incomes. Under reforms, the government sharply raised price levels of most agricultural products collected from peasants, including staple foods, cotton, vegetables and fruits. Such increases were often in double-digits and made several times. By 1984, the average national price level for all agricultural products had a 53.6% increase over the 1978 level, and the costs of these price rises were over 4 billion yuan.

Another boosting measure was to reopen rural markets. Under people's communes, trading of surplus farm produces was prohibited and sellers punished for doing their exchanges. Under the new household responsibility system, farmers felt a growing need to trade their surplus produces and increase their incomes along the way. The government made concessions to have these rural markets reopened and no longer banned local trading of agricultural goods by individual farmers. By the end of 1982, over 40,000 rural markets opened, and their trading helped raising household incomes of rural population.

The focus of reforms up to 1985 was on agriculture. With institutional changes and a series of remedial measures targeting the countryside, agricultural production achieved remarkable growth in those years. In 1984, despite a reduction in total farmland acreage, total grain output increased by 33.6% over that of 1978. In the same period, total value of agricultural products increased 1.13 times, an average annual increase of 13.4%. Taking away price increases, net growth rate is 7.6%. In comparison, average growth rate for years between 1952 and 1978 is 2.7%. Productivity, in grain output per Chinese *mu* of land, rose as well, averaging 4.1% in these years. Other agricultural products and sideline products achieved even faster growth. Good harvests and higher selling prices lifted growth rates and income levels of rural households. Average per capita income value increased 1.65 times between 1978 and 1984, an average annual increase of 17.6%. The real income increase, without price rises, is 14.9% annually. This sharp increase once made farmers one of the richer groups in the country, until further reforms enriched residents in urban centres.

Rural reforms till 1985 achieved the initial goal of increasing total agricultural production and bringing wealth to millions of farmers. These reforms also laid solid foundations for further experiments later in urban areas.

Reforms in Industrial Sectors and Urban Centres

Industrial reforms were undertaken early in 1985, and they are not officially completed until the issue of state enterprises is solved. Encouraged by successful rural reforms, the central government decided to introduce a **contract responsibility system** to urban industrial and commercial enterprises. This decision was put into the Party resolution in October 1984, which announced the beginning of comprehensive reforms to economic systems in the country.

The initial response was to grant factory managers more freedom and authority to do business in the market. The first step was to make managers the real executives of their enterprises, freed from supervision of party secretaries. From 1981, early responsibility contracts were signed between managers and the government bureaux in charge. A typical contract contained items as the follows:

> The manager should fulfil their responsibilities prescribed, such as completing tasks and production targets set by the state, and submitting set quotas of taxes and profits. The enterprise managers bear the consequences of profits and losses incurred from their enterprises. They have the rights to run their own businesses, including buying, manufacturing, selling, exporting and R&D. Enterprises can retain surplus profits and make pay schemes to employees at their discretion. Managers also began

to receive rewards for their management performance and extra work.

Although there was no market economy to speak of at this early stage of reforms, the government still attempted to push for enterprise restructuring and make them operate in a more independent way. The rationale was to increase efficiency and revenues, and thus reduce pressure on government coffers. Bonuses to managers would induce them to work harder to seek market opportunities. Within their enterprises, they would be more diligent on cutting down waste and losses. Employees would also benefit, as a reward system would provide them with higher salaries and incomes if they work harder.

A further reform measure was "**profits to taxes**" ("substituting taxes for profits"), started from 1983. Profits made by state enterprises used to be handed up to the State Treasury. After this significant change, profits drew state taxes instead, and income taxes are the main part, initially set at a rate of 55%. This is an improvement in enterprises' status, as corporate taxpayers, rather than separate units in a government bureaucracy. They have more say in allocating the rest of funds and make business decisions on their own. In the long run, this change from profits to taxes made managers increasingly motivated to earn higher returns.

To prompt managers for higher output on their initiative, the government implemented a **dual-track price system** for industrial goods. Enterprises sold key goods under state control to the state at set prices, but they were allowed to sell above quota goods on the market or to their connected clients at much higher price levels. Earnings from the second category sales flowed back to enterprises as their own incomes. This allowance gave much needed incentives to managers to grab market opportunities and seek for maximisation of profits in their business operations. Unfortunately, the gaps between state and market prices were so huge, that speculators, traders and unscrupulous officials took up the opportunity to make millions from this experiment. The way to operate was to obtain official permits for state controlled goods at low prices and sell them on the market. Officials in charge could easily make money from giving out permits and splitting the profits earned. This system thus signals the beginning of official corruption in China, allowing exchanging official power for cash incomes. This dual price system was eventually abolished in the mid 1990s when market prices in effect covered most goods traded in the economy and when price controls virtually ceased to exist.

The People's Congress passed the Enterprise Law in 1988. The law is in fact a law regarding state enterprises. Since state enterprises at the time took the dominant position in the economy and were the targets of industrial reforms, the law had a wider cover over economic and business units in the economy, not just on a particular type of enterprise. The law stipulates a list of rights enterprises are entitled to, thus providing legal foundation for state enterprises to have a more independent status away from government intervention. The Company Law, passed in 1993, covers all types of enterprises in China, provides legal protection, and regulates business operations of commercial firms. In 1988, the Bankruptcy Law was also passed, starting a process of enterprise bankruptcy, though with little real effect till the late 1990s.

Reforms to state enterprises will be discussed in more detail in a following chapter.

The government began to implement reforms to price and wage systems from the mid 1980s. These would directly affect the interests of most urban residents. The wage system had not been modified for decades and proved rigid and discouraging. Most employees had not received pay raises for years. With the introduction of wage system reforms in 1985, urban residents began to enjoy higher living standards, receiving more incomes from pay raises, pay by unit of work, more generous bonuses and rewards. In the meantime, they had to cope with price rises for the first time, which came with market activities and loosening of state control on consumer prices. Price rises of agricultural and industrial products impacted hard on urban consumers and offset their recently increased earnings. Inflation also became a fact of life, with the changes of CPI closely linked with real living standards of urban residents. Reforms in industries and urban centres later touched upon the critical issues of unemployment and social welfare covers. It can be said that without right solutions to these issues, the reforms are far from reaching the point of complete success.

Decentralisation of Authority

From the outset, the central government recognised the negative effects of central planning, and local initiatives were keenly encouraged. This consensus was based on hard to reach balances among regions and on the failures of the previous planned economy. Local governments made many first moves in early reforms, and unorthodox measures were tried and tested to improve local economies. The tested models in different regions were then accepted by the central government, and new policies formulated for the national economy. The household responsibility system and similar schemes in state enterprises were all conceived in regional economies and adopted by the central government when the benefits became apparent and convincing.

In this process of decentralisation, authority was given back to provincial leaders and local officials, in order to give local governments more incentives to restructure local economic systems and make their own adjustments. An important aspect of this decentralisation is the power to make investment decisions. The central government shifted this power down to provincial authorities, leaving itself with only key decisions on strategic sectors and goods. Provincial governments obtained more power to decide on investments within their jurisdictions. More categories and types of investment projects could now get permission directly from provincial bureaux. Only those national projects and projects over an investment of 30 million yuan required approvals from the central government. Some heavy investment projects, such as energy and mining, required an even higher ceiling of 50 million yuan. On production, the central government was only to give guidelines on the total national scale, and regional governments could compete to raise their own production levels. The central government also tried to change the investment structure, shifting from one single investment source to investment by the central, provincial and local governments. Provincial governments also obtained power to approve foreign investment projects within their territories, without the need to consult the central government or get prior nod. This general trend of decentralisation ignited a fierce race among regions, especially among coastal provinces, to put priority on drawing foreign investment and enlarging local revenues. Certain powerful provinces gained superior status of being asset and cash rich, and became more influential on national policies than other poorer regions. This imbalance was gradually corrected and smoothed out since the late half of the 1990s.

Another line of decentralisation was the reforms to fiscal allocations. With the passing of annual budgets, the central government held the purse string and was in a commanding position to decide on fund allocations. Under reforms from 1980, a responsibility system was set up to replace that central planning. Similar to agricultural household responsibility system, the central government and provincial governments signed contracts one on one on their rights and responsibilities. Provincial governments were obliged to submit a certain amount of revenues to the central government, on the basis of their current revenues, and could retain surplus in their own coffers. Provincial governments had the rights to use and dispose of these funds for various purposes after meeting the set quotas to the central government. The rate of submission and the quotas were negotiated between the central government and individual provincial governments, and each contract had a duration of five years. The central government allocated certain funds back to regions if they suffered losses in revenues. If the economy in a province developed faster and revenues increased dramatically, the provincial government concerned enjoyed more benefits and faced little threat from the central government on taking away the surplus. In a major adjustment in 1988, the central government granted the retention of certain lucrative taxes to provincial governments, such as taxes on urban commercial businesses and personal income taxes. This further improved the financial state of many provincial governments and opened more channels of revenues.

The above major changes during the decentralisation had early positive effects, on development of local economies and on increased local incomes. The negative effects, however, are long term, resulting in a weak central government with shrinking financial resources and a serious imbalance between rich and poor regions. In 1983, total funds in budgets of local governments already equalled that in the budget of the central government. This situation had to be modified, and taxation reforms of 1994, called tax sharing schemes, made another turn in the course.

Permission for Private and Collective Enterprises to Operate Commercial Business

Small collective and private businesses were allowed to operate during the early stage of reforms, as a supplement to production and service provided by state enterprises. Individual businesses could now get their registrations from government offices and thus gain certain recognition. Most early private businesses were in urban centres and in service industries. They gradually moved into commerce and manufacturing sectors after they accumulated sufficient assets and capital. Initially, the official line was not to let private business owners employ a large number of workers, thus limiting the size of their business. The fear was about a breach of socialist doctrines on labour exploitation. This ideological line was soon crossed in reality, and private business took a bigger share in the economy as a result of further reforms.

Collective enterprises received protection and priority in operations in many regions, since local governments were eager to promote local business and make local economy more prosperous. With semi-official backing and without many restrictions on their operations, collective enterprises, especially those in rural areas, boomed, and gained large market shares in many industries.

Opening to the World

Special Economic Zones

The central government made early opening experiments with a designed blueprint of economic zones in coastal regions. The original ideas intended to copy the models of open zones in South-eastern Asian economies and to fully utilise the overseas Chinese connections widespread in southern provinces.

The first group of **special economic zones** included four localities: Shenzhen, Zhuhai, Shantou (all in Guangdong province) and Xiamen (in Fujian province). Shenzhen is next to Hong Kong, and Zhuhai next to Macau. Shantou (Swatow) is famous for its overseas Chinese network, and Xiamen is facing Taiwan and has close ancestry and dialectal links with the latter.

These zones in southern provinces are geographically far from political and economic centres of China, so the leadership considered it safe to conduct reform experiments there. The choice of Shenzhen has also served another purpose, which was not apparent at the beginning. As a new powerful city in the southern province, Shenzhen could well balance the clout of Guangzhou (the provincial capital), which had been reluctant to follow the lines of the central government and often expressed the will to run its own course.

The setting up of these special zones aimed at introducing market operations, capitalist production and foreign investment. The initial sizes of zones were small, but they swelled to big cities once capital and labour flowed in. Ironically, early capital inflow came from other regional governments and state organisations, in hope of getting favourable treatments and investing for higher returns. By the end of 1980s, these domestic investors poured in over 8 billion yuan in Shenzhen alone. Foreign investment, especially which from Hong Kong and overseas Chinese, moved in later.

These economic zones are special not only for their formation, but chiefly for the favourable policies they were granted. Policies were generally flexible and supportive. Take Shenzhen for example. In taxation, there were exemptions on export tariff and local income tax, and enterprise income tax for companies in Shenzhen, foreign or domestic, was at 15%, while state enterprises elsewhere paid 55%. In land use, developers could get land cheap and turn land to money after development of various forms, such as industrial, tourist or housing projects. Real estate development became a major sector in Shenzhen's economy, and the municipal government received huge revenues from land lease. Regional governments in other cities followed Shenzhen's example and leased out land under their control to raise revenues. In foreign exchange, the central government allowed Shenzhen enterprises to enjoy generous rules, for them to retain surplus foreign currencies from their business dealings. In other parts of China at the time, all foreign currencies were handed in to relevant government bureaux. In making local regulations, the Shenzhen government had few interventions from the central and provincial governments to its running of the zone. Its foreign investment and fiscal management were quite independent, and this government had the right to choose its own personnel of the bureaucracy, selecting from recruits all over the country. This freedom attracted many talents and adventurers who disliked the existing rigid personnel system and ubiquitous control over labour mobility in other parts of the country. To many, Shenzhen was a new frontier city of the Wild West.

In 1988, **Hainan** Island was officially declared as Hainan province, the fifth and the biggest special economic zone, and perhaps the last one. Hainan has a size of Taiwan and possesses numerous advantages in development, such as potential for tourism and energy industries.

All these five special economic zones enjoy similar favourable policies and have benefited from their unique special status till the end of 1990s.

Shanghai Pudong New Zone

There is no more special economic zone being set up after Hainan. An exception is Pudong in Shanghai (the east bank of Huangpu River). As a remote part of Shanghai in the past, Pudong had been a backwater for centuries. The Pudong New Zone was officially established in 1990 and designated as a new development zone. It gained an official status quite similar to the Shanghai municipal government, its head being at the official rank of deputy Mayor. The Pudong New Zone is in effect a new Shanghai, in comparison with Shanghai *per se*, which is at the west bank of Huangpu River and has long been an internationally renowned metropolis. Since Shanghai is unable to gain a special economic zone status, Pudong takes its place. In terms of treatment, Pudong has enjoyed more favourable policies and freedom in running business, even more than those established special economic zones. These included revenue retention, tax rates, high-tech imports, foreign investment in previously prohibited areas (for example, banking and retail chains), and relaxed rules on labour market. Today, figures and surveys put the population of Pudong at over 4 million, and numerous foreign multinationals set up their headquarters there. Pudong New Zone is truly a new Shanghai on the rise.

Open Cities

Following the first wave of special economic zones, a group of coastal cities were opened to the outside world. In 1984, the central government named these 14 coastal cities. They are, from north to south, Dalian, Qinhuangdao, Tianjin, Yantai, Qingdao, Lianyungang, Shanghai, Nantong, Ningbo, Wenzhou, Fuzhou, Guangzhou, Zhanjiang, and Beihai. These zones are all with ports for export/import, and have more links with international markets than other cities. They enjoyed more favourable policies than did inland regions, but were not given the same status and treatments as those special economic zones.

Foreign Direct Investment (FDI)

China had a state ministry to handle foreign trade, but none for foreign investment, since this was not an issue for consideration, and there were no ready models to introduce. Under reforms, the need for capital emerged, and the initiatives for attracting funds from overseas Chinese and foreign investors were put forward by local governments in the south. The central government began to search for alternatives to their tested model of foreign funding, by getting foreign loans, and realised the urgency to experiment bolder measures. This led to the early trials of foreign direct investment.

In 1979, the Law of China/Foreign Joint Ventures was passed. The law allows foreign capital to flow in, mainly through joint ventures, and the first such venture was a limited company providing airline foods. The forms of FDI include joint ventures and foreign-controlled companies, as oppose to portfolio investment. In early years of foreign investment, joint venture was a model preferred by the Chinese government, and Chinese majority shareholding was strictly observed. Foreign-controlled enterprises became more common in later years. At this early stage, capital from Hong Kong and Macau took the biggest shares, and average sizes of ventures were small. Two exceptions were Beijing Jeep, which was a joint venture between American Motors and Beijing Motor Work, and Shanghai VW. The lasting quarrels and troubles from the first venture have since been thoroughly examined in business case studies. Special economic zones and open cities attracted most foreign investment. If foreign investors had doubts over the business environment of China, they would conduct tests in those zones to feel more secured about operating in these designated areas. On foreign investment in China, there are separate chapters in following texts.

Road to a Market Economy

Breakthroughs

In a general review of reforms in China, several key hurdles had to be cleared along the way. These may be ideological or practical barriers. Once a hurdle was cleared, the process of reforms evidently quickened.

Making these breakthroughs appear vital to the direction of reforms in China. The general trend of reforms is from a planned economy to a market economy. This goal initially was not fully recognised by the leadership. It was only in the 1990s and after the 15th Party Congress in 1997, that this trend was accepted and put as the official guiding principle. There are several aspects worth noting during this course toward a market economy.

Land Rights in Rural China

An early ideological barrier concerned land use by rural population. The collectives and communes dominated rural life for about three decades, and the existence of these social organisations were protected by socialist doctrines and principles of the Party, which derived its legitimacy from a triumphant peasant revolution. Early reformers in the Party had to explain away the opposition to any changes to the commune system and to granting land use to individual farmers. The central leadership leaned heavily on provincial authorities to make trials and produce proofs of workability of new models. The outcome also depended on successful results in agricultural production, a continued and sharp growth, which finally silenced the critics. In theory, this move is a breach of socialist ideals and the Chinese practice of collectivism. The Party leadership under Deng, however, adopted a pragmatic approach to break this barrier and won political approvals from the vast rural population. This political vindication compensated somewhat for the loss of faith in guiding socialist doctrines.

Foreign Investment

Another early hurdle related to the introduction of foreign investment and joint ventures. The Party leadership had implemented a self-reliance policy amid foreign embargos and blockades. The industrial and financial systems of China had managed to retain its independence from external pressure and intervention. To introduce foreign capital and grant a sharing deal to foreign investors drew loud criticisms. It also reflected a clash between domestic and foreign interests. Experiments of foreign investment took place in special economic zones, and Hong Kong and overseas Chinese capital moved in to soften resistance. In practice, joint ventures and foreign companies did face recurring troubles with their domestic Chinese business partners. In the end, attracting foreign investment was taken as a key part of the opening policy, and foreign capital became a valuable source for China's economic growth. On this particular barrier to reforms, China simply followed practice and success in other newly industrialised economies, which allowed foreign direct investment to play a role in their domestic economies.

Price Controls

The next formidable barrier to reforms is price controls. Socialist doctrines give prominence to social and economic equality, and these are achieved through price controls and equal distribution. China had practised such controls vigorously and continuously in previous decades. Furthermore, the issue of prices is often linked with inflation, and the Party had a deep fear of a repeat of hyperinflation in the years of the Nationalist rule. These price controls, however, run counter to market mechanisms and price signals to supply and demand. The Party leadership opened up both wage and price systems, in order to loosen price controls and keep a right balance. Their decisive assault on price controls, however, failed in 1988, and the political upheavals in 1989 led to more cautious steps towards a free market price regime. In the 1990s, numerous changes to prices of various goods and relaxation of price controls became widely accepted. Despite inflations and widening income gaps, price fluctuations are no longer an intimidating factor, and price rises are often accompanied by wage increases as compensation. By the end of last century, very few goods in China were subject to fixed prices by the state.

The "Southern Tours" by Deng Xiaoping

In 1992, the late paramount leader Deng Xiaoping made his final push for deepening reforms during his tours of southern cities of Shanghai, Wuhan and Shenzhen. In his strongly worded speeches, he criticised left wing and conservative ideas becoming influential during the austerity period, and made it clear to all that transforming into a market economy is not an issue for debate and is the central part of the entire reform effort. On the ideologically charged debate of socialism or capitalism, Deng urged to talk less of this division and more of reform experiments toward a market economy as the goal. This was a turning point in reforms, following which the central planning was discredited publicly and a market economy widely accepted by most people. Party resolutions and official policies all turned to endorse reform measures for achieving the goal of a market economy.

Economic Management

In a transitional economy, such management was new to the central leadership, and the 1993 overheating and inflation gave them a rare chance to achieve an important breakthrough. Accustomed to a planned economy and having experienced a round of recession after 1989, the government faced economic cycles under a more market-orientated environment. This may be their first taste of economic cycles common in Western market economies, and their rudimental trials of fiscal and monetary measures, plus traditional application of administrative measures, won the day and led to a soft landing in 1996-1997, against many pessimistic predictions of foreign observers. The satisfactory outcomes gave them much needed confidence in improving macro management of a market economy and in handling following crises. The central government began to consider economic issues and problems increasingly according to accepted economic models and practices. A more detailed discussion of this course of management is given in a following chapter.

From Public to Private Ownership

The first step was to allow private ownership to come into form. This was initiated in early years of reforms, and large numbers of urban residents began to conduct private business of their own. However, even if the private sector was growing fast, the government saw no threat if they had maintained public ownership to large industrial and commercial corporations. To the central government, domination by public-owned enterprises in the economy was not regarded as an issue for debate, and the remaining question is how to draw the right balance between public and private sectors. This mentality changed dramatically in the late 1990s, as private and foreign enterprises performed better than did state enterprises, and financial burdens incurred by these public corporations grew heavier. The new policy of "grab the big, release the small" indicated the change of mind, and in following years a series of measures from the central government were implemented as possible solutions to woes of state enterprises. The government became determined to shrink further the total shares taken by state enterprises in the economy, to withdraw from commercial businesses, and to carry out massive worker layoffs. Despite the protests from the unemployed and sporadic local chaos, the government seems to have made this trend a definite path towards a market economy.

The WTO Accession

Reforms in China have been in two aspects of internal reforms and opening. The Chinese leadership tended to view internal reforms as their own doing and opening as a supplement of more capital inflows and export earnings. The negotiations of China's accession to the WTO fundamentally changed this mindset. By the late 1990s, it had reached such a stage that whether China could maintain the good trend of growth, to a great extent, hinged on its commitment to following international rules. Under WTO rules, many domestic regulations and rules have to be changed or modified in compatibility with internationally accepted practices. Well-established systems in China, even after extensive reforms, may not meet the standards set by the world body. China's economic growth, in particular in import/export, is to be influenced more directly by international recognition and pressure. Two categories of WTO rules, transparency and national treatment, have the widest impact on domestic industries and on government functioning in many sectors. Numerous government regulations and internal rules have to be revised, and government efficiency and effectiveness in implementing set laws are also in question, judging by international standards. In other words, with the WTO accession, business environment in China will have to improve rapidly, in case penalties and retaliation ensue.

The critical question in reforms is reforming to what extent and according to what rules. Reforms up to the WTO entry were taken as internal issues and came with government initiatives and approvals. It is clear, however, from the tremendous effort to enter the WTO that China will not just make internal reforms by their own standards, but also work to become a full market economy by international standards. Subsequent changes must be made to comply with WTO requirements.

At this junction, China's internal reforms and opening merged into one, and an application of international rules would lead to the final goal of market economy. After this breakthrough in guiding principles, the following path is clear to all, and the transformation would go ahead with little possibility of reversal. A significant outcome is marked improvement in business environment for domestic and foreign investors after the accession.

Regional and National Markets

The move towards a market economy has increased market activities and trade volumes. This process has yet completed. A blocking issue is that there are strong tendencies for local governments to foster regional markets and protect local interests. Provincial boundaries form barriers to traders and producers from outside, and local products enjoy huge subsidies and almost guaranteed leading positions in sales. Local and provincial governments carried out retaliatory actions against each other to ensure the market shares of local companies. Regional markets exist to discourage interaction, capital and goods flows, and nation-wide commerce. As a consequence of previous decentralisation, local trade barriers have become a serious challenge to the central leadership and also to the operation of a national market.

On the other hand, a national market is forming, and many nationally well-known brands and products are sold to all corners of the country. Consumers' demand for better goods and services draw in products from other regions, and leading manufacturers have their national networks of distribution and logistics. Some examples are top household appliance and electronics manufacturers Changhong and Haier. Their products entered all regions and received acceptance from local consumers. The central government is also making rules of business and commerce applied to all regions and enforcing the opening of local markets. The entry to the WTO provided the central government with yet another tool for removing barriers, making internal opening in line with implementation of WTO rules.

The above major issues troubled the leadership one after another during the course of reforms. There are countless problems waiting to be solved, but these key issues need to be properly handled as priority. The ideological implications attached to certain issues increased the difficulty levels, and they could be cleared off the list of hurdles only by a pragmatic approach and a long-term vision for future development. As Deng summarised, reforms will prevail if there are hard facts of solid development and, subsequently, wide-ranging benefits for the people.

Consumption and Consumerism

A vital change of mind is the recognition the government gave to the positive impact of public consumption on commercial business and the economy.

Under the planned economy, the government focused on production and distribution as key economic issues. With equal distribution and government allocations, consumption was considered insignificant. By socialist doctrines, consumption created no real value and over-consumption was even close to waste. Frugality and saving were encouraged, similar to the mode in other Asian economies, but with distinctive Chinese socialist characteristics. With similar levels of income, people also did not have big gaps in their consumption or for extra spending. Subsequently, tertiary sectors and service industries received less attention and funding in pre-reform China. Instead of GDP criteria commonly adopted in other economies, China emphasised the combined total of agricultural and industrial output in their national statistics.

Following policy changes and a drive towards a market economy, the government realised the need to promote consumption. Based on simple economics rules, when people spend more, manufacturers would have more sales, and employees receive more pay, and these people in turn have more money to spend. This typical cycle in a market economy of supply and demand was also emerging in China, and in its effort to reform state enterprises, the government saw the need for more consumption, so that these enterprises could make more sales. It is a realisation made under new thinking and setting of reforms.

Another factor is the adoption of international rules in statistics and GDP criteria. The standard formula for calculating total output of an economy is:

$$GDP = C + I + G + NX$$

Here GDP comprises consumption (C), investment (I), government spending (G) and net export (NX). Thus, an increase in consumption represents an increase in the total GDP of a nation. In a developed economy such as the US, consumption forms the bulk of GDP, sometimes nearly 70%. This standard certainly gave the Chinese government some extra incentives to encourage more domestic consumption.

Numerous measures have been put into practice to increase consumption. First it was the change of mind on consumption itself, and the new message from the government and think-tanks was that consumption is good for the economy. A new fashion is consumerism, where consumers see spending on all goods as a natural fact of life, and buying of new goods to replace the old is done at a fast pace. To consume is to live happily. Consumption items soon swell to include most goods and services on the market, from early electrical goods, to electronics, digital devices, motor cars, real estate property, to travel, entertainment and education. Chinese consumers now can enjoy what foreign residents do, and have become more selective in spending. The emerging middle classes, including white-collar workers and private businesspeople, form the main groups in these consumption waves.

Even spending on exclusive top-end luxury became acceptable. Previous public disdain of such extravagance now does not bother those who can afford. This change of attitude has led to some extreme kinds of consumption. Conspicuous consumption, wasteful spending, and luxury consumption have become the norm and are popular in big urban centres, and the new rich are less humble and more used to show off their riches in various ways. A latest sign of this extreme luxury consumption are the purchases made by a number of Chinese of top-line Bentley and Maybach cars without slightest hesitation. Foreign luxury brands sold very well in China in past years.

The government encouraged spending also through creating demand and discouraging high savings. In an economy of relative surplus, any consumption would benefit product and service providers. Measures included lowering bank interests, which would pull out more national savings into the market and make more spending possible on consumer goods. Interest levels in China are as low now as in other developed countries. Although this was chiefly aimed at fighting deflation, the government seemed to understand that boosting consumption is an approach they could apply in ending deflation earlier and gaining growth.

The government also turned to encourage consumption of various kinds, both high and low-ends. With a widening division between the wealthy and the poor, the government promulgated regulations aiming at those lower-end consumers, providing subsidies and minimum wages for them, so as to increase money spending by these social groups. Government spending on these categories grew bigger each year, for the purposes of social stability and an additional source of consumption as well.

Political Reforms

Political reforms in China have been less dramatic and reflected the gradualist approach more faithfully than economic reforms do. In comparison with Eastern European countries, China is still officially a socialist country with an economy in transition. Judging by other criteria of democratic structures and press freedom, China has retained political systems significantly different from those in the West.

Political reforms have concentrated on institutions, rather than structures. The Chinese leadership made the reform undertaking primarily in areas of their own concerns, and improvement, rather than replacement, is the key in all measures taken. Political structures based on the model of the US have been rejected repeatedly by past and present leaderships, and economic growth boosted their confidence in developing a system of their own which does not impede development while being non-Western.

Changes have been made to the Party and government institutions, which can be loosely put under the term of political reforms.

Decentralisation of Authority

This line of reforms was carried out in a similar way to the decentralisation in economic reforms. In essence, the central government gave away more authority to provincial and local governments and allowed them to act on their own initiatives. The right to experiment on political and institutional reforms could be carried out first in regions. In both political and economic areas, regional competition became common, and there has emerged a divergence among regional governments on the direction of reforms and related issues. They could move toward different directions, based on their interest and judgement of situations. Ideological taboos could be easily broken amid this competition, and pragmatism prevailed in the running of local administration. The central government would have to respect the will of influential regional authorities on national policies and general guidelines.

During the critical period of 1992, debates on future direction and pace of reforms heated up between two camps, and the central issue of retaining economic planning or establishing a market economy drew clashing opinions from various regional leaders. Shanghai and other southern provinces advocated for more market functions and minimising state control on production and consumption. They lost no time voicing their concerns and finally received approval from Deng, during his southern tour, on faster growth and bolder moves towards a market economy. For state enterprise reforms, the policy of disposing of small- and medium-sized enterprises also caused great stirs. Local governments by and large harbour less fear than the central government of this giving away of state assets. Their neutral stand derived from their understanding that many state enterprises made little contributions anyway and that selling these assets would bring short-term benefits to local economy. Local interests outweigh their concern over transfers of public ownership. The central government, on the other hand, had more worries about the impact of state asset disposal and the overall shares state sectors would keep in the economy.

It is often the case that the central leadership succeeded in formally laying down certain reform policies in Party and People's Congress resolutions that had been strongly recommended and put to trials by local authorities. All these are possible because the central leadership from the outset made a crucial decision to decentralise powers, drawing from the hard lessons of centralisation in pre-reform years. This decentralisation is of course not nearly compatible with democratic systems in the West, but the decision gave chance to a more balanced political power structure and heightened political participation from all interest groups.

Legal Reforms

In a socialist or authoritarian country like China, the government bears the ultimate responsibilities of holding up and executing laws. The Chinese government had maintained its rule through state control in pre-reform years. A sharp change in policy came in reform years, which illustrated that the government had to rely on legal means to run the country. The emphasis is on "rule by law", typified in the 15th Party Congress resolutions in 1997, with the government classifying things as legal or illegal, so the society would follow the set rules. Although this is far off from the common practice of "rule of law" in developed economies, it is a distinctive departure from the long tradition of "rule of man". In running the country, the first step must be abandoning rigid ideological doctrines and zealous personality cults.

Reforms to the legal systems covered the following four areas:

1. Property rights: from emphasising socialist public ownership to protecting private ownership, the Party made a great leap in faith and offloaded enormous burdens of ideological baggage. This dramatic turnaround was done through amendments to the Constitution and to Party principles. Personal and public property rights are declared protected by law, thus reducing the risks of doing business and making money.

2. Lawyers: lawyers are again allowed to practice in China. Big efforts have been made to improve quantity and quality of lawyers, with many training and exchange programmes. These included training projects by the UN and the US. Hong Kong professionals offered training in common laws, in contrast to continental laws. Chinese lawyers are governed by the Law of Lawyers, and are given more freedom to fulfil their duties to their clients. They are not always being seen as part of state prosecution teams, as was the case before. The numbers of people in the legal professions have increased sharply in recent times. By September 2004, there are over 100,000 registered lawyers practicing legal services and over 11,000 law firms in business.

3. Business laws: more business-related laws were passed in recent years. The purpose is to improve business environment and perfect legal protection of business practice. It is also partly made in compliance with the WTO rules, under which business dealings

The latest Law of Administrative License, passed by the People's Congress in August 2003 and was effective from 1 July 2004, has particularly positive implications for business, since it promulgates the proper ways for getting official permission and making appeals. The law in effect limits the government's power in authorising projects, thus leaving more space for unhindered economic activities and reducing opportunity of rent seeking.

There will be many government regulations that are to be challenged in court on the basis of this particular law, and those regulations judged illegal would have to be withdrawn. For example, the Shenzhen government has examined several local regulations regarding hotel, real estate and elevator sectors, and they are to be abolished as being deemed against this License law. In Sichuan province as well, the government suspended 122 categories of charges on residents, covering permits for a couple of dozens of small business trades. Apparently, many of these categories were based on draconian local regulations, and this suspension could save local taxpayers over 70 million yuan.

Immediate effects of this new law on business doing are smaller numbers of business ventures subject to government permission and drastically shortened time for official approvals. With more checks and balances, and clauses on compensation to individuals, this law would lead to minimising red tape and official abuse of power.

are to be standardised. Relevant laws include the Company Law, the Banking Law, the Foreign Enterprises Law, the Law of Consumption, and a series of other laws regarding business practices. Government regulations, from either the central or local governments, on the other hand, are also important for business doing. These official regulations could be in various forms of ministry document, directive, circular, guideline, etc. and they are issued several times each year to keep pace with evolving events and emergencies. Investors are to watch closely the changes in business laws and regulations. There has been a growing need in the country to amend laws and issue new regulations in a fast-changing situation.

4. Legal proceedings: to make "rule by law" applicable in economic and social life, the government began to put emphasis on legal procedures and due course, in contrast to past practice of prosecution without procedures. With court rulings and lawyers' defence, the accused and people involved in legal cases can have more protection of their legal rights. For business people, their

asset ownership becomes secured with proper channels provided to have their cases heard and disputes solved. Recent moves included improving the quality of proposed legislation, which demands careful drafting and wording of the bills tabled and discourages the rushing of legislation process. The People's Congress is to screen bill proposals and reject those that potentially infringe on people's constitutional rights.

Government Structures

The government itself was a major target for reforms, and has been subject to rounds of changes to its structure, size and operations. Reforms have included:

Reduction in Size and Changes to Bureaux

Reforms began in restructuring of central government bureaux. Comparing the ministries under the current State Council and those before 1978, a striking feature is that industry-related ministries are now few in number. There had been eight or more ministries of machinery industries under the State Council. Those ministries were in charge of industries from heavy to light, from metals to energy, from machine tools to national defence equipment. The government managed all industrial production in a planned economy. From the first rounds of institutional reforms to the government, many of these ministries were forced to merge or cease to exist. Those machinery industry ministries turned into controlling companies of the industries concerned, and took off their caps bearing government insignia. For example, the Ministry of Metallurgy changed to the national general company of metallurgical industries, and this institution now oversees both steel production and non-ferrous metal production in the country. Large state enterprises, which were subject to relevant industrial ministries, are now the sole responsibility of the State Owned Assets Administration Commission. In the current State Council, only a handful of ministries are industry-related, such as the Ministry of Information Industry, or the Ministry of Construction.

Another line of restructuring is the reduction of workforce within the government. The government acknowledged from the outset that overstaffing was a serious obstacle to raising efficiency in administration. Several rounds of downsizing were carried out in the past 25 years, starting from 1982, to 1987, 1993, 1998 and 2004. Departments, even ministries, were abolished or merged, and large numbers of government employees were transferred or retired. The 1998 restructuring cut the size of the central government by one third, and 20 million workers were made redundant from state organisations.

Unfortunately, bureaucrats managed to create new departments and bureaux and increased staff in total numbers. This resembles closely the situation depicted in the famous British TV series "*Yes, Minister!*", where bureaucrats viewed the growing size of departments under their charge as a sign of success. Although the Chinese government now accepts the idea of small government, previous downsizing did not work as planned, and the numbers of government employees remain large. The latest round of job cutting focuses on those semi-government institutions, such as publishing houses, academies and universities, schools, hospital, etc. These institutions have approximately 30 million employees and 300 billion yuan in assets. The sizes of these institutions have grown bulky due to taking in layed off employees from government offices in previous rounds of downsizing. This is considered the final phase of restructuring in term of size reduction. The approach adopted is to make these institutions more market-oriented and receive less government subsidies.

A Public Servant System

There have been efforts to turn former government officials and employees to public servants. This is borrowed from developed economies, where the system of public servants provides stability and high quality of service to the society. The Chinese government had an urgent need to shift from a place of Party officials to a place of public servants. This need led to the passing of a new government regulation in 1993 on the establishment of a public servant system. The previous internal appointment and promotion systems continued to be the mainstream, however, hiring new personnel through open recruitment began to take place. Many government bureaux employed university graduates in a similar way as private and foreign companies, and middle-level positions are open to competition among professionals from outside the bureaucracy. A contract scheme is applied to public servants, which would be terminated according to set conditions. Drawing on experience from developed economies, the government conducts regular unified examinations for people to take and selects those who pass as qualified public servants. It is likely that in future government functionaries will perform as public servants based on Western models, though the power of decision-making remains in the hands of higher-level party officials.

Retirement Schemes

The trend of making regular retirement a permanent feature of the government began with elder leaders and officials from the 1980s, as illustrated in the setting up of the Party's Advisory Committee. The trend was later reinforced by wide application of compulsory retirement to all government employees. Officials over the age of 60 without being promoted to ministerial levels must leave their current posts. With certain reluctance, the former State President Jiang Zemin retired at an advanced age and passed that top position to the current President Hu Jintao. His departure gave the final approval to the retirement system, and government employees and officials across the country are strictly put under this uniform system. A good example is former Foreign Minister Qian Qichen, who left that post at the age of 70, and is now having no official duties except writing memoirs. As discussed in other chapters, this compulsory retirement caused certain problems of corruption, as officials in power may not willingly relinquish their duties and choose to take bribes before their retirement dates come.

New Generations of Leaders and Officials

At the beginning of reforms, the central leadership consisted of mostly old revolutionaries. A first shift of power occurred in the mid 1980s, with Hu Yaobang as the Party's General Secretary. With a brief stay by Zhao Ziyang, the next in line for the post was Jiang, taking over in 1989 and remaining in the post till 2002. Hu Jintao was officially declared the General Secretary in 2003. In the State Council, the line of succession ran from Zhao, Li Peng, Zhu Rongji and to Wen Jiabao as the current Premier. After these rounds of replacement and new appointments, it is apparent that the central leadership is getting younger, with higher education levels and more administrative experiences. A prominent change happening is that new leaders have commonly less revolutionary background and credentials, are less ideologically tuned and more enlightened in policy making. At medium-ranking levels, the government is filled with people who have satisfactory education and sufficient experience of international environment. As the retirement and public servant systems work longer, the central and regional governments could soon be the places for professionals and technocrats, rather than party officials.

The Jiang-Hu succession also marks a turning point in the history of the People's Republic. Based on past examples of internal frictions and purges of the Communist Party, most foreign observers made pessimistic predictions of a messy transitional process and instability for a couple of years in the country. In the end, this transfer of top power went through peacefully and caused no evident disturbance to the economy. In fact, the new leadership demonstrated its flexibility and open-mindedness in handling the SARS crisis and economic overheating between 2003 and 2004. Their performance exceeded expectations of them even in years without crisis.

The Sun Zhigang Case

In March 2003, a young temporary resident of Guangzhou was detained by police for not carrying his identity papers. He was then transferred to a halfway house for detained migrant labourers and was beaten to death there three days later. The news report and open debates on Internet sites forced the central government to investigate the case, over the objection of local governments. In June 2003, Guangdong High Court sentenced criminals involved in Sun's death and ordered a large amount of compensation from the state to the victim's family. The debates went beyond the legal case and focused on the basic rights of migrant workers and the due process in police actions. It was indicated that a person could sue state organisations for abuse and malpractice. The national and provincial regulations, which allowed such detention to happen, were also harshly criticised. In the end, Premier Wen on 20 June 2003 signed a new State Council regulation on assistance and support to urban residents in need. The regulation superseded the previous regulation, which had been practised since 1982 and created multiple problems in dealing with the urban poor. This case demonstrates a growing understanding that the state is responsible for its proper treatment of citizens, and that actions against law by governments should be punished according to laws and principles of rights.

Relaxing Controls on Media and Public Opinions

As expected, information and public opinions were strictly monitored in a socialist country. Reforms of over 20 years, however, have eroded the overwhelming supervising power of the government. Part of reforms began in relaxing controls on information and news, and debates on policy and regulation matters became common. The Party's bureaux with supervision tasks have lost their influence in imposing certain accepted modes.

Recent application of Internet technology provides a new channel of news and public opinions. Even with regular checking by government inspectors, Internet sites increased in number rapidly, and their contents cover wide-ranging topics, many of them current and sensitive. A good example was the extensive discussion on the Internet about a young migrant who died of abuses at a detention centre in Guangzhou in 2003. The public outcry forced the central government to promptly annul a decade-old regulation regarding treatment of floating labourers.

In the meantime, the government has allowed non-state newspapers to enter the market, and they flourished indeed. With a keen eye for commercial benefits and for readers as customers, many newspaper groups have grown super rich and influential. Shining commercial buildings in many cities, in fact newspaper headquarters, testify to this. Commercialised TV channels also obtained permits from the government and are receiving huge revenues from selling commercials. Under a relaxed control, media in several forms entered the phase of competition and commercial business.

Open Elections

This experiment has been done at two fronts. One is the so-called "democracy within the Party", where party organisations attempted to establish balanced mechanisms of collective decision making. From the central bureaux to grassroots units, efforts have been made on limiting the power of party bosses and supervising the running of party organisations. Such moves have the particular urgency since widespread official corruption hurt the Party dearly, especially its credibility and effectiveness to rule.

The other front concerns the People's Congress and its selection of delegates. It is on this note that most progress in democratising has been made. Local elections have been routinely carried out, and residents in rural and urban areas have the right to vote for their candidates at village, township and county levels. In a direct election, local candidates would have to compete for their nominations and selections, and some of them, though named by government officials, face the consequence of being voted out. The central government has allowed elections to the county level but steadfastly rejected national direct or indirect elections, and elections at provincial level. Such schemes are certainly not on the agenda, and a fear of losing control and widespread chaos drives this line of reckoning. For local elections, candidates come from individuals and community units, but political parties and their nominations are prohibited. This is the Chinese type of political representation and participation, quite different from the Western models of parliamentary democracy.

Further to this trial run of elections, a more significant trend is the increasing role of supervision by the People's Congress on government administration. One channel of supervision is through budget approvals, which the government needs to obtain formally. More vocal complaints and "no" votes have become common at national and local Congress meetings, and the government has to tackle the task of revising their budgets and plans under public pressure. The end results are often more sensible and balanced budgets for the economy. If Congress delegates used to be seen as nominal representatives for rubber-stamping, their strengthening roles in approving government budgets and making legislative proposals now prove some worthiness.

It should be emphasised here that political reforms in China focused on institutional changes and improvement of governance. Sweeping political liberalisation was substituted with a gradualist approach. The concentration of political power has been loosened in a controlled manner, so that structural shocks to the whole nation could be cushioned. In comparison with bolder economic reforms, political changes are much less dramatic. This is due to the pragmatic attitude of the Chinese leadership, which seek tangible benefits rather than grand plans of social remoulding. Short of Western-style parliamentary democracy, progress in other areas have been made spreading a longer time span and without a big fuss.

Outcomes of Economic Reforms

From information available, we can make a preliminary progress report of reforms so far. This assessment will cover the following aspects:

1. Non-state Businesses and Market Activities

State enterprises now count only about one third of market share and total output, moving down from their previous overwhelming position. This process has been quickened since the late 1990s, and firm government measures to shrink the size of state sectors made the reduction in size possible. Private and foreign enterprises take up some equal shares of the other two thirds. It is likely that domestic private enterprises will grow strongly, in competition with state and foreign enterprises. China has changed to a mixed economy after reforms, and the rise of private sectors is a clear sign of a market economy in the making (see Figures 12.6 to 12.8, on pages 452–454).

2. Economic Growth and Social Stability

The rate of economic growth on average is high, through a process of early double-digit growth and steadier growth under management. In the meantime, the economy passed a few cycles and stabilised. China is now one of the safest places and a hot spot for investment. There are separate chapters of discussions on this aspect.

3. Increasing Trade and Foreign Investment

In terms of trade volumes, China is the third biggest trading country in 2004, and China was the number one country in taking in foreign direct investment in 2003. These issues will be discussed in a later chapter.

4. A Society with Diversity

A number of recent trends in China indicate the growing extent of openness and social diversity. NGOs (non-government organisations) began to emerge and have their say on issues of their concern. Most prominent are environmental protection groups, such as "Green Homes" and "Friends of the Nature". These groups have gained certain inroads and access to government organisations and bureaux, and had their voice heard and issues discussed at People's Congress. Chinese environmental groups even made their public presentations at the bid for the Beijing Olympics. The emerging of Chinese NGOs began with the fourth World Women's Conference held in Beijing in 1995. Some other groups are concerned with AIDS. In previous years, these groups met certain suspicions and rejections from government as well as from the general public, but they were eventually accepted more widely in the country. Premier Wen and Ms. Wu, the woman State Councillor, visited AIDS patients at Beijing's hospitals and showed their support for campaigns against the spreading disease. More recently, anti-Japanese groups gained prominence in news reports on their protests, aiming at Japan's territorial claim over Diaoyu Island and their denial of past war crimes against Chinese people. These groups are certainly not government-sponsored, and their activities sometimes draw official harassment. This is a new development in Sino-Japanese relations, noticed by Chinese and Japanese scholars, and both governments feel the pressures from these determined groups.

The Du Jiang-yan Weir, a world heritage site and the ancient water works built 2,500 years ago in Sichuan province, was under threat in 2003 from a new dam construction work nearby. This threat was first investigated by a volunteer environmental protection group, "Green Homes", and members of the group, as journalists and experts, exposed the project in news reports and ignited heated public debates in all types of media. There were apparently internal tussles among local and provincial governments, which wavered on the basis of their own interests. With the combined forces of the media, the environment group, public opinion and experts' recommendations, the relevant central government agency, the State Environmental Protection Administration, finally took action and persuaded the provincial government of Sichuan to seal off the site and suspend the dam construction project. In early 2004, this group again got involved in public debates on the relocation of 100-year-old Beijing Zoo and lobbied successfully for a shelving of the original plans. The central issue is that, for potential commercial interests from this relocation, the municipal government kept their plans in secret and failed to go through proper consultation procedures in urban planning. Once their intention was exposed by the NGO group to the public, the government' move was clearly seen as an abuse of power.

Public Opinions and Interest Groups

There are more channels for public opinions to be expressed. Newspapers and TV stations bear the main responsibility of letting out ideas and complaints, and Internet sites provide additional channels of feedback and updated information. Public debates have grown in a number of topics and gained higher intensity. In the first years of the 21ˢᵗ century, public debates on newspapers and Internet forums have led to a number of changes to official lines and reversal of government decisions. The Sun Zhigang case, as described above, the Liu Yong case, the eviction by force of local residents to make room for property development by the richest man in Shanghai, who was later charged for frauds, the massive eviction and demolition in similar manner by county officials in Hunan, which led to drastic revisions to government regulations in order to protect residents' rights against draconian government actions, and many other cases, all of them bear witness to active participation of and extensive public debates by people from all walks of life. Internet is now seen as the place of democracy for ordinary citizens. The point is not that these public debates have led to certain legal cases being reversed, but that unjust cases were exposed, and the public had a chance to make their own judgement from the point of view of their rights and common moral standards. Subsequently, the government is now subject to mounting pressure to make their administration more sensible and defensible.

The Liu Yong Case

A local Mafia boss was arrested in Shenyang in August 2003 for a series of criminal activities including murder. The Provincial High Court gave him a death sentence with two-year suspension. This is a light sentence according to Chinese criminal laws.

The sentences caused outcry and heated debates on newspapers and Internet forums, and under-the-counter deals were exposed. The defence for the accused was questioned severely. This case had to be transferred to the Supreme Court in Beijing, and Liu was then sentenced to death and executed by the end of 2003. This case gives a good chance for people to discuss on the functioning of a justice-based legal system and the increasingly vital role played by lawyers. The focal point is whether people who can afford to hire renowned lawyers are subject to different rules from those who cannot.

Special Interest Groups

These could be groups bonded by commercial interests and industrial connections, or groups with political and social purposes. Groups in the latter category are close to lobbyist groups in Western countries. Those in the former have clear goals in their forming and functioning. Their coordinated work could put considerable influence on rules and plan decisions of local and central governments. A recent example is the clash between government actions and response from real estate developers. In June 2003, the People's Bank issued No. 121 circular to tighten bank lending to property development and demand higher levels of self-funding by developers. This sent out strong shock waves, since most property projects in China, from the beginning to the end, rely on bank loans for normally over 70% of total funding. Restricting bank credits would mean to cut off their lifelines. Developers would also lose potential profit gains if the size of their development were curtailed. Developers as a group moved swiftly to respond and defied almost collectively this new government rule. They organised public forums for leading developers in Beijing to voice their opposition and dissatisfaction. They also received a favourable hearing and support from their direct supervisory body, the Ministry of Construction, which worried more about a slowdown in an industry under its charge. This interest group succeeded in pushing for a revised government directive, and they got it in the form of "State Council Document No. 18", issued in August of the year. The new directive made modifications to the circular from the People's Bank and gave a balanced assessment of the situation, after broad "consultations". The impact of the first government directive was largely mitigated, and observers viewed this round of battle as a success of the lobbying campaign by property developers.

In another example, domestic retailers were deeply worried by the rushing in of giant multinational retail chains like Wal-Mart and Carrefour. They complained that foreign retailers received preferential treatments from both central and local governments and entered the China market ahead of the WTO entry schedules. Their fast expansion brought them dominant positions in the market, and domestic companies found it hard to compete. Several local retailers formed an alliance and drafted regulation proposals in an attempt to limit the expansion and oligopoly of giant foreign chains. Such drafts were drawn on the existing models of developed economies in restricting large retailers, and they put the drafts forward to Congress delegates to have a favourable hearing. These proposals have now been submitted to the Ministry of Commerce for consideration.

Other special interest groups function following the same logic, to protect their vested interests and lobby authorities to favour their stands. This diversity of individual and group interests makes the government's tasks and administration more complex throughout the country.

The Rise of Middle Classes

Along with prosperity and rising incomes, middle classes are growing rapidly in number. A preliminary study conducted in 2003 put the number as over 100 million, by Chinese standards. They are mostly urban residents, white-collar workers, golden-collar staff (people who take upper-middle and top positions in business corporations), and government employees and business owners. With economic independence, these groups tend to keep a distance from official lines and show their opposition to official policies if those tread on their interests.

5. Widening Social Divide

China is now divided along several key lines. One is the line between urban and rural regions. For many public issues, official policies may just prefer one to the other, such as decisions on food prices. Another is the line between the poor and the wealthy. A smaller number of people amassed huge fortunes, in contrast to large numbers of people at or below official poverty lines. One indicator is that a high percentage of the national bank deposits belong to a small number of depositors. To a lesser degree, a dividing line is also drawn between people with average incomes and those super rich. The third is the line between prosperous, powerful coastal regions and poorer, remote inland regions. The divergence was so evident and contrasts so great that the central government was roundly blamed and forced to make remedies from the late 1990s onwards. Discussions on these topics will be in other chapters.

6. Social Security Issues

Since reforms sped up economic growth and widened the gaps in income, previous socialist principles have in effect been abandoned, and traditional state protection of workers has also gone in a competitive market. When the government undertook the daunting task of reforming state enterprises, they expected the benefits from laying off workers but failed to foresee the high costs, economic and social, in doing that. It was the widespread unemployment and workers' protests in the late 1990s that woke up the government. Without sufficient welfare covers, economic growth would halt and social unrest would wreck the country. Emulating developed economies, the central government established the new Ministry of Social Security and allocated more funds for a comprehensive social welfare net in the country. It has been agreed that this social security issue will make or break the government's effort on reforms, and the system is apparently not sufficient to cover the people in need, despite the fact that the costs already enlarged government deficits.

7. International Competition

Ever since the early opening, China has faced growing international competition. With cheap labour and low costs, Chinese companies may have increased their exports to developed economies, but international competition in all forms has come right back to their doorsteps. Especially since the WTO entry, Chinese enterprises encountered stricter rules on business operations, labour standards, environmental protection, intellectual property rights, etc. While China's economic development has created a higher level of dependence on overseas markets, strong protectionist swing in developed economies may prevent China from following the successful path of those early dragon economies. Anti-dumping measures have considerably raised barriers to Chinese goods in overseas markets, and the WTO entry has yet to relieve this pain. In a worst case scenario, the Chinese economy may even face sanctions and blockades from developed economies and find it tremendously difficult in recovery.

On the other hand, foreign multinationals moved into the China market in droves. With China's favourable policies toward foreign investment, foreign companies have established their bases and expanded ever deeper to all corners and markets. Industrial leaders in many sectors are foreign multinationals, and domestic companies collapsed in an alarming rate in front of this assault. Most of them have no clear advantage in an open market competition, and their market shares would shrink consistently. With less revenues and earnings, domestic companies would have to spend less on technological and industrial upgrading. This, in turn, would further drag down the level of competitiveness. In an economy dominated by foreign players, the government will find it extremely hard to manage over a financial or economic crisis.

For each outcome listed above, there is a corresponding chapter in the following for a more detailed discussion. These outcomes could be put into two groups. Items 1 to 4 represent certain positive effects of the reforms since 1978, while items 5 to 7 perhaps represent some negative consequences or potential trouble spots in the economy. This division will be discussed in regard to future prospects at the end of the book.

Key Concepts

The Chinese gradualist approach and the application of shock therapy in other transitional economies
Rural household responsibility system
Dual track price system
Decentralisation in fiscal and investment authorities
Special open economic zones
Issues of reforms towards a market economy
Issues in political institutional reforms
Major aspects of reform outcomes

Discussion Questions

1. On the basis of the texts and additional information you gather, discuss the process of economic and political reforms, and evaluate their results, in consideration of the gradualist approach.
2. What is your opinion on the degree and extent of this market economy? How do you term (give a definition of) this economy? What are the aspects that move towards the direction of a market economy you understand, and what are those dissimilar to one?
3. Match the aspects of political reforms in China with your own understanding and criteria, find discrepancies and give explanations.

4. Will decentralisation boost democratic trends or create barriers to them? Is decentralisation a necessary condition for democracy? What will be the plausible ways of democratisation in China under the current political systems and economic development?

Related Readings

Lubman, Stanley, *Bird in a cage: legal reform in China after Mao*, Stanford, Stanford University Press, 1999.

Naughton, Barry, *Growing out of the Plan: Chinese Economic Reform, 1978-1993*, Cambridge, Cambridge University Press, 1995.

Perkins, Dwight, *Market control and Planning in Communist China*, Cambridge, Mass., Harvard University Press, 1966.

Riskin, Carl, *China's political economy: the quest for development since 1949*, New York, Oxford University Press, 1987.

Selden, Mark, *The political economy of Chinese socialism*, New York, M.E. Sharpe, 1988.

Story, Jonathan, *China: the race to market—What China's transformation means for business, markets and the new world order*, London, Prentice Hall, 2003.

5

State Enterprises and Other Players in the Economy

China at the current stage of transition has an economy of mixed natures. From its socialist roots, the economy has not rid itself of public ownership and state planning completely. The idea that state-owned assets should be the backbone of the economy has not been entirely discredited and abandoned. In the meantime, other types of economic forces are allowed to play a role during the reforms, making it possible for the economic landscape to shift and remould. Under these circumstances, there are the ubiquitous signs of dominant state sectors in the economy, while different forms of enterprises quite freely operate and expand. This makes the economy of China quite stimulating and vigorous, nothing short of being eventful, and gives hope for a more promising future.

Business enterprises working side by side in China's mixed economy include state-owned, collective, private and foreign types. This chapter will give brief description of three of them, while foreign enterprises will be discussed in other chapters.

State Enterprises

This unique identity used to exist in many socialist countries, and now it remains a formidable force in the economy of China. In general, there are quite distinctive features of enterprises under a market economy and those under a planned economy.

Enterprises in a market economy have their legal entity, which implies legal protection for the assets and ownership from the demands of the state, and the responsibilities are borne by enterprise owners. They normally have shareholders and proprietors of the enterprises, who have a stake in the business and share mutual benefits and risks. They have a common objective, which is commercial and profit-driven. This objective is totally different from that of government or charity organisations. Means are applied freely to achieve this goal within legal, and sometimes ethical, boundaries. Enterprises in operations deal with their suppliers and customers, and seek as higher profit margins as possible without severing the links with either of these groups. Relations between enterprises, and that between an enterprise and its suppliers, are based on equal commercial status rather than political or social status. Legally, there are no difference in status between a company and another, though in real life, certain enterprises such as a monopoly command higher prices and fees. All enterprises are bound by contracts in their deals and transactions.

In contrast, enterprises in a planned (or command) economy are in effect units of the state. They can be seen as production units, administrative units and educational units for various political purposes. The term "enterprise" in fact does not apply to these entities; they are rather organisations under the control of the state. All these enterprises have public ownership and therefore lack clear legal status. They receive capital investment for their establishment and operation, and are continually financed by state fiscal allocations, without resorting to fund raising or private investors. They have little commercial interest to pursue, and as such see little reason to put in their own initiative and improve overall performance. The ultimate goal is to meet the targets set by higher authorities. There are no real commercial relations between an enterprise and its suppliers and distributors, since official ranking and status are behind these units and issues are dealt with in a way similar to that for administrative matters. For this reason, written contracts with partners and dealers may not be honoured. There are also little concern regarding customer needs and service.

The above major features describe differences between enterprises under the two economic structures. Former socialist countries such as the Soviet Union operated their enterprises in such ways. For Chinese enterprises, they slightly deviated from the common model and allowed certain initiatives to be made. However, the category of state enterprises had its roots firmly planted, and central planning directed operations of most, if not all, enterprises in the country before the time of reforms.

State-owned enterprises came into being in China from government funding in previous decades. There is a difference between state enterprises funded by the central government and those funded by provincial governments. The key and backbone enterprises are under the central government, catalogued in national budgets, and they first emerged from the 156 key projects under Soviet aids in the 1950s. Provincial governments, on the other hand, funded their own projects and enterprises to serve the regions under their charge. Local governments support enterprises of even smaller sizes.

According to official definitions, state enterprises in China today cover state-funded enterprises at the county level and above. It is estimated that state enterprises directly under the central government number 196. They are handled and supervised closely by the State Asset Supervision and Administration Commission, which acts as the owner and sole guardian of state assets on behalf of the whole nation. There are around 9,000 enterprises directly owned by the state, and the total number of "state enterprises" was 174,000 in 2002 and around 160,000 in 2003. This picture illustrates the classifications of small, medium and large state enterprises and their respective sizes. This distinction is crucial, since measures to reform the state sectors have to draw a line along which to determine the policies and treatment. In various scenarios, policy makers need to identify the enterprises to support and those to be disposed of, for the sake of future survival of the state sectors. It is also a rule of thumb in any analysis that problems generally associated with state enterprises have a lot to do with large numbers of enterprises at provincial and local levels.

Major Roles of State Enterprises in the National Economy

Industrial Output

State enterprises used to be the backbone of the economy and had near total share of the national production and distribution. In total industrial output, they produced over 90% in 1978. Since the reforms began, other types of enterprises have emerged strongly, and financial losses caused by state enterprises led the government to lower the proportions of state sectors. State enterprises now produce less, and their output total is down every year. It was already down to 40% of total industrial output in 1998 and is in a steady process of reduction. In 2002, in all the enterprises with 5 million yuan or more annual sales, state enterprises produced 52.8% of industrial output, collectives 8.8%, and the rest was produced by private and foreign industrial enterprises. This indicates that, in manufacturing sectors, medium and large sized state enterprises are able to produce more industrial goods than small collective and private enterprises do, with the latter two groups relying on their large numbers and commercial businesses to make up the one third share they have in total output.

Revenue Provider

State enterprises are major revenue providers to the national treasury. Even after the reduction in industrial output, they still contribute large amounts of financial revenues to the central and local governments. Other types of enterprises pay taxes, and tax collection in China are full of loopholes and uncertainty. State enterprises pay most of their earned profits to the government, as well as taxes, and these are secured sources of government revenues. This contribution is routinely made on the premise that the state had set up these enterprises and accordingly holds full ownership of them. In 2002, state enterprises paid two thirds of total taxes from all industrial enterprises in the country, and the 196 large enterprises attached to the central government paid 64% of taxes from a total of 160,000 state enterprises. Combined taxes paid by the top two taxpaying enterprises, Da Qing Oilfields and PetroChina, were 28.2 billion yuan. In comparison, combined taxes paid by top 50 private enterprises altogether were a mere 1.24 billion yuan. As a whole, state enterprises of all types provided 42% of total revenues the government received in 2002, well above those from private or foreign enterprises.

Employer

A prominent feature of a planned economy is full employment. It is for state enterprises to provide most employment for urban residents. They played such a key role in the past, supporting almost all workers and managers. After two decades of reforms, they are still the employers of large numbers of urban residents. The total numbers have declined in recent years, from 103 million in total workforce in 1990 to 71 million in 2003, about 20% of total urban employment. In the absence of a comprehensive social security system, state enterprises have to support those old, retired and disabled workers and their families, paying for many kinds of costs in life.

Asset Investment

State enterprises embody fixed asset investment made by the government. Despite a shrinking share in total national GDP, this asset value has moved steadily upward, from 4 trillion yuan in 1995 to 7 trillion yuan in 1998, and to 11 trillion yuan in 2003. Increases in value are due to operational efficiency and improved profit margins in the market by the largest state enterprises. These big corporations are also the receivers of huge government contracts and projects. For example, PetroChina holds the contracts to lay cross-country pipelines from western regions to eastern coastal regions of China.

Infrastructure

Large state enterprises are the ones chosen for infrastructure work and other long-term investment projects, such as railways, telecommunications and pipelines. One consideration is that some projects may lose money in the first few years of construction, and only state enterprises with government backing would take on the projects that do not look commercially attractive. A typical example is China Telecom, which has to lay lines to all remote rural areas following government plans for a national communication network. This task is very similar to that of Australia Telecom (now Telstra). From a pure business point of view, it is not hard to see that company profits come mainly from large urban centres.

Industry Leaders

The top 500 large state enterprises are industry leaders, by the technology they employ and introduce, and by their commanding market shares. Large state enterprises are leaders in many industries, for example, Sichuan Changhong Electronics, TCL and Konka are regularly the top three TV set makers, and Baosteel in Shanghai is the country's number one steel maker.

Major Problems Facing State Enterprises

Debt Situation

A large number of state enterprises are debt-ridden, and debts owed by them are widespread and interlocked.

These debt burdens are caused by two major factors:

1. Insufficient funds as initial investment

   As public projects, they received state funding under the previous economic structure. A new enterprise requires a certain amount of money to set up and operate. At the beginning of industrial and financial reforms, the government policy shifted from unquestioned fiscal allocations to state enterprises to offering only bank loans. This is called "**allocations to lending**". This new policy is especially unfavourable to new state enterprises, as they received no start-up investment but had to rely on bank lending. In consequence, they are in debt from the first day of establishment and subject to bank charges and heavy interest payments regardless of the state of their operations. Interest payments form a big part of their annual expenditures, and subsequently, they even pay off interests by borrowing more from the lending banks. In retrospect, the government only temporarily lowered its financial burdens when this shift was implemented, since in later years, state investment of hundreds of billions of yuan were urgently required to maintain those enterprises and reduce their total debts. In 1995, the government reversed "allocation to lending" policy to a milder "**lending to investment**" policy, mobilising billions of yuan in public funds to finance existing and new state enterprises.

2. Triangular debts (inter-enterprise debts)

   It is a form of indebtedness initially among state enterprises. Since they are all government-owned and owe debts to state banks, state enterprises disregard their serious obligations to pay back bank loans and owed debts to other state enterprises. Among manufacturers, suppliers and end users, delayed payment and even non-payment after delivery has become very common, and an enterprise, which has not received payment from another one, will stop making payment for the goods received from the next supplier. This chain reaction accumulated to a crisis of business trust, and the whole delivery and payment system was near the point of collapsing. The interlocked payment problem was called "triangular debts" among state enterprises, and this later spread to other types of enterprises in China, seriously affecting business deals in general. The issue of triangular debts came to its peak in the late 1990s and was prominent in government programmes to revitalise state enterprises. This particular issue remains acute, as shown in the two trillion yuan of bad loans at the four state banks, which are to be disposed by asset management agencies as part of reforms to those state banks (see a separate chapter on the banking industry).

Loss Making

State enterprises have been identified by outside observers as embodiments of low efficiency and loss-making machines. There are internal and external conditions conducive to this outcome, and reforms so far have not fundamentally changed that.

Poor Management

A top item on the checklist is the quality of managers. Top executives are appointed by supervising government departments or bureaux in charge of related industries and report to these organisations as a result. They bear official ranks and status similar to those working in government bureaucracies, and some are important figures in both business and government circles. Leaders of large state enterprises can also be appointed as heads of government bureaux. For CEOs of the two giant Chinese petroleum corporations, one from Sinopec was appointed vice minister at the State Asset Supervision and Administration Commission, and another from China National Offshore Oil Corp. became the governor of Hainan province. Large numbers of managers of state enterprises come from official ranks, and are apparently not qualified for positions in commercial business with their background and skills. With so much attention paid to career prospects in government bureaux, these managers are distracted from their business tasks and poorly equipped for handling company operations. Selection, training and replacement of managers are imperative for state enterprises to survive in the new market economy.

The slow pace in decision making is another common shortcoming in management of state enterprises. Managers as semi-officials routinely follow orders from government bureaux they report to, and even if some do have their own initiative, complexity and red tape in bureaucracy put great restraints on managers to act on and respond to market changes in a timely manner. This leads to lost business opportunities or market shares. It was a general rule that overseas investment by state enterprises over the value of 50 million yuan should be reported to, and approved by, the Ministry of Foreign Trade, and even the State Council in some cases. After the first Gulf War, Sinopec obtained the rights to explore an oilfield in Kuwait at a very reasonable price, but its application for allocating funds delayed the payment, and it subsequently lost that deal.

As official staff, managers of state enterprises often lack the sense of market operations, particularly in profits, investment, and prices, and often treat capital investment from government and bank loans as their own revenues. Market opportunities are less vigorously sought after, and these managers are not able to find ways to minimise wastes. Government funding and targets are the main factors they consider. When targets are not met, enterprises put in more resources, thus creating more wastes and costs. It is common to practise bad accounting, making books pleasing to their superiors and inspecting officials. Few adopt international accounting standards, and if they do, serious problems in finance and accounting will surface. Large state enterprises that went to IPOs (initial public offerings) overseas faced this particular enquiry and encountered tough questioning from foreign analysts and investors before they could be listed. A poor state of management is often then exposed to outsiders. Some bad cases and scandals occurred in recent years and have tarnished the image of listed state enterprises, as in the case of the Bank of China branch in the US, which received warnings and were fined twice by the Securities Commission there for their operational irregularities. State enterprises of smaller sizes perform even worse than those listed large enterprises.

Production and Marketing

Managers of state enterprises rely on routine orders and directions from government bureaux, and their eagerness to develop new products is low. They continue to produce those unsuitable or unwanted goods as before, are slow to change production technology and designs, and are slow to recognise the need to meet customers' demands and increase customers' awareness of their new products. All these would only add up their stock volumes, without earning real incomes to the enterprises. The more open an industry is, the more competitive state enterprises become. The household appliances and electronics industries went through tough and fierce competition, and certain state enterprises, such as Sichuan Changhong Electronics, are now used to face market changes and upgrade their products regularly to please customers. They then become market leaders, not the less fortunate ones. Most state enterprises maintain their reliance on government directions, and their production remains uncompetitive in the market.

Marketing and product promotion are the weak points of state enterprises. Since they invest less on product development, their lines of products are short and sales less. Long life cycles of products make them feel less urgent to adopt market promotion, and their marketing strategies become less effective. Even if advertising is applied, the combination and synergy of products and advertising are weak. Lost market shares make them feel less intent to invest more on marketing, in the face of competition from foreign and private enterprises. As a result of shrinking market shares, many state enterprises operate below production capacity, receive fewer orders and have their machines and equipment idle.

Costs and Financial Burdens

State taxes and levies are higher than that laid on other types of enterprises. They pay standard tax rates, while foreign enterprises in special zones enjoy low rates, and private enterprises manage to hide most of their taxable incomes. These burdens take away a significant part of incomes of state enterprises. As shown before, they are the major revenue providers of governments, central or local, and as such hand over a large chunk of earnings to government coffers. Many local governments rely on this kind of revenues to meet the demands from local communities and organisations. Key state enterprises are also routinely forced to reallocate funds to places designated by the government. Their expenditures may not be purely for commercial business, but for political purposes and national interests. For example, Chinese national airlines made purchases of Airbus planes from France or Boeing planes from the US, depending on particular demands from the central government at a particular time, which in turn are decided by political relations and diplomatic strategies with those countries. These extra expenditures come on top of their initial purchasing plans and budgets. Many state enterprises are also asked to make regular or occasional donations to social welfare programmes and public works in their regions.

Senior Chinese Managers

Constraints and Autonomy

Unlike those working in private sectors, managers of state enterprises have their appointments made by government departments in charge of industrial production. They thus face certain constraints in their operations and decision making. Most constraints derive from comprehensive government rules and regulations, plus internal rules of the Communist Party. Business choices made have to subject to screening by people with higher ranks, and out-of-bound actions need implicit permissions or risk drawing unwanted attention. It is therefore better for these managers to be cautious, conservative and follow directions from above.

It is undeniable that there is also a side of autonomy for these managers, who have come to enjoy certain rights during the reforms to undertake tasks and changes according to their own agendas. At one stage, the officially sanctioned responsibility system granted managers ultimate power to run enterprises and get results, even without consensus from party secretaries of similar ranks. As long as they deliver revenues to state bureaux, they can take the enterprises very much as their own. This change of setting has proved problematic in later years, since many managers simply sell assets and enrich themselves with state properties. In general, the performance of an enterprise depends on the CEO's own capabilities and personal characteristics. When the situation is particularly bad, the authorities may more willingly part away with power and care less about procedures of appraisals and approvals. Managers under these circumstances are given a free hand to run. If the situation is improved, the manager is rewarded with more freedom and authority. One case at hand is the household appliances giant Haier, where a Mr. Zhang Ruimin took the appointment as the head of that near bankrupt factory and was given the authority to do whatever necessary to change that place. He moved swiftly to implement his bold plans and ruled the company at will. Today, the corporation has been one of the world's top ten manufacturers of household appliances for years. Selection of right people to the job proves vital to the end results of an enterprise.

After two decades of reforms, restraints have been lessened a great deal and autonomy increased, resulting obviously from the responsibility system. During the same process, however, another problem emerged, namely a lack of long-term planning and strategies. Managers may pursue short-term gains above healthy progress of an enterprise, and exhaust available resources, natural or human, to reach targets set by the authorities. They become risk-taking and profit-maximising in a market setting. They could meet the requirements in their responsibility contracts by overspending and over-stretching, and leave messy burdens behind, including heavy debts and worsening pollution. Since only state assets and expenditures are involved, not their own holdings, they have little hesitation in using up all the resources at hand. In recent years, this unchecked power held by top managers has led to numerous frauds, through which managers in effect steal public property and transfer public assets out to their own accounts and companies. It is under this context that reforms to state enterprises have endured several start-and-halt phases, deriving chiefly from the government's fear that state assets will be depleted and that the system feeds a group of people who get rich through their sole power to distribute these state assets.

Due to their insufficient training and knowledge in doing commercial business, few managers are able to establish effective and unique corporate culture for their enterprises. The old culture of socialist planning is gone, and the hard-edged competitive Western corporate culture is difficult to swallow and follow. Managers swing between the contradictory patterns and trends in business, and inevitably bend to the pressure of meeting short-term goals. A few relatively successful state enterprises such as Haier have developed their own identity and corporate culture, on the basis of certain Chinese and Western models, but their records are still to be tested in the long run. The issue of building a strong corporate culture troubles many enterprises, and a large number of them have only a short life span in business as a result.

Incentives and Incentive Packages

Under a semi-market economy, talents and knowledge begin to have a price. The field of human resources is now wide open, led by foreign and private enterprises. State enterprises stay put with more rigid wage and bonus systems, which need approvals for pay increases and higher salary scales. The gap has been widened between state and other enterprises on this front, and it has been a shared view that insufficient rewards do not encourage better performance from managers. More seriously, poaching by other sectors creates instability and brain drain on the part of state enterprises. Effective measures and flexibility are needed to raise expectations and keep managers at their post.

There have been trials on generous pay packages to managers, especially senior managers of state enterprises. A new approach is to offer annul base salaries to senior managers, plus incentive offers linked to their performance, whether it is satisfactory or exceeding expectations. Since most listed A share companies are state enterprises, these managers receive company shares as a means to entice them to work more diligently. For managers of listed companies overseas, such as those in Hong Kong (H shares and red chips), they have to receive nominal high salaries that match their status as industrial leaders, though their real incomes are made lower than the publicly announced figures on paper, taking account of their home incomes and benefits. Even after these sharp deductions, their incomes are way beyond those earned by managers of domestic companies. For example, the chief of Bank of China, Hong Kong, earned several million HK$ a year, while his counterparts at mainland offices earn a fraction of that amount. This situation in Hong Kong is treated as a special case. Another manager at a Chinese enterprise listed in Singapore had a nominal pay check of 16 million yuan a year. In general, the system of annul pay package has effectively lifted up the real income level of enterprise managers and given them additional incentives to improve company performance and earnings.

In 2003, this system was fully implemented in Shenzhen, a special economic zone and a large city next to Hong Kong. CEOs of 35 municipal state enterprises began receiving annul salaries, and they are paid at the end of financial year on the basis of performance of the enterprises under their charge. It is regulated that bonus pays are not to exceed four times of base salary and performance pays 1.5 times. The CEO of Shenzhen International Trust and Investment Co. received close to 1 million yuan, the highest figure, and the CEO of an electronics company received only 108,000 yuan, in fact his base salary. The average was 516,000 yuan, a figure not extremely high by the standards of Western corporations, but sufficiently attractive to many managers of state enterprises, considering low living expenses in China.

Another aspect of concern is the retirement policy for state enterprise managers. Annual pay and bonus packages are applicable to those at work, while in retirement those managers lose their pay and benefits, abruptly being put into another category. It is often a painful transition to many managers who had one day held great power and enjoyed wide-ranging benefits and the next day reverted to being an ordinary retiree. With inflation, the salaries they earned are much less than their successors. Official appointment to post could offer them power and incomes, but could also deprive them of those privileges at a stroke of pen. Due to these considerations, managers of state enterprises harbour great fear of approaching retirement age, and there have been numerous cases of the "**Threshold of 59**" phenomenon. State enterprise managers are supposed to retire at the age of 60, if they do not get promoted to senior government positions. Many began to plan for their retirement to ensure that their assets would guarantee their good living when the government cannot. They focus on their personal gains and even accept bribes to compensate for insufficient salaries. These occurred a couple of years before their formal retirement year, perhaps at the age of 59, and their economic crimes gathered pace within that period of time.

A telling example is Mr. Chu Shijian, a former CEO of number one tobacco maker Hong Ta. He built up that tobacco empire and the brand name from scratch, and paid billions of company taxes to the government. With a meagre pay and occasional bonuses of 200,000 yuan at one time, he felt unsatisfied and fearful of retirement, and finally committed economic crimes of taking bribes and transferring company funds into his own bank accounts. For this blunder he was put in jail. This case sent shock waves across the country and led to fierce debate on how to treat top managers of key state enterprises, especially how to handle the issue of their retirement.

In another example, the CEO and chairwoman of the board of Shenzhen Energy, a listed public utilities corporation, was arrested in 2002 for economic crimes, after she had led that company to grow from 3 million to 10 billion yuan in total assets over 10 years. Her downfall occurred at the age of 59, near her retirement time. For executives at high positions, their larger than average annual pay and incentive packages can solve part of the problem, but it is obvious that adequate superannuation schemes are essential to wooing top executives of state enterprises. Such a reward system nationwide has yet to be devised, let alone implemented.

Employment Situation

Unpaid and Underpaid Employees

Due to low efficiency and loss of market shares, many state enterprises are unable to pay employees on a regular basis, or to pay them salaries.

Failure to Keep Talents, Technical Staff and Skilled Workers

The turnover rate is high for many state enterprises, and employees with particular skills leave for higher pay and better career prospects at other types of enterprises. It is common that private and collective enterprises hire technicians and engineers from state enterprises nearby and turn around to compete with them later.

Lower Efficiency and Overlapping Work Assignments

Former State Premier Zhu Rongji described at a news conference that in most state enterprises, three workers are doing the job that is for just one worker. This points to a widespread redundancy.

Obligations to Workers and their Families

Workers of state enterprises had rights to be employed, and they continue to be cared for by their employers, for life and death. Retired and deceased workers are still responsibilities of enterprises, the former enjoying housing and medical benefits till they die, and the latter having their family members taken care of in many ways including being employed at the same enterprise.

Burden of Social Welfare

Employment and Related Benefits

State enterprises have one particular function that is to provide employment for people when other types of enterprises are not able or willing to do so. Each employee also receives the benefits from being employed. All medical, housing, and educational care are provided and managed by state enterprises. From all the revenues gained, an enterprise pays taxes and profits to the government, and allocates funds to support those services for employees. These expenditures were budgeted in the previous year and received permission from higher authorities. In order to provide comprehensive services to benefit their employees, state enterprises built housing blocks, schools and clinics (hospitals) for all their staff and employees. These people were then firmly attached to enterprises for their whole life and saw little need to seek services from outside the boundary of their work units. For example, the Wuhan Steel Works had its own hospitals, kindergartens, schools, colleges and bus companies. As enterprises provided welfare schemes to employees, employees in return took enterprises as their own communities. In 1995, people working for such welfare services in state enterprises numbered 20 million, and total benefits including housing and medical for workers amounted to 300 billion yuan. By early 2004, state enterprises still own and run over 11,000 schools and over 6,100 hospitals. Such universal benefits in state enterprises aimed at upholding public ownership and making production and society as one. Employee reliance on state enterprises have been reduced significantly since reforms, yet they still have the officially sanctioned rights to claim their housing and medical benefits, though in reality they may not be able to do so since many enterprises are themselves nearly bankrupt.

Unemployment and Xia Gang

As a result of redundancy and reform measures to remedy it, workers of state enterprises have been pressured to leave and find employment elsewhere. This move is one type of unemployment, but from its state nature, a special Chinese term "*xia gang*" is put into official language and categories. These workers do leave enterprises, but they are still attached to their work units, and receive basic minimum living expenses, of one third or one fifth of employees' income. As one more category on top of retired and deceased workers under enterprise's care, *xia gang* workers are often not paid for months and most neglected by managers. They are encouraged to take another job, doing small business or being labourers, but many stay supported by their nominal employers.

A more drastic measure has been taken to cope with increasing number of *xia gang* workers. Enterprises in different regions began to offer one-off lump sum payment to these workers and cut the links with them for good. In one example, workers at a large motor works in Beijing receive their lump sum payments calculated at 1,500 yuan per working year, plus 20,000 to 30,000 yuan base payment. On the other hand, workers at a heavy machinery company in Wuhan City receive around 1,000 yuan per working year. Many employees in other small urban centres get even much lower offers than this. Since payment amounts are arbitrarily decided by managers and are often far from being a reasonable compensation, this measure has caused deep resentment among veteran workers who feel they are betrayed and abandoned after decades of work. The plight of *xia gang* workers taking this one-off payment has caught the attention of the central government, and the seriousness of social unrest is not lost with the new leadership.

Transforming State Enterprises

As the dire situation of state enterprises came to a critical point in the late 1990s, the central government finally moved to rectify the previous orientation and mistakes. Several key measures were designed and implemented in the following years.

The Three-year Period of State Enterprise Revitalisation—1998-2000

This period was an initiative by the central government under the leadership of the then Premier Zhu Rongji. The goal was to rescue the majority of large state enterprises and make them reasonably profitable. A key measure was the "**Debt equity swaps**" programme. Selected state enterprises had their debts owed to banks converted into company shares and passed them on to newly established state assets management agencies. State enterprises permitted in this programme were able to offload huge debt burdens and save on interest payments. The four state asset management agencies are empowered to conduct the following businesses relating to state enterprises concerned: acquisition and merger, debt collection, transfer and sale, enterprise revamping, bond issuing, business borrowing, refinancing, investment consulting, asset evaluation, auditing and liquidating, direct investment, stock market listing, etc. At the end of Premier Zhu's term, he reported to the People's Congress that technically the goal of revitalising state enterprises was achieved.

Measures taken also included injection of more funds into state enterprises as state investment, amounting to hundreds of billions after 1997, and special State Treasury bonds were issued for this specific purpose. This move coincided with the policy change of "**lending to investment**", making the government a more responsible investor and putting state enterprises on firmer financial ground.

"Grab the Big, Release the Small"

This guideline for state enterprise reform was officially issued in 1995 in a Party plenary resolution, and was widely implemented in the final years of the 20th century. The rationale is to consolidate top and key enterprises, and to put small- and medium-sized ones on the market. This is summarised in the Chinese phrase "grab the big, release the small". It is necessary to distinguish between enterprises of large and small sizes. Common problems associated with state enterprises exist mostly in small ones, and they are the least efficient and most costly to run. Local governments back them for the sake of local economy while being wary of them for their awful performance and depleting funds. On the opposite side, large state enterprises on average perform better and maintain their positions as industry leaders. The new policy reflects this divide and makes a general distinction between the two groups.

In the phrase, "grab" indicates the retaining of ownership and control over large and super large state enterprises. In a breakdown, it could mean to retain and manage 196 centrally controlled enterprises that have been identified and designated, and to include around 1,000 large enterprises at ministerial and provincial levels. Of the total number of enterprises in the "state" categories, these corporations take a very small percentage and would be managed relatively efficiently. The government will concentrate on the state of these enterprises, supporting them with policy, finance and other resources. The exclusive territories for these corporations are backbone and monopoly industries, such as national defence, key public goods and services, resources and high-tech.

The phrase "release" refers to the rest of so-called state enterprises and shows an intention to leave them on their own in the market. They are in large numbers and mostly at county level. They embody the common woes of state enterprises and eat up budgets of local governments. Since the guideline of "grab the big, release the small" was announced in the late 1990s, the number of small enterprises has been steadily reduced, for example, 174,000 in 2003 and around 160,000 in early 2004. In a business sense, this trend of releasing state enterprises from the care of the government could mean merger and acquisition opportunities for external investors, either private or foreign.

Local governments found extra incentives to dispose of these small enterprises, namely refilling their coffers and possibly enlarging personal wealth during the transactions. With little encouragement from the central government, local officials often make quick sales of a whole set of enterprises within their regions, to private companies and to some officials themselves. This imitates a traditional attitude of "**selling family silvers**", and bribes and corruption emerged. The central government had to restate the purpose of "grab" and "release" under the pressure of public opinion and unrest derived from unemployment, and called for ways to improve performance and to sell, if necessary, with transparency and at fair prices.

From early 2003, the municipal government of Xian, Shanxi province announced their plans to sell state enterprises worth of 50 billion yuan in two years. In the meantime, the municipal government of Chongqing, a new directly administered major city in the west, made public of their plans to put state assets on the market worth of 100 billion yuan. This sale is supposed to complete in three years. To counter zealous local governments with their rush to sell, the central government set up three ownership trading centres in Beijing, Shanghai and Guangzhou in 2004. Every deal and transaction involving large state enterprises should be done at one of these three centres under the close watch of state assets authorities.

Under official guidelines, state enterprises face several options. Bankruptcy and takeovers are now common. The Bankruptcy Law was passed by the People's Congress in 1986, but had little effect in early years for its vagueness and resistance from all quarters. This approach has been applied more widely in recent years, with 3,307 enterprises declared closed and bankrupt by the State Council between 1994 and 2003. In 2001, the government allocated 50 billion yuan as the funds for asset write-offs and employee settlements after enterprises became bankrupt.

The official push to dispose of small enterprises has led to some wholesale liquidation and indiscriminate house clearing by some regional governments. This not only causes panic among locally owned state enterprises, but also proves that judging on size alone is not fair to many well-managed enterprises. Small enterprises can still achieve high level of performance and become strong competitors in the market. For example, a small state enterprise in Zhejiang province was a company at the bottom of national ranking for manufacturers of chemicals in the 1980s. In early 21st century, the company was a top producer of washing powders and soaps, and it gained the number one position in washing machine detergents in just over one year's time. In these industries, the company has become a major competitor to multinationals such as P&G and grabbed considerable market shares from them. Local governments using the size as the key criteria for selection often ruin valuable assets and enterprises with potential. It was planned by the central government that by the end of the first decade of the 21st century, courts would pass judgement on enterprise bankruptcy and closure, not state authorities.

As selling state assets and bankruptcy spread into a frenzy and asset losses piled up, the government responded by setting up an overall state asset authority. The State Asset Supervision and Administration Commission was established in April 2003. It is given the power to have oversight for state enterprises across the country, and particularly for those large ones. Restructuring planning and regular inspections are the responsibilities of its 18 regional offices, and approvals must be obtained from the Commission before large enterprises are given major shake-ups.

Getting qualified enterprises listed on the stock exchanges and making them public corporations is another option. This will introduce external investors and press for more vigorous performance appraisals, as well as raising more funds.

A microeconomic measure is to improve corporate governance and set up operational mechanisms of checks and balances, including board of directors, shareholders meetings, external non-executive directors, etc. This issue refers essentially to the relations among the management, shareholders and employees. It is crucial in particular to large state enterprises, and is closely linked with the efficiency and performance of stock markets.

As China has opened its doors to overseas investment, and foreign companies have entered the China market in large numbers, state enterprises have the option to find partners and form joint ventures with selected, complementary foreign investors. For the restructuring of state sectors, introducing foreign players and gaining access to foreign capital have been key considerations from the beginning. Outcomes not always meet the expectations, and this will be discussed further in the sections on foreign direct investment (FDI).

Positive Factors for Enterprise Reforms

In comparison with early periods, restructuring of state enterprises has reached a critical stage, and the overall environment has become more conducive to wider and further reforms. There are several positive factors that drive the momentum.

Minimised Government Interference

The ideological obstacle of socialism has been overcome after the 15th Party Congress, and the urgent changes to total public ownership of state enterprises have been accepted as a reality and the direction forward. The moves toward decentralisation have created a new balance of power, which increased local initiatives and made the central government more tolerant towards sharing authority. The tight control over state enterprises is loosened, and direct interferences, which proved ineffective in many cases, are not welcome.

A Process to Establish Comprehensive Social Welfare Programmes

State enterprises remain heavily burdened by welfare benefits provided to their employees. In market competition, to match the agility of private companies, they need the flexibility to fire unproductive workers, as well as hiring capable staff. This had been the weak point of state enterprises that were bound by the responsibility of lifetime care for employees. The official ban, however, was broken during the three-year revitalisation when the government gave permission for state enterprises to reduce their workforce and become lean as soon as possible. Bankruptcy has also become common. The layoffs gathered pace, and the government suddenly faced millions of unemployed workers who abruptly left their stable jobs. Scattered social unrest was in the making, especially in those regions with concentration of heavy industries. To minimise negative impact of restructuring and cushion workers from this shock, wide social safety nets are essential.

Although the government was slow to respond to the backlash from large numbers of layoffs, a social welfare system on the models of Western countries is in the process of building and expanding. A new State Ministry of Social Security was set up, and compulsory contributions are collected from various sources, individuals and enterprises alike. Certain percentages of proceeds from selling state enterprise shares on stock markets are also deposited into the National Social Security Fund. In 2004, the fund has pooled 133 billion yuan, and it made a profit of about 4 billion yuan from its investment portfolios. This state fund is for related expenditures, including unemployment benefits and basic covers for workers' families. For this reason, investment strategies by fund managers are understandably conservative, focusing on blue chip shares, government bonds and long-term infrastructure projects. With the backing of a huge, though rudimental, social security system, restructuring of state enterprises can move forward with less ramifications and shocks. Especially for top executives, they now have less worries about backlash from workers and the unemployed, and could take timely actions to improve overall efficiency.

Equal or Preferential Treatments

While state enterprises enjoyed certain protection by governments in the past, they also suffered certain disadvantages as a result of reform. In particular, they have been subject to the standard, in other words high, tax rates and seldom received waivers. On the other hand, foreign companies were welcomed with open arms and generally subject to favourable tax rates. If they bargained hard, they were even allowed to pay no tax at all for a number of years. Private companies found their own ways to dodge tax payments and are notorious for their scams. This unequal treatment will be rectified to a certain degree, with all enterprises, including state enterprises, paying about similar tax rates when the national treatment clauses of WTO agreements take full effect. Discrepancies in this regard could be more readily taken care of, and discrimination eliminated.

A Larger Reserve of Professional Managers

An open and more efficient nationwide labour market is now developing. Talents and professionals shift among regional markets and sectors to find their places, and restrictions on mobility are fast declining. In a competition for talents and top executives, state enterprises are relatively disadvantaged due to their less attractive pay packages and lack of flexibility. But they are able to pick capable managers and professionals from a much bigger labour market, and could search for those with experience in Western market economies and those who worked for foreign and private companies. For example, a former Microsoft China CEO left the company for TCL, a state shareholding company in Guangdong. The pie is getting bigger, so state enterprises have more choices if they find the need to employ high calibre executives to lead their businesses.

Certain Negative Factors

Official Corruption

On the basis of one party rule and a semi-market economy, rent seeking is inevitable at all levels of the government. Members of the bureaucracy have the power to halt any project if their personal gains are not increased. Bribes and kickbacks are common, making doing normal business more difficult. Since state enterprises are the major sources of government revenues, any restructuring and limiting of authority would meet resistance from officials concerned.

Unscrupulous Managers

In the current market, the performance of a particular state enterprise primarily depends on the person in charge, on his or her vision, ethical standards and commitments. Without professionalism and reasonable incentives, most managers of state enterprises, especially small ones, take their jobs lightly and run the business in a way that leaves much to be desired. They may take the job for their official promotion or personal gains, and not for the interest of shareholders, investors and employees. This widespread attitude affects the general level of performance of state enterprises. Large enterprises may have more comprehensive systems of checks and balances, and are subject to close scrutiny of government departments.

Outflow of Enterprise Assets and Money Laundering

With certain empowerment, managers of state enterprises have ample opportunities to shift public assets to their own accounts. Outflows of state assets in various forms have been a serious issue in China, resulting in billions of yuan to disappear into black holes and personal bank accounts overseas. The new State Assets Commission is directed to deal with this problem, making greater use of state assets while not giving profiteering managers too many chances. The trust in managers has been badly shaken after scandals emerged non-stop, and this suspicion affects managers in general and the restructuring process in particular.

Overwhelming Foreign Competition

The restructuring of state enterprises has been undertaken in a situation where foreign multinationals already moved in and taken high grounds. The WTO agreements signed by the central government allow foreign companies almost an entirely equal status to domestic companies. State enterprises have little room to retreat and are unable to hold the onslaught. In many industries, leaders come from foreign entities, and previously all powerful state corporations offered token resistance and are relegated to the position for minor players. The "grab the big, release the small" policy is in a way a response to this situation, making efforts to maintain the leading position of domestic enterprises. Since wholly foreign-owned companies now have few restrictions, domestic companies cannot even rely on joint ventures to survive. State enterprises in this fierce market competition do not have the luxury of time and pace; they need to face up to that competition while restructuring and transforming. The tasks are multi-faceted and complicated.

Future Prospects of State Enterprises in China

The question asks if state enterprises will survive and stay in business at all, after further opening and reforms. One scenario is for them to become more efficient in a market economy, similar to those public corporations in Western economies. In areas of public utilities, a public corporation has sufficient ground to stand. Even in manufacturing sectors, state owned or controlled corporations will hold important positions in key industries, those which the state has to take a big stake for the interest of the whole nation, such as military, energy, and advanced technology. Recent efforts have been made toward this direction, shrinking in size while focusing on a few essentials. The pessimistic view, however, is that they will be eventually obsolete, sold and extinct, all taken over by private and foreign enterprises. This view is based on observations that the inefficient operations of state enterprises simply cannot be transformed and that an open market will allow no barriers to private enterprises. The future economy of China then will not have state sectors any more. These two views regarding the future status of state enterprises lead to different recipes and scenarios in reforms.

Collective Enterprises

Since the Communist Party's 15th National Congress, other types of enterprise ownership have been recognised as equals to state enterprises in rights and status. Among them, collective and private enterprises have risen to make more profound impact on the economy.

In essence, collectively owned enterprises included those not owned by the state. They have existed since the time of the founding of the Republic. The term "collectives" implies they are not included in the government's budgets and fund allocations, and all assets and responsibilities are borne by participating members in the collectives concerned. In a sense, this is a form of not so secured ownership, with risks and without the backing of the state. The category can be further divided into urban and rural collectives. In urban collectives, they are formed by lower levels of the government, such as district and prescient offices, by local communities, or by auxiliary units of state enterprises, which provide extra employment for workers' family members and increase their incomes marginally. In the first and third cases, they were called "large collectives" under the former planned economy. In the second case, they were called "small collectives" and were genuine collectives coming from participating members with their combined funds.

Rural collectives included work units that specialise in certain areas related to farming. They were closely linked to sub-county authorities such as town and village committees. Rural collectives produced mostly farming tools and other necessities for rural population, and their production had the mixed features of manufacturing and handicraft. In a comparison with farming, rural collectives produced more goods and incomes for local communities, and this is the reason that they survived through all the political turbulence and tight state control.

Collectives existed under the planned economy mainly because the government was unable to provide all the goods for people's consumption and that collectives could fill in the gap by producing daily necessities. Therefore, collectives used to be in light industries and service industries, leaving key industries and projects to state enterprises.

Since the beginning of reforms, rural collectives first emerged strongly, making big impact on the country's industrial output. The TVEs (Town and Village Enterprises) mushroomed under more tolerant official policies and soon took strongholds in many industries, especially light industries in early periods. Recently, rich peasants tended to invest their money in local collectives and expand into manufacturing businesses. An example is southern Jiangsu province, where surplus capital and labour moved into factories at a fast pace, forming large numbers of TVEs and churning out huge quantities of manufactured goods to supply for consumption across the country. In the middle of 1990s, TVEs made a huge impact on the national economy, taking two thirds of industrial output of all rural regions and one half of national industrial production. These collectives employed around 135 million workers in 1996, where it peaked. In 2002, TVEs numbered 21.3 million, with 133 million employees and 3.24 trillion yuan worth of GDP.

Advantages of TVEs

Flexibility in Business Operations

Unlike state enterprises, TVEs enjoy enormous freedom and flexibility in business operations. They are not subject to strict rules applied to state enterprises, and they receive certain assistance from local authorities, which private enterprises did not at early stages. In decision making, it is for TVEs to make on commercial considerations, and they are quick to grab opportunities, enter an industry, make a killing and exit if results are unsatisfactory.

Protection from Local Authorities

With the guidelines of reforms, local governments had to support any business that could boost local economies and increase employment. TVEs provide extra input to the economy and their business activities enlarge markets. In the meantime, they do not require capital injection and money pumping as those state enterprises do. Many local governments see TVEs as their separate revenue sources and are happy to see them flourish and expand.

Human Resources and Technology from State Enterprises

A simple approach adopted by many TVEs is to attract technical and management staff from state enterprises and make them work for you. Since TVEs normally had low starting points and an urgent need to fill in the gap, they tend to grab required talents from state enterprises in the same industry and business, with markedly higher pay and extra bonuses. In many cases, engineers working in state enterprises help collectives to upgrade their production and receive remuneration several times of their normal salaries. This has led to the situation where state enterprises lose customers and sales, while nearby TVEs in the same business thrive.

Local Markets

With increased production capacity and local protection, TVEs can acquire large market shares in certain regions. Their focus is normally on local population, and not the national market, giving them a manageable pace of development and fitting well with their gradualist strategy.

Negligible Social Welfare Burdens

TVEs rely on rural labour to operate production lines, as their salaries are low and benefits few. Large labour pools in rural regions guarantee that TVEs can find workers at any time without considering pay increases along with higher returns and productivity.

Disadvantages of TVEs

Management Problems after Rapid Growth

When they grow in size, they come with many symptoms and problems similar to what state enterprises have, namely confusion in authority, and low efficiency, flexibility, and responsiveness. They will have to face the ownership issue and more interference from local authorities that assisted them. In general, TVEs have lower levels of management efficiency than large state enterprises. They gradually lost their real competitiveness in later years of reforms as fairer policy adjustments took effect and other types of enterprises expanded.

Quality Problems

These are inherent with their type of production. TVEs have been from time to time synonymous with poor quality goods and little after-sales service. They also form the majority of those manufacturers who copy brand name products and churn out large quantity of fake goods. This has much to do with their swift response to market demands, in order to grab business opportunities.

Pollution

They are the major contributors to pollution, especially in rural areas. They became the top targets when the government enforces environment laws, and their polluting factories are the first to be closed down.

TVEs in China, and collective enterprises in general, have reached a critical stage in development. As the business environment is transforming every now and then, TVEs are moving either to be private enterprises or to revert to state enterprises. TVEs are described by many as bats, taking a cover of collectives and belonging to neither private nor state camps. This has helped them before, since private businesses found little protection from authorities, and genuine state enterprises were bound by the government in business doing. For many entrepreneurs, they started with the "red cap" of a collective name and built a contract relationship with local authorities. As the Chinese economy is becoming more open and private property rights more secured, chiefs of TVEs turned to get rid of that collective "red cap" and change to private enterprises of their own. In the meantime, TVEs can also change back to their true status of state enterprises, since many were established with funds from state organisations at lower levels. When this deep myth of ownership is cleared, many collectives, especially TVEs, will become one of these two categories. As a result, collective enterprises will have a less significant role to play in the Chinese economy in future.

Private Enterprises

Private enterprises are non-state, non-collective enterprises run by individuals. Unlike in a market economy, private enterprises were banned in China for over three decades since the mid-1950s. Restrictions remained on private business in the early years of reforms. The government first allowed individuals to run small businesses, mostly in handicraft and trade. Official guidelines allowed these small entrepreneurs to hire seven workers, but not over eight. The number indicates the ideological line they would not cross, since exploitation by capitalists is in the form of hiring large number of workers to earn profits. This line barred many entrepreneurs and pushed them to use collectives as cover for their business operations. This line, however, has been eroded continuously, and official policies have given more room for genuine private business.

In 1987, at the 13th Party Congress, the position of private business was confirmed in the Party Constitution. In the following year, the People's Congress amended the Constitution and officially guaranteed the protection to private sectors.

Following the shift in official policies, private enterprises can get official recognition in forms of legal rights, business licence, and taxation.

❑ Their legal status is formally protected in official regulations and in the Constitution;

❑ Their operations and business dealings are legal after formal business registration is done and licence obtained;

❑ The paying of taxes to the government is another way to assert their legal rights as taxpayers and as legitimate business owners.

With these changes in regulations and procedures, they receive official recognition for opening their business and entitlement to legal protection, though insufficient in many cases. They also obtained the right to employ workers. The initial cap of less than 8 workers in the early 1980s soon became impractical and was abandoned quietly.

These new regulations gave green light to private enterprises, and they mushroomed across the country. Under Deng's motto "**to get rich is glorious**", this particular business group emerged to take a key position in the economy, on a par with state and foreign enterprises.

Recent moves include the opening of industries to private enterprises. Areas of business previously closed to private enterprises and only accessible by state enterprises are now open, such as car manufacturing, telecommunications and aviation, and the right to trade directly with foreign companies are granted. This latter opening is in line with WTO agreements and considerably increases opportunities and profitability for private businesses.

In 1997, private sectors (traders and enterprises) paid total taxes of 54 billion yuan. In 2000, the number of private companies was 1,761,300, with 25 million employees and 1 trillion yuan of GDP. In 2002, there were 2.43 million companies, with 34 million employees (the state enterprise and government employees were 105 million). These private companies had registered assets of 2.47 trillion yuan. Their industrial output value was 1.53 trillion yuan, and their total taxes were near 100 billion yuan. The average years of operation was seven, which indicates that their operations are similar to those in other market economies, with new business openings and closures as market conditions and economic cycles change. Among private enterprises, 26% of them were transformed from state enterprise, after change of ownerships or takeovers. One third of private enterprises are owned by a single investor, and many have joint ownerships.

Wanxiang Group from Zhejiang province is a privately owned corporation and a top auto-parts maker. It started as a workshop making farm tools in 1969 with 4,000 yuan of assets. The owner Mr. Lu made a strategic decision in the 1990s to make auto parts, mainly universals and bearings. The products were exported to the US from 1994, and the company has become a major parts supplier to the big three carmakers in the US, through importers and wholesalers. In August 2001, the company acquired a NASDAQ listed US company UAI (Universal Automotive Industries Inc.), a major parts maker. Wanxiang took 21% of UAI shares and now controls the distribution networks, assets and clients UAI holds. Wanxiang also acquired two other American companies to form Wanxiang US company.

Family Business

In the category of private business, a new type of enterprise emerged and grew strongly in recent years. This is family business, similar to those in Hong Kong and Taiwan. They maintain distinctive features:

❏ Tight internal structure and family member shares;
❏ Employment of family members a priority;
❏ Less transparency

The rise of family business in China is identified by quick capital accumulation based on family members' common interest and effort. They demonstrate quick response and decision-making in their management, and usually have strong internal cohesion. One feature of family business is the trusted and reliable executives, who demonstrated loyalty and commitment to the family business. On the other hand, it is generally hard for family business to attract talents and managers in demand. People they hire may be less professional, since there is a tendency to distrust non-family members and even workers from other regions, let alone putting them into senior company positions.

Large Chinese family businesses are now seeking stock market listings, for the purpose of more prominent social status and legitimate fund-raising. Stock listings used to be offered mostly to state enterprises, and private enterprises had to seek funds from other sources, even illegal ones.

The power of running family business remains in the hands of first generation enterprise owners. Family businesses in China have not reached the stage when their lasting stability is tested and family assets divided. There has been little chance to observe how second generation owners lead the business and carry on the family name.

> **Case: Shenzhen Taitai Pharmaceutical Industry Co.**
> The company is owned by the Zhu family, which started in 1992 as the couple's private company. Its main products were traditional Chinese herbal medicine from a secret recipe blended with health and nutritional ingredients. With smart marketing and attractive packaging, their products appeal to urban residents and in particular beauty conscious women. In 2001, the company was listed on the Shanghai stock exchange. Since Mr. Zhu owns over 50% and his family 74% shares of the company, he became an instant billionaire worth over 5 billion yuan. The Zhu family still tightly controls the company, and there is no serious contender to his position as the majority shareholder. He even signed an agreement with strategic investor Merrill Lynch that his shares will not be lower than 50% in any future company shake-ups. This company is relatively open. For example during its listing, it received assistance from a securities company and allowed audit by a Hong Kong professional firm. With large amounts of funds from the stock market, the company has undergone mergers and acquisitions to build a top enterprise covering health products and medicines.

Shareholding Companies

These are the companies based on the prescriptions in the Company Law and following models of modern enterprise of the West. Under the government direction of "**merging into international tracks**", which implies adopting international standards and practice, Chinese enterprises are encouraged to transform to shareholding companies with clear divisions of owners, shareholders, investors, the board, management and employees, as those in Western economies, particularly those in the US. Corporate governance is especially emphasised, though most Chinese enterprises lack the sense and urgency of implementing it, and recent corporate scandals in the US, such as that of Enron, have seriously damaged the confidence of people on the effectiveness of governance models.

This category of shareholding enterprises is not limited to a particular group. State enterprises are being pushed hard to move along with their transformation. Plans have been drawn to form shareholding companies step by step. Among 1,200 listed companies in China, over 900 are state owned and controlled, and these are taken as the right targets to become shareholding companies. Over 200 of them have been engaged in internal restructuring towards mixed shareholding, and nine of them obtained approvals from the Ministry of Finance by early 2004. Family businesses are also showing the tendency of moving towards multiple shareholdings as their enterprises grow. Changing shareholding structures is seen as an effective means to transform both state and private enterprises and make them more efficient and responsive in the market.

Management Buyout (MBO)

This is an increasingly common practice to restructure a company's shareholding. Through the management team's investment in the company, they become part owners or even majority shareholders. Their funds can come from financial institutions like banks, investment banks and other lending bodies, as well as their own funds from personal savings, salaries and bonuses. This requires involvement of financial management firms, business consultants and accountants to calculate how the shares should be counted and divided. A specialist firm involved in such MBO process normally receives a retainer as pay for their work. Outside investors can also take their shares of a particular company.

The purpose of an MBO in China is, in particular, to introduce and implement modern forms of corporate governance. The targets could be state enterprises, private enterprises, and township enterprises. For a family business, this is a way to reduce the family's involvement in business and improve overall performance. For state enterprises, this is to make clear distinctions between state investment and individual investment, so the management is more motivated to achieve goals while state assets are protected.

The MBO approach has become trendy in recent years, especially for large state enterprises where the management is keen to acquire part ownership as their guaranteed rewards for their work and effort in the enterprise. However, the state assets authority was concerned over quick transfer of ownership and diminishing state assets. It called for a halt to a nationwide and wholesale MBO process in 2003 and in general prefers limited numbers of approvals to selected cases.

Major enterprise types in China evolve as reforms take place. The previously dominant state enterprises are on their way to adjust and reduce in proportion, and private enterprises now have equal status

Case: TCL Group

The **TCL** Group, a top maker and major exporter of electronic and tele-communication goods in China, has completed its transformation into a shareholding company through a complicated process of MBO. This state enterprise under Huizhou government in Guangdong province has gradually reduced the holdings by the initial government investor. A turning point was when the municipal government granted the management rights to company shares if the enterprise achieved set targets. The TCL Group also acquired a major European TV maker Thomson in 2003, making its own shareholding restructuring imperative.

The management increased their holdings through adding up their own equities (from their bonuses and borrowed funds). The company expanded its market shares and total assets dramatically; thus the management has room to demand more say in decision-making and in changing shareholding structure. The initial investment (registered assets) becomes insignificant in comparison with the company's current total holdings.

In 1998, the management put in over 20 million yuan as their own equity, and the shareholding structure was as such: the state investor held 91%, the management 8% and the union 1%.

In January 2000, after increasing total registered assets, the state investor held 80%, the management 15.4%, and the union 5.6%.

In November 2000, the state investor held 58%, the management 20%, and the union 22%.

In December 2001, the state investor held 54%, the management 24%, and the union 23%.

In 2002, 12.4% of state holding and 6% of union holding were offered to strategic investors.

(The percentage figures are approximates, and other minor shareholders are not included).

State shareholdings have been decreasing in this process, and the overwhelming shadow of the state investor is fast fading.

In January 2004, the TCL Group was listed on the Shenzhen stock exchange as a shareholding company, and the CEO Mr. Li Dongsheng holds 5.6% of the total shares, making him a major shareholder and also an instant billionaire. In total market capitalisation, the management team as a group of individuals holds 32.5% in total.

and share in the economy, after the socialist doctrines are marginalised over past decades. The state will hold on to key and large state enterprises as the pillars of national economy, while private and foreign enterprises gain wider openings in most industries. This transition implies emerging business opportunities, in both market shares and released state assets for acquisitions by external investors.

There are large numbers of foreign enterprises operating and expanding in China since early reform years that have become a group of key players in this market. This will be discussed in the sections of Part Four on foreign direct investment.

Key Concepts

State enterprises, TVEs (collectives), private, family, and shareholding enterprises
"Allocation to lending", "lending to investment"
State welfare benefits and *xia gang*
Debt equity swaps
"Grab the big, release the small"
MBO

Discussion Questions

1. For the two opposite views of the future of state enterprises, what is your choice and what plausible reasons do you have to support this choice? What proportion would you suggest to be owned by state enterprises in the economy? Is the "grab the big, release the small" a policy of privatisation? What will be the major impact on the economy while it is implemented? If you have certain information or experience of such transformation in other economies, make relevant comparisons.

2. As an employment provider, state enterprises played and are playing a special role. How do you see the link between state enterprise reforms and unemployment? Are private and other types of enterprises sufficient in filling the gap and making up for lost jobs? A market by definition is shifting labour and capital to places with demand, and the current social security system relies on state enterprises. In this situation, what will happen if state enterprises are shedding jobs and the welfare net is strained with smaller funds? In the similar vein, how to replace the roles played by state enterprises in other areas (referring to their major contributions to the economy)?

3. With prohibitions on private business being removed, what will happen to collective enterprises, as well as most state enterprises?

4. How do you see Chinese managers in general? What are the major differences between managers of state enterprises and private entrepreneurs? What do you see as the prospects for private enterprises, in particular, for family businesses in China? For an assessment of business efficiency, do you see major differences between a state-shareholding company and a private company?

6

Economic Growth and Management

This chapter will discuss the two major indicators which form a crucial part of a general evaluation of business environment in an economy. An assessment of the performance of an economy and of the government in office will include the following:

1. **Economic performance**, which chiefly covers growth rates, wealth creation and distribution. Economists and the general public draw on tremendous volume of statistical data to make their judgements on the performance and efficiency levels of an economy.

2. **Economic management**, which examines how the government designs economic policies and handles economic fluctuations and crises. The government bears the ultimate responsibility of making the right decisions, and in many cases, they must possess strong political will to devise and implement economic policies which they see fit.

The Case of China

As we can see from other texts on the course of China's reforms, the ruling Party and the government, from the outset, adopted a **gradualist** approach, typified in Deng's famous phrases "seeking truth from facts" and "groping stones while crossing river". This approach essentially implies that the central leadership moves cautiously and learns the ways of economic management step by step. Apart from the cardinal principles of reforms and stability, there is no dominant model or doctrine for economic transformation. This cautiousness, or early ignorance of Western economic management, has, to a certain degree, made reforms in China move ahead at a relatively steady pace. In comparison with the **shock therapy** hastily executed in Russia, the Chinese economy has travelled less bumpy roads and negotiated tough corners with relative ease.

As a result of reforms and opening, China faces both growing internal tensions that demand constant adjustments and external pressure for becoming compatible with international standards. There is no doubt that China desires to be recognised as a major player in the world economy; the concern is the pace of change. Every move impacts on a series of issues in this huge country, and repercussions are often unexpected by bureaucrats or technocrats in Beijing. This reality reinforces the gradualist approach and has led China to adopt certain measures in dealing with economic problems, which sometimes differ from conventional Western economic theories and practices. It is thus worth emphasising here that China is not a typical market economy that we learn in textbooks, but a **transitional** economy—one that is gigantic in size and with many huge baggages. Numerous tested economic theories in the West may not be readily applied in China, and if China solves economic problems successfully, that may well be a great contribution to economics in general, especially in studies of transnational economies.

One way to gauge the results of reforms in China is to see how market sectors are in place in the economy. On this note, from April to June 2004, New Zealand, Singapore, Malaysia, Thailand and South Africa, in this order, formally recognised China's market economy status, and negotiations with Australia on status recognition are underway. By early September, all 10 countries of ASEAN recognised this status in their agreements with China. Brazil is the latest to join this queue in making an official recognition in November. The US is debating on this issue, with the EU indicating their intention to object. It will be a tough choice for the US to grant the status to China as a public recognition. There are enormous national economic interests under consideration. The US, as well as the EU, grabbed a concession from

The Hearing and Judgement of the US Government on China's Market Economy Status (2004)

The US Commerce Department held a hearing on China's market economy status in early June. The assessment was based on estimates in **six** areas: free currency conversion, industrial relations, setting up of joint ventures and foreign enterprises, government control over production, government intervention over resources allocation and prices, and other factors the Department of Commerce sees fit. The Chinese delegation was headed by government and trade association officials, but their application to obtain the desired status was met with strong opposition from US politicians, trade unions, small businesses and lobbyists. The overall background for the hearing was the loss of US jobs, particularly in an election year, and China's non-market economy status was a key factor in forming the American opinion that increased exports from China quickened this trend of job loss.

China has yet obtained this status, so for anti-dumping cases against China, a substitute economy was chosen to make estimates of real costs for goods made. The chosen economy was Singapore, and, more recently, India. If the selling prices in the US are lower than those assumed costs, the US government could make the ruling that Chinese firms conducted dumping activities in the US markets, and thus charge heavy penalties in the form of high tariff rates on imported Chinese goods. This market economy status thus becomes a major barrier to the normal trading of goods in many categories. The Chinese government and Chinese exporters see such a comparison as unfair and have launched campaigns to have this definition removed. Since it is only the third year after China's WTO entry, far short of the 15 years agreed upon by all, it is very unlikely that China be granted market economy status any time soon. As the US Secretary of Commerce, Mr. Donald Evans stated, "The bottom line: until market forces set economic decisions—including labour and currency rates, China will remain a non-market economy".

China during the WTO accession negotiations that they can use the non-market economy status to shut out Chinese-made goods in the following 15 years. This status issue is now partially merged into American strategies used in trade disputes and wars, in particular anti-dumping actions. There are also underlined political and strategic considerations that the granting of market economy status to China will foster a world power rivalling the US in the near future. In spite of these external suspicions and predictions, the Chinese economy is getting more and more market-oriented each year, particularly under the WTO resolutions and schedules. It seems that the last thing the Chinese government wants to do is to reverse to the previous pattern. How to reach an acceptable and right balance between market sectors and those areas under government control is another matter.

As an indicator of the extent of economic reforms, economic fluctuations occurred in China more often in recent years and bore certain similar symptoms to those economic cycles in the West. The common tracks of inflation-overheating-recession-recovery is happening in China now. With little experience of such fluctuations in previous socialist years, the leadership of China has learned to cope and gradually improved their macro-management practice. Economic, monetary and fiscal measures are taken more often than administrative measures in controlling both inflation and deflation, and lessons and precedents of other economies are watched closely. In a general review, the effectiveness of economic management is on the rise, with no serious breakdowns or hard landing. China is an economy with steady growth, in contrast to many other economies inundated with bubble bursts and jobless recovery.

This is perhaps a little hard to explain, since mature market economies do not escape from cycles, and a Chinese economy in transition must also be vulnerable to economic shocks. Such a phenomenon against conventional wisdom draws more interest from researchers on China's characteristics, and hidden weaknesses in the economy have been revealed in extensive studies. Some worry that this calm surface hides deep crisis in the near future. There have been plenty of predictions of a coming collapse of the Chinese economy, based on data of financial woes and severe disparity. For example, a recent book by Gordon Chang gives the year 2005 as the possible time for a wholesale collapse to occur. Part of the reasons for these pessimistic predictions are doubts over the ability of the Chinese leadership to handle crisis and manage the economy as expected. There is also a deeper concern over the pace and security of a nationwide transition. It is therefore logic to have a general review here of past economic performance and management in China.

Economic Performance

This issue can be probed from the following angles.

1. For average rate of GDP growth, China has had an annual increase of 9.4% from 1978 to 2002. The GDP total in 2002 was 10.2 trillion yuan (US$1.3 trillion). In 2003, the total was 11.7 trillion yuan, equivalent to US$1.4 trillion. This takes a 3.9% share of the world GDP total (see Figures 6.1, 6.2 and 6.3).

2. By GDP calculations, which add up all goods and services and use the US$ as the value ruler, China was the sixth largest economy in the world in 2002. This GDP figure is generally seen as an indicator of the size of an economy. However, in 2003, China took the seventh place. With a respectable 9.1% GDP growth, China's ranking is lowered. **Why?** A simple answer will be currency value. Euro had appreciated strongly, and the US$ lost considerable ground after the tech bubble burst and a brief recession. Since the RMB is officially linked with the US$, the GDP total of China in US$ is lower in value in comparison with EU countries. Italy moved ahead of China in the 2003 ranking. Apparently, exchange rates play a big role here in determining the size of different economies, and GDP figures for an economy are not absolutely reliable indicators.

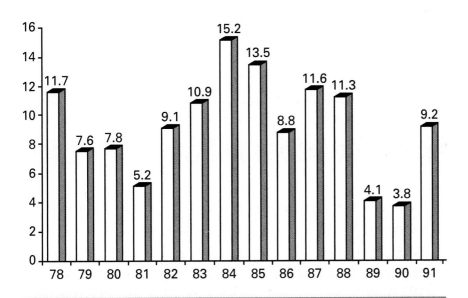

Figure 6.1   China's rates of economic growth

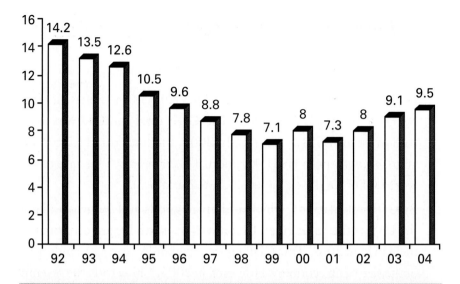

Figure 6.2 China's rates of economic growth (continued)

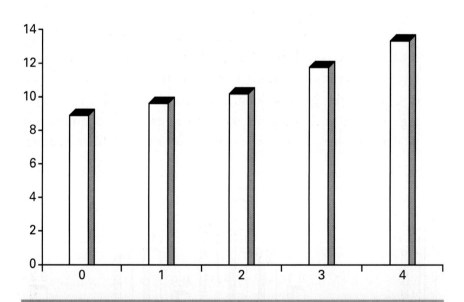

Figure 6.3 GDP figures (trillion yuan)

Naturally, the next question to ask is: what is the real size of an economy?

3. Simply put, economies outside the US cannot accurately measure their real sizes by the current US$-denominated GDP criteria. It is therefore logical to apply another criterion, the **PPP standards** (purchasing power parity). The criterion states that one unit of currency must be able to buy the same goods in all economies. In

reality, it could be said that a US dollar should be able to buy a similar burger everywhere. Taking away the artificially set foreign exchange rates and counting the amount of goods one unit of currency can buy, the PPP can make modifications to GDP figures and give more accurate estimates of the real sizes of economies. In 2002, the World Bank estimated that China's real economic size, using the PPP, was US$5.6 trillion, taking over Japan and second to the US. This indicates the extremely low prices, labour and production costs in China, which would normally drag down China's GDP figures in an international comparison. On the other hand, these estimates reveal the huge potential in domestic markets of China, where local firms trade mostly among themselves and have less dealings with international markets, as well as little involvement with foreign exchange regimes. This reinforces the impression of a huge consumer market for foreign players.

4. On growth contribution, China made up 17.5% of world growth volume in 2002. This indicates an improvement in recent years. In particular, China's economy has been growing while some other economies shrank or slowed down. As a new player, the Chinese economy has made up for some lost growth in other countries. Once this economy moves on a growth track, its huge size promises a consistent vibrancy and an upward trend, with few halts. Growth markets generally draw external investors, who chase for more sales and higher returns, instead of moving to an economy in recession.

5. Foreign exchange reserves in China were over US$600 billion in early 2005. This rapid build-up from previous low bases is the direct result of favourable policies to domestic and foreign exporters. Increases in foreign exchange reserves come from net export, which ballooned in recent years, from foreign direct investment which increased steadily, and from government schemes which direct all surplus foreign currencies into the central Treasury in exchange for the local currency, the RMB. A discussion on China's trade and foreign exchange reserves appears in a later chapter.

6. GDP growth and inflation:

   When goods and services produced are measured at higher prices, the economy sees a high growth rate. The real growth, however, is lower, due to the inflation factor. There is a tricky question about the real benefits of high growth rate if inflation rate is also high. Governments release both GDP growth and inflation figures to the public, so people can have some idea about these inter-related economic aspects. It is often the case that governments face twin highs: high growth and high inflation, or vice versa, twin lows: low growth and low inflation. These are tough choices, and fierce policy debates never end. The preferred combination, high growth and low inflation, is hard to achieve, and this combination will make growth more meaningful and beneficial to the general public. To deal with this dilemma in China, the government has passed a few hurdles and inevitably encountered twin highs through the course of reforms.

7. Total Factor Productivity (TFP):

It has been a long-running argument in the area of economic history that, despite early prominence in economic development, the Chinese economy basically followed a path of extensive growth, except during a few brief historical periods. On the contrary, modern European nations followed a path of intensive growth. The difference is in total amount of inputs against outputs. In other words, more labour and resource inputs created an extensive growth and a bigger economy in size, while more assets and capital accumulation created an intensive growth, leading to sustained growth with fewer resources inputs.

In today's world economy, this contrast is shown by the different levels of TFP, which calculates the efficiency of resources consumption, including changes in technology and creativity. Inputs in production are measured against end output, and a real growth is shown in increased total productivity. The point of input-driven growth in newly industrialised countries was highlighted by several scholars before the Asian financial crisis. The East Asian economies are generally regarded as pouring more input to achieve high growth rates, and this would eventually lead to an end of growth itself.

China is in a similar situation, with the economy growing chiefly on the basis of huge government spending and foreign investment. A national survey in 2004 indicated that the share of contribution from capital accumulation, labour force and TFP to the average annual growth of 9.3% between 1978 and 2002, was 5.5%, 0.8% and 3%, respectively. The first item, which includes investments from government, private and foreign bodies, stands as the major contributor to past growth. The third item indicates certain improvements from the late 1990s, and that resources allocation has been more efficient as a result of the shocks of the Asian financial crisis and of wide application of more advanced technology and management. However, the overwhelming factor of investment has not been reduced in importance, and in macro-economic areas, growth in China relies heavily on consumption of resources such as crude oil, coal, power and steel. Size matters more than efficiency does. This pattern of relatively low TFP growth may still affect sustainable development and harbour potential for future crisis.

8. Per capita incomes:

China practised socialism, which advocated equality among citizens, and government planning was to guarantee this fair distribution. After two and a half decades of reforms, this managed equality has given way to income gaps and divide between the rich and the poor. The general levels of incomes have, however, improved, as a result of quick wealth creation, more job opportunities, and more income sources. By the end of 2003, average per capita income level in China stepped across a key line— over US$1,000. This standard is generally regarded as one of the signs that an economy has moved into an early phase of being a developed economy.

Economic Management

We will review the following cases in the course of past economic growth and also examine government responses and handling of economic fluctuations (see Figures 6.4, 6.5 and 6.6).

Case 1: Deregulation and Inflation

This phase of economic management occurred in the mid- and late-1980s. Economic reforms had just been formally declared as the new direction of the ruling Party, and initial opposition to changes began to subside. The government faced problems at two fronts: to release

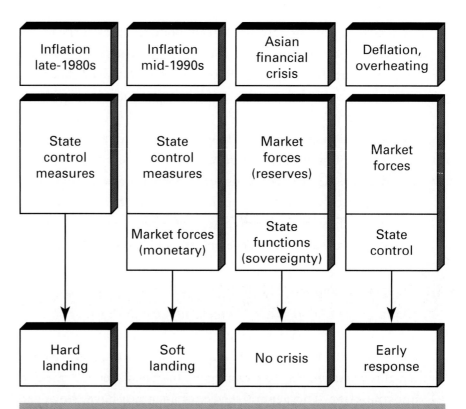

Figure 6.4   Macroeconomic management against inflation and deflation

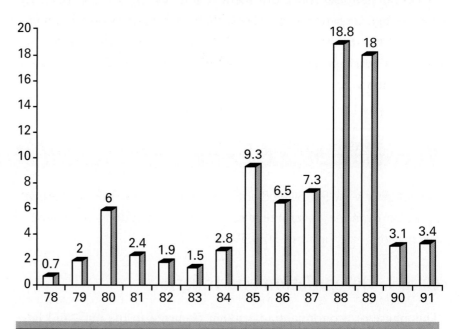

Figure 6.5   China's inflation and deflation

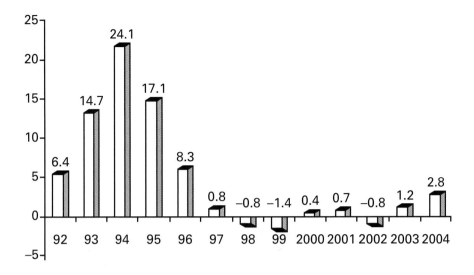

Figure 6.6   China's inflation and deflation (continued)

production factors from the planning, and to open up to early waves of foreign investment. As cornerstones of socialism, price control and public distribution had been the means to maintain social stability and fair share to all. On the back of successful agricultural reforms, which made rapid growth in rural production and income possible, the government began to introduce experimental reforms to urban centres. This included partial ending of price control, flexibility in employment, more authority granted to enterprise managers, and more business opportunities for those who positioned themselves well.

As the economy moved towards a market-oriented path and early rapid growth appeared convincing to all, an overheated economy began to emerge. Double-digit growth led to increased investment and consumption. Economic expansion saw more loans being lent out to enterprises and greater demand for investment from all sources. Incomes also increased, in the form of higher salaries and household earnings in both rural and urban areas. Money supply from the central government rose rapidly, doubling in two years between 1983 and 1984, to keep pace with market demand. It is generally understood in economics that an increase in money supply is a key factor to inflation. In the case of China, the economy then faced the possibility of inflation perhaps for the first time since 1949.

Rapid economic growth put great pressure on prices. Growth rate was 12.8% in 1985, with a CPI of 8.8%. In 1988, growth rate was

11.3%, and CPI rose to 18.7%, reflecting enormous aggregate demand over supply. The government faced twin deficits (trade and fiscal) and had to resort to printing money, issuing bonds and mobilising foreign exchange reserves.

Income gaps soon widened after reforms began, and sharp price rises occurred as a result of early economic growth. This was further compounded by the rash decision of the central leadership in August 1988 to clear, once and for all, the hurdle of rigid price systems nationwide. Accustomed to stable price levels for decades, urban residents had a rude shock of unprecedented price hikes, and shops soon lifted their prices whenever possible. To those who had fixed incomes, this sudden price increase meant devaluation of their savings, and paper money lost its value. This had not happened for three decades, and the horrible experience of hyperinflation under the previous Nationalist regime came back to their minds. In response, panic buying became widespread, and most goods in shops were completely cleared off the shelfs in a short period of time. There was a sense of urgency to turn paper money into whatever solid goods available. Banks faced large numbers of people making withdrawals, which were rare after socialism was established in China. People felt extreme uncertainty about their future and the capability of the government to rule effectively. Coupled with early waves of official corruption and disdain towards the new rich, public sentiment turned from bad to worse, and this frustration in part led to the tragedy at the Tiananmen in June 1989.

Government Responses

On its first battle against inflation, the central government had to handle the issue mainly with administrative measures. At this early stage of reforms, a half-opened economy still under much central planning had no effective means to correct itself, and the central authorities lacked experience and the mechanisms to put inflation under control. The final decision on curbing inflation had to be made by the ruling Party and the State Council.

Measures Taken

❑ Suspend and cancel large numbers of development projects, strictly control the permits for newly opened projects, order local governments to surrender rights of granting permission to the central and provincial governments;

❑ Restrict the size of lending, inspect all banks for lending records, approve no loans over given quotas;

❑ Restrict spending by government organisations and institutions, arbitrarily order all of them to cut down spending by at least 20%, with no exception. This is to reduce consumption by public sectors, so as to reduce demand;

❑ Limit the scale of pay rises, allocate less funds for employees' salaries;

❑ Close down large numbers of investment companies and funds, which had freely made their own lending choices;

❑ Implement price controls and ceilings, charge special consumption taxes on big sales items such as colour TVs and cars;

❑ Raise interest rate to 11.34% in 1989.

Consequences

Except the last measure of raising the interest rate, the central government, in coping with the overheated economy, fully applied administrative measures in their disposal at the time. Most of the measures could be implemented in a planned economy as well, and they were what the government understood for solving the problems they faced then. There were no other alternative means available to the government. Even for the interest rate option, there was no central bank to pass that through, so the central government simply directed the People's Bank to raise the rate and ordered other banks to follow. The authority behind all these measures was the effective power still held by government bureaux and party apparatus.

With these mostly administrative control measures, the economy came around the first inflation in three decades. Prices fell to acceptable levels and stabilised in the following years, much to the relief of most urban residents. The CPI dropped slightly in 1989 to 17.8% and continued to fall.

The phase of panic over inflation passed on to an austerity period, which resembles a recession in a market economy. Market activities became lukewarm for a few years. Complicated by political conflicts, this halt can be seen as a hard landing. To a certain extent, economic management by the government at this stage was old-fashioned, as in the socialist mould, and rudimental. However, it is a positive sign that the Chinese economy seems to be moving along the course of economic cycles common in Western economies, especially in the areas of money supply, inflation and interest rate.

Case 2: Soft Landing

Background

The austerity period of the early 1990s were lean years and produced low growth rates (4.1% for 1989, 3.8% for 1990, and 9.2% for 1991). To rejuvenate the economy, the patriarch leader Deng Xiaoping gave a firm push for further reforms during his southern tour in early 1992, and the general direction towards a market economy was subsequently written into the Party's doctrines. The 14th Party Congress announced the long-term goal of establishing a socialist market economy, and market forces were to be utilised fully in economic development. This indicated, in particular, more significant roles for private businesses to play in future. Market competition was no longer viewed with suspicion and began to be encouraged. Bolder reforms to many state institutions were carried out, such as the coordinated reforms to the banking industry, foreign exchange and stock market in 1994. In addition, faster economic growth was preferred to the then slow pace of development.

The Chinese economy again rebounded. Provinces and regions competed to race ahead of others, in growth and in numbers of big projects. Loosened control and monetary policies led to rising investment and spending. Economic growth rates rose dramatically, at double-digit levels for four consecutive years (14.2% for 1992, 13.5% for 1993, 12.6% for 1994, and 10.5% for 1995). China became the number-one steel producer of the world and consumed large quantities of other resources such as coal and crude oil, in order to meet the demand from an expanding economy. Government actions played a key role in this expansion, through setting up numerous large projects, mostly pushed by local governments, and through making bank credit easily available to business borrowers. This upsurge of economic activities and high liquidity eventually led to an overheated economy.

The symptoms of a runaway economy are in a number of highs. High fixed asset investment created huge gaps in government budgets, and demand for money flow led to high money supply from the central bank. A new factor is that local competition created duplicated investment and over investment for local interests and moved out of the control of the central government. The worse situation is having high inflation. In comparison with high growth rates, the CPI figures surged even higher (6.4% for 1992, 14.7% for 1993, 24.1% for 1994 as the peak, 17.1% for 1995). In addition, high imports from overseas to meet domestic demand created enormous trade deficits. This is a typical example of **twin highs** (high growth and high inflation), coupled with **twin deficits** (fiscal and trade deficits) in the economy.

Government Responses

Between 1994 and 1997, the government carried out a contraction policy and adopted a variety of measures to cool the economy down. Unlike the crisis in the late 1980s, this one in the mid-1990s illustrated a mixed nature of market and government controls. As a result, macro-economic management contained more market-oriented tendencies.

In the area of monetary management, the government let more market forces play. China had then established an improved banking system and reformed the central bank, the People's Bank of China. The government announced a credit-tightening policy, and that policy was carried out chiefly by the central bank this time around. The bank conducted open market operations, common in other market economies, issued government bonds, raised bank reserve requirement levels, and raised interest rates. Deposit rates reached high levels, plus favourable bonus rates for those who kept their money in banks over two years. The effective savings rates could be in double digits. This, to a large extent, offset the negative effect of double-digit inflation and increased total personal savings in the banks. Money supply and liquidity levels were reduced dramatically.

The government also tightened its own budgets, cut down the numbers of investment projects and increased revenues in the Treasury. On this issue, the central government relied on its recent reforms to the taxation system in 1994. The new system divides tax revenues into two separate categories: the central and local taxes. The ratio was approximately 70:30 in favour of the central government, but the central government promised to return certain portions of tax revenues to local governments to fund investment and development. Tax bureaux across the country were divided into two lines, state taxation offices and local taxation offices. (A more detailed discussion on taxation issues is in a following chapter). This move significantly changed the previous precarious situation of fiscal imbalance, in which the central government was losing control of national development and of local authorities. In this combat against inflation, a financially strong central government had more means to reign in inflation and effectively cool down an overheating economy.

It is inevitable that administrative measures were also adopted by the central government, including routine suspension of spending by government organisations and institutions, in order to reduce group purchases, which had pushed up demand and prices. Zealous local initiatives to claim large areas as "open zone" or "development zone" were arbitrarily halted by official directives from the State Council. Potential bubbles in real estate and construction industries were deflated early.

Consequence

In typical market economies, economic cycles include a number of stages, and inflation at a high rate is normally followed by a slowdown. If the government handles it badly and puts a lot of pressure on the economy to slow down, the result may be a recession, and the size of the economy will shrink and the level of economic activities become low. Common consequences are close-down of large numbers of businesses and high unemployment rates. According to the Phillips curve in general economics, there is a trade-off between inflation and unemployment, and this has troubled economists and policy makers for the past half century. A recession as the consequence of inflation control is called "hard landing" or "crash". On the contrary, a "soft landing" is the situation in which high inflation is countered by government budgetary and monetary policies to lead to a slowdown of the economy, but not a recession. Whether it is a **hard landing** or **soft landing** depends on the ways the government manages the economy. There were great expectations among Western observers that inflation in China in the mid-1990s would not lead to a "soft landing".

At a later stage of this inflation, the economy cooled down. Growth and inflation rates were 9.6% and 8.3% for 1996, and 8.8% and 2.8% for 1997. With hindsight, inflation in effect disappeared in China at the end of this cycle, and is still very modest in the first decade of the 21st century. The control measures led to a reduced level of economic activities and made the economy proceed onto a steady path. The government declared the goal of a soft landing achieved in 1997. In this round of combating inflation, the government adopted both market-driven measures and traditional administrative measures. The difference was in the degree. The central intention was to apply more market measures, as shown in utilising the role of the central bank and the interest rate mechanism, while in reality the implementation of control measures surely relied on the effective channels of government and Party bureaux. In comparison with the first experience of inflation in the late 1980s, this mixed approach proved to be a marked improvement and showed the viability of new institutions and reform policies established during this period of time.

A significant aspect of curbing inflation is the elimination of enormous wastage in the economy, since high growth in China often comes with irrational investment, duplicated investment and investment without any meaningful feasibility. Most of these investments have little prospect of earning reasonable returns, on top of their effects in creating false demand and bubbles. An investment-driven growth is conducive to unsteady economic development in the long run. Inflation generally devalues people's savings and eats up people's earnings, and after these two phases of inflation, the government realised that growth alone cannot bring real wealth and benefits. This led further to the question of generating extensive or intensive growth. In fact, Chinese government think-tanks and scholars thereafter talked more about the negative effects of **extensive growth** — growth in size, and advised to reduce the plays by the government in the economy and focus on TFP and efficiency.

Case 3: The Asian Financial Crisis

From 1997 to 1998, many East Asian countries suffered an unprecedented financial crisis. Their continuous economic growth in the previous decades was abruptly broken, and huge losses occurred in all of these economies. They were hit by massive capital flight, severe currency devaluation, evaporation of foreign exchange reserves, and lost values of fixed assets. Financial institutions from Western economies succeeded in making these Asian currencies devalue dramatically and even become worthless. Wealth was sucked away at alarming rates, and business closure and unemployment abound. A weak recovery emerged only in the first decade of the 21st century.

Many of these economies suffered heavily during this crisis partly because of their common pattern of extensive growth and an over-reliance on exports to Western markets. As discussed earlier on TFP, some economists had pointed out that this type of growth could not sustain for long.

China was in the same category of extensive growth and sought the same export markets, as did those East Asian economies. China, however, was generally unaffected by this crisis, at least not directly, and the economy did not encounter problems such as currency devaluation or capital flight. There are some reasons for this exception.

Monetary and other related reforms in the previous battle against inflation had created a much healthier financial system to cope with another external shock. Great emphasis on domestic economic restructuring reduced wastage and increased efficiency. One important asset was the rapidly enlarging foreign exchange reserves after the financial reforms, which reached US$51.6 billion in 1994, US$139.8 billion in 1997, and US$154.6 billion in 1998. These enormous financial resources provided much-needed funds at the government's disposal when facing a potential crisis and made foreign speculators exercise caution in their planned attacks. Revenues in the hands of the central government also increased considerably as a result of extensive taxation reforms.

Above all, the financial system of China operated independently from international financial markets, and foreign capital and money flowing in and out of China were under the control of the central government. In particular, China's stock and foreign exchange markets prevented foreign speculators from freely selling down the currency or stocks and transfering their profits out of the country at will. These barriers essentially put a stop to an onslaught by foreign speculators and made the occurrence of capital flight out of China nearly impossible. As a result, the RMB currency was stable at around 8.3 yuan to a US$ during and after this crisis.

For China, an added factor in this financial upheaval is Hong Kong, which returned to Chinese sovereignty in 1997. As a sovereign country, the Chinese government took on the responsibility to assist the Hong Kong Special Administration Region to fend off any attacks from foreign speculators. As such, economic management by the government was shown mainly through its firm support to Hong Kong in defence of its currency.

The Hong Kong dollar, before and after the handover of sovereignty, was linked with the US$, at approximately HK$7.8 to a US$, under the peg system. As a fixed foreign exchange system, it is subject to great external pressure to appreciate or depreciate. Its stable value depends heavily on the state of the economy, health of the financial system, and sufficient foreign exchange reserves. The Hong Kong government relies on its huge foreign exchange reserves and land funds to support this peg system, making timely adjustments (buying, mostly) to keep the currency value within the acceptable band. On this note, the central government provided much needed assurance during the crisis that the foreign exchange reserves in China can be used, if necessary, to help the Hong Kong government fend off attacks on its currency.

Since Hong Kong is an open free market, foreign capital can move in and out of it without any impediment. After attacking other East Asian economies, foreign speculators, in particular international hedge funds, intended to make the peg system of Hong Kong collapse in 1998. They sold heavily on foreign exchange and stock markets, attempting to devalue the currency and sell off Hong Kong stocks at low prices, in order to gain in futures markets. The Hong Kong government decided to avoid the fate of other East Asian economies and to meet the challenge head on. It bought up the Hong Kong dollar when there was heavy selling, and bought up whatever blue chip Hong Kong stocks that were on sale in the market. In the end, the government spent tens of billions of Hong Kong dollar to save its currency and stock market.

It also took other effective measures to make it harder for foreign speculators to borrow and gain profits, such as the measure to raise overnight money rate sharply to 300%, thus raising the costs of borrowing the Hong Kong dollar locally by foreign speculators who would sell on the market the next day. After several rounds of spectacular selling and buying, foreign speculators finally retreated, with certain undisclosed losses, and the Hong Kong dollar stayed at about the same level in value. The Hong Kong government became the holder of large amounts of blue chip stocks, which were sold to Hong Kong residents at a steady pace in the following years. With international hedge funds also suffering heavy losses in Russia, the battle to save the peg system in Hong Kong in effect spelt the end of financial crisis in Asia.

The Chinese government and economy were not directly affected by this financial crisis. Their major contributions can be categorised as follows. First, an improved domestic financial system guaranteed that sufficient financial resources could be mobilised. Second, the government held firmly to the stand that the RMB would not devalue, which proved critical when other Asian currencies were in collapse. Third, the government backed up the Hong Kong authorities in its fight to keep the peg system, through official public statements and readily available foreign exchange reserves.

An Issue for Discussion

There are opinions that the devaluations of RMB in 1994, from 5.7 yuan to 8.3 yuan a US$, made Chinese goods more competitive on international markets, and Chinese exports to industrialised economies jump sharply afterwards. Since the southeastern Asian economies exported to the same markets, the surge of Chinese exports took over the markets previously held by these economies. This shift reduced the real value of currencies in those economies, and speculators spotted this discrepancy, in addition to the belief that the NICs relied on investment and inputs for growth. They then seized the opportunity to attack the currencies of these economies. The financial reforms and RMB devaluation in China are thus considered by some as one of the causes that led to the Asian financial crisis in 1997.

In the years following the crisis, southeastern Asian economies grew to rely more and more on the market and growth in China. Exports to China helped to maintain favourable trade balances in these economies, and Taiwan, Korea, Malaysia and Thailand were among top 10 places China had trade deficits with. This indicates a growing pattern of interlocking relations between China and these economies, and a general trend to focus on the China market for continued growth at home. China is also working to enter a free trade zone with the ASEAN countries.

Case 4: Deflation and Overheating in 2004

There are several causes for the deflation period in China from the late 1990s to early 21st century. The double impact of a domestic soft landing and the Asian financial crisis dampened consumption. The US and other developed economies were experiencing recessions as well, thus putting pressure on Chinese exports. Domestic production capacity had grown rapidly and churned out huge quantity of goods into the market. China officially turned from an economy of shortages to an **economy of surplus**. Market competition and overcapacity continued to drive prices down, and big sales campaigns by manufacturers met with fewer buyers. Supply overtook demand by a large margin, and CPI figures were lowered year by year. China also faced, for the first time, serious problems of unemployment, as a result of open labour market and massive layoffs at state enterprises. Job security became low, and this affected consumers' purchasing decisions. Without adequate social security covers, spending on consumer goods unavoidably shrank.

Western governments had little experience in dealing with a deflationary economy. They had been combating inflation most of the time after WWII. One tool at their disposal was the interest rate, which was lowered by their central banks. Although the zero or negative interest rate set by the Japanese government did not seem to work in pulling the economy out of its decade-long recession, the lowering of the interest rate was a step Western governments had to take. It was after a few years that this monetary policy worked the economy towards a recovery.

The Chinese government did not expect to encounter a deflationary economy either. In practice, they applied the same approach as that taken by the US Federal Reserve. The official interest rate in China was lowered several times from 1998, from a high of 12% to combat inflation, though it was still slightly higher than the US rates. The government also adopted a pro-active approach in their fiscal policies. From 1998 to 2003, the government issued bonds worth 800 billion yuan specially designated for long-term reconstruction. The rationale was to raise funds this way to fill the gaps in state budgets, spend the money on infrastructure and increase total state investments. Money was then allocated to numerous state investment projects, and the government was hoping to stir up economic activities in other sectors and provide strong impetus for more consumption. The official slogan at the time was to induce aggregate demand in domestic markets. Even with heavy government debts incurred, this government-led campaign was seen as one of a few viable options in an economy with deflation. Another means was to encourage more exports, in this case allowing more tax rebates to be granted to those exporting firms. In other words, government, public investment and exports powered the growth of the Chinese economy in these years.

The situation finally turned around from 2002. Another economic expansion commenced, and a new wave of heavy investment began. The previous situation of oversupply changed to a shortage of equipment in all projects. As the economy picked up pace, consumption of energy and natural resources jumped sharply. Subsequently, power-generating equipment also sold well. Output by heavy industries increased by 20%. Exports by more foreign multinationals, which took China as a favoured production base, increased as well and consumed more natural resources in China. In 2003, the economy expanded by 9.1%, while in previous years, it was between 7% and 8%. In the first quarter of 2004, the economy grew by 9.7%, a near double-digit growth. This was mainly in the forms of increases in fixed assets investment, which in 2003 was 26.7% and in the first quarter of 2004 reached a whopping 43%.

Banks loans in the quarter increased by 21%, and increase in money supply at 19%, indicating a high liquidity in the economy. The issue of money supply was compounded by China's foreign exchange control. As will be further discussed later, this control system directs all foreign currencies from foreign investment to the central Bureau of Foreign Exchange Administration and sends out RMB funds to investors at a set rate. These foreign currencies became foreign exchange reserves of the central government. As the debate on China's RMB exchange rate heated up in 2003, foreign speculators predicted a RMB appreciation under the pressure from the US government and from China's own trade situation. Anticipating potential higher returns, they pumped large quantity of foreign currencies into China, in the forms of foreign direct investment, QFII portfolio investment, and through other countless channels. Since the central government is obliged to trade RMB for foreign currencies, money flows into the market increased in volume as a result. This loophole in foreign exchange control has not been mended effectively.

One of the most worrying signs was from the real estate industry, with investment rising by 41.1%. This particular sector has been a hotbed for bubbles, in China and in other developed economies. A relatively good sign is that public consumption began to rise, with retail sales increasing by 11% in the first quarter. It has long been the goal of the government that heavy state investment would eventually lead to more consumption. The CPI is still at a modest level of 2.8%.

Government Responses

The central government was alarmed by this widespread upsurge, fearing to fall into another inflation trap so soon after years of deflation. Government officials, from Premier Wen Jiabao down, seem to have reached a consensus that taking actions early could ensure a soft landing, rather than a hard landing when the economy became out of the control. They keenly spread the message repeatedly to the general public and to international investors that an overheated economy did not benefit the interest of all involved.

To reign in overinvestment and duplicated investment, the State Development and Reform Commission was given the ultimate oversight power. It approves or rejects project proposals, and also allocates or withholds funds to all large investment projects. With the authorisation of the State Council, this Commission acts as the top state agent and has decisively cut down the number of development projects in a short period of time. Many of such projects were scraped and forced to close down. One example is a new giant steelwork in Jiangsu province, which required a total investment of over 11 billion yuan. Named by Premier Wen at a State Council meeting, this project was immediately annulled by the Commission, and local government and bank officials who did not report this large undertaking to the Commission were penalised according to state regulations.

In the meantime, the State Banking Industry Commission monitored the operations of banks, and irregularities in lending were punished swiftly. Money credit was thus tightened, easing the urge to invest. The People's Bank also watches closely China's domestic situation and that of the US. It has publicly stated that if there is a rate rise in the US and if domestic CPI creeps over 5% in consecutive months, it will likely raise RMB rates. The People's Bank began to take other necessary actions early from the end of 2003, to raise bank reserve requirement levels, from 6% in late 2003 to 7.5% in early 2004, in effect freezing hundreds of billions yuan in banks. With this concerted precautionary effort to mainly reduce total investment, fixed asset investment in May 2004 dropped 16.4% from the previous month, a clear slowdown in growth.

During this entire economic cycle, the government made choices of different kinds. For stimulating the economy during deflation, the government made big spendings, lowered interest rates like central banks in other developed economies, and issued bonds of large quantity. This pumping of money into the economy created some heavy budget deficits to the government, but the positive effects emerged in following years. At a later stage, the government realised early that the economy was running hot and deflation had ceased to be a central problem. Based on data and advice from all quarters, the government acted quickly to prevent a runaway economy from becoming a reality. Signals of overheating were more closely monitored, and government bureaux in charge were coordinated to respond effectively.

It is interesting to note that market forces were more widely mobilised, and that the macroeconomic management focused on monetary and fiscal measures, rather than administrative measures. These measures include the early warnings to banks on their lending policies, raising bank reserve requirement levels a few times, thus tightening credit and freezing large amounts of money, and publicly discussing the possibility of lifting official interest rates. Since the US Federal Reserve was considering the same option, the discussion and prediction of a rate rise gave people adequately clear signal of the intention to curb the overheated economy. The majority of control measures was handled by the People's Bank, with the Banking Industry Commission, through open market operations. In fiscal policy, the State Council reduced bond issues to 110 billion yuan for the year 2004, reducing government budget deficits and spending as a result.

It is unavoidable that economic management by the government had to be implemented through government bureaux, so administrative measures still have to be applied, to impose measures on government departments and regional authorities. A typical example is to roll back duplicated and low-tech investment projects, in both scale and number, and to cancel land allocations for such developments. Since real estate development took a significant share in all investment, local governments tend to allocate large areas of land for "open zone" or "high-tech zone", selling land for huge profits. During the restructuring campaign, the central government in 2004 ordered to have such zones closed or confiscated. These number over 3,000, half of the total new zones under development across the country. Counting from early 2003, over 70% of new zones were cancelled. Similarly, other government-sponsored projects of golf courses, office buildings and shopping malls came under strict scrutiny and were suspended. All these administrative measures, in addition to monetary and fiscal measures, proved necessary in creating a timely remedy for the economy's needs.

The precautionary control measures are justified for another underlying reason—the country has a much larger unemployed group, numbering tens of millions. While a slowdown of economic growth would be acceptable, a crash could be disastrous for the general public and the economy. The government preferred minor adjustments and early defusing of high inflation, so that smaller scale shocks would affect only portions of the economy, and social stability could be maintained. They did not want to repeat the experience of the late 1980s, therefore the option of early and incremental measures was taken, instead of having to brake hard when a high inflation crisis becomes a reality.

This round of macroeconomic management since 2004 has yet reached its conclusion. Foreign observers have their own views on the possible end result as to whether a crash or a soft landing would ensue. Hopefully the economy would cool down and proceed steadily, without the threat of another high inflation.

Summary

The Chinese economy has become more market-orientated and achieved a respectable average growth rate through the last quarter of the 21st century. However, this average growth did not ease the difficult phases of highs and lows, and overheating recurred. This indicates policy and structural defects in the economy and exposes weaknesses in the government's economic management. The swings of fluctuations appear quite wide, causing high peaks and low troughs to happen within a

span of few years. To varying degrees, a Chinese saying of politics—
"once loosened up, chaos ensue; once tightened, things barely move"—
can also be applied to economic management by the government since
the reforms began.

This is the result of measures available to the government in
resolving potential economic disasters, including financial institutions,
industrial complex and tight control over the bureaucracy, from top
national bodies to local administrative units. It is unavoidable for the
government to rely on one of these means if the economy shows signs
of deviating from the right course. On the other hand, market forces
have penetrated most corners of the economy, and market fluctuations
have become a fact of life. This change causes deep concerns within
the government. Between economic fluctuations in a market economy
and remaining clouts for control, the government often has to make a
tough choice. The way ahead implies a less forceful government
intervention into the economy and a willingness to let market forces
fix certain defects. However, in this transitional economy, the market
cannot function well yet, and the government may be forced to lend a
hand and mobilise the forces under its control to bring back certain
stability in the economy. This internal struggle will continue for a long
while, with a more mature economy coming to form in the near future.

Under the new leadership in the 21st century, the government handles
the current economic upheaval in a more systematic and confident
way. First, predictions of an overheated economy had been made and
early warnings given. This reduced the potential damages a high
inflation may cause. Second, government management focuses on
economic, monetary and fiscal measures, similar to approaches common
in Western economies. Administrative measures were imposed as
secondary means, to those sectors with strong state influence and less
market forces. One similarity between the overheating of 1993 and
that of 2004 is that investment-induced growth formed the core of
potential inflation.

To sum up, the Chinese government has improved on handling
cyclic inflation through monetary controls and grown to conduct
macroeconomic management in a way that is more compatible with a
market economy.

Key **Concepts**

Patterns of economic growth and TFP

Hard and soft landing

Market economy status for China

GDP and PPP criteria

Inflation and deflation

The Asian financial crisis and the peg system of Hong Kong

Discussion **Questions**

1. How do you evaluate China's economic performance in general? What economic indicators do you use and what aspects do you emphasise?

2. What are your views on the sustainability of China's economic growth at current rates? Use growth patterns (extensive and intensive) to explain the possible future of economic growth in China.

3. Examine and evaluate the government's handling of the Asian financial crisis, in both Mainland China and in Hong Kong, using data and information you can find.

4. What are your views on China's market economy status? What evaluation criteria did you apply?

PART III

ONGOING ISSUES OF CONCERN IN THE BUSINESS ENVIRONMENT

7

Financial Systems

This chapter will discuss the crucial issue of financial systems in an economy. These systems are in tertiary sectors, and financial markets quite commonly reflect the state and strength of the national economy. In pre-reform China, central planning regulated capital flows, and budgetary arrangements of the central government replaced the roles played by financial markets. The focus of financial management was to provide funding for designated projects in the country and serve the domestic market. Profound changes since the reforms have made the current financial sector unrecognisable to central planners of the past, and the process has been hastened in recent years. However, it is the common view that inherent troubles in this sector stand as the last few hurdles in the course of overall reforms, and the entire financial structure has not been whipped up to international standards.

The key parts of the financial sector in China, the banking industry and the securities markets, are discussed below.

The Banking Industry

The National Currency

The official currency of China is Ren Min Bi (RMB) which literally means "people's money note". The Nationalist government, which ruled

China before 1949, issued Fa Bi ("legal money note"). Fa Bi ran into serious troubles as a result of shocking hyperinflations, and was soon worth less than the paper it was printed on. When the Communist government secured their rule over the whole country, they issued RMB instead as the new national currency. In a major reform in the early 1950s, the RMB was revalued, at a level of one unit equalling 10,000 units of the note it superseded.

What were the major rationales behind this move? Economic reality, not ideological or dynastic motivations, forced the hand of the government. The move was aimed mainly at giving people sufficient confidence in the new currency and the new economy, and at erasing the sorrowful memories of worthless currency circulated during the previous periods of economic disasters. People could, from that time on, trade and hold a currency which would not dramatically and unexpectedly shrink in value and eat up their real incomes. This change also made it easier for people to do business: a more valuable currency gave people the convenience when making transactions as much smaller bundles of paper notes are required. A stable currency helped stabilise the national economy and heralded the coming age of effective central economic planning.

The basic currency unit is **yuan**, as that of a dollar, with a symbol of ¥ marked in accounting books. It was worth approximately US$8.2 to US$8.3 in 2004. Chinese counting units, including RMB, have special terms for ten cents ("jiao"), 10,000 ("wan") and 100 million ("yi") yuan. The latter two are particularly difficult in translation, when people try to convert English figures into Chinese figures or vice versa. For example, ¥300,000 yuan in Chinese is 30 "wan" (30 ten thousands), which confuses many into saying 30,000 in English.

On the back of unabated economic growth over 20 years since the 1980s, the real value of RMB has come to be a contentious issue in international trade, and there have emerged talks of a single Chinese currency ("Zhong Yuan") for China and for Asia, if China's economy expands to match the Japanese economy in size. The Chinese currency and its exchange rate are discussed in more detail in a following chapter.

Banks in China

The banking industry of China is governed by the "Law of the People's Bank of China" and "Law of Commercial Banks", both passed by the

People's Congress in 1995. There are several layers among banks operating in China. At the top is the People's Bank, followed by four state-owned commercial banks, other commercial banks, foreign banks and credit unions.

The People's Bank of China (the PBOC)

The People's Bank of China was once the only bank in business across the country until 1979. It had numerous branches at all levels of administrative units, and was authorised to perform a wide range of roles, functioning as monetary authority, interest rate and foreign exchange regulator, and carrying out commercial-bank functions. In a centrally planned economy, this was a single bank that operated with simplicity and efficiency, with an ultimate goal of channelling money to the places as directed. There was no real need to create competition or to consider profits or returns for this bank. Accordingly, concerns over improvement in customer service or unit output appeared to be marginalised. The bank acted more as a credit union and a casher for designated projects or maintenance of public works. The normal financing process ran from government collection of taxes, budgeting at the Treasury, allocation of funds, bank deposits and lending out, to end users which were state organisations at all levels. This routine repeated itself through time, with occasional redirections from the government based on its own political or economic priorities. On one hand, the general public had a solid confidence in this single bank, since it represented the state and all public resources, being the only place to deposit and withdraw money for other things in life. There was no possibility of bank runs or credit risks. On the other hand, all suffered from insufficient funding and unreliable services in the hands of the bank.

Due to its mixed nature, the People's Bank stood virtually alone in the financial sector. It saw no need to part from the monopoly and be thrown into a market competition or to take precedent from international practice. It is only after the reforms pushed for market competition that the government realised the existence of the unique and ambiguous status of the People's Bank. Hence the ongoing changes to the bank's functions and authority.

From 1984, the bank has been in a process of being reformed into the **central bank** of China, similar to the US Federal Reserve Bank or the Monetary Authority of Hong Kong. The bank was instructed to withdraw from all commercial operations and turn its branches into representative offices of the central bank. Its commercial and banking functions were attached to other commercial banks, which gained independent status or were newly reorganised to undertake commercial operations.

In 1995, the People's Congress passed a law which formally stipulates the roles of the People's Bank. In April 2003, the central government set up a new **Banking Regulatory Commission**, which is in charge of monitoring and supervising all financial institutions in China (see Figure 7.1). Thereafter, one more function of the People's Bank was transferred to another central authority.

Since the government has not granted permits to genuine private banks, this type of financial institution does not fall under the supervision of this Commission. Approvals given to new banks are issued by the Commission and the People's Bank. The approval

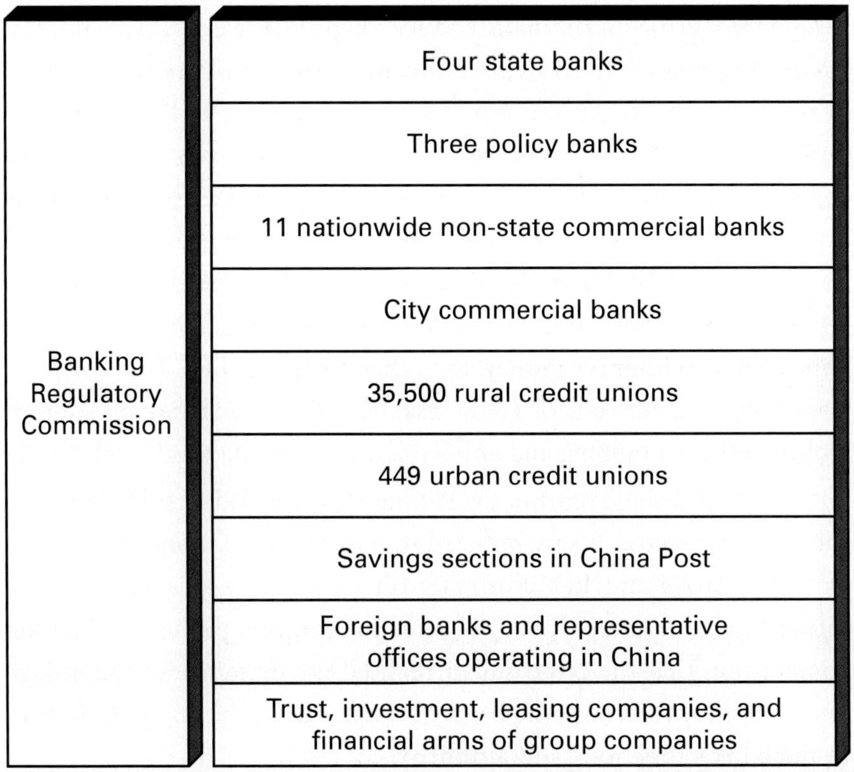

Banking Regulatory Commission

Four state banks

Three policy banks

11 nationwide non-state commercial banks

City commercial banks

35,500 rural credit unions

449 urban credit unions

Savings sections in China Post

Foreign banks and representative offices operating in China

Trust, investment, leasing companies, and financial arms of group companies

Figure 7.1 The target financial institutions under the Commission's charge

procedures include application for preliminary work, application for opening business, review and approval, issuing of permit and business licence, and public announcement. The whole process may take at least one year, if official policies allow.

After this separation of authority, the People's Bank focuses on monetary policy and financial stability. Major functions now include regulating money supply, foreign exchange rate, interest rate, lending to other financial institutions, clearing, and national bonds.

Central banks around the world generally have several measures in their disposal to control money supply. These include: 1) open market operations, such as selling or buying government bonds in financial markets; 2) bank reserve requirements, including setting higher or lower rates to control the amount of money in other banks; and 3) discount rate, such as deciding the cost levels of borrowing from the central bank by other banks.

After years of reforms, the People's Bank of China operates by and large along these lines, to carry out monetary policy and to monitor the financial state of the economy.

In August 2003, the People's Bank raised the required reserve rate of banks from 6% to 7%, effectively freezing about 150 billion yuan of RMB in the country. The move was a response to the overheated foreign exchange market, where dealers and speculators bought up RMB and eyed the rise of RMB value. As a result of that rush, total RMB amount and money supply increased, and risks of inflation and financial crisis emerged. The People's Bank, acting as the central bank, thus ordered the lifting of reserve rate to reduce the total RMB amount circulating in the economy and lower the liquidity in financial systems. For the economy as a whole, such control measures taken by the People's Bank would minimise the threats of either inflation or deflation.

State Commercial Banks

Since the People's Bank of China has withdrawn from commercial banking business, four giant state-owned commercial banks have emerged to fill the void left by the People's Bank. The **"big four"** are described here.

Industrial and Commercial Bank of China (ICBC)

The bank used to take central responsibility of providing credit to urban industrial and commercial organisations, and is now China's largest commercial bank. It has the largest customer base—420 million individual accounts and 8 million corporate clients in 2002. After 10 years of work, it now has around 80 million credit and bankcard holders under its cover.

The bank ranks number one in China, with 25% of China's banking market, and by its US$500 billion in assets, it was the No. 10 bank in the world in 2002.

In 2000, one third of ICBC's new loans went to consumers, mostly for mortgages and consumption, and mortgage lending grew 32 times in the four years between 1998 and 2002. Up to 2003, personal loans took 12.25% of the total loans the bank had lent out, covering 3.39 million borrowers.

The bank reduced its workforce by 75,000 in 2000, made 30,000 more redundancies in 2001, and the current total workforce is around 400,000. This is quite bulky for an international bank, but for this Chinese bank, it has been through some tremendous effort and painful downsizing and has opened the door for a higher efficiency level in future.

Agricultural Bank of China

The bank used to be part of the People's Bank and was concerned with rural credit and lending, covering the majority of rural population and public works. Financial reforms created new business opportunities, and the bank has since entered other sectors of the economy and international trading.

China Construction Bank

The bank took the responsibility of financing key state projects under the People's Bank and was concerned mainly with backbone industrial establishments and state enterprises. It is now a key player in financial markets and lends to all possible clients. One of its functions remains serving state enterprises, whether they are insolvent or competitive in the market. The bank has long planned to be listed on overseas stock markets.

The Bank of China

The bank had a special role to play under the People's Bank. It was the only one to conduct foreign transactions and deal with foreign exchanges. All foreign currencies passed through this bank, and all hard currencies to buy imports were issued from there. After the reforms, the Bank of China lost that monopoly in foreign currency transactions and has to share and compete with other banks in this business. However, the bank gains in getting more overseas business opportunities with its widespread networks. The bank was the first to move into overseas financial markets and the only one listed on the main board of the Hong Kong stock market (stock No. 2388).

Although the names of the big four indicate different specialised services, they are not confined to these sectors and are allowed to enter every area of the banking industry. For example, the Agricultural Bank can operate in all regions, including cities, and they can conduct industrial investment and foreign currency trade as well. Rural regions now receive less service and credit from this "agricultural" bank. Perhaps for this reason of operations without boundaries, large bank lending from the four state banks tends to flow to developed regions to chase profits and has created visible bubbles in industrial and commercial sectors there.

In recent years, the government is planning to get the big four to change into public corporations. They are now fully state-owned, without institutional investors or strategic partners. The first step is to introduce certain qualified external investors, while the state still holds the position of a majority shareholder. Part of the financial burdens can be transferred to others, and more capital will be injected.

The second step is to have the four banks listed on the stock markets for share trading and circulation. They will then become public-owned, and small and big investors have access to hold and trade these company shares. An example of such public corporations with state background can be found in the Commonwealth Bank of Australia, which has passed two rounds of privatisation through public listing and could just be a model for Chinese state banks. As public corporations, the big four will become more accountable, efficient, and responsive to market trends and adequately meet international standards.

Non-state-controlled Commercial Banks

The non-state commercial banks with nationwide business took 13% of market shares in 2002 and include:

- ❑ Communications Bank (Jiaotong);
- ❑ Citic Industrial Bank (Zhong Xin);
- ❑ China Merchants Bank (Zhao Shang);
- ❑ Shenzhen Development Bank;
- ❑ Guangdong Development Bank;
- ❑ Fujian Industrial Bank;
- ❑ China Everbright Bank (Guang Da);
- ❑ Hua Xia Bank;
- ❑ Shanghai Pudong Development Bank;
- ❑ Minsheng Bank
- ❑ Qingdao Commercial Bank

These non-state banks are also called "shareholding commercial banks". They are not directly owned by the state; they are not genuine private banks either, that have particular ministries, provincial bodies or powerful industrial organisations as their key backers. This is especially so for development banks, as they were formed from the initiatives of local governments and received start-up funds from government fiscal allocations. Five of these banks are listed on the stock markets of China, attracting institutional and private investors. As a result, in later years, more and more private enterprises became the shareholders of these commercial banks, lowering the total shares held by state organisations.

The Minsheng Bank is the first Chinese bank that is private in nature. The bank was facilitated and promoted by the All China Association of Industry and Commerce in 1994. The State Council and the People's Bank issued official approval for the birth of this bank in June 1994, and its formal business opened in early 1996. Its major shareholders include Sichuan, Beijing and Fujian private and collective enterprises, and they contributed over 80 percent of its initial funds. The bank was listed on the Shanghai Stock Exchanges in November 2000.

City Commercial Banks

There are other local and city banks operating in various regions, and their number is around 110. These commercial banks emerged out of previous urban credit unions and were upgraded in the mid-1990s to serve local customers and support local economy. For example, Shanghai Bank was established on the basis of 99 Shanghai urban credit unions in 1995. The business scope and scale of these city banks are small, the core of their operations focused on serving local and even district customers. On one hand, they can hardly compete with national banks and expand rapidly. On the other hand, they have very close contacts with surrounding business communities and residents.

Asset Holdings among Chinese Banks (as of 2003)

- Industrial and Commercial Bank of China (ICBC): over 4 trillion yuan;
- The other three state banks: over 2 trillion yuan each;
- Communications Bank (Jiaotong): 600 billion yuan;
- China Merchants Bank (Zhao Shang): 200-300 billion yuan; and
- Other national commercial banks: 50-150 billion yuan each.

In total assets, deposits, lending, network and market shares, the big four enjoy great advantage and leading positions. For example, the big four took 88% of deposits, 88% of lending, and 69% of total assets of the banking industry in 2001. Banks outside the big four take a small total market share. This stark contrast arises mainly from the priority given to the big four by the government and by other state organisations. All fiscal allocations and transactions by the government must be handled by these state banks, and most enterprises of considerable size open accounts with them, either following government instructions or choosing for the sake of convenience. Business opportunities available to non-state banks are thus limited. Despite this situation, these non-state banks lack the heavy debt burdens of state banks and have opted, at their own discretion, to introduce foreign partners and international banking practice into their operations.

Foreign Banks

A summary of foreign players in the banking industry is as follows:

❑ By April 2004, 64 foreign banks had opened 192 operations, and 88 of them were allowed to do RMB business in China. Foreign banks have 209 representative offices across the country;

❑ Foreign banks held total assets of US$49.5 billion, 1.32% of the total in the industry;

❑ Loans in foreign currencies were over US$14 billion in 2003;

❑ More than 25% of bank lending in foreign currencies are made by foreign banks in China.

All foreign banks need official approval from the People's Bank to open their business in China. Although there are no quotas on number of grants and China's WTO entry promises a complete opening in the near future, procedures for application and approval are still in place for the admission of foreign banks. General requirements for foreign banks to get approval include:

❑ Their representative offices in China have been set up at least for two years running;

❑ Their total assets in the year prior to the application for a registered wholly foreign-owned bank are not less than US$10 billion, and their total assets are not less than US$20 billion if applying to open a regional branch of a foreign bank;

❑ Their home countries have proper financial monitoring mechanisms.

To meet the asset requirements, the East Asia Bank of Hong Kong had to take over the First Pacific to be qualified, and Yong Long Bank of Hong Kong did the same by taking over First Zhejiang Bank.

Foreign banks face official restrictions on businesses allowed, branch location, and ownership after merger, etc. They are not allowed to undertake RMB transactions, are confined to foreign currency deals, and served mainly foreign companies in China, instead of Chinese business clients, especially state enterprises. They are given permission to open a few branches in cities designated by the central government, and each time they intended to move to another city or region, they must obtain official approval before moving.

There are several entry modes for foreign banks. They can open their own representative offices and branches. The Hong Kong based HSBC bank so far has the most branches opened on the mainland. Foreign banks can also make joint ventures with Chinese banks, and purchase stakes in Chinese banks.

Restrictions on foreign banks and their business in China stood as major hurdles in the marathon negotiations for China's WTO entry. After the accession, foreign banks have been given more room to manoeuvre and are better positioned to take up opportunities in China according to agreed timetables of market opening.

From 2001 onward, changes have come in a steady progression. The banking sector in China will be completely open to foreign banks in 2006, and foreign banks can operate RMB business with Chinese enterprises in that year as well. These will be done in a selective way, which implies that those banks already operating in China would be given priority.

Early in 1998, eight foreign banks were allowed to join the national inter-bank loans network, as well as borrow and lend RMB in China markets. These banks, however, were only able to lend RMB funds to foreign companies to support their operations, while RMB businesses for Chinese residents were out of their reach. This will change when the barriers to retail business operations are removed in 2006, and RMB transactions will be a major form of business for foreign banks.

Many other restrictions on foreign banks are to be phased out. Regarding location restrictions, foreign banks are allowed to move into all cities and regions, including rural areas, though they are more likely to operate primarily in urban areas. They can take part in handling foreign currency transactions for Chinese companies and individuals, and they can offer a whole range of personal banking services, such as the increasingly lucrative mortgage and credit cards business, to the growing number of Chinese customers with high incomes.

To make adjustment to these changes and meet new demands in a potential market, foreign banks have sped up their preparations for new businesses coming their way. Applications by foreign banks to open branches come in large numbers at the door of the People's Bank, and new partnerships and alliances have been formed. They also need to train large numbers of Chinese employees to provide needed services. For example, HSBC of Hong Kong set up new customer centres in

Guangzhou in 2002, with more than 700 local staff. More customer centres are to be set up in Shanghai and Beijing.

Citibank of the United States has firmly established its bases in China. The bank moved its China headquarters from Hong Kong to Shanghai in 1995. In 2000, Citibank ranked number one among foreign banks in assets, and its RMB deposits and lending were one fifth of the total. In 2002, Citibank was the first foreign bank to get approval to provide services in foreign currencies to Chinese companies and residents directly. The bank also acquired a 5% share of Shanghai Pudong Development Bank in 2003, and made joint launches of credit cards and Internet banking to the market. The joint credit card allows the bank to share RMB retail business with its Chinese partner, in effect crossing the line that marks 2006 as the year for foreign banks to start operating RMB retail business. Citibank is one of the few foreign banks granted permission to carry out QFII business in China. It has received 19 patents of financial products, including applications and systems, from 1996 to 2002. The bank also pioneered personal banking services and, to this end, has hired and trained large numbers of local employees in major urban centres.

Current Issues in the Banking Industry

Bad Loans at State Banks

The industry is one of the few most regulated ones in China. State banks and other banks in the financial systems are heavily controlled and influenced by government regulations and decisions. From a centrally planned economy where all financial resources flowed through government-owned banks, this industry has been undergoing a process of liberalisation, typified by the new roles for the People's Bank of China and by the emergence of various kinds of commercial banks. The industry is also characterised by two major problems, namely the issue of heavy bad loans and the unsatisfactory operational performance of banks in general.

The four state banks bear the burden of most bad loans, as shown in the first debt equity swaps programme which took away 1.4 trillion yuan worth of bad loans from these banks in 1999. The big four have a combined responsibility, under the instructions of the central government, to offer financial support to those state enterprises that face market competition, bankruptcy, and closure. Loans from these banks are lifelines to many struggling state enterprises, to pay for their daily operations, their production materials, and even salaries and benefits to their employees. It is hard for these four banks to refuse lending of this nature. As such, bad loans accumulate, with little hope of being repaid. Provincial and local governments are more eager to let banks inject funds to their own enterprises, in fear of losing revenues and causing local unrest, which would in turn jeopardise their official careers. Since local branches of these four banks are under the dual jurisdictions of their national superiors and local administrative authorities, they have few clouts to resist such lending. Under the direction of the then Premier Zhu Rongji in the late 1990s, the central government was determined to minimise the woes in state enterprises. In consequence, these four state banks bear the double burden of existing bad loans and of additional funds to support the newly established social security systems for the unemployed following the drastic reforms.

The dire situation of the four state banks indicates an unhealthy state of the banking industry and has led to numerous drives to make urgently needed remedies. Top among them, is the emergence of state asset management companies.

State Asset Management Companies

To deal with the common problem of bad loans among state banks, the central government set up four state asset management companies in 1999, to take over bad loans from the big four banks and transform the debts into assets or company shares. The four asset management companies each received initial funding from the central government of 10 billion yuan.

1. Huarong: took over 407.7 billion yuan of bad loans from ICBC, involving 71,000 enterprises; signed debt equity swaps programmes with 330 selected state enterprises valued at 110 billion yuan
2. Xinda: took over 370 billion yuan of bad loans from China Construction Bank, involving 50,000 enterprises; signed debt equity swaps programmes with 168 selected state enterprises valued at 154.5 billion yuan

3. Dongfang: took over 260 billion yuan of bad loans from the Bank of China, involving 20,000 enterprises; signed debt equity swaps programmes with 65 selected state enterprises valued at 63.9 billion yuan

4. Changcheng: took over 345 billion yuan of bad loans from Agricultural Bank of China, involving 195,000 enterprises; signed debt equity swaps programmes with 21 selected state enterprises valued at 12.5 billion yuan

The method used to complete this transfer is called "**debt equity swaps**". After asset management companies formally took over debts owed by enterprises, they shoulder the responsibility of debt collector, valuer, and liquidator. In this way, asset management companies became the major shareholders in debt-ridden enterprises and thus gained the authority to restructure them, in whatever ways plausible. If enterprise performance is not going to improve under the new management, these asset management companies have the absolute right to dispose of the debts, which include bankruptcy, auction, bond issuing, stock market listing, and discount sale. To facilitate the transfers undertaken by asset management companies, government policies allow foreign as well as domestic private investors to buy into the bankrupted enterprises.

Solving the bad loan problem is a task of tremendous magnitude. The total debts taken over from the four state banks were 1.4 trillion yuan in 1999. Since the process went quite slowly in the first few years, disposing of 93 billion yuan worth of bad loans by 2001 and new bad loans adding up every year, the total bad loans reached 2 trillion yuan in 2003.

This debt equity swaps programme was aimed at releasing debt burdens from state banks and state enterprises, and for this reason, many enterprises of central and provincial governments rushed to take advantage of the opportunity and pleaded for special treatments. They passed their debts on to the asset management companies and turned their debts into shares later offered to external investors. Interest payments on existing loans were also waived. To state banks and a large number of state enterprises, this was a newly found bonanza in their territories.

The programme picked up some pace in later years, drawing foreign investors to probe and acquire assets in state enterprises on offer.

Institutional investors such as investment banks and securities brokers show most interest and actively engage in negotiations with the four state asset management companies. The key questions are the discount price the foreign investors pay and ownership issues related to the purchases made. The four state asset management agencies have been in promotion mode to lure prospective foreign institutional investors, and road shows have been staged for sales of enterprise assets overseas. With strengthened effort and more sensible handling, by early 2003, 300 billion yuan of bad loans had been cleared and disposed off.

These four state assets management companies were set up exclusively for solving the bad loan problem of state banks, as such their functions are non-commercial and the duration of their duties are set at a time when bad loans of these banks were lowered to an acceptable level. In view of the current pace of bad loan settlements, these asset management companies could be in the business longer than initially expected.

Another boosting measure is repeated capital injection into these banks by the central government. These include a special Treasury bond issue of 270 billion yuan in 1998, along with debt equity swap moves, to increase capital assets of state banks, and another injection of US$45 billion from state foreign exchange reserves in early 2004 to the China Construction Bank and Bank of China.

By the end of 2003, the average non-performing loan ratio of the four state banks was at 26%. China Construction Bank had 11.8%, and Bank of China had 17%. These two banks may be among the first few to be cleared of bad loans.

In comparison, non-state commercial banks have much less mandatory duties to bankroll state enterprises in difficulty and face few bad loan problems. Minsheng bank has a bad loan ratio of around 3%. These banks have the autonomy to set their own criteria and select lending targets, and commercial interest is high on their list of key considerations. On the other hand, they encounter more challenges in market competition and have to answer to their investors and shareholders. One major obstacle is the size of these commercial banks: they are too small to have a big impact on the industry and on the financial state of the economy. The central government has shown intention to let these commercial banks lead in reforming the industry and experimenting new models of management and ownership structure. In the end, the overwhelming weight of the big four makes many such trials insignificant, since the successful practice from a lean and flexible commercial bank may not be viable in one of the big four.

Financial woes in the banking industry have attracted great attention from observers, domestic and foreign, and these are seen as the final hurdles to China's reform towards a market economy. In the words of some pessimistic Western commentators, the coming collapse of China's economy is after all illustrated here. Such views hold that if financial liability is not handled properly, the whole situation would explode and the economy would suffer sustained damages. These woes have, at the very least, caused resurgent pains and disturbances to the central government and the economy as a whole. Based on this grave concern, the success or failure of reforms in the banking industry poses a real test to the future of China's economic reforms, growth and public welfare.

Opportunities and Market Competition

New Banking Business Opportunities

Some profitable new businesses for banks are mortgage, consumer lending, including car loans, and credit cards. As urban residents seek more ways to spend their money and accumulate assets, lending in these two categories appear on the rise in recent years. Unlike lending to state enterprises and other types of institutions, consumer lending is based on more diligent checking of applicants' credibility and ability to repay. There is much less or no government pressure on loans, and there are no targets to achieve. A fresh start of this service implies a more business-like attitude toward customers, which leads to more careful and accurate appraisals before money is loaned out. Such practices are closer to international standards, and if the proportion of consumer lending increases, state banks could gradually minimise their bad loans incurred from irregularities common in state enterprises.

An essential part of regular bank lending is a comprehensive credit-rating system, where information and bad records are shared among banks, and borrowers with bad reputation would be refused further loans. Financial institutions in China are beginning to submit information on borrowers to a national database, and the government is behind this scheme, spearheaded by the Banking Regulatory

Commission and the People's Bank. A national database of credibility is, of course, also for other industries, but it is extremely important to the banking industry and its daily business. With an improved credit-rating system in place, banking practice can be expected to follow international modes more closely, and users of credit cards will grow in number.

Market Competition in the Banking Industry

Open competition is now common in the banking industry of China, especially after China's WTO accession. Chinese banks generally have the advantages of domestic players over newly entered foreign banks. They enjoy huge benefits of a widespread business network across the country, with over 140,000 branches in cities and rural areas by the four state banks alone. They have the dominant market shares in deposits and lending. They have stable and long standing relations with Chinese enterprises, with strong business and even personal connections. They normally have firm government backing, particularly from regional governments. Even with the WTO entry, this backing is not diminished. In between entry and full implementation, Chinese banks gained a few years of breathing space and have undertaken more vigorous and drastic reforms to gear themselves for the coming competition, including implementing international practice and partnering with certain foreign banks.

For foreign banks, they capitalise on being newcomers and avoid direct frontal attack on the massive market currently occupied by Chinese banks. Despite the withdrawal of a number of foreign banks and a smaller percentage in national total assets (1.32% in 2004, down from 2.42%), foreign banks now adopt more steady strategies in market competition and pursue various types of profitable businesses. The strategies are centrally targeting small groups of customers with high profit margins, instead of setting up wide business networks. The former strategy earns them quite lucrative deals. In banking business, it is a rule of thumb these days that about 80% of bank profits come from 20% of spending customers. There are not many quality business clients for banks in China, and most banks compete fiercely to woo these clients to take up their services. Multinationals, Joint Ventures, and successful big and medium-sized Chinese enterprises are valued customers. Under previous rules, they were exclusively the customers of domestic Chinese banks, in both deposits and lending fields. As rules relax, foreign banks are allowed to poach customers, and they take this opportunity to win over some important clients in the market.

In 2002, Nanjing Ericsson left its Chinese lenders, such as China Communications Bank, for foreign banks, among them HSBC and Standard Chartered Bank. The loans involved were worth about 2 billion yuan. Shanghai Sharp had borrowed from several Chinese banks, mainly from the Agricultural Bank, and then in 2001 it repaid most loans and refinanced with Japanese banks, such as Tokyo Mitsubishi Bank. The services offered by those Chinese banks proved not entirely up to the expectations of Shanghai Sharp, so when it was the right time, the company changed lenders. These cases sent shock waves to domestic Chinese banks and alarmed them a great deal.

The latter strategy made them save considerably on branches and on staff costs. The Banking Commission stipulated on 1 December 2003 that foreign banks must have operational funds in place before opening regional centres. The requirements are from US$300 million to US$500 million per branch. A regional centre requires large office space, fixed assets and a whole set of equipment, and foreign banks have to consider poaching top staff with lucrative salary packages. It is thus sensible for them not to spend huge amounts of time and money on establishing a parallel network as that of Chinese banks. An alternative is to acquire equity in existing Chinese banks and participate in their networks.

Foreign banks also have advantages in human resources and advanced business management models. A relatively simple way to set up a foothold in business is to poach qualified managers from domestic banks, luring them with tempting salary packages and various incentives. The more rigid wage and appointment systems in Chinese banks, especially in state banks, appear powerless to prevent this poaching practice. To a Chinese bank employee with a 50,000 yuan annual pay check, an offer of 150,000 yuan per year from a foreign bank is understandably appealing. The gap is getting narrower, as Chinese banks recognised the serious risk in losing capable managers, but the less flexible human resources management system and wage system, in particular, make them vulnerable in competing with foreign banks over talents.

Foreign banks have extensive experience in offering personal financial management services to high-end customers. They pioneered personal banking centres in China and offered one on one, tailored made services to meet particular needs of customers. This began with HSBC's personal banking "premier" service in 2002. Chinese banks soon followed with their own service schemes and centres led by China Merchants Bank and ICBC, targeting customers with over 500,000 yuan deposits in their banks. In general, a big gap exists in quality and performance between domestic and foreign banks, and foreign banks play the role of pacesetter in the area of personal banking.

Interest Rate Mechanisms

The central bank holds the authority to change interest rates as required by economic conditions. Interests are prices paid on money borrowed. A higher interest rate discourages borrowing of money, reduces the liquidity in the economy and leads to less investments and transactions. The economy then slows down. The central bank uses interest rates to manage money flows in the economy. When it sets a lower interest rate, the common response is that the money (in savings and deposits) flows out of commercial banks to other investment portfolios, such as property, stocks, or funds. Related business sectors get more investment and more returns. Since the central bank is the authority on money supply, it can set rates arbitrarily as it sees fit to suit the monetary policies of the government. The levels of interest rates are responses to changes in economic conditions, which are assessed regularly by the government.

Interest rates offered by domestic banks are basically at the levels set by the state treasury and the People's Bank. For deposit and lending, banks in China are not allowed to set up their own rates, and there are not much differences among banks or big margins over the basic rates, unlike banks in other economies. Currently, savings rate is at 0.72%, one-year term deposit at 1.98%, three-year term deposit 2.52%, five-year term deposit 2.79%, and there is a 20% tax rate on interest earnings. Competition in interest rates is not fierce among Chinese banks because of the state regulations, and higher rates sometimes offered to particular investors are treated as irregularities or illegal operations. These may be investigated by government bank authorities as potential criminal cases. Thus, market competition is mostly in the forms of services offered, rather than in favourable rates.

Negative rates and deflation: China was in deflation towards the end of the 1990s. The government and the central bank followed the US Federal Reserve and lowered the interest rate several times. With savings and term deposit rates at the levels cited above, the 20% tax rate on interest earnings and subsequent price rises led to negative real deposit rates. Under deflation, such low rates would lead to money outflows from banks and into investment. This was expected to happen to boost investment, production and consumption, so that deflation can end.

However, bank deposit figures continued to rise, from 7 trillion yuan in June 2001 to nearly 12 trillion yuan in early 2004. This was a sign of trouble for the government. The government had achieved the goal of ending deflation through other means, but failed in addressing many critical issues in the economy, such as unemployment, dependable social security covers, and wealth gaps. The rising personal bank deposits ominously indicated that consumers were reluctant to spend their money on non-essential goods and kept the money in the bank, since that was safe and could be used to meet unforeseeable difficulties.

These conservative behaviours came from two lines of reasoning. First, consumers' expectation of future uncertainties was strong, based on the near collapse of the former social welfare systems under socialism and the new threat of massive unemployment. These uncertainties pressed the people from the middle-level down to increase their cash options for emergencies. The traditional Chinese wisdom of coping with crisis still cast enormous influence on the population. Lower interest rates or not, many of them intend to hold on to their money.

Second, there was also the issue of very limited investment opportunities in the economy. The stock markets yielded meagre gains, housing properties were sky-high expensive, and few business investment could generate attractive returns to investors, due to ubiquitous and fierce market competition. Under such circumstances, consumer confidence was low, and most of them would rather put their money in the bank and spend less. The end of deflation in China in 2002-2003 depended on many other factors, such as recovery in developed economies and large government spending, while market conditions have not been markedly improved or effectively readjusted.

Government interest rates began to have some effects on bank deposits in 2004, mainly because of price rises, which indicated the coming of inflation, and the lowering of the RMB's real value. Under these circumstances, the central bank refused to officially announce a rise in interest rates. This has caused money (deposits) to flow out of banks into diversified investments. Deposits have increased at a slower rate since 2004, and total deposit figures have dropped. This may be the result of having low interest rates in place for a long period of time.

Summary

The banking industry in China has gone through several tremendous shifts. It is an industry touched by reforms at a relatively later stage, and due to accompanying uncertainties, the seriousness of existing problems in this industry affects all sectors of the economy. The industry has moved closer towards international practices, while the bad loans issue has to be dealt with urgently. The promised opening after WTO accession provides abundant opportunities for foreign banks to grab shares in that market and also for domestic players to raise their efficiency and competitiveness.

China's Stock Markets and QFII

Stock markets in China were suspended after 1949, and during the following decades of planned economy, stock markets lost their edge in raising funds and share trading. Economic reforms from the early 1980s reaffirmed the vital functions of stock exchanges in a market economy. A growing importance is attached to the health of stock markets and of companies listed there.

Some key data relating to the operations of China's stock markets are noted here.

❑ The first stock market, the Shanghai Stock Exchanges, was opened in December 1990. The Shenzhen Stock Exchanges opened in April 1991.

❑ The Securities Regulatory Commission was established in October 1992. Thereafter, the Commission took over the regulatory and supervisory roles over stock markets from the People's Bank of China.

❑ The Securities Law was passed in July 1999.

❏   There were 60 listed companies on Shanghai and Shenzhen stock exchanges in 1991. In 2002, companies listed on the two stock markets numbered 1,224, with market capitalisation at 3.8 trillion yuan (4.2 trillion yuan in early 2004). There are a total of 66 million small shareholders.

Types of Shares

The securities market in mainland China covers two kinds of shares, A shares and B shares. Closely related to China's stock markets and enterprises are H shares and red chip shares traded on the Hong Kong stock markets. There are three types of shareholding on the A share markets.

State Shares

These are held in the hands of state assets management organisations and their authorised institutions. This is a confusing concept derived from the socialist ideas of public ownerships. Since the public and the government theoretically own state assets and enterprises, state shares are in effect held by government departments that oversee listed state enterprises. The authorised organisations include approved shareholding companies, whose executives are appointed by, and report to, government bureaux. In the 21st century, the official body holding state shares is the State Assets Supervision and Administration Commission, at least according to socialist theories and government policies.

Legal Person Shares

These are held mostly by state enterprises. The enterprises that issue company shares hold a proportion of the total as legal person shares, and founding members of the listed companies also have rights to hold such shares.

Public Shares

These are shares put on the markets through initial public offerings (IPOs). Individuals and institutions can buy, hold and sell this type of shares on the two stock exchanges.

Among the three types of shares, the state and legal person shares are not for trading and circulation on stock markets. They form two thirds of the total shares registered. Most listed companies on the two exchanges are state enterprises, and the central authorities are strict on giving approvals to collective and private companies to be listed. In this way, the state is at any time the majority shareholder of the combined total of listed companies. Investors are able to trade only one third of total shares circulated on the markets. The state and legal person shares can be traded outside the exchanges, through deals made between enterprises and institutional investors. This practice involves large amount of shares in any one deal and is common in takeover bids, company restructuring, and introduction of strategic investors. Inspite of these deals and share transfers, these two categories of shares are still not publicly traded on the market.

With limited stocks on offer, buyers pushed up stock prices and P/E values. This created opportunities for early stock buyers and speculators. As stock markets were new to most Chinese urban residents at that time, the government tried hard to persuade and coerce participation, including ordering many government employees to buy. Those who did purchase, willingly or reluctantly, gained considerable profits when stock prices shot up, and an early group of Chinese millionaires emerged from stockholders and traders, especially in Shanghai. In the early 1990s the get-rich-quick sentiment reached a high point, and in a raging frenzy, hundreds and thousands of people rushed to Shenzhen to buy newly offered company shares. Armed police had to be called in to quell chaos and riots caused by disappointed crowds. When sentiments were low and state policies were initiated to pour cold water on overheated stock markets, share prices fell sharply, causing big losses to investors. Price drops also built up resentment and anger towards stock market regulators. In either case, the state as the majority shareholder stands to gain in the market, since these fluctuations can hardly devalue the two thirds of non-trading shares. In both cases, the government bears the blame of not handling the situation better, and calls have been getting louder for the government to protect the interest of small investors, and not just the interest of the state and institutional investors.

After years of development, the total number of shareholders is now over 60 million, and their concerns with the performance of stock markets reflect a wider opinion of the general state of the economy. To make peace with small investors and invigorate stock markets, the government has been planning to release state and legal person shares to public trading. However, bad handling of this issue made the plans backfire. In mid 2001, the State Council announced plans to reduce the shareholding of state shares. The number of shares for trading ballooned, in other words, large numbers of shares were "dumped" on stock markets. In reality, small investors do not have enough financial resources to buy up all these extra shares. Another criticism is that small investors bought shares at much higher market prices after first floating, while state and legal person shares were taken up at low prices before initial public offerings. If these previously non-trading shares were now selling at market prices, the big victims would surely be small investors. In response, panic selling began, and stock indices dropped more than 40% in following months. Under mounting pressure and complaints, the government soon suspended the reduction plans and withdrew the operations completely in June 2002. The stock markets have since been quite sluggish and lacklustre.

Despite this severe setback, the reduction of state shares is apparently the way to move forward. The central questions are how to minimise shocks and compensate small investors fairly. It has been suggested that certain discounts and special dividends be granted. On the other hand, the government has made it clear that the state will remain as the majority or controlling shareholder in most state enterprises, and that reductions will be only in percentage. It is thus not realistic for investors to expect the floating of all state shares in the foreseeable future.

China's stock markets began with state enterprises as listed companies. The initial idea was to finance these enterprises by investors' funds from stock markets. Accordingly, government approvals were issued primarily to large and key state enterprises. At a later stage, private and shareholding companies were given permission to be listed in growing numbers.

In early years of stock market operations, small investors participated very actively, making frequent trading for quick profits. In recent years, while stock markets saw less severe fluctuations, people began to hold shares as long-term investments, a means to offset temporary hardship and to provide some support for their old age.

Share Terms

A Shares

These are shares traded on Shanghai and Shenzhen stock exchanges and open only to domestic investors (Chinese citizens and institutions). Transactions are made in Chinese currency, RMB, and A shares cover all stocks traded in the markets. The state, legal person and public shares, discussed above, are all in this category. A share markets are apparently the centrestage for stock trading in China.

B Shares

These are shares open only to foreign and overseas Chinese investors (individuals and institutions). They are traded on separate boards of Shanghai and Shenzhen stock exchanges, and purchases and sales are made in other currencies (US$ in Shanghai and HK$ in Shenzhen). There are 110 stocks displayed on B boards by early 2004. B share markets are not closely linked with A share markets or follow changes there. With its small number of selected Chinese companies, it cannot be seen as the key indicator of China's stock markets. The introduction of B shares serves the purpose of drawing overseas capital, and Chinese citizens do not have access to these markets. In recent years, however, foreign currencies became abundant in China, as such official rules were modified in early 2001 to allow Chinese citizens with foreign currencies to buy B shares at stock exchanges. So far, domestic financial institutions have been barred from trading B shares.

The A share markets in Shanghai and Shenzhen are much bigger in size than B share markets and absorb most capital. Due to limited stock choices, number of buyers and investors' interest, foreign institutional investors gradually withdrew from this market, and B share markets have been in slow motion and made small trading volumes. Recently domestic investors filled up the vacuum and form about 70% of total capitalisation.

The original intention of attracting foreign capital into B share markets has been completely lost. These markets were even considered for other uses in the early 21st century, such as a place to let loose surplus foreign currencies held by Chinese citizens, at a time of potential trade wars with the United States. After the WTO-initiated opening in financial markets of China, other channels of foreign capital become available. Under these circumstances, there has been a possibility of merging A and B share markets. This merger of the two markets will also mean one step closer to a convertible RMB.

H Shares

The Hong Kong Special Administrative Region was formally established on 1 July 1997, shortly after the British government handed back Hong Kong's sovereignty to China. Many mainland Chinese companies had been actively doing business in Hong Kong, and many more were listed on Hong Kong's stock exchanges after the handover. It is thus necessary to include Hong Kong-listed Chinese companies in a review of China's stock markets.

H shares refer to those mainland companies listed on the Hong Kong stock exchanges. H stands for Hong Kong. Their stock values are shown in Hong Kong dollar, but for asset, profit, and dividend values, these stocks are shown in RMB. H shares include only state enterprises selected and approved by state regulatory bodies. More importantly, H share companies arc subject to Hong Kong stock market regulations, in addition to mainland regulations, while their real business operations are on the mainland. The gaps in operation standards and supervision require the cooperation between regulatory authorities on both sides of the border. Before listing, these state enterprises have mostly been trimmed and restructured, creating redundancies and leaving bulky burdens to the government or other domestic companies. These preparations are crucial in achieving a reasonable level of efficiency and making a good impression on overseas investment banks and funds.

The first H share company is Tsing Tao Beer, and heavyweights now include PetroChina, China Telecom, etc. By early 2004, circulated H shares were worth about HK$300 billion. H shares commonly have low P/E values (8-12), and many companies listed are industry leaders, such as PetroChina, which have great potential for growth and investment returns. In many cases, listed H share companies perform better than their domestic counterparts and are gaining experience in corporate governance and management. These can be valuable lessons in drives to reform domestic state enterprises. Private Chinese companies obtained permits to be listed as H share companies at a later stage.

Since H share companies are formerly state enterprises, they face stringent scrutiny in Hong Kong over their real income-earning capability, performance, management skills, and transparency under Hong Kong regulations. Furthermore, small investors in Hong Kong have unyielding faith in their own blue chips companies and focus on trading in that sector. H share companies therefore attract less interest, set at lower price levels and show low P/E values. A good example is PetroChina, which is a top oil producer, the biggest tax payer on the mainland, and number-one profit earner among listed Hong Kong companies, yet its stock price after initial public offering was merely HK$1.5 a share. Its low stock price shot up in late 2003 only after American billionaire Mr. Warren Buffet bought over 13% of its shares.

For those companies listed on both A share and H share markets, there are wide gaps between their prices. In general, H share prices are more affordable than A share prices. Shrewd investors would appreciate the differences and gain on the margins. Along with widening reforms of stock markets and China's unabated growth, this discrepancy has drawn more attention recently from international investment houses on H share companies.

Red Chips Shares

These are the stocks issued by mainland companies that are listed on the Hong Kong stock exchanges. These companies come with the backing of mainland governments at different levels and have trade and business operations in Hong Kong and mainland China. One way to get listed is to buy shares of a listed Hong Kong company (buying a

Gaps between some Share Prices in A and H Share Markets (February 2004)

(A: RMB yuan; H: HKD)

China Eastern Airlines	A: 4.8	H: 1.37
China Southern Airlines	A: 6.06	H: 3.6
Sinopec	A: 5.33	H: 3.25
Shanghai Petroleum	A: 6.67	H: 3.475
Jilin Petroleum	A: 5.33	H: 1.54
Nanjing Panda Electronics	A: 9.46	H: 2.175
Anshan Steel	A: 6.42	H: 3.975
Jiangsu Highways	A: 9.6	H: 3.7
Guangdong Kelon Electric	A: 7.9	H: 4.375

shell) and become majority shareholders. After changing company name and legal documents, it turns into a red chips company (back-door listing). An example of red chips companies is Citic Pacific (stock number 267). It originated from Citic China, a government investment company based in Beijing. Citic China bought a 50% of stake in a Hong Kong company, changed the company name, and became one of the top listed companies in Hong Kong. A criterion by Hong Kong regulatory authorities to define a red chips company is whether mainland enterprises or financial institutions are majority or controlling shareholders.

The leading red chips on Hong Kong stock exchanges are giant mainland enterprises such as China Mobile and Shanghai Industries. With certain investment projects and interests in Hong Kong, these red chips companies undertake their main businesses on the mainland and draw the bulk of revenues there. With the negative effects of the Asian financial crisis from 1997, the Hong Kong economy shrank and business revenues fell. Many red chips companies turned around and moved their main business to the booming mainland economy. For example, China Overseas (stock number 688) came out of China Construction in Beijing and had extensive real estate projects across Hong Kong. From 1999, the company quickly decided to suspend major investment in Hong Kong projects and focus on mainland property projects, including residential and commercial blocks.

Although the rising tide of H share companies brings some challenges to red chips companies, the latter, in comparison, are more internationalised, transparent and efficient in business. They are thus still treated more favourably by foreign investment banks and traders.

Get Listed

Chinese enterprises view stock markets as one of their fund raising sources, hence their eagerness to get listed. There are certain rules and regulations over the listing process. General requirements include:

❑ Total share value is not less than 50 million yuan, and founders take no less than 35% of shares;

❑ The company has had continuous earnings for three consecutive years;

❑ Shares offered to the public are not less than 25% of total share value, and for total value over 400 million yuan, shares offered to the public are not less than 15%.

Application Procedures

1. Restructuring:

   The company needs to undertake restructuring, in order to be a standard shareholding company. This implies that shareholdings and shareholders within the company are clearly defined and identified. This is particularly acute for state enterprises, for they have a structure of public ownership that grants all company shares to the state. At this stage, the overseeing authorities would get involved and appoint certain enterprise executives to be part owners of the company. The state organisation above the enterprise would act as the majority shareholder on behalf of the state.

   Another important task is to decide what assets and businesses are to be associated with the listed company. To appeal to external investors, especially to overseas institutional investors, the government tends to select quality assets and the most efficient production sections as assets of the new listed company. Those inefficient and obsolete sections, financial liabilities and other burdens are left behind. The relations between the former state enterprise and the new listed company are similar to that between a group company and a subsidiary. However, since the listed company has outside investors and shareholders, they also report to the company board and general meetings. This creates some conflicts between the two entities, in strategies, management and profit sharing.

   For private companies, they also need to pass through this restructuring stage, to make clear their shareholding structures. Normally, the central issue is how the founding members of the original company got their shares in the A listed company. An example is the top Internet portal company Netease, which was founded by a young engineer named Ding Lei. After a series of restructuring, he became the majority shareholder of the company, with over 50% of total shares. This made him an instant billionaire after Netease was listed, oddly, on NASDAQ (special arrangements and approvals had to be made and obtained from Chinese authorities to get listed on overseas stock exchanges).

2. Training:

This refers to the stage when a company appoints an authorised and qualified consultant firm to act as its sales agent and to assist in preparations for listing. For large state enterprises, chosen consultant firms are usually internationally renowned investment banks such as Morgan Stanley. The Securities Commission and other authorities would examine the work done and certify the results before moving to the next stage.

Training and preparations generally include:

- To affirm that past records of the company are legal and in order;
- The company has its own independent functions such as finances, asset holding, production, sales, human resources, etc. from the group company;
- All executives, board members and major shareholders learnt laws and regulations regarding securities;
- Systems for general meeting of shareholders and the board are adequately established;
- Systems of disclosure for public interest and transparency are established.
- The duration of this training is from one to three years.

3. Formal application

All required documents for applications are submitted to the Securities Regulatory Commission, on the official forms issued by this authority.

4. Approval

The application is assessed by a panel consisting of securities-related organs under the State Council and external experts by invitation. The panel casts their votes, and the State Council issues official approval.

5. Public announcement

The company publishes its prospectus and company constitution, and makes them public on newspapers designated by the Securities Commission.

6. The company starts public offering and signs contracts with stock selling agents.

7. The company makes application to the stock exchanges and gets listed on stock markets on the designated date. The company has a choice to select either Shanghai or Shenzhen stock exchanges, but after official approval is given, it will be listed on the stock exchange they applied for. The considerations of which stock exchange to choose are generally the size, turnover volumes and number of small shareholders of a particular exchange. The two exchanges have begun competing to get more companies listed on their exchange by offering certain incentives.

Get Delisted

When listed companies show signs of irregularities, the Securities Regulatory Commission will take actions in accordance to existing laws. One measure is called "**Special treatment**", shortened as "ST". Their stocks and derivatives are all marked "ST", and the margins for price rise and fall cannot exceed 5%. Although their stocks are still meant for normal trading, listed companies with this "ST" sign will be viewed warily by traders and investors. This is a kind of soft warning from the Commission, and time is given for "ST" companies to restructure, reorganise and eliminate irregularities.

The signs of irregularities include negative net profits after audit for two years, net asset value lower than share value on initial offer, and that accounting firms refuse to sign audit reports, etc.

Listed companies can have their "ST" signs removed if their restructurings are successful, and if the considerations behind "ST" sign are sufficiently explained and cleared off.

A more serious matter is to delist a company. This will happen when the company is in loss for three consecutive years, in serious violation of laws, has falsified books or has fundamental changes to its shareholding structure. In 2003, 12 listed companies were delisted. In 2004, at least 21 companies were delisted due to their status in the "ST" category and their continuous losses. These companies can re-apply for listing in future, after the above matters are cleared and remedied. In particular, a company in loss can be relisted once it achieves net profits for a year. As such, the Chinese term for this situation is "suspension of listing", which implies temporary delisting.

Corporate governance is relatively new to Chinese enterprises. After two decades of economic reforms, most enterprises have only preliminary grasp of this concept in their operations. This insufficient understanding also affects listed companies, with numerous enterprises placed under "ST" or even delisted. More seriously, the relations between group companies and their listed companies are very murky and unstable, leaving ample room for financial scandals. A common practice is that group companies suck funds from listed companies and inject them into their own operations. As such, listed companies play a role of ATM machines, depleting funds and earnings from small investors and shareholders. Transfer of assets and capital in this way often create big black holes for listed companies. On the other hand, listed companies may grow more powerful and independent, and have deep business conflicts with group companies.

The QFII Regime

The A share market is closed to foreign investors, and the B share market has not preformed well to appeal to investors from overseas. Between the two types of foreign investment, direct investment and portfolio investment, China has focused on the former since reforms began, partly due to an underlying fear that portfolio investment by foreign financial institutions may cause financial risks and disturbances to financial management by the state. A way to get around the stumbling blocks in stock markets was then devised in the early 21st century—the **QFII regime**, which stands for **"qualified foreign institutional investors"**. The new regulations took effective in 2003 to allow selected and approved foreign investors to hold A shares in China's stock markets.

The whole idea is that foreign institutional investors, such as funds and investment banks, can buy shares of mainland listed companies on the two A share markets. They can also buy into Chinese funds and participate in IPOs of Chinese companies. Deals and transactions are done through these approved QFII agencies, and individual small investors are not able to buy A shares by themselves. This is thus an indirect approach to conduct foreign portfolio investment in China and provide a slightly open window to overseas investors.

Foreign financial institutions need to make applications to the **State Foreign Exchanges Administration** to be qualified; on the other hand, the government selects the QFII agencies they prefer. European, American and Japanese financial institutions are, of course, the major contenders.

The first group of QFII agencies approved by the Administration include UBS (Swiss), Citibank, Morgan Stanley, and Namura Securities of Japan.

At this early stage of trial opening, the government grants QFII agencies certain **quotas** for their investment total in A share markets. The quotas are determined and announced by the Administration. If investment opportunities arise and QFII agencies reapply for quota increases, the authority in charge will raise their quotas. In general, foreign QFII agencies tend to ask for more quotas once their existing funds have been spent on the A stocks. For example, the UBS exhausted its initial quotas in three months, after spending on nine Chinese A share companies across sectors such as energy, ports, finance and telecommunications. The bank then seeks a further quota of US$500 million. On the other hand, rules demand these QFII agencies to transfer funds in full to the designated accounts; otherwise their quotas will be reduced. The Dutch bank listed below had its quota cut in half for this very reason.

Under the QFII regime, foreign institutional investors have a limit on their total spending on China's stock markets, but they are now facing a new market with over 1,200 listed companies to choose from in their investment strategies. Many of these companies and many

Quotas Given to QFII Agencies (2004)

UBS: 600 million USD

Namura Securities: 50 million

Morgan Stanley: 300 million

Citibank: 200 million

Goldman Sachs: 50 million

HSBC: 100 million

Deutsche Bank: 200 million

Dutch Commercial Bank: 100 million

Morgan Chase Bank: 50 million

Swiss Credit First Boston: 50 million

industrial sectors cannot be found on B or H share markets, or markets anywhere else. The QFII regime increases investors' choices and makes it easier for them to adjust investment directions to follow the growth in companies, industries and in China's economy as a whole. As RMB is currently inconvertible, this regime offers a way to bypass the currency issue and make it possible to invest with foreign currencies. It also increases the total foreign-owned assets in China. In a following chapter, we can see that foreign investors have opportunities to use QFII mechanisms to pour US dollar investment in the Chinese economy, in anticipation of a RMB appreciation.

The number of QFII agencies so far (as of October 2004) has reached 25 and their total approved investment quotas reached nearly US$3 billion. Comparing with the size of Chinese stock markets (25 billion yuan approximately against total market capitalisation of 4.2 trillion yuan), this foreign capital injection has not caused extensive shocks or enabled foreign players to manipulate the market. The likelihood of financial instability and risks from this external source is quite low. This is the reason the government devised and implemented the QFII regime, making a controlled opening while not causing significant changes to the current A and B share markets. It is expected that at a later stage, the implementations of QFII will eventually change B share markets, leading to standard portfolio investments into A share markets and to the mergers and reorganisation of China's stock markets.

Summary

Stock markets in China have been through certain turbulent phases. These markets are under the influence of government policies and sometimes directions. Whether it is a bull or bear market depends to a large extent on how the government views the situation and intervenes. This is because the state controls a huge chunk of company shares which are not in circulation, and the sentiments of investors are in response to prospects of economic growth and monetary policy. In stock market circles, it is often referred to as a "policy market". This has left a great deal to be desired for smoother operations in future.

Unlike stock markets in other Asian economies, China's stock markets are closed, therefore there has been no chance for foreign speculators to use them and derivatives trading to manipulate markets and suck funds away, as they did during the 1997 financial crisis. On the other hand, foreign investors and funds have no access to Chinese companies and their equities, and domestic companies are short of one important channel of financing. This tricky situation is partly improved by the QFII regime, which allows limited and controlled volumes of overseas funds to flow into the stock markets. Since the WTO agreements have little to do with securities and company shares, an open, well-managed and smooth-running stock market is to be in shape well after other financial reforms, including banking, monetary and foreign exchanges, are sufficiently implemented.

Key Concepts

The People's Bank of China
State commercial banks
State assets management companies and debt equity swaps
Opening under WTO rules
State, legal person and public shares
A, B, H and red chips shares
QFII

Discussion Questions

1. How do you see the roles played by the People's Bank of China in the economy, and particularly in monetary management? Find examples of actions taken by the People's Bank to fulfil its roles, in interest rate, money supply controls and other areas. Search for related news reports or analyses.
2. What are the future prospects for foreign banks competing in the China market after the banking sector is fully opened in 2006? How will the balance in banking sector be changed?
3. What effects would you expect the QFII regime to have on China's financial markets? How would foreign investors take part in new opportunities and caution themselves?
4. Make a brief assessment on the state of the banking industry and, based on that, evaluate the views of the industry's coming collapse or moving out of crisis? Assess whether the debt situation can be improved and suggest remedial measures.

Related Reading

Lardy, N. R., *China's Unfinished Economic Revolution*, Washington, D.C., Brookings Institution Press, 1998.

8

Regional Development and Disparity

*T*his chapter covers the two major issues of regional diversity and wealth, each with numerous implications. Problems caused in relation to these two issues would affect the long-term prospects of economic development and subsequently impact on major investments of foreign companies.

Introduction

National or Regional Markets?

In general, China is seen by many as a huge market for business. Looking closer, there is a distinction between a national market and numerous regional or local markets of China. For foreign businesspeople, the perception of a national market is based predominantly on policies of and formal agreements with the central government of China. It is essential that accepted rules be established for normal business activity to start rolling. This is why foreign governments have actively pursued World Trade Organisation (WTO) agreements and other bilateral treaties with the Chinese government. With such treaties and agreements signed, the central government bears the ultimate obligation of universal implementation and enforcement within the country.

China is indeed a vast country, approximately the size of Europe, with regions and provinces as large and populous as major European countries. The effectiveness of administration by central authorities has been a lasting and chronic issue in history and is particularly acute since China's reforms began with a trend of decentralisation, as described in previous texts. While a great number of national policies and laws come out from the central government in Beijing, there are even more regulations and by-laws from local governments and authorities. The central government promulgates official national policies and issues guarantees to foreign governments and corporations, while local governments add more to the range concerning their own development plans.

From foreign investors' point of view, this lack of an effective national standard and market may not necessarily be a bad thing, since most regional and local governments are eager to attract foreign direct investment to territories under their charge and will push very hard for more projects by offering enticing terms. In many cases, generous offers and waivers from local governments are tailor-made for giant foreign multinationals to move in and set up their business. The grey areas in policies give certain local authorities considerable leverage in granting their own permits and approvals. This point can be illustrated by the well-known examples of explosive expansion of foreign soft-drink brands and food chains in China.

In addition, with the huge size of China, many foreign companies are only able to enter selected regional markets at certain stages and could plan further expansion to more regions when their supply and distribution capacities permit. Regions and macroregions of China have sufficient numbers of consumers and purchasing power to meet multinationals' sales targets. These multinationals therefore appear content with running existing core businesses in a number of regional markets and do not often wage an all-out offensive aiming at the national market at once. Wal-Mart's cautious expansion and steady growth in China best illustrate this strategy.

On the other hand, the failure of universal implementation of policies and rules gives overseas investors headaches, since their projects may face local barriers, and strong protectionism makes their products fall well short of penetrating local markets. Such protectionism derives from desires to maintain local revenues and employment, and its unilateral nature contravenes the central government's policies for a free flow national market. Officially, practices of preventing the entry of products from other regions are illegal and should be minimised, but in the foreseeable future, trade barriers will continue to cause great harm to domestic and foreign companies doing business. Western scholars have examined this particular aspect of market conditions in China and raised doubts on an effectual national market and the high costs of inter-regional trade. This issue is a crucial one in considerations of entry strategy and market positioning in China.

Go West or Stay in the East?

Multinationals and small foreign investors alike would take footholds and establish selected subsidiaries at an early stage, and then fan out to wider markets with sufficient support. Considering the geographical features of China, it is a common practice for foreign investors to step in initially on coastal territories. This, combined with China's official policy of opening to the outside world, has created a much more prosperous eastern region after two decades. The next step of expansion could be towards interior territories, but due to vastly different conditions there, foreign investors would weigh the choices of moving further inland or staying in the localities they have established business. To many, the coastal belt, from Dalian in the north down to Shanghai

Local Protectionism in Action

In July 2001, the local government of Wuxue, in Hubei province, issued a directive to call on all residents in the region to support their own beer brands and producers. They forced each and every government employee to buy at least six cases of local beers each year. In the meantime, distributors of other beer brands were summoned and penalised by various bureaux of the local government in the forms of fines and extra taxes. This kind of action is similar to the "buy local" campaigns in many countries yet different in its nature, since initiatives and actions were taken by governments rather than by a popular civil movement.

A well-known battle was fought between Hubei provincial government and Shanghai municipal government over market access for cars. Both regions have carmakers: Hubei has a joint venture with Citron; and Shanghai a joint venture with VW. The Shanghai government imposed an 80,000 yuan surcharge on buyers of Hubei-made cars. In retaliation, the Hubei government invented a 70,000 yuan fee payable when buying Shanghai-made Santanas. Cars made in these two regions failed to enter the other's market.

in the middle and to Guangdong province in the south, represents the real Chinese economy after reform and provides a mature market and sophisticated production base for their needs. This costal belt is still vibrant and growing, being the favourite site for foreign direct investment and the foundation for the grand economic plans of the central government.

Beyond this promising land lie the inland provinces that present a different picture. Here, regional diversity shows its full width. Policies and regulations adopted by regional governments are varied and complicated. Contrasts in development strategies and levels are extraordinary. The western regions are both rural and heavily industrial, producing a smaller percentage of the total GDP and receiving a tiny share of the nation's foreign direct investment. Indicators of production, consumption, trade, and export are lower than along the eastern coastal belt. Even basic transport lines and communication facilities are problems for normal business activities in some western regions. To realign this huge economic imbalance, the central government initiated the "Developing the West" (or "Go West") campaign in recent years and has poured in huge state funding to improve infrastructure and the business environment there. Things will change after some years, and there are both opportunities and risks arising from this campaign and its aftermath. The question to foreign investors is how to assess the benefits and costs in business operations in the east and the west of China. Or, if business in the east is well established, whether there is a plan to expand and move to the west?

The Pearl River Delta (PRD) or the Yangtze River Delta (YRD)

Foreign investors may quite likely need to make a decision on picking one of these two key macroregions of the nation for their main bases. The PRD and YRD have their own merits and drawbacks. The former has the enviable blessing of the central government for early trials of reform measures and has been a major operating base for many foreign companies. Its proven experience and highly commercialised environment are well suited to foreign business operations. To date, the PRD leads in export and consumption, and in several other areas of economic activity. Most importantly, the regional and local governments there are more familiar with international business practices, under the enormous influence of the nearby Hong Kong economy.

The YRD has long been the commercial and industrial centre of China, with a complete set of manufacturing bases and a skilled workforce, and its attractiveness to foreign investment increased significantly with the grand plans to revive this macroregion. Combined with the belated blessing from the central government, the YRD, in particular Shanghai, has made an effort to catch up and open up. Its rise in the 1990s was stunning to many—transforming a heartland of the planned economy to a vibrant and competitive market economy in a decade. Indicators of economic activity give this macroregion more clout in the national economy, especially in consumption, export, finance, foreign investment and technology transfer. This has allured many Hong Kong and Taiwan investors to move north in recent years and caused a great stir to the PRD that had dominated the economic scene in the 1980s and early 1990s.

The pace of development between the two macroregions is not a great divide, since both have displayed potential business opportunities and future prospects. The rivalry, however, exists and poses a serious question to foreign investors in terms of choice. Gigantic foreign multinationals are of course capable of taking on projects in both macroregions, but investors in general need to make astute assessments and decide on their preference.

The Rich or the Poor?

Forbes magazine began to publish a list of China's richest people in 1999, under the shrewd management of a Putonghua-speaking British pollster Mr. Rupert Hoogewerf. Such media hype aside, the general impression is that Chinese citizens are getting higher incomes on average, and their purchasing power has increased dramatically. The rise of a middle class has been anticipated since the beginning of the reforms, and now there are strong signs of this phenomenon. Such changes and information form the basis for marketing campaigns of multinationals in China, targeting those who can now afford foreign products, brands and luxury.

On the other hand, income gaps are getting wider in China. With the elimination of price controls and guaranteed jobs, income levels are generally raised, but more people fall into the social groups whose earnings cannot adequately cover their spending on necessities. These groups include the newly redundant state enterprise workers and the large number of migrant workers from rural areas. One urgent task for the government is to establish a viable social security system to handle increasing demands from the poor and needy. A great social divide is in the making and may cause serious consequences to future economic prosperity. This is, of course, a thorny issue mainly to the central government, but in the meantime, an urban centre with large groups of the poor would be unable to generate much purchasing power and desire to spend, so the sales targets of multinationals may be affected adversely. It is a crucial task to estimate the income levels and consumer behaviour of a particular region for the business to operate and stay in good shape.

The above issues will be discussed in detail in the following prargraphs, and they are the main themes for an understanding of regional diversity and markets in general.

Regional Environment: Economic Development in the Western Regions

In consideration of China's geographical features, the national territory is officially divided into three groups: the eastern, central and western regions. This division was initiated in the 1960s and further detailed in the 1980s when regional diversity was formally recognised.

❏ **Eastern:** Beijing, Tianjin, Shanghai, Liaoning, Hebei, Shandong, Jiangsu, Zhejiang, Fujian, Guangdong, Hainan;

❏ **Central:** Heilongjiang, Jilin, Shanxi, Anhui, Jiangxi, Hunan, Hubei, Henan;

❏ **Western:** Inner Mongolia, Sichuan, Shaanxi, Gansu, Guangxi, Ningxia, Qinghai, Xinjiang, Xizang (Tibet), Guizhou, Yunan, and Chongqing (after its separation from Sichuan province in the late 1990s).

Such classifications are also based on past bureaucratic customs, economic development and living standards. "Western" is synonymous with remoteness, a lower GDP output and higher level of poverty. Thus, there is apparently room for negotiations to have a region's status changed. For example, Guangxi province in the south is not a closed inland province, with its own coastal lines and proximity to the prosperous Guangdong province. Since the province is not a well-developed economy and suffers from poverty in numerous counties, and also because being in the category of western regions means certain financial benefits under the new policy, the province appealed to the central government and had its status changed to a western province.

Causes to Gaps Between the East and the West

Historic and Geographic Factors

1. Economic centres and modern industries in the south and the east:

   The modern history of China is marked by foreign influence on the costal belt, with the first and second waves of foreign concessions and open cities situated mostly along the coast, and early commercial and industrial centres fanned out to some inland regions gradually. Major cities are nicely located at these places, and business and production bases were set up by central authorities to take advantage of convenient import and export facilities. Even under the planned economy, which relied on domestic markets, there were huge investments in coastal urban centres, and industries in Shanghai produced the bulk of the nation's manufactured goods.

2. Natural and transport conditions:

   Eastern and coastal regions enjoy a high population density and a bigger urban sector, thus even rural areas there are close to large urban centres. The urban and rural residents in these regions have easier excess to commercial markets nearby and those at higher (provincial and national) levels. The consumer market is thus large and extensive, and this in turn encourages more production and sales in eastern regions. There are also widespread and interconnected major water and land freight lines for easy transport of goods and people, such as the Yangtze River, the Beijing-Guangzhou and Beijing-Shanghai railway lines. The only relatively isolated region is Fujian province, which is blocked by land barriers from Zhejiang province at the north and Guangdong province at the south. It, however, has a full length of coastal line for importing and exporting, and receives large amounts of investment from

Taiwan across the Taiwan Strait. Western regions, in general, lack easy transport to major domestic and foreign markets, except some cities along the main east-west railway lines and the Yangtze River.

Other Factors

The gap between eastern and western regions has been further widened in the 1990s due mainly to the following two factors:

1. Foreign investment and capital injection

   These include government, private and foreign funding, as well as investments from overseas Chinese. Eastern regions have more access to these types of investment, especially for those open economic zones, which are the first to benefit from reforms and foreign trade. Government funding helped build infrastructure in open zones and other facilities for modern-day business. The southern part of the coastal belt, in particular, draws enormous amounts of hard currency and investments from overseas Chinese who prefer to invest in their home village or county of their ancestors and relatives. Western regions lag behind chiefly due to early neglect in reforms and lack of personal networks of overseas Chinese. When early opening and production improved the overall environment in eastern regions, the tendency to invest there, rather than to enter new territories, was reinforced. Even government funding flowed in that direction. State funding and capital often seek better projects and higher returns, so the central and provincial governments are more likely to approve projects in the east and invest their funds there, despite the guidelines for more balanced investment strategies. Surplus and unused funds in inland provinces have since been used to inject capital into eastern regions. The more the economy booms in the east, the more business opportunities and choices emerge there, and the more funds the east draws from the rest of the country.

2. More flexible policies

   Coastal regions enjoyed earlier preferential treatments in reform and were allowed to experiment with new measures in the national economy. These include taxation, tariffs, approval of joint ventures with overseas companies, flexible land use, etc. Governments and businesses of eastern regions benefited greatly from such freedom and advantages, and the average living standards were improved in a short period of time. Such generous offers offended many inland governments and businesses. They demanded to have the right to enjoy similar treatments, and claimed repeatedly that if they received the same offers, the regions under their jurisdiction would have achieved the same goal. A sharp debate erupted in the late 1990s on how long Shenzhen, as a special economic zone, should enjoy the benefits it had had for about two decades. Although the Shenzhen authorities defended their position fervently, the general impression around the country was that something must be done to minimise discrimination and restore the balance. This led to a policy change in 1998 to address the issue of regional disparity that had become quite serious and profound after years of "tilted" reforms.

A comparison of preferential treatments in zones:

- Special economic zones: 15% tax rate, lower tariffs
- Coastal open cities: 24%
- Open cities along major rivers: 24%
- Coastal economic development zones: 24%
- Economic and technology development zones: 10-15%, right to pass local laws to suit their needs
- National border open cities: 24%
- Hi-tech industrial development zones: 15%, concession in land acquisitions
- Others: 55% till 1993, 33% thereafter

Government Investment Strategies

In the 50 or so years of rule by the communist central government, the investment strategies have changed a few times. The latest strategic plans are a collective response to the situation in the late 1990s and also the growth prospects of the 21st century.

Early Industrialisation

There were early twists and turns in government strategies. Aids from the Soviet Union in the 1950s guided the central government, and industrial bases were set up in the northeast and the east. Progress was clearly shown by steady growth in industrial production. Due to the worsening relationship with the Soviet Union, the central government initiated the strategy of "the third frontier". This strategy had its historical urgency and was aimed at reducing the impact of military threats (such as surgical strikes) from the Soviets. According to the plans, major industrial and military complexes were to be rebuilt in remote, almost inaccessible inland provinces to protect them. State investments in western regions of China flowed in from the Treasury continuously, and huge projects were built at sites away from major road systems and large urban centres. These projects were mainly heavy industries and the defence industry, drawing large numbers of employees to remote western regions. Even during the turbulent Cultural Revolution, building of the third frontier projects did not stop. In retrospect, many observers today view this strategy as one of the forces that dragged China's economy down. This was one time the central government had put great emphasis on western regions and provided real funding to support industries there. The priority was mostly military in nature, and that this strategy could be carried out for years was only possible under a planned economy and effective central administration.

The Reform Era

Since reforms began in the early 1980s, the central government publicly reversed many previous policies, including the priority of state investment. The initial plans were to have trials in places more likely to have contact with the outside world. The obvious choice was to select coastal regions for experiment. This led to a resetting of places for capital injection and a flow of the lion's share of investment into eastern regions—a major shift in policy priority. Another consideration was to depart from state-run businesses typified by huge projects in the northeast and the west and to encourage other types of businesses in the commercially active eastern regions. In 1998, state investment in western regions reached the highest percentage of 14.5%, at 1/4 of eastern and 1/3 of central regions, indicating that the average ratio of state investment in the west had been quite low. As a result, western regions are short of state funding and have fallen back in pace of development.

General Conditions in Western Regions

Structure of Industries

Western regions rely mostly on agriculture and manufacturing industries, and depend heavily on state enterprises (65-85%) in comparison with eastern regions (30-60%). A large part of these enterprises are in the defence industry, a legacy of the previous strategy of "the third frontier". Although some defence manufacturers made a successful transformation to civil-use production—an outstanding example being Changhong group in Sichuan province, the No. 1 television set producer in the country—many suffer problems and cannot sufficiently support their employees. In 1998, the level of industrialisation in western regions was at 30.3%, 43.9% in eastern regions and 42.1% the national average. Non-state sectors (collective and private) gained much higher shares in regional economies of the east.

Lower Levels of Urbanisation and Education

The number of large cities with key commercial centres is small, with only a few provincial capitals qualified to be regional centres and transport hubs. These large cities are so few that they are buried in the vast land of the west. Subsequently, the number of tertiary education institutions is also small, admitting fewer students and supplying fewer graduates to the market. In 1998, the number of tertiary institutions, high schools, and teachers in the west was around 20% of national totals. The central government has continued to try to raise the level of education in the west, enticing and even forcing many teachers to relocate to western universities to teach and work, but flow of education staff in the opposite direction also happens. Some key universities there receive adequate funding and attention from the central government and are ranked as the country's top universities, but many others are in a poor state.

In 1998, urban population in western regions was 17.9% of the national total, while in eastern regions the percentage was 28%. While a few big urban centres hold millions of residents, large numbers of towns there have small populations on average. This lowers the proportion of urban residents in the total.

(The figures for 1998 are presented here for the reason that this was the situation before the new policy of the central government had been initiated, and these are the very figures that led to the change and shift in policy and strategy. Figures after 1998 require a further study.) (see Figures 8.1, 8.2, 8.3, 8.4).

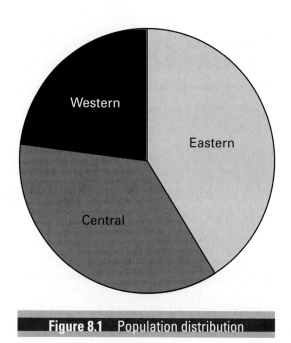

Figure 8.1 Population distribution

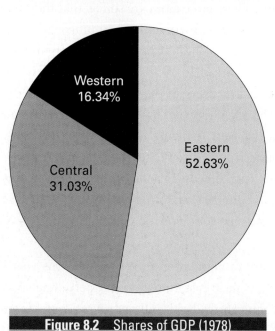

Figure 8.2 Shares of GDP (1978)

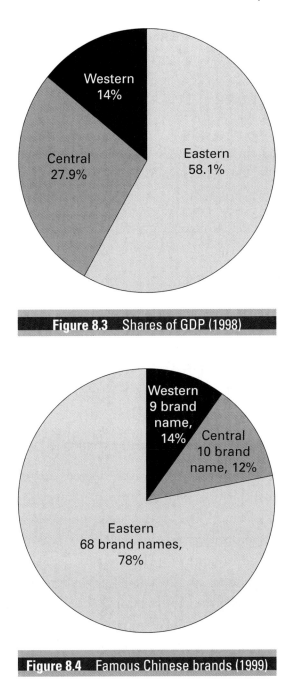

Figure 8.3   Shares of GDP (1998)

Figure 8.4   Famous Chinese brands (1999)

Government Responses

The response by the central government has been twofold. One response was the traditional intervention in structure, finance and personnel. The other was letting the invisible hand make the market work and improve the business environment. With the demand from western regions for more equitable treatment, the policies finally adopted by the central government appear more in line with the current market forces.

Routine Assistance

This is a tested way of assistance. From 1997, developed eastern regions were instructed to form regular one-on-one cooperative links with western regions. The relationship implies partnership or sisterhood. The pairings are as follows:

- ❑ Beijing——Inner Mongolia;
- ❑ Tianjin——Gansu;
- ❑ Shanghai——Yunnan;
- ❑ Jiangsu——Shaanxi;
- ❑ Zhejiang——Sichuan;
- ❑ Shandong——Xinjiang;
- ❑ Liaoning——Qinghai;
- ❑ Fujian——Ningxia;
- ❑ Dalian, Qingdao, Ningbo——Guizhou;
- ❑ Xizang (Tibet)——from all over the country.

In their set relationships, the "Giver" regions are to offer concrete support to beneficiary regions, in terms of financial, personnel and technological assistance. They are, in return, able to explore certain business opportunities that exist in their sister regions, such as rich natural resources. Examples of such assistance are Shanghai's projects of water supply systems and hospitals in Yunnan and Xizang. This move is not different from the traditional state assistance in the past and contains a little more of local initiatives.

Policy Shift

When the imbalance became serious enough for everyone to see and with the concern of the concentration of industrial bases along the coast, which would prove vulnerable in a major conflict with foreign powers, the central government began to implement a wholesale campaign aimed at this great divide. This led to the inception of the **"Developing the West"** strategies from 1998. The package included the following:

1. Adjustments in investment focus

    State funding for western regions was increased by a big margin, and key investment projects were to be opened in the west. Transport, power, natural gas, and tourism became the industries of priority. These key projects and more generous funding form the core of the "Developing the West" campaign and received speedy approvals as a late compensation for past neglect.

    These include the following:

    -   10 key projects began in 2000, an investment of over 100 billion yuan (US$12 billion approximately);

    -   Other key projects began in 2001, with total investment of over 300 billion yuan, and the government issued treasury bonds of 50 billion yuan to support part of these projects;

    -   In 2003, a further 130 billion yuan was poured into 14 key projects;

    -   By late 2003, a total funding of 700 billion yuan was allocated to the west.

    These huge projects will continue for up to 10 years and thus provide job opportunities for large numbers of workers in western regions. The contractors of these huge projects are large state enterprises, and they take the lion's share of the total investment. This is an opportunity for the central government to offer large state enterprises long term work and profits. The state projects would keep many state enterprises in good shape financially and escape the fate of bankruptcy awaiting many small state enterprises. The new strategies therefore serve two purposes: improving infrastructure in the west and feeding major state corporations. For example, PetroChina took over oil and gas pipelines running from central Asian countries and Russia to China's coastal regions and is in a favourable position to offer partnerships to foreign petroleum giants such as Shell and BP. Subsequently, other foreign companies find it difficult to participate in these major projects, a possible alternative being acting as partners or sub-contractors of large state enterprises who hold contracts.

    -   Other types of special government bonds were issued for the sole purpose of developing western regions.

    -   60% of international funds and low-interest foreign government loans were allocated to the west.

2. Improve investment environment and offer preferential treatments

    The above measures followed past experience of assistance and aimed at solid targets such as infrastructure. The other line of assistance runs along improving business environments, considered as soft targets. In many cases, this is in response to calls from the west to get similar treatments granted much earlier to eastern regions. The rationale of adjusting regional balances allows the tested models and practices to be transplanted to the west, in the hope of introducing market systems, generating more output and increasing efficiency. The central government is now more confident to grant more authority and leeway to local governments, since the same experiment in the east had been deemed successful.

    Under this guideline, new offers from the central government to western regions include the following:

    *   Preferential company income tax rate of 15% was granted for 10 years (to 2010), which would allow enterprises in the west to enjoy the same favourable rate as those in the east;

    *   Relevant authorities in western regions have the power to approve foreign investment projects in service industries;

    *   On-the-spot visas are now issued to foreign tourists and these tourists, in organised groups or individually, do not need to apply for visas before their flights in. This change greatly benefits tourism in western regions, since there are numerous world famous tourist sites, and foreign tourists and agencies are less likely to be deterred from visiting by 'red tape' and complicated application procedures.

    *   Adjust prices of minerals and railway transport

        A central rationale for developing the west is to be able to utilise its rich natural resources. Therefore, development strategies may not be exactly the same as in the east, and emphasis is placed on those areas with certain advantages. Western regions produce huge quantity of minerals to feed industries in other parts of the country, and prices were previously set low by the central government to supply cheap resources for industrial development. Benefits from selling these minerals proved inadequate to support local economies. On the other hand, charges on transportation were set relatively high, adding more costs to enterprises in the west. In the long run, such practices will lower the efficiency and exhaust the enterprises in such businesses. New government guidelines have made necessary adjustments to these prices and charges, as a late move to compensate enterprises there and increase their profit margins.

- Improve education and technology research

  These include setting up hardship allowances for talents in demand, support from central government funding, relaxing *hukou* (residential registration) regulations and allowing experts with job offers to move in or out of western regions. The central government also increased quotas for admissions to tertiary institutions in the west.

Potential and Opportunities

The "Developing the West" campaign attempted to realign regional balances in the national economy. Along with government initiatives and investments, market conditions are in a constant process of change, and there are new potential and opportunities emerging in the west.

1. Natural resources and energy industries will gain:

   These western regions contain 40% of national mineral reserves, 86% of natural gas reserves, 64% of coal reserves, and 73% of the national total of hydro power.

   For example, the project of building a 4200-kilometre natural gas pipeline from Xinjiang to Shanghai was to be shared by PetroChina, BP and Shell. In the end, PetroChina completed the project by itself and began to supply gas to coastal regions, including Shanghai, in 2004.

2. In the developed coastal regions, there are problems of oversupply of goods, shortage of natural resources, insufficient power supply, market saturation and fierce competition. Coastal regions need

The Asia-Europe Land Rail Links

From Lianyun port in Jiangsu province to Rotterdam, Holland; passing major cities of Xian, Lanzhou, Urumqi, Moscow, Minsk, and Berlin.

The rail links running in China's territories cover 4131 kilometres, 40% of the total length.

room to expand and require new market for sustainable development. Western regions with abundant natural resources and unexplored markets would be suitable in this regard, and transfer of production capacity would benefit both parties.

3. Extremely low labour costs:

    Low labour costs have been a key consideration of investment planning, and the wage levels in western regions appear affordable to both foreign and domestic companies in eastern regions. For example, the top television set producer, Changhong in Sichuan, pays assembly workers several hundred yuan per month, while TCL in Guangdong is paying more than double this wage because of the generally higher living standards there. Since the production lines in both places are imported and similar, Changhong has a definite advantage in production and is maintaining its leading position in the industry amid fierce competition.

    To minimise the effect of this wage differential, some manufacturers in coastal regions have begun to cooperate with inland companies, in the form of assembling products in western production sites and putting on their own labels for sale in the market. This will reduce the costs spent on labour and gain certain advantages ahead of competitors. Another major TV set producer, Konka, has its headquarters and part of its production facilities in Shenzhen while using a factory in Xian to make TV sets. The subsidiary employs local workers, and the products are sold under the Konka label.

4. Certain large urban centres in the west have huge consumer markets and strong purchasing power, and, with numerous tertiary institutions, these centres have high quality employees and engineers, from whom a middle class is emerging even in the west. Urban centres in this category are Xian (population 7.4 million), Chengdu (12 million), Chongqing (31 million), Lanzhou (3.14 million), and Kunming (5.78 million). Retail sales in these cities are on the rise, and foreign and domestic brands have already gained wide acceptance. Major foreign multinationals are not going to ignore these cities in their marketing and sales campaigns in China. In addition, numerous higher education institutions in western regions are nationally renowned for technological research and tertiary education.

Case 1

A Hong Kong company owned by Mr. Wong Min-gang has invested mostly in tourism in the west. These include hotels and travel services near Dunhuang caves in Gansu, and in Qinghai and Xinjiang along the ancient Silk Road sites. The total investment to date is over one billion yuan. Mr. Wong personally directed investment projects in the west for over ten years. The company is now firmly established in the west, with steady revenues, good business reputation and wide connections. (A major Hong Kong TV network, Pearl, featured him and his company in several documentaries.)

Case 2

The Chung Kong Group is a giant conglomerate in a variety of businesses. The group has its major stake in Hong Kong, while eyeing possible investments in the mainland. It now has three billion yuan of investment in western regions, approximately 5% of the total investment in China. This is practically a fixed percentage of total investment, showing the group's intention to participate. Although the company's chairman, Mr. Li Kai-sing, is regarded as supporting the central government's new policy by investing in the west, the projects selected primarily reflect his business sense.

Case 3

The Shui On Group is a construction company with many mainland undertakings. With sprawling and successful real estate projects in Shanghai and Beijing, the company boss, Mr. Lo, directed investment in Chongqing in a number of cement plants. His prediction is that there will be housing booms in the following years, and people with average income will be able to get reasonable accommodation, so the demand for cement will increase steadily. Producers of cement have enjoyed booming business in recent years, and this Hong Kong company is going to produce high grade and high quality cement to meet the increasing and specific market demands.

Hong Kong Investment Experience

Hong Kong is a major source of overseas investment in mainland China, and Hong Kong businesspeople have established production and marketing networks across the entire country. With a common cultural background, language advantage and particular skills in adapting to national conditions, Hong Kong companies present a good example of how to do business in China. While their business activities are concentrated along the coastal belt, many Hong Kong companies have managed to set up production and sales branches in the west. Their experience can be shared with foreign investors in general to examine precedents and a working process.

Points for Caution Regarding Investment in Western Regions

The issue of a great divide between the east and the west of China has caused serious concern to those who gauge macro-trends of economic development. The newly implemented "Developing the West" strategies commencing from 1998 will change many aspects of the economy in coming decades. For prospective investors, an improvement in market conditions and better infrastructure in the west will be realised at a later time, and their planned investment or expansion of business there may make sense. As with any investment in China, a caution is warranted. There are particular aspects to heed in any consideration of investment in the west.

Government Actions Influence Enterprises

This implies that regional and local governments in the west have more power of persuasion on local businesses and enterprises. This is in contrast to the commercialised and flexible environment along the coastal belt, especially that of the freewheeling Guangdong province. The relationship between the government and enterprises are intertwined, with enterprises relying on government permission and promotion, and with the government at times enforcing its own will on enterprises. The separation of government action and business activity is minimal, and business decisions are often made under the direction and duress of government bureaucrats. This is mainly due to the fact that so many state enterprises are operating there, and the private sector has yet to gain prominence in local economies. A related question is how open is the market and how effectively the government enforces those rules benefiting business.

Credibility Problem and Heavy Reliance on Guanxi

With lasting cultural customs and less intrusion of outside influences, local networks are alive and strong, and supplement incomplete and insufficient government regulations. Business is often done through *guanxi* network, and informal deals take precedence over formal contracts. Credibility in business runs in a circle: people do business on the basis of trust, but they cannot trust anyone unless they know someone. A handicap for outside investors is the lack of adherence to legal contracts and the belief that *guanxi* and informal means can fix things if needed. Investors thus have less protection for themselves and little confidence in dealers and partners whose credibility is on shaky ground. In comparison with more sophisticated market mechanisms in eastern regions, the west suffers from this shortcoming, and the appeal to outside investors in general tends to be weak. From past records and anecdotal experience, it is evident that even domestic investors often feel confused and frustrated when doing business in western regions, let alone foreign investors.

Local Protectionism and Levies

To enter a local market with established brands and new products is still an option full of uncertainty, since local authorities will attempt to block your entry one way or another. This is not a matter of personal dislike, but mostly out of a concern over how to keep local enterprises and employees happy. Local firms may have to be closed down because of strong competition from other regions, and local workers may become redundant due to less sales and profits. On top of this situation, local governments are getting less revenue from the enterprises under their control. A common response is to block entry, with regulations and standards specifically targeting outsiders. These include technical standards, environmental standards, customer complaints, etc. A loud call of "**buy local**" can also raise people's awareness and arouse public anger against products from other regions. Similarly, laying more charges on outsiders will increase the latters' costs and reduce the impact of competition. This last option is also frequently taken by local governments for the purpose of filling local coffers.

Shortage of Qualified Professionals

As a matter of fact, western regions lose their talents and experts due to higher wages and better career prospects in coastal regions. University graduates tend to find opportunities somewhere else. Similarly, few talents and experts move in from other parts of the country to live and work in western regions. As this imbalance continues, western regions face the danger of brain drain as a long-term problem. Subsequently, it becomes harder for investing companies to find suitably qualified personnel in the local labour market; and for new and specific business areas, specialists must be brought in from coastal regions, Hong Kong or the home countries of multinationals. For a certain position, human resource managers face fewer choices in their selection, due to the smaller pool of qualified professionals and even fewer applicants.

Limited Purchasing Power in Many Regions

Although a number of urban centres in the west are quite large and relatively commercialised, purchasing power on average is weak. This makes it harder to sell manufactured goods and keep profit margins at reasonable levels. When multinationals did enter western regions, they tended to concentrate on major cities, such as provincial capitals, and seldom ventured into second-tier cities, namely regional and county centres. The revenues coming from areas outside major cities often fail to offset the costs of setting up business operations there.

There are other concerns which investors may have over the business environment as a whole and in particular cases. After the "Go West" campaign started in 1998, early optimism has not led to expected booms and a flood of investment from outside. Both the government and investors in general realised that the process of improving market conditions in the west had to be a long and arduous one, while business opportunities over there could be seized only after patient search and careful planning.

In a nutshell, the first line in the new policies on western regions— direct state investment on key projects—would lead to marked upgrading of the infrastructure, an essential part of overall business environment, and is less likely to provide many concrete opportunities for foreign investors. The second line—improving market conditions— may create more business opportunities and attract foreign investment, if obstacles there are handled skilfully.

The Pearl River Delta and the Yangtze River Delta

William Skinner's Macroregions Model

Professor William Skinner applies a macroregion model to treat regional issues in Chinese studies. The major regions of economic activity are divided into eight macroregions, which are formed around core centres of intensified economic activities, with high population density and convenient transport networks, and are surrounded by peripheral areas.

These eight macroregions fit well with the administrative divisions of China during the Qing dynasty (1644-1911). One macroregion covers roughly the same amount of territory under the jurisdiction of a governor-general (or viceroy), from one to three provinces. In fact, the model focuses on commercial and market networks; on economic forces rather than political divisions and movements. Attention is paid to business activities, how close farmers are to a certain market, and how geographical features such as natural barriers, land and water affect trade and commerce. It is through merchants and commercial firms that farmers are connected to local, regional, macroregional, and finally, the national market. The particular conditions in a macroregion determine the way of doing business, and economic activities within the macroregion circle around the centre.

The model is followed by the majority of China scholars in the West and led to comprehensive studies of regional economies of China in recent decades. The two macroregions under discussion below (the PRD and the YRD) fit well with this model. The overall conditions in these macroregions have the following characteristics.

Reforms in China Evolved Around Zones

These zones were selected by the central leadership, zones such as the special economic zones in Guangdong and the New Pudong Zone in Shanghai. The central leadership gives the permission for certain zones to be set up and rejects proposals for other zones. The early focus was opening windows to foreign investment in the south, therefore most zones were set up in southern coastal regions. To balance the economy and promote development in other regions, Shanghai was later given permission to set up the New Pudong Zone, which enjoys some of the most favourable policies and treatments. These zones offer better conditions and facilities to foreign companies, and they project an image of an improved business environment in China. In a sense, these zones are insulated from the rest of the country and make it relatively easy for investment projects to operate. There have been frank comments and criticisms from returning Chinese students and investors that they could not do business smoothly outside their zones and have had to rely on zone officials to make arrangements on their behalf. Business environments in zones and in other places are perhaps different.

Reforms so far have led to decentralisation, regional competition, rivalry and protectionism. Regional interest, in many cases, has overwhelmed the will of the central government, and created its own momentum and tendencies. This demands greater attention to be paid to segmentation in marketing.

The Reshaping of Economic Gravity

Regions compete to gain advantages over others, and some traditional centres of economic and political activities have given way to new centres. A number of provincial capitals lost their charm and appeal, despite the full support of their provincial governments. Many local governments promoted local economies and improved the business environment there by their own initiatives. As a result, many new economic centres emerged to replace the old ones. Examples of areas of waning influence are Wuhan, Jinan, Nanjing, Tianjin; and those of growing clout are Shenzhen, Suzhou, Dalian, and Qingdao. The latter three—Dalian, Suzhou and Qingdao—are often mistaken as the *de facto* capitals of their respective provinces, due to their economic progress and prominence; while Shenyang, Nanjing and Jinan are, in fact, the real seats of government of the respective provinces.

The Redrawing of Mega Economic Circles

This is a new trend in the 21st century and goes beyond provincial or even macroregional boundaries. One circle combines a number of regions and represents close economic ties and integration among local economies. Common purpose and cooperation are needed to coordinate economic activities and reduce inefficiency within these circles. The first of the three circles is the Bohai Sea economic circle, which includes cities from Dalian, Tianjin, Beijing to Qingdao, covering three provinces.

The second is the Yangtze River Delta (YRD), which covers two provinces and one municipality. The third is the Pearl River Delta (PRD), which is basically Guangdong province, and it enjoys close ties with Hong Kong and Macau.

The PRD and the YRD are essentially macroregions on their own (see Table 8.1); and the Bohai Sea circle is a new cluster with looser connections among the participants.

Table 8.1 Comparisons between the PRD and the YRD		
	PRD	**YRD**
Cities	9	15
Land	42,000 km²	90,000 km²
Population	33 m	74 m
GDP (2002)	1 trillion yuan	1.9 trillion yuan

The Pearl River Delta (the PRD)

Hong Kong's Role in the PRD and in China

We will deal with the PRD first. This region is essentially Guangdong province; however, it is impossible not to draw Hong Kong into this equation. To a certain extent, economic development in the PRD has a great deal to do with Hong Kong's involvement, and Hong Kong's contributions to China's national economy are chiefly reflected in the phenomenal rise of Guangdong as a major powerhouse of the country in generating GDP and exports. The following data demonstrate the clout of Hong Kong in this macroregion and beyond.

❏ Hong Kong has made up nearly half of overseas investment (FDI) in mainland China;

❏ Hong Kong is one of the biggest trading partners of China;

❏ Hong Kong is in a dominant position in regional markets where Cantonese and other dialects are popular. This includes Guangdong and some areas in the Guangxi and Fujian provinces.

❏ Success of Hong Kong businesses has made Cantonese one of the three mainstream business languages in China (together with Putonghua and Shanghainese—the former being spoken nationwide, and the latter amongst Shanghai businesspeople).

❑   Hong Kong had early contact and trade with the mainland from 1979, being taken as the major transhipment port, with transactions reaching US$1.5 billion in 1987.

❑   Investment from Hong Kong has continued to flow to a number of coastal open zones. Due to the close proximity and early opening of such zones, many small- and medium-sized Hong Kong companies were able to invest in Guangdong and other parts of the mainland. As a result of certain restrictions, many Hong Kong businesspeople and companies also used others' names to invest, for example, mainland relatives' names or foreign companies' names respectively. Investment from Hong Kong has been extremely widespread and well exceeds the official figures.

Hong Kong and Guangdong

A close bond between Hong Kong and Guangdong has been forged, with the former as the shop front and the latter as the backyard factory. This form of cooperation involves companies in Hong Kong getting orders, manufacturing in Guangdong factories, and delivering goods through Hong Kong ports to overseas customers. Both sides have been accustomed to this type of operation, and numerous obstacles have been worked out and removed in the past two decades or more.

❑   Migration of Hong Kong manufacturing sectors to the mainland: While the "shop front/backyard factory" formula enhanced cooperation between Hong Kong and Guangdong, this made it unnecessary for Hong Kong to keep massive manufacturing bases there. Hong Kong turned to concentrate on paper work, finance and coordination; and the dramatically increased labour costs also forced the movement of most manufacturing facilities to Guangdong where low labour costs made possible by migrant workers could be fully utilised. Attractive terms offered by local governments are key factors to Hong Kong companies' northward relocation as well. Such terms include tax waivers, less restrictions on land use, and permitting larger operations (often many times above their original size in Hong Kong).

❑   Hong Kong companies have invested heavily in key infrastructure projects in Guangdong: highways, freeways, bridges, container ports, power plants, and even the Luohu border and customs complex. BOT (build-operate-transfer) projects were adopted widely. Hong Kong investments are concentrated in the business areas where they have good experience and certain advantages over local companies.

❑ Real estate, retail, and banking are business areas where Hong Kong companies have a strong presence in the mainland. The first two are traditionally the top choices for Hong Kong businesses, for example, the Orient Square built and managed by the Changjiang group in Beijing's central business district. The banking industry in Hong Kong has long been deregulated and is exceedingly competitive. Hong Kong banks are quick to enter the mainland market, to support Hong Kong businesses there and to reach for larger markets and more customers. For example, the Bank of East Asia has established extensive network and customer bases on the mainland and operates much like a local Chinese bank.

Contribution of the PRD to China's Economy

With the huge inputs from Hong Kong and overseas, coupled with internal reforms, the PRD in turn has earned itself a top ranking among all regions of China, in terms of economic might. The PRD has the following to offer:

❑ 11% of national GDP (2001)

❑ 35% of the national total of foreign trade (2002). It was only in early 2004 that the foreign trade volume of the YRD overtook the PRD on a quarterly basis.

❑ US$200 billion assets, in the form of factories and fixed investments

❑ 2.5 million technical professionals

❑ 2/3 of the total number of overseas Chinese living in China

❑ Three currencies in circulation and business transactions: RMB, US$, and HK$. These three currencies are openly accepted and traded, not only in business deals, but also in daily retail sales (HK$ trading perhaps being more conspicuous than US$ trading). This flexibility is convenient to many business operations in the region.

❑ The PRD is 80% dependent on foreign trade, and the region is most open to international markets. Their main targets are international buyers, and they receive orders from overseas customers and produce mostly for export, obviously with the assistance of Hong Kong middlemen.

❑ Large numbers of non-state enterprises (private, foreign, Hong Kong, and Taiwan).

❑ Well-established manufacturing and logistics bases:

Complete production and supply chains are set up, and there are close relations between manufacturers and suppliers, as well as between parts producers and end-users. The PRD has good transportation networks and logistics supply capabilities, and is able to provide any product to meet the orders from any buyer.

❑ Flexibility in policy and administration:

Open-minded authorities offer room for improvement and flexibility in business operations, and most are eager to meet special demands from business sectors. They tend to provide the most help possible under the current official policies, and in some cases work eagerly to protect FDI interests against central government directives. Since these local governments were the first in the country to be allowed to test new models of business and management, the central government tolerates certain pro-business actions in the PRD.

❑ Entrepreneurship, adventurism, and highly developed business culture:

The PRD is certainly the most commercialised region in the country, with mature business groups and a high level of entrepreneurship. People are willing to take risks in business, seek opportunities and seize them. They also honour contracts, while relying on trust to make deals.

❑ Training of modern enterprise managers and skilled employees for other regions:

The PRD is filled with migrant workers who moved there to seek employment. Enterprises hire large numbers of employees and train them into managers and skilled workers. These people become the core workforce after moving to other regions, so the PRD is a huge industrial and business training school and offers millions of people basic work experience in manufacturing and management.

Potential Risks and Issues

After 20 years of growth and pace setting for the whole country, certain weaknesses in development potential in the PRD were exposed. As other regions imitate and catch up, the existing problems in the PRD may become worrying and threaten its leading position in the future.

❑   Conflicts and non-coordination among city and local governments:

The PRD cannot decide whether Guangzhou or Shenzhen is the leading city, and many second-tier cities compete fiercely among themselves. Guangzhou keeps its status of provincial capital and holds enormous political capital. Shenzhen fuels hi-tech expectations and boasts direct links with Beijing, with many of the big companies there having ministerial support. These twin giants and other cities all desire expansion of their local economies, and they have minimal intention and drive to faithfully follow directives from the Guangdong provincial government. Coordination among them and in particular, persuading someone not to participate in certain projects, prove to be difficult.

❑   Unhealthy or even hostile competition in resources, projects and foreign investment:

Governments have the priority of obtaining the best opportunity for their own areas, disregarding others' interests, and rushing to grab foreign investment, even if it is to take these away from other cities or towns of the PRD. There is a serious lack of a cooperating spirit.

❑   Nearly identical products, overlapping in production, surplus capacity:

Enterprises in the PRD enjoy greater market freedom and are well exposed to competition. Therefore, they tend to catch market trends very quickly, copy the hot-selling and popular products, and others' technology and production process, and put their investment in the projects that bring quick returns. As a result, there are bountiful supplies of identical products and designs in the PRD; and an oversupply of similar goods on the market leads to price cuts to outsell others. In doing so, enterprises show disregard of profit margins and give priority to market share. This leads to over capacity and reduced sales for most producers, and they would then seek new products and markets, and repeat this cycle all over again.

❑ Barriers to economic expansion and influence radiation:

Traditionally, the PRD was a market for itself, blocked from other interior markets by natural barriers (mountain ranges and narrow passages) in the north and east of Guangdong. The PRD economy does not have great influence on the economy north of the border and can only have limited links with the two neighbouring Guangxi and Fujian provinces. Other neighbouring provinces such as Jiangxi and Hunan look eastward to the YRD and particularly Shanghai, essentially relying on cheap water transport along the Yangtze River for close links. In a more recent move, these provinces tied up with Guangdong and Hong Kong in the so-called "9+2 arrangement".

❑ Concerns over infrastructure:

The PRD boasts extensive and advanced means of transport, including land and air travel. Infrastructure works have been a priority in the government's development plans, chiefly for the purpose of meeting demands from Hong Kong and Taiwan investors. Completed highways, freeways and airports are numerous, and freight transportation and travel have become easy in comparison with many provinces. The problem, however, is the fragmented planning by different local authorities, and competition between them makes coordinated systems hard to achieve. There are numerous highways and freeway systems initiated and funded by local governments, three international airports in the PRD (Guangzhou, Shenzhen, Zhuhai—each city demanding to get their own), modern port facilities in many places (that compete by lowering unloading charges). The talks on a cross harbour bridge linking Hong Kong, Zhuhai and Macau have been delayed by regional and local rivalries, despite the consensus that this project will greatly benefit the greater PRD (Guangdong, Hong Kong and Macau). It took the central government and a new leadership in Beijing to officially put this crucial project on the table, and the interested parties reached an initial agreement in 2003. (The dire state of the Zhuhai airport as a result of competition is a case study).

❑   Quality of workforce:

There is a general concern about the quality of the workforce in the PRD, especially when a comparison is made with the YRD. The central issue is education level. The workplace is filled with migrant workers, mostly from rural areas of western regions. They lack basic school education and remain at low literacy levels. They need extended training to do factory work, but most of them perform processing and assembling tasks, so training is minimal. Managers from Hong Kong often complained about these workers with their slow pace of learning and inability to master the required skills. It is a difficult task to find and hire qualified personnel in management and technology fields. One possibility is to hire people from other regions and provinces of the country. Since the PRD's priority is production for overseas markets and orders, the goal of developing local R&D is largely neglected. When there are enough orders to fill, the enterprises lack the incentive and will to plan for the future and invest in new technology. The PRD is generally in shortage of qualified management executives and is weak in technology development. Shenzhen, with its wider view of the national market, has made serious attempts to turn the city into a hi-tech centre of China, with hi-tech fairs on the city's calendar every year. In spite of this, the municipal economy is dominated by traditional manufacturing and real estate businesses, and in hi-tech fields, Shenzhen this far is not a serious challenger to Beijing or Shanghai.

❑   Problems in human resources management:

Thanks to plentiful job opportunities in the PRD, turnover rate is high, and employees typically work short-term for a company. Senior and experienced managers are easily poached by other firms in the industry. The range of fringe benefits offered to employees is not adequate to woo them, though this has been addressed in recent years. Companies in the PRD mostly lack an established corporate culture, leading to low levels of employee loyalty and cohesion. The workforce there is highly mobile and unstable, and executives may jump ship with company secrets and a group of colleagues who used to head company divisions.

❑   Soft environment—government services to commercial business:

Complaints about government services and performance have been growing in number and scale in the PRD. Business operations are not isolated from government functions, and actions by authorities in charge have a direct effect on business activities. There are frequent charges and levies on business. Financial burdens on business also include fines (expected and unexpected), occasional donations and contributions, regular bribes and protection fees. Since there are many grey areas in government functions, rule bending and breaking is common. Irregularities pose a serious problem for businesses in terms of obtaining permits and approvals. A particular issue in the PRD is an overwhelming reliance on *guanxi*, which often decides the conditions and outcomes of running a business. Many experienced Hong Kong and Taiwan businesspeople conclude that in Shanghai you can obtain official papers in a certain period of time, with or without *guanxi* with relevant authorities. In the PRD, without *guanxi*, you may obtain official papers in months rather than weeks, even though you have everything ready and the official regulations require a quick response.

Another grave concern of investors is the worsening social disorder and public security in the PRD. Criminal activities are on the rise, with organised and individual crimes threatening their personal safety. Cases of murder and kidnapping of wealthy investors appear more frequently in local news reports, and overseas investors have less confidence in local police and legal protection. This is a thorny issue for the PRD governments when the situation there is compared unfavourably with the YRD, which is largely untouched by serious crimes in general and those crimes against overseas investors in particular. This security factor will tilt many prospective investors toward locating their business and operation bases elsewhere.

The Yangtze River Delta (the YRD)

This macroregion includes the Shanghai municipality, Jiangsu and Zhejiang provinces. The rise of this macroregion was preceded by flourishing economies of the two provinces, typified by booming private and collective enterprises. The real turning point, however, came in the early 1990s when Shanghai received the auspices of the central

The Pudong New Zone

The zone is at the west side of the Huangpu River and opposite the established metropolitan areas of Shanghai. It had 2.53 million residents in 2000 and a land size of 522 square kilometres, including a number of specialised zones such as a financial and commercial zone at Lujiazui, a hi-tech park at Zhangjiang, and an export processing zone at Jinqiao (Golden Bridge).

government to push ahead bolder reforms based on the earlier PRD experience and with their own initiatives. The rise of Shanghai is the focus of the next stage of economic development, and the key indication of this move is the Pudong New Zone, which in effect has become a new Shanghai.

Positive Aspects in Business Environment of the YRD

❑   Law and rule abiding culture:

Local residents have demonstrated their mainstream tendencies to follow rules, respect authority, and work within the boundaries of current laws. This is in contrast to common behaviour in the PRD where many seek to gain within or without the boundaries of laws. Shanghainese are well known in the country for law-abiding behaviour. Two factors contribute to this trait. One is the foreign influence from the colonial era, which taught many in Shanghai to honour contracts, respect legal proceedings and courts. The other is, ironically, the planned economy, under which Shanghai followed the tight control and planning of the central government. As the key industrial base of the country, Shanghai was organised according to socialist ideas, and workers and managers were used to carrying out strict orders in production and business. Even at the early stages of reforms, Shanghai did not make bold attempts in restructuring; it fully opened itself only after the central government laid down new development strategies. These two factors combined to reinforce the abiding of laws and rules.

❑   There are clear and standard government procedures dealing with business affairs, and government functions are less influenced by *guanxi*. Government bureaux set out clear rules and procedures, and they follow these procedures in application and other matters. Steps and timetables for the completion of procedures are also openly displayed, so applicants have little trouble or uncertainty about the process. This relative efficiency and transparency in administration benefit business and reduce the need to rely on *guanxi* in the process.

❑ Education institutions and quality of workforce:

The level of education in the YRD is reflected in wide school networks, large numbers of tertiary educational institutions, and a high average literacy level in this macroregion. Elite high schools and top universities in the region are undisputable proof of education levels, and they supply many engineers and experts in all areas of economic development. Accordingly, workers there mostly have sufficient school education and technical skills, and with effective training, they are quick to learn the required techniques. Quality of workforce is one key factor for multinationals in choosing the YRD as their manufacturing base.

❑ Division of labour and coordination among regional centres:

Shanghai is the clear and undisputed economic centre of the YRD, and there is no real challenge to her leading position. Other cities in the macroregion willingly follow Shanghai's lead and make their goal of economic development that of serving her in many areas. The relationship between Shanghai and other cities is complementary in production and sales, and other major cities with rich resources still see Shanghai as their target market, rather than a rival. Although nearby Suzhou has absorbed a greater share of foreign investment in recent years, the position of Shanghai as the "dragon's head" is still in no doubt. This situation and an orderly structure make coordination and planning a relatively easier task in the YRD.

❑ Expansive inland regions to sustain future growth:

Traditionally, the YRD has had close economic ties to many inland provinces, and transportation from the YRD to other major regional markets is convenient and frequent. One obvious route to take is along the Yangtze River all the way up to Sichuan province. The gigantic hydro-power project at the Three Gorges further facilitates closer links of regional economies from Shanghai to Sichuan. The YRD enterprises could thus tap the natural and human resources of many regions and enter many considerable inland markets. This is the reason many multinationals chose Shanghai and the YRD as their stepping-stones to penetrate the national market of China.

❑ Urban centres, matured urban culture, huge purchasing power and consumption potential:

In the YRD, many urban centres have existed for centuries, and they form a wide network of cities and towns, not far from each other. This is a highly urbanised macroregion, with an established urban culture. This is also an ideal place for consumer markets and new fashion products. The macroregion has a high population density and urban sectors, with a sizeable middle class and many high-income groups. Being coastal regions, residents there harbour a strong tendency to follow new trends, keep close contact with foreigners and are under strong international influence. Large numbers of foreign companies in the YRD pay relatively high salaries to Chinese employees and make consumption of "large item" goods possible, such as cars and household electronics.

❑ Weakening Shanghai-centred attitude and discrimination against migrant workforce:

Shanghai used to be a closed community, separate from other parts of China by language (dialect), behaviour and the *hukou* system. Now many restrictions are relaxed, and it is far easier for people to live and work in Shanghai and surrounding areas. The YRD can now get talented and qualified personnel from all over the country, in order to meet the growing demand in business and R&D. More migrant labourers are allowed to work there, so as to provide unlimited reasonably-priced labour for ongoing construction and factory work.

❑ Increasing internationalisation to attract more foreign companies: This is shown in the moves after China's WTO accession. Learning and communication in English became more widespread, contact with foreign persons more common, and rules and regulations were modified or changed to be similar to that of international standards, especially in financial and services sectors.

❑ The already complete industrial structure and formidable production capacity in Shanghai are further reinforced by key projects of the central government, in the industries of energy, steel, automobile, petroleum and machinery. Many industrial reforms to state enterprises have been experimented here, and large corporations in Shanghai have managed to turn themselves into efficient and flexible conglomerates, for example, Bosteel.

Issues of Concern in the YRD

❑ Strong government interference and guidance in economic spheres: Shanghai's reform and rise are coordinated by the central and municipal governments, and initial changes and following stages are carefully planned by government bureaucrats. The government gives clear signals for allowing or rejecting certain changes, and economic development of the YRD responds sensitively to guidelines from the government. The rise of the YRD is also based on heavy investment from the government, particularly in infrastructure, and today, the municipal and regional governments have enormous financial resources to promote a certain district or sector. Businesses thrive in the YRD under the strong influence and protection of regional governments.

❑ Heavy state investments on major projects:
Major projects of infrastructure, power, and transportation are all government projects, funded by state resources. These projects provide much employment for workers and business for contractors. Through major projects, cities have changed faces, and governments then have the incentive to raise money and collect fees from the public.

❑ Overflows of capital and FDI pushing up prices and costs:
An improved business environment attracts many FDI and domestic investments into the YRD. Investors see the macroregion as a favourable manufacturing base and consumer market, and they want to set up offices or factories there, for fear of lagging behind. This sentiment creates strong demand and pushes up price levels and living costs in the YRD. In future, high costs and prices may discourage investors and reduce the total volume of investment.

❑ "Bubbles" in property market and other consumer markets:
In particular, property prices in Shanghai keep rising and reach levels which are not justifiable. Property booms have occurred in Shanghai and other YRD cities in recent years. Construction of

high-end apartment buildings in Shanghai took one-third of total funds in late 2002. Similarly, property prices in Hangzhou rose many times in five years. This trend is created by speculation and a flood of foreign and domestic capital into the region, and has caused grave concern over the huge bubbles building up in the real estate sector. Living costs and rental on office space are also dearer than before. Shanghai now ranks as one of the most expensive cities in the world to live.

❑   Similar industrial structures and products among many cities in the YRD:

Since foreign investors see the YRD as essentially a manufacturing base, they have introduced many production lines and facilities to this region. As a result, industrial structures and products made are quite undistinguishable among producers there. This has led to an oversupply of goods on the market, confused consumers, and buried brand names.

❑   More domestic sales rather than exports to developed economies:

The YRD has great influence on domestic markets and is the focal point for internal commerce. Many products made there are sold to domestic customers. On balance, the YRD gets more income from domestic markets, and is not highly dependent on exports, in comparison with the PRD. Shanghai is one of the key ports for exports, but its foreign trade was US$33.2 billion in 2001, 6% of the national total, with exports worth US$27.6 billion. In comparison, Guangdong (the PRD) had a foreign trade volume of US$176.4 billion, 35% of the national total, and Shenzhen's exports alone amounted to US$37.4 billion.

❑   Non-convertible RMB:

State regulations and restrictions are against Shanghai becoming a true international financial centre. In a comparison with Hong Kong, Shanghai has definite disadvantages in free currency conversion and in other areas of financial management. These are issues for the central government to consider and decide, and Shanghai is at best a trial base for any new policies on finance and foreign exchange. Shanghai and the YRD in general cannot remove these negative effects in the near future, and their links with international financial markets are indirect. This handicap worries many multinational corporations which have an intention to operate in the region.

Shifts of FDI from the PRD to the YRD

Recent moves by overseas investors to shift investment and operations from the PRD to the YRD caused a great stir to governments in both regions. Faced with healthy competition, regional governments are to respond by evaluating their strategies and thoroughly examining defects in their own business environment. The capital flight is more urgently probed by the PRD. Since 2002, net utilised FDI in the YRD has overtaken that in the PRD, and more fresh university graduates have rushed to the YRD for employment.

❑ Widespread concerns over soft environments:

Disadvantages in this region include but are not limited to: higher costs, higher government charges, fiercer market competition, limited future potential, unpredictable government regulations, corruption and *guanxi* pressure, safety issues, pollution and industrial safety.

The above disadvantages involve costs in business. Even corruption and *guanxi* pressure require constant payments to be made, so there is an intangible and sometimes unbearable pressure on the part of businesspeople, foreign or domestic. Many came to invest with an expectation of growth based on *guanxi*; however, they later realised that the costs from irregularities could exceed the benefits from *guanxi*. The more standard practice and rule-based environment in the YRD then becomes more appealing.

❑ Moves by Taiwan companies:

They are big investors in the PRD, now numbering in the thousands. They have moved in groups or are planning to move to the YRD, and many have found a better business environment in that macroregion. In particular, large and dominant Taiwan microchips companies have signed contracts and set up bases in Shanghai and Suzhou, and large numbers of medium-sized companies have built factories in other YRD cities close to Shanghai.

Taiwan companies used to carry on similar businesses on the mainland as Hong Kong companies, such as restaurants and real estate, but in recent years they have switched to introduce IT and computer-related manufacturing into mainland China, for which they have virtually no domestic competitors. Even Hong Kong companies will not be seen as compatible rivals in these industries.

Taiwan companies have also moved the complete value chain production to the mainland, involving many suppliers at different stages and end users. If one major manufacturer relocates, its suppliers and end users will also have to follow. This is happening to some Taiwan companies previously operating in the PRD, which have since shifted to the YRD, and it is a common phenomenon for a group of Taiwan companies to move in the same direction. For example, Mr. Guo, head of the Taiwan business association in Dongguan of the PRD, moved his furniture business to Shanghai and Jiangsu provinces after a dispute with local officials, and this caused a number of other related companies to move there as well.

❑   Language is a factor for moving north. Taiwan businesspeople speak Putonghua with local partners in the YRD quite comfortably, while their communication with partners in the PRD is often hampered by the local Cantonese speaking environment.

❑   For Hong Kong businesses in the PRD, a TDC (Trade Development Council Hong Kong) survey conducted in 2002 shows that 75% of them see the PRD as the first choice site of investment, while 21% see the YRD as the first choice. Although there are no restrictions on locations for Hong Kong businesses on the mainland, close ties with the PRD and preference for its rules cause the majority of them to stay put and do business in that region. Companies surveyed have all set up business in the PRD and put priority on the proximity to their Hong Kong headquarters as well as language convenience (Cantonese speaking). The surprising indication in this survey is that a bigger proportion of Hong Kong companies is playing with the idea of business expansion into the YRD.

In comparison, Taiwan companies see little difference between travelling to Shanghai and Hong Kong; therefore moving to Shanghai seems a reasonable option. For Hong Kong businesses, however, the short distance to the PRD is a key consideration in their business and investment decisions; having to drive only a few hours to your factories is a better way to justify the investment there. Some researchers have developed a three-hour drive rule:

when choosing sites, Hong Kong businesspeople would most likely pick a place within the radius of three-hour drive from the boundary of Hong Kong.

In addition, Hong Kong companies are operating in a friendlier environment in the PRD, speaking the same dialect (Cantonese) and sharing many cultural traits with the locals. On the other hand, Taiwan companies may feel the YRD is a better environment culturally, because Mandarin is spoken and local customs are similar. These linguistic and cultural preferences may help decide whether a company moves away or stays in a region.

❏ **Movements of foreign companies from Hong Kong to the YRD:** There is a parallel line of northbound movement. Some foreign multinationals have moved their functionaries or operations from Hong Kong to the YRD, mainly to Shanghai. This is essentially based on their projections of future growth in these two macroregions. The PRD has northern barriers to markets in inland provinces, and this may affect future growth for investing multinationals. In this regard, multinationals' decision to move north is not based on how Hong Kong performs, but primarily on their overall estimates of market potential in different regions. Hong Kong is still closely connected with the PRD, and how the PRD grows in future will have some impact on how foreign investors view Hong Kong. The Hong Kong economy has had a minor fright over the unexpected rise of the YRD, and it needs to act quickly to seize opportunities in both macroregions.

Long-term Prospects

Without considering the YRD factor, the right solution for Hong Kong investors would be a further integration of the PRD, forming a greater PRD with three zones and five mega cities—Hong Kong, Macau, Guangzhou, Shenzhen and Zhuhai. The market size of this greater PRD is already much bigger than the entire YRD, and will grow even bigger if internal barriers are removed or minimised. It is essential to start with coordination, positioning these five mega cities at the right market places and assigning different tasks to them. Efficient and close networking can be in many forms, for example, the cross-harbour bridges and highways linking Hong Kong and Zhuhai. These links will fully explore the market potential in the western wing of the PRD, which has been outpaced for many years by the eastern wing.

An obstacle to the emergence of a greater PRD is the ambition of the Guangdong provincial government. The government may take up the option of setting up the provincial capital Guangzhou as the centre, and seek comprehensive cooperation with neighbouring and inland provinces. Four provinces—Guangxi, Hunan, Fujian and Jiangxi—are supposed to line up behind Guangdong, and Guangzhou will have its left arm stretch to Shenzhen and Hong Kong, and the right to Zhuhai and Macau, and the southern ends will be linked by the proposed cross-harbour bridge. Guangzhou would without doubt sit comfortably in a commanding position in this setting, leaving Hong Kong on the sideline. Under the urge of the central government, this alternative scenario of a greater PRD and a disconnection from Hong Kong is less likely to happen. The new CEPA agreement enhanced Hong Kong's status as the only international financial and trade centre in southern China; and Guangdong provincial officials began to consolidate Guangdong as an established production base for international trade. The second round of "front shop/backyard factory" has begun on a mutual understanding of benefits between Guangdong and Hong Kong.

(Note: A pan-Pearl River Delta regional cooperation framework was formed in June 2004, with Fujian, Guangdong, Guangxi, Guizhou, Hainan, Hunan, Jiangxi, Sichuan, Yunnan provinces, Hong Kong SAR, and Macau SAR. This is called "9+2" in short, indicating closer cooperation among these regions. This framework is an extension of the Greater PRD, with Guangdong province and Hong Kong SAR being the major economic powerhouses).

On the other hand, Hong Kong businesspeople need to consider the YRD for future growth and utilise the industrial potential and human resources there. These can be achieved under the WTO rules and with more cooperation between Hong Kong and the YRD. Many Hong Kong investment projects can be placed in the YRD when time and conditions are right. Such moves are logical, following increasingly common shifts of FDI to the YRD in recent years and positive projections of future growth trends in the region. Hong Kong businesses can adopt both strategies and seek business opportunities in either of the two macroregions. A new beneficial arrangement (CEPA) was signed in 2003 for Hong Kong to enjoy wider opportunities on the mainland that were expedited by the central government. (CEPA is further discussed in the next chapter.)

Disparity in Living Standards

The central rationale for reforms is to rid China of poverty and life at subsistence levels—consequences of the previous rigid planned economy. The means applied is a market economy, which has proved effective in producing more goods and services for the populace. While more people are receiving higher incomes and consuming more products, the seemingly equal society in the old days is being replaced by a sharp contrast between wealth and poverty. Ever since the early years of reforms, the divide between the rich and the poor had been emerging, and it is now getting to the stage of ripping the entire society apart. Amazing economic growth lifted many to the levels of the middle class and the wealthy, while many more got the taste of being left behind in this drive to achieve economic goals. The alarming inequality shadows many success stories and causes deep resentment and grievances. Another aspect of concern is the widening divide between urban centres and rural areas.

Income Gaps

The Good News

Benefits of ongoing reforms are primarily shown in increases of average incomes and an emergence of a middle class, similar to other newly industrialised countries.

❑   Average annual salary levels in top four cities (2002):
  • Shanghai: 49,180 yuan
  • Shenzhen: 47,943 yuan
  • Beijing: 46,611 yuan
  • Guangzhou: 41,377 yuan

❑   In 2002, incomes rose in 35 major cities, and the list of cities with an average income of 10,000 yuan per person is topped by five cities—Shenzhen, Guangzhou, Shanghai, Ningbo, and Beijing. This data shows an underlying difference among regions, in that people in some cities are able to get extra income on top of their salaries, so that their real incomes are not affected by their lower average salary rankings.

The Middle Class

❑   Estimates of the size of the emerging middle class indicate that many groups of people enjoy high salaries and purchasing power, numbering between 100 and 150 million;

❑   Surveys on millionaires in Beijing in 2003 show that the number is between 1.5 and 2 million (including their property values);

❑   Surveys in 2002 on average asset value of urban households present a figure of 228,300 yuan. If a household asset value between 150,000 and 300,000 yuan is set as the standard for the middle class, then about 200 million Chinese are in this band, or 18% of the total population.

These cursory results demonstrate considerable increases in income for urban residents and for many groups of people with secured employment. These are the essential information for multinationals' estimates of the potential and consumption of the China market.

The Not So Good News

On the other side of the story, many more groups of people are near or falling to the official poverty level, including both urban and rural residents. Growing gaps in income between rural and urban areas have emerged. From statistics, incomes in rural areas show slower growth rates in the 1990s and early 21st century (see Figure 8.5). Consumption by rural residents has fallen from 40% of the total value of consumption in 1996 to 38% in 2000.

In 2002, income by migrant workers took 70% of the share in income increase for rural residents. Migrant workers from rural areas find employment in urban centres and post part of their income back to their families. This kind of income is counted as rural income and compensates for the insufficient income generated from local agricultural production. The percentage of this contribution is growing.

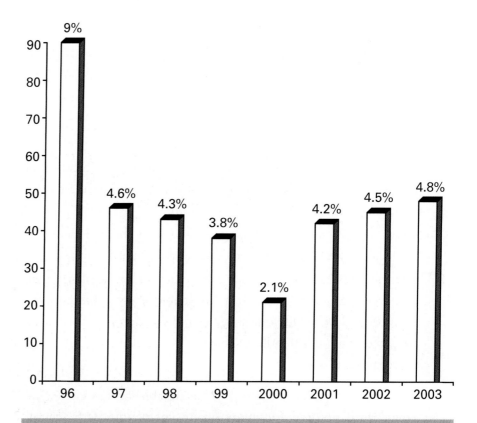

Figure 8.5 Income growth rates in rural areas

Poverty Line

There is an official poverty line set for people who earn negligible incomes. This line was set at an annual income of 625 yuan per capita. By this criterion, official figures put the rural population living in poverty at 28.2 million for 2002. If this standard is raised to 825 yuan, as it has been in more recent years, there would be 90 million rural residents in poverty. There have been active discussions within the country on this poverty line and the application of the United Nations' definition of one US$ income per day, which is about 3000 yuan per year. The new yardstick will definitely put more Chinese residents, rural or urban, into the impoverished group.

Unemployment

The official definition of unemployment covered residents in cities and towns, and those who registered at state job centres. From 2003, this official definition was clarified as including those within working age (between 16 and 60 years old for males, and 16 to 55 for females), are capable of working but unable to find employment. This is closer to the term "unemployed" adopted internationally. Under this guideline, official unemployment rate for urban residents was announced at 4.3% for 2003. Rural labourers, who are underemployed or migrating, are excluded from the calculations of this category.

Official figures also do not include workers in the category of *xia gang*.

State statistics show that there were 4 million *xia gang* workers in 1995, 8 million in 1996, 12 million in 1997, 16 million in 1998, 20 million in 1999, and 11 million in 2001. The surges in 1998 and 1999 corresponded with sweeping state enterprise reform under the watch of Premier Zhu Rongji, as discussed in the previous chapter on state enterprises.

Since the official figures of the unemployed do not cover many categories, it is a common understanding that the real number of people who are unemployed is much higher; with some observers suggesting a 10% unemployment rate. These unemployed may well be the people who are in the poverty groups.

Xia gang: Redundant Workers Mainly from State Enterprises

This is a special Chinese term, invented by bureaucrats to describe the above-mentioned group, without directly classifying them as the unemployed. *Xia gang* workers are officially attached to their work units or enterprises, and they continue to receive basic minimum subsidies for their living and medical expenses. These workers are encouraged to take another job, search at state-run job and re-employment centres, or set up their own small business.

The official term "unemployed" was used from 2001, and *xia gang* workers, implying state enterprise workers, is still used in another category in general statistics. In 2002, *xia gang* at state enterprises numbered 4.12 million.

Labour Flows and Movements

The total labour force in China was estimated at 740 million in 2002, among which 347 million were in the urban labour force.

The category of work unit (*dan wei*) employees amounted to 105 million. This category covers all those who receive salaries from governments at all levels, including government employees, teachers and professors, party and military personnel, etc. This category does not include those working in private, collective and foreign enterprises and organisations.

From the official statistics available, we observe certain indicators of labour supply and movements in the country.

First, the Chinese economy faces a 10 million annual increase of labour supply. This is based on the prevailing levels of population growth and of school leavers. This increase has set in as a near constant factor in labour market and economic forecasts.

In the vast countryside of China, there exists a surplus rural labour of 150-160 million people, and annual floating rural labour is estimated at 60-80 million. Rural migrant workers who are employed in or around urban centres amount to over 110 million. Since this trend of migrating and settling in has continued unabated, the central government set the target of moving rural labour to urban centres at 12-15 million a year. A shift of such a magnitude is considered a necessary step of modernisation and also an acceptable price to pay for reducing rural poverty. As a result of this ongoing shift, the official urban population reached 353.4 million at the end of 2002, about 30% of the total population.

Structural Change

Structural change refers to the trend of labour flow from primary industry to secondary industry and then to tertiary industry. This has an implication in the history of economic development that developing countries would release the bulk of rural labour from land and thus provide a sufficient workforce for industrialisation. This change occurs again once labour flows from traditional manufacturing industries to services (tertiary) industries. Developed economies of the West have completed structural changes in history from agricultural production to industrial production and to services. Each stage involves dramatic changes in balance and labour distribution in the economy, and the shifts made great impact on the society as a whole. Developing countries, including China, are on the path to such significant structural change at this stage, with massive flow of rural labour to markets in urban and manufacturing centres.

Labour flow was allowed in early reform years, and now it is relatively easy for people to seek work and employment in all regions of the country. The obstacles are mainly from the urban residential registration (*hukou*). This restriction separates rural and urban residents and justifies the benefits provided by the state to the latter group. Since there is a great need for more labour to do the work in cities, municipal governments have bypassed the *hukou* system through issuing temporary working permits and residential papers to migrant labourers from outside their cities. The *hukou* system was further eroded by the nationwide ID card system. Citizens of China with their ID cards hold theoretical rights to live and work in any part of the country, and many supervisory functions, such as police work, can be done by checking their ID cards. The remaining functions of *hukou* are for certain medical, educational and old-age benefits offered to urban residents, and many of these benefits are not so exclusive and privileged any more since migrants could purchase such rights if they had the financial means.

The *Hukou* System

It came to shape from the directives of the State Council in 1958, which stipulated two categories of residents in China. The purpose was to maintain a dual structure and prevent the rural population flocking to urban centres. Under the *hukou* system, it was extremely hard for rural residents to do so before the reform years. The channels available were tertiary education, marriage, official promotion, and selection after army service, etc. The Ministry of Public Security issued new rules in 1995, giving temporary certificates to rural labour staying in urban centres. The certificate is valid for one year and needs renewal thereafter. Without this certificate, rural labour cannot be hired in urban centres. Since the incidents of rural labour being abused by local authorities increased, when they fail to produce certificates, there have been official and unofficial discussions on treating these rural labourers more humanely, through formal legislation. The State Council in 2003 formally revoked measures previously taken to round up migrant labour in urban centres who were without proper certificates.

The transformation from the *hukou* system to a nationwide ID system indicates the contradiction between residential restrictions and labour mobility, and labour flow in China today is by and large unhindered by past barriers.

Social Security Systems

Social security is a relatively new area of government responsibility. Similar departments were named as "civil affairs" (or the like), and they dealt with the old and the sick. A national system providing universal safety nets had not been conceived. From the 1990s, the central government began to explore the possibility of such a system and sought information on this practice and experience in Western economies. (The author received and guided a visiting Chinese delegation from the Ministry of Labour and Personnel in 1992. The sole purpose of the delegation was to watch how the social security system worked in Australia and how the Australian government handled a variety of issues arising from this system. The delegation met with senior officials of the federal government in charge of social security and visited a number of local offices in Sydney and Melbourne to see how the system operated. They were extremely interested in all facets of social security in a market economy).

With the growing concern over redundant workers and the effects of medical system reform, the central government realised the need for a national social security system under a market economy. The new Ministry of Labour and Social Security was established in 1998, taking over some responsibilities from the Ministry of Civil Affairs and former Ministry of Labour. Its top priority is to set up funds to provide assistance to the needy, and more importantly to establish comprehensive mechanisms for the collection of payments especially for the purpose of social security for citizens.

Following the available models in the West, the central government stipulated the items of social insurance and instructed enterprises and organisations to pay for their employees. These compulsory items of payment include:

❑   pension
❑   medical expenses

- ❑   unemployment benefits
- ❑   industrial accidents insurance
- ❑   maternity leave insurance

These five items form the bulk of social security revenues the government receives. Enterprises in China, domestic or foreign, state or private, are all required to make regular payments under these categories for their employees. Failing to do so will incur heavy fines, public warnings in the newspapers and even suspension of business licences. For example, Shanghai newspapers regularly publish a list of enterprises that do not make such payment on a monthly basis. Often, the sum of these five payments can amount to half of employees' salaries. Some unscrupulous employers have evaded their obligation by labelling company employees as temporary staff, who are not eligible to enjoy the above benefits. Regulations and rules are expected to be tightened in future to extend the cover to all working employees. In 2002, government statistics show that those who have basic pension insurance consist of 111 million employees and 36 million retired workers; and 94 million had basic medical insurance. Under the new system, urban groups with the lowest income receive minimum living assistance from the government, from 36 yuan per month in Hebei province to 233 yuan per month in Beijing. The total number of people under this scheme was 21,824,915 in 2003.

The collection of these five types of social security is done by government bureaux at all levels, and the money is transferred to the central treasury for future payments to employees. The official recipient is the National Social Security Fund. For pension payments, the peak pay-off time is far from now, since the system is newly established, but this could be a serious problem in future years when large numbers of employees retire. Due to the accumulation of the amount payable and the untested performance of pension funds, there is no certainty that payments can be made in full to retired workers. Pension schemes in other economies face the same payment problem in future, and this uncertainty could also cause trouble to the whole social security system in China.

Key Concepts

Macroregions
"Developing the West"
The PRD and the YRD
Guangdong and Hong Kong
Xia gang and unemployment
Middle class and poverty line
Social security payments
Migrating labour

Discussion Questions

1. What do you think are the opportunities and risks in doing business in western regions? Are they any different from those in the east?
2. Do you agree that the government drive to "develop the west" will narrow the gap between eastern and western economies?
3. With your understanding of the issues of income gaps, poverty and floating labour, etc., what is your view on doing business in China?

Scenario Assessment

Suppose you are making proposals for your company to expand its business in China: first decide on the need for expansion (market shares and potential), then decide on which region to invest, giving brief lists of pros and cons.

Related Readings

Enright, M., *The Hong Kong Advantage*, Hong Kong, Oxford University Press, 1997

Forbes, 1999, the list of China's richest.

Gilley, B., "Provincial Disintegration", *Far Eastern Economic Review*, 22 September 2001

Hong Kong Economic Daily, Hong Kong, 23 June 2003, pA32.

Jing Ji Can Kao Bao (Economic Information Daily), Beijing, 24 September 2003.

Nan Feng Chuang Biweekly (Window of Southern China), Guangzhou, China, No.1, 2002, pp30–33.

Nan Feng Chuang Biweekly, Guangzhou, China, No.11, 2002, p24.

Nan Feng Chuang Biweekly, Guangzhou, China, N.10, 2002, pp24–27.

Riskin, Carl, Zhao Renwei, Li Shi, ed., *China's Retreat from Equality: income distribution and economic transition*, New York, M.E. Sharpe, 2001.

Skinner, G.W., ed., *City in Late Imperial China*, Stanford, Stanford University Press, 1977.

9

Foreign Trade and China's Customs

This chapter will focus on trade issues in the Chinese economy. Reforms in China have proceeded chiefly along two lines: internal restructuring and the open door policy. International trade and investment form the major parts of the second line of movement, and they are also the foremost indicators of the degree of market openness. As China's economy grows at a steady pace, China's international trade increases at an even faster rate. International trade now has more impact on China's economy, and trade related changes exert a deeper and more extensive influence on the domestic economy and society. Trade makes China more integrated into the existing international systems and creates a more secure future for China.

Open Door and Trade in General

The open door policy was initiated in the late 1970s as a principal part of government reforms, and this fundamental change from previous closure and self-reliance has stimulated foreign trade to grow at a rate of 15.2%, much higher than that of GDP in the past decades.

Four key elements—market opening, technology transfers, export drives, and foreign currency earnings—were the original objectives of government policies on foreign trade from the 1980s, based on urgent needs and high expectations for a revamped economy.

Export-oriented Economic Approach and the East Asian Models

The official policies focused on opening up and trade, especially exports, to generate much economic growth. In this regard, the government took a serious look at the experience and success of other East Asian economies, including those of the four "tigers" before the Asian financial crisis. East Asian economies utilised the advantages available prior to the 1990s and took great gains in free exports to America and other developed markets. Through exports, they achieved stunning economic growth and rising incomes. Drawing from these models in nearby Asian regions, the Chinese leadership foresaw great benefits if China took the same path. From the beginning of the open door era, government policies offered favourable terms to domestic companies operating in foreign trade and export.

It has been a concerted effort to follow the East Asian model of development and seek bigger overseas markets for Chinese-made products. Two typical expressions at the time were "**both ends outside**" and "**international circulation on a grand scale**". The first refers to a pattern of drawing foreign capital and technology into China and then exporting manufactured goods to foreign markets. The second refers to making Chinese manufacturing a set phase in constant international flows of goods and capital. The Chinese economy is thus a huge work platform for goods targeted mostly at foreign buyers. These policies have the apparent advantage in using the inflow of foreign capital to reach the goal of huge export volumes, within a relatively short period of time. These policies, however, tend to ignore the domestic market and economy, especially domestic consumption. The rationale behind these policies are perhaps to take an easier course of development and leave more complicated and tougher internal reforms to later stages. As a result of this outward-looking approach, China witnessed spectacular growth in trade and export, leading to massive foreign exchange reserves and trade surplus with developed economies. Unexpectedly, the export-oriented model of economic development lost some appeal during the Asian financial crisis of 1997. Serious structural imbalances emerged in the Chinese economy, in the form of unusually high dependence on foreign trade and problems arising from an overflow of foreign investment. The need to modify the official policies and emphasise domestic markets and demands is widely recognised by the new national leadership in the early 21st century.

Positive Factors to Growth in Foreign Trade

Several crucial changes have contributed to the phenomenal growth in China's foreign trade in the past 25 years.

Loosening of State Monopoly on Foreign Trade

Previously, state foreign trade agencies held exclusive rights to conduct foreign trade, and trade deals and procedures had to pass through them. The export of manufactured goods in China to the US, for example, was handled by such government agencies. Even after reforms began in the 1980s, Chinese enterprises had no right to make contact directly with foreign buyers or sellers. They took business orders from government agencies, delivered the goods, and received fixed payments. Government agencies handled the whole process of export and import, acted as middlemen, and grabbed fat commissions.

Reforms in this aspect proceeded in two phases. First, some enterprises were given rights to conduct foreign trade by themselves, not through state agencies. These enterprises were mostly large state enterprises, and later such rights were extended to more enterprises, even private ones. Business deals and trade agreements can now be made between Chinese and foreign companies directly. Only the issue of foreign exchange in these deals is still handled by state bureaux.

Second, in recent years, there is a trend in policy to abolish the granting of rights to foreign trade completely. The government bureaux had the authority to grant such rights to certain Chinese enterprises, but in accordance with the WTO rules, enterprises will have such rights as a matter of course. Their business operations naturally include conducting import and export activities, and they are free to explore opportunities in overseas markets. The state will thus minimise its authority over the control mechanisms of foreign trade, and the granting of such rights will no longer apply. This new rule is in the process of being implemented in China (see Table 9.1).

Table 9.1 Chinese domestic companies authorised to conduct foreign trade										
1978	1985	1986	1988	1996	1997	1998	1999	2000	2001	2004
12	800	>1,200	>5,000	12,000	15,000	23,000	29,258	31,000	35,000	Open to all

These companies may enjoy legal rights of import/export of certain products or technologies, but not the overall trading rights.

Devaluation of the National Currency RMB

The value of the national currency, RMB, has been in a process of adjustment and devaluation since the beginning of the reforms, and this devaluation has contributed to export growth substantially. The currency and foreign exchange rate issues will be discussed in more detail in a separate section.

Tax Rebates on Exports

As a form of tax incentive, the government allows exporting enterprises to have part of their taxes reduced and repays the collected taxes to these enterprises. This rebate policy has given those enterprises more incentive to increase volume of exported goods and gain export earnings. Along with rapid export growth in recent years, there is also a rise of fraudulent reporting of export gains by Chinese enterprises, especially by those in southern regions, such as the Wenzhou region. The issues of export rebates and latest policy changes will be dealt with in another section.

Market Competition and Government Promotion

Governments at all levels seek export opportunities for the enterprises within their territories, and they conduct promotional campaigns, overseas tours and exhibitions to ensure those goods are manufactured locally. In doing so, under a decentralised structure, government actions and promotions may cause competition between regions and conflicts in business interests.

Reduction in Import Tariffs

The central government bears the responsibility of regulating tariffs on imports. As a result of China's accession to the WTO in 2001, import tariffs have been reduced in recent years, and imports from foreign countries have increased. Reduction in import tariffs is reciprocal, so such actions taken by the Chinese government will provide Chinese enterprises with more export opportunities and less discrimination from foreign countries. The issue of tariffs is discussed in another section.

Growing Market Size and Potential

Due to higher income levels and growing market size, China attracts more imports and investment from foreign countries. The increase in imports reflects the understanding of foreign companies of the market potential in China's economy, and it also shows the government's intention to allow more imports to balance huge increases in exports. If this balance is not maintained, it will be more difficult for Chinese companies to enter foreign markets and enjoy export growth in future.

Supplies for Multinationals Operating in China

A large part of exports to foreign markets are produced by multinationals in China. These multinationals set up manufacturing bases, hire Chinese workers, import materials and equipment, and produce goods mainly for foreign markets. The need to support their China projects has caused imports to rise and indirectly benefits exports by those multinationals. Consequently, foreign trade rose sharply in recent years. Favourable terms and improved investment conditions contributed immensely to this rise.

Latest Trade Situation of China

As an outcome of opening up and export-oriented strategies, China's foreign trade sector in the 21st century has presented some remarkable figures:

❑ Reorganisation: The Ministry of Foreign Trade and Economic Cooperation was merged into the Ministry of Commerce in 2003, in a recent restructuring of the central government. This implies a strengthened hold of the Ministry, especially its foreign trade offices, on domestic production and distribution. Those offices are not merely part of a sector, but form a coordinating hub for overall production and exports of the country. The clout of the Ministry and its foreign trade core is vividly demonstrated by the long delayed policy change and legislation on tax reforms. The Ministry made publicly known their fear that a unified tax rate for both domestic and foreign enterprises would scare foreign investors away.

❑ Export growth has contributed around 20% to China's economic growth; for a 10% annual growth, 2% came from exports (see Figure 9.1).

❑ In 1978, foreign trade was US$20.6 billion, 0.78% of world trade volume (in 32nd place), and exports in terms of total GDP was 5.6%.

❑ In 2003, the total trade volume was US$851.2 billion, with imports of US$412.8 billion and exports of US$438.4 billion, representing an average growth rate of over 15% from 1978 (see Figure 9.2).

❑ China was in 11th place in world trade in 1997, 9th in 1999, 7th in 2000, 6th in 2002, and 4th in 2003 with US$851 billion. With a total trade value of US$1.1 trillion, China reached third place in 2004.

❑ Total trade surplus accumulated from 1994 to 2003 was US$228.9 billion; but annual surplus is on the way down (see Figure 9.3).

❑ Foreign exchange reserves have increased from US$21.2 billion in 1993 to US$439.8 billion in March 2004 (due to speculation of RMB appreciation and inflows of foreign currencies, reserves reached over US$600 billion by the end of the year).

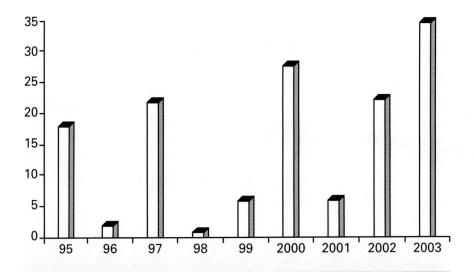

Figure 9.1 Export growth rate (%)

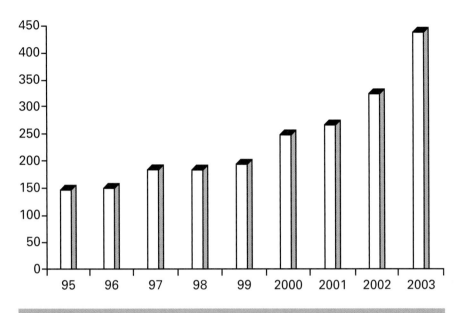

Figure 9.2 Actual increase in export (in billion US$)

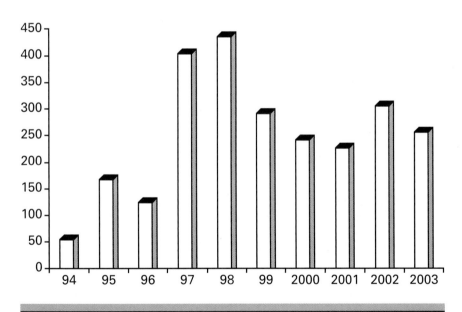

Figure 9.3 Trade surplus (in 100 million US$)

❑ Dependence on foreign trade is the total trade value in the total GDP figure. Since total foreign trade in US$ is converted to RMB value, this trade thus takes a big share in China's total GDP. The dependence rate has been high from the 1990s (see Figure 9.4). Whether this is healthy or risky is an issue for concern, and such

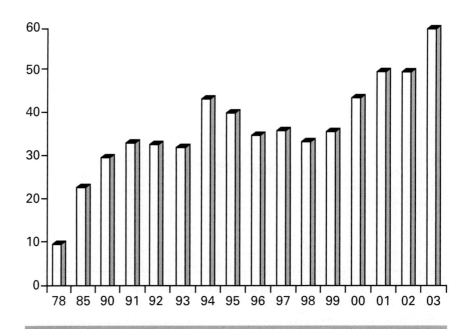

Figure 9.4   Dependence on foreign trade (trade/GDP)

rates are close to or higher than the rates in many Asian economies prior to the Asian financial crisis.

❑ According to statistics and calculations, for an export value of 100 million yuan RMB, state tax revenues increased 35 million yuan (not counting tax waivers and rebates). An export of 100 million yuan of manufactured goods creates 12,000 jobs in China, and an export of US$100 million creates 100,800 jobs. These jobs deriving from exports further create other indirectly related jobs and increase total consumption.

❑ Since the mid-1990s, foreign companies' exports are about 50% of the total volume of national exports (see Figure 9.5). For 2003, the ratio is 53%.

FDI's Contribution to GDP Growth

From March 1986 to March 2003, approved FDI projects were 426,020 in number. Contracted investment reached US$834.9 billion, and FDI in industrial growth, tax and export were 23%, 18% and 53%, respectively, of the totals.

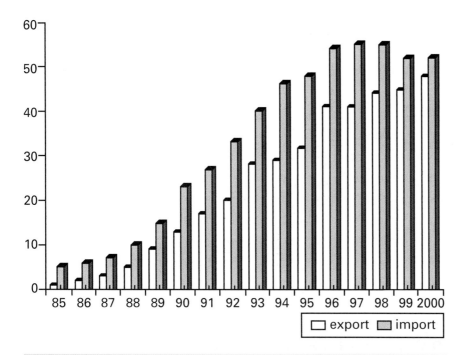

Figure 9.5 Share of import/export by foreign-owned enterprises in China

The calculation of GDP is illustrated in the following formula:

$$GDP = C+I+G+NX$$

In this equation:

❑ FDI projects pay wages to Chinese employees thus increasing consumption potential;

❑ FDI are investment on projects thus increasing total investment volumes;

❑ FDI produce for exports to overseas markets thus increasing net export.

The leading sources of investment include Hong Kong, Japan, the US, Taiwan, Singapore and South Korea. China has been the recipient of the largest foreign direct investment among all developing countries for the seven consecutive years since 1993. In 2002, China took over from the US as the recipient of the largest foreign investment.

WTO and CEPA

International trade and investment in China deal directly with foreign economies, investors and markets. These contacts have made the Chinese leadership more aware of trends and moves in the international arena and have led to enormous effort being made on conforming to international norms and rules. The World Trade Organisation has established commonly accepted rules and regimes for international trade, and the Chinese central government has been keenly seeking the accession to such international bodies and access to the related benefits and protection. Conversely, the open door policy and a membership in the international trade organisation provide tremendous stimulus to domestic reforms in every aspect of China's economy, including the trade sector.

Reforms in Foreign Trade Sector Prior to the WTO Entry

This sector has been under the most comprehensive reforms, which have taken many forms. These have created the outcomes of vibrant and positive-looking foreign trade, in contrast to faults and halts in internal reforms.

Decentralisation of power in foreign trade:

❑   Establishing provincial trade agencies to divide authority from the 12 state agencies under the Ministry of Foreign Trade, which previously held exclusive trade rights;

❑   Granting the rights to conduct foreign trade to selected large state corporations, most of them enterprises under other ministries;

❑   Granting economic zones and open cities the rights to conduct foreign trade, such as Shenzhen's trade with Hong Kong.

❑   Number of companies with foreign trade rights increased to over 2,200 in 1987.

❑   The responsibility system:

The central government has, since 1988, signed agreements with provinces and cities on trade rights. These agreements included items and targets of foreign exchange earnings from exports and set the amounts that should be transferred to the central government. Surplus foreign exchange earnings above the targets and quotas could be retained in the hands of local governments and exporting companies. This was to encourage local initiatives and efficiency in trade, and enterprises in export business began to enjoy more trade rights and income after the set targets were reached.

From the early 1980s onwards, central government directives on trade targets were abolished, replaced by indirect control measures on tariffs, quotas and permits.

❑ Lowering trade barriers and increasing transparency:

From the early 1990s, tariffs have been lowered in steps, and the range of permits issued was narrowed. Foreign exchange rate control was relaxed, with flexible management and fixed fluctuation margins. With the negotiations on a WTO entry under way, foreign trade management moved towards international standards and practice, transparency and accountability. By following WTO rules, rights to import/export will be granted to all firms in China, domestic or foreign, state or private. These changes in the trade sector were initiated primarily for compatibility with WTO rules.

Foreign Trade Law (1994)

This law was passed by the National People's Congress in 1994 and a review is currently under way for amendments. Without delving into details, comments will be made on a few articles in this law which relate to foreign trade and investment in China.

In general, mandatory planning of foreign trade by government bureaux ended, and indirect trade management mechanisms, such as tariffs, quotas, and permits, replaced administrative restrictions and government directives.

Article 2 of the law defines foreign trade as covering import/export of goods, that of technology, and trade of international services. This goes beyond import/export of goods and their total volumes, as calculated at customs. The first category of trade figures highly in China's exports, and exports in goods have drawn scathing attacks from certain protectionist sectors in developed countries. If import/export of technology and trade of services are counted, developed countries turn out to be winners with big margins, since the China market is nearly a pure receiver. Technology transfers in the forms of patents, permits and software yield big incomes but are not counted at customs. Services provided, such as accounting, management consulting and banking, are high valued-added, but are not counted at customs either. These are typical exports from developed economies to developing economies such as China's. This Foreign Trade Law in 1994 therefore included the trade of all the three categories.

Article 9 stipulates that foreign-invested companies would be allowed to import non-production goods, equipment, raw materials and to export finished products. These lawful activities give them the right to conduct foreign trade; a right denied to the majority of domestic companies at the time of this law becoming effective.

Articles 16 and 18 grant the authority for the State Council to limit import or export of certain goods under specific circumstances. The State Council is able to restrict the export volumes of certain strategic resources, such as crude oil. In 2004, China and the EU were at odds on the issue of charcoal, which is crucial to steel making, and exports of charcoal from China were sharply reduced by the government due to domestic shortage.

Articles 29, 30 and 31 provide legal basis for the government to conduct anti-dumping investigations and implement counter-measures. At the inception of this law, the issue of anti-dumping remained obscure in foreign trade. Since the late 1990s, domestic companies and government bureaux have filed more cases against dumping by foreign importers, and these articles are increasingly applied in legal disputes.

WTO Negotiations and Accession

The fundamental principles of the WTO are "mutual respect, equal opportunity, sharing of advantages, open trade and shared prosperity".

Major WTO Principles

- ❏ Non-discrimination: Members will not discriminate against products from other member countries.
- ❏ Preferential treatments: Members give preferential treatments to products from other member countries, in comparison with products from non-member countries.

❑ National treatment: Members allow enterprises from other member countries to enter their market and offer the same treatment in all aspects to these foreign enterprises as to their own domestic enterprises.

❑ Tariff reductions: Members lower their import tariffs on goods from other member countries at levels according to agreements.

❑ Mutual benefits: Members pursue mutual benefits in bilateral trade and offer benefits to the other side.

❑ Transparency: Members should make their regulations and rules public to all members and provide up-to-date information for other members on all changes and revisions.

Key WTO Agreements

❑ Trade of manufactured goods: Tariff reductions move down to the level of 5%, for developing countries.

❑ Agricultural products: Tariffs and subsidies are to be lowered.

❑ Textile products: This concerns market opening and reduction in quotas. The relevant agreement was previously under the name of "multi-fibre agreement".

❑ Rules of origin or country of origin: The relevant authorities are to guarantee the transparency of the process and the accuracy of country origins.

❑ Anti-dumping: This gives countries permission to respond to under-priced imports flooding domestic markets. The WTO allows retaliatory measures to be taken on importing countries if dumping actions and scales are established. Responses can be punitive tariff imposition and denial of market entry. This is an exception to general WTO rules on tariff reductions. The WTO set up commissions and tribunals to handle dumping complaints and make judgements that are binding.

❑ Trade of services: These are new areas under WTO structure (as a result of the Uruguay Round, 1994), carrying similar requirements to those for trade of goods.

❑ Intellectual property protection.

Anti-dumping Cases In and Against China

"The first important anti-dumping case in China was newsprint (paper) imports from several firms in the US, Canada, and Korea. In November 1997, nine Chinese domestic newsprint producers applied to the Ministry of Foreign Trade for an anti-dumping investigation. A huge surge in newsprint imports had taken place, starting in 1996. Imports rose from 74,000 metric tons to 356,000 tons, an increase of 660% in a single year. Imports from the US, Canada and Korea in 1996 increased 1,335%, 743% and 1,566% respectively. After reviewing the evidence presented by domestic and foreign firms, the Ministry in July 1998 announced anti-dumping margins and imposed temporary anti-dumping duties."

Nicholas Lardy

By 2002, there were 557 anti-dumping and market protection cases against Chinese companies and their exports. From 1997 to 2002, there were 21 anti-dumping cases against foreign companies and their export to China.

China's Application Process and Deadlocked Issues

❑ China formally lodged application for re-entry in July 1986 to the GATT, the predecessor of the WTO.

❑ China completed the Uruguay Round talks and signed agreements, but did not get permission to be a formal member of the newly established WTO. Instead, China was offered an observer status.

❑ China continued WTO negotiations with 36 countries, and signed agreements with the US in November 1999. Agreements with the EU followed. The last round of negotiation was conducted between China and Mexico.

❑ The final accession was officially announced on 11 November 2001.

Deadlocked Issues in Negotiations

Over 15 years of negotiations were focused on key issues, during which course these issues were kicked back and forth. It is no easy task to convince the counterparts to soften their stance on major obstacles.

China's status: A developing country or a semi-developed country?

The position defined for China has many implications in relation to other issues below. There are two sides of the debate on China's status.

With indicators of income per capita, people in poverty, average education levels, average financial assets, China is to be in the category of a developing country, and she has been in this category for many decades. This is China's position in negotiations, and she wanted to enter the WTO as a developing country. With indicators of economic growth, total GDP, total trade volumes, China could be put into the category of a developed country, and this is the view of the US and many of the EU negotiators. In the end, compromises were made, and China entered the WTO as a developing country, but is treated quite differently in some aspects from other developing countries. China accepted some tight conditions, and the commitments made are far beyond those by any country that has joined the WTO after 1995. For example, the US and the EU are to make a 36% reduction in value on agricultural export subsidies, and developing countries a 24% reduction. China instead agreed to eliminate all subsidies on agricultural export. For anti-dumping clauses, China allowed the US and other WTO members to treat China as a non-market economy in such cases for 15 years. This will make it easy for others to apply anti-dumping actions and thus jeopardise China's export growth. The final decision to enter under such restrictions was a political one made by the Chinese leadership, opting to enter the international body earlier with some cost to their own economy.

Length of transition periods

As a developing country, China could open some industries to foreign investors after a longer grace period. However, since certain special terms apply to China, a shorter grace period is set, and Chinese markets will open to foreign investment earlier, say in 5 years, rather than 8 years in the case of other developing countries.

Tariff reductions

Negotiations dragged on concerning how low tariff levels are to be set at and in how many years for tariffs to be lowered to the agreed levels. Since China had set higher levels of tariffs to protect domestic industries, agreements on this issue mean more drastic reduction of tariffs and a shorter period of time for this process.

Non-tariff barriers

Since China built up a planned economy and still has a large economic sector with many state enterprises, government actions against imports take many forms. In addition to tariffs, the government issues quotas and permits to enterprises for import and export, and it also provides subsidies to domestic enterprises. All these will give them more advantages in a competition with foreign companies. Imports from foreign countries would thus be limited or reduced. To address this issue, China agreed to lower non-tariff barriers, for example, to reduce the scope and number of permits and approvals issued by the government.

Service industries

China has an economy with large shares of assets in the primary and secondary industries. Service industries are relatively small, and many enterprises in this sector are state owned and closed to the outside. Foreign multinationals have great advantages and expertise in service industries, and the opening of service industries thus becomes one priority in their negotiations with China, as well as with other developing countries. To protect infant industries and service enterprises, such as hi-tech, banking, telecommunication, retail and wholesale, the Chinese government negotiated for more and longer protection, but in the end, the timetables for the opening of service industries provide only shorter grace periods for China than for other developing countries. For example, the banking sector will be completely open in 2006, rather than the 8 to 10 years normally granted to developing country members.

Intellectual property rights

For service industries, intellectual property rights (IPRs) are increasingly more important in trade negotiations. Since China has few IPRs to protect, government actions against violations are slow and piracy is widespread. Developed countries pay much more attention to IPRs and demand these be respected and protected. As a result of the WTO accession, the Chinese government agreed on IPRs rules and promised to strike hard on IPRs violations. The actual effect of IPRs protection is an issue for debate, and foreign companies operating in China are now allowed to lodge lawsuits at court for such violations.

Compliances

China's WTO accession means its regulations have to be revised, and if non-compliances are found, legal action can be taken at the WTO to redress the issues. Trade disputes need to be put to WTO bodies, with tribunals, rulings and arbitration on particular cases. There is a greater chance that the Chinese government can be sued for some wrongdoing, because after signing the agreements, the Chinese government has the obligation to follow and enforce WTO rules within its territory. On the other hand, if Chinese enterprises and exports suffer unfair treatment overseas, they could also use the WTO mechanisms and arbitration to solve trade disputes, instead of relying solely on bilateral negotiations.

Obligations and Changes in Investment Environment following the WTO Accession

On the signing of the WTO agreements in 2001, the Chinese government not only was committed to WTO principles, namely free trade, but also made public their commitments to undertake prescribed tasks within certain timetables. This then started the phase of implementation.

❑ Increasing transparency in trade and revising laws and regulations: The government is to revise and modify many laws and regulations, to be consistent with WTO rules. These laws and regulations need to be made public and transparent in all processes. So far more than 3,000 laws and regulations have been revised. In particular, those laws and regulations regarding FDI are at the centre of this process. The Foreign Investment Law was revised in 2003, making a few key amendments to the law. With WTO rules widely accepted in China, the business environment will steadily change for the better.

❑ Tariff reduction: Average level of tariffs is to be lowered to the required target by 2005.

❑ Non-tariff barriers: By 2005, the government is to eliminate all import permits and limit control on quotas, permits, foreign exchange and subsidies.

❑ Opening domestic service markets: By 2005, the government is to open industries of banking, insurance, transportation, construction, tourism, education, telecommunication, legal service, accounting, consulting, retail and wholesale etc.

❑ Protection of intellectual property: Legislation and enforcement are required.

❑ National treatment:

Foreign companies are to enjoy the same treatments as those offered to domestic enterprises. This means the opening of many industries to foreign investors, and the previous protection to state enterprises will not apply. Market competition will be more intense, and closing down of domestic enterprises will become more common.

❑ Enterprise share holding:

In a reform of Chinese enterprises, the number of shareholding companies will increase, and foreign companies have more opportunities to invest and become large and even majority shareholders of domestic enterprises. They will look for well-run companies and participate in and then control such companies. For Chinese companies, this provides a better channel for capital injection and for restructuring.

❑ Opening more industries:

This is to follow the national treatment principle, and the government is obliged to have less control of the economy and let many sectors open. Foreign companies will move into many newly opened industries and sectors.

❑ Market access and exit:

Foreign investors will get more market access in different regions, and if the business environment is not desirable and failures occur, they can easily leave the market and withdraw investments from regions and even from China as a whole. There will be fewer restrictions on their movements and capital flows. In the end, the business environment will mirror those in western countries where you can open a business and exit the market according to your own planning.

❑ Private businesses obtaining rights to undertake foreign trade:

The state monopoly on foreign trade will finally be removed, and the granting of rights by government bureaux will not be required. State, foreign and private businesses all acquire rights for foreign trade and conduct their import/export business without government supervision. In this situation, private enterprises are expected to obtain more shares in foreign trade than state enterprises.

CEPA (Closer Economic Partnership Agreement)

The Origin of CEPA

CEPA derives essentially from a response by the Hong Kong business community to China's WTO accession. The major facilitator was the general chamber of commerce of Hong Kong. In the face of a mainland economy open to all international trade partners, Hong Kong business communities proposed a quasi-free trade agreement to the central government, in order to gain significant benefits to offset the impact of post-WTO entry competition.

Under "one country, two systems", Hong Kong is a special administrative region of China. The new arrangements thus cannot take the form of a formal treaty of free trade between two countries; it instead takes the name of "closer economic partnership" to indicate that this is an inter-regional framework within the country of China.

The agreement was signed by the central government and the Hong Kong SAR government on 29 June 2003.

Two Key Parts of CEPA

Zero tariffs are applied on goods originally from Hong Kong. The catalogue contains 273 items. With CEPA, 90% of Hong Kong domestic exports to the Mainland can enjoy zero tariffs. It takes effect from 1 January 2004. The level of contents required for being classified as Hong Kong goods is to be negotiated, and it would likely be between 25 to 30% of Hong Kong inputs to the total value.

The mainland opened service industries and markets to Hong Kong businesses prior to the overall opening to international businesses required by WTO rules. The 17 open industries listed in CEPA include: management consultant services, exhibitions and conventions, advertising, accountancy, construction and real estate, medical and dental services, distribution services, logistics services, freight forwarding and agency services, storage and warehousing services, transport services, tourism, audiovisual, legal services, banking, securities and insurance.

Projected Benefits

Zero tariffs offer advantages to Hong Kong-made products in entering the China market, and CEPA offers a wider definition of being a Hong Kong company. This would attract international investors to inject capital in Hong Kong's manufacturing and other sectors. They could list as Hong Kong companies and gain mainland market access under Hong Kong origin rules. This would raise capital accumulation in Hong Kong and strengthen Hong Kong's position as a bridge between mainland and international businesses. The previous reliance on *entrepot* trade with China will be reduced.

Zero tariffs for Hong Kong would reduce tariffs on imports from Hong Kong, and the savings for Hong Kong businesses are estimated to about HK$4.3 billion per year. Since the products in the 273 items include those in large quantities and high value, the impact is profound and extensive. For example, watches made in Hong Kong currently have an 18% tariff, and jewellery has a 35% tariff. With CEPA rules, these types of Hong Kong brand products could be sold directly to mainland customers in larger quantity resulting in bigger market shares.

Hong Kong businesses could establish closer ties with Shenzhen and Guangdong on the basis of proximity and logistics. With the reputation of quality products, Hong Kong goods without tariffs would be more competitive in the market and popular to mainland consumers, and increased flows and sales could benefit Hong Kong and regional economies of the Pearl River Delta. This would strengthen the cohesion of the greater PRD as a major financial and manufacturing centre of China. It is also a boost to Shenzhen and Guangdong for their sustainable development.

There are benefits for earlier movers of Hong Kong businesses in mainland markets, particularly for those in service industries. Being two years ahead of other international competitors, Hong Kong businesses could set up branches, networks and customer bases for their services. For capital intensive industries such as banking and insurance, Hong Kong companies need an early start to make preparations to face later competition from multinationals. For professional services such as legal, accounting and consulting, Hong Kong firms could be well ahead of competitors and grab considerable market shares with their high quality services. A less optimistic view is that if Hong Kong businesses do not take actions quickly in response to CEPA provisions, two years is not adequate for business expansion and would not make a big difference.

Some industries could plan to shift part of their operations back to Hong Kong and create more job opportunities. Since Hong Kong is a free port and the mainland maintains a tariff regime even after accession to the WTO, it is more cost-effective for those products with imported components and technology to be shipped back to Hong Kong and, after local inputs, sold to the mainland without paying tariffs. This situation would make the manufacturing of certain value-added products in Hong Kong, rather than on the mainland, more appealing to businesspeople.

On 27 August 2004, the second round of CEPA was concluded with the signing of agreements between the central and HKSAR governments. These agreements include:

❑ The further opening of the market to eight service industries (airport, trade mark, culture, information, patent, headhunting, etc);

❑ Zero tariff treatment to more imported goods from Hong Kong, after which almost all types of goods produced in Hong Kong can be exported to the mainland with no tariff.

❑ Individual HK businesses are allowed to enter more mainland regions. Hong Kongers can now open their business on the mainland as mainland residents do.

With this round of CEPA agreements becoming effective, Hong Kong business sectors have obtained what they could ask from the central government on trade and investment and have received a head start of one and half years in enjoying such treatments. In 2006, when the WTO rules are fully applied in China, this CEPA business framework will lose its uniqueness and be compatible with the WTO rules.

Foreign Exchange and the Currency RMB

Foreign exchange controls are trade-related issues and have considerable impact on import/export. In general, a currency of low value (low exchange rate) reduces export prices, raises competitiveness, and increases export volumes. It also reduces demand for imports, makes it more expensive to import and less possible to buy needed foreign goods, equipment or technology. The foreign exchange rate of a currency is decided by many factors such as inflation rate, interest rates (comparing with those in other economies), trade and budget deficits, foreign exchange reserves etc. Its value is basically subject to supply and demand.

China's Foreign Exchange Markets

Strict and Rigid Foreign Exchange Control in Pre-reform Years

The only bureau dealing with foreign exchange was the state bureau of foreign exchange in Beijing, and the Bank of China had the sole responsibility of handling foreign exchanges.

The state fixed exchange rates at an over-valued level to subsidise imports of sought-after goods and equipment from international markets. It was also a response and remedy to the extremely weak Chinese currency under the previous Nationalist government. A higher value of the currency was set to give people confidence in the new economic systems.

Circulation of foreign currencies was banned, and institutions that held foreign currencies in their operations had to submit all such currencies to the central government. Any use of foreign currencies for any justifiable purposes had to be approved by the authorities in charge.

Foreign exchange inflow was encouraged, but outflow of foreign currencies was restricted by state directives and regulations.

Changes in Foreign Exchange Control to Date

In pre-1994 years:

❑ Foreign currency transactions and exchanges were allowed.
❑ Exporters and importers (state or authorised dealers) had a right to retain surplus foreign currencies made from business deals. Foreign companies could decide what to do with their own foreign capital and currencies.
❑ Other state banks, in addition to the Bank of China, were allowed to conduct business in foreign currencies, and they could keep their

earnings from transactions and deals with overseas investors (Hong Kong investors included). Foreign investment increased circulation of foreign currencies in the market, and financial institutions tried to get a share of this activity.

❑ Individuals were allowed to hold assets in foreign currencies, and private transaction and exchange became common.

❑ Swap markets for foreign exchanges were set up and open to people and companies who trade RMB for foreign currencies and vice versa. Banks were normally the place for swaps, and trade activities at banks at certain official rates were legal. Along with official swap centres, there was a black market of foreign exchange.

❑ Exchange rates fluctuated and moved away from the official rates. Supply and demand determined the rates and margins. RMB was seen as overvalued and needed to move down to a more realistic level. The plan to promote exports and reduce imports also demanded a re-evaluation of RMB and relaxation of foreign exchange control. RMB had been officially devalued (depreciated) steadily by the government, adjusting to changes in open swap rates.

From 1994 onwards:

In 1994, the foreign exchange regime was further reformed and has since continued to function in that way.

❑ Two rates (official and swap) merged and there will be only one foreign exchange rate for the market.

❑ The RMB, at the time of merging the two rates, was devalued from 5.8 yuan to 8.7 yuan to one US$, the latter being the swap rate.

❑ Foreign exchange control evolved into a system of managed rates with floating margins based on market conditions.

❑ Designated banks handle foreign exchange and offer such services to customers. Banks post their rates within the range (band) set by the State Administration of Foreign Exchange and the People's Bank of China. Institutions, enterprises and individuals can make exchange deals at banks freely, though in reality, banks would more likely accept foreign currencies from individuals and provide RMB notes. For individuals to exchange RMB for foreign currencies, they need to provide certain reasons, such as overseas education or travel, and the daily exchange amount is limited according to banks' rules.

❑ Domestic and foreign enterprises in China need to sell their foreign exchange income (above a set limit) to designated banks, and, when needed for payment in foreign currencies, buy foreign currencies from banks with their RMB notes, together with proper official documents. This is called conditional convertibility of RMB under current accounts. The central government can now receive large amounts of foreign exchange for other purposes, and foreign reserves of the country increased rapidly after this reform in 1994.

❑ 14 Chinese banks were authorised to open foreign currency accounts for enterprises, and later, foreign banks in China and other types of financial institutions could also open such accounts after approvals were given.

❑ Foreign exchange deals between commercial banks were allowed at the Foreign Exchange Centre in Shanghai, set up in 1994.

The State Council stipulated most of the measures and changes listed above in the regulations on foreign exchange management, issued in 1996.

Foreign Exchange Controls and FDI

Foreign companies operating in China have two main responsibilities regarding foreign exchanges.

Foreign investments are put into capital accounts, and investing foreign companies are required to open a foreign exchange account after receiving official approval for their projects in China. Investment in foreign currencies is exchanged into RMB at set rates at the branches of the People's Bank of China, and the RMB funds foreign companies receive are for their subsequent operations in China. This is one of the three key requirements for foreign investment, together with a business licence and tax number. Relevant authorities (the Administration of

Designated Banks

The Bank of China, the Industrial and Commercial Bank, the Bank of Agriculture, the Bank of Constructions, the Bank of Communications, the Citric Bank, China Everbright Bank, Guangdong Development Bank, Shenzhen Development Bank, Fujian Industrial Bank, China Merchants Bank, Hua Xia Bank, Shanghai Pudong Development Bank, and China Investment Bank (closed down in 1999).

Foreign Exchange bureaux and the People's Bank) are to inspect and certify that those foreign companies did transfer funds in foreign currencies into their accounts in China, and then issue them with a foreign exchange certificate. After this, the FDI application process is complete and foreign companies' operations in China are legal.

According to foreign exchange regulations, foreign companies need to hand in their surplus foreign currency earnings under current accounts to designated banks and receive RMB in return. They also pay RMB at those banks to obtain requested foreign currencies for their purchases and operational needs. In this way, foreign companies are frequently involved in the foreign exchange regime of China and trade in this market. Their business is thus under the influence of fluctuations in international currency rates. Under these regulations, domestic Chinese companies can make such trades as well.

Two Consequences of Foreign Exchange Reform

Total trade volumes and particularly export volumes jumped, based on competitive prices and goods exported by foreign companies investing in China. The former condition is a result of cheap labour being available in China and a depreciated RMB in comparison with US$. The latter condition is due to multinationals taking China as a manufacturing base for their export business, after considering labour cost and industrial capability. The US had enjoyed a long period of economic boom in the 1990s and a strong dollar was the government policy on foreign trade. The depreciation of RMB and increasing exports to the US are the results of American economic strength and policies.

Foreign exchange reserves increased steadily first and then dramatically since 1994, from US$21.2 billion in 1993 to over US$500 billion in September 2004 (see Figure 9.6). Depreciated RMB and increased exports provide enterprises with more foreign currencies from their international deals, and the regulations regarding these foreign earnings direct them to flow into the central treasury. All enterprises could sell their foreign currencies to designated banks, and since they could easily get capital in foreign currencies from banks for their subsequent projects, selling to the government did not represent an unbearable burden. This situation leads to more money flowing to the central government and the rapid increase in total foreign exchange reserves.

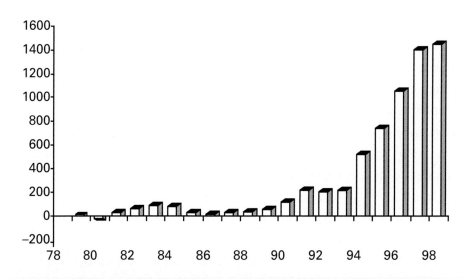

Figure 9.6   Foreign exchange reserves in 20 years of reform (in 100 million US$)

The RMB Rates and Trade-related Issues

The currency rate is a complex issue connecting both foreign as well as domestic markets. Many other issues came into play in recent years, testing the handling skills of the central government of China.

Interest Rates, Foreign Exchange Rates and Foreign Trade

Financial markets in an open economy link interest rates with foreign exchange rates. A change in domestic interest rate can affect foreign exchange rate and then affects imports/exports. A higher domestic interest rate increases savings and reduces money circulation in the economy. This higher rate also attracts foreign investors, who come to buy domestic assets and earn higher returns. Foreign investors need to exchange their currencies into domestic currency, and demand exceeds supply. The domestic currency is more valuable and the exchange rate is raised. Thus, a higher interest rate leads to a higher foreign exchange rate. A higher exchange rate then makes domestically made goods more expensive compared with foreign goods. Exports will fall, and imports will increase, as they are less expensive. A lower interest rate will lead to a lower foreign exchange rate, more exports and fewer imports. These apply to open market economies.

In China, interest rate and foreign exchange rate are kept low to boost exports. When there was high inflation in China and bank deposit rates reached over 10%, the official exchange rate remained the same. The government adopted a few measures to maintain a low exchange rate and support exports. The official rate has a floating band of less than half a percentage. The official rate has been up from 8.7 yuan to US$1 in 1994 to 8.2 yuan to US$1 in 2004-2005. This is an acceptable appreciation of the currency. The government also bought up all extra foreign currencies coming into China. This reduced demands for RMB and kept the exchange rate at acceptable levels. Extra RMB in money supply was absorbed domestically by the government in other ways. Before China's entry into the WTO in 2001, the financial system was largely closed to foreign investors and speculators, and foreign currencies in China were mostly in FDI and easy to monitor. Since 2001, China has been in a deflation, and interest rates have been low, down from previous inflations. The close links between interest rates and foreign exchange rates have not been thoroughly tested in China in practice. The last measure taken by the government to prevent exports from being affected by inflations and higher interest rates was export tax rebates, which will be discussed later.

The Asian Financial Crisis

After initial devaluation, the RMB was stable prior to the crisis. An observation made by some Western analysts is that the devaluation of RMB from that time on might have made Chinese exports more competitive in comparison with goods from Southeast Asian economies, thus causing many Asian currencies to be overvalued and triggering the crisis three years later.

The financial systems in China were mostly closed to foreign investors and speculators, and such interested parties could not trade Chinese securities or currency. The only option for foreign currencies to be exchanged into RMB was through direct investment. Thus, speculators could not sell the Chinese currency at open markets, unlike what they did in other Asian countries.

Fast-accumulated foreign exchange reserves after the 1994 reforms provided sufficient financial resources for the central government to hedge risks and deal with sudden crises. The central government moved in to back the Hong Kong dollar peg and halt the spreading panic over collapsing currency values and stock markets by not devaluing the RMB.

The Hong Kong Dollar Peg and Hedge Funds

In 1998, international hedge funds sought to chase the Hong Kong dollar down in value, in order to gain from their futures contracts. If the Hong Kong dollar collapsed like other East Asian currencies, these funds would reach their maximum targets and receive large sums of money. The sale orders from these funds and purchase orders from the Hong Kong government formed the battleground in Hong Kong's foreign exchange markets, and hedge funds did have a chance to maximise their gains according to their plans. Certain external conditions shifted to favour the other side and interrupted hedge funds' assaults on the foreign currency market.

These new conditions included:

- The collapse of the Russian bond market after the Russian government refused to honour its obligation on national bonds, which minimised the gains hedge funds could collect;
- The crisis faced by the US Long-Term Capital Management Fund (LTCM), whose heavy losses in the bond market alarmed its lending banks. These banks then had to lower lending to other hedge funds and this greatly reduced the funds' ability to influence international financial markets;
- The tough measures taken by some Asian governments to safeguard their currencies, which included the measures and enforcement in Malaysia to suspend outflow of foreign currencies, and those by the Hong Kong government to defend the Hong Kong dollar peg. The Hong Kong Monetary Authority raised rates on Hong Kong dollar borrowing, increased the funds' costs on borrowing Hong Kong dollars from local banks, and thus made it less possible for speculators to continue to sell down the currency.

With these unexpected events, the hedge funds had to cease their selling bids and pulled out of the market.

Such decisions require the backing of reasonably abundant foreign exchange reserves.

Japanese and International Pressure on China for RMB to Appreciate

Since the RMB is not officially convertible, the value of RMB is not freely tested in the market, and there is always pressure being put on the government to float the yuan. The RMB could appreciate or depreciate after floating under market influences.

In the year 2003, foreign governments and interested groups chose to focus mainly on pushing the value of yuan upwards, since this move would in effect depreciate foreign currencies and lead to more imports to the China market. The Japanese government has been asking for an appreciation of yuan against Japanese yen from the beginning of the 21st century, claiming that the yuan is too low for its real value. The American and the European governments have joined in this request and have ratcheted up the pressure. The Chinese government has not yet been convinced by such a call for an appreciating yuan, and has refused to bow to various pressures from the outside.

In a market with free trading, the RMB could appreciate or depreciate. Except for fund injections conducted by foreign speculators, there has been only modestly greater demand for the RMB in international markets. In an economy with certain foreign currency controls, the government decides currency values in relation to its own national interests. In both cases, the current price of RMB seems a reasonable one for the economy and for foreign trade. The central government thus far has only offered very gradual, long term readjustments of the foreign exchange regime, and it indicated on various occasions that major readjustments and a subsequent revaluation of RMB was likely only when speculative hedging by international financial institutions subsided.

The Linked Currencies of RMB and US$

A key component of the 1994 reform is to link the Chinese RMB to US$ at a set level. This level has been stabilised at around 8.3 yuan a dollar, with a narrow band of floating margins. This is similar to the Hong Kong dollar peg. Since the Bush administration in the US has moved away from the previous strong dollar policy and the dollar has been depreciating, the RMB link with US$ made it depreciate in real value against other currencies as well. This link-up strategy has annoyed the US government and some industries deeply, since their trade deficits with China have not improved or have even increased, and the depreciating US dollar has not caused the appreciation of the yuan. The US government has joined other governments to demand a revaluation of the yuan—up at least 20% against the dollar. The demand is based on China's increasingly bulky foreign exchange reserves and huge trade surplus with the US.

On the prospects of the yuan:

The Chinese government is unlikely to make the yuan appreciate following repeated and concerted calls from foreign governments. In response to foreign pressure, Premier Wen Jiabao has given the stability of RMB a high priority, and the governor of the People's Bank also stated that the Chinese government would not consider a revaluation of RMB in the foreseeable future.

The major concerns behind this decision are factors in the domestic economy. Exports should continue to grow, so a dearer RMB will reduce competitiveness of goods made in China.

A yuan at higher exchange rates will not help solve unemployment and other internal problems during a transitional process.

The consequence of an overvalued yen for the Japanese economy is an alarming example to the Chinese government not to take that option. Lifting RMB value by the central authority would only inflate the currency and create economic bubbles.

An independent foreign exchange policy is the key for the stability of the domestic financial market, and fair trade in essence implies that the parties involved will not accept unilateral demands or instructions. Acting on requests from other governments will hamper this independence and cause further chaos in future.

As for the main factor behind the calls—rising trade deficits on the side of the US—there are clear indications that this is not the main cause for more exports from China; it is the low labour costs in China, which have made Chinese exports decidedly competitive. A rise in RMB value will cause some goods to be more expensive, but in comparison with similar goods made in the US, they are still a lot cheaper.

There have been increased foreign currency inflows to China, with anticipation of an RMB appreciation. If this appreciation is now sanctioned by the central government, the expectations of speculators will be realised. In that case, speculators would start selling RMB to turn their profits into US$ and move them out of China. A concerted selling wave will lead to financial market fluctuations and RMB depreciation after a short period of appreciation. An early move for an appreciation certainly plays into the hands of external speculators.

Due to these considerations, the central government will not act under the urge of foreign governments to revaluate the RMB or float the yuan in the near future. On the other hand, of course, RMB appreciation will bring benefits to China in terms of cheaper imports of hardware, raw materials and natural resources, especially under the circumstances of an energy shortage and a surge in prices of crude oil in recent years. The likely policies to be adopted are to use the huge foreign exchange reserves in many other ways, including encouraging overseas business expansion by Chinese companies, and encouraging more deposits and spending in foreign currencies by ordinary Chinese citizens. In the area of imports, Chinese companies will be able to purchase more equipment and materials from Western economies, including the US, and seek advanced technology for achieving higher levels of productivity when restrictions on the US side are relaxed. The tendency will be to widen the band around the foreign exchange rate to defuse pressure on a full float and maintain a healthy balance in foreign trade through more imports.

Foreign Exchange Reform and Risks in Financial Management

Even if China was not directly affected by the Asian financial crisis and is not going to be influenced by foreign demands for a dearer yuan, the reforms in 1994 still increased the risks in domestic financial markets. These risks came from the increasing flexibility in foreign exchange controls under reform. As required by state regulations, foreign companies could sell foreign currencies to the Chinese bank and also sell RMB they hold to get foreign currencies. Each time they sell US$, the government has to pay them an equal amount of RMB, and when they sell RMB, the government pays them US$. In these transactions, there is a possibility that foreign money can cast a certain influence on domestic markets and exchange rates. When a large amount of US$ is presented at banks for exchange, a huge amount of RMB must be produced to make the transaction. This would cause a demand for RMB and indirectly increase the supply of RMB. The central bank controls money supply and prints the money to meet market demand. Excessive money supply in the market is a cause for inflation, and an overflow of foreign currencies makes it possible for an inflation to occur. Thus, foreign money has an indirect way to influence domestic financial markets. Under the current foreign exchange control systems, continued FDI inflow by foreign businesses in China have generated demands for huge amounts of RMB to be provided to keep the balance.

Also in these transactions, an extraordinary demand for RMB will have the effect of making this currency dearer. If foreign speculators, rather than average investors, gather huge amounts of US$ and demanded RMB payments in return, this would lead to a higher value of RMB in exchange. Even though the official rate is fixed, floods of US$ put great pressure on RMB to rise in value. To counter this, the government has to print more RMB for the payments, and this would lead to the possibility of inflation. It is a choice between inflation and RMB appreciation, and if the later is chosen, the official exchange rate could be raised. In this scenario, foreign speculators have a chance to put the stability of the RMB to the test. FDI, in practice, may not cause unusual trouble to the current foreign exchange regime, but an organised campaign by speculators could have more serious effects on the official rate.

Furthermore, over 70% of foreign exchange reserves in China are mainly in the form of US dollars, and the benefits from these reserves are quite low, mostly being spent on buying US Treasury bonds. China is the second largest holder of US bond after Japan, amassing US$119 billion worth of bonds in 2003. Such a concentration of US dollar reserves and overseas assets contains potential risks. As the US dollar has depreciated over 20% in past years, the face value of China's reserves and assets has dropped dramatically, in billions of US dollars. There have been questions raised about the wisdom of holding such huge amounts of foreign exchange reserves and, in particular, about the losses incurred from the US$ holdings.

It is suggested on the basis of these assessments of risks that the existing foreign exchange control systems need to be modified as situations evolve, and a more flexible management of foreign currency flows in the economy will remedy certain defects inherent in current systems.

Bilateral Trade

The open door policy allows China to break the barrier and establish normal and regular trade relations with major economies of the world. In the areas of import and export, China enjoys vast benefits from free trade and open markets abroad, as a result of bilateral trade agreements as well as its multi-nation treaties, such as the WTO. China has come to terms with playing the rules of international trade, while her growing size and weight in trade also cause concerns for her major trade partners. China in the 21st century is facing a nearly completely different world of international trade from her isolated situation in the 1980s.

Common Trade-related Terms

Balance of Trade

❏ Trade surplus (value): export > import

❏ Trade deficit (value): export < import

❏ **Terms of trade**: price of export/price of import

This benchmark indicates the real state of foreign trade of a country. When the figure increases, the net value of exported goods has increased, with same quantity of exports exchanged for higher values than that of the previous year. Improved terms of trade come from an increase in value per unit of exported goods and in wealth-making to the exporting country. In the case of China, despite the fact that the country is now the world's number three trading entity in total value, terms of trade have been worsening, since more exports are required to earn the same amount of money in return. Causes of this worsening situation are low prices for exported goods due to cheap labour and market competition, low exchange rate of RMB, and high value-added products imported from developed economies. The more Chinese companies export to overseas markets, the lower the figures in terms of trade and the less real benefits to the Chinese economy. Lack of core technology and brand names caused exported goods to be sold cheap. Additional side-effects include exhaustion of resources, environmental deterioration, and worsened workers' social welfare. This is a direct consequence of export-oriented policies taken by the government since the opening up.

Trade Prices

❏ FOB price: It stands for "free on board", indicating that the seller handles all the costs before goods are loaded on the ship, and bears all risks.

❑ CIF price: It stands for "cost, insurance, and freight", indicating the buyer handles costs, insurance and freight charges, and bears all risks before goods reach the designated port.

There are certain obligations borne by buyers and sellers under FOB or CIF trade terms (see Table 9.2).

With considerations of obligations and costs involved, the importing and exporting companies would prefer to choose one of the trade terms for their business, and their governments would also encourage certain ways of trade. For a developing country like China, a FOB term on imports would mean that their trading companies have the choice in selecting insurance and shipping companies that are cost effective, in comparison with a CIF term, in which foreign exporting companies choose services carriers and would most likely incur higher charges. A Chinese shipping company, such as Cosco, may charge less on its freight lines than a foreign carrier, such as the Danish carrier Maersk. Conversely, a CIF term for exports would also give Chinese trading companies choices to select the best options with lower costs. The home government would certainly desire such a practice, for the reason that this would offer more business and contracts to their domestic companies. In the case of Cosco, a Chinese trading company taking a CIF term for export would provide orders for Cosco's freight services, and many Chinese shipping and insurance companies would benefit from this.

Types of Trade

There are several types of trade options for traders and producers. Some types of trade are less explored by Chinese companies, such as leasing trade, while others were encouraged by the government since the beginning of opening up.

Table 9.2   Obligations in trade (A: importer; B: exporter)

Trade terms	Risk After goods on board	Procedures Who books freight ship?	Who handles insurance?	Costs Who pays for freight charges?	Who pays for insurance?
FOB					
CIF					

Processing trade

Domestic companies import raw materials, parts, equipment and technology, and manufacture to fill overseas orders. Their operations include mostly producing finished products and exporting them to overseas markets.

In China, processing trade includes three categories commonly applied by domestic and foreign companies. They are: (1) import of material for export of finished goods; (2) manufacture according to specific designs and modes for export; and (3) import of parts and components, assembly and export.

All these three types of processing trade can be seen as forms of OEM (original equipment manufacturing) production, utilising existing manufacturing facilities and capacity in an economy for exporting goods to overseas markets.

Compensation trade

Domestic companies import equipment, technology and other components on loans from foreign companies, and within a set period of time pay back the loans on instalments with finished products or services. Foreign companies act as both lenders and buyers. Domestic companies can continue to use the manufacturing capacity for their production after the full amount is paid. This type of trade meets the demand of those companies that lack financial resources to purchase equipment and thus face obstacles in increasing their production capacity.

Leasing trade

Domestic companies lease equipment or products from foreign companies, and within the lease term pay rental to the lending companies. The items leased are normally heavy equipment, ships or airplanes. For example, Chinese airline companies may be engaged in this type of trade and lease airplanes from foreign firms. This option is particularly attractive to newly established airlines or regional airlines, due to their limited financial resources and the uncertainty in entering the aviation industry. A good example is Dragon Air of Hong Kong, which leased airplanes at its founding stage to compete with the almighty Cathy Pacific.

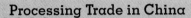

Processing Trade in China

Over half of China's trade is processing trade. Such trade brings to China meagre added value and income from local manufacturing processes, while, on the basis of rule of country origin, the total value of exports are considered China's exports to developed economies, such as the US's. For example, a globe newly designed by American companies is for developing children's learning skills, as well as for playing. An American importer sends an order to a Hong Kong agent at a price of US$40 per piece. The Hong Kong agent passes the order to a Guangdong trading company at US$20 per piece. The Guangdong company gives the order to some manufacturing companies in Guangdong and Jiangsu at US$15 per piece. The basic cost for the globe is US$12 per piece. When the American importer receives the finished goods, it sells to American retailers for US$72 per piece, and the retail price on supermarket shelves is US$88 per piece. The bulk of the revenues in this value chain are taken by American and Hong Kong middlemen, while the manufacturing stage in this processing trade generates the least added value.

Barter trade

Domestic companies exchange goods of **equal value** with foreign companies according to mutual agreements and estimates. This type of trade is adopted particularly by those economies that are not able to pay for imports in hard currencies or foreign exchanges. For example, to pay for industrial equipment from Russia in the 1960s, China exported a huge quantity of agricultural products to that country. Similarly, to pay for imports of various goods from China in the 1990s, Russia exported crude oil and military hardware to China.

Patterns of Trade in China

Early exports concentrated on agricultural products, petroleum, and raw materials. Exports in these categories amounted to over 80% and industrial goods less than 20%. The main place for foreign trade deals was the annual Guangzhou Trade Fair, which offered a rare opportunity for domestic and overseas traders to meet and negotiate. Under state control, those trade deals were handled by authorised state trade agencies, and Chinese companies at the Fair could offer limited variety of products and were subject to approval from state bureaux for deals made with foreign companies.

With the reforms and more liberal trade policies, exports in labour-intensive manufactured goods have grown rapidly. These include textiles, apparel, footwear, toys, and lately, electronics. In 2000, primary products took 10% of the total, while manufactured goods took 90%, among them machinery and electrical goods making up 44%. In 2002, primary and manufactured goods were 20% and 80% of the total volumes respectively. This is a complete reversal from the trade situation in the early 1980s.

The top five export categories are apparels, crude oil, textiles, household appliances, and steel. The top five import categories are equipment and technology, chemicals, fertilisers, crude oil, computers. The export categories illustrate the advantages China has in labour cost and mass production, while the import categories show the need to achieve higher productivity and to acquire advanced technology. For the category of crude oil, China has become a major oil importer of the world; however, its own oil production makes it possible to export crude oil for hard currencies. This may change very soon as a result of a severe shortage of oil for domestic use. PetroChina announced in November 2003 a reduction of the export of petrol for that month. Similar reduction or suspension of oil exports may happen more frequently in future.

Processing trade has been about 50% of total exports, and exports by foreign companies operating in China have reached about 50% of this processing trade.

Exports of electronics and high-tech goods have gradually increased. In 2000, hi-tech export was a record US$37 billion, 15% of the total export. In 2002, hi-tech export was US$67.8 billion, over 80% of which was made by foreign companies in China.

Imports of heavy, advanced and precision equipment and production lines have formed the bulk of the total volumes. To save time and money on indigenous R&D, many Chinese enterprises adopted the convenient approach of importing, especially for purchases of complete sets of manufacturing projects and heavy, advanced machine tools.

It is estimated that China spends over 1 trillion yuan (US$122 billion approximately) each year on equipment investment, and over 60% of this investment is spent on importing heavy equipment in key projects.

As a result of this import priority policy, heavy industries and machine tools industries in China are about two decades behind developed economies. Imported equipment takes 100% market share in fibre optical manufacturing, 95% in mobile communication, 80% in integrated circuits, 80% in petrol-chemicals, and 70% in textile equipment, motorcar, and computer-controlled machine tools.

With urgent demand for advanced technology and equipment, and with unsatisfactory supply of domestic alternatives, China will be seeking more imports of foreign equipment for a long period of time. This will open tremendous business opportunities for enterprises in the developed economies. If this demand is handled skilfully, the issue of trade deficits with China, which troubles many Western governments, will be relegated to a much less prominent position in their policies.

Top Trade Partners

By 2002 figures, China had her most trade deals with the following economies, ranked by the value of total bilateral trade.

1. Japan
2. USA
3. The EU
4. Hong Kong
5. ASEAN
6. Taiwan
7. South Korea
8. Russia
9. Australia
10. Canada

These ten trade partners make up 85% of China's total external trade in 2002.

If individual economies are counted, then among the EU countries, Germany took the 6th place, the UK the 8th place, France the 9th place, Holland the 10th place, Russia the 12th place, and Italy the 13th place. Among ASEAN countries, Singapore took the 7th place, Malaysia the 14th place, and Indonesia the 15th place. Hong Kong, Taiwan and South Korea are to take the 3rd, 4th and 5th places respectively, after a re-arrangement in ranking.

Top Ten Export Markets (2002)

1. USA
2. Hong Kong
3. Japan
4. The EU
5. ASEAN
6. South Korea
7. Taiwan
8. Australia
9. Canada
10. Russia

Top Ten Places of Exports to China (2002)

1. Japan
2. The EU
3. Taiwan
4. AEASN
5. South Korea
6. The US
7. Hong Kong
8. Russia
9. Australia
10. Canada

China has trade deficits with many of her major trade partners. The reasons for these deficits are not the size of the other economy, or how big the trade volume is, but some specific conditions in bilateral trade. For the trade between Taiwan and mainland China, it is a rather political situation in which mainland China opens much of its markets to imports from Taiwan, while Taiwan imposes many restrictions on goods from the mainland, even after the accession to the WTO by both parties. This is out of Taiwan's primary concern for the politically sensitive issue of reunification and the concern of the overwhelming economic power the mainland possesses. For trade with other economies, the issue is the demand on China's side for several types of imports, such as technology from Germany, crude oil and military hardware from Russia, timber and natural resources from Malaysia etc.

Bilateral Trade with Major Economies

Apart from general trade agreements and WTO rules, China has had more focused bilateral trade with major trading partners. In fact, this kind of bilateral trade took the centre stage, whether China was isolated or had begun normal stable trade with a few key economies. Only in the age of globalisation of the 1990s, did the central government realise the implications of multilateral trade arrangements and international rules.

China's Trade with the US

❑ Official trade began after the normalisation and formal treaties were signed in 1979, and trade growth has been over 18% every year since then;

❑ China is the US's fourth largest trade partner, and the US is China's second largest trade partner;

❑ In 2004, trade was estimated at US$169 billion, with exports totalling US$124 billion and imports US$45 billion;

❑ The US now buys more than one third of China's exports, a large portion of these exports being made by US companies in China.

❑ The US figures show that trade deficits with China are growing fast, overtaking deficits with Japan in 2003. The figures put the deficits for 2002 at over US$100 billion (see Figures 9.7 and 9.8).

The US is a big market for Chinese exports, incurring the cited trade deficits above, and large numbers of US companies have invested in China. This intertwined situation creates some problems in foreign trade between the two countries. On the one hand, huge trade deficits with China cause anxiety in the US, and conflicts with China have the potential to lead to trade wars and sanctions. On the other hand, American businesses in China have vested interests in maintaining good relations between the two countries. In particular, a large share of China's exports to the US market come from American companies operating in China. These companies therefore tend to mediate between the two governments and push for more stable and formalised trade relations.

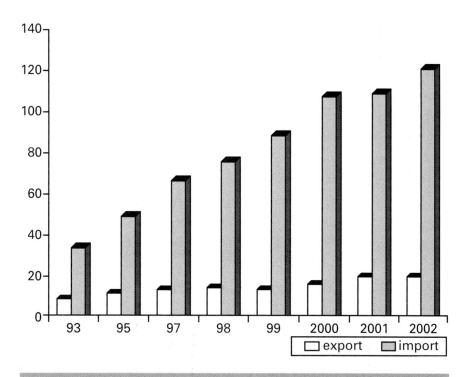

Figure 9.7   The US's trade with China (in billion US$)

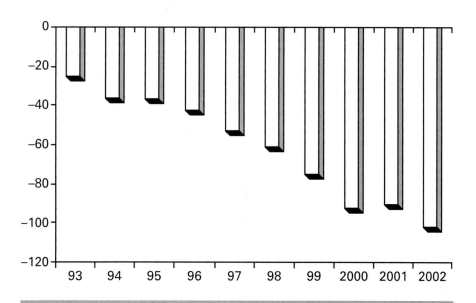

Figure 9.8   The US's trade with China (in billion US$)

Furthermore, a large part of exports to the US was through Hong Kong. The Chinese statisticians see this as exports to Hong Kong and do not include them in the bilateral trade with the US, but the US figures do. Thus, the Chinese figures on exports to the US is smaller than the US figures. The US sees any imported products with the label of "made in China" as direct imports from mainland China, and it does not see American products sold to China by other countries or regions as US exports to China. The pictures of the US trade deficit presented by the two countries are quite different, with huge gaps in trade figures. This has caused widespread confusion and frequently surfacing accusations in bilateral relations. There have been proposals in the US to revalue the yuan upwards or to splash high tariffs on Chinese imports, in order to contain the rising deficits. A more plausible approach would be to encourage more exports that meet the huge demand in the China market.

There are certain benefits to be gained from trade deficits endured by an economy. The existence of deficits implies that domestic residents have taken advantage of more imported goods and additional production capacity somewhere else. They are able to enjoy extra natural or human resources and capital outside the borders of their own country. This is suggested as one major benefit of free trade, and bearing trade deficits enables the US economy to do just that. Moreover, American consumers now have wider buying choices and need lower expenditures on necessities. By spending less on the same goods, the economy can have a slower CPI rise and subsequently cure the high inflation.

There is another way to view the alarming trade deficits the US has. Overseas investment and operations have long been a central strategy for many US multinationals. FDI by these companies in other economies and markets have accumulated huge assets and are generating stable, significant returns for these multinationals. Such overseas earnings flow back as real profits for US headquartered companies and thus for the economy as a whole. The total earnings by these multinationals and overseas companies more than offset the deficits the US consumers incur for their imported goods. Again, US multinationals utilise a variety of overseas resources and grab business opportunities in many other markets, while also making up for the overspending of their home economy.

The legal framework for China-US trade was the most favoured nation (MFN) status, which was included in an agreement signed in 1980. The US Congress debated every year on the issue of granting the

MFN to China and renewing the status. Under this framework, Chinese exports to the US enjoyed some preferential treatments, especially in tariff levels and quotas. For example, the US tariffs on imported carpets from China was 46%, but fell to 6% under preferential treatment.

Due to the trade volumes and importance of China trade, the MFN was in no real danger of being rejected. However, the annual MFN debate gave cause to many troubles in bilateral trade relations, and it was often under the influence of political and ideological forces within the US. This short-term arrangement was very fragile, giving American businesses in China little confidence in their operations and long-term commitments there. The US business sector and particularly those working in China had pushed for a permanent status for China, but this was only possible when China's WTO entry was secured. Following the US agreements with China on the WTO accession, the US Congress finally debated and passed a new law to give China permanent normal trading nation status and solved the problems caused by the MFN debate. The new law provides a long-term basis for China-US trade instead of the annual extension of trading rights.

Top US exports to China:	Top US imports from China:
Power generation equipment	Electrical machinery & equipment
Electrical machinery & equipment	Power generation equipment
Air & spacecraft	Toys & games
Medical equipment	Furniture
Plastics & articles	Footwear & parts
Oil seeds & oleaginous fruits	Apparel
Fertiliser	Leather & travel goods
Organic chemicals	Plastics & articles
Iron & Steel	Iron & steel
Raw hides & leathers	Medical instruments

The above columns indicate various market demands from one economy for products from the other and comparative advantages in production in each economy. In many categories, exports from the US clearly include high tech, high value-added goods, and those from China are products of general use. For example, the power generation equipment the US exports to China are hydraulic or thermal power stations (the US government forbade exporting nuclear power station or equipment to China until 2004), while those exported by Chinese companies are small power products for household uses. Similarly, the US exports sophisticated machine tools and manufacturing equipment to China, while Chinese exports to the US are small machine tools such as electrical chainsaws. This exchange pattern is also shown in other categories of exported goods from these two economies.

In addition to the overall concern of trade deficits with China, there are other specific concerns inherent in this bilateral trade.

Textiles exports to the US

China is a major supplier of textile products to the US, and the US domestic textile industry is shrinking fast. The US has reduced quotas for textile imports from China since 1980 and enforced control on the "country of origin" rule. The Commerce Department of the US government put further limits on certain categories of textiles from China in 2003.

Imports of agricultural products from the US

The products in this category have been a priority in most US negotiations with China, and the US government acted swiftly to promote American products and protect their farmers' interests. Any problem or delay in opening the market to such imports from the US causes a quick response from the US government. In one such case, when agricultural exports to China were halted due to unsatisfactory quality and new Chinese regulations on genetically modified foods from abroad, the US government issued statements to warn of the consequences of this delay. Agricultural exports to the China market have increased, especially after China's WTO accession. However, this is still a thorny issue, due mainly to the US's stand that is deeply influenced by domestic policies and the political clout of those farming counties.

Restrictions on export of advanced technology to China

An effective way to reduce trade deficits with China is for the US to sell more advanced technology and even military equipment to China. The US government has not given this option any serious consideration, and the strategic interests of the US make it unlikely for them to relax restrictions any time soon. Restrictions are imposed on advanced technology, supercomputers, precision machine tools, military use technology and many categories that may be interpreted by the US authorities as vital to their national interests. Taking these categories away, what the US is able to sell to China includes commercial airplanes, food and fruit, civilian use technology and equipment etc., many of which are neither extraordinarily competitive with the European and Japanese products, nor happily accepted by Chinese customers.

China's Trade with Japan

Japan is the number one trading partner of China, with trade volume of US$102 billion in 2002, and this figure reached US$130 billion in 2003. China is Japan's second biggest trade partner.

Japan has gained trade surpluses with China four years in a row, and benefited from large exports to China. Imports from Japan take the number one spot in China's total imports, and China is the second biggest export market for Japan, after the US. In 1990, exports to China took 2.14% of Japan's total exports, while in 2003, this share rose to 12.18%.

Trade with Japan has been in two parallel lines, with primary products exported to Japan, and Japanese manufactured goods (in particular electronics) exported to China.

With many Japanese and international companies investing in China, exports to Japan were recently changed to manufactured goods, and imports of equipment and machinery increased. Prominent Japanese corporations, from the late 1990s, began to move core operations and production bases to China, following international trends. Although this move caused domestic outcries of "hollowing out Japanese industries", Japanese corporations gain from manufacturing in China and exporting finished goods back to Japan.

❑ Long-term trade deficits in trade with Japan: From 1978 onwards, China has had only four years of trade surplus with Japan, and each time the surplus was an insignificant amount. In 2002, China had a trade deficit of US$5 billion with Japan.

❑ Trade barriers in Japan: There are high Japanese tariffs on particular Chinese goods, especially on primary and agricultural products. These are subject to stringent examinations at high technical and health standards. Primary products from China also often face quarantines.

❏ Trade conflicts emerged in certain categories when Chinese imports increased markedly. A decade of recession in Japan led to stronger protection of local farmers and industries against imports from China.

❏ Exports to China are primarily manufactured goods, to be sold to Chinese customers. Japanese corporations appear extremely conservative in introducing and transferring key technology and advanced equipment. They have a well-known reputation in the China market of not being keen on offering technology and know-how, but being eager to sell. A pointed example is the car industry. Japanese carmakers avoided setting up joint ventures or foreign-owned projects in China, since they reckoned the China market would only be big enough for imported cars, and would not be able to manufacture for domestic demand. While Japanese cars sell well, their production capacity and market shares are way behind German and American carmakers. It is until the beginning of the new millennium that Japanese carmakers made a reversal and rushed to invest in the China market. The experience and

Is Japan or the US the Number One Trading Partner of China?

This question seems redundant, since the lists presented above show that Japan is almost always taking the top spot. However, there are discrepancies in the figures. The Japanese figures show that they reached US$102 billion in 2002, giving them the top position in the list. Interestingly, the figures provided by the US government show that their trade deficit with China was already US$103 billion in the same year, and the total trade volumes were US$120 billion. Based on these figures, the US is clearly the leader in trade with China. These discrepancies occur because the list was composed by Chinese authorities, based on their customs statistics. The trade deficits the US had with China were estimated at US$42.7 billion in 2002, rather than US$103 billion as claimed by the US government. There are further reasons for these contradictory figures, which we have discussed before, including the issues of Hong Kong re-exports, processing trade, exports by US multinationals etc. These discrepancies and confusion about the top trade partner make it abundantly clear that trade issues are complex and that you need to look behind published figures.

hesitation of Japanese carmakers in China is a good example of making a strategic decision in entering a new market.

China's Trade with the EU Countries

Overall, China's total trade volume with the EU (15 countries) was US$86.7 billion in 2002.

The EU was the third biggest trade partner of China. After a dramatic expansion that added 10 new members and thus ten new economies to the EU in April 2004, the EU as a whole, technically, became the number one trading partner of China.

The EU is in second place for China's imports, and transfer of technology is nearly half of the total contracts signed with China.

The overall picture for the 1990s was described by some analysts as "fairly dismal", "taken at face value, the aggregate statistics ... appear to indicate that China-Europe trade and investment flows are relatively unimportant". The EU has been in a constant competition in many categories with two of China's major trading partners, North America and Japan, and the EU has its own internal squabbling among over two dozen members. Major EU economies thus developed their own trade ties with China and strategies for the China market.

Germany

Germany is China's biggest trade partner in the EU, making one-third of the total trade volumes and taking sixth place in the overall list of trade partners. In 2001, the trade volume was US$23.5 billion, with Chinese exports of 9.76 billion and Chinese imports of 13.7 billion. Germany is the second EU country with the largest FDI in China. In 2001, signed contracts of technology transfer with Germany accounted for 20% of all the contracts.

Since Germany has a neutral position in world politics, a good relationship with China, and its industries and advanced technology are highly respected in China, Germany is a big provider of technology to China, especially industrial technology. When China-US relationship becomes strained for various reasons, China could seek alternatives from Germany and get similar technology for her own enterprises. Thus, technology transfers from Germany have been in large numbers and growing. In 2003, Germany sold US$6.8 billion worth of machine tools and other equipment to China.

France

Trade between China and France has been steady without many fluctuations, but also shows no sign of huge potential to expand dramatically. The increase in trade volumes is modest, and, in comparison, the total is lower than those of other major European economies. Trade between China and France is marked by two issues listed below.

❑ Marred by political issues:

Weapons sales to Taiwan in the late 1980s, including submarines and Mirage jet fighters, brought the mutual relationship down to the lowest point. China, in retaliation, suspended many business negotiations and cancelled contracts with France, for example, the bidding for subway projects in Guangzhou. Trade with China dropped between 1990 and 1992. China also downgraded diplomatic relations with France, closing the French general-consulate in Guangzhou. This messy situation was reversed only after France promised never to sell weapons to Taiwan in the future.

❑ Benefits from China-US trade and political disputes:

In trade disputes between China and the US from the mid-1990s onwards, France has been in an advantageous position, along with Germany, to receive benefits in trade with China. China could turn to France to buy Airbus airplanes, while cancelling orders of Boeing airplanes from the US as an instant measure of retaliation. China could also show to the US that they do not entirely rely on trade with the US and on technology transfer, so as to increase their bargaining power in negotiations.

The major French exports to China are airplanes and nuclear power plants. Airbus deals take about one third of total trade volumes between the two countries, making the Airbus fleet on a par with Boeing among Chinese airlines. French industrial technology transfers and equipment take a major share in trade, in particular the nuclear power station at Da Ya Bay of Guangdong, which is the biggest in China. More stations will be built by French companies in other regions. Recently, French retail chains and environmental protection industries are gaining market shares in China.

The United Kingdom

The UK is among the first EU countries to recognise China after 1949, and is now the number one country in that bloc with the largest FDI in China. Like France, the UK faces no serious problems in trade with China, other than the political issue of Hong Kong's return to China.

Trade between the two countries was hampered by the political atmosphere and tough negotiations on Hong Kong's return to China in the final years of British rule.

From the early 1990s, the Hong Kong issue has been one intruding part of trade relations between China and the UK. British companies could still operate normally in China, but in the final years of British rule in Hong Kong, the push for democratisation and other last-minute changes led to the deterioration of their relationship and swift reactions from China. Certain forms of "sanctions" were put into place to discourage British companies doing business in China, including exclusion of bidding projects, reduction in imports, cancellation of orders etc. The worsened trade relations forced British Prime Minister Mr. John Major to visit China in 1997 for conciliation.

Improvements and normalised trade relations ensued after the handover, and trade between the two countries now continues without the hazards caused by the Hong Kong issue.

For trade between the EU and China, two issues are prominent, with the potential to block the flow of goods in these two huge markets:

❑   Anti-dumping: The EU has clear rules on import dumping activities, and because the EU functions as a collective group, any member can ask the EU council and the trade commission to start an investigation of and take action on Chinese imports. The EU lawsuits and dumping ruling have cost Chinese exporters over US$3 billion in past years, in the forms of lost business opportunities and blocked market entry. Even if the EU did not object to China's WTO accession, anti-dumping laws are frequently used to check imports from China. For example, Chinese TV manufacturers received permission in 2003 to re-enter the EU market after being under strict restrictions in the previous 15 years.

❑   High levels of technical and environmental standards: The EU has set up high standards of technical requirements, safety requirements and particularly for environmental protection. The EU standards are in many cases tougher than the US ones, and environmental requirements in emissions, residuals, and anything related to human conditions are very high for most Chinese companies and their exported products. Chinese goods can easily be legally excluded from the market on the basis of violation of the EU regulations in these respects.

On the other hand, the EU has a less strict policy on exports of technology and equipment to China, and on FDI in China.

As an indication of the effect and distribution of foreign trade on China's domestic economy, the performance by major regional economies is listed below.

Top ten trading regions of mainland China (in millions of US$, 2002):

1. Guangdong: 221,105
2. Shenzhen: 87,219
3. Shanghai: 72,640
4. Jiangsu: 70,297
5. Beijing: 52,508
6. Zhejiang: 41,961
    Ningbo: 12,263
7. Shandong: 33,935
    Qingdao: 13,721
8. Fujian: 28,399
    Xiamen: 15,183
9. Tianjin: 22,754
10. Liaoning: 21,738
    Dalian: 14,600

It is clear that the top performers are the open zones and coastal cities, those regions with large shares of FDI and manufacturing bases, and those with smaller shares of state enterprises. It is also clear that a number of cities implemented open policies to encourage trade and thus their performance could match those by the whole province.

Customs and Taxes

The open door policy has given tremendous boosts to China's foreign trade and exports. Specialised zones play a crucial role in trade, and in tax and customs areas, these zones enjoy favourable treatments. It is essential for overseas investors and traders to have some knowledge of Chinese customs requirements and operations in general.

Trade Zones in China

❑ Special economic zones and open coastal cities: They are listed in Part II, Chapter 4.

❑ Open Yangtze River cities: Wuhan, Chongqing, Chengdu, Yueyang, Jiujiang, Wuhu, Hefei, Nanchang, and Changsha.

❑ Export processing zone: This is a designated area, within which the government builds infrastructure and facilities, and provides tax and tariff free measures to encourage foreign companies to invest, manufacture in the zone and export finished goods to overseas markets.

   Export processing zones in China (2000) are: Dalian, Tianjin, Beijing, Yantai, Weihai, Kunshan, Suzhou, Shanghai, Hangzhou, Xiamen, Shenzhen, Guangzhou, Wuhan, Chengdu, and Huichun.

   All these national-level zones and proposed zones in future need approvals from the central government. Local governments could set up their own zones, with much less appeal to foreign investors. Foreign companies in these zones enjoy tariff waivers or reductions, tax waivers, minimum foreign exchange controls and legal investment protection etc., while being subject to government regulations on investment project selection, target markets (domestic or overseas), local employment, wages and benefits.

❑ Bonded area: Also called a bonded warehouse, this is the area set up or permitted by the Customs, within which foreign imported goods can be stored for a period of time without being subject to customs declaration or import tariffs. These goods are subject to tariffs if they are later moved into domestic markets. Goods for general import purposes are not allowed to enter bonded areas. A bonded area serves as a point for transhipment and provides certain benefits for importers. For example, car importers can store their import cars at the Tianjin bonded area, wait for rises in car prices in the China market, and then sell to Chinese car buyers. The same strategies are also practised by crude oil and raw materials traders. A new function of a bonded area is for enterprises to set up factories and undertake processing trade for overseas markets. Bonded areas with manufacturing facilities are then similar to export processing zones. The biggest bonded area with favourable conditions in China is the Waigaoqiao bonded area in Pudong, Shanghai.

Customs Duties or Tariffs

They are taxes charged by state customs on imported and exported goods and collected from trading companies.

❑ Import duties: These are charged on importers for foreign goods imported to the country. The purposes of import duties are to limit flows of imported goods, to protect domestic markets and to raise the competitiveness of domestically made goods.

❑ Export duties: These are charged on exporters for their goods being exported to foreign countries. Since export duties reduce the competitiveness of locally made goods in international markets, most countries make ways for export duties to be minimised or eliminated. Export rebate is just one form of this reduction in export duties. Such duties are still charged by governments for the purposes of protecting domestic environment and natural resources, or of raising state revenues.

❑ Protective tariffs: These are charged on imports, for the purpose of protecting domestic industries and markets. The rates of protective tariffs are unusually high on imports in order to achieve the intended goals. Protective tariffs are adopted by developed economies to counter cheap imports into domestic markets, and by developing economies to foster their infant industries.

❑ Retaliatory tariff: These are charged at high rates on imports from the country that practices discriminatory treatments to goods exported from this country. When the opposite side withdraws their discriminatory practice, retaliatory tariffs are accordingly cancelled. One such example of retaliatory tariff is the average tariff of 27.5% proposed by some US senators and congressmen to be imposed on Chinese imports if the RMB is not revalued upwards or floated.

The Chinese Customs

As a country with a long history and frequent contact with neighbouring and foreign traders, China has had a complete system of customs and tariff collections. An obvious example of this system in pre-modern times was the Guangzhou customs, which contributed a significant part of revenues to the imperial Qing governments (1644-1911), and whose implementation of blockades to opium trade conducted by Western merchants led to the infamous Opium War in 1841. After trade with Western countries was allowed and trading ports were forced to open, the customs of the Chinese governments and the collection of tariffs were in the hands of foreign powers. An Irish civil servant, Sir Robert Hart, was in charge of the imperial customs and carried the title of Inspector General from 1861 till his retirement in 1908. Hart expanded the customs services across the country and collected customs duties to meet the demand of the imperial court on many new modernisation projects. He introduced Western trade and customs systems to China and ran the organisation under his charge as an efficient civil service of the imperial government.

In the following decades, the Republican governments continued to rely on customs duties to pay for many budgetary expenditures and wars. The People's Republic, from 1949, was under an international embargo and blockade led by the US, and normal foreign trade and customs duties shrank rapidly. From the 1980s, reforms in China revitalised trade and made it necessary to re-establish customs and tariffs regimes. The State Administration of Customs was set up under the State Council in 1980, taking direct charge of all lower levels of customs across the country.

The customs law stipulates that the importer should make declarations to the customs within 14 days of the carrier's arrival date, and should make the tariff payment within 7 days after the date the customs issues tariff payment notice. The customs imposes a daily surcharge of 1‰ on overdue payments.

Non-tariff Trade Barriers

Non-tariff trade barriers are more selective, direct and discriminatory than general tariffs, and they are more effective in curbing floods of imports. They can come in different forms.

Import Quotas

These are amounts or volumes of certain imports set by the government for a period of time (a year), over which a ban on imports is initiated, or a retaliatory tariff is imposed thereafter. The overall purpose is to limit the scale of imports.

Import quotas are divided into two categories: global quotas and national quotas. Global quotas are the maximum amount or volume allowed for certain imports, and all countries could export until the quotas are reached. National quotas are defined specifically for imports from one economy, and this economy cannot export above the quotas and cannot use quotas allocated to other economies.

China imposes import quotas on certain bulk goods. The two categories are electrical goods and machinery (see Table 9.3), and general goods.

The final decision on import quotas and allocating of quotas is exclusively in the hands of the State Economic Commission, the State Development Commission and the Ministry of Commerce. Relevant departments in local governments are to assist in managing and distributing quotas in their regions, without any say in the process of deciding on quotas.

"Voluntary" Export Quotas

Export quotas are to prevent excessive export of precious natural resources or specialised goods. They also serve the purpose of abiding

Table 9.3 Quotas for electrical goods and machinery in 2002	
Motorcar and key components	US$7.9 billion
Motorbikes and key components	US$380 million
Car cranes and chassis	US$120 million
Cameras	US$133 million
Watches	US$482 million

by international trade agreements between exporting and importing economies. If an importing economy considers the exports from one particular economy excessive, trade disputes and wars may follow. To prevent such disputes, export quotas are agreed upon. Many export quotas take the form of "voluntary" controls on the part of the exporting economy, under pressure from the importing economy or from the fear of losing export markets completely. For example, Japan had undertaken "voluntary" export quotas on its cars to the US, and China also signed agreements with the Common Market to "voluntarily" limit the export of paint brushes to 22 million pieces a year in 1987.

Import Licence or Permit

These are certificates issued by state authorities to importers, without which foreign made goods cannot enter domestic markets.

In China, import quotas are to deal with imports with national quantity limits, as shown in Table 9.3, and import licences are to deal with certain categories of imports, without quantity limits.

Organisations in the central government, under the State Council and other state commissions, apply for import licences at the Ministry of Commerce. Organisations at the provincial level apply for import licences at provincial bureaux of commerce. Organisations in the 14 coastal open cities apply for import licences at the representative offices of the Ministry of Commerce in their cities.

In 1992, state authorities handled 53 categories of goods subject to import licences. In 1997, there were 34 categories, and in 2003, there were 12 categories.

Foreign Exchange Controls

This type of non-tariff trade barrier has been discussed in previous sections.

State Monopoly of Foreign Trade

This refers to bulk and specific types of goods, such as alcohol, tobacco, agricultural products and military hardware. In a reform towards a market economy, China's state monopoly has been disappearing fast in recent decades and civilian goods are no longer subject to such monopolies.

Government Procurement

Required by law, governments at all levels must purchase domestically made goods for their regular procurements. Government organisations and institutions are often big buyers of a variety of goods, such as office equipment, and buying orders from governments mean ongoing business for many manufacturers and companies. For example, Microsoft has been involved in a long-running battle in China to win contracts from municipal governments of major cities; but the company lost opportunities in the past in Shanghai and Beijing to local Chinese software companies.

In addition to non-tariff barriers, the state can also influence foreign trade by undertaking policies that encourage more exports. Such policies include:

Export credit

Banks provide loans to domestic exporters or foreign importers, or the state provides guarantees to such loans for export businesses. These types of credit are common in developed and developing countries.

Export subsidies

The government provides financial subsidies directly to exporters of certain types of exports. The government also uses special funds to compensate losses incurred during competition for more export markets. Other indirect forms of export subsidies are financial assistance provided by the government, such as tax waivers and allowances. Export rebate is common in developing countries, and its application in China is to be discussed in the following portion.

Tariff Rates in China

From the early reform years, general levels of tariffs in China have been consistently lowered (see Figure 9.9 and Table 9.4). They were more drastically reduced in the late 1990s, in line with China's accession to the WTO.

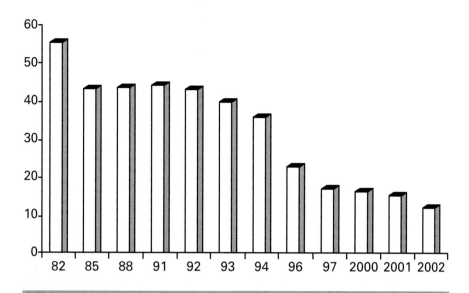

Figure 9.9   Average statutory import tariff rates

These nominal rates are perhaps high, as required by official regulations, but the real tariff rates are calculated by dividing the total import value with the total revenues from tariffs collected. The real tariff levels are much lower, for example, from 1991 to 1995, the levels were 9.2%, 8%, 6.6%, 4.9%, and 4.7% for each year respectively. The reasons behind this gap are that in the export processing trade, imported materials need not be declared or taxed, and the central and local governments offered considerable tariff waivers to foreign companies to attract investment, and inevitably, large scale smuggling.

In general, revenues from tariffs are in decline, especially from the years of lowering tariffs. In 2001, revenues from tariffs took a mere 5.7% in total government tax incomes. In contrast, the same revenue source contributed 38% to government incomes in 1930.

General Procedures of Customs Clearance

❑   Before the goods arrive: Apply for an import licence or permit from relevant authorities. For those companies without import/

Table 9.4   Average tariff rates

1982	1985	1988	1991	1992	1993	1994	1996	1997	2000	2001	2002
55.6	43.3	43.7	44.1	43.2	39.9	35.9	23	17	16.4	15.3	12

export rights, find an authorised trade agency to handle the procedures on your behalf.

❑ Customs clearance: People are to make declarations with proper forms, certificates, import licences and other paperwork. At various busy border customs, such as at the Hong Kong-Shenzhen borders, declarations can be done electronically. Electronic forms are recognised and accepted by the Chinese customs.

❑ Inspection: Inspection is carried out by customs officers on imported goods.

❑ Tariff payment: The importer pays tariffs required at the customs, after receiving the form of payment from them. Payment is made in RMB.

❑ Certification and pass through: The customs reaffirms the procedures and stamps on forms. The importer can then pick up their goods.

For those importing and exporting companies without regular customs clearance staff, they can hire authorised professional clearance agencies to handle the procedures.

There are also customs inspections on imported goods in the areas of quality, weight, safety, sanitation, disinfection etc. These inspections are carried out by agents from the State General Administration of Quality, Supervision, Inspection and Quarantine at the borders.

❑ Customs clearance for foreign companies investing in China: They should fill the clearance forms specifically designed for them and provide certificates and licences etc. Other procedures are similar to those applied to Chinese companies.

From 1 April 1996, such newly approved companies must pay tariffs at statutory levels on imported equipment and raw materials, even if the value of these purchases is within the amount of their total investment in China. Previously, such purchases were considered part of their investment and were not subject to statutory tariffs.

These companies are exempt from export duties if they export locally produced goods, except for those goods prohibited by national regulations from being exported.

From 1 January 1995, these companies no longer enjoy favourable tariff treatments if they import office equipment and stationery. They are encouraged to buy domestically made cars and enjoy favourable tariff treatment. All imported cars and motorbikes are subject to statutory tariffs.

Export Rebates

Export rebates are commonly adopted by exporting economies to prevent double taxation on exported goods, so as to raise the competitiveness of their manufactured goods in the international market. The government waives **value-added tax (VAT) and consumption tax** on such goods and allows taxation departments to rebate equivalent sums to exporting companies after exports are delivered.

China began to test export rebate measures in 1985 and, during the financial reforms of 1994, the government adopted an indirect tax system on the basis of VAT and implemented policies of "rebating full taxed amounts", making exported goods bear zero tax. The top rebate rate is 17%; the lowest is 5%. The government modifies rebate rates in response to changes in the markets and the economy. During the Asian financial crisis, the government upheld the official RMB exchange rate, while raising rebate rates from 9.3% to 15% for the purpose of promoting exports.

Export rebates cover domestic tax categories of **VAT** and **consumption tax**. The range of VAT rebates covers goods exported by domestic enterprises or by those trading companies on behalf of domestic companies; goods purchased in China and then exported by foreign-invested companies or through their trading agencies; goods manufactured and exported by foreign-invested companies established after 1 January 1994 and with trading rights, or through their trading agencies.

The range of consumption tax rebates covers exported goods purchased by local companies that have trading rights and have paid consumption tax at the time of purchase, and consumer goods exported by foreign companies on behalf of other trading companies.

From 1999, all foreign-invested companies in China have rights to enjoy rebates on their exports, and this move puts them in the same category of enterprises covered by export rebate policies.

Procedures for Export Rebates

After clearing customs for exported goods, companies fill in the application form for export rebates, provide certificates including special VAT invoices, detailed logs of exported goods, clearance forms for exported goods, and receipt of foreign exchange payment for exported goods etc.

The customs then certifies the application, and local trade and economic commissions stamp on the application. The application and related documents are then transferred to certain sections of taxation departments that handle rebates and authorise money transfers to exporting companies.

Issues of Concern in Export Rebates

1. The procedures take a long time to complete, and the forms and documents required are too complicated in practice. Exporters need to prove their goods cleared the Customs before lodging claims. Average rebate time is over a year, and a large number of exporting enterprises receive rebates within three years.

2. The funds for rebates come from the central treasury and this causes a heavy burden on government budgets. The central government factors export rebates in its annual budget, but this is far below the claimed amount. The current deficit is about 300 billion yuan in unpaid rebates.

3. Business frauds abound in cheating rebates. Companies involved could claim large amounts of rebates on goods not exported, and forged invoices are widely used to support such fraudulent claims. Export rebate frauds are a major type of financial crime and prevalent in southern China where many trading companies operate.

4. Export rebates have also led exporting companies to lower prices to their bottom line or even at cost, then to rely on rebates as company earnings. Even if they suffer losses in production and export, they can legally claim 15-17% in tax rebates and make overall profits. This scheme has provided enormous incentives for trading companies to export cheap and in large quantities, thus subsidising consumers in foreign markets at the expense of local industries. The government is indirectly involved in this subsidy

by paying out rebates. Rapidly growing exports also cause conflicts with developed economies, and rebates in general clash with China's WTO obligations to reduce and eventually eliminate export subsidies.

New Initiatives on Export Rebates

On 13 October 2003, the State Council issued new regulations on export rebates. These regulations became effective from 1 January 2004. They include:

❑ Lower rebate rates: These on average are 3% lower for exported goods, and rebates on exported natural resources are annulled. The new rebate rates are: 5%, 8%, 11%, 13%, 15% and 17%;

❑ Increase funding in the state budget for rebate payments: In 2004, the central government paid 420 billion yuan for this purpose. Among these budget allocations, 200 billion yuan was earmarked for paying off all tax rebates accumulated in previous years.

❑ Share rebate burdens with local governments: A 75:25 ratio between the central government and provincial governments was fixed;

❑ Strike hard on export rebate frauds.

The long-term goal is to eliminate export rebates completely and revamp export industries.

This chapter deals with trade-related issues of import/export, foreign exchange and customs. Since the opening is one of the two wheels which have driven China's economic growth, the export-oriented strategy has, by and large, paid off, creating increased national wealth and mirroring past success stories of some East Asian economies. It can be said that reforms in trade-related areas have been most effective and comprehensive, and these received a further boost from China's WTO accession early this century. With a few exceptions such as the RMB's exchange rate, changes in trade-related areas have maintained momentum and move the economy towards meeting international standards, as obliged by WTO agreements. However, the deeper the Chinese economy is integrated into the international trade system, the more conflicts and problems emerge, and issues such as non-tariff trade barriers require the involvement of international institutions.

Key Concepts

Export-oriented policies and the East Asian model of economic development

High dependence on trade

China's WTO obligations and relaxation of trade regulations

CEPA

Foreign exchange controls and FDI

Trade terms (FOB/CIF)

China-US trade patterns and balances

Export processing zones and bonded areas

Non-tariff trade barriers

Customs clearance

Export rebates regime

Discussion Questions

1. Describe the causes for the rapid growth of foreign trade in China.

2. Explain foreign firms' need to conduct import and export in China and their shares in trade.

3. What benefits or problems do you think are caused by the Chinese economy's high reliance on foreign trade?

4. Identify those WTO rules that are closely linked with foreign investment in China, and describe how the application of WTO rules would benefit China's foreign trade.

5. Describe the key contents of CEPA; choose a particular Hong Kong industry and make a brief summary of the expected benefits or otherwise that CEPA would bring to that industry.

6. For FDI in China, which issues are related to foreign exchange management?

7. What are your predictions of RMB convertibility in the near future (considering the supply and demand of foreign currencies and the likelihood of state controls being relaxed)?

8. What are your predictions on the appreciation or depreciation of the RMB against US$ (considering economic strength, trade deficits, alternative foreign currencies for transactions and reserves)?

9. Describe the trade patterns and top items of import/export in China, and explain the comparative advantages the major trading countries have. In other words, explain the reasons certain goods are exported to China and imported from China.

10. Share your views on trade deficits of various countries. Do you think these deficits are reasonable, acceptable and sustainable, and if not, what do you think would work to balance trade deficits?

11. Explain why governments encourage trade companies to adopt FOB terms for imports and CIF terms for exports.

12. Explain the major forms of non-tariff trade barriers and devise ways to enter a market with such barriers.

13. Explain the export rebate system and its application, and analyse its impact on foreign trade, especially on exports.
14. Explain the differences in customs clearance between a domestic enterprise and an enterprise in an export processing/bonded zone.

Related Readings

Cass, Deborah, Williams, Brett and Barker, George, eds., *China and the World Trading System: Entering the New Millennium*, Cambridge, Cambridge University Press, 2003.

Dixon, John E., *Entering the Chinese Market: the Risks and Discounted Rewards*, Westport, Connecticut, Quorum, 1998.

Enright, M. J., Scott, E.E. and Dodwell, D., *The Hong Kong Advantage*, Hong Kong, Oxford University Press, 1997.

Fung, K.C., *Trade and Investment: Mainland China, Hong Kong and Taiwan*, Hong Kong, City University of Hong Kong Press, 1997.

Kelly, Land and Yadong Luo, eds., *China 2000: Emerging Business Issues*, Thousand Oaks, California, Sage Publications, 1999.

Lardy, N.R., *China's Unfinished Economic Revolution*, Washington, D.C., Brookings Institution Press, 1998.

Lardy, N.R., *Integrating China into the Global Economy*, Washington, D.C., Brookings Institution Press, 2002.

Li, F., and Li, J., *Foreign Investment in China*, New York, St. Martin's Press, 1999.

Overholt, W., *China: the Next Economic Superpower*, London, Weidenfeld & Nicholson, 1993.

Rosen, D.L., *Behind the Open Door: Foreign Enterprises in the Chinese Marketplace*, Washington, D.C., Institute for International Economics, 1999.

Strange, Roger, Slater, Jim and Wang, Limin ,eds., *Trade and Investment in China: the European Experience*, London, Routledge, 1998.

Yan, Yanni, *International Joint Ventures in China: Ownership, Control and Performance*, London, Macmillan Press, 2000.

10

Government Functions, Leadership and Political Balances

This chapter covers issues of efficiency in government administration and leadership. The Chinese economy is moving forward under policy control and is influenced heavily by administrative and political forces. Uncertainties in FDI and prospects of future economic growth are all related to the nature of and changes in this political structure. Whether foreign observers foresee a coming crisis or viable development, they tend to view the quality of the administration and that of the leadership as major indicators. These issues thus have high relevance to the business environment and to investment decisions of foreign enterprises. The appeal of a potential growth market may just be offset by a hidden crisis and chance of mismanagement. Apart from the sensitive issue of parliamentary democracy, political stability and administrative efficiency are key criteria in investment decisions.

In addition to pressures from outside, China has long been plagued by imbalances between the central and regional authorities. This had been a recurring issue long before Western impact was cast on modern China, and a choice between a centralised or a federal structure has repeatedly troubled Chinese leaderships. As conflicts grow among various interest groups, the Chinese government needs masterful skills and intelligence to solve these challenging problems.

As briefly touched upon previously, political reforms in China have been in a less dramatic fashion under the guideline of gradualism. Reforms also touched more upon institutions and administration. This chapter will provide more details on related issues and deep-rooted problems in political development, and estimate potential risks and prospects.

Relations between the Central and Regional Governments

A key part of economic reforms is a decentralisation of authority. This has boosted local initiatives and growth in regions with favourable conditions. The fundamental issue in administration, however, remains. It is about how the central government effectively implements its national policies, without stifling regions' desire to flourish. It is a matter of loosening or tightening central controls. For a country the size of China, this is not a trivial issue to deal with. Chinese emperors failed in regard to handling the relation. Although many would blame recurring social upheavals on the iron fist control of the imperial state, numerous eras of disintegration have created crises of similar magnitudes.

China remains an authoritarian state in the sense that there is only one political party in power and no other political forces could possibly be seen as viable contenders. At present, an alternative ruling force is even more unlikely, given the growing economic might and sense of nationalism. Although, to many Westerners, stability sounds like an odd notion in China's reforms (since reform implies changes made to a stable status or equilibrium), it is a critical issue not only to Party and government leaders but to millions of Chinese who have enjoyed this rare period of uninterrupted progress in the history of modern China. The question is then how to adjust and fine tune the relations between the central and regional governments, without igniting an explosion of deep conflicts which would cause irreparable damage to stability.

China has been, is and will remain a centralised state. In the foreseeable future, power centralisation is not an option, but a necessity. The nation building process of China was sudden and brief under extreme pressures from external powers, Western and Japanese; as such, there were no similar gradual stages of nation states as in modern

Western Europe. This vast land has been held together by one authority, whether imperial or political. Western scholars observe some occasions of declared "independence" by provincial authorities during the dying days of the Qing dynasty (1644-1911) and explored the possibility of this scenario replaying in China in the 21st century. That "independence" proved to be a convenient tool for local groups to emerge, and they subsequently worked towards a new stage of national unification. Under the current established national sovereignty, regional independence is out of the question, even when border regions such as Tibet are concerned.

As a federal system and independent separate states are excluded as plausible options in the foreseeable future, the question regarding the direction of China's political development returns again to the relations between the central and regional governments.

In a centralised country like China, there are government apparatus from the central level, down to provincial, regional (city), county, and town. Local governments are the extension of the central government, and their legitimacy comes from the orders of the latter. As set out in the Constitution, these regional governments, provincial or county, are simply outposts for officials assigned and directed by the central government, and their roles are basically agents or inspectors on behalf of the central government. There is a single command chain and one-way control. The central government can arrange local jurisdictions, grant or take away authority, and instruct programmes of the central government to be implemented. This situation is reinforced by the Party structure, which emphasises the same principle in administration. The central government holds the authority to appoint and remove provincial leaders. Local affairs below provincial level are handled by provincial authorities, on behalf of and following instructions from the central government. There were times when a mega-regional Party office stood between a number of provinces and Beijing. The central government dealt with these Party offices directly and controlled the provinces indirectly. This practice proved potentially risky, since a mega-regional Party office administered land areas larger than a number of medium sized European countries combined and enjoyed enormous political and economic clout. This threat to the central authority was removed by the Cultural Revolution, and from then on, individual provinces have been directly responsible to the central government.

On another front, in recent years, regional governments immediately below the provincial levels have been changed in name to cities, having authority over surrounding urban districts and rural counties. This is in line with China's urbanisation and structural changes, where the bulk of rural population are to be gradually merged into urban population.

Under this set of central-regional relations, the central government is in charge of macroeconomic management, foreign affairs, national defence, customs, post and communications etc. Responsibilities for education, science and technology, culture, health, sports, environmental protection, urban development, finance, civil affairs, ethnic affairs, justice, supervision, population planning, are shared between central and local governments. The major means of administration are through "rule by law" and executive orders. National laws and executive orders from the State Council overrule those from local governments, and the central government demands full compatibility of local rules to the national rules.

In these relations, there seems to be no room for local manoeuvring or initiatives. In reality, local authorities hold more power than they do on paper. An important factor is that they are in a local environment and have to respond to local conditions and demands. There is room for local authorities to waver between instructions from Beijing and local concerns. Priorities shift at times according to situations and changes. Another key factor is the trend of decentralisation since the reforms began. Throughout the 1980s, the central government delegated numerous authorities to provincial governments. That complemented the process to dismantle the planned economy and the move towards a market economy. This trend proved more beneficial to regional authorities than to the central government, and the latter soon found out about the tyranny of threats from this practice during early stages of reforms.

Two Phases in the Central-regional Relations

From the viewpoint of the 21st century, we can summarise the central-regional relations in China as having passed two major phases. The **first** phase is of decentralisation, which allowed room for early regional development and has left visible marks in the political and economic life of today. The most significant impact came from the reforms to the taxation system and fiscal policies. Under the guidelines of decentralisation, a number of regional authorities were granted the rights for their own budgets and financial management. In 1979, Guangdong and Fujian provinces in the south obtained permission to experiment with a financial responsibility scheme, similar in form to the rural household responsibility system. The scheme included measures to "draw up set figures of revenues and expenditures, hand in set quotas of revenues to the central coffers, and fix the quotas for five years". Negotiations proceeded between the parties involving terms and numbers. A base figure was set as the minimum financial obligation these provinces have to bear. From the central government's point of view, its tight budget status would improve with guaranteed revenues from local governments. From these provincial governments' point of view, they would benefit from the extra revenues they could collect above the quotas, if they adopted more aggressive reform policies in their territories. This trial scheme was adopted nationwide from 1985. Guangdong and Fujian provinces continued to operate the scheme, and they succeeded in enlarging their own coffers many times over the set quotas of revenues delivered to the central government.

Along with a series of opening policies in coastal regions, this quota scheme gave provincial and regional governments tremendous incentives and sources of revenues to develop their own economies. Southern coastal provinces became less willing to obey instructions from Beijing. Foreign observers frequently talked about several *de facto* "kingdoms" and a disintegration of territories of the early 1990s. The hot spots were identified as Guangdong and Fujian, the latter being close to Taiwan in economic terms. The central government lacked sufficient financial means to counter this tendency, relying on revenues from local governments while spending more on increasing budget outlays. The ratio of government revenues to total GDP dropped from 31.2% in 1978 to 11.8% in 1994; and in 1993, total local revenues were more than double the revenues the central government collected. Budget deficits became a regular feature of the central government from 1979 to 1992, with the only exception of 1985. The budget deficit in 1994 was over 63.8 billion yuan. Furthermore, this quota scheme created problems of regional disparity and uneven financial burdens. Guangdong province achieved first position in GDP output in 1992, while its revenue quota to the central government was 300 million yuan, being one-eightieth that of Shanghai, which was ninth in GDP output. Quota negotiations often involved hard bargaining, favours and special considerations, causing headaches to the central government.

This situation made the central government a less viable provider of nationwide public social welfare. A strong need grew for the central government to achieve a right balance between decentralisation, which played a key role in stimulating the economy, and the designated functions of a national government. In developed economies, a financially weak federal government is not a preferred option. In fact, it is often the case that federal governments hold the vital financial resources and distribute them to regional authorities according to their own schedules. In Australia, for example, the federal government in Canberra collects the lion's share of tax revenues and allocates funds in its budget. The amount of funds one state can receive is decided at the annual conference of the Prime Minister and state Premiers, and each state vies for the best deal for its own interests and population. The federal government clearly takes a commanding position in this distribution process and is not worried at all by threats from certain powerful regions. The financial reliance of states on the federal treasury is evident, not the other way round.

After years of decentralisation and suffering from lack of financial means, it was apparent to everyone that decentralised structures created a financially weak central government and a growing imbalance between coastal open regions and less developed inland regions. From the early 1990s, the central government made a crucial policy turn, moving into the second phase of changes in central-regional relations.

The **second** phase was marked by an effort from the central government to recoup revenue losses and regain control. The central government devised and implemented a new dual taxation system, or tax sharing, in 1994 under which the revenues for the central government and those for local governments were redefined and fixed. The central government maintains the right to collect most taxes and takes approximately 70% of the total taxes in value. Through transfer payments, under which the central government allocates certain portions of tax revenues back to local governments to fund investment projects, the central government again holds the key to financial resources and sets itself in a commanding position above any regional authorities. To carry out the tasks, tax bureaux across the country were reorganised into two lines—state taxation offices and local taxation offices. These offices were responsible for collecting different types of taxes and handing them into different coffers. Despite early sluggish actions by local authorities, due to their overall consideration of local revenues, state taxes collected increased dramatically, reaching 1.41 trillion yuan in 2003, well over local taxes of 630.3 billion yuan.

The second phase proved not to be a complete re-centralisation. It only increased the financial capability of the central government in handling nationwide problems. A number of provinces, especially the southern provinces, showed early resistance to this taxation reform, since it meant curtailing their own financial resources. To compensate this loss, the central government made promises of further benefits, in the forms of retention of certain categories of collected revenues and allocating sufficient funds when possible for local needs.

This change in the taxation system provided much needed and stable revenues to the central government for its macroeconomic management. From then on, the central government did not need to engage itself in one-on-one negotiation with provinces, and a systematic process of taxation was in place. The quota and responsibility system was terminated. Moreover, the central government could now collect increasing amounts of taxes when there was steady economic growth.

Taxes and Budgets

The taxation system of China today has been in operation since the crucial revisions in 1994. The central government collects major categories of taxes, which include tariff, consumption tax, corporate income tax from central government-owned enterprises, income tax from local banks and foreign banks and other financial institutions, income tax from rail road companies, banks headquarters, insurance company headquarters, and tax on profits from central government enterprises.

Local governments receive revenues from a dozen of other minor taxes, which include business tax, income tax from local enterprises, tax on profits from local enterprises, personal income tax, urban land tax, fixed investment direction adjustment tax, urban construction and maintenance tax, vehicle license tax, urban real estate tax, vehicle tax, stamp tax, land appreciation tax, slaughtering tax, agricultural tax, cultivated land occupation tax, and contract taxes. There are also taxes collected and shared by the central and local government, which are value-added tax (in a 75:25 ratio), natural resource tax, and stamp duties from the stock exchange (in a 50:50 ratio).

The value-added tax is the biggest category of tax, reaching 734 billion yuan in 2003. With consumption and business taxes, they take up half of total tax revenues the government collects. This value-added tax is shared between the central and local governments, in a ratio of 75 to 25. Personal income tax is a major category in developed economies; it is increasingly becoming a similarly important category in China, with a sum of 141.7 billion yuan in 2003, though its percentage in total tax revenues remains small, being approximately 7%.

Under the current taxation system, the central government has reaffirmed its leading position and keeps huge financial resources for policy implementation. Government budgets cover the five layers of the government structure, from the central government down to township governments. The national budget is to be approved by the National People's Congress each year, and it needs to cover major areas of concern and provide financial assistance to designated regions. In 2003, the central government made a transfer payment of over 800 billion yuan to local governments. Of this, 300 billion was tax retention to regions. In 2002, the central government collected revenues of 1.89 trillion yuan and had expenditures of 2.2 trillion, creating a deficit of 308.8 billion yuan. In that year, government spending on national social security was 136.8 billion yuan, 264 billion yuan on education, 100 billion yuan on government procurement, and 167.5 billion yuan on national defence. Local governments have their share of local taxes as designated after the 1994 financial reforms, receive transfer payments and other assistances itemised in the national budget from the central government, and have their rights to collect additional revenues in their territories. Local charges are not included in the formal budgets presented to the local People's Congress, and more developed regions hold considerable financial resources generated from these charges. The car registration fee in Shanghai, as mentioned above, is one of the forms of these extra-budget revenues for local authorities.

Years after the 1994 taxation reform, the central government has spent more on public goods and macroeconomic management. Enlarged financial capability, to the tune of an annual 100 billion yuan in extra revenues, proves vital to the government's numerous ventures. Even with these huge increases, the central government has been running budget deficits for years (see Table 10.1).

In 2003, budget deficits of 320 billion yuan and a GDP of 11.67 trillion yuan result in a ratio of 2.74%.

The government bears its obligations to the public in the form of increased expenditures on social security and other payments. In particular, the government's major weapon to fight deflation from the late 1990s was **proactive fiscal policies**. These included more government spending on key projects, large amounts of government bonds being issued and increased export rebates. These macroeconomic policies were adopted in order to boost the economy. Apart from lowering official interest rates, the Ministry of Finance issued government bonds in large amounts—an average of 150 billion yuan each year in the past six years. The money from issuing bonds was in turn spent on major investment and infrastructure projects. This spending spree created contracts for enterprises and jobs for workers, and it was hoped that consumption would recover soon. This proactive fiscal policy is now under more scrutiny, as deflation gave way to a growing prospect of an overheated economy and mild inflation in 2004. The Finance Minister announced at the end of 2004 that the fiscal policy would shift from proactive to moderate, keeping the budget deficit at a level of 300 billion yuan and reducing the amount of bonds issued. This will be the main trend in the coming years.

Issues of Central Control

The 1994 financial reforms effectively shifted power back to the central government and represented an "empire strikes back" syndrome, but it has yet provided a final solution to the problems in central-regional relations after years of decentralisation. Local authorities have been encouraged by the relaxation of rules and have made extra effort to pursue their own goals. This has a negative impact on implementation

Table 10.1 Budget deficits/GDP (%)									
1990	1991	1992	1993	1994	1995	1996	1997	1998	1999
0.79	1.1	0.97	0.85	1.23	0.99	0.78	0.78	1.16	2.12

of national policies and stands as a serious obstacle to effective government administration.

This tendency to prioritise local interests remains strong despite a central government with enlarged financial resources. In recent years, numerous cases have indicated the extensive influence of a number of powerful provinces on national policy, and economic fluctuations were caused by self-serving provinces. Tension between the central government and provincial governments has not been completely defused. It has merely taken a different form—not in open rejection of or challenge to central directives, but in implicit discontent and delaying tactics. Local governments at different levels have learned to ignore national policies and regulations. They have grown the bad habit of "countering policies from the top with locally designed measures". Local governments tend to pay lip service to central policies and take no real action and follow-ups. Policy implementation is often selective, with local governments carrying out tasks that fit more of their own interests. Refusal to implement central policies is based on excuses of local conditions and uniqueness.

In an extreme case reported by the media in 2004, officials from a local government in northeast China disobeyed the instructions from the central government on rectifying certain abuses of power. In the face of direct orders from Premier Wen and investigation teams from Beijing, local officials succeeded in deception and continued to guard their interests. They reported to Beijing that the matter was duly dealt with and that the officials involved were dismissed. These deceits almost worked. It took more written directives from Premier Wen and more investigating teams to expose this scam and bring down that local government. The nation was shocked to learn how easily local authorities fooled the State Council and defended their own interests despite state regulations. There naturally arises a question mark on the effectiveness of government administration and the chances of national policies being implemented.

Another sign of unsolved problems in this relations is the urge of local governments to override economic policies from the top. As in FDI, local governments in competition usually offered unbelievably favourable conditions to prospective foreign investors and were eager to get things underway, while being fully aware of making a clear breach of official regulations. Large foreign investments received extra tax benefits for projects, and stores and factories were in operation without official approvals from Beijing. The two coke makers, Coca-Cola and Pepsi, obtained permissions for the opening of their bottling factories mostly from the governments of the respective territories. The French retail chain Carrefour signed numerous agreements with local governments to open its stores at a fast pace; it was only caught and fined for regulation violations by the central government much later. Before the central government could act, foreign-invested projects had long been set up and running. These happened more often in the middle and late 1990s, when nationwide uniform rules had not overpowered local initiatives which had blossomed under decentralisation and the quota system.

In the area of macroeconomic management, which is the domain of the central government, Beijing faces many hard choices. The central government issues economic policies which control the direction and pace of economic growth. Unfortunately, it has been interrupted and upstaged by local initiatives a number of times. The latest round of economic boom and subsequent cooling down in 2004 is best summed up as a response by the central government to frenzied overinvestment by local governments. The terms used to describe these drives are "blind" and "duplicated" investment, which result from competing provinces pushing to have everything other players have. These include motor car factories, power plants, financial centres, hi-tech centres; even university towns are used as a new excuse for acquiring land and establishing industrial zones. This frenzy made the central government act in order to slow down the runaway economy.

The overheated economy in early 2004 brought high growth rates, larger investment spending, and a severe shortage of energy supply. As a result of high growth, coastal regions and urban centres began to suffer from power blackouts and rotating power supply, something long forgotten in people's memory. Many manufacturing businesses suffered losses and faced the consequence of having to move to another region. The warning sign came in late 2003, but it was ignored by most due to their singular focus on growth. The central government had to tighten bank credit, write off large numbers of development zones in localities and punish local officials who approved large investment projects. The net result was a mess, causing great wastage and hurting many innocent businesses. A worse consequence could have been a "hard landing". A loss of balance in central-regional relations certainly led to defects in administrative control, such as hard to implement national policies and local initiatives which overrode national schemes.

As a result of this round of economic fluctuation, the central government is exploring new investment systems. Since the bulk of collected revenues flow to the central government, and local governments are not allowed to issue their own bonds, they have strong incentives to persuade the central government, chiefly the State Development and Reform Commission, to grant permits to projects in their own territories. Once a project gets off the ground, it is hard for the central government to stop funding until it is completed. The central government thus bears huge risks in approving local projects, while local governments tend to drag the central government in to shoulder the costs. In a new State Council circular issued in July 2004, it was stated that a new investment system is in place. It follows the guidelines of "whoever invests makes decisions, enjoys benefits and bears risks". Investments made by enterprises do not need any approvals; enterprises only need to submit their proposals and reports for record keeping. The system includes divisions between the central and local governments in their investments, and the central government is not responsible for investments made by local governments. These changes would encourage more market competition and private investment; rather than having only the government to fund large projects.

There is also an interesting twist on this issue of political relations. Local protectionism hampered effective implementations of national policies and laws from the central government. At the time of China's WTO accession, the central government suddenly realised that their hard-earned international agreements with foreign countries might not have real effects in different localities and therefore began to re-examine the consequences of decentralisation in terms of a national market. Protectionism in the name of local interests had grown into stubborn barricades to efforts creating such a national market. In various official investigations and surveys, over 20 provinces reported their products being blocked in local markets, and two-thirds of enterprises acknowledged their business operations being affected by discriminatory local treatments. Important WTO terms such as free trade and national treatment may not be even applicable to producers from another region. This has pushed the central government to deal with the issues of protectionism and local interests more seriously. There have been more directives and circulars on faster flows of trade and transportation through regions. Local governments have been under pressure to rectify or revise their local rules and bylaws. In 2004, under the direction of the State Council, seven national authorities, including the Ministry of Commerce, the Ministry of Finance, and the Taxation Bureau, issued a joint circular to all local governments, demanding that they complete a thorough inspection of protectionist activities and rectify them by the end of the year. All local regulations and restrictions which obstruct the building of a national market were to be abolished.

In a nutshell, a well-balanced set of central-regional relations would improve government administration significantly, and decentralisation has been gradually modified to setting up a structure for the central government to lead and guide. The efficiency of national administration depends to a great extent on a smooth managing of this set of relations. There is still a question of whether regions can pursue their own goals and make their own economic plans, as long as these do not violate national policies.

In 2004, the Ministry of Commerce clashed openly with the Shanghai municipal government on auctioned car number plates. Publicly, the Shanghai government was concerned with congested roads and pollution due to increasing numbers of motor cars, so they charged hefty fees on plates through auctions. According to principles of supply and demand, a scarce resource should draw high prices on the market. The municipal government has collected over 10 billion yuan from Shanghai car buyers since the practice of auctions began in the late 1980s. The Ministry of Commerce, on the other hand, was concerned with consumers' rights, which go against any unreasonable, unfair and unnecessary charges by authorities or by manufacturers. No other municipal governments charge similar fees. In addition, the Shanghai auction charged more premium on cars made in other regions. This smacks of discrimination in business and indicates a common protectionism. The two sides have yet to reach an agreement; it seems that the local interests in this case will prevail, because of the unwillingness to forfeit millions of yuan as revenues.

Government Ranks and Public Servants

A government is essentially a bureaucracy, consisting of large numbers of state employees performing designated tasks. The whole burden is borne by tax-paying citizens, and the public has the right to make enquires about government policies and the performance of these state bureaux.

Ever since the first unified Chinese empire was established, there have been continued debates on the size of government and acceptable or optimal numbers of officials. This debate has focused mainly on reducing financial burdens on the rural population, and the best practice in pre-modern China was to announce tax reduction or exemption. The combined pressures by officials and clerks in government bureaux often pressed the rural population to revolt. Such debates have little to do with the western concept of "small government", advocated and implemented by right-wing political figures such as Margaret Thatcher of the UK. The Chinese perception on the size of government is more straightforward, counting the costs of administration and reducing the number of bureaucratic layers.

The government structure of the People's Republic of China in effect follows that of imperial China. This implies an ever-growing size as the economy grows. A skeleton of government bureaux in the early years of the Republic quickly exploded to bulky sizes, as demands for administrators and new governing functions grew. The factor of the ruling Communist Party should be taken into account as well. The Party has its own departments and employees for tasks. Although party officials commonly take government jobs, their subordinates and associates are also put on government pay rolls.

As estimated, government employees, those people who are on government pay rolls and counted in official budgets bearing the name of "cadres", currently number over 40 million nationwide, and those working in government offices and departments (including Party organisations) number around 7 million. This gives an average of 32 persons per government employee. As nearly 30 million of these people in fact work in government-related sectors, such as school education, hospitals, science and technology, culture and sports, they are employees in public services. This distinction is similar to that of developed economies, where the government supports employees in such public services as well. If this number (30 million) is taken away, the remaining 7 million personnel are cadres in a genuine sense. The ratio between government employees and total population will then be 7:1300, at 185 persons per government employee. This is an increase from the 1949 figures (1:600). A major item of government budgets is spent on paying these employees. At local levels, wage payments to these employees have taken the bulk of government budgets, leaving less for public service expenditures. Spending on maintaining offices, facilities, transport and other benefits for these employees takes nearly 40% of the total national budget, and government vehicles cost over 300 billion yuan annually, well over the total spending on national defence.

There is also the category of employees who are not on pay rolls. Different levels of the government keep their own secret safes for paying for various items, including hiring staff. Another expenditure is the occasional task when an emergency occurs, such as SARS and crime raids. Auxiliary personnel perform some tasks and require payments on an irregular basis. These expenditures would make the total budget spending even larger.

In the current government or public servant system, the real number of formal government employees is 7 million; they are usually called "cadres" and work in various government offices and departments. These are the employees with official ranks to identify their status.

Official ranks in the public servant system (15 ranks):

- ❑   Premier
- ❑   Vice premiers/state councillors
- ❑   Minister/governor
- ❑   Deputy minister/vice governor
- ❑   Bureau head (central)/ department head in provincial governments
- ❑   Deputy bureau head/deputy department head
- ❑   Office head/county chief
- ❑   Deputy office head/deputy county chief
- ❑   Section head/district head (rural)
- ❑   Deputy section head/deputy district chief
- ❑   Section member
- ❑   Clerk

The 15 ranks are mixed among these 12 levels, with some titles such as section member or clerk crossing two ranks. Except for the level of Premier and clerk, each category may cover up to four ranks. For example, a deputy minister could be at a rank from bureau head to minister. A routine practice is to grant a higher level rank to the person with the official post. A deputy bureau head often bears an official rank of bureau head.

Government employees had been a privileged group in the society, with lifetime employment, fringe benefits and frequent promotion. But with the implementation of the resignation and dismissal system in 1998, over 50,000 government employees have left under these two conditions. Many others lost their places during reshuffle and restructuring.

Hiring of educated people from outside to be public servants has been part of a policy to fill vacant posts with more skilful employees, and thousands of people sit for annual public servant entry examinations. New college graduates are also encouraged and persuaded to enter government offices. The wage levels and benefits for newcomers have been raised to increase appeal. These people would have certain conflicts with existing employees who are under previous pay scales.

The morale of public servants had been lowered dramatically by wealth gaps and high incomes earned by private entrepreneurs and foreign company employees. To boost their morale and efficiency, the government began to raise salaries in recent years. In 2004, the Beijing municipal government decided to revise wage systems for government employees under its charge. It was to merge all kinds of incomes, including bonuses and allowances, and fix the formal wage levels for them according to their ranks. Several rounds of pay rises were carried out, and middle level government employees, even without taking bribes, have risen to be in the middle class.

To deal with chronic bureaucratic problems in administrative efficiency, the central government has conducted several rounds of institutional reforms. The major measures are downsizing and merging. The following is a brief review of government reshuffle and restructuring in the past two decades.

1982-83

This was the first major shake-up of the central government after the Cultural Revolution. The number of vice premiers was reduced from 13 to 2, and several state councillors were added instead. A system for retirement of officials was established at fixed age levels, making it mandatory for ministers and provincial governors to retire at the age of 65 and vice ministers at the age of 60. Officials at lower ranks had their retirement ages set accordingly.

1988

This round of reshuffle focused on separation of government offices and departments from those semi-government organisations such as schools. The number of ministries was only slightly reduced, and their functions redefined. There was also the separation of government organisations from Party organisations.

1993-96

This round weakened the government's authority to approvals and permits, and clarified functions of government departments. It also reduced the number of government employees and departments. For various reasons, the initial goals were not achieved and the reshuffle became ineffective.

From 1998 on

It turned economic departments into macroeconomic management departments, and carried out the reorganisation of ministries and commissions. Many ministries were merged and some abolished.

The ministries of Railway, Communications, Construction, Agriculture, Water Conservation, and Foreign Trade remained as they were.

The ministries of Post and Communications, Broadcasting and TV, and Electronics Industry were merged into a single Ministry of Information Industry.

The ministries of Coal, Machinery Industries, Metallurgy, Domestic Commerce, Light Industries and Textiles were turned into bureaux, under the State Economic and Trade Commission.

The State Electricity Corporation and Grain Reserves became bureaux. The Ministry of Chemical Industries, the State Oil and Natural Gas Bureau, and the Petrochemicals Bureau became state-controlled group companies. The National Forestry Bureau, the Education Commission, the Ministry of Labour and Social Security were reset as new ministries. The Ministry of Geology, the Land Bureau, and the Ocean Bureau merged into the new Ministry of National Land Resources.

By 2004, the State Council had 22 ministries, 5 commissions and 28 bureaux, plus the People's Bank and the National Audit Office.

Organisations under the State Council cut their ties with large state enterprises previously under their direct control, and these enterprises are still subject to inspections from representatives sent by relevant ministries and commissions.

All of these rounds of restructuring have not prevented an upward move in the number of government employees. There are repeated processes of downsizing and ballooning in size. There are repeated processes of merger and separation in government organisations and functions. There are also repeated processes of delegation and withdrawal. These attest to a state of contradiction in policy and control by the central government.

At local levels, provincial governments reduced the number of departments, from 53 to 40 on average, reduced the number of sections at county and district levels, and turned county towns into cities (for the purposes of replacing previous regions as one administrative level, urbanisation and controlling nearby rural areas).

Leadership Transfer and Top Leaders

Officially, the leadership of China has passed four phases. The **first** generation of leaders was headed by Mao Zedong and other early revolutionaries. The leadership laid down the foundations of economic systems and early industrialisation, and their rule was maintained through war-time mentality, Party disciplines, and the introduction of socialist ideals. Free market and capitalism gave way to political ambitions and ideological doctrines. This generation of leaders ruled till the late 1970s.

The **second** generation was headed by Deng Xiaoping. He was a member of the first generation and fought through revolutions and wars. His rule of the country, however, differed from the Mao leadership. After years of running the economy first-hand and encountering economic problems which could not be readily solved by revolutionary movements, Deng and his followers decided to change tracks and started the reforms from the late 1970s. They were in fact the first group of state bureaucrats/technocrats, with experience of economic management, as well as revolutionary credentials. To these second generation leaders, reforms were logical solutions, following the principle of "seek truth from facts". Based on this pragmatic approach, ideological doctrines and taboos formed no serious barriers to reform initiatives. Even market forces could be harnessed after trials and experiments. Early success of reforms derived from the determination and clear goal-setting of this second generation of leaders.

The **third** generation of leadership emerged after the 1989 Tiananmen Incident and was headed by Jiang Zemin, the Party's General Secretary. There was more practical pressure on them to manage the economy well and less political or ideological constrains. This group consisted more of technocrats and administrators, with extensive interaction with the outside world. They had to deal with foreign countries and international affairs more directly than before, since China's economy was moving into the world economy. They ruled at a time when the influence of Western economics and political sciences grew fast in China, so that imitating models of the West in many fields became unquestioned. The guiding ideas for running China's economy very often came straight from economics textbooks and theories, mostly American, and overseas-educated economists became important members of state think tanks or advisors to top decision makers. The push to enter the WTO at much cost received solid support from this leadership, especially at the final stages of talks. It is apparent that the leadership sought an opportunity to engage China closely with international markets and expected that this entry would eliminate many of the existing domestic troubles. Economic growth, in terms of GDP growth, proved satisfactory or highly successful at times, making China a country with consistent growth in spite of financial crises and recessions in other economies.

Internal restructuring was also a top priority to this group. Reforms to state enterprises and to social welfare probably increased efficiency in industries, but the social costs of this rapid marketisation were high. Unemployment abounded, and materialism and official corruption became widespread. Tension between developed coastal regions and poorer inland regions sometimes reached flash point. Poverty emerged as a serious social problem as millions of people were thrown out of the state's social welfare net. Deflation occurred in China for the first time, as people's consumption expectations dropped. By the end of the twentieth century, China was presenting a mixed picture of remarkable growth and deep-rooted problems. This is perhaps the main reason for the upsurge of writings on a coming crisis or collapse of the Chinese economy. It is clear that the Jiang leadership attempted to run the country and economy as other state administrators did elsewhere, with strong political motives but little ideological passion.

The **fourth** generation of leadership took over the reign from Jiang in 2002 at the 16th Party Congress after he retired. His quiet exit surprised many Western observers and pundits, since Jiang was widely described as a person with an intention to stay in power at all costs. On 19 September 2004, Jiang relinquished his last key post as the Chairman of Central Military Commission, against all speculations. He was perhaps seeking to equal Deng's precedent and status in the Party's history. With this gesture, the new leadership had full control and authority over the country, including the domain of the military. What this transfer means to leadership in China is that for the first time the process of power transition followed some regular and accepted patterns, and that the sometimes unbearable influence of a strongman in the Party's history had faded. With a more collective leadership style with each generation of leaders, the transfer of power will become steadier, with less shocks and turbulence.

This fourth generation is headed by Hu Jintao, the current President and Party General Secretary. The inception of this group illustrates a complete different set of images from that of the first generation. Hu and others in the top echelon of government grew up in an age of socialist doctrines and technology training. They received recognised education in their formative years—Hu, for example, studied at the prestigious Tsinghua University in Beijing—and further benefited from the opening of China when they began to move up the career ladder.

They are more exposed to the outside world and embody the essence of technocrats. In some way, they might be the faithful executors of policies of the previous generation of leaders, who had a pragmatic approach towards internal restructuring and foreign influence.

The direction, however, has been adjusted under this new leadership of the 21st century. The imperatives in the society have forced their hands. They take on the unenviable task of dealing with imbalances and irregularities in the economy accumulated from previous years of high growth and marketisation. First on the list is unemployment coming primarily from reforms to state enterprises and structural change; second, poverty and wealth gaps derived from a lack of social security supported by viable financial resources. Discontent, protests and near riots all sound alarm of an economy hampered by severe imbalances. It is for this new leadership to announce a new priority in government policies—from growth first to living conditions first. The previous emphasis on economic growth at all costs created heavy casualties in terms of low wages (for export competitiveness), wastage of natural resources and pollution, stagnant consumption and tension between haves and have-nots. The cycles of economic fluctuations, such as overheating and prospect of a hard landing, have threatened growth sustainability. These issues have been addressed by the new leadership, and visible adjustments and realignments are made.

One sign of adjustments is the effort to "squeeze out the water" in growth statistics. Local governments have plenty of incentives to falsify figures and show their improved performance to the central government. This action is for their own promotion and also for more local investment projects to be approved by the central authorities in charge. The new Premier Wen is known for his no-nonsense work style and attention to details. He has managed to expose problems at lower levels of the government during his frequent inspection tours. Some of the consequences of this pragmatic approach are the handling of SARS in 2003 and a more practical view of Beijing's Olympic construction projects, the latter having led to major revisions to, or even suspension of, construction of new stadiums and sports venues.

Unlike the third generation of leaders, whose broadside restructuring stimulated growth and optimism at the time, this new generation of leadership faces tougher choices, many of them inherited from the previous administration. The upside is that they hold no illusions and make no unrealistic projections of China as a strong power any time soon, simply because of high growth rates on paper. They plan to narrow down their scope of tasks and achieve reasonable goals, especially in maintaining social stability for sustainable economic growth.

The backgrounds and average age of this new leadership (this refers to the Politburo members) have been marginally improved. Education backgrounds range from college degree holders to MA degree holders (three of them with associate degrees), and their career paths include engineers, teachers and state administrators. This shows more versatile selection criteria, a shift from the traditional emphasis on party workers and military men. The average age of the Politburo at the time of the 16th Party Congress in 2002 was 60. With their high positions in government and the Party, these members are able to serve two terms before reaching their official retirement age (70).

According to Party traditions, promising leaders are to endure a phase of local administration and hardship attached to their appointments, before they can prove their worth and move back to Beijing to enter the top echelon. President Hu, for example, was assigned to Guizhou province in 1985 as party chief, from his leisured position as the head of the All China Youth Federation. He was assigned again from this region to Tibet as chief officer and party secretary. From there, he was transferred back to Beijing to work as a member of the Party Secretariat. The rest is history. These procedures are applied to many of the current leaders to test and justify their promotion to key Party and government positions. It is not a coincidence that two top leaders, President Hu and Premier Wen, came from posts in two of the poorest provinces in China. Philosophically, this trial is consistent with Confucian rationale that "before a great man is to accept the most important responsibilities from Heaven (to rule), he must fatigue his body and endure hunger".

The current generation of leaders have improved their image among the public. Excesses from previous years are being curbed, including conspicuous consumption and neglect of rights of millions of sacked workers. A more recent focus of attention is the treatment of millions of migrant workers from rural regions. Even the sudden shock of SARS in their first year of administration was handled in a more sensible and transparent way. The transition of authority was smooth and free of violent confrontations for the first time in the Party's history since 1950.

The willingness of Jiang to step aside and Hu's years of internship made the power transfer less dramatic than many China watchers expected. This is a good start, providing a crucial precedent for later generations of leaders and transfer processes. It also proves that ideological and political elements are receding in the leadership, and with each new generation, the influence of communist doctrines is getting less detectable. On the other hand, the guiding principle of pragmatism from Deng's era continues.

Official Corruption

In transitional economies, corruption occurs most rampantly. In the case of China, this has become a major issue often at the top of agenda. Official corruption is a form of **rent-seeking**. It takes place when business is blocked by regulations, and certain officials hold the key to a path or to permits. These officials in charge could demand fees (as rent) to be paid before procedures can go ahead. The fees charged take the form of bribes, kickbacks, and other "under the table" deals. Official corruption in general raises transaction costs and increases financial burdens on businesses.

In a centralised country like China, official corruption has been widespread and deep-rooted. The Nationalist government which ruled China before 1949 was known for its hopeless state of thorough corruption, and the administration allowed millions of American dollars to be held by a few powerful families while the whole country was in a dire situation. This was a main reason for the Communists' sweeping victory over its ruling political rival.

Corruption had been suppressed quite effectively under the first generation of leaders. There was strict discipline (Party and government) over officials' behaviours, and severe punishments were given to any violators. This followed the Chinese legalist tradition, which saw the application of harsh laws as the only way to keep the country in peace. Another factor was the centralised economic planning, under which official's wages and amount of consumption were pre-determined. There were huge differences between benefits for officials and that for ordinary people, but there was little chance for officials to grab large financial gains for themselves in this rigid economic system. The way for officials to have a better life was through promotion to higher positions, and receiving a million-yuan reward by making a special deal with merchants was unimaginable. Officials were routinely sacked or executed for stealing from their offices several thousand yuan. Punishment was harsh and swift.

The opportunity for government officials to engage in rent-seeking came with the reforms. It happened when officials in charge of authorising or approving businesses colluded with business people, private or overseas. There emerged a chance to trade their authority for money. The interrelations between government offices and businesses usually occur in **four** types of deals. These are the times when officials approve bank loans to businesses, approve investment or construction projects, issue permits for land acquisition, and issue formal certificates and approval papers. It is evident in these types of deals that one side has authority and the other, money.

Corruption also provides officials with channels to get their bribes out of the country, to escape confiscations and to plan for their retirement life in future. Between 1998 and 2003, the Party's central commission for discipline inspection filed charges against ministerial and provincial level officials in 74 cases of economic crimes. Recent sensational news reports recorded numerous provincial leaders and ministerial level officials being jailed or executed for economic crimes, while many others sneaked out of the country and moved to developed countries like Canada and the US. A new report from the Ministry of Commerce estimates that over these reform years, about 40,000 corrupt officials abused their offices and transferred money out of the country to the tune of US$50 billion.

Even the education and academic sectors are not immune to corruption and are affected by this urge to make money. Methods taken are mainly through charging hefty fees on those entering education institutions and trading the legal right to education for money. In 2003, the Ministry of Education estimated that schools and universities across the country had overcharged fees of 853 million yuan, and 359 principals were subsequently sacked. The latest scandal exposed by the media traces the routine practice of employees of the renowned Beijing Aerospace and Aeronautics University to charge over 100,000 yuan each on students whose tertiary entry scores hovered around the set thresholds.

In the last ten years, more than 500,000 cases of graft and corruption have been investigated. More than 64% of them involve international trade and foreign companies in China. Many of these involve project bidding and tender, equipment and production line purchases and imports. The well-known case of Lucent Technologies in China in 2004 exposes the approaches widely adopted by foreign companies in dealing with their Chinese clients and government offices which hold the key in major projects. The methods used are increasingly similar to the "revolving door" in the US, which provides secured benefits for retired government officials in private corporations that obtained commercial benefits from close relationships with these former officials. In China, officials in charge are often offered positions of senior advisers, share options or offshore bank accounts. From the opposite perspective, foreign companies also would like to hire senior officials to be managers of their public relations and other areas. The benefits coming from these connections and past networks are enormous. As a result of growing corruption in business deals with foreign multinationals, the US law against offshore corruption will be extended to American companies operating in China, as reflected in the Lucent case. Four members of top management of Lucent China—the CEO, COO, a finance manager and a sales manager—were sacked during a SEC investigation of the conduct of the home company.

A major approach against corruption is to reduce officials' chances of rent-seeking. The State Council annulled and revised 795 items of permission by administrative officers from 2002 to 2004. Provincial governments were ordered to have their own number of administrative permissions sharply reduced. This is to produce disincentives to officials who had authority in granting permits and thus minimise the chance of under the table deals. The most significant move is the passing of the Law of Administrative License in late 2003. As briefly described before, this law pushes governments at all levels to limit the number and scope of administrative permits and make it easier for businesses and the general public to appeal and challenge illegal and unfair administrative actions. This will have profound impact on the business environment in the country.

As a long-held tradition, the government also waged repeated "strike hard" campaigns to fight rampant official corruption. In recent times, many provincial level officials were indicted and jailed. It is getting so serious that some local governments need to be completely overhauled, since top officials there are all involved in corruption and new officials from outside have to be sent in to fill the vacancies. Even with this harshness in one round of campaign, the general public is getting more suspicious and less confident over the capability of the Party and the government to rid of official corruption any time soon. It is on this basis that a talk of a multi-party political system could receive some positive response. By and large, the talks on corruption focus on transparency and public supervision, rather than a change of the ruling party. It is clear to the Party that their rule may fade as rage over corruption is rising, similar to the situation before 1949, when the Nationalist government failed to heed these problems.

Crisis Management and Handling of Long-term Planning

Government functions cover many areas, but the responsiveness of a government is most clearly demonstrated by its ability to handle sudden crises in the society, whether social, economic or political. The performance of a particular government can be more accurately evaluated by its showing in such crises. This attests to the effectiveness of its decision making and leadership quality.

A crisis may bring unpredictable and potentially negative results to a society or organisation. The crisis and its aftermath may cause tremendous damage in terms of lost values in products, services, and financial soundness. In a broad sense, an incident disrupts a component or a sub-system; an accident causes physical disruption to the whole system; a conflict disturbs the symbolic structure; and a crisis physically affects the whole system and threatens its basic operations. Crisis also refers to man-made "disasters".

A key consideration in crisis management is negative publicity. While disclosure and transparency are imperative, keeping a positive public image would raise confidence, reduce panic and stop government branches and offices from falling apart. At a time of crisis, news conferences urgently need to be called to give the public a clear picture and minimise unhelpful rumours. Effective communication with the media would rally support from this sector of influence and reduce their hostility. It is important that the messages delivered maintain their consistency and provide uniform responses to questions. The Chinese leadership and the government have endured trials of crisis management in the past and gradually caught up with the sophistication of media campaigns in a crisis. This can be shown during the SARS crisis.

In a centralised country like China, the decision making process implies the command from the top to the bottom of the government. The central approach is to follow instructions and national laws. As the top member of the management is the one to make decisions, there is little interaction in decision making, and the quality of decisions are questionable. Decisions are often swift, with little consultation and communication.

Communication in Organisations

Four basic types of **communication networks** are common in organisations, businesses or government (see Figures 10.1 to 10.4).

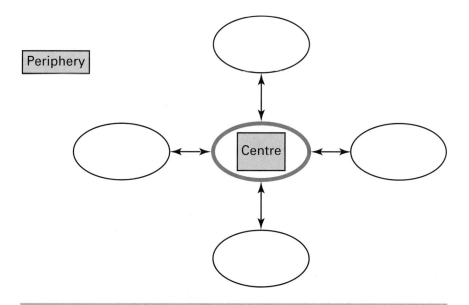

Figure 10.1   Wheel network

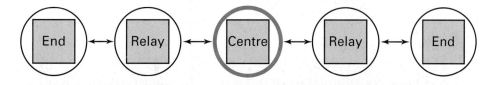

Figure 10.2   Chain network

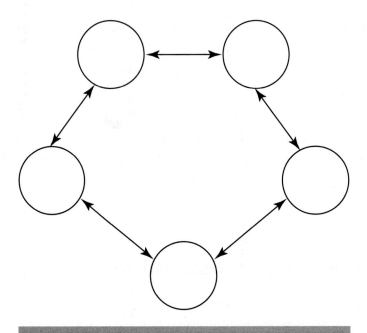

Figure 10.3   Circled network

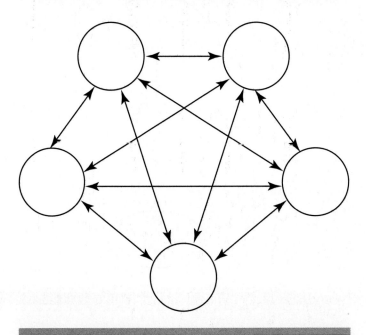

Figure 10.4   Completely connected network

1. Wheel network—It is a clear centre-periphery relationship and the most common structure type. It is the centre which directs all communication and controls the flow of information. This is most efficient for routine decision making.

2. Chain network—Information from end persons is passed through relay persons and up to the next line of communication. The centre person connects with all persons through the chain, similar to the wheel network; but relay persons have more responsibilities.

3. Circle network—Information passes through the circle and every person receives and decides on matters, having his or her role to play. The circle network calls for participation, but may be more time-consuming for decision making.

4. Completely connected network—Members form their own ideas and view alternatives. This mode is with least restrictions and widest share of information. It takes longer time to pass information, and information is likely to get blurry during the process.

Although the Chinese leadership has been following the pattern of collective decision making—decisions are made by the core in the Politburo, rather than a single dominant leader—problems in decision making remain, most prominently in the areas of making right judgements of the situation and in underestimating threats. Their communication network remains in the first two modes.

Problems in Policy Formulation

Information Distortion

Top decision makers receive false information and distorted figures from their direct subordinates or officials at lower levels. This arises mostly out of a desire for advancement in political career. Figures can be inflated if growth or a boom needs to be shown, or minimised if the crisis situation is to be downplayed. Cover-ups or hiding threats serve the purpose of escaping responsibilities and penalties. Decisions made on the basis of this distorted information would lead to serious disasters and miscalculations.

Lack of Due Process

The absolute power in the hands of top leaders makes it possible for some to exert their own will and preferences in decision making. There is also a lack of professional and independent consultations, and officials behave irresponsibly and fail their duties.

Vested Interests

Great influence comes from vested interest groups. These include sectoral interests, monopoly, regional interests, and protectionism. Their contest to more power gives them incentive to promote and advocate their own agenda, rather than providing objective views.

Improvement in decision making in China derives from recent relaxation of the political environment. The process has moved towards being more transparent, and public opinions have greater influence on decision making bodies. As briefly discussed in a previous chapter, media attention and exposure led to laws and regulations being revised and redrawn, such as in the case of migrant workers' rights. Consultations are more common, and the impact of media reports and investigations is felt. There are now the departments of protocol or a policy research office in each ministry or commission of the central government, which raise questions, collect information, set targets, draft official papers, screen options, submit documents to chiefs of organisations, and launch new government regulations or policies. Learning from the West, the governing body, the Development and Reform Commission, stipulated in 2002 that public hearings on important public concerns could be held. Such hearings have become a regular feature in public life, such as annual hearings on long-distance train fares, which drew large audience from the travelling public.

The following two cases are included here as examples of crisis management and the efficiency of government administration.

Case 1: The SARS Crisis

The atypical pneumonia outbreak started first in Guangdong province in November 2002. It is also called severe acute respiratory syndrome (SARS) for the symptoms of the disease. It is atypical, as it is different from known pneumonia and there is so far no vaccine for the disease. It is highly contagious, spreading through contact and air. The most effective way to beat the disease is to quarantine the infected and treat them with intensive care. This requires firm actions by the authorities and wide cooperation of the community. Both were lacking in China when the disease was first spreading. By the end of April 2003, most provinces and autonomous regions of China reported cases of atypical pneumonia.

The government reacted to this spreading disease initially with little concern and saw it as a local epidemic in Guangdong. The central government was tightly bound by the annual National People's Congress and other agenda. The health minister dismissed worries about the disease and assured the audience at a news conference that foreigners and Chinese citizens were safe living and working in China. The Mayor of Beijing also pointed to the reported official number of cases by early April as proof that a city the size of Beijing was largely unaffected.

Two issues are related to the SARS crisis here. The first is the transparency of government and actions taken. The central government was certainly not aware of the extent of damage this new disease caused. It did not have accurate information of the scale of the disease spreading and received false figures. The number provided by the Beijing mayor later proved a long way off the real figure. Local governments, including Guangdong's and Beijing's, tended to paint a less threatening picture to minimise the shock. Consequently, the number of infected and confirmed cases reported were at acceptable levels. Local governments and the Ministry of Health also kept these figures away from the general public. Local governments did receive more information on the disease within their territories, but their response was low key and leaned towards waiting for the central government to declare the existence of this new epidemic disease. As it was truly an unknown type of disease, the central government failed to pay enough attention and find the right way to combat it. The fast spreading disease was still dealt with by local governments separately, on their own initiatives. Without coordination from the top, official moves to contain the disease lost precious time at the early stages.

The second issue is international involvement. The disease in Guangdong and then Hong Kong was reported and discussed by foreign media and experts, and the World Health Organisation made enquires about the disease to the central government. Initially, authorities in charge of public health resisted such concerns and declined to follow advice from this international organisation. They were even more opposed to travel warnings issued to tourists and businesspeople by the organisation about certain regions of China. They chose not to cooperate. For all these occasions, the handling of the situation was behind the scenes, and no public announcements or notices about the disease were made. The main rationale was that this international organisation could not offer much real help. There was perhaps also a factor of pride behind many denials of existence of this disease. In the end, pressure from outside, in the form of cancelled international conferences and tourist groups, and quarantines to Chinese citizens entering foreign countries, among others, eventually caught the attention of the central government.

A major negative consequence of this belated response was that the disease infected more urban residents without the general public noticing the spreading danger. Hospitals did not take proper actions to contain the disease and report an accurate number of cases. This made quarantine more difficult at later stages.

The day of 20 April 2003 was a turning point in governance and crisis management in China. An official news conference was called in Beijing, which announced many critical changes regarding atypical pneumonia:

- ❑ The State Council demanded all local governments and hospitals report any cases of atypical pneumonia in their areas to the central government, and any actions of non-compliance, including false and delayed reporting, would be punished;
- ❑ The government admitted that there were much more cases than previously known, that previous numbers were not accurate, and that the supervision and reporting systems had faults;
- ❑ All reported cases would be checked and publicly announced on a daily basis to the nation and to the World Health Organisation. This was the beginning of the first public disclosure system;
- ❑ Officials who made mistakes previously were to be disciplined. Among them, the Minister of Health and the Mayor of Beijing stepped down immediately. A headquarters office was set up and headed by a female vice premier to take full charge of the nationwide campaign against atypical pneumonia;
- ❑ The government sought cooperation and assistance from the World Health Organisation and had an understanding of the travel warnings on China issued by the organisation.

These announcements formed an official apology to those affected during the government's initial handling of the disease. With this gesture of transparency, the reported number of infected victims jumped many folds. A further problem was the panic caused by official announcements. People locked themselves in to avoid any contact with others; one infected victim would cause the whole neighbourhood to panic and flee; and those sent to hospitals considered themselves as facing a certain death. Urban residents began panic-buying of necessities off supermarket shelfs. Large numbers of people fled major cities like Beijing and returned to their home regions. This increased the possibility of infection at an even larger scale. Some mainland students studying at universities in Hong Kong, where the disease had grown extremely deadly, hastily withdrew from classes and flew back to their home cities. Following this panic, many business sectors were affected badly, since business activities came to a halt when no one wanted to make face to face contact with anyone else. Foreign multinationals rescheduled their operations plans and sent many of their expatriate employees home. Only a "skeleton" of staff stayed behind.

The government was in a difficult position to respond. A more transparent approach would cause major disturbances and business losses as a result of panic, while a secretive approach would make the government lose credibility with the international community and acquire a bad image. The new leadership (five months old) chose the first option and mobilised the state machine to contain damage. Thousands of infected people were sent to isolated hospitals to be quarantined, and infected areas were segregated. Despite huge difficulties in calming the community down, these actions were executed across the country.

By July that year, the situation shifted back to normal, as the infected people recovered and left hospitals, and medical sites for this purpose closed down. Estimated numbers by the end of June were 5,326 infected and 347 dead in mainland China. Beijing, as the most affected area, received the removal of a travel warning at the end of June. During the crisis, the government allocated 13.6 billion yuan to a disease prevention fund.

In handling of this sudden crisis, the government performed very differently at early and later stages. Crisis management requires quick response and high transparency, in order to gain confidence and minimise the loss of credibility. The Chinese government followed past experience in early responses, with neglect and very low transparency in their handling. Regular bureaucratic muddles and the falsifying of numbers were exposed at this stage. This did not work when the scale of threats reached beyond the capacity of local governments. Then the central government shifted gear to follow a more internationalised approach, including publicising actual figures and seeking direct assistance (even supervision) from the World Health Organisation. The government began to be more open and seemed genuinely determined to take full responsibility. Most surprisingly, high ranking officials in SARS-related posts were removed quickly, paying the price for their poor handling and purposefully misleading the country. This was unprecedented. The government showed that it was willing to sacrifice certain officials in order to overcome this crisis. This move markedly enhanced the status of the new central leadership and made subsequent measures more legitimate and coherent. The reputation of the leadership was in fact boosted by this dramatic change.

There have been many discussions on the performance and improvement in crisis management by the government. The new leadership is widely seen as passing its first serious test with flying colours. Another positive effect is that the leadership recognised from this experience that economic growth alone could not fix everything, and that major policy shifts and adjustments needed to be made, in order to maintain stability.

Case 2: Power Shortage in 2004

In the summer of 2004, many regions in China faced severe power shortages affecting industrial production and the daily life of urban residents. A total of 24 provinces and autonomous regions implemented rotating power shutdowns, and the gap between supply and consumption of power was estimated to be as high as 25 million kW.

This traces back to strategic decisions made some years before. In 1998, with the effects of the Asian financial crisis and contraction of the domestic economy, there was a power surplus across the country. Many power generation plants had 50% idling capacity. Since the power industries had been reformed to meet market demands, their profit-making depended on how much power they sold to users. Previously, these plants had taken a near monopoly position, and they sold their power to users as though they were providing a favour. In boom years, users begged hard to have power connections and supply. When these plants could not sell power quickly in other times, they incurred huge losses and were unable to pay bank interests. Coal mines faced the same problems as power plants.

In response, the national bureau in charge of power supply and grids made a plan to reduce total capacity. In the following years, plants producing a total of 10 million kW of electricity were closed down, and further investment and construction of power plants were strictly regulated. More unfortunately, the national bureau planned for future power supply on a very conservative basis, predicting that future consumption would be moderate and surplus power inevitable. In discussion and evaluation with other government offices, this view was passed as a consensus in the official government policy on power supply of the nation. Obviously, this plan underestimated the surging demand for power and overinvestment in general of the country in following years. Power consumption rose 12% on average between 2001 and 2003, while new power capacity increased at an average of 7%.

As China's economy turned the corner from deflation to recovery or even overheating, there was a huge gap between power supply and the existing capacity. This caused serious disruption to manufacturing industries in coastal regions and to the lives of millions of urban residents. Foreign companies in Suzhou even threatened local authorities with shifting their production to nearby regions, if power shortages and random blackouts were not solved. Thousands of enterprises in Beijing and Shanghai were ordered to leave their production lines idle at the designated time slots and let their employees have holidays in rotation. Large numbers of enterprises scrambled to buy their own diesel generators to supply electricity for their business. Urban residents had to resort to a life of candles and no TV. Ironically, this widespread power shortage may turn to power surplus again in a few years as the result of the current rush by the government to issue permits to build more power plants due to this shortage.

This case primarily shows the government's decision making process and response to crises. With a lack of long-term planning, industrial fluctuations occurred and cause unexpected troubles and losses to businesses.

The above touches upon several aspects of government administration in China. In regard to business operations and environment, we should pay attention to the shifts in the central-regional relations and the issue of a national market. Official corruption has become common in business deals, thus causing considerable costs to prospective investors. The direction under the new leadership is important, since their performance will be a key factor in any assessment of the future business environment in China.

Key Concepts

Central-regional relations and phases of change

Taxation and budget allocations

Official ranks and rounds of government restructuring

Leadership generations and transfers

Official corruption and rent-seeking

Types of communication networks

Crisis management and issues in policy formulation

Discussion Questions

1. What are the major characteristics of a centralised political structure of China? How do the central-regional relations work in a centralised country and a country of a federal system?

2. How can a central government effectively control localities and run an administration when it conducts decentralisation policies? In your opinion, should the decentralisation in the first phase continue, and if so, what would be the long-term prospects?

3. With respect to the 1994 changes to the taxation system, what are your views on their consequences (both positive and negative)? What would you suggest to reach a right balance in the central-local relations, in regard to issues of central control as discussed in the contents?

4. Do you think the idea of "small government" is the right solution to problems linked with the bureaucracy in China? Take reference from government downsizing in other economies.

5. Assess government handling of emergencies and leadership quality, based on the examples in the text and from other sources.

6. What are the major causes of corruption in China? What would you suggest to prevent corruption activities at Chinese operations of foreign multinationals?

Related Readings

Harding, Harry, *China's Second Revolution: Reform after Mao*, Sydney, Allen & Unwin, 1987.

Lam, Willy Wo-Lap, *The Era of Jiang Zemin*, Singapore, Prentice Hill, 1999

Lieberthal, Kenneth, Oksenberg, Michael, *Policy making in China: leaders, structures and processes*, Princeton, New Jersey, Princeton University Press, 1991.

MacFarquhar, Roderick, ed., *The Politics of China: 1949-1989*, Cambridge, Cambridge University Press, 1993.

11

Incomes and Consumer Market

his chapter will discuss issues of incomes, purchasing power, consumer spending, and retail business in China. It attempts to draw a picture of private spending and consumption in the China market and hopefully throw some light on market potential. This chapter also includes some discussions on marketing and advertising in the context of consumer spending.

Average and Disposable Incomes

The population figure in an economy is a key indicator to economists of the scale of potential consumption and the size of a particular market. A market needs to have some considerable size to be resilient and to generate profits for manufacturers and retailers. In an overall estimate of market potential, highly relevant issues include wage levels and disposable incomes. As a developing country, China is widely identified with low income levels and poor living conditions. Since the reforms began, total national output has increased, and people were allowed to grab employment and business opportunities to enlarge their incomes. Average incomes for Chinese families have been on a steady rise from the late 1970s (see Figure 11.1).

Along with the rise of incomes, people's purchasing power grew, and a wide variety and large quantity of goods are now consumed by

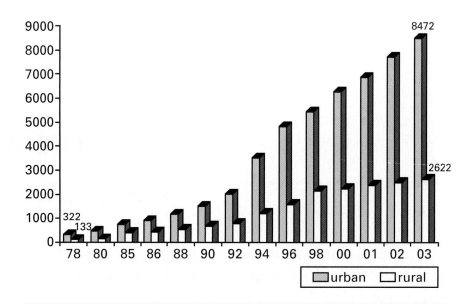

Figure 11.1 Average disposable income per capital (in yuan)

more consumers with more money to spend. Consumer markets of different goods flourished, and retail sales figures rocketed. The retail sales figure for 1978 was 152.7 billion yuan, and for 2003, it was 4.58 trillion yuan (approximately US$5,585 billion). A clear sign of this dramatic increase is that many foreign companies initially invested in China to export finished goods to markets in developed economies; but they now turn to sell more goods to the domestic market of China.

From the above figures of average disposable income per capita, we can see that rural household incomes rose rather sharply and gained on the urban household incomes in the 1980s. The rural population became big spenders and snatched up consumer goods available in cities in those early years. From the 1990s on, preferential policies and treatments given to rural areas became less effective, and urban residents found numerous ways, legal or illegal, to increase their incomes. As such, the gap between the two groups in income has grown wider instead of narrower. Purchasing power in these two groups also diverged, with rural consumption falling quite a distance behind urban consumption. Retail sales in the countryside are normally not the focus of marketing campaigns by domestic or foreign companies. This shift and the resulting lackluster rural retail consumption stands as a hidden problem to future growth and will be discussed next.

A few figures are listed below for illustrating average incomes and consumption:

- ❏ In 2002, urban residents had an average annual income per capita of 8,177.4 yuan, while their consumption amount was 6,030 yuan. In the meantime, rural households had an average income per capital of 2,475.6 yuan and a consumption of 1,834 yuan. These show that a high percentage of their incomes were spent on buying goods for their livelihood.

- ❏ In 2003, urban residents had a disposable income of 8,472 yuan, while for rural residents it was 2,622 yuan.

- ❏ In April 2004, average urban residents had 980 yuan monthly real income per capita, 895 yuan disposable income, and 689 yuan as consumption.

- ❏ An indirect sign of income growth in the country is that China's GDP per capita passed the US$1,000 mark by early 2004.

Personal bank deposits have increased steadily and unabated in recent years. By April 2004, it reached 11.2 trillion yuan (see Figure 11.2).

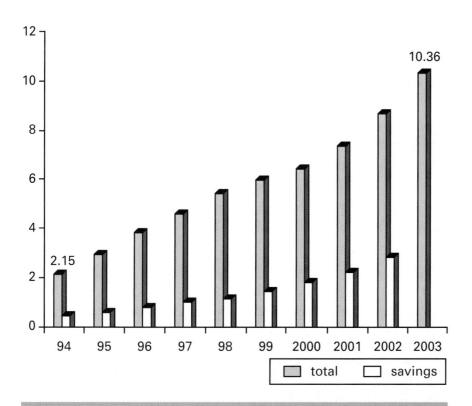

Figure 11.2   Personal bank deposits (in trillions of RMB yuan)

It is interesting to note that the Chinese economy underwent a period of deflation in the first few years of the 21st century, as discussed in a previous chapter. To boost consumption and the market, the Chinese government adopted measures similar to those by the Federal Reserve Bank of the US—to lower interest rates a number of times. This was supposed to encourage people to withdraw money from banks and spend on buying consumer goods and other properties. It achieved some results, but not in the area of total personal bank deposits. These figures continued to rise, from 7 trillion yuan in June 2001 to the above-cited figure in early 2004. This was a sign of trouble for the government, which was unsure of the effectiveness of interest rate mechanisms and of the impact of such huge amounts of money pouring into the market at an unexpected moment of time.

Wage Levels

China's GDP figures have more than quadrupled since the reforms began, while average wage levels have risen as well, though unevenly. In one of the latest surveys conducted in 2004, Shanghai retained its leading position as the place where average annual salary was the highest in the country at 47,634 yuan, with Beijing at 44,626 yuan, Guangzhou at 39,471 yuan, and Shenzhen at 39,305 yuan. Shenzhen fell from the top spot in past surveys. This signals a sharp turn in a long process of wage increases. With the most favourable policies in the country, Shenzhen had been a city of both growth and high incomes, appealing to large numbers of venturers and talents, and its standing in past wage surveys stayed high. It was in 2003 that Shanghai first surpassed Shenzhen in this key category of economic development. This reflects the facts of increased foreign investment and steady wage rises in Shanghai, which makes the city attractive to job seekers, resemblant to the status of Shenzhen.

In another category, however, Shenzhen is the place with the highest average disposable income in the first half of 2004, at 12,373 yuan per capita, followed by Guangzhou and Shanghai. This ranking order indicates that in many southern urban centres with large shares of private and foreign businesses, people's basic salaries are often complemented by bonuses and extra incomes from various sources.

In a research report by the State Development Research Centre released in 2004, 71% of Chinese employees in various types of enterprises have average salaries of between 800 and 2,500 yuan per month. If the lower end of base salary is taken as a reference, then increase in wage has been slow in the past 10 years or so. Migrant workers from rural regions are in the same situation. Their average annual income from their urban employment, including manufacturing, construction and services, is around 8,000 yuan for long hours of hard labour; and it becomes even less after their living costs are deducted.

An estimated 180 million rural residents have moved to urban centres and settled down for employment or business. They are permanent urban residents without formal urban household registrations. Floating rural labourers working in industrial enterprises send back between 350 and 400 billion yuan to their home areas every year. These large additional funds increase rural income levels significantly and have made it possible for many of the remaining rural population to buy consumer goods that they need.

At the other end of the spectrum, in major cities such as Beijing and Shanghai, top and middle level managers gained an average 8% pay rise in 2003; and section heads, professional and technical experts gained 7.2%. It is estimated that by the end of 2003, probably over 100 million people were earning an average annual income of 60,000 yuan or more, which is a level for people to enjoy a reasonably comfortable life in China. The income gap between the bulk of the working class and those at management level is evidently widening.

In 2002, five groups of people in the upper middle-class are commonly regarded as having the highest growth rates in income. They were executives in technology companies at a time of high-tech boom; private business owners; managers in finance and securities firms; representatives and executives of foreign companies; and professionals in specialised firms, such as lawyers and accountants. Apart from these groups, officials with certain authorities, scholars in areas of economics and finance, and heads of state enterprises have become newly rich with rapidly rising personal wealth.

Wage increases in the Chinese economy have contributed to a vibrant and growing consumer market. With more disposable income and purchasing power, Chinese consumers, especially urban consumers, are now able to spend money on numerous kinds of goods, from necessities to luxury items. There are, however, deep-rooted defects in the general trend of income increases. One seemingly unrelated factor is the official policy in the past decades of promoting exports to developed markets. Large quantities of goods are made in China by cheap labour and exported to the markets in the US, the EU and Japan. For the sole reason of competitiveness, goods made in China are marked considerably lower than goods from other economies. Chinese workers are therefore hard pressed to keep their wages and production costs low.

In the most concentrated areas of exporting manufacturing in the Pearl River Delta, wages of migrant labourers, who form the main workforce, have hardly been raised, and assembly workers routinely receive a few hundred yuan a month for back-breaking factory work. As observed by Chinese academics, in over 20 years, average labour costs in the region have consistently been 500 yuan per month, not much higher than the official level of minimum wage, while prices for most goods and services have risen sharply. In 2002, the average monthly salary for workers in a major industrial city in Guangdong province was 731 yuan at American or European enterprises, 718 yuan at Japanese or Korean enterprises, and 571 yuan at Hong Kong or Taiwanese enterprises. In 2003, average workers' pay rose 6.7% as a result of labour protests and pressure from local authorities.

Top executives of listed Chinese companies now have a large amount of paper value. In 2003, the top 50 senior executives of listed companies made large gains from their share holding of the companies under their management. The top executive has a market value of 1 billion yuan, and the last in the list has a market value of over 50 million yuan. 37 of these executives have market values of over 100 million yuan.

With a recent change to the rules regarding listed companies, top executives can now hold company shares as a natural person, giving them opportunities to be major shareholders of the companies under their charge. A recent sensational event is the TCL listing, during which the CEO of the company obtained 144 million shares. His market value after floating reached over 1 billion yuan, in effect becoming richer than the top executive on the above list. Other senior officers of the company also became large shareholders and multimillionaires.

Across the nation, workers' pay remains low. A report by the Ministry of Labour and Social Security in 2004 concludes that in 24 major cities, new workers receive on average 660 yuan a month, and those working in the regions around Shanghai receive wages that are 8.5% higher than the average. With low average salaries that compare unfavourably with other regions, migrant labourers flow to the Pearl River Delta in smaller numbers or leave the region after working there for a short time. A consequence is that the Pearl River Delta in early 2005 had an estimated labour shortage of over 2 million workers in its manufacturing industries—the industries which have sustained the region's growth and prosperity for the past two decades.

This low wage situation is not confined to the southern cities of China. Under the guideline of "exports first", keeping labour cheap is commonplace in coastal regions which make the bulk of exports. This squeeze on workers' pay in exporting manufacturing industries influences other types of enterprises, and general levels of work wages are kept low on purpose. With a continuing supply of cheap rural labour, this trend will be maintained. It is therefore justifiable to say that the export-driven policies have had a key part to play in making average wages low for Chinese workers.

What does this situation mean to consumption and consumer markets? It is clear that the society has divided into two parts: with middle-level and above groups receiving higher pay and consuming better goods; and with average workers getting low pay and being unable to purchase goods other than necessities. Since the people in the latter groups make up more than two-thirds of the total population, it is quite conceivable that consumption often just inches ahead, rather than grows steadily. This is a crucial question to foreign investors, who may feel confused by this situation. While it is often heard that

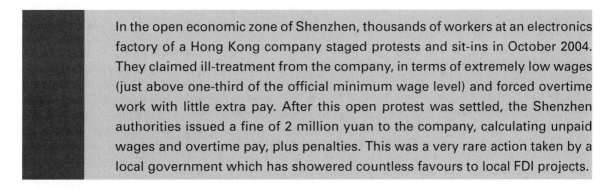

In the open economic zone of Shenzhen, thousands of workers at an electronics factory of a Hong Kong company staged protests and sit-ins in October 2004. They claimed ill-treatment from the company, in terms of extremely low wages (just above one-third of the official minimum wage level) and forced overtime work with little extra pay. After this open protest was settled, the Shenzhen authorities issued a fine of 2 million yuan to the company, calculating unpaid wages and overtime pay, plus penalties. This was a very rare action taken by a local government which has showered countless favours to local FDI projects.

the middle class in China is growing fast and people have money to spend, there are unsold goods everywhere, and the economy of shortages under socialism has long been replaced by an economy of oversupply. This should be seen as a superficial oversupply, since large numbers of people are only supposed potential buyers with little extra money for purchases. This low wage policy has also caused headaches to the government, in terms of lacklustre performance of enterprises and huge bank deposits which cannot be efficiently utilised for investment.

Divisions of the Society

China used to be divided into two main classes: workers and peasants; and capitalists. The reforms since the late 1970s have caused a fundamental transformation of the country, creating more subclass social groups. The main class lines are thus largely blurred. With dramatic changes in incomes and social status, people in the society now belong to numerous groups distinctive from others. It is no longer applicable to identify someone as either proletarian or capitalist; and it is time to reclassify and establish new categories of social groups, as the course of development demands. A cornerstone research was completed in 2001 by scholars and surveyors of academic institutes in Beijing, chiefly the Chinese Academy of Social Sciences. Their research was based on extensively collected data over three years and set up major criteria based on economic, organisational and culture (educational) resources. The ten major social groups identified in Chinese society are as follows:

1. State and society administrators, with organisational resources;
2. Managers, with culture or organisational resources;
3. Private entrepreneurs, with economic resources;
4. Professional and technology experts, with culture (educational) resources;
5. Office clerks, with some culture or organisational resources;
6. Small businessmen and traders, with small economic resources;
7. Commercial and service industry employees, with very little of the three resources;
8. Manufacturing industry workers, with very little of the three resources;

9. Rural labourers, with very little of the three resources;

10. Vagrants, unemployed, under employed, with no resources.

These major categories are relevant to economic analysis and marketing research. As indicated in the categories, the groups from the middle level down form the bulk of the population, and their disposable income levels decide the total consumption and sales of manufactured goods. Despite certain luxury purchases by the rich and super rich group members, the purchasing power of other social groups is the key to sales volumes and, subsequently the success of certain manufacturers. It is clear that the Chinese economy has yet to solve its current problems and bottlenecks in raising average income and creating market forces for sustainable economic growth.

Consumption

During the transition from a planned economy to a market economy, consumption patterns and major items of goods for sale have changed dramatically. Such changes spell business opportunities to smart manufacturers, and timely upgrading in products and production is essential.

In an economy of shortages, Chinese consumers were satisfied with occasional purchase of durable goods, on top of their daily necessities. There were so-called "big four items" on their lists—a bicycle, watch, sewing machine, and radio. This early consumption wave began before the early 1980s, and each item cost a few hundred yuan. These four were major items considering the wage and disposable income levels at the time.

This phase was followed by the next purchasing wave of "new big six items"—a colour TV, washing machine, tape recorder, fridge, fan, and camera. This was the time from the early 1980s to the mid 1990s; and each item cost up to a few thousand yuan to buy. The "big four items" had long been common in rural areas, and the "new big six items" are near saturation in most urban centres.

The third phase saw the trend to purchase "new big four items"— a motor car, air-conditioner, computer, and audio/video equipment. This happened from the late 1990s and will continue to the early 2010s; and each item could cost at least over ten thousand yuan. During these phases of consumption waves, people concentrated on buying major home appliances for their families, and manufacturers of household appliances have made huge sales to those consumers. From consumption of these major items, several domestic companies have become market leaders in these industries.

Policy Changes on Consumption

Stage One

Dramatic changes occurred from "investment first" policies to policies encouraging consumption, as described in a previous chapter. Due to free competition and relatively lower entry barriers, consumer markets have become the most open and competitive markets in the economy, and they signify the real market competition. State, private, collective and foreign companies are all engaged in these markets and provide a large quantity and wide variety of goods to Chinese consumers. Many consumer goods became accepted by consumers and sold well after patient market nurturing and education by manufacturers, such as DVDs and digital cameras. From the late 1990s, this consumer market has grown to a considerable size and increased its appeal to foreign investors.

Stage Two

With conservative consumer behaviour and more serious economic conditions under a deflation, retail sales have been slow, with growth rates at worrying levels. The following figures show the mild growth rates in retail sales in recent years after the Asian financial crisis.

- ❑ 1995: 26.8%
- ❑ 1999: 10.1%
- ❑ 2000: 9.7%
- ❑ 2001: 10.1%
- ❑ 2002: 8.8%
- ❑ 2003: 9.2%

These figures indicate certain problems at the current stage of consumption. Although consumption was placed as one of the key components of modern GDP, recent economic growth in China has been driven chiefly by investment and exports. As shown by government efforts in fighting deflation, state investment projects and export drives at all costs helped the economy move out of the last deflation, while consumption levels remain low and less finished goods were sold to consumers. The concerted efforts in 2004 to cool down the economy took the form of curtailing bank lending and cancelling huge investment projects. This exposed the existence of serious structural problems in the economy. A chief concern is the insufficient demand for consumption, as shown by the slowing down in retail sales. From 2004, the government has been making adjustments and turned to consider consumption as a key factor in achieving economic growth, an even more significant priority than investment and exports. This follows the examples of developed economies, where consumption routinely takes over 60% of total GDP; and taking reference from the bad experience of deflation, when private consumption dragged down growth rates in those years. It is now more accepted by the government and Chinese academics that consumption, especially private consumption, should be the primary driving force for GDP growth.

This turnaround demands a complete rethinking of development strategies and calls for decisive actions by the central government. **First** of all, reasonably high consumption requires the support of adequate income levels of the populace. To consolidate this basis, the government has to change consumption related policies. It has to find ways to boost average income levels of the biggest social groups—the rural population and manufacturing workers. These two groups have been badly disadvantaged in the process of economic development and have lost enormous benefits to other social groups. The failure of these two groups to be in the range of lower middle classes demonstrates a weakness of previous consumption booms. From the above listed social categories, the current middle classes engaged in non-labour work are less than 10% of the total population, though the absolute number of 100 million is comparatively huge, and they are not able to carry consumption through to high grounds by themselves. Conspicuous consumption by the rich has its limits and targets particular luxury goods. The main forces of consumption have to come from these two largest groups. As such, their inadequate incomes and spending power have prevented consumption figures from climbing higher.

Second, making consumption a top priority would imply changes to past emphasis on exports and investment. Export-driven growth would be downgraded, and cheap exports would become undesirable and unrealistic, since wages to manufacturing workers would have to be raised to reasonable levels, in order to increase their real incomes. Exporting firms, whether overseas Chinese or foreign, would have to abandon their past practice of keeping wages low and unchanged. Also, investment by the government should be reduced in proportion, and private investment encouraged to make their own market decisions. More importantly, if the focus shifts to consumption, there may be a certain slow-down in economic growth, since a reduction in government spending and export volumes directly impacts on headline growth figures. There are some political prices to pay for this change, and whether the government is able to fend off blame for a slower growth remains a question. In a review of macroeconomic policies, this role change among investment, exports and consumption will definitely cause some disruptions to drafting new policies and to implementation.

Regardless of the consequences of a major policy shift, consumption has been clearly a chronic issue in China's economic development, and a public consensus has been reached that consumption has dragged down economic growth considerably. It is time to see whether consumption can be placed in its rightful position in government policies in the following years. As one indication of this consensus, a central government conference held in early December of 2004 declared a continuation of realignment of investment and consumption, and lifted consumption to be a more important driver to GDP growth.

Common Behaviours of Chinese Consumers

Consumer behaviour in different cultures generate different trends. In China, there are some clear trends people largely follow.

First, they are under the influence of traditional thinking, which places high priority on thrift, saving, and preparations for the worst scenario. Public opinions are generally against conspicuous consumption, and even with the emergence of the newly rich today, the media and people by and large do not shed much sympathies on them, despite some admiration toward some who went on eccentric spending sprees for luxuries. Conspicuous consumption a few years ago shocked many and drew sharp criticisms in response. The recent media frenzy on Bentley purchases by a number of wealthy Chinese soon met with inquiries and accusations of waste.

There are also deep concerns for old age insurance. Extraordinary attention to saving has been for a certain financial guarantee for old age life costs. This was a serious concern in pre-modern China and is considered by many scholars as a main cause for population growth. This concern seemed to have evaporated during the socialist era, since the government provided covers of various kinds to the public under the planned economy. The expectation of a secured old age life disappeared soon after the reforms began and was entirely wiped out by the shocking magnitude of unemployment in the late 1990s. People now recognise that the government is no longer an effective manager of old age insurance, and with some more income being earned, it is up to the people again to plan for their future life after retirement. With such a mindset, and after the purchase of major items, individual consumers began to turn back to their old beliefs and spend cautiously on goods. It is then hard for manufacturers to entice them to spend money freely.

The second factor is that consumers are getting more rational. In an economy of shortages, people were easily getting excited by the prospect of buying something new. The situation in the first decade of reforms confirms this. People were willing to spend money on major items, and new generations of products were favoured. This has to change after the economy shifted to be one of oversupply. Chinese consumers have so much to choose and so many categories to select from. The pace of individual spending has slowed down.

During the early years of consumption waves, manufacturing companies began to apply marketing and promotion techniques learned from foreign-invested companies. Hong Kong and Taiwanese companies simply transplanted their market promotion campaigns to China and gained outstanding results. Foreign multinationals, such as P&G, are masters and pacesetters in this field, giving Chinese consumers something they never experienced before and exerting much influence on them to buy products. Their marketing and branding strategies dazzled many and made those consumers dedicated buyers of their products. With domestic manufacturers catching up on this and using more promotion and advertising, Chinese consumers grew fed up with non-stop sales pitches almost everywhere. This used to be exciting, and people did spend after being influenced by such pitches, but they soon grew weary and learned to pick genuine bargains from inferior products. They now tend to buy what they desire, not because of advertising. Their consumption behaviours are more rational, analytical, and sometimes opposite to what manufacturers want. Manufacturers made matters worse by engaging in long price wars, under the threat from competitors in an economy of oversupply. Price wars worked briefly, increasing sales, but people began to understand that they could wait for the prices to drop even further. Thus, they would hold their money close to their chest until prices slid down to an accepted level.

This happened to the motor car market. Chinese car buyers paid ridiculously high prices for cars sold in China, often double the prices in developed economies. This was due to both high import tariffs and the large profit margins carmakers set on their cars for sale. People began to realise this money-grabbing activity on the part of carmakers and turned to buy domestically made cars that were cheaper. When sales figures were down, large carmakers began to lower prices a little, causing a flood of sales and annual returns to them. When further price cuts were announced, people's enthusiasm to buy a car faded, and they wanted to see the final results of competition among these carmakers. Price drops or price wars give people the idea that they are the ones who can afford to wait it out. In the current car market, people often do not spend their money on buying a car immediately and prefer to wait till the right time to buy. This attitude has caused great difficulties to some large carmakers, since they have accumulated a large car inventory and face financial strains.

In addition to response to price wars, Chinese consumers are also getting savvy about quality, service, and consumer rights issues. There are more and more news reports on consumer complaints about defects and undesirable treatments, and even products made by foreign multinationals cannot escape the fury of Chinese consumers. They are more choosy and demanding, doing their best to speak out against manufacturers of defective products. The government has an annual date for dealing with consumer rights and complaints, which is on 15 March every year. Problems reported on this day receive more attention from government bureaux in charge of quality and public safety. At other times, Chinese consumers would have to resort to all kinds of pressure on manufacturers of faulty products, including the media and court. They are more concerned about complaints on products made by foreign companies, because in general, those products and companies have better brand names and reputation, so consumers assume they are better protected. When some problems are reported and this trust is shaken, those foreign companies are very often in hot water due to their mishandling of the complaints. Refusal to provide service or rejection of a replacement or refund only makes the matter worse for the foreign companies involved.

All these in fact are good examples of consumers getting more rational; and their purchasing behaviours have a big impact on domestic and foreign enterprises in this market.

In more recent years, Chinese consumers, especially urban residents, have begun to let up in spending through bank and credit cards. They are attracted by the cashless convenience these cards provide, and commercial banks have made continued system upgrading to meet rising demands for such services. Cards issued by major banks now allow consumers to withdraw money and make payments in most cities. By mid 2004, it was estimated that there were over 700 million bank cards and credit cards issued to Chinese consumers. Among them, bank cards, which require deposits in customers' bank accounts, are the majority. Credit cards are less used, due to inherent problems in credit rating and risks. Over 18 billion yuan was swiped away from these cards in 2003. Personal spending and consumption have been boosted remarkably by growing numbers of card users.

In a recent survey conducted in late 2003, Chinese consumers with sizeable disposable incomes are put into five groups. The purpose of the survey is to investigate how these people tend to spend money. A key indicator is how they see wealth, and their actual purchasing decisions would be influenced by their views on wealth. According to the survey, the categories include:

1.   Indifferent to wealth (15%): These people do not see money as a major criterion of success. They have minimal interest in investment options and follow others in consumption of certain goods.

2.   Average investors (36%): These people long to enjoy a good life, but do not chase it at all costs. They tend to change their living

conditions when possible and are cautious in spending, for the sake of saving.

3. Careful investors (24%): These people are rather conservative, very cautious in spending money, trust brand names and services by foreign companies, such as banks or insurers. They would make purchases at stores they trust, based on past experiences.

4. Wealth pursuers (18%): These people are willing to try new wealth-creating means, are adventurous, and tend to enjoy a quality life. They accept new ways of investment or insurance and are eager to build up assets in property and cars.

5. Wealth keepers: These people have made money for a good life and see money as a key sign of success. Their central concern is to maintain the value of their assets, so in investment they are rather conservative. To safeguard their wealth, they prefer to send children overseas, trust foreign banks, and stay away from domestic stock markets, for fear of big losses.

Current Levels of Consumer Goods Ownership

Consumer markets in China have developed for over two decades, and consumption of many products and manufactured goods has been in large scale in many regions. The following are some collected data on the penetration of goods and perhaps signs of saturation in some markets.

Average durable goods ownership by rural residents (per 100 households) in 2002

- ❑ Washing machine: 31.8
- ❑ Fridge: 14.8
- ❑ Motor bikes: 28.1
- ❑ Colour TV sets: 60.5
- ❑ Black/white TV sets: 108.6
- ❑ Tape recorder: 20.4
- ❑ Camera: 3.3

Average durable goods ownership by urban residents (per 100 households) in 2002

- ❏ Washing machine: 92.9
- ❏ Fridge: 87.4
- ❏ Colour TV sets: 126.4
- ❏ DVD/VCD player: 52.6
- ❏ Camera: 44.1

In June 2004, in a nationwide survey conducted by the State Statistics Bureau, the number of motor cars per 100 urban households was 2, and the number of mobile phones per 100 urban households was 106. The number of travels taken per 100 urban residents was 64.

From the above figures, we can see that Chinese households, especially those in urban centres, have purchased and acquired most consumer goods available on the market. It is estimated that the urban population, 40% of the national total, generates 65% of national retail sales. Major purchasing items are no longer their main purchasing targets; and for household spending, there are some uncertainties on the next wave in consumer markets. These situations are crucial indicators to manufacturers' market strategies. As one market reaches a certain point of sales, there is a possibility of saturation, and no matter how hard an enterprise tries, sales figures would not match those in previous years when consumers had just began to spend big on certain major items. This quieting down often causes some enterprises to panic and even collapse, and this is also the main reason why many enterprises seek a diversification strategy to enter certain potential markets early. Staying in the same industry with a coming saturation means stagnation and a plateau in sales and revenues. Company CEOs are supposed to watch the figures in each category of consumer goods closely and find new markets to enter. In the case of China, many domestic enterprises had been forced to take such actions for survival. For example, the top household appliances maker, Haier, moved into other industries as far away as pharmaceuticals and computers.

Next Trend of Consumption and New Hotspots of Money Spending

After previous stages of consumption, which focused on the purchase of major items, consumer markets in China had been drifting without clear directions. People had probably acquired all household appliances they needed, and domestic and foreign enterprises have to invent new hotspots and encourage consumers to spend money. From 2001, there have been moves toward new ways of consumption. The following areas of spending will be thriving in the near future.

Motor Cars

There has been a major change in trend from making cars for officials to making family cars. Motor cars used to be a symbol of authority and wealth. With higher income levels and carmakers' urge to sell more, they are now more affordable to average households and a variety of models are laid out for buyers to choose from. Since 2002, car sales have risen an average of 50% per year, and major carmakers gained 13% annual profit growth on average. By late 2003, China had over 10 million private car owners. The average household income level for these car-buying families is around 40,000 yuan per year.

Cars used to fetch high prices due to tariffs and carmakers' markups, but the prices dropped sharply in recent years. Even European makes from Chinese joint ventures, such as VW, began to make unprecedented price cuts to their mainstream models on the market. Pressures come from small domestic carmakers that launched cheap small cars to price-conscious buyers, and from consumers in general who wait to see the best value for their money. These caused considerable numbers of unsold cars in stock and forced major carmakers to unload their cars at lower prices. The most acceptable price level is around 100,000 yuan, for an affordable family sedan containing essential equipment. As shown before, in 2004, the average number of car owners per 100 urban households was 2. Assuming that this covers 400 persons, it is then one car per 200 persons. If this is increased to one car per 100 persons, with an urban population of 500 million, the demand for cars will be 5 million vehicles. It is therefore likely that car buying will be a major area of consumption in following years, when average incomes rise and cars are made more affordable.

Housing

This is a type of consumption which emerged even earlier than the booms in car sales. It still has huge purchasing potential. The sales figures (in yuan) and space sold (in square metres) in 2003 rose 45% and 35%, respectively, over that of 2002. Since buying a house (an apartment in most cases) involves an investment of a large amount of money, the sale process would be slow yet lucrative in the long run.

There were early property purchases from the 1980s onwards, first by the early groups of people who made money from business. The real house-buying waves started with the housing sector reforms in 1998-99. From that time, the government announced that public housing would give way to private property ownership, and new employees in government organisations, including those in state offices and enterprises, would not receive free dwelling or housing. They must pay for their own properties at market prices. To compensate those existing employees who had served long term, the government offered a one-off lump-sum payment to assist their purchase of the properties they lived in. This compensation is usually above 50% of the value of the property, and the people who lived there came up with the rest of the money. Since the implementation of this housing compensation scheme was in the hands of individual organisations, many of them provided very generous funds to their employees for this purchase, and an allowance could be up to 90% of the property value. Large numbers of government employees and officials became property owners as a result of this housing reform. This change cost the government large sums of money, but in the meantime triggered housing booms.

Another key condition for the housing market was the introduction of mortgage payment as a new option from 1991. This follows the common practice of developed economies and is aimed at encouraging spending on properties. With this new source of finance, consumers have become more willing to make purchases and to borrow money. The push factor on consumption is apparent. For bank finances, a mortgage has been a more reliable loan type than business loans, since the income and credibility levels of a borrower are generally carefully checked before a loan is made, and the bank can get its hand on the property if repayment is not made.

There are still many buyers on the market, seeking affordable housing or to upgrade to a bigger space. Many of them are currently halted by high prices in major cities, but with economic adjustments and more rational policies in the housing and construction industries, prices will become more sensitive to market demand and slide to reasonable levels. The current sky high prices are more common at upper levels and luxury houses. This situation has made developers unwilling to make price adjustments. Since most real estate developers received bank funding for their projects and paid little with their own money, they are less concerned with huge property stocks. Unsold apartments and buildings are in fact liabilities to the banks. The total bank loans to this market, including loans to developers and to mortgage borrowers, amounted to 1.6 trillion yuan in 2002—12.45% of total loans from financial institutions. By the end of 2003, this ratio rose to 15%, and it was estimated that unsold stocks reached over 100 million square metres. Once the government revises its regulations and forces developers to put their own money in, large numbers of them would not be able to withstand losses and have to cut prices. The government issued such a crucial regulation in 2004 to make developers pay for their projects, and this caused uproars among developers. Even with a watered down version of the regulation as a concession to developers, it is clear that real estate developers can no longer be exempted from their responsibilities, and it is likely that ridiculously high prices in this market will be reduced to more sensible levels.

In the long run, this sector of the consumer market has enormous potential. Rural regions will release large numbers of migrants to cities, perhaps in hundreds of millions. All of them need accommodation and housing eventually, so the market is not likely to be short of buyers. This push factor will decide the trends of consumption in the housing sector in future years.

Education

This is a newly opened area of consumption with great potential. A priority of family life in China is children's education. This has been the case in traditional China, and under the official one child policy, a good education for the only child in the family is certainly a paramount concern of millions of parents. These children are often the centre of activities and attention, and their requests for receiving better education have seldom been refused by their parents, rich or poor. Child products and services are usually hot selling items in total consumption. These include toys (educational or otherwise), baby care, tuition fees paid for getting into reputable education institutions from kindergarten, primary school to university—these are often at a premium if academic scores of a child are not meeting entry requirements—tutoring fees, talent development such as piano playing, boarding fees, various kinds of contests and overseas trips, etc. Since 1996, the Chinese government made a critical move to change universities from free public tertiary institutions to fee-collecting institutions, starting at around 4,000 yuan per year and rising. Parents are ready to pay for this and many other fees charged by universities. In recent years, large numbers of families spent money on sending children to overseas schools. Tuition and boarding fees charged are often well beyond the level of income a Chinese family has. Numerous foreign education institutions have taken this opportunity and expanded their recruiting campaigns in China. Private consumption in areas of child education would continue to be on the rise.

For people in other categories, spending on individual education and training are also high on their agenda. Large numbers of people attend wide-ranging courses to obtain recognised certificates of qualifications. China has established systems of such vocational education, from correspondence courses, distance learning, TV courses and continuing education, plus numerous schools teaching specialised skills such as English, computer and accounting. These would help students in their further development and employment. Fees paid on these forms of education and courses are considered worthwhile. With more leisure time and adequate income, education on a variety of personal preferences and hobbies would also draw people to spend.

Travel, Holiday and Leisure

As China adopted a five-day work week some years ago, people have got more leisure time for themselves. With adequate incomes and a growing range of hobbies, people tend to take more vacations and travel to other places. Chinese citizens spend a lot of money on travelling now, from domestic travel to international travel. Many tourist agencies are busy handling waves of tourists. China initiated a "golden week" system from June 2000. Three big Chinese holidays are named "golden weeks", which include the Chinese Spring Festivals, May Day (1st of May) and National Day (1st of October). These three public holidays each last more than one week and give people plenty of time for their travel and other leisure activities. As at early 2004, it is estimated that the past ten "golden weeks" generated total tourist revenues of 321.2 billion yuan. Consumption during these weeks benefited numerous industries, including tourism, transport, restaurants, telecommunications, hotels, and entertainment. In 2002, total revenues from domestic tour trips were 387.8 billion yuan, and US$20.4 billion from international tour trips. In the first half of 2004, 5.6 million mainland visitors flocked to Hong Kong in a variety of tour groups and spent a huge amount of money in that Chinese territory. Chinese tourists are now given permission to visit 12 EU countries. Consumption on leisure also spreads to many other areas, such as fishing, and brings benefits to restaurants, entertainment, transport, and advertising industries.

Information

On top of standard household appliances, Chinese consumers now tend to upgrade their information related products, such as mobile phones, computers and audio-video products more frequently. There were nearly 90 million Internet users in China by the middle of 2004, and 300 million mobile phone users. Chinese consumers have some late-comer advantages in getting in touch with brand new products available on the market. Since many products have been launched by manufacturers within a short period of time, Chinese consumers have the chance to select the more advanced ones to their liking. In a sense, they have been able to be in a faster upgrading process than people in developed economies. For example, Chinese consumers can choose to buy VCD/DVD players rather than VCR players, and digital cameras rather than conventional cameras. The availability of new and old generations of technologies gives them a chance to move directly to a more advanced level. The average time for a certain product to command a large market shares is getting shorter every year. New designs and functions are added to products by manufacturers to appeal to more consumers. There is a general trend for Chinese consumers to buy new generations of digital products.

"Grey" Consumption

Along with the greying of the Chinese population, the market for about 130 million elderly people will become huge and profitable. Products in health care and nursing would be popular; hospitals and medicines would be in big demand; and new businesses in housing specially designed for the aged would have great demand and prospects.

These categories cover some large scale markets in the near future that have great potential. There are more segments and niches of smaller scale in the China market, such as those that cater to specific demands from women consumers—for example, cosmetics. It is for manufacturers to search for market opportunities and manufacture goods to meet customers' demands.

Advertising and Consulting in China

Before the late 1970s, commercial advertising was considered as evil tricks employed by capitalists to swindle people of their money. Even without official denunciation that this was a non-socialist activity, its importance to trade and retail sales was largely downgraded. This has since changed dramatically and has probably moved towards the other extreme. Commercial advertising is used everywhere and in every form conceivable. Chinese consumers face a continuous bombardment of advertising, mostly from TV channels and newspapers.

Advertising Revenues

The advertising industry of China generated revenues of 50.6 billion yuan/US$6.1 billion in 1999, and 80 billion yuan/US$9.7 billion in 2000, an increase of 36%.

In 2003, advertising revenues reached 154.4 billion yuan. This figure covered only TV and paper media, at 120 billion yuan and 33.5 billion yuan respectively. Radio media had 1.2 billion yuan, and outdoor advertising (signs, vehicles, etc.) had 3 billion yuan. Corresponding figures for 2002 are: 87 billion for TV; 24 billion for papers; 0.7 billion for radio; 1.35 billion for outdoor advertising.

These revenue figures have made mainland China an advertising market second only to Japan in Asia. This is also a fast growing market, based on those sharp increases from 1999 to 2003. Considering that China suffered the shock of SARS in 2003, future growth in commercial advertising is expected to be in double digits. In fact, advertising revenues in the first half of 2004 reached 102.7 trillion yuan, an increase of 35% over the same time span in 2003.

The top five industries which spent the most money on advertising are: cosmetics, foods, pharmaceuticals, retail, and housing. This indicates that commercial advertising in China targets the sale of retail consumer goods.

Among the top ten advertisers of 2003, four of them are foreign multinationals in household cosmetics industries, but they did not reach the top positions.

TV commercials are still the most popular and effective means of advertising, since most Chinese urban households have at least one TV set. Advertising revenues from TV takes up 78% of total advertising revenues in 2003. For this reason, the central TV network (CCTV) controlled by the government moved quickly into commercial advertising as its main financial resource, in addition to government allocated funds, and it now takes the most advertising revenue, averaging 3 billion yuan a year. In comparison, advertising revenue from Guangdong TV stations was 260 million yuan in 2000. The CCTV also has wide reception in the country, and its many programmes are broadcast to all the corners of China. It is thus able to charge premium rates on its time slots, especially the slots after the daily evening news reports. Advertisers have the same idea and consent to pay the required prices. Auctions of prime time slots are routinely held, and advertisers and manufacturers bid fiercely to get a piece of the time slots they desire. The CCTV is a sole beneficiary of this competition, and its leading position in drawing in advertising money has met no serious challenge in the country. Most recently, China P&G paid 380 million yuan for the most sought after time slots of CCTV programmes at an annual bidding meeting on 18 November 2004. Previous top advertisers at this meeting were all domestic Chinese enterprises.

Newspapers are strong contenders for top places in advertising, and their widespread networks help them reach millions of readers. These are good sources of advertising revenues, as well as of information. Some predictions were made: first, paper media would lose out to online news; and second, Chinese newspapers would be phased out as they primarily serve political purposes. Contrary to these early predictions, newspaper groups and networks are growing so powerful and rich that they have become the places with high-tech and well-paid jobs. All these are derived from their ability to draw advertising money. Many old-fashioned Party newspapers changed their form quickly and grabbed market opportunities swiftly. Their transformation has been nothing short of remarkable, and through commercialisation and realistic approaches, they hold onto readers. Their focus is now more on public life and pressing issues. It is not uncommon that many of them insert sensational tabloid stories into their reporting and fan up curiosity. Occasionally, they would stir up some controversies and benefit from a larger number of readers who pay attention to certain current affairs stories. The leading newspaper publishers are Beijing Youth Daily Group, Wenhui-Xinmin United Press Group of Shanghai, and Nanfang Daily Group of Guangzhou.

Online advertising emerged strongly in China in recent years, following the high-tech boom in the US. Chinese Internet companies transplanted the business models of Yahoo! and AOL, and relied heavily on online commercial advertising (banners, pop-ups etc.) as their main sources of revenue. At the beginning of their business, they used investment money from foreign venture capital and poured money on equipment and commercials to attract users and increase the number of page views. It is quite ironic that the new economy media relied almost solely on old economy media to promote themselves. The top three Internet service providers are Netease, Sohu and Sina, which have all been listed on the NASDAQ board. Their business models were badly damaged after the high-tech bubble burst in the US, and Chinese online service providers faced tremendous difficulties in gaining enough advertising money as revenue. Timely rescues came from the short message service (SMS), which allows mobile phone users to send text messages, and online games. There are about 300 million mobile phone users in China, and they soon caught up with this new fashion in information and communication. Online service providers quickly expanded their services into these new areas and gained sizeable revenues for their survival. Their business recovered in 2003-2004, with more Internet users and increased investment from conventional news media. Now, online news websites takes a large share of the audience in China, provide news, chat rooms and other services, and receive online advertising revenues in the process.

Outline of Regulations for Advertising

Advertising in China is under the regulation of the Advertising Law, passed by the National People's Congress in 1994, and central authorities, in particular the State Administration of Industry and Commerce, are given the power to supervise and impose penalties on those firms violating the relevant regulations.

Key points in the Advertising Law on the contents of commercials include:

❑ Must not contain false information or deceive or mislead consumers;

❑ Must not use the national flag or emblem of the People's Republic of China;

❑ Prohibit the use of names of government, military, and police organisations;

❑ Provide accurate data to support the claims in commercials;

❑ Must not use exaggerating terms such as "national or international standards", "the number one", or "the best";

❑ Must not contain racial or sexual discrimination;

❑ Must not contain comparative advertising or belittle or insult others in the industries concerned;

A large foreign multinational in the fast food business once produced an impressive TV commercial. It showed Chinese restaurants offering traditional and popular Guangdong cuisine attracting few customers, since they all rushed to enjoy tasty dishes at a nearby store under this foreign restaurant chain. Eventually, those Chinese restaurants closed their doors, and their century-old business signs fell down in the cold wind. The commercial was roundly condemned and caused a public outcry. Regardless of the hurt feelings of Chinese restaurant goers for their beloved Chinese cuisines, this commercial obviously broke the rule which forbids any belittling in commercials of other players in the industry. The foreign food chain initially resisted pressures from the public and local authorities, but the TV commercial soon disappeared without a trace.

❑ Tobacco advertising is not allowed in any media;

❑ Must not contain messages against the communist morality, or include "bad manner" images.

In the official report of the fourth quarter of 2003, the State Administration of Industry and Commerce provided the results of its inspections of all commercials appearing in the 63 largest provincial newspapers and on 64 TV channels on a number of pre-determined dates. They found 8.2% of print commercials violating the laws, and 9% of TV commercials guilty of violation. The main charge was misleading consumers in various ways; and the main areas of false commercials were medicines and food.

In the advertising industry, cultural misunderstandings could easily surface. A practice or perception which is quite acceptable in one culture or one region, may not be acceptable in another place. A TV commercial for a Japanese car brand featured obedient dragons in front of the car, in effect projecting one of the symbols of Chinese culture in a humiliating way. The new Nike sneaker TV commercial of 2004 featured NBA star Lebron James effortlessly beating several Chinese-looking opponents, and state authorities took action to suspend the broadcasting of the commercial after receiving torrents of complaints from viewers across the country and from Singapore. Even Hong Kong and Taiwan advertisers have some difficulties in adjusting to the environment and rules in mainland China. Despite sharing the same language, these advertisers would encounter misunderstandings and ill feelings if they adopted the same advertising strategies from back home without considering local customs and environment. A typical gimmick for promoting real estate projects in Hong Kong, for example, is to apply the words of "royal" or "imperial" to the names of the buildings for sale. This wording often meets with suspicion and rejection from local authorities, who feel uncomfortable toward these words based on their own socialist training in the past. A commonly used phrase "off the building jumping prices" (meaning selling at suicidally low prices that incur big losses) in Hong Kong is viewed, on the mainland, with some intention to mislead and cheat customers. These subtle implications are hard for outsiders to comprehend at first, and some of the direct application of past practices would lead to wasted time and money on advertising campaigns which are not allowed to go ahead. It is paramount for advertisers from overseas to do their homework and get used to the rules before launching major advertising campaigns.

The advertising industry of China has grown to a considerable size, similar to Germany's or the UK's, in terms of total revenues. Its further growth depends on the rate of economic growth, increase in disposable income and volume of consumption. This industry has been open to foreign advertising firms since 1986, and foreign agencies have formed strategic partnerships with domestic firms. They are the leaders in creative designs and brand names, and they serve mainly foreign multinationals operating in China. Powerful commercials for Coca-Cola and P&G products, for example, are the outstanding results of work done by foreign advertising agencies, such as WPP. They now provide services for domestic companies as well. Chinese enterprises increasingly employ their services to promote their products. On the other hand, Chinese consumers still have some misguided ideas of the roles of professional advertising agencies, such as how creativity really works and how advertising is to be valued. They have also grown fairly resistent to excessive commercial advertising and promotion, as discussed in another section of this chapter.

Market Research

Market research and management consulting are two of the business services introduced to China by foreign firms. The world leaders in these two fields have entered the China market for a long period. It was hard for them to sell these services to domestic companies, so, as in advertising, they started by providing services to foreign companies in China. Comparatively speaking, market research is more widely accepted by Chinese companies in later years, since this service supplements the official statistics and provides crucial information and key figures to manufacturers. Their targets may not be the macroeconomic data but key industry-specific information. These prove extremely important to the players in the industry concerned. These firms also provide survey results about markets, consumer preferences and product sales. For these purposes, they are regarded as reliable and useful sources.

Top 10 market research companies (2000):

1. AC Nielsen

2. Central Viewer Survey and Consulting Centre
3. RI China
4. Asia Market Intelligence
5. Gallup China
6. Taylor Nelson Sofres
7. Lantian (blue sky) Marketing Research
8. East Marketing Research
9. X & L Marketing Services
10. All China Market Facts

Views of Enterprises on Market Research

Chinese companies have their fixed perceptions of market research, especially those which have dealt with foreign agencies in the past. In a 2000 survey, they made their points in several areas:

❑ Market research obtains data, which can facilitate decision making if clients know how to use them—64%

❑ Market research firms should provide services from consulting to sales—53%

❑ Results published by market research firms will help establish brand names—35%

❑ Enterprises will not sponsor market research which presents a negative image of the clients—13%

Causes of Errors in Market Research

It is evident that there are gaps between Chinese clients' expectations and the services provided by market research firms. The major causes of the discrepancies may be one of the following:

❑ Rapid changes in market and business: The fast changing economy has made many projections by domestic and foreign agencies quickly irrelevant.

❑ Research methods adopted from developed economies need to take into account local conditions in order to reduce chances of errors.

❑ A lack of business ethics leads to collection of false data; this implies false reporting and covering up unfavourable figures.

❑ Chinese customers are not yet used to Western ways of market surveys and respond to questions with confusing answers. For example, to avoid causing a loss of face, respondents may choose an option at the middle level, instead of an extreme option, even if he or she dislikes the product or service under survey. They prefer not to publicly claim the existence of faults and reveal their disgust.

❑ Published rankings and related data may be the result of manipulation, and consumers lose confidence in them and manufacturers stop taking them as useful information for their operational plans. In recent years, many industry rankings or top ten lists have been proved false, since sponsoring enterprises exerted pressure on the surveying agency, or the list was just a closed-door deal among a few players. These attempts at manipulating public views for corporate benefit have largely damaged the reliability and credibility of many surveys and that of market research as a whole.

Management Consulting

Management consulting provides enterprises with analysis and programmes for improvements in efficiency. The range of services cover customer relations, business solutions, e-commerce, supply chain management, business expansion and restructuring etc. Major foreign firms in China are Andersen Consulting (which is separate from the defunct accounting firm Arthur Andersen), Boston Consulting, McKinsey, and A.T. Kearney. They focus on big projects and foreign multinationals; and local Chinese firms tend to serve small- and medium-sized companies, with lower commissions.

Different in some ways from market research, management consulting has met stronger resistance and suspicion from Chinese clients. Foreign firms, with their world renowned business reputation, have encountered countless difficulties in winning domestic clients and focus instead on serving foreign multinationals operating in China. A typical view among domestic enterprises can be summarised in the words of a CEO of a construction company in China's northeast: "We know the problems and the solutions in our company better than those coming from outside." A top executive of Founder, a leading Chinese IT corporation, reveals that the company has declined numerous offers from management consulting firms of services in planning future strategies. The company believes that it has clear vision and thorough knowledge of itself. Another issue is the true value of business consultations to the operation and development of an enterprise. There is more mutual understanding and acceptance between management consulting firms and foreign multinationals than that between the former and Chinese enterprises. The example of McKinsey Consulting in China is given below to illustrate general perceptions of and problems in management consulting in this market.

A widespread joke of McKinsey is on the Internet in China. It describes that a man in suit proposed to a shepherd: "If I tell you the number of sheep owned by you, would you give me one sheep as payment for my service performed?" The shepherd agreed. The man in the suit used GPS, laptop and other tech gadgets to calculate and told the shepherd: "You have a total of 720 sheep". The shepherd had to give up one sheep as payment. He then asked the man in suit: "If I tell you which company you are working for, would you give that sheep back to me?" The man in suit agreed. Then the shepherd said: "You are from McKinsey". The man in suit was very surprised and demanded to know how the shepherd could tell. The shepherd explained to him: "First, you came to offer your service without my invitation. Second, you told me something I knew all along and charged me for that. Third, you do not know this business. The thing you are holding is not a sheep; that is actually my German shepherd".

McKinsey is a world renowned business consulting firm, with over 4,000 partners who have MBA or PhD degrees. The firm is a top provider of business solutions and management consultations. McKinsey entered the China market in 1993 and has built up its reputation in the consulting business. It has trained local Chinese partners, who can provide more regional-oriented plans to deal with local demands. McKinsey used to serve foreign multinationals in China, and then it expanded to the field where domestic enterprises became its major clients. In 1998, domestic clients surpassed foreign clients in number, and in the following years, Chinese corporate clients make up over 70% of the total. Demands from these clients focus on overseas market entry, expansion and diversification strategies, or internal problems and restructuring. As state enterprises have been under pressure to transform and perform, McKinsey saw the opportunity to offer solutions in stock market listing or debt conversion. These have some appeal to state enterprises. Among others, a top Chinese insurer Ping An and a beverage maker Robust both employed McKinsey to provide solutions to their problems.

McKinsey also got involved in government planning and redevelopment. A typical example is the firm's cooperation with the Shanghai municipal government to transform the famous Nanjing Road commercial district. The century-old commercial boulevard had been the centre of Shanghai's consumption, but was in decaying in the 1980s. The municipal government made great efforts to revitalise the area and transformed it into a pedestrian shopping zone. The project created a mess, with large crowds, fewer sales and loss of stylish high-end shops. McKinsey was called in by the government in 2001 to present a new redevelopment plan. With 13 weeks of intensive survey and brainstorming, McKinsey produced a grand new blueprint of and an ultimate solution to Nanjing Road. The road was to be divided into three sections, with "Occidental flavour", "prosperous metropolis" and "bright future" as the main themes. The whole project of revitalisation would cost 18 billion yuan, a dear sum even for a cash-rich municipal government like Shanghai's. After initial loud praises, this plan is getting less attention in following years, and the municipal government seems to be waiting for more foreign investment to fund this gigantic project. McKinsey received several million yuan as fees.

McKinsey has maintained its unique work style in different countries. It intends to apply standard work processes and solutions universally. In different areas, such as market entry or restructuring, McKinsey offers schemes to clients from its pre-tested cases. This guarantees the uniformity of solutions from McKinsey, with little modifications. The firm does conduct detailed, and sometimes exhaustive, examinations of the enterprise in question and get practical knowledge, but their final solutions to the problems are chosen from the categorised archives. The focal point is not the particular problems in an enterprise, but what solution at hand **usually** deals with those kind of problems. McKinsey also sticks to its principle of providing consultations only, not engaging in implementation. In order to have their plans work in the target companies, their consultants play the role of tutors to company employees. Another feature of McKinsey routines is, of course, that it charges fees for field work, surveys and produced reports. The fee levels are not affordable to many small- and medium-sized Chinese enterprises, and their suspicion of the effectiveness of a McKinsey touch makes it more unlikely for them to be clients.

Case: The Start Technologies Project

A case of management consulting, which hurt McKinsey's reputation in China dearly, is the restructuring of **Start Technologies**. This is a computer and high-tech company registered in Fujian province and is listed on both Shanghai and Hong Kong stock exchanges. After rapid market expansion and growth, the group company faced pressing problems of managing numerous subsidiary companies in the country.

One of the two central problems was the expansion and diversification into many new industries. The group company received huge financial resources after being listed and began a process of rapid diversification, entering areas of VCDs, printers, e-commerce, real estate, import/export etc. Among these diversified businesses, only the computer and printer businesses made reasonable gains.

The other problem involved management. The group company had more than a couple of dozen subsidiaries. Many of them were set up to operate new businesses, and these sub-companies gained their independent status in following years, especially those with excellent performance records and sales. The group company came to lose control of its subsidiaries in finance, operations, marketing and distribution. Many subsidiaries worked out their own market plans and did not follow the directives from the group company. Some sub-companies even grew financially stronger than the group company, while others made big losses and affected the group company's overall performance.

The top management of Start made a critical decision to initiate an internal restructuring for the coordination of all projects and subsidiaries within the group. At this point, Start turned to international models and signed a contract in 1998 with McKinsey Consulting to design a new management structure.

McKinsey recommended the adoption of company structures of top international IT companies and provided Start's top management with two sets of plans: one gradual and one radical process of implementation.

Start adopted the radical plan in 1999, which included actions as follows:

❑ Transform subsidiaries into units under separate departments of the group company, a centralisation of power and authority;

❑ Leave marketing function in the hands of the group company and not delegate this to sales divisions and to subsidiaries. This means that product strategy, launch, and promotion would be handled and coordinated by top management of the group company;

❑ R&D and sales were similarly handed back to the group company for direct central management.

The central theme was to break up subsidiaries and enforce a centralised control over individual subsidiaries. As part of their routine work procedures, McKinsey consultants moved into Start and formed project groups. They conducted lengthy interviews with company employees and staged numerous problem-solving conferences. They provided many operational procedures for the company to adopt, in order to have a standard process for smooth company operations. These consultants spent two months on the job and received 3 million yuan in fees. Start tried to implement many of these procedures, for example, rotating job posts for thousands of employees, but found it difficult to complete the process while facing various problems and stiff resistance.

After six months of a trial run of McKinsey's management models, Start changed course and returned to the previous subsidiary structure. During the restructuring and confusion, the group company lost market share and employee morale, had a 55 million yuan loss in 1999 and a 267 million yuan loss in 2000. Worse, the group company was given "special treatment", which implies delisting from stock exchanges if operational losses were not fixed soon.

The group company and subsidiaries are now run separately. Under this decentralised structure, subsidiaries have their own boards of directors and decision-making authority, and some sub-companies succeeded in certain areas, such as printers and PCs. Revenues from these two sectors effectively support Start as a viable high-tech company. This is an indication that the McKinsey plan for a centralised structure may not have the benefits desired, and the question is whether a centralised structure is really needed to change the situation of the group company.

Judging by McKinsey's own criteria that clients' performance grades its consultations as successes or failures, the Start project proves to be an unsuccessful case for McKinsey. This is a widely agreed verdict among Chinese managers and analysts, while McKinsey maintains that through consulting work, standard Western management practice can be adopted by local Chinese companies.

Issues Related to the Start Case

1. Problems in strategies and transformation of Chinese companies:

    The Start group company typified the general strategies of many Chinese companies at the time: rapid expansion, diversification, loss of focus in long-term strategies, losing control of subsidiaries and networks in the process. These are typical of most private businesses in China in the 1990s, when the economy boomed and more business opportunities emerged. Market forces pushed companies along, and top management made rash decisions to expand and to grab emerging market opportunities.

    Top executives of Chinese companies tend to underestimate the difficulties in restructuring and in adopting a more radical approach in transformation. Start selected the more resolute plan from McKinsey consultants, rather than the gradual one. The main reasons for this move was that they could not stand waiting for positive results of the restructuring to come, were eager to fix urgent problems and move on to make significant gains in business. With such a mentality, Start managers were urgently called back to headquarters to attend countless training and re-education sessions. Their usual tasks in sales and services were left unattended. The switch of direction from decentralised to centralised and back to decentralised structures seriously disrupted normal business operations and made sales and growth goals unattainable. This illustrates the neglect of top Start management to the gravity of fundamental changes to internal systems and structures.

2. Foreign organisational models and Chinese business practice:

    The model of centralised management was copied from large foreign IT companies, with an intention to transplant the practice of successful foreign companies to this Chinese company. The whole process was an experiment of tested management models, and the consultants had less time to examine the company's real problems. As mentioned before, consultants often bring out specific solutions to one category of problems in the target company from their database, which catalogues all possible solutions in various formats. These may not be up to the demands and expectations of local managers. A leading industrialist, the CEO of Legend Group, speaks from his own experience: "Advices from management consultants come from case studies of established corporations. They have their merits, of course, but if we just follow and copy what is shown to us on those Powerpoint slides, we will never grasp the essence of enterprise management and improve our capability of strategic thinking and planning". Legend received little concrete help from management consultants at the critical point of entering the Internet business.

Foreign models would invariably encounter certain resistance from vested interests within the target company (major shareholders, managers, employees). These would make the implementation process more complicated and disrupt routine business and sales. A fundamental restructuring requires work on new procedures, training, and problem solving. These processes cannot be rushed.

3. The timing of this transformation at Start was also a questionable point. The group company needed consolidation, after a time of rapid expansion, not a complete overhaul or excessive restructuring.

Other Factors to be Considered

1. Differences in corporate cultures and cultural interaction: Significant differences in corporate cultures existed between this Chinese private company and Western trained consultants who knew more about international standards and practice. Their interaction seems inadequate due to the short time spent by McKinsey consultants at the group company.

2. Gaps between expectations and assistance offered: Start may have wanted quick short-term solutions to the current problems, while McKinsey consultants are used to offering long-term services and advice. The time those consultants spent on the project appears insufficient for them to make a comprehensive and effective contribution to solving problems. There is also a question about the level of commitment on the part of the consultants, since they

did not have follow up inspections of the implementation process, which they routinely offer to many other clients.

3. Balance between centralised operations and delegation of authority: Consultants saw the urgent need to curb the decentralisation tendency, so a restructuring plan was presented. By doing so, they provided some solution to the immediate problems, but failed to recognise the balance between centralisation and delegation and the need for subsidiaries to operate with less intervention and more freedom. A number of subsidiaries in fact achieved quite satisfactory results in their business and contributed large sums of revenue to the headquarters.

4. Problem diagnosis: Consultants provided some solutions to the existing problems in the company. Their selection was primarily based on comparisons with well-studied international models and practice. It was through case studies of Western companies, many of them large multinationals, that these consultants reached conclusions on how this particular Chinese company should be restructured. Their problem diagnosis seems to have been based more on model compatibility than on the real situation of the target company. Furthermore, the chosen models or schemes may not be applicable to small- and medium-sized Chinese companies.

This case covers two types of strategic decisions: diversification and restructuring. The decision by Start to diversify was made in a rushed manner, typical of many Chinese companies, and the decision to restructure was made rationally, though the result was far from their expectations. The issue of how foreign consulting firms work on Chinese companies emerged to have significant impact on the final outcomes of restructuring.

Retail Business and Enterprises

Domestic commerce in China has the following six key characteristics:

1. There are clear regional differences in income, purchasing power and patterns. There has never been a uniform national market, and sales of goods show vastly different trends in regional markets. Even mighty foreign retail multinationals have to modify their strategies to meet challenges in regional markets.

2. A general situation of oversupply has been in place since the late 1990s, and inflationary pressure remains weak. This is now a buyer's market, with a slight possibility of boosted consumption in the near future.

3. There exist much diversified commercial operations, such as department stores, supermarket chains, shopping malls, boutique shops, discount shops, convenience stores, warehouses, wholesalers, direct selling, TV commercial selling etc. In this segregated market, sales by large retail chains and groups take small shares of the total retail sales figures (see Figure 11.3).

4. Retail sales figures show a stable trend of growth, averaging 9.7% in the 1990s and at a level below 10% in the first few years of the 21st century. These consistent figures worry many in the government, since consumption has not been able to play a key role in economic growth, and people seem to have held back on spending. The consequences on manufacturing and service industries would be negative.

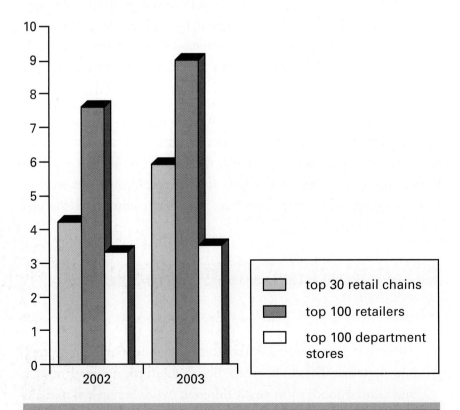

Figure 11.3 Top retailers in total sales (%)

5. Supermarket chains have gained great inroads and have become the main form of retail sales to residents. The First Shanghai Department Store used to be top in the city in sales, customer numbers and reputation. Since 1999, it has given way to Shanghai Lianhua Supermarket Chains in retail sales. In 2001, Lianhua had over 1,000 outlets and over 10 billion yuan in sales, making it the number one in supermarket chains. The market for department  stores is near saturation, while supermarket chains are on the rise in major cities. In 2003, the Ministry of Commerce published a list of top 30 retail chains in China. Shanghai Lianhua and three other Chinese companies took the top four position; Carrefour was number 5; with Wal-Mart at the 16th place. Foreign retailers made up 20% of the top 30 players on the list in sales figures.

6. There emerged specialised chains. These include retailers of electronics and electrical goods, building materials, furniture etc. The top household appliance retailers are Gome Group and Sanlian Group. They specialise in electronics and electrical goods and command extensive distribution channels. Gome was the number three retail chain on the above list and has expanded to Hong Kong to set up three stores there selling cut-price wide-ranging household appliances and electronics products. One of the advantages of these specialised retail chains is that they can bargain hard with manufacturers and get the best deals. As effective wholesalers, they offer large orders to household appliances manufacturers, such as TV set maker Changhong, at negotiations and demand favourable discount prices. In return, they can sell goods at their stores at lower retail prices. Manufacturers would have to take their orders while reluctantly accepting their price offers. Specialised retail chains in other sectors work in similar ways, though they lack the monopolising power of these two household appliances retail chains.

Foreign Retail Multinationals

Foreign retail chains were first approved to operate in China in 1992. The State Council officially approved 28 retailers in the form of joint ventures by the end of 1999, but local governments approved 277. Large foreign retail chains such as Carrefour made extraordinary efforts to woo regional authorities and obtained business permits from them. The French retailing giant of course received penalties from the central government for its breaching of rules. By early 2004, about 300 foreign retailers had entered the China market, with over US$5 billion in investment. This amount covers only the registered capital and assets, not other types of spending in operations. The number one retail chain in the world, Wal-Mart, has so far invested over US$200 million and opened 40 stores in China. This store number is less than Carrefour's 49 outlets, but it plans to reach 100 stores in total in three years. With its enormous outsourcing volumes, Wal-Mart is in effect China's 8th trading partner and takes over 10% of China's total exports to the US. In 2003, Wal-Mart made a procurement in China of US$15 billion. Carrefour plans to open 10 new stores each year, in addition to its 49 existing outlets. These top two foreign retail chains in China employ over 42,000 Chinese workers and managers. The German retailer Metro has opened nine stores in China and plans to reach 40 stores in three years.

According to China's WTO agreements, official restrictions on foreign retail business are to be removed completely from 1 January 2005. Those restrictions are in the areas of locations, number of businesses to be opened, levels of share holdings, and modes of operations. Foreign retailers have already obtained rights to take controlling shares in any joint venture companies with Chinese partners and are now able to expand their business to all provincial capitals.

In fast expansion processes, large foreign retailers applied a variety of price strategies to beat local competitors. These include super low every day prices (a trademark of Wal-Mart), bulk buying and discount prices paid to suppliers, and fees imposed on them as well. The first store is normally opened with full funding from a retail multinational, providing capital injection for a large site for sales. Subsequent stores may not be opened with their own funding; since the existing store can generate revenues, payments to suppliers can be delayed for a few months, and suppliers who sell their products in the new store have to pay entry and other fees. It has become a standard practice for retail multinationals to utilise the revenues from one store to subsidise expenditures on the next store, and so forth. This rolling process has enabled major foreign retail multinationals to set up a number of new stores in a short period of time, without detectable financial strains.

As a leader in supermarket retailing, Carrefour has encountered certain problems recently with its local suppliers. The key issue is the charges Carrefour collects from suppliers who wish to have their products put on shelves in Carrefour supermarkets. This is called entry fees and is standard practice in Carrefour shops. The problem is the high charges, which often force suppliers to take a loss and withdraw from the business.

A routine list of fees at Carrefour includes:

❑   The French National Day contribution (100,000 yuan/year);
❑   The Chinese National Day contribution (300,000 yuan/year);
❑   New store opening (20,000 yuan);
❑   Posters (2,340 yuan/store/round);
❑   Best display spot (2,000 yuan/store);
❑   New product entry (1,000/item);
❑   Manufacturer's discount (8% of sales);
❑   Services (2% of sales);
❑   And other miscellaneous items or fees.

The troubled relations between Carrefour and local suppliers came to a head in 2003. A business association of fried dry foods suppliers in Shanghai negotiated with Carrefour and demanded a 50% reduction in fees. After the refusal from Carrefour, the members of that association withdrew their goods from all Carrefour stores in Shanghai. As a common practice, supermarket chains collect fees from suppliers for various purposes, including promotion campaigns. This practice has saved them significant funds and assisted the opening of more outlets.

Wholesale Business

This sector has been a strictly protected area, in the hands of state-run companies. After China's WTO entry, foreign companies could enter the wholesale business and set up joint ventures with Chinese companies. The first such approved joint venture was between the Shanghai First Department Store and a top Japanese firm. Their cooperation in fact has little to do with WTO rules. The negotiations had been on for five years, and the initiative for a joint venture in the wholesale business came from the reforms under the Ministry of Commerce. Shanghai First was under threat from the emergence of supermarkets and failed in its transformation from state enterprise to a shareholding company. The cooperation with a foreign wholesaler was seen as a way out for this troubled company.

The proposed joint venture received support and approval from the authorities in charge, namely the Ministry of Commerce and the State Administration of Industry and Commerce. The negotiations went through several rounds in both China and Japan.

After expressing interests and intentions, both sides set up task teams, signed a framework agreement, and selected key personnel for this round of discussions.

The Japanese side sent executives to take field trips to Shanghai, Tianjin, Shandong, Guangdong and Fujian, assessing possibilities and risks. They examined retail and wholesale businesses in these regions and discussed issues with suppliers and manufacturers. They finally selected the Shanghai company as their partner.

Heads of the Japanese firm met the Mayor of Shanghai, thereafter starting the formal application process. On the Chinese side, the State Economic and Commerce Commission, the then Ministry of Domestic Trade, the State Administration of Industry and Commerce, the Ministry of Foreign Trade, Shanghai's Foreign Investment Commission, and Economic and Commerce Commission were all involved in the negotiations. After the proposed project from Shanghai was approved by the State Commissions, the two sides engaged in negotiations on the contract for the joint venture. The contract was approved by the national authorities in charge.

The project then became official. More procedures for registrations and other matters followed. The Japanese side took 49% of shares and the position of chairman of the board. The managing director is a Chinese, with two Japanese and one Chinese assistant managing directors. The time for final procedures for this joint venture came as

China entered the WTO. This coincidence has some significance in that foreign companies began to enter previously prohibited sectors, and their early endeavours and experiments prove not to be in vain under this new WTO framework.

Key Concepts

Disposable incomes, wages and other sources of incomes

Migrant workers, export manufacturing and cheap labour

Current social divisions and criteria

Major consumer behaviour patterns

Future consumption areas with potential

Advertising industry and management consulting services

Retail industry opening, retail chains and wholesale business

Discussion Questions

1. What do you see in the rising personal bank deposits in China? What are the main causes of this trend? What effects would such huge, stable deposits have on the economy (positive and negative)?

2. What are the major factors influencing consumption? What do you think are the right ways of boosting consumption; and which groups do you think are crucial for raising consumption levels (top, middle and low)? What would you suggest to lift incomes of lower groups and narrow the gaps?

3. Do you think it is plausible to place consumption as the key to GDP growth? In the case of China, what do you think is the right mix of the four components of GDP in development? What are the benefits of export-driven growth and of domestic market-driven growth? Are pro-consumption policies the right direction for economic development in the 21st century?

4. How would you describe and categorise Chinese consumers? How do traditional and contemporary ideas influence their purchasing behaviours? What areas of consumption do you think have future potential? Make comparisons with the trends in developed economies.

5. In the areas of advertising, market research and management consulting, what effects do cultural factors have on these businesses? Give examples.

6. Present your views on the Start case and the consultations by McKinsey.

7. What are the prospects of the retail market in China? What would be the future shares for domestic and foreign retailers?

Related Readings

Davis, Deborah, ed., *The Consumer Revolution in Urban China*, Berkeley, University of California Press, 2000.

Yan, R., "To reach China's Consumers, Adapt to *guo qing*", *Harvard Business Review*, September-October, 1994.

Yau, Oliver, *Consumer Behaviour in China*, New York, Routledge, 1994.

PART IV

FDI,
JOINT VENTURES
AND
MULTINATIONALS

Objectives of FDI and Growing Weight in the China Market

*F*oreign investment is an essential part of studies of China businesses. The contents of discussions focus on two major themes: foreign direct investment (FDI) and multinationals in China.

Foreign Direct Investment

In the present world markets, capital, technology and talents flow virtually freely among individual economies. Investments are frequently made by external investors, and businesses expand or contract in response to changes in a particular economy and business environment. Foreign investment has two major forms: foreign direct investment and portfolio investment.

Foreign direct investment (FDI) implies direct capital investment and set-up of projects in another economy. It requires official registration of business there, regular business operations and production or services provided in that economy.

Portfolio investment in foreign assets implies foreign investment made indirectly through financial institutions such as banks or funds. Investors put money in established funds as an initial investment, and fund managers invest the money in a combination of projects in other economies. The selected stocks and companies form an investment portfolio. Such investment involves foreign currency trading as well.

FDI focuses on investment in industrial or commercial projects, and it requires direct capital input and on-the-field operations, and is thus a riskier kind of investment. FDI, however, makes it possible for investors to enjoy the full benefits of smooth-running business and market expansion directly, so this is a preferred approach taken by foreign multinationals and companies with international exposure. Portfolio investment, on the other hand, presents less immediate risks, since fund managers could set up conservative targets and gain from the portfolio through risk spreading. Investors receive dividends and certain increases in asset value, instead of direct business returns, and losses made by managers are ultimately borne by investors. In the end, foreign portfolio investment is seen by foreign investors as just one more investment option to their domestic investment portfolios.

Objectives of FDI

The reasons for a foreign company to enter a new market are diverse. It generally follows a line of profit maximisation and business expansion. When a corporation reaches a certain level of dominance in domestic markets and foresees market saturation, it may consider expanding its business operations farther to another market. The incentives behind this move include enlarging the number of customers, saving on resources and transportation, searching for cheaper suppliers, seeking more talents, and finding new sources of income. Extra market potential, lower production costs and more income sources are the top considerations driving an expansion out of the boundaries of domestic markets. To many foreign companies, this is simply an extension of their current production and distribution lines, and their established business models can be applied to more markets with minimum modifications. The results would be more buyers and larger markets, as added bonuses to their present operations. Under such circumstances, foreign companies hold a strong desire for making FDI. Two examples are Coca-Cola and McDonald's. Based on their need for sales and their basic formula of costs and returns, the central goal is to get more people to consume their products, regardless of whether these people are in the US or in Uganda. Opening more shops or bottling factories means near certain enlarged returns in just a couple of years. These companies have thus engaged themselves in FDI in many countries to chase local customers and bigger sales figures.

In a similar vein of rationalising, foreign companies seek lower costs in their production through using cheaper labour and resources available in other economies. In a market economy, an enterprise can gain advantages in the market by being the industry leader in cost cutting. This principle also applies to businesses overseas and has been practised faithfully by multinationals. Production capacity has been shifting since the 1960s from the US to Japan, and to Taiwan and other East Asian economies, and then to South East Asian economies, and then to mainland China and Vietnam. Western European production capacity flowed to eastern European countries after the end of the Cold War in the same pattern. To manufacture one unit of product with the same assembly lines, the labour costs in the US is a few times above that in Singapore; and such costs are perhaps ten times higher in Singapore than in mainland China. The gaps in labour costs are so obviously wide that it is hugely attractive for multinationals to make FDI and sharply lower their total production costs.

In addition, FDI has become an important way of raising efficiency in an increasingly globalised world, and the desire for FDI will grow stronger if domestic competitors intend to make the same moves. In many industries, leading firms have gained dominant positions in the market, in the form of an oligopoly, and an overseas expansion by one leader would inevitably force the other to take similar action, for fear of losing the edge in a global competition. There is a strong desire among foreign multinationals to cultivate a new market and share the returns, rather than to face threats from other competitors which undertook successful overseas expansions. A good example is the rivalry between Coca-Cola and Pepsi, which follows the same pattern in China as that back home and in other markets.

Making FDI proves to be a convenient way of prolonging product lifecycles. A new product or model comes out on the market with considerable costs involved, and the manufacturing company would keep it on production lines for as long as possible. This is getting hard in a market economy where competition forces constant upgrading and offers widening choices for consumers. As market saturation is near, manufacturers have to abandon obsolete models and products.

With FDI in developing economies, manufacturers are able to reuse old models and prolong product lifecycles. Their designs, production lines, moulds and software could be transferred to another economy and continue to churn out products for the market there. Sales generated from a new market bring returns well above the initial costs for developing the product, and there is normally a standard fee charged on product transfer to a new user. One example is the car model Santana, from VW, which was a mature model introduced to China in the early 1980s and had taken a large market share for over ten years. It was superseded by new models only towards the end of the 1990s and is still in production.

A more recent occurrence is outsourcing, in which multinationals delegate most production and packaging to countries with a low cost labour force and satisfactory education. The home company works largely on design, financing, marketing and sales. Capital invested overseas result in finished goods exported back to domestic markets. In this case, there is a clear separation between the bulk of production activities and the overall management of business. The labour costs at home can be kept minimal, and greater profits from overseas operations flow back to the headquarters. FDI in this form are chiefly to set up the required production facilities and maintain routine operations. Outsourcing is growing in shares of total FDI, especially in countries like China and India. Inevitably, outsourcing touches on social and political issues in the domestic environment, namely loss of jobs and reduced domestic investment; and rising imports and trade deficits lead to a deterioration in trade relations with supplier economies. To sum up, the reasons behind the rise in outsourcing are precisely the reasons for FDI in all these processes.

FDI Policy Matters in China

Following the initial opening, the Chinese government in the 1990s worked expeditiously on improving FDI-related laws and regulations, and these improved the business environment especially for foreign companies operating in China. In 2000 and 2001, the National People Congress passed amendments to the laws of "Foreign-Invested Enterprises", "Foreign Joint Ventures", and "Foreign Cooperation Enterprises". Detailed rules regarding foreign enterprises had been issued in the 1990s, as supplements to the already published laws. The tax treatments to foreign enterprises were unified in 1991, and foreign firms and foreign employees began to bear uniform income tax rates afterwards.

More industrial sectors and regions were open to foreign business, and the 1995 industry catalogue from the State Council gave clear guidelines for FDI . The catalogue contains three categories of FDI. The "prohibited" areas of entry include those damaging national security, national economy, public interest, natural resources and the environment. The "restricted" areas include those where domestic enterprises have ready and matured technology, where monopoly is likely to emerge, duplicated investment, over capacity investment etc. The "encouraged" or preferred areas include new agricultural technology, energy, power, raw materials, infrastructure, electronics, motor cars, petrochemical, advanced technology, new technology, energy-saving technology, production for export, high value-added, and recycling technology.

In October 2003, the National People's Congress made the latest amendments to the three laws regarding foreign enterprises in China. These contain three major changes. The first was to remove the requirement on foreign enterprises to balance their own foreign exchange funding. The second was about the requirement on purchasing raw materials first within China, and the third was about the requirement on foreign enterprises to meet export quotas. These three were core requirements in early years before the government approved a foreign-invested project. The first one indicates the government's intention not to provide funds in foreign currencies to these projects. The third one shows an intention of protecting domestic markets and allowing FDI to be set up mainly for export purposes. Under previous rules, foreign enterprises had to export about 70% of their products to overseas markets, and sales to domestic markets were strictly limited in volume. Along with China's effort to enter the WTO, these requirements have been consistently modified and softened, till their final removal by the amendments in 2003.

The favourable treatments FDI projects received are often called "super national treatment". Obtaining national treatment was a key issue before China's WTO entry; in reality, due to policies of opening up and preferential treatments, foreign firms have enjoyed better terms in their operations over domestic Chinese firms in many areas, including tax rates, getting approvals, export incentives, labour requirements, and bank loans (see Table 12.1).

Table 12.1 Super and sub-national treatments to foreign and domestic enterprises		
	Foreign Enterprises	**Domestic Enterprises**
Operation and Management	Full rights to produce and export, no social welfare obligations	No full rights to produce, very few rights to export, many social welfare obligations
Foreign Exchanges	Holding all earned foreign exchange, free trading, direct borrowing from foreign banks	No rights to hold all earnings in foreign currencies, no choice in trading, limited borrowing from foreign banks
Approval Procedures	Agree to capital injection: set up business, then invest capital, instalment payments allowed	Capital injection certification: capital investment, then set up business, upfront payment
Credit and loans	Simple application and quick approval	Complicated and long approval process

FDI in China

FDI in China has grown in an uneven manner, with a sharp rise in the early 1990s and a plateau since the late 1990s, especially in utilised FDI.

❑ By July 2004, the total number of registered foreign-invested enterprises in China was 490,494. This figure is the aggregate of newly opened foreign businesses each year. It is inevitable that some foreign businesses later closed down and withdrew from the China market. The total number of foreign companies currently operating in China will be lower than the total registered number.

❑ By July 2004, the total utilised FDI in China reached US$540 billion and contracted FDI US$1,026 billion (see Figures 12.1 and 12.2).

❑ In 2003, 41,081 new foreign investment projects were approved, in comparison with the 2002 figure of 34,171.

❑ In 2003, China absorbed US$53 billion in utilised FDI, overtaking the US for the first time (see Figures 12.3 and 12.4). The US received FDI of US$40 billion, drastically down from the previous year of US$72 billion.

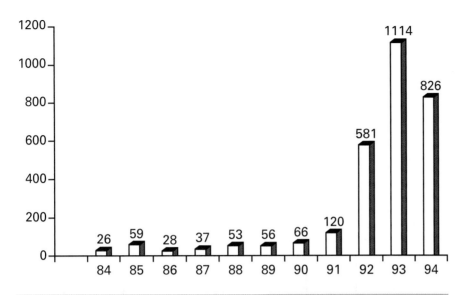

Figure 12.1   FDI in China (contracted, in 100 million US$)

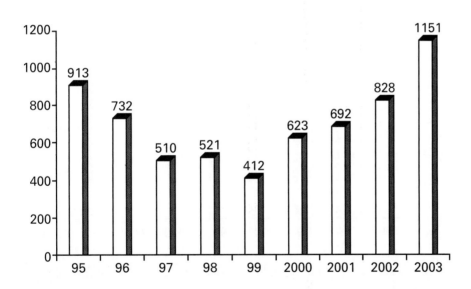

Figure 12.2   FDI in China (contracted, in 100 million US$)

❑   The first quarter of 2004 saw contracted FDI at US$34.3 billion and utilised FDI at US$14.1 billion.

❑   Foreign multinationals have set up over 600 research centres in China, with estimated R&D funds of US$4 billion.

❑   Over 90% of FDI is concentrated in eastern coastal regions, and a number of inland regions even registered negative FDI growth in 2002.

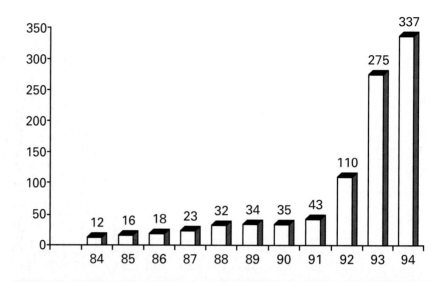

Figure 12.3 Utilised FDI (in 100 million US$)

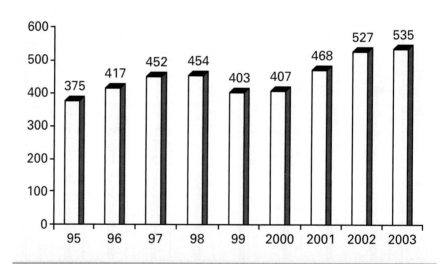

Figure 12.4 Utilised FDI (in 100 million US$)

❑ FDI from Hong Kong and Macau takes a share of over 40%. FDI from developed economies (the US, Japan and the new EU) has a total share of 25%. Although the above two regions returned to Chinese sovereignty in 1997 and 1999 respectively, investments from them are counted as FDI, and their investing companies enjoy preferential treatments in mainland China from being classified as foreign companies. Combined with investment by overseas Chinese, capital injection by investors of Chinese origin counts for over 60% of total utilised FDI.

❑   Investing countries or regions: Top FDI players in 2003 were Hong Kong, the Virgin Islands, Japan, South Korea, the US, Taiwan, Singapore, West Samoa, the Cayman Islands, and Germany. This ranking is based on the utilised FDI from these places.

In Figure 12.5 of **discrepancy**, there is a time gap between the signed contract of investment and the capital injection into the proposed project. In the past, some foreign investors took advantage of this time difference, making business deals while not making real capital injection as required by the contract. "Fake" foreign investment also occurred as some companies had no intention to invest, but only to change the status of certain domestic companies to joint ventures on paper, so as to enjoy those preferential treatments designed for foreign companies. The Chinese government later corrected this loophole and tightened rules on this matter. For example, in Shanghai, you can get business registration done and start business operations after the contract is signed. Within six months, the promised capital in foreign currencies, such as US$, must be deposited into the account of the local bureau of the State Foreign Exchanges Administration. A special team there is charged with the duties of certifying your deposits and issuing official receipts. At the end of six months, you get a warning for not making the required deposit, and your business will be suspended. At the end of the 12th month, if your capital investment is still not made, your business registration, previous contracts and business deals in China

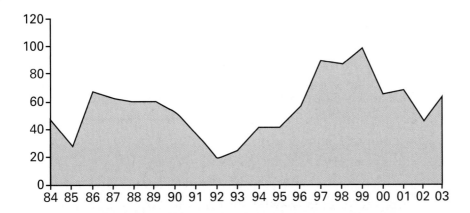

Figure 12.5   Margins between contracted and utilised FDI (a full compatibility at 100)

will all be cancelled. You have to start a new process to register a business and make the investment as required. Needless to say, your second business registration will be extremely difficult with bad records of previous non-compliance.

The figure of discrepancy also tells us something about the investment environment and investors' intentions. At its highest point in 1999, there was a near 100% compatibility between contracted and utilised FDI. This indicates that, as the Asian financial crisis spread through Asia and posed threats to other developed economies, capital flight turned to capital inflows to the Chinese economy—an economy considered safe under those circumstances. Swift capital injection after FDI contracts shows a sign of urgency on the part of foreign investors to seek a haven for their money quickly. Gaining higher returns was perhaps moved to the back burner. In contrast, the low point in 1992 indicates a slow process of capital injection by somewhat reluctant foreign investors, when the Chinese economy was undergoing a period of austerity, and Deng's southern tour had not revitalised the economy. Prospects seemed quite gloomy, and investors were less committed to their proposed projects in China. After this point, capital injection compliances increased remarkably till its peak in 1999. In the following years, the compatibility reached a stable level, and investment decisions were made by investors on the basis of their own business plans and financial resources, being less influenced by a sudden desire to rush in.

Types of FDI in China

There are several common types of FDI in China, and Chinese laws have been passed in regard to four of these types.

Equity Joint Ventures (JV)

The joint venture type includes the following contents. Investments are approved by Chinese authorities, foreign businesses are allowed to operate in China, and foreign investors are to make joint capital investment with Chinese partners, shoulder risks, and receive gains according to the agreed shares. The joint venture is a limited company, with the foreign partner making no less than 25% of the total investment. In the early years, due to the extent of market opening, foreign partners could not take more than 50% of total shares. This has been changed since the late 1990s, and many multinationals now acquire a share higher than 50% or hold controlling shares. Legitimate gains and profits can be transferred back to the country of the foreign partner or for reinvestment in China. Tax breaks and other incentives are provided for such reinvestment. The Chinese law of Foreign Joint Ventures provides detailed rules in regard to joint ventures in China.

Wholly Foreign-owned Enterprises (WFOE)

They are foreign companies approved by Chinese authorities to have business operations in China, with full ownership of the business and full capital injection from foreign investors. The Chinese law of Foreign-Invested Enterprises gives the full descriptions of rules in regard to wholly foreign-owned enterprises in China.

Contractual Joint Ventures

These are companies operating in China, with government approvals and foreign investment made by foreign investors. Cooperation is at the core, indicating that most capital, technology and equipment are provided by foreign investors, and the Chinese side largely provides land, labour, factory space and natural resources. Such a company is formed because of the perceived mutual benefits to both sides and the advantages held by each side. This type of enterprise is bonded chiefly by the contract, under which each side performs certain required duties. Unlike an equity joint venture, each company in the joint venture pays taxes separately, with foreign companies paying their own taxes in China according to relevant rules.

Joint Exploration

By definition, joint exploration is the oil and natural gas exploration on land and sea by business partners.

In a brief period up to 1992, foreign capital into China was mainly in the form of loans. FDI came into the mainstream after 1992, with equity joint ventures and wholly foreign-owned enterprises as the most common. Since 1999, mergers and acquisitions have been on the rise, leading to increasing numbers of wholly foreign-owned enterprises. The other two types are less common, especially the fourth type of mostly huge energy projects involving both governments of the FDI partners. An example of such an investment is the natural gas pipeline from China's western regions to coastal regions, over a distance of 4,000 kilometres. The project was undertaken by the biggest Chinese oil producer PetrolChina and Royal Dutch/Shell Group companies. This gigantic joint exploration project needed the firm backing of both Chinese and British governments and has endured numerous clashes of interests in the process.

FDI in China's Economy

FDI is a major source of growth in China's GDP.

Capital injection from FDI increases the total investment in the economy, thus enlarging total GDP (see Figure 12.6).

$$GDP = C + I + G + NX$$
$$= \text{Consumption} + \text{Investment} + \text{Government Purchase} + \text{Net Export}$$

In recent years, foreign enterprises delivered more than 60% of exported goods to their home economies, in a pattern of outsourcing as described above. As a result, the item of net exports jumped, so FDI has an indirect impact on GDP through increased exports. FDI also

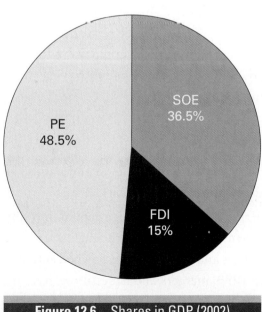

Figure 12.6 Shares in GDP (2002)

adds to total investment. It is estimated that between 1983 and 1999, FDI made a contribution of 27.8% to China's average GDP growth rate of 9.7%.

Through operations and hiring local workers, FDI also injects certain percentage of taxes into the government's coffers (see Figure 12.7). From 1986 to 1995, taxes collected from foreign-invested companies totalled 150 billion yuan. In 2003, the annual corporate income tax from foreign-invested companies was 70 billion yuan. To regional governments, taxes collected from locally operated foreign companies figure heavily in their budgets, hence the earnest effort to attract more FDI projects. For example, P&G Guangzhou has regularly made tax payments of 1 billion yuan per year to the municipal government.

FDI has made a profound impact on China's economy in the areas of technology, management, marketing, work ethics and efficiency. Foreign companies have provided established models in these areas for Chinese managers and employees. The lifting of technological levels is done through introduction of new production lines, equipment and manufacturing standards. Management skills and work ethics have been vigorously taught in training schemes and in business practice. Chinese managers also learned the ways of conducting marketing

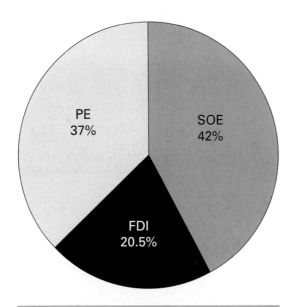

Figure 12.7   Shares in tax payment (2002)

campaigns and increasing efficiency from the operations of foreign companies close by.

❑ Employment:

At the end of 2002, foreign companies in China directly employed 23 million Chinese workers. From 1997, foreign enterprises annually created 1.1 million jobs on average. Since FDI projects provide salaries for Chinese employees, job opportunities offered by foreign companies also contribute to the total of GDP by increasing consumption. It should be pointed out that despite a smaller percentage in total employment numbers, foreign enterprises have hired that particular part of the workforce that are mostly well-educated and skilful workers through selection and training. Foreign multinationals enjoy the privilege of choosing the cream of talents from university graduates. On the other hand, domestic state and private enterprises hire large numbers of employees of various levels of qualifications. It is basically a contrast between white-collar workers and migrant, peasant-turned-workers (see Figure 12.8).

❑ Competition with domestic enterprises:

Foreign companies pose a formidable threat to the very existence of domestic companies. First, they introduced market competition

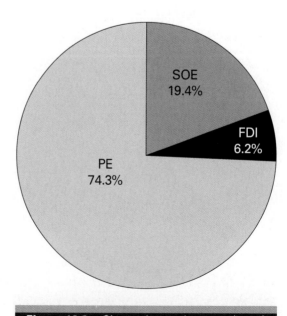

Figure 12.8 Shares in employment (2002)

at the early times of reforms when state enterprises received sufficient protection and private enterprises were in infancy. Second, market shares gained by foreign enterprises are those lost by domestic players. Although the markets increase in total size, making a bigger "pie", foreign enterprises succeed in entering permitted sectors and squeeze out previous participants. The idea of market competition has been widely accepted by domestic enterprises, and a number of them turned the idea around and achieved better performance in various industries in the face of the onslaught of powerful foreign multinationals. On the whole, the entry of colossal foreign multinationals proves devastating to business operations of many domestic enterprises.

❑   Domination in certain industries:

This issue is closely linked with the point just mentioned. Through fierce competition and with advantages in technology and management, foreign companies often reach the top position of particular industries in a short period of time, and leave a large distance between them and domestic companies. Monopoly or oligopoly now exists in a number of industrial sectors, and the Chinese government has not effectively dealt with this problem. The following contents on foreign multinationals will provide further discussion on this point.

Latest Trends of FDI in China

From Joint Ventures (JV) to Wholly Foreign-owned Enterprises (WFOE)

Along with China's WTO entry and relaxation of legal restrictions, WFOEs are fast increasing in number as the new focus of FDI projects, replacing joint ventures. From 1997, the number of WFOEs has overtaken joint ventures in newly approved foreign enterprises in China. From the point of view of cross-cultural management, this change also indicates that foreign multinationals have acquired sufficient knowledge and experience of doing business in China, so that they no longer require the service of their former Chinese partners and instead intend to go ahead alone in business operations. For example, Siemens, the giant German manufacturer, now has 59 individual enterprises in China. Among them, 12 are WFOEs, and 45 joint ventures are with controlling shareholdings by Siemens. In Shanghai, over 80% of newly registered FDI projects in 2003 were wholly foreign-owned.

Setting up WFOEs

With fewer restrictions, foreign partners of a joint venture could set up a separate wholly owned subsidiary and then transfer major business operations to that subsidiary. Eventually, foreign partners would withdraw from the joint venture and make the switch to control a new WFOE. To a certain extent, VW is doing this by establishing a wholly owned car sales subsidiary, which will take over all distribution and sales of cars from Shanghai VW, and the previous extensive distribution network of Shanghai Automotive Industry Corporation will have little control over car sales.

Injecting Funds to Become Majority Shareholders

Foreign partners adopt this strategy of increasing funding in the joint venture, so that they can get a majority shareholding. In the example of Shanghai VW, VW decided to pour in Euros 5.3 billion from 2003 to 2008 as new investment. This would make VW shareholding in Shanghai VW well above 60%, and SAIC will become a minority shareholder. Kodak also invested US$100 million and a new production line in its Chinese competitor, Lucky Film, to obtain 20% shares, making it a strategic shareholder of the company. In the Siemens case, most of its controlling shareholdings in joint ventures came from its increased investment and the giving up of shares by Chinese partners.

Technology Transfer and Setting-up of R&D Centres

Multinationals hold core technologies in their FDI projects in China, and these business advantages are subject to strict supervision and tight control in a supplier economy. Even for joint ventures, foreign partners have complete control over core technologies, while production lines are open to their Chinese counterparts. As FDI increases, transfer of technology becomes an increasingly troublesome issue in achieving growing operations and mutual benefits. Multinationals began to set up their R&D centres in China from the late 1990s. Nortel of Canada was the first to set up an R&D centre in Beijing in 1994.

Such centres have benefits in three aspects. They service local operations and can solve many problems in production quickly. They are able to utilise a large local talent pool and draw in professionals of higher education for extensive research work. Microsoft established a central research institute in China, with about 200 staff from the best university graduates and even with a number of renowned scientists working there on a regular basis. These centres are also close to local markets and customers' needs and have a shorter response time. In these R&D centres, new products, designs and patents are still the properties of the investing company and registered under their name. By June 2002, foreign multinationals had set up over 150 research institutions in China.

Entry to Previously Prohibited Areas

These areas include service industries, such as banking and wholesale industries. Foreign banks and retail chains have gained great inroads to the China market after the WTO entry, and have established solid foundations for their quick expansion. For government-controlled sectors, such as municipal utility projects, trial runs of foreign participation are under way. These projects cover water, gas and electricity supplies and were subject to direct management by government agencies. Changes in rules regarding foreign involvement, for example, have led to foreign shareholding in Shenzhen's gas supply networks. In 2002, a French water company purchased a water supply factory and network in Pudong, Shanghai, paying 2 billion yuan for 50% of the shares and the right to operate for 50 years. Beijing has also offered shares for participation by foreign investors in its projects of energy, heating, recycling and tolled roads. It is likely that some foreign enterprises are to be listed on domestic stock markets. The first entry is perhaps Unilever, which has submitted a formal application to Chinese authorities. Other foreign heavyweights such as Ford, have obtained their shareholding in listed domestic companies, so there is a possibility for them to be listed.

Transforming Indebted State Enterprises

Policy shifts since the late 1990s have allowed foreign companies to participate in restructuring of state enterprises and to become part owners or even majority shareholders of these enterprises. In particular, large numbers of insolvent state enterprises in the hands of the four State Asset Management Agencies are to be disposed of in acceptable ways. Selling part of or most company shares to foreign companies in the same industries would be a preferred option. This spells out enormous business opportunities for potential foreign buyers. The Japanese carmaker Suzuki was the first to take action in buying 25% shares of Beijing Travel Group in 1995.

Recent Allowances Made for FDI

From 2003, revised rules gave more room for FDI to enter China. The required 25% minimum share of capital investment in a joint venture has been readjusted, and joint ventures with lower than 25% of foreign capital investment are now able to get business registration and enjoy certain favourable tax treatments. New rules from 2003 also give investments made in RMB the same status as that of foreign currencies. This applies especially to reinvestment of earned profits and dividends in China projects. Since China has accumulated a huge pool of foreign exchange reserve, mostly in US$, there is no longer a shortage of foreign currencies, and the focus has shifted from earning hard currencies to providing more funds, even in RMB, to enterprises operating in China. The RMB, after all, is the currency vital to most business operations in this economy. Foreign enterprises may benefit from this change through easier financing and less trouble in making hard currency transfers.

Analysis on Establishing Joint Ventures in China

The following is a brief description of considerations from both sides on a joint venture in China. The key questions to be asked are why foreign companies come to invest in China and what both sides expect from their counterpart. For joint ventures and wholly foreign-owned enterprises, all parties involved need to lay out their objectives and considerations before making FDI and proposing business strategies.

Foreign Partner's Objectives in a Joint Venture

A Presence in the China market

This is particularly crucial if your competitor has built up a sizeable presence there.

Generating Profits in China

This relates to the issue of income sources. Investors prefer a strategy that creates more sources of profits instead of one source.

Rationalising Production by Making the Best Use of Location Advantages

This is to move closer to your markets and customers. You get feedback and respond to them more quickly. In addition, transportation costs will be minimised.

Lowering Labour Costs

As discussed above, cost cutting is a central rationale in all overseas expansion, and utilising a cheaper labour force has positive effects over the entire production process. China is known for providing low-wage yet well qualified workers for assembly lines. A comparison between wages in China and Singapore shows a ten-fold difference in general.

Risk Diversification

A typical business saying is that you don't put all eggs in one basket. Risks increase as your investments concentrate in one market, even if that is your home market. The purpose of portfolio investment is essentially to even out risks. For multinationals, their needs to diversify are so strong that overseas expansion and outsourcing have been regarded as the main forms of risk diversification. For small- and medium-sized foreign companies, they harbour fewer urges to expand outward, but they follow the general rule of risk diversification as well.

Overcoming Trade Barriers in China

This is based on practical needs. It was a common practice that domestic markets were tightly protected by high tariffs and other treatments to deter imports. Even with foreign trade liberalisation, trade barriers to imported goods can be seen in all countries. This kind of unfair rule also applies to Chinese companies that have moved overseas. To counter this restriction, an effective way is to set up business in that country and produce and sell locally. With this strategy, joint ventures appear more appealing to local authorities than wholly foreign-owned enterprises, due to their cooperation with local partners and mutual benefits that are generated from such projects. More favourable treatments are thus provided for foreign partners in joint ventures. Foreign multinationals have successfully tested this strategy in China and made a consistent effort in seeking suitable partners. On the other hand, Haier, the Chinese household appliance manufacturer, entered the US market with the same approach. However, a related consideration is that when tariffs are sufficiently low, locally made goods would sell at price levels not much lower than those for imported goods. Foreign partners in joint ventures will soon have to face this new dilemma.

Building a Base to Access Markets in East Asia

A foreign multinational often sets up regional headquarters in an attempt to get access to most markets in that region. With China's central location in East Asia, with Japan to the north and Singapore to the south, a business stronghold in China will project influence to neighbouring economies and help gain access to more markets in the region.

Gaining Access to Natural Resources

Locally operated businesses would have ready access to natural resources such as crude oil, gas, minerals, and raw materials. Such operations would lower transportation and production costs considerably.

Chinese Partner's Objectives in a Joint Venture

Their objectives and considerations often reflect the original rationales of the government behind the open door policies.

Obtaining Technology Transfers

Foreign investment was seen as a major source of introducing advanced foreign technologies. In a joint venture, both sides are supposed to share capital, costs, profits and technologies.

Learning Management Skills

This aspect became more important at later stages when Chinese partners realised that management skills and practices enhance total performance and increase operational efficiency. These are perhaps more crucial in production than equipment imported.

Utilising Foreign Capital

There was a wide shortage of capital for investment, upgrading and production for China in the early reform years. Foreign investment, whether from overseas Chinese or developed economies, was seen as crucial in attracting needed capital into the economy. Joint ventures would serve this purpose by getting more capital injection into investment projects.

Penetrating Foreign Markets and Generating Foreign Exchange

This is part of export strategies. Early joint ventures aimed at overseas markets, and foreign investors provided capital for enlarged production and then exported finished goods to developed economies. It was the common thinking that foreign partners bore the responsibility of selling to foreign customers. Earnings in foreign currencies would be shared by Chinese and foreign partners. Before the end of the 1990s, this had been a central rationale for the government to encourage foreign investment and exports in many ways.

Improving Employment Situation

The Chinese government expected to provide more jobs from approving more foreign-invested projects. This strategy has worked only partially, with foreign enterprises hiring more people each year, while more domestic firms having closed down in the face of unprecedented market competition. Local governments continue to advocate this strategy, since more investment projects in their own regions will surely increase employment for the time being.

Developing Independent R&D

This has been an undaunted goal of the government in opening markets to foreign investors. Advanced foreign technologies come along with imported equipment, and trained Chinese engineers will later master the introduced skills and technologies. For this reason, joint venture contracts often contain demands from Chinese partners on setting up R&D centres or facilities. Being aware of the sensitive issues of core technologies and copyright protection, foreign partners have adopted various tactics to delay compliance of or simply refuse such demands. In recent years, foreign multinationals have sped up their process of setting up R&D centres in China, as one of the new trends discussed above. The Chinese strategy has worked to a certain extent, as shown in quality products from Chinese parts suppliers to major motor car manufacturers. This strategy can also be seen to have failed, since core technologies in many industries are still in the hands of foreign multinationals, and research patents from those R&D centres legally belong to their investing companies.

Investors' Major Concerns

There are common concerns from investors who may or may not have full knowledge of the business environment in China. FDI to them is perhaps simply an investment option, among others, and business expansion seems a logical solution to many. As the process of FDI moves forward, investors increasingly confront interlocked and complicated issues. As a preliminary plan, investors would like to search for answers to some basic questions. These include:

Rule of Law in the Business Environment

This is particularly crucial to investors from rule-based economies, where parties involved in business enjoy legal protection and rights to appeal. This gives great confidence to business people who intend to invest. If the target economy is not a rule-based one, particularly where it is not a common law environment, then the top priority is to gather information on formal laws and regulations in regard to investment and business activities.

Governing Skills of Government Officials

The outcome of investment in a non rule-based economy depends largely on how effective the government handles the problems and whether officials have the required skills and quality. In open coastal regions of China, things have improved remarkably, with streamlined procedures and helpful officers to guide investors. When the government takes a pro-active approach towards FDI, investors are able to leave many tasks to them and save time on getting around all kinds of procedures. The Chinese concept of *guanxi* provides added bonus for foreign investors to smooth things out. Government officials are also the people who bridge the gaps between foreign investors and local players. Increasingly, conflicts between domestic and foreign enterprises are mediated by government bureaux to find a resolution. Multinationals have learned quickly the subtle ways of persuasion of government officials in charge and get results they desire.

Continuation of Preferential Treatments

In the case of a late mover, knowledge of other businesses receiving preferential treatments would encourage the making of investment decisions. The concern will then be whether such favourable conditions will continue to be in place at the time of investment and afterwards. This also applies to existing players in the economy, as their established positions and investment may be affected by adjustments imposed.

Industrial Bases and Suppliers

This refers to general conditions in industrial production. Foreign investors mostly aim at an extension of production, thus the level of industrial development, in terms of large industrial bases and availability of a supplier network, is essential. This determines the involvement and smooth running of a business after initial FDI is made. The choice made has much to do with this level of development, and foreign investors prefer a particular region to invest in simply because there are ready suppliers to provide quality parts and prompt delivery. There is a common saying that in particular towns in the PRD or YRD macroregions, you can find all the parts and machinery for your business needs from suppliers in a radius of, say, 50 kilometres and you get prompt door-to-door delivery seven days a week.

After these questions regarding general conditions are examined, investors need to consider further factors in detail, for a real investment project. These are related to business costs and the size of the budget for initial capital injection.

Cost Factors to be Considered

Negotiations

There are costs involved in business negotiations. These include flights, accommodations, transport etc. Business trips to China will incur further unexpected expenditures, as the practices there are different. It should be pointed out that negotiations have multiple rounds and may lead to no immediate conclusion. It is not uncommon that the Chinese partners come back to you for a concrete deal after a few years have passed.

Construction

A FDI project, industrial or commercial, requires land and space acquisition. For this, investors should consider getting official permits, ensure clearly marked boundaries, making required compensations to local residents if the project leads to eviction and resettlements, expect delays in construction, which may come from contractors' misconduct or from natural causes, and get water, power and gas connections etc. These are normal tasks to undertake for a foreign-invested project and incur corresponding costs. For FDI in housing projects in particular, these are routine procedures and practice.

Equipment

Investors need to plan for the quantity and value of imported equipment and key parts for their industrial projects. Costs involved may be considerable.

Transportation

These cover the ways your materials and products are moved. You should consider the use of available means of transportation, and for bulk goods, to use containers for external transportation, and other means for domestic needs. The factor of convenience also includes the customs. Foreign enterprises are able to choose their ports of import and export, not necessarily the one closest to the site. Many choose a port on the basis of their assessment on how efficient and fast the customs are cleared. For example, in southern China, you can choose from Hong Kong, Shenzhen, Guangzhou and Zhuhai. Depending on what impression you get, you may choose one of them because of friendly treatments and time saved there. These should be all factored into cost calculations.

Employees

Foreign investors need to hire both expatriate and local employees. The wage levels for expatriates are higher than those for staff at home sites, and their package includes basic pay, bonus, hardship subsidies, accommodation, transport and communication expenses. Foreign nationals are employed as managers of projects to ensure quality of products and smooth management of projects. Local employees would cost more to hire than those in domestic enterprises, in order to give incentives to and attract suitably qualified employees from other types of firms. As a common practice, local employees are also provided with fringe benefits, pensions, and training costs. In recent years, the government enforced social securities payments more systematically and vigorously, and those companies that failed to oblige, foreign or domestic, were punished accordingly. Foreign investors should take this into account.

Sales

Foreign investors also need to spend on marketing and sales. This includes setting up distribution networks, at least shop fronts, or making deals with wholesalers or retailers. Extra budgets must be set aside for advertising and promotion of new products and brands. Ongoing costs will be incurred for maintaining brand image.

Operating Capital

Foreign investors have to ensure sufficient operating capital and take into account delayed lending, payment for goods delivered, and chasing of debts owed. All unexpected trouble will mean slower capital circulation and cause difficulties in business operations.

Raw Materials

The normal operations of an investment project require stable supply of raw materials, and foreign investors need to pay attention to price changes. Some are quite sensitive to market fluctuations, and price increases hurt the bottom-line of many industries. A precaution is to store raw materials in warehouses in bonded areas near customs. These raw materials can be shipped in right away if there is a shortage.

Rights Protection

Multinationals in China spend huge amounts of money on protecting their brand names and chasing copyright violators across the country. Since intellectual property rights is a serious issue and fake goods are aplenty, foreign investors would have to spend considerably on counter-measures. The US giant P&G spends about US$3 million in China on eliminating fakes and carries out hundreds of raids each year. The compensation P&G receives from court cases against fakes are often meagre.

Law Suits

Now foreign companies are used to suing in Chinese courts for violations and illegal activities. Big companies with sufficient funds would be able to bear the costs of lawsuits, but these are heavy burdens on smaller companies. A serious problem is that even if they win legal cases, compensation for their losses may not be sufficient and enforcement takes a long time.

Others

There are other relatively minor costs to be considered. On top of taxes, enterprises have to pay for surcharges and levies from various authorities. Occasional fines and donations to certain institutions also have to be made. It is always a good practice to keep extra room for meeting such demands.

Recent Re-evaluation on FDI in China

The Chinese economy has undergone fundamental changes in the past 25 years, and new challenges have impacted on government policies and regulations. It seems that the initial rationales behind its opening up have lost certain plausibility. Rethinking of FDI in China has emerged and will bring about more changes.

A central understanding regarding FDI is to attract foreign capital for China's reconstruction. Capital shortage was severe at the beginning of reforms, and the central government pushed hard seeking alternative sources of capital injection. Under this thinking, a series of preferential policies were proposed and implemented across the country. The number of projects and quantity of FDI flowing in were even placed as major criteria for the promotion or demotion of local officials. Over the years, this previously crucial issue has lost its urgency. Capital is no longer in short supply, in terms of total GDP figures, as there are increased government revenues, an ever growing amount of foreign exchange reserves and huge personal savings sitting in banks. The focus turns to how efficiently funds are utilised, rather than how large the total quantity of FDI is. Many cases of official malpractice coming from pressure of FDI quotas, such as offering extraordinary deals to prospective foreign investors against government rules, and selling local land and factories at low prices, have cast doubts on the worthiness of FDI. The direction of FDI in following years will be closely scrutinised and modified.

In a macroeconomic review, it is clear to all that increased FDI is a result of market shares being given out. Part of official policies toward FDI included opening markets, allowing foreign enterprises to operate in many sectors. To domestic enterprises, their market shares have been traded for an increase in FDI. The end result is a monopoly by foreign enterprises in many of these opened industries. There is a simple switch of places between state enterprises and foreign enterprises in this monopoly.

On the issue of technology transfer, the original goal of the government has not been achieved. Foreign multinationals continue to dominate in many industries with their tightly held core technologies. Labour-intensive production facilities and assembly lines are widespread in China, with little advanced technology used. Core technology and key parts are imported from overseas to make completed final products. With a growing percentage of outsourcing, technology transfer is becoming even less likely. The Chinese government and many industry analysts hold the opinion that giving out market shares has not brought in the technologies they wanted.

As the total foreign trade volume rose sharply, the Chinese economy faces an awkward situation. High percentages of exports are made by foreign enterprises under their outsourcing strategies—about 55% in 2003 (see Figure 12.9). In addition to trade disputes between China and developed economies, this kind of exports also creates a complicated problem for the government. Since low costs and high mark ups are the common practice of multinationals, there is only small room for high value-added production, and growing exports bring back relatively small earnings to domestic manufacturers. This situation has been

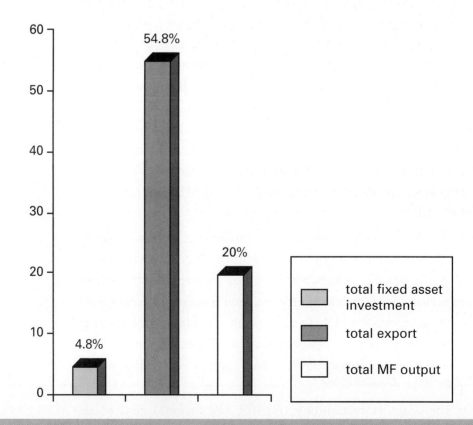

Figure 12.9 FDI in total fixed asset investment, exports and manufacturing output (2003)

discussed in the sections on China's foreign trade. FDI, in this case, generates fewer real returns than expected.

Under the policy of opening up, the government granted various forms of preferential treatments to FDI and has through this improved the general business environment. Under the WTO agreement on national treatment, many of these preferential treatments are now in question. They are legal breaches of the WTO rules and discriminate against domestic players. In recent years, calls to limit super national treatments to foreign entities have grown louder, and top authorities have begun to look at this issue more seriously. In an effort to bring all players to an equal national treatment, some preferential treatments and favourable deals negotiated between individual foreign firms and governments at all levels may be scaled back. In this relationship between FDI policies and the WTO rules, the trend will be to follow the latter and make adjustments to the former.

The above is a summary of recent changes to FDI and some general reviews the government has made on FDI. Foreign investors, however, may still have their troubles and complaints on the actual business environment and demand improved FDI regulations to better service their investment projects. With steady economic growth, the government may see FDI as just one of the issues in the Chinese economy, rather than a top priority. It is then vital for foreign investors to follow closely the changes and revisions, and realign their investment plans accordingly.

Key Concepts

FDI and foreign portfolio investment
Objectives in FDI
Three categories of FDI in official guidelines
Types of FDI in China
FDI contributions to the Chinese economy
Major concerns and cost factors in FDI

Discussion Questions

1. What are the top objectives of FDI from the viewpoint of multinationals? What do you consider are the most important factors in a business environment for an investment decision?

2. In the case of China, explain the areas in an economy in which FDI has impacted on.
3. Considering cost factors and policy matters, give the reasons for your choice on joint venture or wholly foreign-owned as the preferred type of FDI.

Related Readings

Ambler, Tim, Morgen Witzel, *Doing Business in China*, 2nd ed., London, Routledge/Curzon, 2004.

Harwit, Eric, *China's Automobile Industry: Policies, Problems and Prospects*, New York, M.E. Sharpe, 1995.

Huang, Yasheng, *Selling China: Foreign Direct Investment during the Reform Era*, New York, Cambridge University Press, 2003.

Kelly, Lane, Shenkar, Oled, eds., *International Business in China*, New York, Routledge, 1993.

Mann, Jim, *Beijing Jeep: the Short, Unhappy Romance of American Business in China*, New York, Simon & Schuster, 1989

Strange, Roger, *Management in China: the Experience of Foreign Business*, London, Frank Cass, 1998.

Strange, Roger, Slater, Jim, Wang, Limin, eds., *Trade and Investment in China: the European Experience*, London, Routledge, 1998.

Strasser, Steven, "China: Rules of the Game", *Newsweek*, 21 February 1995, pp 44–49.

Walker, Danielle Medina, Walker, Thomas, Schmitz, Joerg, *Doing Business Internationally: The Guide to Cross-cultural Success*, 2nd edn., New York, McGraw-Hill, 2003.

13

Procedures and Adaptation in FDI

umerous Chinese laws and regulations have been promulgated in regard to operations of foreign enterprises. Before business operations can begin, foreign investors are to have their business legally registered in China. This process involves multiple procedures and approvals. In addition, internal government rules have been stipulated for bureau officers to follow in handling applications. Under these general guidelines, regional authorities have their power to set up their own rules, to speed up the procedures or add more enquires, depending on their intentions. It is for the foreign investors to successfully clear these procedures and then work on their intended investment projects. It should be pointed out that there are many detailed rules, and the actual application process may be quite tedious. As such, we can only offer a summary here of the most common procedures as a reference guide.

General Procedures for Joint Ventures

Selecting Your Joint Venture Partners

Foreign investors now have a discretion in choosing Chinese partners. They were often not given such a chance in the past, since the government tended to appoint a partner for the venture, from state enterprises in relevant industries. This is not solely to control foreign businesses or necessarily a bad thing. It is partly for the benefit of foreign investors, since they had little knowledge of the business environment there and how a company functioned in China. The partner chosen was often a top enterprise in that industry and had compatible size and financial strength. Especially for those national level joint ventures, the Chinese side would most likely provide an industrial giant with firm government or ministerial backing. One example is the venture between VW of Germany and Shanghai Automotive Industry Corp., both in the top three positions in the automobile industry of their own countries.

This early practice, however, had many defects. The chosen Chinese partner, though considered suitable by the government, might not be the right type for the venture. Foreign investors, needless to say, preferred to get their own choices. Now they are able to do just that and select state, collective or private companies to be their partners. This relieves the responsibility on the part of the government, but puts pressure squarely on foreign investors, testing their searching and evaluating skills. The doubt over whether they picked the right partner in an unfamiliar business environment is surely a heavy burden they have to bear.

In their preliminary searches, foreign companies must examine the attributes of their potential local partners. They need to investigate diligently whether the Chinese partner has an acceptable position in the market and the industry concerned; whether that enterprise is a business of long standing and has considerable connections to authorities and other key players; and whether its corporate image and distribution networks would benefit the venture. Since large Chinese state enterprises have their chiefs bearing official ranks, the strength and standing of these enterprises can be detected by checking out these ranks. If an enterprise is attached directly to a ministry of the central government or the chief of that enterprise has an official vice-ministerial rank, this entity would have more clout and resources of all kinds available for the venture.

Foreign companies would also need to ask the question about their partners' exposure to foreign trade and overseas markets. A previous experience in doing business with a foreign entity would prove valuable for the venture, raising the likelihood of a smooth relationship in future cooperation. In addition to these efforts to get a general picture, foreign companies also need to make detailed studies of figures, checking out financial resources, asset values and liquidity. Since these figures are also requested by government offices at the stage of application and approval, Chinese partners would have to reveal relevant information and data about the state of their operations to their foreign partner.

Partner searches for a joint venture can be through many channels. Interested foreign companies could make contact with Chinese diplomatic missions (there is always a section for business affairs), Chinese bank branches and overseas representative offices of provincial governments. Numerous formal newspapers contain regular listings of investment projects open to public tenders. *The China Daily* and *Hong Kong Commercial Daily* are just two of these publications. Online information abounds, one of the main sources being "www.fdi.cn", the official website under the Ministry of Commerce, which delivers its routine service of listing and promoting major projects to prospective foreign investors. Foreign companies could also conduct their searches in conventional ways, through industry exhibitions, clients' networks or overseas tours.

Criteria for Selecting a Joint Venture Partner

As a necessary step in setting up a joint venture, foreign investors will have to search for their Chinese partners that meet their criteria. Some generally accepted rules apply here.

❑   Strategic compatibility: This implies that the relative sizes and positions in the industries concerned should be compatible between the two partners. It is common for two leading companies in separate economies to form joint ventures, in order to enhance performance of both companies. For a large company to join hands with a medium-sized company creates a great deal of uncertainty. The strategies of both companies are to be compatible as well. In a FDI scenario, this implies a positive approach towards FDI on the part of the domestic company and an expansionary strategy from an investing company.

❑   Complementary skills and resources: The two partners should have mutual expectations of the other, making the venture beneficial to both. A shortage or lack of certain skills, or resources, could be compensated by the other side, thus creating strong bonding effects.

❑ Compatible management teams: Top executives of both partners should have similar vision and understanding in their management, so that communications between the two are likely to be direct and smooth. It was common in early years of reforms that executives from foreign multinationals found it difficult talking with executives of state enterprises. With great effort from both sides, communication can be improved; but for a competitive enterprise in a market economy, a shared value, management philosophy or vision could significantly boost partnership and cooperation.

❑ Mutual dependency: The purpose of a joint venture is for both sides to complement each other in production and services. It is crucial that one side has some dependence on the other side, in areas such as technology, distribution network, *guanxi*, raw materials, target customer groups etc. A partnership without certain interdependence would work only for a short period of time and lead to eventual parting. A Chinese phrase of **"chicken bones"** makes a good point on this situation. "Chicken bones" are that part of a chicken which you have little appetite to eat but feel it is a waste to throw it away. The joint venture between American Motors and Beijing Auto Works in the early 1980s exemplifies this somewhat awkward situation.

❑ Communication barriers: This includes the influence of language, culture and training on communications. It is quite often that language appears not to be a serious problem, but background, training and management styles stand as more stubborn barriers. At the negotiation stage, communication barriers could lead to a breakdown and eventual failure.

❑ Trust and commitment: Business trust can only be built up gradually; but for a joint venture, basic trust on the other party appears crucial at the outset. Trust is the foundation of continued contact and cooperation. Once a decision is made, the parties involved should show commitment to the project and continue to work toward the final goal.

Negotiating a Letter of Intent

This is the initial stage of cooperation, and it confirms the intention of both parties to conduct further business deals. Legally, a Letter of Intent has no bonding effect on parties involved, and they can leave this relationship and find other partners. It is for a contract to set cooperation on course and formally establish a venture project.

A Letter of Intent, however, covers some basic ideas for later development. Its contents normally include:

❑ Business scope: This is about which industrial sectors they are going to enter and specific requirements on production.

❑ Corporate control structure: If a joint venture eventually materialises, the structures of that venture and personnel arrangements to be made are listed.

❑ Foreign exchange and export: Both parties make it clear on the issue of foreign exchange about who supplies the foreign currency and the amount. There was also a requirement on the finished goods for export, but this is not strictly enforced now, so a clause would be included on whether export is an issue.

❑ Production scale: This is about the size of the project and the projected quantity of output.

❑ Source of technology: Foreign investors are normally the suppliers of technology, and this will be made clear in the letter, including the specific type and level of technology introduced.

❑ Source of production inputs: This is about other factors of production, namely land, labour, and raw materials. Chinese partners would promise to take responsibility of sourcing for these supplies.

❑ Markets: Some observations on market potential would be included in the letter, and a distinction on domestic or overseas sales will be made.

❑ Disposal of assets on termination of the joint venture: For the sake of precaution, the letter would have to include distribution of items on termination and the ways of asset disposal.

❑ Settlement of disputes: It is commonly stated in such letters that when disputes occur, parties involved should seek settlement at industrial tribunals and at court. All cases should be heard and settled according to Chinese laws and regulations.

After these early preparations and negotiations, a joint venture has passed its first phase of cooperation. These preliminary meetings and talks are essential, since the Chinese and foreign parties are to provide various documents to relevant authorities at the next stage. Without agreement and consensus between the two parties on the form and future of the proposed venture, the procedures will be much harder to get through.

The following steps are formal procedures and involve government authorities. These are crucial matters for the outcome of a venture. Many foreign investors found these steps troublesome and typical of bureaucratic red tape. In facing mounting complaints, the government has strived to minimise obstacles and streamline procedures. Certain regional governments achieved better performance in this area, especially in Shanghai, and some local authorities have even placed officers from several bureaux under one roof, so that applicants would save time by not having to run from one government building to another. To a certain extent, favourable treatments to FDI in China cover not only preferential regulations, but also speedy procedures in getting approvals out. Whatever the efforts to cut red tape, a number of basic steps in the process are uniformly applied and followed.

Submission of a Project Proposal by Chinese Partners for Approval

An approval for a joint venture requires certain formal documents to be submitted to relevant authorities. Foreign partners need to provide documents regarding their identities and background, with acceptable certifications. Chinese partners carry out the main tasks. They are to hand in applications and project proposals to the government departments in charge of their industries. These will then be transferred to the authorities handling affairs of trade and foreign projects. These authorities were formerly the local branches of the Ministry of Foreign Trade, and are now branches of the Ministry of Commerce.

Preparing the Feasibility Study

What is a **feasibility study**? It is a general description of the technical and financial aspects of the proposed project including costs, income sources and projections. The purpose is to present an overall picture of the project and examine its feasibility from many angles. Major indicators are calculated, such as costs and returns, and potential contributions to local economies. It is also a key document that central and provincial government departments, those under the Ministry of Commerce, will use as a basis for consideration and approval of the project. In reality, feasibility studies tend to provide glowing comments on the projects concerned and mostly recommend approvals. This practice is understandably common given that getting FDI in has been a central part of the government's work. In recent times, many of the government departments provide the service of drafting feasibility study for your project within a promised time limit, and they charge a fee for this service. With this new government function, the phase of feasibility study would not be a difficult barrier to intended investment projects.

Drawing up a Contract

When both parties decide to form a joint venture and get official approval, they need to draw up a formal business contract for their joint venture.

Principal matters addressed in the joint venture contract include:

❏ Setting out the objectives of the joint venture: scope of business, production capacity, size of workforce, scale of production and export volumes etc.

❏ Total investment and equity structure: This is to make certain investment capital and shares for each party. For foreign investors, their shares are generally over 25% of total capital, as required by law. Below this level, the venture is considered as being without a foreign entity.

❏ Responsibilities of each party: This is to divide work between domestic and foreign parties. A common practice is to let domestic partners deal with internal issues and government regulations, and let foreign partners deal with overseas markets and exports.

❏ Board of directors and organisational structure: Both parties should agree on the personnel appointments for the venture. Important positions are chairman of the board, which comes from the majority shareholders; board members, which are major shareholders; and the CEO. A common practice is to have the biggest shareholder as chairman of the board and the second biggest shareholder as CEO. If there are only two parties involved, the Chinese party would most likely get the position of chairman, and the foreign party gets the CEO position. Important positions also include directors in charge of personnel and finance. These must be stated clearly in the contract.

❑ Transfer of technology: This is a specific requirement that puts an obligation on the foreign party.

❑ Marketing and export: These two areas are normally handled by the foreign party, though the Chinese party would claim that they understand local markets better and their connections with local export agencies would work wonders.

❑ Procurement: This is about the purchases for equipment, raw materials, land, factory space etc.

❑ Labour management: This involves hiring local employees and filling management positions. The task is more complicated than it sounds. For a state enterprise partner, it would have to consult with its higher authorities on the selection of employees to work in the new venture, on wage levels, on treatments to remaining workers, and on social security payments or owed payments. Local authorities would not be happy to have a new venture with capable workers and a local company left with debts to pay and less qualified workers to support it. This has been a thorny issue in many FDI ventures, and both sides would have to heed the concerns of the other side and make compromises. There is also the issue of keeping good relationships with local labour bureaux and unions. For difficult situations, local governments have to get involved and allocate funds to workers as settlements. Since labour management is a complicated task, foreign investors in a venture leave this largely to their Chinese partners to handle.

❑ Life of joint venture: This is to set a tenure for the proposed venture, and the time could be as long as 30 years.

❑ **Exit clauses:** For the purpose of legal protection, the contract should include exit clauses, listing the options if the joint venture business fails. Matters such as how to end the contract legally, responsibility of each side, asset liquidation, and the right to seek legal means in solving disputes, are crucial clauses in the contract. Many foreign companies have opted to quit from the China market in the past, and an exit clause enabled them to end the venture smoothly when their investment yielded little returns and was not retrievable. It should be pointed out here that all contracts include the clause of abiding by Chinese laws and regulations. In legal disputes, the court would automatically regard any activities following the laws of other countries as illegal.

Most of the contract contents could be a confirmation of the original Letter of Intent. From the late 1990s, the government began to provide a standard format for joint venture contracts. Venture partners simply need to pick up a contract document from a government office and fill in the information on all listed items.

Approval and Registration

Completed documents, including feasibility study, contract, company constitution, name list of board members, are to be submitted to relevant authorities for official approval. Chinese partners bear the responsibility of getting through this process and answering enquires from all related official bodies. There are different government bureaux to get approvals from.

Approvals of First Degree Importance

The Foreign Economy and Trade Committee

This is the key official body in the application process. The purpose is to get official approval (certificate); without it, no further business can be done. FDI projects can be approved by provincial level committees.

The Bureau of Industrial and Commercial Administration

FDI applications must pass through this bureau to get formal business registration (licence); without this, your business is illegal. After obtaining official approval from the above Committee, the next step of getting this registration poses no serious difficulties. Your business will be subject to annual inspection and occasional audits from this bureau as well.

The Taxation Bureau

This is the place you get a taxation registration series number for your business, and the bureau charges taxes according to their database which contains your taxation number. Your business must pay taxes to the bureau, normally on a monthly basis, and is subject to regular tax inspections.

Approvals of Second Degree Importance

The Planning Committee

This is to get permits for certain construction and real estate works. The committee is to guarantee that your proposed projects do not interrupt the overall planning for urban development. The function of this committee is similar to that of council committees on zoning regulations in developed economies. In fact, with this authority, planing committees in many regions have created numerous cases of official corruption, including receiving large bribes from developers.

The Industries Committee

This committee works to guarantee that proposed industrial projects adhere to specific industrial standards and rules.

The Labour Bureau

Approvals are to be obtained from this bureau, so that the new project can hire employees legally. In particular, foreign enterprises are to get permission from this bureau (local branches) each time they hire new employees and advertise through mass media. The bureau is also to oversee that your firm follows labour laws and regulations, and pays workers the required compensation and social security charges.

The Bureau of State Land Administration

This bureau has taken on heavier responsibilities because of a recent sharp reduction in total acreage of state land and booms in urban development. If your proposed projects are in real estate business, including housing and office buildings, you must obtain permission from this bureau. Industrial projects that require land for factory floors and warehouses will have to do the same. For many foreign companies that require only office space in existing commercial buildings, permission from this bureau is not applicable.

The Bureau of Environmental Protection

Your need to obtain permits from this bureau for your manufacturing business, especially if it is a chemical related business. If your business is in some service industries, such as restaurant and hotel industries, you must obtain a permit from this office and are subject to frequent inspections by bureau officers. This rule is not applicable if your investment is not in the above categories.

Some minor tasks

Project managers need to go to the local police station to register company staff and Chinese employees. For the former, expatriate employees need to obtain official permits or work visas to live and work in a Chinese region. Employers bear the responsibility of providing appropriate documents to support expatriates' visa applications, including information on employment contract, position and salaries. For the latter, police also need to check employees' identity papers and certain work permits. For an enterprise with import/export operations, project managers need to check with the Customs and get relevant documents done for later trading activities. You are also required to open bank accounts for RMB and foreign currency transfers. The State Bureau of Foreign Exchange Administration monitors your capital injection to the designated bank account, but you can start your business operations without approval from this office. Only when the capital injection is not made in six months will this office notify other authorities and have your business suspended.

Official approvals in the first group are top priorities for proposed investment projects, and no business can start without approvals from these relevant authorities (see Figure 13.1). Approvals in the second group are less important, since only a certain proportion of FDI projects need to acquire them. It is a common practice that after obtaining your approval certificate from the government bureau in charge of FDI, the rest of the procedures become routine, without a high degree of uncertainty.

The formal process of application and approval for FDI ends after approval certificate, business licence, and tax registration are properly dealt with. The application for wholly foreign-owned projects is in a similar process but even simpler, without the early stages of selecting

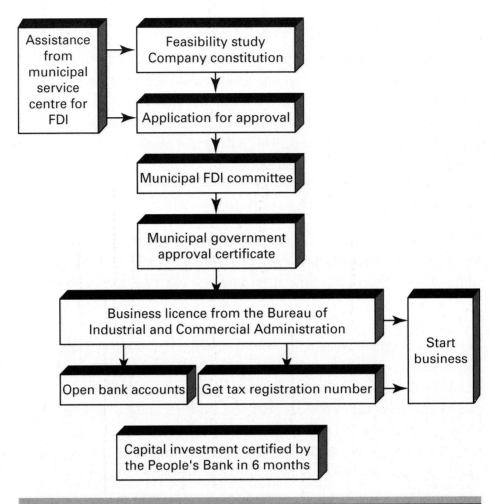

Figure 13.1   Application and approval process in Shanghai

and negotiating with Chinese partners. Foreign investors work out their own application documents, submit these to relevant authorities (again, the Ministry of Commerce), obtain official approval certificates, business licences, and tax registration numbers. A step omitted in this process is that for the contract between Chinese and foreign parties. As a general rule, a project with a total investment of less than US$3 million will get approvals from regional authorities, and above this amount, the project needs approvals from the relevant bureaux in the central government. There are rules regarding the time limit for handling a specific task in the process, say 10 days for a duty officer to reply to a submitted document. It is often the case that, for a small-sized foreign company without serious troubles along the way, an approval process from the time of handing in formal documents would take about three months.

A Case of Petrochemical Joint Venture

China National Offshore Petroleum Oil Corporation (CNOOC) and Shell

The joint venture involves CNOOC and Shell to build a giant petrochemical complex. It is a business of 50/50 shares, costing a total of US$4.5 billion. The project is claimed as the largest FDI and joint project ever in China.

This project has taken 12 years to complete its process of application and approval. The first letter of intent was signed in 1988 between the two partners. At the time, several Chinese enterprises showed interest in being a partner, including PetroChina. In the end, CNOOC stayed as the only Chinese partner in the venture.

Since this is a very large FDI project, a specially set up state international projects consultants company carried out an evaluation and reported to the then State Planning Commission. With this evaluation, the State Council officially approved the project in principle.

The first feasibility study was conducted in 1991, testing and assessing oil quality and costs. It was only until the third feasibility study in 1996, that they gave the project its approval. Both sides invested in this study with a total of US$30 million, again in 50/50 shares.

Partners on both sides engaged in long-running negotiations for a formal contract. They also signed numerous subcontracts concerning patents, tech-support, sales etc., at the end of the negotiation stage. The central problem was profitability, with a return of 10%. Shell initially demanded at least 12%, and wavered on this prospect, but eventually both sides reached an agreement in 1996. Its final decision hinged on China's WTO accession. They made a business projection of annual sales of up to US$1.7 billion. The contract was signed on 28 October 2002 and is for a 50-year operation.

The municipal government of Huizhou, where the site of the project is located, also got involved in talks and negotiations. The plant site takes up 4.3 square kilometres of land there and requires world class port facilities. Many other issues required the cooperation of local governments for a smooth-running project, such as power supply, water supply and quality, resettlement, dredging, environmental impact etc. The evaluation report on environmental impact needs approval from the State Administration of Environmental Protection.

At the end of 2002, the Ministry of Commerce issued an approval certificate and the State Administration of Industry and Commerce issued a business licence to this project.

Tax Treatments

For foreign-invested enterprises, including joint venture and wholly foreign-owned enterprises, an income tax rate of 15% is applied to them in the five special economic zones; while in the 14 coastal open cities, the rate is 24%. In more recent times, many open zone authorities managed to obtain permission from the central government to collect taxes at a rate lower than 24%, as an added incentive for foreign investors to come to their established zones.

Uniform discounts offered by the central government to FDI projects include tax exemptions in the first two years, and a further 50% reduction in tax from the third to the fifth year. In addition, foreign companies enjoy numerous benefits offered by local authorities, often as the result of hard bargaining between them and local governments. On the basis of national preferential tax rates, local governments attempt to attract FDI to their regions by further extending the period of tax exemption, sometimes over five years, and by dramatically lowering land sales prices in bargaining with prospective investing multinationals. These irregular activities are against the rules set by the central government and have created a large number of duplicated investments in many regions. Since FDI has been one of the criteria for officials' promotion, it is hard for them to stop competition in cutting deals on tax breaks with foreign investors, even if these deals are incompatible with national regulations.

Another favourable tax treatment is exemption of tariffs. For production equipment and other required goods, foreign companies could import them from overseas as tax-free goods. These include many categories, such as office items, furniture, computers and even motor cars. In the mid 1990s, the government resumed charging tariffs on imported equipment, in anticipation of the coming WTO accession. This action caused loud complaints among foreign investors and, through them, the foreign media. It was seen as a step back from past preferential tax treatments to FDI, and foreign investors felt it harder to do business and earn high returns from the China market. The Chinese government later made modifications to the new rule, in order to pacify some growling foreign enterprise representatives.

In more recent times, in view of the WTO entry and discrepancy between several types of enterprises, the central government has considered to merging various income tax rates paid by domestic and foreign enterprises. It has been suggested that a unified tax rate would be between 25% and 28% for all enterprises. This change will be part of a drafted new law on enterprise income tax, and that draft will go through formal national legislative procedures. If passed and enacted according to plan, the law will be effective from 2005. For those foreign companies who had obtained preferential tax treatments for their existing investment projects, the government will allow a grace period, in order for them to enjoy the benefits in full. Due largely to the reluctance of the Ministry of Commerce and concerted campaigning by foreign multinationals in China, no such bill was tabled for legislation at the Congress meeting in early 2005. The move to unify tax rates was delayed. However, it is still very likely that, in the near future, foreign and domestic enterprises will face the same tax rates, as a proof of universal implementation of national treatment in China.

Several Aspects Worth Noting for a Joint Venture

Technical Feasibility

❑   Product: The proposed investment is to put final products on the market. It is crucial that a proper assessment is made on technical figures of the product and whether the product can be successfully mass-produced.

❑   Equipment: This is to arrange equipment to be sufficient in number and in quality for the production.

❑   Technology: This is to decide on the level of technology adopted, neither too high nor too low for the final product. In some cases, Chinese partners would view certain imported technologies as having not much use at the current stage of production, and foreign partners may introduce technologies at relatively low levels that their final products have little competitiveness on the market.

❑   Training: This is about the quality of employees, which often does not match the standards at the time of hiring. Investors need to decide on how long and what types of training should be provided for workers.

❑   Infrastructure and plant: Investors are to make sure that the infrastructure around and the plant itself are both up to the requirements, so that production and transportation would not be hampered. This includes roads, power, water and telecommunications.

❑ Environmental protection: This is to make sure that your production lines pose no serious threat to the surrounding environment and the pollution levels are below the standards set up by environmental protection offices. This has become a serious concern of the government, which put projects with heavy pollution on the list of prohibited FDI operations.

Financial Soundness

❑ Market and sales projections: Both parties should make careful calculations of market potential and sales volumes. Even with a feasibility study attached to the application of a joint venture, the partners should have realistic surveys and estimates for their overall plans.

❑ Exports: They also need realistic projections on export volumes, since most FDI in China is accompanied by an intention to export, and foreign enterprises now increasingly work towards the direction of outsourcing. Chinese partners have relatively less pressure and responsibility on export drives.

❑ Pricing: Right pricing puts more products onto the market and leads to more sales. It is the balance between costs and sales that decides the pricing. Foreign multinationals normally have two strategies at their disposal. One is to occupy the high end, marking up prices for their brand products. The other is to undercut others by supplying and selling in bulk.

❑ Sources and costs of production inputs: This refers to the sources for labour, raw materials and other factors such as energy. Managers are to secure these sources, and the total costs from these inputs are calculated against total sales.

❑ Financial projection and statement: Investment projects need an overall financial projection, for the authorities in charge of approvals and for the joint venture concerned. Foreign investors should obtain a formal statement on the financial situation and then strive to secure the financing for the project.

Socially Beneficial to the Host Economy

❑ A new project should have positive impact on the local economy, creating growth and wealth, and lifting general standards of living. This appears to be the idea of the government and does not apply to commercial interests. In reality, however, many foreign multinationals have done just that, making considerable contributions to the Chinese economy, as briefly described in Chapter 12. The point is that, by introducing FDI, the government expects to gain in capital, technology and growth.

❑ The employment effect: This is not an easy goal to achieve. It is the initial desire of local governments to increase employment by attracting more FDI. Even if this is realised, with newly opened projects hiring local employees, the overall picture is not that rosy. The Chinese government and think tanks now recognise that FDI has created less job opportunities than expected. The figures of FDI employment in Chapter 12 show just that. In addition, FDI projects produced a "**squeezed out**" effect, causing many local enterprises to close down under market competition. Creating more jobs and high efficiency at multinationals are self-contradictory, and the first things a foreign enterprise does are to screen employees and reduce total number of employees to levels acceptable to them.

❑ Projected earnings and tax contributions: In contrast to FDI's minor contribution to employment, foreign companies are often big corporate taxpayers in the industry to which they belong. They are particularly friendly to local governments, which under the taxation system receives a large chunk of local taxes from these enterprises. Their ability to earn and to pay taxes in a consistent manner impressed local authorities, and for this reason, local governments have tried many ways to prevent them from leaving the territories under their jurisdiction. An example is a P&G venture in Guangzhou, which pays more than 1 billion yuan of annual tax, and the Guangzhou municipal government offered other incentives to discourage P&G from moving to Tianjin.

❑ Compliance with Chinese laws and regulations: Foreign enterprises are expected to observe established Chinese rules and carry out no illegal activities in their business. These include activities in taxation,

Carrefour in China

The French retail giant Carrefour expanded way too fast in the China market, gaining annual sales of up to 6 billion yuan in 2000, only five years after its initial entry. This caused great concern from the central government. In a following inspection, Carrefour was found breaking the rules set by authorities. Its 27 outlets in China were set up by its contract signings with local governments, without formal approvals from the central government. This has violated the regulations in regard to the retail market and proceeded way ahead of the opening schedules China formally promised at the time of WTO entry.

Carrefour was then penalised in 2001 from opening 10 new stores. To smooth out the relationship with the Chinese government and reopen retail outlets, the CEO of Carrefour visited Beijing to apologise and promised to regulate the firm's business activities more strenuously. Many months after the imposition of penalties, Carrefour was allowed to open more stores and warehouses in China.

labour rights, or pollution. This is the case even if these rules are not totally compatible with those of their country and might change later.

A Review of Joint Ventures in China

On the basis of past records and cases, some general observations can be made on joint ventures in China and certain patterns summarised.

Identifying Key Success Factors

Top Management Commitment

A key element in a successful joint venture is the strong commitment from top executives of the two parent companies. This would usually diffuse troubles and eliminate divergence. In the case of Shanghai GM, despite many doubts on a new motor car joint venture in an already competitive market, the CEO of GM, Mr. Wagoner Jr., consistently affirmed his commitment and funding of over US$1 billion for the project. The Chinese chief at SAIC made a similar effort in securing support and funds from the Shanghai municipal government. Shanghai GM is now overtaking Shanghai VW as the top car manufacturer in China, and the unspectacular Buick brand sells well to Chinese car buyers.

Solid Feasibility Study and Pre-departure Training

This refers to preparations made before a plan of joint venture is decided. Staff need to gain basic knowledge through proper training, including cultural background and business environment. The central themes are that rushing into a joint venture is always a bad idea, and that the business models at home are not readily applicable in another economy.

A Good Local Partner

This has been discussed in previous texts. This selection was perhaps assisted mainly by Chinese authorities, but in more recent years foreign investors have gained greater freedom in choosing the partners they intend to work with. This, however, in a way increases the risks in searches, since the final decision is made by foreign investors alone, and a mismatch in size and expertise could result. Experiences prove that a good local partner could make an immeasurable contribution to the joint venture in question and to foreign investors involved.

Building Mutual Trust

This has been discussed as a key element in a successful cooperation.

Effective Human Resource Management

This will be discussed in the sections on cross-cultural management in foreign enterprises. This issue arises from the acute need for foreign companies to hire Chinese employees and therefore the many problems in effectively managing a new workforce.

Patience and Perseverance

Many foreign multinationals have made long-term development plans and sufficient budgets available to sustain initial losses in the China market. While a few of them achieved their goals after a few years, such as P&G and Shanghai VW, many cultivated their market patiently till reaching their targets in sales and market shares over a longer period of time, as long as 10 years. From the opposite perspective, some foreign companies withdrew from the China market after a few years of operations and decided to re-enter in more recent years. This turnaround may be purely a company strategy based on their estimates and projections, but it also indicates the degree of patience in entering a new market. Strategic decisions of certain foreign multinationals will be further discussed in other chapters.

Effective Use of Intermediaries of Chinese Origin

This issue relates to both market entry and cross-cultural management. Expatriate executives normally form the top management of foreign enterprises in China. Their work and effectiveness depend much on how they grasp the situation and find the niche. Another problem is in how to successfully connect to Chinese counterparts. Employees of Chinese origin can often offer valuable services and break the ice. Hong Kong and Taiwan businesses have led the way into the China market and shown their agility and flexibility in operations. Foreign multinationals tended to hire employees of this background to work in their China projects and have achieved remarkable results. An additional aspect is that increasing numbers of employees with a mainland Chinese background have taken top positions in foreign enterprises in China. This rather significant change occurred in the late 1990s and has evidently enhanced the performance of multinationals in the China market.

Brand Image

It appears that most successful multinationals in China focus on maintaining and promoting their brands. In this respect, foreign multinationals hold wide experience and are pace setters in the market. From many surveys, foreign brands stand at the top of the charts, and their marketing and brand strategies shed great influence on domestic companies.

A side effect of these brand strategies in China is some negative impact on joint ventures. Foreign partners would emphasise their own brands while relegating local Chinese brands to obscurity in the market. A prominent case is the experience of Unilever with Maxam in Shanghai. The Chinese brand began in 1912 and had been the market leader in tooth paste and facial cream for many years. A joint venture with Unilever was formed in 1994, and Chinese partners received a one-off payment for their Maxam brand. In following years, Unilever gave full attention to their own brands through marketing campaigns and promotions. In contrast, Maxam products were left aside and sold at lower prices. The market shares for Maxam dropped dramatically. Chinese analysts called this a **"freezing"** of Maxam. After seven years, the Chinese partners decided to pay back 360 million yuan for the buy back of the Maxam brand. This joint venture formally ended. Such a conflict of brands has happened in many other joint ventures, and, with the general trend towards wholly foreign-owned enterprises, foreign products would seek their own standing and establish their distinctive brands.

Identifying Potential Trouble Spots

Conflicts in Goals

A joint venture should aim at a win-win situation, with mutual benefits instead of just gains for one side. Many joint venture partners in China have separate goals in business, ranging from inputs, earnings to market shares. This initial divergence would inevitably lead to conflicts in subsequent phases of the venture.

Incompatible Management Skills and Quality

The gap in management styles could be huge. In reality, the foreign side could easily show their lack of respect or impatience when introducing their business models, and the Chinese side could similarly stick to their own ways of operation. Two joint ventures set up by the same foreign company can have quite different outcomes, and the key is the quality of management teams sent to work and the effort from both sides in adaptation.

Conflicts on many Details

There are many issues that could spark serious confrontations within a joint venture, such as assets evaluation, which decides the input on the part of Chinese partners. A higher evaluation of assets including land, factory floor and inventories gives them more claims for profit sharing, and foreign investors would have to pour in more capital to maintain a reasonable level of equity ownership. As the Chinese side usually prefers to inject less cash input, inflated figures in evaluation are common. In this case, asset evaluation is better done with the involvement of an independent third party, and foreign accounting firms should take part. It has been a standard procedure these days that renowned international accounting firms, such as the big four, are hired to do the job of asset evaluation. In any case, it is unavoidable that each side may attempt to downgrade the asset or capital value of the other side in a joint venture.

Some Common Mistakes made by Foreign Companies in the Past

Underestimate the Extent of Competition in China Market

Many foreign companies saw this market as a quiet one, a market easy to be taken if their business strategies were applied. They did not expect much competition and took the decision for expansion into this market lightly. Their failure came from insufficient understanding of the business environment and from lagging behind the changes in the process. They missed the signs that the Chinese economy is moving towards a market economy with wide-open competition. These flawed perceptions were very common before China's entry to the WTO and began to fade afterwards.

Market competition in China, in fact, comes from all directions. **First**, it comes from domestic producers, which were inspired by the business models of foreign multinationals and then worked to catch up. Emerging domestic challengers forced foreign giants such as Unilever and P&G to fight an all-out war in order to preserve their leading market shares in the industry. An obscure local company from Zhejiang has successfully grabbed the number one position in sales of washing power, beating Omo of Unilever and Tide of P&G. Other producers are steadily eroding the remaining market shares held by foreign multinationals.

Second, competition comes from other foreign companies operating in China. Competitors at home tend to move to a new market together and engage in a lasting rivalry. In the China market, there are perhaps few industries that do not see a battle on many fronts. In the motor car industry, three foreign giants are fighting for their shares. In the soft drink industry, Coca-Cola and Pepsi are competing as usual. P&G and Unilever seek to keep their top positions. In this growth market with many new entries, a foreign company cannot afford to underestimate the degree and extent of competition, and it can no longer be overconfident of its own advantages in this market. The Danish beer producer, Carlsberg, rushed into the China market in the early 1990s, anticipating high returns from a large beer-drinking population. In the end, Carlsberg found it so hard to keep up with numerous domestic and foreign competitors, that it sold its Shanghai beer factory to Tsing Tao Beer Group, a top Chinese beer maker.

Provide Less Advanced Products and Keep a Slower Pace of Upgrading

Many foreign companies began to enter the China market with low-end products or products that were being phased out. These products could satisfy local customers in early years but soon lost their appeal. Foreign companies failed to provide advanced or upgraded models to replace the old ones, even when Chinese customers earned more income and faced more choices in the market. As a result, these products were seen as obsolete and out-of-date, and their sales went down dramatically. An example of this kind of mistake was from Peugeot, the French carmaker, which entered the China market and produced the F505 model car for many years. The Peugeot experience will be discussed in a later case study.

Send in Less Experienced Expatriate Executives

This mistake was common in early years. To save costs and in underestimating market competition, many foreign companies sent expatriates in to their Chinese operations who were near retirement age, recent graduates or new recruits, or those chosen only because of their adequate Chinese language abilities. They were not fully equipped with skills and training for the important task of competing successfully in the China market. Company headquarters, of course, could replace them fairly quickly, but damages to business operations had been done. Many foreign companies later recognised the adverse effects of this approach and began to send in higher-ranking, experienced executives to oversee their China operations.

This practice, however, is still an option to many foreign companies in China. A recent case is **Morgan Stanley** in China. Morgan Stanley formed a joint venture with an experienced loan restructuring and disposal firm and sent in an *ad hoc* team of three members, with authority to make major business decisions. The team leader was a Ming China historian and spoke fluent Putonghua. The second member was his student, and the third a relative of his with some accounting training. Judging from the very daunting and complicated task of disposing bad loans of state enterprises, these team members did not have the matching credentials and experience. Their Chinese partners had more required expertise than the team. Despite their inadequate qualifications, the team managed to take over the firm and squeezed out their Chinese partners, backed by solid financial investment from Morgan Stanley. The take over was successful, but the Chinese partners took Morgan Stanley to court for breaching contracts. Domestic business analysts made further enquires on whether the restructuring of state enterprises could rely on big name foreign financial institutions that do not have practical experience and applicable solutions. Public debates and media investigation on such issues would damage Morgan Stanley's business reputation in the China market. As will be discussed in another chapter, some heavyweight foreign firms endured similar gruelling treatment and had their image tarnished.

Adaptations in FDI

Under the opening-up policies, FDI has entered China for over two decades. Foreign companies have made impressive progress both in gaining significant market shares and in adapting to a vastly different business environment in China. Their adapting process is shown most clearly in the shift of trend from joint ventures to wholly foreign-owned enterprises and in their consistent effort on localisation of business.

From Joint Ventures to Wholly Foreign-owned Enterprises

There are two sides of this shift. Foreign companies tended to familiarise themselves with Chinese rules and follow the set regulations cautiously. At this stage, the Chinese government was uncertain about the best ways of utilising FDI, and an acceptable option to them was to limit FDI to joint ventures. On the other side, foreign investors had little confidence in their Chinese ventures and mostly made investments on a trial and temporary basis. Foreign companies also had little knowledge of the characteristics and internal mechanisms of the China market—a market largely not rule based at that time. Under such circumstances, joint ventures appeared to be a right way ahead. Their Chinese venture partners could be their best guides, providing necessary conditions such as labour, land, factory space and, more importantly, local distribution and sales networks. This created a certain guarantee to doubtful foreign investors, and joint ventures became the mainstream of FDI.

From the 1990s, Chinese rules on FDI have been relaxed steadily, and many more sectors have opened to FDI under the urge of the government. Forming a wholly foreign-owned company no longer met with official barriers and early discriminations. Foreign companies themselves have gained plenty of experience in dealing with Chinese suppliers and customers, and their confidence in operational performance has grown high. Within existing joint ventures, there have been recurring troubles and conflicts in many areas. Disagreements with Chinese partners often delay plans on expansion or investment by foreign partners. Benefits from a joint venture have been downgraded, and setting up a wholly owned enterprise with full authority turned out to be a better option to many foreign companies. Success by early players encouraged late comers, and as figures show, more foreign investors opted to set up wholly owned enterprises in China. This shift from joint venture to wholly foreign-owned enterprises essentially represents recognition by most foreign investors of an improved business environment, market opening, government efficiency, and an established legal framework.

Along with their tendency towards wholly foreign-owned projects, multinationals made urgent drives to **restructure** their operations in China. Under previous regulations on FDI, foreign companies set up numerous joint ventures and a few wholly foreign-owned enterprises in different regions of China, and these entities served the main purpose of targeting local markets. This segmentation has proved inefficient and has not met the needs of those super multinationals. Many of these multinationals worked to reorganise their framework and command systems. The central idea is to link all separate entities across the country and put them under one new controlling or group company. The normal practice is to construct a chain of production across all regions for the manufacturing of final products and establish a commanding headquarters in Beijing or Shanghai. This way, many duplicated and competing projects can be effectively streamlined, and wastes and losses in the whole production process can be minimised. For example, in 2003, Panasonic established a wholly owned company of Panasonic China, which is authorised to reorganise all 50 separate local operations bearing the Panasonic name. Unilever reorganised its 14 joint ventures in 1999 and refocused on three major areas: personal care, food and drinks, and ice cream. The fact that these and other restructurings by multinationals were possible indicates the extent of changes to FDI rules and their increasing desire to achieve economies of scale in China operations.

Influencing Policies and Public Acceptance

Foreign companies have practised various strategies to enhance their interests in an environment they have grown to feel comfortable with. The initiatives from multinationals have led to modifications to government regulations and more effective preferential treatments. In 1995, the central government decided to review tax exemption on equipment imported by foreign companies for their production. The result was the removal of this exemption. This official regulation, however, only lasted for 6 months. Existing and investing foreign companies made their case to the highest levels of the government and threatened to withdraw investment in China, on the basis that their contracts and negotiations of potential investment gave them rights to enjoy tax exemption in this area. The State Council balked and reversed its decision, in response to unexpectedly fierce reactions from foreign investors and concerns from local governments. Another example is the abolished articles in the Foreign Enterprise Law, which previously required foreign companies to fulfil their duties in providing foreign exchanges, priority purchasing of local raw material and exporting to meet set quotas. Despite the fact of growing FDI projects for outsourcing, foreign companies benefit from this legal revision through having more freedom in selecting suppliers and in selling more products to large groups of domestic consumers. They have been able to achieve this goal by persuading central authorities and citing WTO terms in all negotiations.

As an indication of growing influence, company chiefs of foreign multinationals have been invited to be senior advisers of Beijing and Shanghai municipal governments, being consulted on strategic matters and policy feasibility. At this point, foreign companies have turned from simply following the set rules to participating in drafting new rules that would allow them more room for expansion.

In cultural aspects, foreign multinationals have made great strides in adapting to local ways of doing business and managing local operations. Many of them relegate their universal models and eagerly adopt local customs. This is part of the localisation process and has proved essential in winning business. The Chinese concept *guanxi* was picked up and used effectively on government authorities and local Chinese players. Foreign multinationals cultivated good relationships with officials in charge and have established regular contacts with senior leaders in the government and the Party. They are also generous donors to schools and poverty regions. During the SARS crisis in 2003, multinationals made a large amount of donations to medical institutions in China—most prominent among them being the GM team headed by Mr. Wagoner Jr. himself. All of these boosted their standing in industries and won praises from Chinese consumers.

Ironically, their PR skills have improved so much that some activities border on lobbying through bribes. In import/export, market entry and FDI, foreign companies need to keep a good relationship with authorities for granting of favourable treatments. The many ways of cultivating such a relationship include sponsoring scholarships for children of officials, appointing retired officials to senior company positions or as advisers, doing business with companies owned by relatives of officials, depositing money into overseas bank accounts for officials, and offering special club memberships as a way of transferring money. In many cases of official corruption in China, foreign companies, through their local Chinese managers, are involved in providing the bribes. In 2004, the CEO of Lucent Technologies China Limited had to be sacked by the parent company for being indicted in corruption cases, which exposed under-the-table deals of money for large business orders for telecommunication equipment from Lucent. This is the first case of a major foreign multinational being exposed for unethical behaviour in China and has caused rising concerns for formal legislation to deal with similar practices in business.

The familiarity of the business environment of China led to another downside—**tax evasion**. Foreign companies routinely report losses and few claim that they make profits. This has puzzled foreign and Chinese analysts alike. One of the plausible reasons is an excuse to pay fewer taxes. In a nationwide inspection by the State Taxation Bureau for four years from 1991 to 1995, the bureau audited over 47,000 big and small foreign companies operating in China and dug out over 4.2 billion yuan worth of unpaid taxes. Of all companies under investigation, 35% were found engaging in tax evasion or avoidance. Combined with transfer pricing (to be discussed later), foreign companies could easily find themselves in a position of posting losses on paper.

Localisation of Foreign Operations

This is shown in large numbers of local suppliers for foreign multinationals and in appointments of Chinese staff to senior or top executive positions. The first kind of localisation can be illustrated in the level of locally made contents in foreign brand cars sold in the China market. Take Shanghai VW for an example. The first model of the Santana, though fairly out-dated, dominated the industry for about 10 years. During that time, the level of local contents reached nearly 100%. That means almost all parts and components were sourced from local suppliers. The second model 2000 had a slightly lower level of local contents, and the recent Passat model had an even lower level. This may be due to more sophisticated designs and computerisation of many parts in the car. It, however, indicates that multinationals seek higher levels of local contents for their production while keeping a firm hold on design and core technology. From previous discussions on outsourcing, it is clear that a localisation of production is inevitable if foreign multinationals desire to achieve success in their FDI.

The process of localisation in human resources has been on for an even longer time. Expatriate executives are still sent to a FDI project site, but eventually they have to delegate authority to their local employees. In the case of China, hiring local staff to work for your project proves vital to the end results. It is not simply a matter of the main workforce, with floor or office workers and middle level managers, but a more decisive matter of having Chinese executives at higher levels.

The term "**Chinese**" here includes those with mainland Chinese background, those hired directly from local employment agencies and those who studied overseas and were hired for a company position in China. This term thus does not cover those executives who are residents of Hong Kong or Taiwan. In more recent times, Chinese executives have made immeasurable contributions to the performance of China operations of multinationals. Their inputs are chiefly in breaking through various local barriers with their knowledge and *guanxi*, in making timely adjustments to corporate strategies in China, and in effectively running an organisation of nearly 100% Chinese employees. It has been evident in many cases that the battle is often not fought between a foreign multinational and a domestic company, but in fact between a Chinese executive in a foreign company and his Chinese counterparts in a domestic company. The advantages on the side of foreign company are therefore numerous.

These professional managers undertake tasks of various kinds, such as lifting sales or cutting losses, for the multinationals they work for. A

A List of Senior Positions held by Chinese Executives (Past and Present)

CEO of Shanghai GM

CEO of VW China Investment Limited

CEO of Pepsi China

Deputy CEO of Wal-Mart China

CEO of Microsoft China

CEO of Motorola China

CEO of Electrolux China

Vice Chairwoman of Kodak China

CEO of Lucent Technologies China

CEO of Danone China

CEO of Nokia China Investment Limited

CEO of Dell China

CEO of SK & F China

CEO of LG China Limited

CEO of Compaq China

CEO of HP China

Senior Vice President of Siemens Mobile Phone China

Vice Chairman of Panasonic China Limited

Vice President of GE China

CEO, Vice President of Philips China

brief description should be made here about the long learning curves of **Microsoft** in China. This giant multinational has gained relatively little from the China market, with negligible sales figures compared to its world total. In the 12 years since the opening of its first office in Beijing in 1992, it has widely irritated its Chinese customers, even government departments, by focusing on short-term sales and dragging domestic producers to court to face piracy charges. Visits by Mr. Gates often caused heated debates about his real intentions, and even the introduction of some new products met strong opposition from domestic players in relevant industries. One such occasion involved the Venus project, which is a Microsoft-designed box connecting computer and TV and gives users more choices. Industry analysts hailed it as a smart move to gain millions of dollars, since China at the time already had a large urban population with TVs. However, it did not sell in China at all. The public image of Microsoft was of monopoly and greed. The Chinese government began to lean towards the Linux operating system, a serious blow to Microsoft. In a software public tender for government procurement in 2002, the Beijing municipal government did not give a single order to Microsoft among a number of bidders.

The business model brought over from Microsoft did not work well in China, and the corporate culture of Microsoft was a formidable obstacle. Successive CEOs of Microsoft China were Chinese, with or without overseas education. These Chinese CEOs understand the huge differences in situations and business environment and have worked hard to realign the firm's China strategy from confrontation to cooperation. A number of them left the post disappointed and in disagreement with decisions wired over from the headquarters. The overall strategy finally shifted at the end of the 1990s. Microsoft China has now markedly improved its relationship with the government, domestic manufacturers and Chinese consumers. It has turned its focus from sales, revenues and high-profile copyright lawsuits to real inputs and investment, such as in Microsoft's R&D centres in China. In return, it has improved sales prospects. For some lost bids and orders, it gained other contracts from government and business clients. In the words of some Chinese analysts, Microsoft China has transformed from a **"problem kid"** to a corporate citizen.

Key Concepts

Feasibility study

Three key government offices for approvals

Preferential tax treatments to FDI

Common mistakes in FDI

Localisation of operations and human resources

Discussion Questions

1. What major issues would a foreign investing company face in initiating a joint venture with Chinese enterprises?

2. For formal approval and registration, what key offices do you have to get through and what favourable treatments can you get?

3. What major issues of concern lead to failure, success or unsatisfactory performance of a foreign enterprise in China? What measures would you suggest for an improved adaptation to the business environment and competition?

14

Success and Setbacks: Multinationals in China

*L*arge numbers of small- and medium-sized companies have involved in FDI, but most prominent among them are large foreign multinationals. They are the pacesetters in the market, and their performance and manoeuvrers are closely monitored by other players in the field, as well as by business analysts. These multinationals are a key component of this study on FDI in China.

Foreign Multinationals

The definition of multinationals is that they are groups of large companies, with one headquarters in the form of parent or holding companies, and their subsidiaries spread across several economies. These are in the category of multinational corporations (**MNCs**). A similar term "transnationals" simply refers to companies doing business outside their own country, as well as inside it. Multinationals control integrated production and services of their subsidiaries in these economies and conduct internationalised businesses operations. Their activities are the major forces driving the process of globalisation and create the massive flows of capital, goods and, to a lesser degree, labour around the world. Regional operations of multinationals have their legal entities and complete management structures, but these are the subsidiaries of multinationals, and are therefore tightly controlled by their overseas headquarters and shareholders. In China, for example, IBM has its operations as IBM China, a legally registered company.

There have been recent debates in China on whether subsidiaries of multinationals should be counted as domestic enterprises. Top executives of these subsidiaries prefer to be placed in this category, for the benefit of bearing less hostile treatment from local consumers. With national treatment rules offered to FDI, multinationals do enjoy local status in many areas, such as the right to sell to domestic buyers. Under their localisation policy, their operations connect with local suppliers and staff, thus contributing considerably to GDP, business and wages in the host economy. This situation, however, does not change the nature of multinational subsidiaries. Their profits flow back to headquarters and to shareholders, and the overall decision-making power is in the hands of top management at multinational bases. Even if profits were reinvested in local projects, it is still counted as asset accumulation for the investing multinationals. This increases the net foreign investment total and the national wealth of the home economy.

Multinationals are able to coordinate their production and supply chains around the world, and FDI brings about sought after benefits of reducing waste and increasing overall efficiency. A good indication of this control mechanism is that once a multinational decides to streamline its workforce, all of its subsidiaries the world over receive instructions and quotas of employee sacking. Subsidiaries in a local economy have no right to object or even to suggest a smaller scale of retrenchment. In this age of outsourcing frenzy, more emphasis is laid on local manufacturing and exporting finished goods to the designated markets according to plans drawn up at the headquarters. As multinationals expand to all corners of the world, intra firm trade has become increasingly significant in total trade volume. From these aspects, it is clear that the nature of multinationals has not changed to being a local company, despite increasing local inputs and outputs.

Multinationals in the China market have several considerations for their entry (see Table 14.1).

First, multinationals aim at global markets and right positioning, and globalisation brings production facilities of the world into orderly line-ups for the purpose of dominant market shares. China is by and large seen as one spot in their global networks. Multinationals initially regarded China as a place for industrial manufacturing, and their increased activities has made China a major workshop of the world.

Second, multinationals have a general aim at the high growth China market. This was not the initial aim, since foreign companies did not see China as a potential market of consumers, with its low per capita income. This perception has changed gradually in recent years, and foreign companies are able to sell both production and consumer goods of various kinds to this growth market. As such, their FDI in China now aims at **future** growth in sales and profits.

Third, many foreign multinationals had a history in China operations, from the early period of the last century. Companies like GE and Siemens were quite active in this market since the 1920s, and the re-entry simply implies resuming their business lost some 50 years before. GE was once China's largest foreign company in the 1930s. Two particular companies, HSBC Corp. and AXA Insurance, were founded in Shanghai, China and expanded business from there to other regions. When reforms and an opening up began in the 1980s, these two multinationals made the sensible move to come back to Shanghai and the China market. AXA even reacquired its original headquarters building at the Bund, but HSBC failed in moving back into its former office building. That building is now occupied by Shanghai Pudong Development Bank.

Other considerations are common ones as previously discussed in an early chapter on FDI objectives.

By the end of 2003, more than 400 of the world's top 500 foreign multinationals had made an investment in China.

Table 14.1   Key factors in multinationals' decision to invest in China (based on a survey in the late 1990s)

Huge market:	92%
Low-cost and abundant labour supply:	84%
Large profit margins:	71%
Displaying superior technology:	50%
Prolonging product lifecycles:	33%
Having market shares earlier than competitors:	37%
Knowing the market and exploring other products:	24%
Part of company's global strategies:	19%
Others:	26%

Stages of Entering the China Market

Market Exploration

Multinationals got in touch with the China market first through selling products to limited numbers of Chinese customers. Their beachheads were in the form of representative offices in different localities. These offices had the duties of contacting potential buyers of imported products, gauging responses, and building up reliable contacts and early networks of clients. Japanese electronics giants Sony and Sharp made big sales to Chinese urban families and started the first wave of consumer goods purchases. On the other hand, used production lines and facilities were sold to Chinese manufacturers for local production, thus prolonging product lifecycles. At this stage, foreign multinationals widely considered the low income per capita in China a major obstacle to sales, and a consumer market would take a long period of time to mature. As such, they did not see any urgent need to set up large industrial projects. This cautious and gradual approach can be seen in the course of Siemens' entry into China. The German multinational set up its Beijing representative office in 1982 to handle sales, set up joint ventures only in the 1990s, and became wholly foreign-owned from 1994.

FDI was normally on a small scale at this stage, and traded products were mostly foreign brands that commanded high prices. The mainstream FDI came from Chinese investors in Hong Kong, Taiwan and overseas Chinese communities. These investment projects focused on low-end and labour-intensive manufacturing. These investors enjoyed the advantages of their connections with mainland enterprises and of shared language and culture. Very few large foreign multinationals made industrial investments, and their chosen type of FDI was joint ventures. Examples are VW and P&G, which invested capital in major China projects and stayed on in the market to operate their businesses.

Multinationals' early entries suffered from some teething problems and faced difficulties in adjusting to the business environment and in winning government support. There are some well-publicised examples of troubled joint ventures. A top story in the 1980s was Beijing Jeep—the joint venture between the American Motors and the Beijing Auto

Works. The American company did invest early and introduced its Jeep models to the China market. There were multiple problems for this joint venture. There was disagreement on what generation of car model to introduce. Technologies in these models are vastly different. Division on capital investment was also serious, since the American side invested in cash and the Chinese side mostly held tangible assets and labour. Early production relied on importing parts and assembling. This required the Chinese partners to pay hard currencies for imported parts, which went against their initial desire to save on imports. The American side opposed the common practice at the time for foreign companies to target mainly overseas markets and increase exports. Finished Jeeps were sold primarily to local Chinese customers. The levels of local components for Jeeps rose slowly. The government of the day had only vague ideas of how this joint venture should run and stuck to the guiding principle that the Chinese partner should be able to obtain key technologies from this project.

In addition to confusion over regulations and production, the American side chose the wrong target customers. Jeeps by and large were not popular with Chinese customers, who preferred to own a stylish sedan. This perception derived either from officials, who are conscious of their formal status, or from a few newly rich, who could not stand driving a cross-country or military type of vehicle. This perception receded only in the late 1990s, when the fever over SUVs spread from the US to China. The success story of VW's Santana brand in China, which is in a standard sedan shape and used as a government vehicle, highlights the faults in the Americans' choice of car models.

This early joint venture by a large foreign multinational became the focus of extensive studies, and the case exemplifies the mounting troubles and unexpected difficulties in FDI. One could probably pick out many mistakes foreign investors committed, as listed in a previous chapter. Although higher authorities of both countries got involved, this joint venture was widely seen as an unhappy marriage. It staggered along, with negligible outputs and sales volume, and the bad experience alarmed American carmakers as a whole. They collectively hesitated for about ten years before moving into the China market *en masse*. Chrysler later took over the project and placed it into an overall restructuring under Daimler-Chrysler in the late 1990s.

More Aggressive Strategies and Expansion

At this stage, after the early 1990s, perseverant foreign multinationals had confirmed the positive results of their entry and gained adequate confidence. Early FDI in joint ventures provided them with valuable learning experience, making them used to the business environment. With the need to service increasing numbers of Chinese customers, who were allured by successful marketing campaigns, they adopted an expansion strategy to sharply increase their investments for bigger production capacity. Increase in sales volume and promotion campaigns followed. Competition in this market has forced them to strive for leading positions in their industries and to beat off challenges from domestic and foreign competitors. Foreign multinationals had moved from tentative trials of FDI to a keen pursuit of market dominance.

Examples of this transition are Coca-Cola and Kodak. Coca-Cola undertook its aggressive expansion deep into the China market and negotiated with local governments for the right to establish bottling factories. It is out of its own necessity that the company has a bottling factory in a large region to service massive distribution channels to all localities. If two or more regions rely on one bottling factory, the costs in delivering the drink to local customers would be huge, making their operations uneconomical. After Chinese customers began to catch up with the new trend of drinking Coke, the next problem for Coca-Cola was to have more bottling facilities in locations close to target markets. This required huge amounts of investment, but the multinational had to carry out this business undertaking. By 1994, Coca-Cola had 16 bottling factories around the country. By the end of the 1990s, it had 28 bottling factories, despite the unofficial objection from the central government to its quick expansion. In the new century, this multinational planned to spend US$150 million on six new factories, taking up most regional markets in China. At this stage, this giant multinational in fact does not need to make fresh investments on new facilities; its earnings from its China operations provide adequate financial resources for new spending.

Kodak, meanwhile, realised the huge potential in the China market. Low average figures of film consumption indicated to Kodak that this could compensate for the losses in saturated markets of developed economies. Kodak made the strategic decision to invest in the China market and compete head on with the leading firm, Fuji. This fascinating battle will be discussed in detail later.

In the same period, some multinationals made strategic decisions to quit the China market. Their major concerns were fierce competition, heavy losses, small market shares, and no near future of recovery and expansion. Two prominent examples of exiting foreign multinationals at this stage are Whirlpool and Peugeot. Their experience and choices will be later discussed in case studies on strategies.

A spectacular exit happened in the beer industry. Many foreign beer producers entered the market in the late 1980s and 1990s. They spotted the wide gaps in average beer consumption between developed economies and China and also the increasing demand for beer as a common drink, in place of traditional fiery Chinese alcohol. They made huge investments in joint ventures or in wholly owned projects, in anticipation of big sales in following years. Carlsberg invested over 1 billion yuan in two breweries, and Foster's of Australia did the same. In bitter competition with domestic producers and with other foreign brands, many beer companies encountered serious problems and could not reach the original goals in sales and profits. Eventually, many of them cut their losses and exited the market in the late 1990s. Carlsberg, Bass, and Foster's sold their breweries to the remaining domestic producers. Tsing Tao Beer Group, under an over energetic CEO, who later died of a heart attack, acquired many small- and medium-sized beer factories, including foreign ones, and built up its leading position in the industry. Industry analysts called this round of retreat from the beer market in China as the **"great escape"**, and the lessons learned serve as good reminders of earlier experiences of market entry by foreign players. By the time of the early 21st century, three major domestic breweries dominated the market, and some new foreign heavyweights, such as the American firm Anheuser-Busch and South African firm SAB, moved in for a new round of complicated mergers and acquisitions.

Market Leaders and Earning Rewards

From the middle of the 1990s, foreign multinationals have gained considerable market shares and returns in the China market. Statistics show that foreign-invested companies in China earned US$6 billion as profits in 1996 and US$27 billion in 2000. Based on their tax reports, experts estimated that profits from FDI in China was over US$20 billion in 2003, and taking in the value of FDI stocks up to that year (US$250 billion), the average return rate on investment was between 8% to 10%.

A white paper published in 2004 by the American Chamber of Commerce in China concludes in its survey positive business results for its members. About 75% of American multinationals in China were profitable in 2003, and 10% of them achieved large gains. The levels of profits from China operations exceeded their world average. About 40% of these multinationals had their revenues rise sharply in 2003 over that of 2002. The main areas in which foreign multinationals gained profits are: household consumer goods, heavy equipment and machinery, motor cars, mobile phones and computer hardware. Retail and household appliances are the industries where losses are common due to fierce competition from domestic manufacturers.

In response to increasing business demand, more aggressive multinationals quickened their pace of setting up regional headquarters in Beijing or Shanghai, shifting from Hong Kong or Japan. By the end of 2003, Shanghai had 56 regional headquarters of foreign multinationals, and Beijing had 24. This move is based on their projections of more sales and local demand for their services. They also face the tasks of effectively coordinating and supervising all subsidiaries from a closer and more convenient location. The leading position held by foreign multinationals can be demonstrated by the following summaries of various industries.

Multinationals' Market Shares and Domination in Industries

Since the late 1990s, foreign multinationals have held large market shares and, in some industries, they have simply dominated.

Motor Car Industry

This is the one industry foreign multinationals hold a clear advantage in technology and production. Domestic carmakers failed to compete and maintain their previous shares. Over 80% of market share belongs to major world class carmakers. Among them, Germany's VW used to take nearly 70%; it still commanded a respectable share of about 30% in early years of the 21ˢᵗ century. VW achieves this through its two huge joint ventures and a complete line-up of models from luxury to small sedans. VW is closely followed by Shanghai GM and Dongfeng-Nissan-PSA. Shanghai GM has made its Buick brand a formidable contender to VW's Audi and Passat, and finally outsold VW in June 2004. China's Dongfeng Motors had relied on French models of Citroen to compete, and once it foresaw the risk of being marginalised by the top two, it conducted a complicated merger deal with Nissan of Japan and formed the current triangular strategic partnership. There is a fourth contender, Honda of Japan, which made profitable business in a joint venture with carmakers in Guangdong and has linked up with Toyota of Japan. Apart from top luxury cars such as Mercedes and BMW, most sedans running on China's roads are from these four joint venture motor works. The remaining shares are taken up by minor Chinese players, including state enterprises and private enterprises. This distribution of shares is likely to continue, with little prospect of foreign multinationals giving up the shares they have gained.

Telecommunications

In fixed line phones and cordless phones, Chinese manufacturers take the most shares, TCL being a long time leader among many small players. Foreign multinationals have not vigorously pursued leading positions in this industry. They instead concentrated on mobile phones, an industry with a promising future. The first analog network was established in Guangzhou in 1987. Multinationals ruled the market and allured Chinese consumers with their exclusive technologies and brashy advertising campaigns. The big three—Motorola, Nokia and Ericsson (now Sony Ericsson)—took over 80% of market share in 1999. It is only in recent years that sizeable Chinese manufacturers made their brands known to customers and grabbed considerable market share from multinationals. They adopted new designs, marketing campaigns and price cutting, some of which were learned from leading foreign firms. TCL is a formidable challenger in this battle, along with a number of other domestic brands on the market. In 2002, Motorola saw its share drop from 40% in 1999 to 26% that year, and Nokia suffered a drop from 32% to 18% in the same period.

Telecommunication Equipment

Multinationals had clear advantages in this sector. Motorola, Lucent, Ericsson and NEC used to command the market and received most equipment orders, particularly in digital switching machines. Government policies favoured local makers and ceased to grant preferential treatments to foreign makers in 1995. A top Chinese company Huawei in Shenzhen began to grab orders and now takes 50% of market share. Its biggest client is China Unicom, a competitor to the giant China Telecom (and its detached section China Mobile). As a whole, foreign multinationals dominate in this tech-intensive market, especially Motorola, which enjoys a good relationship with the government and receives a stream of lucrative business orders.

Drinks

In the soft drinks industry, it is the familiar situation that two foreign multinationals dominate and compete between themselves, like in all other developing and transitional economies. Coca-Cola has over 50% of market share, and, with Pepsi, these two giants command over 80% of market share. Their distribution and sales networks cover all large and medium sized urban centres. To secure their current standing, they also engage in a series of takeovers, share holding and buying up local makers, so that competition with this oligopoly is more unlikely. A few Chinese producers remain in the market, making soft drinks blended with unique flavours to appeal to local customers.

In the beers industry, it is a totally different situation. Many foreign beer makers came in to set up joint ventures, but they found a very fragmented market with different rules of the game. Local customers also had their own preferences. Fierce competition made gaining profits nearly impossible, so that many exited this market. In the current market, the Chinese brand Tsing Tao holds the number one position, and China Resources is another top player, through many mergers and takeovers in the past. In September 2004, China Resources bought out the China interests of Australian top beer maker and a long time China player, Lion Nathan, for US$154 million. This figure includes US$71 million as cash payment and US$83 million as debt obligations taken over from Lion Nathan. Foreign beer makers such as SAB, AB and a few Japanese firms conducted a series of mergers as well, bringing them into the top league. Under these leading firms, numerous beer producers carve out local markets and are hard to recognise as nationwide competitors. The beer market is more chaotic than others, and constant mergers and takeovers make it easy to change market shares. Since China Resources is officially a listed company in Hong Kong, though it originated from mainland China, a general assessment of the beer market indicates that over 70% of breweries with over 50,000 tons of production capacity in the country are joint ventures with foreign partners.

Films and Printing

It has chiefly been a battle between Kodak and Fuji. Kodak achieved its goal as the number one film provider in the China market, with over half of the total sales. Kodak also took over numerous domestic film manufacturers and faces little competition from them. Fuji lost the leading position to Kodak, but has made inroads in digital products ahead of Kodak. It is a near total oligopoly situation in this industry, with Fuji's shares shrinking. The only domestic manufacturer Lucky Films still held about 20% of market share in 1999 and provided its own films to customers. Since Kodak successfully acquired 20% of share holding in Lucky Films in 2004, it is hard to expect the Chinese firm to be a serious challenger to Kodak.

Household Appliances

This is perhaps one of the few sectors in which domestic manufacturers are industry leaders. Several top Chinese brands take the lion's share in the market and have forced early foreign players to minor positions. Since 1997, four or five Chinese fridge brands held over 95% of market share, and Haier took the number one position. The American firm Whirlpool lost its share and exited in 1997. In air conditioners, Haier again takes a dominant position with its quality products and after-sales services. A number of Japanese players remain in the market, such as Sharp and Hitachi. In television, Changhong from Sichuan province dominates the market, with its economies of scale and price advantages, and Konka has made a series of market expansions as well. Japanese TV makers used to dominate the market, but now they focus on high-end and digital TV sections. It should be pointed out that some foreign multinationals are still active players in these industries, such as Electrolux, and in many electronic products, Japanese brands still have strong appeal to Chinese customers. It is in terms of total sales and volumes that domestic manufacturers reach the top positions. Viewed from another angle, top domestic manufacturers in fact suffer losses in all out price wars, while foreign multinationals gain from smaller sales numbers but large profit margins.

Household Chemicals

Foreign multinationals moved into these industries early and quickly. In toothpaste, the top three brands are from P&G and Unilever, despite many low and middle level local brands. In personal hygiene products, P&G alone takes 50% of market share. In washing powder, the market was until recently controlled by joint ventures and wholly foreign-owned enterprises. Some domestic producers managed to reach the top group, flooding the market with low price products.

Retail

From 1992, the government granted permission for foreign retail chains to set up and operate in China. The French firm Carrefour entered in 1995 and swiftly expanded its operations to major cities. By the middle of 2004, Carrefour had 49 hypermarkets and 90 Dia discount stores. The total sales in 2003 was 1.33 billion Euros. After Carrefour served the penalty period for its past violations of market entry rules, it has now established a stunningly good relationship with government departments in charge.

Wal-Mart is a latecomer and an extremely cautious player, starting from the southern city of Shenzhen in 1996 and limiting its operations there for some years. The entry strategies of this mega retail multinational puzzled many business analysts. Apart from its snail-like pace, Wal-Mart chose some provincial capitals and second-tier cities as their choices of locations. This strategy was termed by analysts as "**encircling cities from the countryside**", a famous Mao strategy in revolutions.

It has, however, changed to a faster expansion strategy since the beginning of this century. It now has operations covering department stores, supermarkets, boutiques, convenience stores, warehouse-style markets and wholesale depots. Two logistical distribution centres, one in Shenzhen in the south and one in Tianjin in the north, service its stores across the country. A distinctive feature of Wal-Mart is that sales in China serve its ultimate purpose of global supplies. Wal-Mart has a huge sourcing business in China through the two centres and in 2003 exported US$15 billion worth of Chinese products to its stores worldwide, taking around 10% of China's total exports to the US. Its sales in China, however, were only 5.85 billion yuan, at 16th place in the market. Its supermarkets in China sell at low prices to customers and are unlikely to make large profits at this stage. It, on the other hand, buys low from local suppliers, making favourable deals with them by throwing in big orders. The overall strategy focuses on sourcing and exporting cheaply to overseas markets. This forms the main source of their profits. Current losses at regional supermarkets appear small in comparison with the huge gains from outsourcing. Low retail prices in a way force down the procurement costs and weaken competitors. Wal-Mart could maintain its large gains in its exporting business and turn around at a later stage to take over those debt-ridden competitors. In short, Wal-Mart has a market strategy unlike others, and its expansion or investment serves its own goals of a worldwide network.

Several Chinese players also made huge sales and take up top positions in the market, with Shanghai Bailian Group as the number one retailer; but foreign retail multinationals, such as Carrefour and Wal-Mart, pose serious threats to domestic players.

Multinationals' Brand Strategies

Foreign multinationals adopt a variety of strategies for their brand promotion. In developing economies such as China's, brands command much higher values than normal mark ups over costs. A group of foreign brands could establish a good corporate image and influence consumers' purchasing preferences. Brands have lasting effects on consumer behaviour, and many consumers stick to their regular buying habits without frequent changes. These behaviour patterns would elevate good brands and seriously marginalise many other non-brand products on the market. Multinationals have utilised this advantage to its full and mostly occupy high-end markets. This choice has saved them from unsettling price wars, and they can maintain higher profit margins that domestic manufacturers cannot reach.

There are a number of brand strategies common to foreign multinationals in market entry.

Standard Brands, Promotion, and Production

Multinationals make a product sold and used everywhere, universally promoted, with globally recognisable logos. A brand name claims world class quality and unique image. This is the strategy adopted by most multinationals in their push for sales. One example is the Tide detergent from P&G. Kodak has all of its printing shops decorated with the same styles and logos. Shanghai GM claims that the Buick sedans made there meet the GM standards in the US, so that Buick buyers in China could rest assured of the quality, safety, technology, and comfort attached to this brand. Shanghai GM achieved dramatic sales increases soon after its assembly lines started rolling and began to outsell German models in 2004. These brand claims give customers the impression of assurance coming from that manufacturer, so that their purchasing decisions are justified. Foreign multinationals also make Chinese customers pay more for their brand products, because of the common recognition of better quality and value for money from these brands.

Modifications Under Localisation

Foreign multinationals do not fail to notice the differences in market conditions and in consumer behaviours. To make a brand and product accepted by local consumers, they also provide brand products with certain modifications. It is a choice between a standard brand name and local ingredients. In many cases, these modifications were made under certain pressure from customers. A good example is Citroen cars. From its joint venture in Wuhan, the French carmakers launched a hatchback car model to the China market. This type of car had been very popular with young European families and others. Citroen hoped to catch more market share in China with this model. Many Chinese buyers made the purchase for the reliable engine of the car, but the common perception was that this body shape (hatchback) was unsuitable for families. Chinese car owners normally think a car should be sedan-like, representing some status, and a hatchback is only suitable for teenagers. In the end, Citroen changed its design and replaced the hatchback with a conventional booth at the rear of the car. This is perhaps not as stylish, and goes against the original concept, but this new model sold well and has been accepted by more Chinese buyers as their family car. Necessary modifications enhanced the brand and sales, instead of damaging them.

Another example is Coca-Cola. Despite its sweeping success in taking most market share in the soft drinks industry, its expansion was seen as intruding and threatening to many local manufacturers. There were strong nationalistic feelings toward Coca-Cola, and media reports tended to label it as an overwhelming force gobbling up domestic businesses. In regular public relations campaigns, Coca-Cola reaffirmed its goal of localisation, from producing locally, employing local workers to serving local customers. It launched new bottled drinks of traditional Chinese styles, with genuine local inspired packaging. It also made special issues of Coke, with accompanying themes of Chinese Spring Festival, Beijing Olympics, or the 12 Chinese animal symbols for different years. The central idea was to make Coke drinks as local as possible, without giving up Coke's flavour and brand. The Chinese CEO of Coca-Cola China even argued forcefully in public that their company is more Chinese than other Chinese soft drinks producers are. These efforts on localisation and branding achieved the desired results of increased sales and softened resistance from Chinese customers.

P&G learned from surveys that Chinese consumers, unlike American consumers, preferred smaller packages of shampoos to large packs for a whole family. The company subsequently changed its packaging and provided many categories of small packs. Similarly, Unilever made its products to suit different kinds of demands from customers, such as hair types, climates, hand or face skin types. These many modifications in fact do not change essential ingredients or formula, but they sell well to targeted consumer groups and enhance people's confidence in these brands.

All of these modifications are part of the localisation strategy adopted by foreign multinationals. They stick to the brand names as universally as possible, but responded to local demands with needed modifications. Such moves essentially represent an extension of business and do not hurt their overall brand strategies. On the contrary, they have created new sources of income and brought home larger returns than expected.

Maintaining Brands' Market Dominance

There are some common approaches for foreign multinationals to maintain the dominance by their brands.

They make their products suit different markets and segments, targeting at particular groups, and tailor-making them to suit special needs. Some customers groups include children, yuppies, or **dinks** (double incomes no kids). Some niche markets are often ignored or overlooked by domestic manufacturers.

They make an ultimate guarantee on product quality, even if this would push prices higher than the average. This is to protect brand image and promote wide recognition. Chinese consumers received such perceptions of quality from the TQM systems of Japanese companies and the universally renowned German technology and craftsmanship. Complaint and refund policies give customers further assurance of the quality goods produced under those brand names. This wide recognition spread to other well-known brand names from foreign multinationals.

They also promote the green factor in more recent times, obtaining ISO1400 certificates for their products, in order to allay customers' fears. They are also the leaders in reducing waste and pollution and in encouraging recycling. On these issues, they follow the rules in their home countries and are apparently way ahead of domestic Chinese enterprises.

Dealing with Local Brands

Foreign multinationals have to deal with existing local brands. The extension of their own brand names often clash with Chinese brands of long standing. They have different ways of dealing with this. An obvious choice is to force local brands out, through all kinds of competition and reducing their sales. Coca-Cola and Pepsi drove out most local Chinese drink producers, except for a few which are severely marginalised. Another choice is to form joint ventures and then legally buy out the Chinese brands their Chinese partners held. Under coordinated management, Chinese brands would become less recognisable and gradually disappear from the market. This aim can also be achieved through takeovers and mergers. The experience of Shanghai toothpaste brand Maxam and a number of washing powder brands are the examples of this strategy. In the course of brand name expansion, many traditional Chinese brands have ceased to exist. On the other hand, some new Chinese brands, such as Haier in household appliances industries, stand out in recent years as new competitors to foreign multinationals. Since a status quo has been reached in many industries and foreign multinationals mostly achieved their desired positions in the market, previously urgent needs to eliminate local brands have given way to maintaining current brands on the market.

Product Life Cycles

Foreign multinationals desire to fully utilise developed technology and to prolong lifecycles of products, in order to get more returns on R&D costs. They would launch their older and matured products in the China market and keep production lines running, so that products of the previous generation could be sold to local buyers. This practice would continue until the next model is launched. Even with upgrading, multinationals could keep wide gaps between new products in developed and in developing markets. This has been the approach adopted by many in China. A typical example is the Santana sedan introduced by Shanghai VW. It topped the motor car sales for about 15 years, and today, it is perhaps two generations older than other car models available on the market. Early models from other joint ventures, such as the F505 from Peugeot, are also the result of this strategy of prolonging lifecycles of products.

Facing mounting market competition, foreign multinationals have made certain revisions to this practice. They now introduce new models only a short period of time after their launch in developed economies. And in some cases, new models were launched at about the same time. This new activity aims at grabbing big market shares ahead of competitors with new technology and models. In this case, their main target is the other leading foreign competitor. For example, VW launched the Audi A8 to the China market soon after a similar move in the European market. It was concerned that BMW was going to form a joint venture with a Chinese partner and build luxury cars in China. VW is also vulnerable for not having a top-line luxury car model to compete successfully with Mercedes and BMW. Its Audi A6 is seen as a middle level executive car, and without the Audi A8, VW cannot escape being regarded by Chinese consumers as only a family car maker.

For these changes, foreign multinationals need to set up new production lines and introduce new technology. It is inevitable that they would have to upgrade more than they did before. This is perhaps contrary to their initial goal of prolonging product lifecycles. The shortening of these cycles in China happens only when the market is fast getting matured and demands are more versatile, and when competition among leading multinationals heats up.

Multinationals' Distribution Channels

All foreign multinationals operating in the China market face the same inescapable issue of distribution networks. One of the important needs of getting a local Chinese partner is to use existing distribution channels for products made by joint ventures. However, existing channels had problems in several areas. They lacked the capital for setting up sufficient channels to meet requirements from multinationals, affecting quantity delivered and timing, and the infrastructure was also insufficient, including transportation and capacity of delivery. Government regulations were also rigid, providing little guidelines and protection. They often obstructed the business rather than supported it, since wholesale and logistical businesses were officially closed to foreign firms. What Chinese firms had then were small sized, segmented and multiple levels of distribution, and disconnection between wholesalers and retailers. Under such circumstances, foreign multinationals had to seek different ways of dealing with the problems in distribution.

Multinationals' Response

They could take in existing middle dealers and their networks, and place them under their own management. This approach requires sending in expatriate executives and restructuring of the system. The overhaul has to be done through major efforts in training and supervision. The tasks in selection and coordination are formidable. Motorola has adopted this approach and relies on authorised agents to sell its wide varieties of products.

They could select and establish new dealerships and sales teams, and establish a completely new network under their full control. This creates opportunities for smoother operations under the headquarters, but involves more funding and investment. It also makes the operations more subject to market risks. Business failures would make these investments sunk costs. Large multinationals would be able to afford this expenditure, and they often prefer to have their own means of transportation and storage facilities. For GM and Honda, as late comers in China's motor car market, they adopted this approach of setting up brand name showrooms for selling their cars. They have spent large amounts of capital on their own distribution network, thus controlling sales, services and returns.

They could opt for cooperation and share distribution networks among a few multinationals. This way, they collectively save on funding and have a more economical and secured network for themselves. In China, Colgate and Johnson & Johnson share their warehouse and sales facilities. This obviously does not apply to long time rivals in the same industry. It is hard to imagine Coca-Cola and Pepsi sharing their distribution networks for soft drinks.

According to a survey conducted at the end of the 1990s, the majority of multinationals in China take advantage of existing dealers and networks, and a third of them have established their own networks. The second option was taken up by some multinationals apparently due to the huge sales volume involved, which cannot be effectively handled by local distributors or through sharing with other companies.

With growing sales and demands, multinationals saw the urgent need in expanding distribution networks and in penetrating more localities. More extensive covers and operations under one's own control were paramount. Subsequently, more investment is needed to cope with rising demands. There would be a new phase during which multinationals move to complete their network building and handle distribution by their own teams.

The UK multinational Unilever had set up distribution centres in 129 cities by 1995, but they pushed to cover more county towns and countryside. So by the end of that decade, Unilever had greatly extended their distribution network and sub-distributors to more than 1,500 counties and one-third of county towns. Kodak made a similar effort to place more localities under the cover of their service network, with over 10,000 film printing shops across the country.

Foreign multinationals also introduced more advanced distribution channels to replace existing ones. In the place of traditional shops and department stores in the old distribution system, they set up mega chain stores in large urban centres. These retail chains operate with quick buying and selling processes, lower prices, wider selection of goods, and more importantly draw more suppliers to provide products and thus bind with retail multinationals. Through lower wholesale prices and more variety of goods, retail chains speed up transactions in distribution channels and raise efficiency. The old distribution system was then marginalised. Top retail multinationals also introduced warehouse style mega stores. These are favourite sites for large numbers of local consumers, who can find almost everything there for their needs. The recent trend is for such mega stores to open in more places and to replace many small shops and even large stores. Multinationals use such super stores to revamp the distribution network and build up their total assets in the China market. This trend has been going on in developed economies for a couple of decades and is now emerging in the China market.

The unique business model of direct sales by Dell is favoured by many Chinese computer users and has achieved unexpected good results in China. Dell has passed many previous computer giants to become a market leader. In 2002, its annual revenue was 17.57 billion yuan in China and it employed over 3,000 staff. Dell introduced its model to China in 1998 and quickly set up representative offices in the four directly administered municipalities and sales offices in all major cities. Through its free hotlines and website, Dell can take orders from individual buyers and clients, and deliver the goods within one week. The main competitor is the Chinese manufacturer and brand name Legend, which has its own extensive distribution network, many layers of dealers and sale agents, and round-the-clock services and support.

Dell is fighting with this domestic giant with its direct sales model, and this could be an uphill battle for Dell China. Recent problems for Dell include growing customer complaints on quality, service and delivery, and this direct sales model conflicts with the common habits of Chinese to have a look at the product before buying, and the tricky issue of payment by credit cards. With few assembly plants, it is often hard for Dell employees to fulfil the promise of prompt delivery. There are also numerous local companies copying its direct sales practice. Despite these problems and concerns, Dell has consolidated its position in the industry, and its direct sales model has made the company a new force to be reckoned with.

Multinationals and Local Distributors

Knotty problems existed between these two parties that are closely linked but hold different positions. Multinationals need to develop and maintain good business relations with local distributors, and both sides maintain mutual commitment to the general goals. After decades of reforms, many local distributors are sizeable companies themselves, state or private, and their decision on accepting dealership of a particular multinational is made on a purely economic basis. Multinationals need to consider offering price discounts and special rates to local distributors, for them to share certain profits. They also pay for commercial and displaying fees etc. to support local distributors. They need to conduct adequate training and retraining, and provide genuine products, parts guarantee and other extra support in service. Once there is a problem of defects, distributors expect prompt response from the multinational that made the product. On the other hand, multinationals respond to those distributors who do not cooperate with lower margins, delayed delivery, and threat of termination.

By the end of the 1990s, foreign multinationals recognised that all competition narrowed down to the competition in distribution channels, so that they needed not only to provide quality products but to deliver them to end users. A number of manufacturers could provide similar products, but distributors decide which to sell to customers. They also have the choice of selling products from competing companies, as long as those products sell. This caused certain troubles to multinationals which tended to have a firmer control over distribution. Shanghai VW

Example: P&G

P&G delegates its distribution and delivery to Wal-Mart in many other markets in the world. Since Wal-Mart cannot legally operate its logistic systems in China under previous regulations and did not even enter the market when P&G did, P&G had to rely on a local logistic company in Guangzhou for its business. This small company, Baogong Logistics (literally P&G Supplier Logistics in Chinese) caught this precious business opportunity and, with its reliable services, has grown to be a top logistical operator over many previously dominant state companies.

Over 80% of P&G products are sold in China by its distributors. To P&G, these distributors are its major clients. P&G entered the China market with its own distribution model. It followed the common practice in the US: providing distributors with goods and passing the sales responsibility on to them. How those distributors sell to customers is a decision made by distributors and wholesalers. P&G simply receives payments for goods it delivers. In the China market, P&G carried on with this practice and resisted pressure and demand from its distribution network. Its hardline standard practice created an unpopular impression, such as the name play of P&G by some distributors as "**Push & Grunt**".

P&G achieved early success in sales and market shares thanks to its brand names and consumers' loyalty. As its sales covered wider territories and the numbers of distributors increased, P&G faced mounting problems in coordinating this huge network and maintaining brisk sales. Its disregard of sales pressure on distributors did not help. It had to change from the standard practice to a more helpful approach to distributors, through sending product experts to assist sales, training of sales representatives, hiring staff to draw clear market zones among distributors, handling bonuses, granting incentives to distributors who handed in payment within 14 days of sales, promoting digitalised operations and raising management efficiency etc. These resulted in a network of between 300 and 400 distributor companies in 1997 and top sales volume in the industry for P&G.

A drop in P&G sales following this peak came with a multi-layered network of distributors and their actions to lower prices in market competition. P&G as a market leader attracted many willing distributors, and they all desired to sell more by selling low. Sales figures and average profit margins dropped at the end of the 1990s as a result. Some distributors had to sell other foreign brands or domestic brands to breakeven. This was not allowed by P&G; its distributors were supposed to be exclusive dealers of P&G products. P&G thereafter implemented a "**downsizing**" project. It cut down the number of distributors by 40%, stripping away some marginal and small distributors and focused on strengthening more cooperative distributors. It installed a computerised system to control delivery, sales and payments of all distributors in the network. The central idea was that along with spreading retail chains, the role of distributor will diminish, and P&G needed only to keep core and top-end distributors within its massive delivering system.

This hardline approach upset many distributors and led to lower loyalty from them. Some of them relinquished their P&G dealerships, and the number of distributors dropped to over 100 in 2002. The computerised system of P&G is exclusive, so that distributors could not effectively sell other brand products. Many of these distributors are companies of considerable size and top wholesalers in their regions. Their dissatisfaction and resistance eventually forced P&G to adopt a milder approach in late 2003. The computerised system is now recommended, but not compulsory, though the distributor companies that remained working for P&G responded positively. P&G also made room for distributors to use this platform to sell products from other manufacturers. It recognised that distributors are dealers the company cannot simply ignore in its sales drives. The issue is instead to select core distributors and offer needed assistance.

The experience of P&G and local distributors shows a learning curve with several twists. The standard sales network of P&G had been tested and under pressure to change. P&G links its sales success with these local distributors, as such the relations between the two ought to be managed with flexibility and an open mind.

as a joint venture has performed well in the market, while its Chinese partner enjoyed the exclusive right to sell cars made by Shanghai VW, with annual revenues of a few billion yuan. VW gave away this right at the early time of the joint venture because they knew next to nothing about the China market and had to rely on the existing distribution network their Chinese partner controlled. The distribution network for VW's joint venture with FAW (First Auto Works) was also held by local Chinese partners. After years of cooperation, the German carmaker VW decided to set up new joint ventures with its two major Chinese partners and get involved in distribution and sales. VW now owns 40% of the venture with Shanghai Automotive Industry Corp. and shares with FAW the distribution network. The sales and services previously provided by Chinese partners are now under joint control, and VW gains on management authority and returns.

Transfer Pricing, Losses and Taxes

Transfer pricing commonly refers to all inter company pricing arrangements between related business entities and to transfers of tangible and intangible property between these entities. These companies are legally and independently registered businesses, but they are in fact subsidiaries of a controlling or group company. The controlling company uses transfer pricing to make internal assessment and adjustments for a balanced development. This transfer pricing follows the rules set by the controlling company and serves as effective tools in lowering total costs and raising performance efficiency.

Transfer pricing has become an important means adopted by multinationals in their global operations. In this world of globalisation, multinationals face the difficult tasks of coordinating operations in vastly different regions, efficiently utilising advantages, and reducing duplications and waste. Their business dealings are now more involved in company transactions across national borders. Transfer pricing offers them a convenient tool to search for the best places for business and lower costs.

Transfer pricing serves several purposes. It enables multinationals to evade high taxes by shifting tax burdens to low tax economies. It makes production costs lower by shifting tax burdens to low cost economies. It enables subsidiaries to increase their earnings, and with certain losses, increase the total earnings for the controlling company, the multinational at headquarters. It also reduces the tariffs multinationals have to pay for their exports to a certain economy.

In practice, multinationals implement their transfer pricing strategy through coordinating payments and transactions between subsidiaries and the headquarters. Exports to a subsidiary in, say, China are marked with very high prices. This will lead to two results. Since the Chinese government encourages foreign investment, imported equipment is subject to low or no tariffs, and the China subsidiary of this multinational saves on tariffs from importing production lines and equipment. In the same scenario, this subsidiary paid a high price for imported goods and parts. When it exports finished goods to the multinational headquarters, counted as part of China's exports to a developed economy, it sets low prices for such exports. On paper, it is a negative figure for this subsidiary, so that it can claim operational losses and pay much less tax to local taxation authorities. The basic way of doing business—buying low and selling high—can be commonly found in transfer pricing between subsidiaries and the controlling multinationals. Regardless of certain nominal losses to a subsidiary, in aggregate terms, the home company receives profits and real earnings out of a particular economy.

Transfer pricing is designed for effective tax avoidance and securing positive business results of the company headquarters. In an economy like China, which promotes FDI with a lasting zeal, transfer pricing proves to be an effective way to transfer capital out of the country. FDI of a multinational is registered and sealed in bank accounts of the People's Bank, but through transfer pricing and regardless of the actual production process, this capital turns to earnings flowing back to the investing multinational.

Numerous cases in China demonstrate the application of transfer pricing by foreign multinationals. Most multinationals keep their accounts strictly secret, and since they are not listed companies in China, they are not subject to transparency and disclosure rules. As in the example of the survey by the American Chamber of Commerce in China, cited above, multinationals seldom reveal detailed figures of their earnings or losses, providing only vague descriptions of whether they have gained profits or not.

It has been a common perception that many foreign companies post massive losses from their China operations. This has made an unfavourable impression that the business environment in China has a long way to go for any business to be profitable there. One of the reasons for this pessimistic picture is that many engage in the practice of transfer pricing, so that those companies incur routine losses. These nominal losses do not necessarily equal bad business. A great deal of losses occurred between a China subsidiary and related companies, mostly other subsidiaries of the multinational concerned. While the company with losses can rightfully claim a tax reduction or exemption, the company that receives the payment offshore reports profits. A recent preliminary study by China's Central Bureau of Tax Administration puts the loss of taxes due to transfer pricing by foreign multinationals at 30 billion yuan a year. For example, a large multinational in the household chemical business in Guangzhou was once caught for tax avoidance of over 80 million yuan through transfer pricing.

Transfer pricing is a practice regularly conducted by foreign multinationals, in their push to maximise profits as well as for tax avoidance. This complex issue involves both real increases in operational efficiency and related taxation matters. Transfer pricing is so common in these days of globalisation and multinationals, that many governments have to revise rules and regulations to deal with this business practice taking place often beyond their own borders. A likely solution to inappropriate transfer pricing is to gauge the large discrepancy between product price levels and enact rules to narrow them down to reasonable levels.

Competition between Leading Multinationals

Many foreign multinationals have shifted their past competition to this newly opened field in China. Rivals soon realised that the most challenging task was to fight the old devil they knew. This is true for many sectors in the China market. Here is a brief review of the all too familiar competition between Kodak and Fuji.

Case Studies: Kodak and Fuji

Kodak in fact reacted to challenges in China following Fuji's initiatives. It had concentrated on markets in developed economies and found it hard-going in near saturated conditions. Fuji moved quickly into the China market, built a respectable image for its products, and took a leading position in sales and networks. Kodak initially failed to see market potential in China, citing low average income levels and meagre demand for cameras and films. It, however, changed its mind after surveying this market more thoroughly. The difference is in potential. Average annual film consumption per capita in developed economies is now 4 to 5 rolls, while in China it is only 0.14 roll. Assuming that the low Chinese level rises near the level in developed economies, sales and returns would be enormous.

Kodak adopted a more aggressive approach from the early 1990s. It set up a total of 18 representative offices in China and moved its Asia-Pacific regional headquarters to Shanghai. In six years, Kodak established over 5,000 printing shops in 500 cities, and radiated its services to surrounding areas. It also achieved the satisfying result of lifting market share from 26% in 1993 to 53% in 1999, thus grabbing the number one market position from Fuji. Furthermore, sales from the China market rose from 17th place in 1996 to the second place in 2001 among the markets where Kodak sells its products.

As a result of this offensive from Kodak, Fuji lost its leading edge and large market share. It made a series of mistakes in strategy and management. The principal strategy was a cautious and inflexible approach to investment, which maintained sales figures but delayed adequate services to customers. Fuji had a weakness in decision making. Its China market management was run by Fuji's subsidiaries in Hong Kong. Local dealers had little say in products and sales, and the average response time to market changes was rather long. The common distrust of Chinese staff by Fuji executives also dragged efficiency down. Its negotiations with some Chinese enterprises on joint ventures fell through for this very reason.

To secure their leading position once and for all and to minimise the chance of a Fuji comeback, Kodak made an extraordinary move to initiate an all-out campaign. This was a grand strategy approved by Kodak top management, namely former CEO Dr. George Fisher and current CEO Daniel Carp, and executed meticulously by the Kodak China chief of Chinese origin.

"The 98 Agreement": A Wholesale, Cross-industry Deal with the Central Government

After four years of exhaustive negotiations, Kodak reached an unprecedented and comprehensive deal with the Chinese central government in 1998. The deal allowed Kodak to take over several insolvent domestic firms in the same industry and to make them profitable. Kodak was to pay about US$1.3 billion for these takeovers, R&D, and operating funds for all production and facilities under the name of Kodak thereafter. The only Chinese film maker to stay in the industry was Lucky Films, which demonstrated some strength to survive on its own, so that the central government was reluctant to give it away.

In return for these heavy investments and obligations, Kodak obtained from the central government exclusive rights to three years of making and selling films in China. According to the agreement, no more foreign firms were allowed to build film printing facilities in these three years, and no Chinese firms were to form new joint ventures with other foreign companies. Kodak was the only authorised foreign firm to do business, and Fuji was of course excluded, unable to set up new projects or to expand. Several attempts by Fuji to form joint ventures with small Chinese enterprises had to be aborted after Kodak lodged appeals to authorities.

This groundbreaking deal gave Kodak a precious opportunity to reshape the film industry in China, according to its own plans. Kodak effectively used these three years and the government authorisation to reorganise the six Chinese film companies, making them integral components of the Kodak production chain. Coordinated division of labour designated one factory for film making and another for printing paper, and these separate factories under Kodak service customers in localities across vast territories. With this restructuring, Kodak achieved near total market dominance in a short period of time and made Fuji a largely negligible competitor. At the expiry of this agreement, Kodak has an enviable position where no serious challenger or threat is in sight. By the end of 2003, Kodak had a network of about 10,000 printing shops in 700 Chinese cities. Its hold on market shares is so enormous that its long time rival Fuji would almost give up conventional films and have to seek other approaches to compete, namely in digital products.

The "99,000 Yuan" Project

Kodak realised that after solving the problem of production, the next key issue was a distribution network for sales. Unlike the cross-industry deal with the central government on film factories, Kodak did not set up such a network with its own funds alone. It designed a smart scheme called the "99,000 yuan" project. A standard Kodak film printing shop would require an investment of at least 100,000 yuan. This includes the printing equipment from Kodak, materials, operating costs and shop decorations up to Kodak standards (logos and signs). Kodak promised to provide films, training, support and advertising. This is a typical business model of franchising, but the Kodak difference is that it promised those participants a full return on their capital investment in three years, calculated on the basis of the Kodak brand and projected sales. This scheme appealed especially to small investors in Chinese cities, who found it hard by the end of the 1990s to get a really reliable investment opportunity and a new source of income. The number of Kodak film printing shops shot up.

This scheme also proved to be an excellent public relations campaign for Kodak. Large numbers of unemployed urban residents also sought to be a Kodak shop owner and through this to change their life. Many such printing shops were later run by previously unemployed workers. Kodak reached agreements with municipal governments for local banks to grant loans to those prospective shop owners who lacked financial means. These loans were backed up by Kodak, thus providing an additional indirect support for shop owners.

This scheme was very successful, and its benefits to Kodak are obvious. Kodak achieved the goal of a widespread network for selling products and servicing customers. Kodak provided only part of the funds for this extensive network, with small investors making up a significant part of finance. Kodak also utilised bank lending for its scheme, thus saving on real capital investment. Its support for the unemployed was a genius public relations move, which in particular won praises from the government, which was concerned about social instability. Through providing opportunity for self-employment, Kodak also won loyalty from Chinese customers and enhanced its image as a responsible corporate citizen in China, not just another intruding profit-seeking foreign multinational.

Localisation

Unlike Fuji in early years, Kodak adopted a more thorough localisation strategy. This is shown in many areas of operations. The "98 agreement" in fact reinforced Kodak's localisation process. After over a half-dozen Chinese firms were transformed to be subsidiaries of Kodak, this foreign multinational would have little worry over tariffs or trade barriers, since most of its products are now made in China. Kodak operates in a thoroughly local process: local factories making films, delivering to local Kodak shops and then selling to local customers. The bonding effect impacts on all involved.

In decision making, Kodak drew positive lessons from Motorola and delegated authority to its 18 regional offices. Their decisions would follow market changes more closely, in comparison with the offshore offices of Fuji. Kodak China relied heavily on local staff and talents for its operations. Kodak provided generous pay packages to Chinese staff and attracted many experienced engineers and managers to work on a Kodak project. Many Chinese managers reached the top of Kodak China, and many more transferred from the Chinese firm Lucky Films to work at Kodak. The wage levels were vastly different; for instance, one engineer earned a salary six times his pay at Lucky. Kodak selected the most capable and experienced employees from those working at the nearly collapsed Chinese firms.

Kodak's Shareholding at Lucky Films

As a logical sequel to the "98 agreement", Kodak continued to work on mergers after that agreement expired in 2001. Lucky Films still commands 20% to 25% of total sales in film rolls and paper. Fuji had conducted negotiations with Lucky Films to form a joint venture to counter the dominating Kodak, and it was near the closing phase by the end of June 2003. A news conference was going to announce the joint venture between these two companies. In the end, Kodak spent US$100 million to buy 20% of Lucky Films in October 2003, becoming a strategic shareholder of that Chinese company. This is a considerable back down from Kodak's original offers of over 50% controlling shares and changing to the Kodak brand. Kodak also promised not to increase shareholding or buy shares on the stock market from small investors. The deal is for a term of 20 years. Kodak seeks a strategic balance among major players for the simple reason, that when others cannot threaten your current leading position, there is no need to disrupt this equilibrium for the sake of change.

Kodak succeeded in achieving this crucial deal with the blessing of the Chinese government, which recognised that Kodak had fulfilled all its obligations stipulated in the "98 agreement". Lucky Films obtained a certain assurance by this purchase and sees no immediate risk of being taken over. In the meantime, since Fuji failed to form a joint venture with Lucky Films, it has little opportunity to wage a comeback with help from a sizeable domestic or foreign player. The biggest beneficiary of this situation is Kodak; and a stable China operation would give Kodak precious time to compete with Fuji in the digital field for the future.

Kodak's market strategy in the China market is a textbook case of how a multinational operates successfully in another business environment. Its rule-abiding activities and perseverant negotiations with the government on key projects are especially commendable.

Fuji's Counter Strategies

As a formidable force in the film-processing industry, Fuji has not retreated completely from market competition. It lost valuable time in forming crucial partnerships with Chinese players and failed in securing the deal with Lucky Films. The "98 agreement" in effect blocked Fuji's expansion plans in the China market, and it saw its shares in sales of conventional filming products dropping sharply. That official agreement is a barrier Fuji could not get around or remove. This has forced the Japanese multinational to concentrate on developing and promoting digital cameras and other related products.

At the end of the three-year moratorium, Fuji is now free to form new alliances and extend its lines of digital products in the market, including digital camera and video camera, photo imaging and related products. Fuji has built a strategic production base in Suzhou for making Fuji digital cameras. In addition, Fuji has formed a strategic alliance with Xerox, setting up a company of Fuji Xerox China, which controls and coordinates all operations of the two multinationals in China. Fuji draws benefits from this venture of document processing and imaging technology which are specialties of Xerox. Worldwide, Fuji now has applied digital technologies to 60% of its product lines, while Kodak has only reached 30%. Fuji's soft belly is still its distribution network, being hard pressed by Kodak.

At the time of the "98 agreement", Kodak was not worried by the coming of the digital age, due to the initial stage of this new technology and the low consumer acceptance. Kodak had to make an announcement on 25 September 2003 to shift its attention to digital areas and to spend most of its new investments in those areas. This involves investments of several billion US$. In short, Fuji opted to spend a minimum on conventional film products in the China market and moved swiftly into the digital areas, where Kodak currently lags behind. In a newly opened field of competition, Fuji would probably have a chance to fundamentally change the balance to its favour.

In other industries and sectors, we see similar competition between old rivals, and twin market leaders are often foreign multinationals, which have expanded into growth markets. For example, Coke and Pepsi continue their rivalry in the soft drinks business, KFC faces MacDonald's, while P&G and Unilever, Wal-Mart and Carrefour maintain their oligopoly positions. As such, foreign multinationals make similar efforts in adapting to the new business environment and adopt similar strategies. Their market positions in China mirror those in the world market; the one exception is perhaps Carrefour, which overpowers Wal-Mart in the China market while, on the whole, is a minor player in a global comparison with the latter. This indicates the probability of beating a stronger competitor in a new market if the right strategies and approaches are taken. This will be further discussed in case studies of foreign multinationals in China.

Key Concepts

Multinationals

Entry stages

Lifecycles of products

Brand and distribution networks transfer pricing

The "98 agreement"

Discussion Questions

1. Are foreign multinationals local companies? How do they differ from domestic companies, with national treatments applied? What are their major objectives and intentions in entering another economy?

2. Considering the three major stages of entries by multinationals into the China market, what you would consider the preferable time and approach of entry? What are your comments on those who exit and those who stayed? Make certain detailed analyses on particular companies.

3. What are the benefits and drawbacks of market domination to foreign multinationals and to domestic companies? Do you consider this situation to be prolonged and that an oligopoly can be maintained? Use an industry or sector to comment on.

4. What do you think of the losses borne by foreign multinationals in this market? Take one company example and provide at least two qualified reasons.

5. For the rivalry between Kodak and Fuji, what do you think would be the likely scenario in the near future? What counter strategies would you suggest for Fuji?

Cross-cultural Management

ross-culture communication and management have become more relevant at the time of globalisation and multinationals. Large numbers of companies are not dealing exclusively with enterprises and employees of their own economic types and business cultures. There is a growing trend among them to deal with other cultures and growing concerns about the capabilities of managers sent out to handle those offshore operations. This makes cross-culture studies more important to company executives. With an increasing emphasis on localisation, investing companies cannot avoid encounters with local environment and cultures. Studies on cross-cultural aspects are often included in subjects such as international business or international management. These studies broaden the views of managers and provide feedback to their to-be-introduced business models and practice. For multinationals, it is understandable that in many cases, the success or failure of their operations in another economy depends not on how their business model is precisely implemented, but rather how their cross-culture management works. This is also true in the case of China, where an understanding of cultural traits makes or breaks foreign multinationals in the market.

Hofstede's Culture Dimensions

A pioneer study on cross-culture management came from the work of Geert Hofstede since the 1970s. From 1967 to 1973, he conducted research on work-related cultural values in multinationals and analysed data from over 100,000 company employees working for IBM. The samples selected covered forty countries and regions, providing very diverse cultural backgrounds for this research. Based on this collection of data, he established a model with several common culture dimensions as analytical tools for cross-culture studies. These tools can be used to gauge cultural behaviours and propensities, and encourage better understanding of inter-cultural differences. They are also relevant guidelines to multinationals, indicating potential conflicts in their operations arising from diverse cultural traits. To executives of multinationals, these are key reminders that business models and practice can be shared with but not transplanted to business entities under another culture. Modifications have to be made, since behaviours of local employees and partners differ widely from what multinationals have at home.

The Four Culture Dimensions:

1. **Power distance**

    This is "the extent to which the less powerful members of institutions and organisations accept that power is distributed unequally". It is concerned with social inequality and authority in one person over others. This dimension can be illustrated in the difference between two types of societies. One is an authoritarian or centralised political culture, which relates to high power distance. Authority is held in the hands of a few persons, groups or leaders. Other sections of the society are subject to this authority and attach to it with high cohesiveness. Hierarchy gives superiors absolute power over people at lower ranks. Low power distance implies a culture in which authority is regulated, restrained and checked by many forces in the society. Even superiors are equals of their independent subordinates. Using political terms, a high power distance correlates with "rule by rulers", and a low power distance "rule by people and of law". In the case of China, a much generalised distinction can be drawn between a Chinese culture of high power distance and Western cultures of low power distance. It is therefore vital for foreign companies to take heed of behaviours and manners of their Chinese partners and employees that are partly based on this particular cultural dimension.

2. **Uncertainty avoidance**

   This points to "the extent to which people feel threatened by ambiguous situations, and have created beliefs and institutions that try to avoid these". It is concerned with how people deal with conflicts and crisis. In reality, this can be used to gauge people's attitude towards problems and obstacles. Strong uncertainty avoidance tends to edge people towards seeking security and risk-evasion. This is true in the case of China. Problem solving is not a top skill Chinese people and managers master, and many of them choose to avoid trouble by not reporting to relevant authorities or hiding it until it is too late. Risk-taking is another trait apparently lacking among the Chinese. Except for adventurous overseas Chinese who migrate to escape certain hardships back home, most Chinese people prefer getting used to changes and fear disrupting the status quo if unprecedented ventures are made. In managing their projects, executives of multinationals should be aware of this common tendency among their Chinese employees. Certain incentives would help make up for their lack of enthusiasm.

3. **Individualism versus collectivism**

   This shows the position a culture takes on a contradiction. The first is defined as a "situation in which people are supposed to look after themselves and their immediate family only", whereas the second is defined as a "situation in which people belong to in-groups or collectivities which are supposed to look after them in exchange for loyalty". It refers to the degree at which an individual places his or her dependence on the group. By and large, China is still a collectivist society, based on long traditions and established political institutions. Group interests and actions frequently overrule individual preferences and specific desires. This is in stark contrast to individualism which is widely embraced in the West. Behaviours and customs vary significantly, and actions taken out of a collectivist mentality would be hard to be grasped by personnel from a cultural background of individualism. This contradiction is at the heart of many misunderstandings foreign managers harbour.

4. **Masculinity versus femininity**

Masculinity is a "situation in which the dominant values in society are success, money and things", while femininity is a "situation in which the dominant values are caring for others and the quality of life". The difference between China and the West is not primarily in this contrast; it exists between social groups in Western countries as well, as demonstrated by ongoing debates between the right and left wings in Western politics. To a larger extent, even emerging discords between the US and Western Europe derive from this distinction, as shown in their different positions along the PPF curve. A previous section on efficiency and welfare has explored this issue. Despite the wider existence of this contrast, it is a justifiable observation that the Chinese society contains more elements of femininity, with growing elements of masculinity in more recent times.

These dimensions draw a dividing line between two different cultures. The existence of a combination of dimensions in a particular culture is based on past history and other key factors, such as social and political. In the case of China, each dimension has its own background for being different from Western patterns. A large power distance has its unique place in China, evolving from political centralisation, planned economy and traditional Confucian doctrines on the state and authority. This society has been in a process of incremental changes towards rule by law, instead of rule by leaders, and then towards rule of law, which requires fundamental constitutional changes in future.

The high uncertainty avoidance derives from risks and crises common in Chinese business and society, which have been under constant internal and external threats. Normal business operations can be interrupted and seriously damaged by political and other forces. In a sharp observation, the **"European miracle"** is said to have come into being simply because the overall environment of Western Europe had been short of continent-wide shocks. A similar observation cannot be made of China. The traditional Chinese concept of harmony as an ideal status reinforces this strong tendency of risk-aversion.

Collectivism of course runs deep in Chinese thoughts and culture, since family, group, clan and the state are all the forms of collective institutions. Under one single authority, people could grow to rely on that authority or on a particular group close to that authority. There is more thinking of "**group**" than of "**me**". Individualism is seen as encouraging drifting and unstable elements within the society, and a society with dominant individualism cannot resist external pressure and would collapse in the absence of group cohesiveness.

The fourth dimension of masculinity versus femininity has both showings in Chinese culture. The traditional yet popular idea of social equality emerged in each and every Chinese political movement and stood behind the socialist experiments before the reforms began. This idea is particularly appealing when unemployment and poverty become two hot issues in current policy debates in China. Similarly, ill treatment of Chinese employees in foreign-invested companies inevitably cause a loud public outcry. Growing discontent towards official policy failures and widening wealth gaps testify to the lasting influence of this inclination. In the meantime, individualism and personal wealth gained prominence in the media after decades of reforms and internationalisation. A clear sign is the resurgence of conspicuous consumption, in the example of fast selling of super luxury cars like Bentley. Success stories of amassing wealth quickly appeal to many, while the general public are hard pressed in their effort to make a decent living. Both sides of this dimension exist in contemporary China. The point is that executives of multinationals may be confused by this mixed picture, and their operations could be affected if some of their Chinese employees resort to the traditional Chinese ideal of social equality and seek better treatment from the management.

With the guidance of these cultural dimensions, managers from the West would be able to understand that a Chinese culture with its own characteristics is likely to resist some models and practices introduced from the outside, and these clashes are inevitable. Especially in a culture like China's, which has assimilated so many intruding cultures, religions and political thoughts in its long history, accepting a completely alien system is dependent on a variety of factors and justifiable causes. Even as macroeconomic structures and environment have been significantly changed, people's behaviours and cultural norms usually outlast official policies and regulations. Foreign managers of China operations have to deal with these micro management issues and ensure effective interaction.

Furthermore, social and business activities are ongoing processes, demanding long-term views, unlike political moves. Following the venerable tradition from the Chinese classic *Book of Change (Yi Jing)*, the whole universe is in a constant course of change, and the only thing eternal is change itself. In reality, business models and practices introduced from Western economies proved their effectiveness in China operations and raised efficiency levels quite remarkably. To many Chinese, this does not necessarily prove the invincibility of foreign practices. Success of some domestic firms in competition with foreign multinationals and a number of spectacular failures by multinationals in the China market, and in their home markets as well, support this Chinese view of long-term trends. To minimise this suspicion and mitigate resistance, managers of foreign multinationals need to heed the rationale and logic behind certain behaviour patterns and understand the cultural roots of the different views held by their Chinese counterparts.

Key Chinese Cultural Traits in Doing Business

Confusion over a mixed picture of cultural diversity can be lessened by effective cross-cultural communication. There is a growing need to establish regular and healthy communication across cultures, particularly in joint ventures and branches of multinationals, as a result of widespread business operations under globalisation.

The following are some key concepts commonly applied in cross-cultural communication, and an understanding of them is crucial in doing business in China.

Guo Qing

This is literally a Chinese term for national conditions. When this term is used in communication or negotiations, it implies a balanced, not necessarily more favourable, view on unique Chinese characteristics and national conditions, taking them into consideration in business deals. It is a subtle way to make foreigners acknowledge the existence of cultural diversity. The term is perhaps rather close to saying "When in Rome, do as the Romans do". *Guo qing* implicitly creates the impression on the part of foreigners that a practice is **permissible** given the host country's relative level of economic development. On this basis, numerous discrepancies and irregularities can be explained away. In business negotiations, foreign participants are often puzzled by certain behaviours on the Chinese side. The showing of hierarchy, responsibility being eventually shifted to the top, delays in decision making and hints of kickbacks—these are all issues causing anxiety to foreign participants. In many cases, the single answer they receive is *guo qing*. It explains, for example, that at the current status of a developing country, taking certain kickbacks in exchange for business commitments is not totally wrong, hierarchy has existed for generations, and authority delegation is not a common norm in Chinese organisations etc. For state enterprises, a decision has to await a nod from government bureaux since they have the final say and hold access to resources.

The use of this term is usually for defending the Chinese stand in meetings or negotiations. In general, however, *guo qing* represents an unavoidable background for any market planning by foreign multinationals. Success or failure often hinges on their understanding of *guo qing* at a particular stage. An example for this is the estimates on market potential in China. If this potential is either overrated or underestimated, losses would occur. For example, the giant European electronics maker Philips estimated in 1996 that VCD, as a trial technology, would not attract big sales of related products in five years. The multinational aimed at the more advanced DVD technology and market, and thus passed up this opportunity. This is undoubtedly a misreading of *guo qing* in China. Chinese consumers, with their rising incomes and strong desire for enjoying better audio/video entertainment after the age of the cumbersome VCR, embraced VCDs with open arms. The hesitation of Philips opened the door for many local enterprises to grow and take in astronomical sales figures. The number of VCD players sold in 1996 was more than ten times over that in 1995, and in 1997, 10 million sets of VCD players were sold to Chinese consumers. Some of these domestic enterprises built up their later-day business empires in electronics and audio/video from the financial gains of these two to three years. Philips was a part player of this VCD surge only as a chip supplier.

As described above, *guo qing* generally refers to consideration and tolerance of current market conditions in a different economy. This can be further extended to an overall understanding of the fast changing process in China, where market potential is hard to predict and rapid growth in an industry is sometimes unexpected.

Guanxi

Guanxi is a Chinese term for relationships and connections. It may go beyond Western ideas of networking or business favouritism, and may imply the sidestepping of formal regulatory or contractual processes to seize certain opportunities. *Guanxi* requires commitment from both parties and is based on trust from past cooperation. It is the time-honoured tradition that two parties should spend considerable time checking things out and building up preliminary trust. Once this *guanxi* is confirmed, subsequent negotiations are merely rituals and routines. *Guanxi* is reciprocal and needs continuous investment in forms of money, favours, and help in times of emergency. There is a common Chinese saying of "Don't embrace Buddha's feet (beg or pray) when in your hour of need". This testifies to the essence of *guanxi* that maintaining regular and reciprocal contact is the right way for business and that one does not get prompt help from others who see no *guanxi* in the relationship.

Guanxi would cease to function if this investment is stopped by either side. In a way, *guanxi* resembles a bank account, which can be in the black or in overdraft. An overdraft would lead to a much higher final payment or a cancellation of the account. Even a long time camaraderie requires regular association and acquaintance. With this kind of investment, new *guanxi* can be established through introduction by middlemen and after one's trustworthiness is proven.

Guanxi itself derives from traditional concepts of five fundamental relationships, and the upholding of these relationships has been seen as extremely crucial to the survival and resurgence of Chinese civilisation and culture. As such, Chinese people believe that right relationships surpass laws and rules in importance. If formal rules are inefficient or lacking, business can still be done with the application of *guanxi*. It is often seen as an indispensable lubricant in the running of the society.

One cause for *guanxi* to be ubiquitous is century-old social customs. In a culture with large power distance and strong collectivist dimensions, people need to define their places in the society in reference to others. Status and official ranks identify one's place, and relationships decide the distance to other players. This relations-centred mentality is reinforced by mass movements and internal struggles common since the 1960s. The insecurity and turbulence created strong needs for trading benefits and favours among people in different social groups.

For businesses, *guanxi* opens doors to opportunities. It helps get through red tape, since there are plenty of irregularities in rules. *Guanxi* in this case seeks certain regularity in doing business, obtaining assurance out of unclear and uncertain rules. It is a way of working side by side with formal procedures and enforcing business deals when formal rules are ambiguous.

Since *guanxi* is essentially dealing with relations, this Chinese characteristic has certain parallels in Western concepts as well. The often-cited model of market competition by Michael Porter reveals the crucial relations in business. A new company in a particular industry would need to consider its relations with other forces. These include existing competitors, potential competitors who may enter, suppliers, end users (customers) and substitutes which would create new businesses and destroy current ones. Within this five forces model, the relations between a company and its suppliers and customers are most important for its survival and growth; and most management, marketing and brand strategies focus on these two sets of relations. The Chinese concept and practice of *guanxi* have the same implications to this Western market model, since mutual relations with suppliers and consumers cause most problems to enterprises, and well-maintained *guanxi* proves to be an effective means in alleviating some of them.

In regard to customers, *guanxi* has similarities with public relations management in the West. With long time suppliers and customers, stable *guanxi* would withstand certain short term shocks and overcome sudden difficulties. Ignoring this brings serious consequences to a company's business reputation, sales and market shares. A Chinese laptop computer maker refused an offer from a client to give him free repairs within the warranty period and dragged the client to court after he wrote a damning complaint about the company's response on the Internet. The company won the libel suit and financial compensation from the former client to pay for the damage to its business reputation. In the meantime, public opinions on the Internet and in the media focused on consumer rights and responsibilities of manufacturers. This has caused headaches to the company, resulting in a sharp drop in sales and a widely rejected brand name. The company achieved the opposite of its initial goal: the compensation it received for its damaged company image cannot match the following loss of market share and a good company name. A common remark on its hardline public relations moves is that it won the legal case but lost its brand and customers. The company has since become an obscure player in the computer industry. Neglect of well-maintained *guanxi* with consumers has also created public relations nightmares for two large foreign multinationals: **Dell** for its poor services to its computer buyers, and **Mercedes** for its flat denial of defects in its cars sold in China, which led to a number of spectacular scenes and news reports of Chinese owners having their Mercedes cars publicly smashed by sledgehammers. In these two sets of key relations, domestic and foreign companies need to carefully nurture good *guanxi* with their suppliers and customers.

Sufficient attention and care could win over clients and establish stable *guanxi*. Once this *guanxi* is secured, it will be for the long run and can resist shocks of various kinds. It is therefore worthwhile for enterprises to build up and purposefully maintain such *guanxi*, even if that incurs certain costs. A Chinese fridge manufacturer in Hangzhou adopted this approach to their benefit. When fridges sold like hot cakes in a certain year, distributors lined up in long queues at the gates of fridge manufacturers, with loads of cash. Many fridge manufacturers treated them with indifference, making them wait indefinitely or allocating small numbers of units as they desired. In contrast, this Hangzhou manufacturer saw all distributors as their long-term clients and provided as many units as possible to meet the demands. Even distributors from remote inland regions with smaller orders were adequately supplied. Their actions were rewarded by those distributors with a stable *guanxi* network. In following years when fridge sales nosedived and many manufacturers panicked, these distributors continued to choose this Hangzhou manufacturer for fulfilling their orders.

Guanxi has its special place in business also for its potential influence on the government. In developed economies, the government does not often interfere with commercial business, but it holds undeniable influence in areas of setting up standard rules, issuing permits (especially in key industries), government procurement, and offering government contracts to private companies. Maintaining good connections with government bureaux remains crucial, and through these connections, powerful corporations have a chance to influence the government's industrial policies and regulations in their favour. In a collectivist country like China, this management of relations with the government is vital, and it takes the form of *guanxi* in order for enterprises to smooth things out and avoid disasters. Large foreign multinationals have built up *guanxi* with the government in many ways: from public charity, donations, financial support for government projects (such as the **Beijing Olympics**), purchase of government bonds, hiring unemployed workers, and, needless to say, some bribes offered to certain government officials. Ericsson China uses its renowned research institute to offer MBA degrees to many of its big clients, who are government officials and heads of major telecommunications providers in China. Ericsson provides part of the finances for these clients to pay for their courses. This has proved an effective and subtle way of establishing stable *guanxi* with key players in the industry.

In practice, *guanxi* also refers to the persons who attach themselves to an established relationship. Your *guanxi* can be an official in charge or a middleman with certain undisclosed channels of communications. Public relations drives and networking in China aim at utilising *guanxi* and in fact searching for *guanxi* persons who would be an asset of the corporation concerned. In an emergency situation, for example, your *guanxi* would help calm it down in formal and informal ways. In such cases, *guanxi* refers to certain persons, rather than the popular Chinese concept.

Some Applications of Guanxi in China Business

In this evolving market economy of China, official policies and regulations are in constant processes of adjusting, and international standards have been more widely applied in years after WTO entry. What effects would this Chinese *guanxi* have on business? A simple answer to this question is that *guanxi* works things out along formal and informal lines. The following are some suggestions on its effectiveness in certain areas.

Know people in right positions

This has two lines of applicability. One is targeting on particular personnel who hold the key to business procedures and approvals. It is essential for businesspeople to find out the official in charge of the right authorities. A successful tender or application depends on figuring out which bureau has the real authority in approving this, and many foreign companies found out too late which government department had the power to say yes. The other line is an effort on wider networking. A common Chinese saying is that "one more friend means one more way of doing business". This implies making extensive contacts with all kinds of businesses and narrowing down on key players when your project needs a decisive push. It is also an extension of your client base, securing good relations with potential customers.

Get in touch with new clients

Your *guanxi* may be able to direct you to a client when you are new in the industry, or to find new clients for you when you expand. It is commonplace in business that people pass buyer information on to their *guanxi*, who are seeking selling opportunities, and middlemen help both parties of a business deal come together.

Reduce tension and solve disputes

In business negotiations and joint venture operations, there bound to be tension between the two sides. This tension can result from early sizing-up, insensible gestures or remarks, a wobbly trust-building process, and lead to direct confrontation. Despite promises made by both sides, uneasiness and uncomfortable feelings abound. In the case of China, there are also common opposing views, based on ego and arrogance from the foreign team, and nationalism and close-mindedness from Chinese partners. One of the knotty issues is the high wages of foreign executives, which local managers and employees in general often consider too lavish. Misperception and misjudgment from the opposite side quite easily lead to angry outbursts and a desire to quit.

On top of these unhappy feelings, serious confrontations occur when certain business interests are seen as damaged. Issues of share of authority, management control, costs and prices, and distribution of returns make some quarrelling unavoidable. Business partners could even go to court if disputes are not settled in a satisfactory manner. In these situations, *guanxi*, both as an approach and as persons, are crucial in solving urgent problems. A *guanxi* in the right position can be an effective mediator and gives both sides confidence and assurance of acceptable compromises being reached. *Guanxi* in relevant organisations would exert influence on the parties for a sensible solution. In many cases, negotiating parties reached the point of breakdown, only to be persuaded or pressured by *guanxi* to move along and make the deal of cooperation.

Get formal contracts signed

For Chinese executives, signing a contract is a minor formality at the end of negotiations. Since the Chinese place much importance on mutual trust in business, this signing is regarded as a non-priority. This unnecessary waiting, however, hurts business in terms of long delayed formal operations. A delay of signing is also possibly for giving some time to the Chinese side to seek other alternatives. Unsigned contracts have no bonding power. In such a situation, it is again the time to employ *guanxi* to give the final push, close the deal formally, and get signatures on the dotted lines of a business contract.

Receive more business-related information

Information is crucial in a *guanxi*-based system. With an established *guanxi* network, foreign companies get assistance from eyes and ears in the business world and can compete more effectively in the market.

Kodak's "98 Agreement" Negotiations

These negotiations went on for four years. This very complicated and exhausting process involved seven film plants, 10 regional governments and the central government. Clashes of business interests were inevitable, and negotiations were peppered with emotional outbursts and frustration. The key figure was the Kodak team head of Chinese origin. Her central approach was to reach the end goal in the Chinese way—focusing on mutual understanding, sensible rationales, and legal matters, in that order. This is the opposite of the usual American approach that emphasises legality. One round of negotiations on the fate of a particular plant lasted about three days, and a legal expert of the American team had to exit the conference room, since his precise interpretation of legal clauses did not impress the Chinese side; on the contrary, it only poisoned the atmosphere for a sensible dialogue. Kodak's good *guanxi* with the government demonstrated their extensive influence on the final decision of the agreement. The chief coordinator of these negotiations was Vice Premier Wu, with the auspices of Premier Zhu. In one separate negotiation, the Shanghai plant completed its tough talks on a merger with Kodak under the direct instructions of Mr. Wu, who had previously headed the Shanghai municipal government.

Shorten negotiation time

With *guanxi* persons as middlemen, searching for partners and conducting negotiations can go ahead swiftly and smoothly. This saves time and expenditure for the investing foreign company. Accurate interpretation of intentions and helpful sideline dialogue could help quicken formal negotiations.

Get government permits and approvals

Guanxi persons are like guides, showing foreigners the gate to get through, and the right steps and procedures to follow, which save a lot of trouble and reduce the chances of being rejected. It is important not only to know what the government intends to introduce in the various industries, but also to know the more subtle preferences it has in selecting foreign investors. In procedures, people often make minor mistakes and have to reapply. This requires help from *guanxi* who will give detailed instructions to foreigners. Issuing of permits and approvals is a tricky area; you never know when you will get them. Except for a few places, such as Shanghai, there are no clear guidelines to procedures and timetables or schedules for your receipt of official papers. One function of *guanxi* is to ensure you get all required documents and official replies within a certain time.

Face

"Face" concerns one's status and respect received. In a society where people are conscious of their appropriate places, face implies proper relations among people. Face of officials indicates their ranks and positions; of businesspeople their wealth and influence; of professionals their intelligence and reputation. Loss of face implies different consequences of possible demotion, lost business opportunities, or damage to credibility for different groups of people. Major items on your preparation notebook should include proper attention paid to the rank, seniority, and background of the persons across the negotiation table. If you address the wrong person for answers during the dialogue, several of them may feel a loss of face.

From this concept of face, people tend to get first impressions of others and size them up for later judgements. This refers to the behaviour, manners or etiquette someone first shows to others, and, without losing one's own face or causing others to lose face, this person is subsequently regarded as well behaved and possibly the one to conduct business with. A first impression of a person with the opposite kind of behaviour draws distrust and suspicion.

This face concept also requires people to be true to their words. If one is caught taking back words or breaking promises, that person instantly loses face and the confidence of others, and the ones who took these words seriously may also feel they have lost face for being duped. In regard to face, the drinking habits of Chinese have been well known, and foreigners touring Chinese regions now anticipate that they would encounter endless drinking parties and even contests with their Chinese hosts. This custom forms a key part of a face-giving process. To many Chinese, drinking bottoms-up gives enormous face and respect to the other side, and those shirking this obligation are seen as insincere and probably untrustworthy. In recent years, this drinking test has been more restrained and is more popular in the north than in the south of China. It is, in any case, an important face-giving gesture, which many Chinese can readily appreciate.

In business negotiations with Chinese counterparts, causing them to lose face on certain issues is one of the main reasons for disastrous outcomes. This includes publicly showing anger, frustration, disrespect; or being dismissive, mocking and patronising. When your counterparts feel the danger of losing their face right in front of you, a negotiation ceases to be meaningful and cannot proceed. It is doubtful if they would return to the negotiation table, and this would be possible only if a guarantee of no disrespect from your side is made—in this way, face is given back to your counterparts. Since most Chinese desire no public loss of face to their counterparts, even if they see little prospects for cooperation or contract signing, they would be very reluctant to speak their true opinions. Their replies will be far from a blunt rejection or candid admission of dislike. This presents a tricky problem to foreigners who prefer direct answers and are therefore deeply puzzled by mixed signals sent out by Chinese negotiators.

In negotiations, face can be used by the Chinese as a means for getting better deals. Nationalistic feelings help make their case. If a proposed deal is not accepted, they lose face in front of colleagues and superiors, and they tend to blame foreigners across the table for not being willing to enhance China's economic development and national interests. Making certain minor compromises gives the Chinese side face, thus increasing the chance to cut the deal sooner. Even in heated debates over key concerns from both sides, it is a good idea to leave a way out for the Chinese side. When they are in an awkward situation, you may find it hard to resist the urge for further embarrassment or making them feel caught. Such moves easily provoke them by causing them to lose face, and these may just backfire. A rather more effective way is to offer a ladder for them to climb down. This face-saving tactic would be appreciated by the other side, enhance mutual trust, and help make an acceptable deal for both parties.

The above three concepts are crucial in a business environment influenced by Chinese cultural traits. Suggestions have been made on dealing with these concepts in business, and they should be considered as overall background factors. Suggestions focus on precautions, not on uniformity in approaches. An understanding of *guo qing* or *guanxi* does not necessarily imply the making of concessions against company interests or bending backward to avoid direct confrontation. Knowing the tricks of *guanxi* is also not an excuse to use bribes or kickbacks as regular means to get business done, as some multinational executives have done in China. The discussion of these concepts is to present the essentials to those who will work in this environment, so views need to be broadened and cultural values cross-checked in advance. After acknowledging cultural diversity, foreign executives would benefit from a grasp of these three concepts and gain further knowledge of the behaviours and moves their Chinese counterparts make. To know your opponents would mean to have a better chance to succeed and minimise the possibility of frustrating confrontations.

Cross-cultural Communication

Language Barriers

In cross-cultural communication, problems exist even when the same language is spoken by people from both sides. English has been widely used by people in business the world over, so Chinese managers with a broad education may be able to use English in communication with foreign managers. English interpreters are also in bumper supply in

Negotiations Tactics in Review

Negotiation styles of the Chinese and how to counter them have been fascinating subjects in countless China-related guidebooks. A literature review can trace back to the time of China's early opening, or even earlier, to the negotiations proceeding Nixon's China trip in 1972. In political and business deals, negotiations are steps people cannot avoid. Partly due to difficulties at the negotiation table and some experience of business failures, foreign investors grew wary of perceived Chinese ways of tricking or defeating them. It has become widely accepted in the West that the Chinese are negotiation masters and they have 36 stratagems drawn from ancient Sun Zi military strategies. These perceptions have become another category of stereotypes of Chinese culture. Some American academics proposed counter measures, to apply those Chinese tactics on the Chinese. Sometimes these tactics worked, and the Chinese side was deeply amazed by how much foreigners knew about classic Chinese proverbs of wisdom.

Along with smoother communication and wider cultural exchanges between the two sides, there emerged revised observations of the so-called Chinese negotiation styles. It has been proved convincingly by more recent studies that there are perhaps no standard or uniform negotiation styles or formats for every Chinese negotiating team to follow; and the intention, demand and tactics of Chinese representatives are so diverse that a generalisation on Chinese negotiation styles is able only to present a tiny part of the whole picture. (Pye, Lucian, *Chinese Commercial Negotiating Style*, Cambridge, Mass., Oelgeschlager, Gunn & Hain, 1982; Fang, Tony, *Chinese Business Negotiating Style*, London, Sage Publications, 1999)

China, though many of them may not be able to adequately handle technical terms and jargons. Despite this improving English-speaking environment, the crucial factor in cross-cultural communication is not a linguistic one, but of background knowledge and understanding of cultural norms and customs.

Without knowing something of the cultural background, executives of foreign companies find it difficult to figure out the real intention of the other side, at or outside negotiations. Interpreters are up to the standard in getting the conversation going between the two sides, but many cope with "**hard**" negotiation less satisfactorily, due to language skills or their own lack of knowledge of both cultures. In some anecdotal examples, interpreters "**swallowed**" certain contents in conveying the message. To the Chinese side, responses from the foreigners appeared bored and flat, making them doubtful about the joint venture. Once another interpreter came in to work, much more information flowed in, and messages came back with richer tones. It is often the practice of some slack interpreters to deliver only parts of the whole message from negotiators. A good interpreter with adequate knowledge would benefit both parties by providing unfiltered information and minimising confusion. Dialogues would then become direct and genuine.

It is clear that language interpreters have a crucial role to play, and they should be the first to understand cultural differences and to bridge them. Without effective channels, there will be no real communication between the two parties involved, and business deals are hard to begin with.

There are language problems on the side of the Chinese as well, who very often use awkward English in doing business with foreigners. English translation by local Chinese does not always convey the right message to targeted foreigner customers. Subtle hints and special meanings in English are hard for them to grasp, and their standard verbatim translation only complicates the matter and causes more confusion. A regular column in the (now defunct) *Far Eastern Economic Review* collects examples of misused English in many places. The following are a few anecdotal examples of the Chinese usage of English, in order to show the misplaced meanings or lost meanings in language translation.

Language translation proves vital in effective advertising and marketing in another economy. English words may have no or a negative meaning after verbatim translation into Chinese words, and vice versa. This type of translation does not guarantee success if wrong words were chosen. It requires extra effort from the marketing team to find out the suitability of a brand name in Chinese. For example, the first Chinese translation of Coca-Cola in the early twentieth century was in four Chinese characters, which means "thirsty mouth and wax". A more cheerful translation with another combination of four characters gave the meaning as "tasty and delightful". This was much closer to the expectations of Chinese consumers for imported drinks and has made the drink a popular brand ever since.

The most successful and creative translations of foreign brands come from the motor car industry. Except for those Chinese names which adopt their phonetic sounds of foreign brands, such as Audi or

Chinese-style English

- A Hainan airline ticket office has a poster saying: "We take your bags and send them to all directions";
- In a Guilin hotel a notice reads: "Because of impropriety of entertaining guests of the opposite sex in the bedroom, it is suggested that the lobby be used for this purpose";
- Outside a Tianjin clothing shop, a notice reads: "Order your summer suits quick. Because of big rush we will execute customers in strict rotation";
- In a Beijing hotel lobby, a notice reads: "The lift is being fixed for next day. During that time we regret that you will be unbearable";
- A sign in a Hangzhou zoo reads: "Please do not feed animals. If you have suitable food, give it to the guard on duty";
- At a Wuxi dry cleaning shop a notice reads: "Please drop your trousers here for best results";
- An advertisement by a Kunming dentist says: "Teeth extracted by the latest methodists".
- In a Jinlin hotel a notice reads: "You are very invited to take advantage of the chambermaid";
- In a Shanghai hotel elevator, a sign says: "Please leave your values at the front desk".

Buick, many translated names fully demonstrate the love of car buyers and make boring foreign names shine in Chinese. The best examples are Mercedes and BMW, with their Chinese names meaning "gallop" and "treasured champion horse", respectively. The traditional emotional attachment to legendary horses in China has been shifted to the car marques they admire immeasurably. The undistinguishable sound of Volvo came to mean "rich and powerful" in Chinese, which profoundly appeals to those newly rich who eagerly desire a symbol of their new status. Some of the Chinese translations follow the original meanings in English words, such as Jaguar, which has just average appeal to Chinese consumers despite it belonging to the club of luxury cars. On the other hand, Land Rover has been translated into Chinese as "land tiger", which adds some sense of mightiness to these somewhat unglamorous English words.

There are many examples of good and bad translations of brands in English to those in Chinese. It is important for foreign companies to know that their brands may mean nothing to Chinese consumers if they simply copy English names phonetically; or they might send out the wrong signal if the Chinese translations of their brands touch upon some words the Chinese generally dislike.

Presentation Styles

Among language problems, a major obstacle is to find appropriate ways for English-speaking foreigners to communicate effectively with their non English-speaking audience. It may be hard for, say, the Americans to realise that they do not face an audience in China who speak and think the same way as they do. This is because native English-speakers in China are so few that the Americans have to deal with people with varying levels of English proficiency. Even in higher education institutions and government departments with international tasks, few officials or staff members can adequately conduct academically meaningful conversations with native English-speakers. At academic seminars or conferences, senior professors and graduate students are often busy figuring out unfamiliar English words and expressions, rather than focusing on the contents of the presentation. On-the-spot interpreting thus remains a walking stick for foreign personnel who have to do business in China.

Foreign personnel can improve cross-cultural communication through their own efforts in sending out clear messages. This implies making necessary adjustments to their normal speaking styles and raising the acceptance rate of their Chinese audience. In China and in Asia, people tend to remain quiet when they cannot catch up with English instructions or presentations that foreigners are giving. It is the social norm that guests are not to be impolitely interrupted and the audience choose not to raise questions. Acknowledging that you did not understand certain points in the presentation, especially the ones made by foreign guests, is quite embarrassing in front of peers. It is for the native English-speakers to notice and realise that many in the audience may have trouble following their talks. A more accommodating atmosphere would make the audience feel confident and ask questions on particular points more eagerly. Genuine communication begins only when both presenters and the audience feel unfettered in offering their opinions and getting answers.

Effective communicators would adjust their speaking styles when facing a non English-speaking audience. Many Americans, including academics, are used to impressing other people with long-winding and complicated sentences, and when they see puzzled faces in the audience, they tend to explain what they just said with more sentences. The Americans also customarily throw in a few words in their sentences, breaking the pace to demonstrate their versatility. This sometimes works wonders to their home audience, but to listeners in a non English-speaking country, it resembles a gentle torture, as the audience is working hard to follow the theme and pace of the talk, and finds it very uncomfortable and distracting to have to deal with those interruptions. It is essential for foreign presenters to keep their sentences plain, short and clear, and repeating phrases and key words surely helps the audience a great deal.

Native English-speaking executives need to particularly avoid using their usual speaking styles on their Chinese staff. They should slow down the pace of conversation considerably in talks with non English-speaking Chinese. They should also avoid using idioms, slang, and phrases understood only by their fellow countrymen. For those with strong accents, they may have to switch to clear pronunciations in a formal way similar to the standard of radio broadcasters. Jokes normally do not help in making an impression, since these may need translation for the benefit of the audience, during which any humour would be lost. The CEO of Intel once visited the company's chip plant in Shanghai and made a speech to Chinese staff and workers. To his delight, his speech and some humorous remarks in it were well received by his Chinese subordinates, and their laughter and applause to his jokes convinced him of their sufficient English proficiency for work at that plant. While it is a little doubtful how much of his jokes were actually picked up by Chinese workers around, this is a rare occasion of non English-speakers with adequate language skills receiving clear messages from the Americans.

Out of necessity of doing business, foreign executives face an unenviable task of adjusting their speaking and presentation styles. This is an indispensable part of cross-cultural communication, in which native English-speakers have to sacrifice their beloved English speaking habits and make extra effort to convey clear messages to their Chinese partners and staff.

Opposing Perceptions in Cross-cultural Management

Common to cooperation projects between Chinese and foreigners, each side has its old and new perceptions of the opposite side. In business negotiations, joint ventures and foreign-owned enterprises, cultural backgrounds and norms distinguish two groups of people. On the basis of various cultures and their stereotypes, a clash of intentions and initiatives is inevitable. The central issues are how to mediate different views and prevent clashes from wrecking the entire cooperation.

Perceptions of foreign cultures have been formed through education, mass media, and through personal experience working with foreign personnel in business. China has now registered over 400,000 foreign-invested companies, and in major cities, thousands of expatriate personnel live and work there. Encounters and cooperation with foreign multinationals are no longer rare occasions. It is with these changes that stereotypes of the other culture are displayed openly and comparisons made possible.

The following are two lists of perceptions of the other side, from a survey conducted in the late 1990s.

Perceptions of the Chinese on Foreigners

1. No consideration of human feelings—strict, uncompromising, giving no face;

2. Little consideration of human factors in operations: worship of rules, technology and systematic management;

3. Arrogant: self-centred, look down on Chinese staff;

4. Distrust of Chinese people: share little management authority and technology, suspicion over Chinese staff, supervise or scrutinise closely;

5. Hard to figure out their rationales: elusive behind office walls, little communication with local employees, confined to the small circle of expatriates, giving unclear instructions and plans;

6. Dictatorship: make all final decisions, controlling, disregard of other opinions, sack disagreeing local workers and staff at will;

7. Inflexibility: strictly following set rules, even if that incurs extra costs and waste;

8. Extreme concern over money matters: control of finances, tight budgeting, cost cutting;

9. Lack of understanding of China: introduce own models and cultures, see no need to learn from local culture and ignore Chinese cultural norms.

Perceptions of Foreigners on the Chinese

1. Lack of sense of responsibility: disregard of rules and set tasks, no professionalism, no quality control, rushed work, absentism, etc.

2. Conservative: satisfied with current situation, lacking initiative, opposing change and creativity;

3. Dare not make own decisions on the spot when needed: dependence on others, afraid of bad consequences, make others the leaders and blame failures on others;

4. Afraid to offend others: keep harmonious atmosphere, evasive, avoid giving direct suggestions and fear of reappraisal, even if threats are near;

5. Slack practice or laziness: late for work, inefficient, slow work pace, low output;

6. Actions not matching their words: saying something while doing another, break promises;

7. Adherence to small groups: stick to close allies, group mentality, reject non-group members, groupthink;

8. Emphasise sectional interest (over interests of corporation): department and line interests are high priorities, company goals are low priority, and concerns over group benefits.

There are some well-known examples of misunderstanding and clashes. One of these is Beijing Jeep.

In 1984, at an early stage of the joint venture Beijing Jeep, American managers demanded to spend 400,000 yuan on fixing blocked toilets and painting all factory walls. The American side reasoned that an enterprise cannot be managed well if it cannot even have clean and working toilets. A newly painted factory building in bright blue would create a better, more pleasant work environment and be likely to increase work efficiency. As such, the toilets and blue walls were signs of improved management. It was important to let Chinese workers know that they were having a new start. These demands reflected the intention and determination of American executives to implement their management models and practice in this new enterprise.

The Chinese side had other ideas. Their priority was the introduction of advanced car making technology from the US as early as possible. If production lines could be installed early, then car production would begin soon. Spending money on toilets and colourful paint were surely weird ideas. The Chinese side considered it a waste of money and a misplaced priority on exterior appearance. In reality, they did not mind certain unpleasant work conditions as long as finished cars rolled off the assembly lines.

Perceptions and stereotypes reduce the effectiveness of cross-cultural management in business cooperation and joint ventures. Foreign models and practices have been widely introduced and vigorously maintained in most foreign-invested companies in China. The question is not whether to implement these new systems, but rather how to get the best results in face of cultural clashes as well as conflict of interests. Knowledge of culture in the host country is especially crucial in dealing with issues of local sales and marketing. Insistence on particular management and marketing models in the China market has led to certain unexpected troubles and failures. This is evident in examples of misreading Chinese customer behaviours and preferences. Along with multinationals' localisation drives, the mainstream trend needs to shift to grasping and making use of characteristics of local markets, instead of ignoring or denying them. The following is an example of the gaps between foreign initiated planning and market reality.

In the latest comprehensive survey on public opinions and impressions of foreign multinationals in China, conducted by the State

The Myth of Gol

As a hot selling VW model, Gol's world sales record was around 4 million units. Shanghai VW figured that this would be a hot model again in China and outsell other models on the market. German personnel were put in charge of marketing and launching this model in 2003. They essentially implemented the brand and marketing strategies used in other markets.

The Gol model received bad reviews and made miserable sales. The central problem was that they misread the cultural elements in consumer behaviours and made the wrong sales pitch. Gol was first launched as a two-door coupe, which evidently appeals to young and fashion-conscious consumers. Unfortunately, people in this group are on average financially tight, and the number of buyers from this group is small. Those middle-class families with adequate purchasing power apparently prefer more standard and stately four-door sedans as their family vehicle.

Furthermore, to copy the practice in other markets where buyers specify customerised items for their cars, Shanghai VW made the entry level Gol so basic that a radio and air conditioner were not supplied. Many common features on other makes and models were optional, and buyers had to make extra payments for some basic equipment. The end result was a pushed up price for a Gol car, thus losing its price advantage. Worse, consumers were irritated by Gol's bare standard equipment and felt they were intentionally short-changed. "**No air conditioner**" was a common remark when Gol was mentioned in conversations. Buyers for a family car would not give a thought to a Gol, and young people who were supposed to be target buyers could not afford so many additional costs for optional equipment. In the end, Gol achieved unsatisfactory sales and almost ruined the reputation of VW in China. The multinational had to re-design the model, let local staff conduct marketing, and launch a four-door model at a later stage. In the absence of a successful new model, the dated Santana models had to remain on the market.

Gol of VW resembles the experience of Citroen with its own hatchback model, and both suffered from a lack of understanding of the China market, though Citroen's models received a high acceptance rate despite being unique. It is often a mystery to foreign managers why a hot selling model in a market does not repeat its success in another market. The simple answer is a misreading or neglect of cultural differences and varied consumer behaviours under cultural influence. Localisation helps solve many such problems through cross-cultural management and building a bridge between the cultures involved.

Development Research Centre, American, European, Japanese, and Korean multinationals are the four groups of companies under scrutiny.

In the category of overall public image, American and European multinationals take top places as preferred companies. This implies public recognition of these companies in the China market. In corporate culture, they take the same places as well, indicating a matured and multicultural approach in their China operations. Germany's VW is a top player in career prospects, work choice and public image, while Philips, Nike and Mercedes are companies with the worst public image. Among them, Philips played a key role in waging ongoing anti-dumping campaigns against Chinese exports to the EU market; Nike was accused of exploiting child labour; and Mercedes experienced damaging publicity about its smashed cars. From past experience and media reports, the general public form their opinions on whether a foreign multinational should be rated a friendly partner. Categories in this section indicate the degrees of general acceptance of foreign multinationals; and American and European companies certainly benefited from their well publicised charity work, large investments and technology transfers.

Amongst enterprises, however, American and European multinationals fall behind in the categories of internal work conditions, management systems, and corporate culture. These are assessments made by employees in foreign multinationals, therefore the conclusions are quite different from the impressions of the general public. Japanese companies are rated low in public image, for political and economic factors. From internal assessments, however, Chinese employees give Japanese companies higher marks for work conditions, training and benefits, than they give American and European companies.

Korean multinationals are rated low in both public image and internal assessment categories. In particular, Chinese employees consider Korean management by and large arrogant, parochial (pushing employees to speak Korean, for instance), hard to communicate with and unwilling to practise cross-cultural management. They are last in the category of work choice.

As a whole, American and European multinationals have mastered public relations campaigns and have won recognition from the general public. Their cross-cultural communications and management within a corporation have been comparatively unsatisfactory, and it seems that their management model and systems have been overrated. A low rating by Chinese employees indicates the existence of barriers in such communication and reinforces Chinese perceptions of foreigners, as listed above.

Two examples of cross-cultural management are given below.

Motorola

Among foreign multinationals in China, Motorola stands out as a leader in cross-cultural management, as well as in the telecommunication business. It has adopted approaches relatively different from its standard models and encouraged full involvement in localisation. The latter implies emphasis on cross-cultural communication and cultural diversity.

In general, Motorola vigorously promotes its own corporate culture in major areas. These include integrity, participation, creativity, employee satisfaction, empowerment, service and quality. In its China operations, Motorola routinely conducted ongoing training of Chinese employees, inside and outside China, to introduce and reinforce the company goals and rationales. In the meantime, Motorola adds culture-specific guidelines, with publicly announced goals of making China its home and being a 100% Chinese company. Full scale localisation, harmony and trust are particularly emphasised.

Since most company employees are local Chinese, Motorola has made modifications in management to adapt to the environment in China. Motorola provides fixed employment contracts to formal employees, giving them a strong sense of job security and belonging. This is similar to job security in state enterprises and is thus a preferred option for workers. Motorola also provides various fringe benefits to local employees, from medical, transport, to housing. It conducts regular open performance appraisals, in order to create an environment of fair competition and mutual trust. Motorola has undergone a thorough localisation process, placing Chinese staff in key positions from the top to middle management. Senior level positions are for executives of Chinese origin or local Chinese personnel. There are also numerous channels of communication open to employees seeking their input and participation, including regular meetings, dialogues, group discussions, and a company website. Motorola has won high employee loyalty through guaranteeing personal dignity, promising prospects and making employees feel respected.

The Haier Culture in its US Project

Experiments of cross-cultural management have another side. It could be the experience of Chinese companies operating overseas. As a number of Chinese companies ventured overseas to a more open international business environment, there is also the experience of two cultures' interactions. Haier has been a top household appliances maker in China. As part of its expansion strategy, this Chinese company set out to enter the US market. It is there that a cross-culture management of another kind began.

Haier set up its US plant in South Carolina in 1999, costing over US$40 million. The plant manufactures fridges for local markets, through major retail chains such as Wal-Mart and Home Depot.

As a well-managed Chinese company and a quick learner of German knowledge and practice, Haier is confident of its ability to adapt to the US market and customers. It introduced Haier culture and management norms to this US plant, and trained local employees with Chinese concepts and work ethics. It is obvious that some key Haier doctrines cannot be applied in this plant, such as serving the country and developing strong domestic industries, and its emphasis on employee loyalty and submission to leadership has certain problems locally as well.

A few Haier work practices, common to Chinese enterprises, are perhaps new to local American employees. These include pre-shift group meetings to brief tasks and discuss problems. These meetings are also for employees to say what they think and get responses from others. To Chinese employees at local plants, this can be the time to know each other better and foster a sense of closeness. It is somehow odd to American employees who take a straightforward attitude toward their work and do not see much need for this meeting time at all.

Another typical Chinese practice in domestic enterprises is to nominate and vote for the best Haier employees. "**Model workers**" are publicly honoured at assemblies and others are encouraged to learn from them. These non-financial motivation methods receive little response from American employees, who see selecting an employee of the month as an acceptable practice, but disagree with publicly lauding nominated workers. Also, a vote by employees themselves would create attrition and such a selection loses objectivity. All these responses are not what Haier received in its Chinese operations. It has moved to tone down those strong Chinese characteristics and made an effort to assimilate to local American culture and norms.

Haier delegates total authority to American executives, with a small number of Chinese personnel stationed there. Haier America is headed by Mr. Michael Jemal, who is in charge of all production, advertising, technology and sales. Haier America is rather quick in response to consumer demands, designing and making new types of products to suit buyers' specific needs, such as a mini fridge with a fold-down flap for a laptop. Haier products have taken large shares at the lower end of the markets.

Among cultural clashes at Haier's US plant, prominent areas are in management styles. Under the influence of a strong corporate culture, Haier managers have been used to a near autocratic leadership style. They attempted to explain to their US counterparts that in China the leader decides and the subordinates follow. This was something of a culture shock to American workers, and Chinese managers were surprised by the Americans' reaction. Both sides regarded their own routines as normal and saw the other's as unusual. At the US plant, the leader decides, and the staff responds to this with questions and suggestions. This had a profound impact on Chinese managers and made them think of alternative ways of management. In the end, tension subsided as the two sides got used to each other and mutual understanding prevailed. Chinese managers expressed their interest in taking home some of what they learnt at this US plant and planned to experiment with certain two-way management styles.

In general, Haier is operating in a matured market of a developed economy. As such, its own Chinese characteristics and corporate culture have been in stark contrast with the American norms and practices. On this level playing field, Haier is able to absorb well tested Western management models while taking advantage of its strong Chinese traditions.

In a Vroom-Yetton model on leadership styles, there are five basic categories in three groups. The first style implies decisions made by leaders themselves. The second style gives others a limited role in supplying information, with no role to play in decision making. These two styles are in the "**autocratic**" group. The third style gives members an opportunity to learn about problems, and then leaders make decisions without input from those members. The fourth style gives others an opportunity to be informed of problems as a group. Without discussions, the leaders make their own decisions. These two styles are placed in the "**consultative**" group. The fifth style allows the group to be informed of problems and to collectively discuss issues concerned. Leaders and other members reach a consensus. This is called the "**group**" style.

The first two "autocratic" leadership styles are distinctive in Chinese management, as we can see in the case of Haier, in both its Chinese and American plants. The "consultative" style is common in foreign companies, as shown in Haier's US plant, where local American employees were not used to the Chinese leadership and management styles. The "group" leadership style proves rare even in foreign companies, since decision making is often one-way in cases of serious problems, despite common two-way communication between top management and employees. The Motorola practice in its Chinese operations seems to combine "consultative" style and certain elements of "autocratic" style. Motorola, like other multinationals, maintains a direct chain of command in production and pushes hard for quality and efficiency. "Autocratic" leadership is necessary for top management. As in China, they recognised that a more acceptable approach is employing a "consultative" style, in order to increase cooperation and participation of Chinese employees.

Relations between Headquarters and Chinese Subsidiaries

The China operations of foreign multinationals are in effect a multicultural work environment. There are a few types of controls between China subsidiaries and headquarters. Controlling or parent companies set up regional headquarters in China to coordinate country operations. There are also Asia headquarters or Greater China headquarters. China regional headquarters of certain multinationals are under Asia headquarters or Greater China headquarters (see Figure 15.1). In this case, China headquarters serve under and report to its

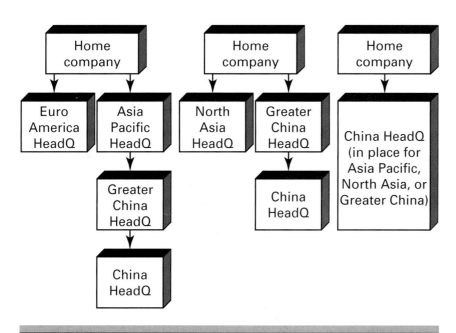

Figure 15.1   Headquarters and subsidiaries

superior headquarters rather than home headquarters. The authority and freedom in decision making by these headquarters are thus limited. Some other multinationals, such as Toshiba of Japan, place their China headquarters as an equal to their American or European headquarters, thus giving it more authority and direct access of communication with home headquarters. This is often out of consideration of business scale. If the China market figures highly in the whole company, foreign multinationals even move their Asia-Pacific headquarters to China, normally in Beijing or Shanghai—such as Honeywell, which moved its headquarters from Singapore to Shanghai. Similarly, China headquarters could oversee operations in Greater China regions or for North Asia, depending on the scale of business done in China.

A major difficulty is organisational relations between China headquarters and Greater China headquarters. The former is doing more business in recent years and is the core of Greater China regions. As such, a strong control from Greater China headquarters over China headquarters tilts the balance towards outer markets, away from the core market. This often causes difficulties and failures in business operations in China. On the other hand, if the China headquarters makes more independent decisions on its own, the Greater China headquarters is likely to lose control and becomes irrelevant.

Foreign multinationals may delegate greater authority to their China headquarters to coordinate all operations within the territory, including production, technology, and sales. The main reason of this overall responsibility is that the China operations are numerous and in a variety of industries, so that a regional headquarters is the ideal way to link them together and achieve high efficiency. A senior Chinese industrialist, the chairman of Legend Group, gave this advice on increasing efficiency: "Legend receives frequent suggestions from people at their workplaces, screens them and accepts those valuable ones promptly. In China operations of foreign multinationals, they implement rules and routines transplanted from their headquarters back in their home countries. Chinese subsidiaries are supposed to follow those rules precisely, and if local staff find things to be improved, they have to report through layers of the bureaucracy and obtain approval from their home headquarters. This handling process not only lowers efficiency but also discourages their Chinese staff at work".

Home headquarters has direct control over this type of regional headquarters through the appointment of CEOs and inspections. On the other hand, this type of China headquarters is able to make strategic decisions in expansion and acquisition as the market requires, and could get financial support from home headquarters. This would cut down response time and increase flexibility in market competition. Foreign multinationals may also just grant certain authority to their China headquarters, while other functional departments at home headquarters, such as R&D or sourcing, have their own offices and authority to operate in China. In this case, the home headquarters takes a global view and makes its China operations serve the ultimate goals of the multinational.

In the process of fast localisation, foreign multinationals have learned good lessons in managing regional offices and local markets in China. A key component in the strategy is hiring local personnel and executives of Chinese origin. The latter include those executives with overseas education, who are assigned to China by the company and come originally from Singapore, Taiwan, or Hong Kong. These personnel may work at the Greater China headquarters or take up positions in China headquarters. In either case, their work focus is the China market. This structure and personnel arrangement would lead to recurring conflicts between overseas personnel and local personnel. To home headquarters, there seems no difference in management, as both work for the company and have similar qualifications. But there are indeed clear differences between the two groups. Overseas personnel have better access to home headquarters, with their overseas education background, language skills and internationalised knowledge. Since they are selected and appointed by home headquarters, they generally earn more trust. Their previous work experience in the company helps them understand more of the corporate culture and internal mechanisms. In terms of office politics, they are certainly better equipped than local Chinese managers.

On the other hand, local Chinese are proud of their first-hand and in-depth knowledge of the China market and of local consumers. They have better feel of market trends and customer preferences, and they receive true market information from buyers. Their contacts and network would function better in obtaining business orders and in making projections more precisely than formal market research is able to. These are the advantages coming with long experience and hands-on operations in the field. Many brilliant plans in marketing, brand promotion and price wars come from their own initiatives. As for disadvantages, their access to multinationals' home headquarters is perhaps more restricted, and their initiatives have to be cleared by executives at Greater China headquarters and are likely to receive less support from the home company.

In this situation with two groups of localised personnel, there is a possibility of conflicts and subsequent damage to company business. In some cases, senior Chinese executives have caused certain delays in their response to problems and even crises. Chinese consumers sometimes wonder why foreign multinationals acted indifferent in the China market to damaging events and bad publicity, such as Toshiba laptop defects and the smashing of Mercedes cars by angry owners. It is particularly irritating to local Chinese managers that the multinationals they work for have made worldwide recalls to certain faulty products, but did not include China in their recall lists. There is a barrier between local managers and headquarters, and signals of market problems may be ignored by executives at Greater China headquarters. This tension would escalate if the situation is not properly handled and adjustments made. Recently, some top Chinese executives quit from multinationals because of complex situations and tension between the China headquarters and Greater China headquarters.

The general trend for foreign multinationals is to enlarge their China headquarters and delegate more authority to executives there. Regional headquarters, in addition to China headquarters, adds more layers in internal communication and has proved ineffective. A more flexible approach is to place China headquarters as equal to Asia-Pacific headquarters and, more significantly, allow it to have direct communication channels to home headquarters.

Managerial Staffing and Local Employees of Foreign Multinationals

Foreign multinationals inevitably face the problem of recruitment of personnel for their China operations. There are in general three types of staffing policy. The "ethnocentric" policy refers to the practice of sending personnel from the home company into the host country. Foreign companies adopt this policy to guarantee their China operations proceed as planned and their investment is protected. This policy usually works well at the early stages of FDI, when only personnel from the home company can be trusted and authorised to set up and manage new projects. Evident drawbacks of this policy include the communication barriers between assigned expatriate personnel and local staff, clashes of two very different corporate cultures, and heavy financial costs for stationing foreign personnel. Making China operations follow home standards is an advantage and therefore a major reason for foreign multinationals to continue sending in expatriate executives, though in smaller numbers these days and chiefly for top positions.

If a foreign multinational decides to stay long in the China market, it soon switches to the "polycentric" policy. This implies an emphasis on the operations of regional headquarters and adapting to local culture. A process of localisation follows, in particular in recruitment and promotion of local managers. Eventually, senior executives at the top management will come from local talent pools. Those large multinationals have extremely wide-ranging human resources bases and thus select the most suitable personnel for their worldwide operations, regardless of the nationality. This is called a "geocentric" policy. Selected executives have extensive work experience and hold versatile skills to handle situations in different countries and markets.

For example, a former Ford CEO was a chief officer at Ford Australia, and Nissan's current CEO, Mr. Gohsn, comes from the French carmaker Renault's Brazil operations.

Expatriate managers need to be adequately trained. Such training should focus on cultural sensitivity and ability to gain knowledge of other cultures. Selected personnel should possess interpersonal skills for conducting meaningful and helpful dialogue with local partners and employees. As discussed previously, people sent to China in early times of FDI were often selected for their language capability and lacked real understanding of the environment within which to do business. These were, of course, contingent plans when qualified candidates were hard to find—those with sufficient industry experience, management expertise and cultural competence. The last characteristic proved most important in a successful local project in China. This shortage has been greatly lessened in recent years, with increasing numbers of seasoned managers of Chinese origin and local managers who grasped foreign cultures and core business management techniques quickly.

Selected foreign personnel, ideally, should possess an open personality and great confidence in dealing with people in a strange environment. Experienced managers with weak communication skills and an emotional personality are not suitable for positions in another culture, since expatriates very often work in an environment alien to their own, and anxiety and loneliness could affect their performance. It is important for these expatriates that they find their own ways to break the ice and resist any depressing feelings. For example, a senior manager of Chinese origin was assigned by a Hong Kong bank to be stationed in Dalian and had only an annual leave to return to his home in Canada. Confined to a top apartment complex in the city, he managed to get rid of ill feelings and loneliness through practising Chinese calligraphy and writing Chinese poems. He also tried hard to learn from his Chinese subordinates spoken and written Putonghua, to complement his own Cantonese. These extra activities outside office hours freed him from miserable feelings and helped him to maintain high spirits at work.

The family factor is a major consideration in selection of expatriate personnel. It is only reasonable that they can take their families along to their work posts. This of course increases the total costs. A package offer also commonly includes a set amount of **hardship allowance**, to compensate for any loss of living standards they would otherwise enjoy in the home country. This is in the form of either a doubled pay or a fixed additional pay on top of base salary. As expatriate executives increase in number, there are many new facilities on offer in major Chinese cities, such as international schools for expatriates' children, household services for foreign personnel, and special accommodations like apartments or villas so that they do not have to live in expensive but impersonal five-star hotels. As average living conditions improve in China, foreign companies tend to lower the amount of or abolish hardship allowances offered to expatriate managers. This is a trend most obvious among Hong Kong and Taiwan companies. Hong Kong managers working in major cities such as Beijing or Shanghai are now seldom offered extra pay and allowances that were previously up to 20% of salary, and their pay has moved closer to that received by local managers.

In managing local employees, foreign multinationals have improved remarkably in their approach. A key component of localisation is recruiting more talented local managers. These managers, in turn, are the ones who are familiar with the local environment and can manage local employees more effectively. In comparison with state enterprises, foreign multinationals enjoy certain advantages in hiring and recruitment. According to regulations from labour bureaux of the Chinese government, foreign companies are not subject to wage guidelines regularly issued by authorities. By the decisions of the CEO or the Board, foreign companies are allowed to set up their own salary scales and negotiate packages with promising candidates. The guideline on wages for employees of foreign companies is to follow the "**market floating**" principle, which in effect means going market rates. As a result, Chinese employees in foreign companies receive on average higher pay than those employees in other types of enterprises. This is a key competitive edge in the hands of foreign companies, which almost guarantees their success in gathering local staff with the most potential. Large foreign multinationals routinely stage recruitment shows in top Chinese universities and have a free hand to pick the cream of talent from thousands of applicants. A side effect of attractive offers from foreign multinationals is the high turnover rate, which cause frequent job switching by experienced Chinese managers who seek even higher pay. Foreign multinationals have since devised numerous ways to retain valuable staff.

Pay for employees in foreign companies consists of salary, bonus, allowances, and extras. Allowances usually cover lunch, uniform, accommodation, child care, pension, transport, hardship, heating, recreation etc. With relatively higher pay, these employees receive less in social securities, which are still the benefits enjoyed by those working in state enterprises. Only a few large multinationals are able to provide accommodations for senior Chinese executives and offer mortgage assistance to company staff.

Foreign companies generally implement two separate categories of salaries: one for Chinese employees, following market rates or higher; and one for expatriates, normally called "**overseas terms**", which even includes tax payment by the company in order to equal or be higher than their pay at home. These two separate categories created wide gaps between two groups of company employees in income. For example, a senior expatriate executive in a foreign-invested hotel in Guangzhou earns HK$140,000 per month, while the top Chinese manager there earns 1,800 yuan per month. This smacks of discrimination to many local Chinese staff. Due to average income levels in different economies, this kind of gap will continue to cause certain troubles to top management of foreign multinationals in China.

Key Concepts

Hofstede's four cultural dimensions and their showings in China
Three Chinese cultural traits: *guo qing*, *guanxi*, and "face"
Applications of *guanxi* in business
Barriers in cross-cultural communication
Perceptions and stereotypes in cross-cultural management
The Vroom-Yetton model of leadership styles
Headquarters and subsidiaries
Staffing policies and managing Chinese employees

Discussion Questions

1. What do you see as the typical illustrations of the four cultural dimensions in China? Make comparisons of these dimensions with another Asian country and a Western country as well.

2.   What are your views on *guo qing* and the saying that "a practice is permissible given the host country's relative level of economic development"?

3.   What are the differences between *guanxi* and public relations in developed economies? What are the inherent links between *guanxi* and "face"? Identify major ways that will not to cause the other side to lose face in negotiations. Make suggestions on establishing and maintaining *guanxi*. Will *guanxi* still be relevant in an environment with improved market conditions and under the rule of law?

4.   What would you suggest to diffuse tension from the perceptions of both sides on their relations, as listed in the texts? Pick one Chinese and one foreign perception and provide possible reasons for their formation.

5.   What would you suggest to improve communication and control mechanisms between China headquarters and greater China headquarters? What do you consider as the best organisational structure to place the headquarters for China operations? Draw up an organisational chart if necessary.

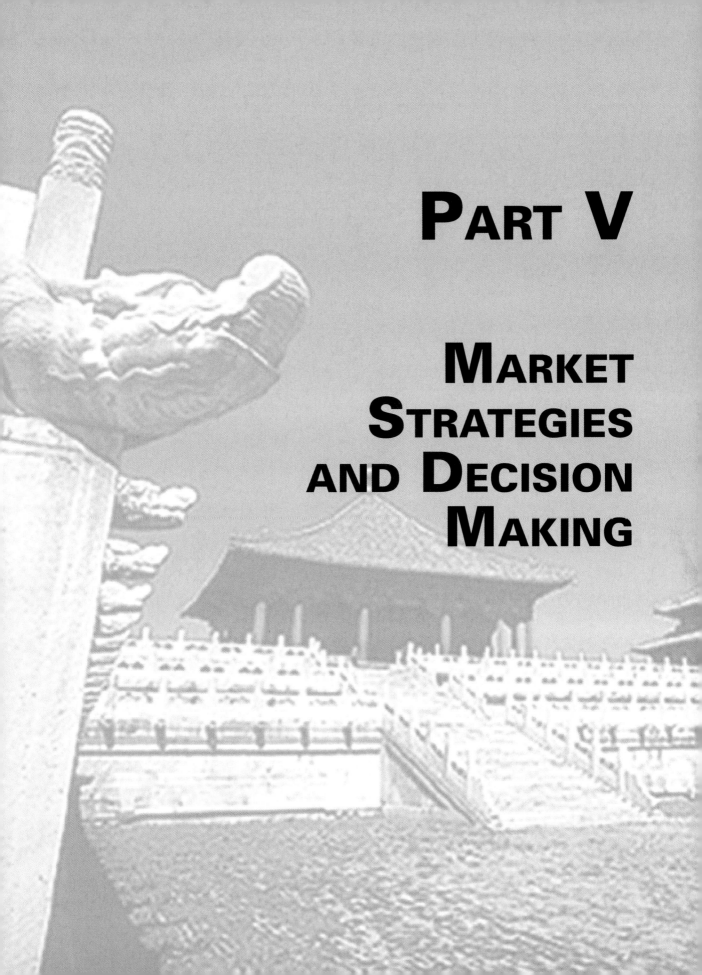

PART V

MARKET STRATEGIES AND DECISION MAKING

Decision Making Studies in General

This chapter and the next relate to the specific topics of business strategies and decision making. In foreign direct investment, market entry and expansion decisions are crucial to all corporations, on top of investment procedures and requirements. Foreign companies have accumulated ample experiences of dealing with the China market and Chinese partners, while some of them prove to be defective in strategic decision making. We will first touch upon major aspects of decision making and strategies, with established concepts and analyses, and then go on to analyse some cases of doing business by Chinese and foreign companies. More detailed case studies will be presented in Part VI.

Decisions and the Process

There are certain general approaches toward the subject of decision making. Three elements in studying decision making include:

1. Decision making as a process of choosing alternatives;
2. Decision maker, with authority, expectations, and particular objectives;
3. The decision itself, with outcomes and consequences.

What is a decision? Put simply, a decision involves choosing between alternatives.

❑ It shows an ongoing process of evaluating alternatives;

❑ It sets a particular objective;

❑ It requires actions to be taken;

❑ It demonstrates the decision maker's authority and expectations.

> "Effective people know that the most time-consuming step in the process is not making the decision but putting it into effect. Unless a decision has 'degenerated into work', it is not a decision; it is at best a good intention."
>
> Peter Drucker

Decision making passes through a series of stages, which take place in the process of managing organisations. The movement of the stages is shown in the following sequences:

1. Identification: This is to monitor the environment and situation, define risks and constraints, and clarify what is to be achieved;

2. Listing of alternatives: This is to search for alternatives, courses of action or solutions, and establish the methodology or criteria for appraising alternatives;

3. Selection of the most beneficial outcome: This is to appraise alternatives, solutions or courses of action, and choose the best from the list;

4. Implementation of selected alternative, solution or course of action;

5. Feedback on the quality of the decision and its outcome.

Decision frameworks are not a magical solution or an excuse for bad decisions. These stages or procedures cannot replace common sense, judgment, evidence, or leadership.

Obviously, it is no use sticking strictly to a set number of stages in a decision framework when the circumstances demand a rapid judgment. Using these frameworks too rigidly merely limits managerial freedom of manoeuvring and hampers decision making.

Analysis of Individual Decision Making

There are in general four types of decisions in life and business, as shown in the chart below.

	Personal	Organisational
Programmed	• Daily routines • Habits	• Standard operating procedures (SOPs)
Non-programmed	• Job choice • Career selection	• Strategic planning issues • Crisis

It is widely assumed in economics and other social sciences that people make rational decisions based on their rational sense and behaviours. This also applies to studies of decision making as a key concept.

What is rational decision making?

❑ When making decisions, people believe they have a firm objective that is completely rational or logical, and there are alternatives from which a choice is made to achieve the objective.

❑ For analysis, individuals follow the set steps, investigate **all** the important consequences and make careful selection of **each** of the alternatives.

❑ Rational behaviour means making a decision after reviewing all the alternatives and aiming to maximise the satisfaction or utility of the decision maker.

The end result of rational behaviour is **maximisation** of profits in the case of business firms and maximisation of utility in the case of people in general.

Programmed Decision Making

This is based on the idea of rational decisions, so that decisions made are predictable and in a set order.

❑ Programmed decisions are repetitive, routine choices, and have a frequent, daily occurrence.

❑ They can be proceduralised, that is to break down into discrete, sequential steps, such as from A, B, and then to C.

❑ The attraction of programmed decisions resides in a reduced need for judgement or **intuition,** both of which are based on ample past experience and intelligence.

Programmed decisions are only viable if a number of basic criteria are satisfied:

a. Sufficient time and money for data collection and analysis;

b. Adequate amount of **quantified** data;

c. Environment is stable and no pressure exists to react constantly to fast changing conditions which prevent outcomes from being finalised; if changes come fast, it is hard for decisions to be programmed;

d. Sufficient skills available to turn problems into well-defined, quantified operational requirements.

Some Examples of Programmed (Routine) Decision Making

Organisations (commercial or others) commonly use standard operating procedures (SOPs) to handle well-defined and well-known problems in their operations. These are rules and standards that have been set out in order to ensure that specific steps and actions are taken. These rules are in the form of manuals and guidelines, and they are highlighted in training instructions. The basic requirement for an employee is for him or her to make programmed decisions, otherwise the whole organisation would be in chaos.

In dealing with customers' complaints, counter staff follow the procedures laid down by the organisation. There are normally a number of pre-set rules for staff to apply, so they have an understanding of the range of potential problems. But they also have to make a particular judgment to respond to varying circumstances. The responses to a demand from a customer could be a full refund, a replacement with another item from the shop, or a rejection of the complaint on certain grounds stipulated by company rules. Counter staff are to make programmed decisions while meeting specific demands.

Non-programmed Decisions

In contrast, non-programmed decisions are novel, infrequent, unstructured and with little predictability. As shown in the above chart, personal decisions such as job searching and career changes involve many uncertainties, and such decisions are not frequently made. There are no standard rules to follow or guarantees for the decisions made.

For organisational decisions, the stakes are even higher, and they are made on a case-by-case basis, thus are most unlikely to be programmed. For crisis management, despite the fact that disasters do happen, they have no fixed patterns that can be studied beforehand, and they come in different forms and natures (natural, man-made, organisational, bad publicity etc). As a result, non-programmed decisions need intelligence, combined with adaptive, solution-orientated actions.

Both programmed and non-programmed decisions exist in business operations, and they are more or less made in turn. The primary task for top management is to open for business and start production or service, and their decisions at this stage are most likely **non-programmed**, with a new market, new demands and new problems to deal with. When the business starts running, they need to set out rules and standards for employees to follow in their routine work. SOPs are then put into practice, and many decisions in business are now **programmed** ones. Well-established companies maintain their operations in clear structures and well-defined procedures. This may cause large corporations to be prone to hierarchical inertia. When business expansion or strategic changes are on the agenda, **non-programmed** decisions again must be made, with little reference to the set standards already in place. This entire process runs in cycles, and both types of decisions are common in business operations. For top management, making non-programmed decisions are their major responsibility, while for employees, they are most likely to deal with programmed decisions in their work.

A good example of the contrast between programmed and non-programmed business decisions comes when foreign companies start their business in a different environment like China's. Programmed decision making procedures back home are what they are familiar with, and they assume that an extension of such procedures overseas would solve problems. In reality, a lot of non-programmed decisions must be made in a new business environment, and their known programmed decision making often runs into trouble in that environment.

Maximising Behaviour

This is to assume, on the basis of rational decision making, that managers without exception will make an effort to achieve maximum results. In business, this means to reach primary objectives such as profit, sales and growth in resources (land, material and personnel). These objectives provide the basic rationale for the existence of private enterprises. The decision maker must pursue schemes and strategies designed to foster greater efficiency in the firm. The maximising of profit is cited as the most influential motivator for business organisations.

In reality, such maximising behaviour appears more an assumption of people's capability, and managers often fail to do so in their decision making process. This is due to the following reasons:

❑ Managers have an inability to search for alternatives or pursue the highest ranking objectives to maximise the outcome. They may just make decisions that satisfy lower objectives.

❑ Limits on the information available to the management makes it impossible for them to perform the precise profit margin analysis necessary for maximisation.

❑ Managers, being human beings, have an inability to comprehend all the relevant variables in a given situation, which is too complex to be handled in all of its detail. For example, a manager may fail to understand the impact of high-tech equipment on productivity or impact of foreign exchange fluctuations on company earnings, since his experience is in unrelated fields.

❑ There are limitations on the cognitive capacity of decision makers, considering their background and outside influences (intelligence level and effort to learn).

❑ Most of all, **maximisation** tends to disregard environmental effects and thus works against long-term goals of the business. It may also cause serious ethical problems such as fraud, cheating, and inflating figures to get rewards in shares and bonuses. The recent

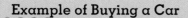

Example of Buying a Car

You need not visit or call every car showroom in town, and after a few visits you will be able to get a good idea of the going market rate and make a sensible purchase. The rational way is to search all prices, but people tend to limit their search and objectives for their final buying decisions.

Example of General Electric (GE)

GE under Jack Walsh set out a strategy that if one of their product sections was not the number one or number two player in the industry concerned, the company would withdraw from that industry completely. This is a rational decision to maximise results and reach the highest level of market share and profit. Very few companies can set this goal in their overall strategies. This is not applicable under current Chinese conditions, since the market potential in many industries is so huge that even a company at the tenth position can be quite profitable.

collapse of Enron of the US reveals serious drawbacks of all-out profit maximisation. This propensity also inhabits financial and stock markets, as profit maximising reigns supreme in these trading places.

From past experience and studies, a majority of managers would not make an ultimate effort and decision to maximise results in business. Their decisions may most likely be in accordance to their assessment of conditions and fall short of maximisation.

Satisficing Behaviour and Bounded Rationality

On the opposite side of maximising behaviour stand these two common tendencies.

Bounded Rationality

❑   There is a likelihood of choosing a particular objective and alternative;

❑   The search for alternatives is limited; choices made are adequate and **acceptable**;

❑   Decision makers' own views outweigh hard information and data;

❑   Final decisions may be based on criteria other than simple optimisation or outcome maximisation.

Satisficing

❑   This is to choose a satisfactory, rather than optimum, course of action;

❑   For a business, a necessary and acceptable level of profit should be sufficient to cover the costs of long-term investment and produce sizeable returns to investors;

❑   The focus is on information and alternatives **at hand**, since the decision maker has difficulty estimating the utility of alternatives not yet available.

Primary Stages of Satisficing Behaviour

1.   Initial search uses simplified strategies, taking reference from similar situations in the past;

2.   The search is kept close to the objective; it is not expansive or wide-ranging;

3.   In the case of unacceptable alternatives, there is the need to make an intensified search and re-examination of them (or to view some of them as acceptable);

4.   Expectation is lowered if necessary, and objectives are modified;

5.   Time pressure and restrictions in different forms are considered;

6.   Once a satisficing alternative is found, the search ends and turns to implementation.

It therefore can be said that these common appearances of bounded rationality and satisficing behaviour are not typical rational decisions. For business, rational behaviour would demand an optimal alternative; while bounded rationality lowers the demand to a satisfactory level, in terms of sufficient returns to investment. In the example of setting out the year's target, the manager would desire to reach an ideal high profit margin, as a rational person would do, yet a 10% profit is a good enough result these days, especially for many small businesses.

Taking into account bounded rationality and satisficing behaviour, one should treat decision making as an art, not a precise science in the real world. As a former senior manager of Ford and Chrysler car companies, Lee Iacocca, put it: "If I had to sum up in one word the qualities that make a good manager, I would say it all comes down to decisiveness. You can use the fanciest computers in the world and you can gather all the charts and numbers, but in the end you have to bring all your information together, set up a timetable, and act". The action taken may not be rational to many other people, as shown in the following examples of intuition.

The main reason for the element of uncertainty in decision making is that it involves the **future**, which is never absolutely certain. Uncertainty is built into the very nature of decision making because it is about choosing between alternatives, and often there is uncertainty about which is the **best** choice. People then have to make a decision by trying to analyse what **might** be the best course of action. Uncertainty is often called "**probability**". As the management guru Peter Drucker put it: "A decision is a judgement. It is rarely a choice between right and wrong. It is at best a choice between 'almost right' and 'probably wrong'. But much more often it is a choice between two courses of action neither of which is probably more nearly right than the other".

The conclusion we can draw here is that a decision made by a company can be portrayed or promoted as the best to achieve the desired results, but in fact, it may just be one of the choices which sounds or looks better than the others. In the subsequent process and with a change of environment, the difference between the chosen one and the dismissed ones may surface and lead to outcomes which were not initially perceived. The chosen alternative may cause trouble and be deemed the "**wrong**" one by studies at later stages, and people turn to think that other choices should have been selected. The judgement made by decision makers derives from current estimates, and it needs to be understood that they are not able to give definite promises and defend their selections convincingly, if the outcomes present a different picture. This is the exact reason we need to conduct studies on decision making and examine the outcomes.

Intuition and Judgement

These two factors are closely related to the ways decision makers behave and act, and they often cast a heavy influence on critical decisions made by chiefs of organisations. As discussed before, a decision involves actions, and it can be made simply on the basis of an individual's judgement with unexplainable intuition. Consequences and outcomes of actions taken depend to a great extent on the intuition and judgement of a particular decision maker.

Intuition

This is a common characteristic of decision makers, and there are numerous anecdotes and sayings regarding intuition.

❑ "Intuition is perception of the possibilities inherent in a situation", said the Swiss psychologist Carl Jung.

❑ "It was a move which in pure economic terms everybody thought was mad, including my closest friend". These are the words from Charles Branson in 1984 on the birth of Virgin Airlines. His tone is very similar to that of Lee Iacocca of Ford.

What is intuition?

❑ Intuition in the philosophical sense is a form of knowledge or cognition independent of experience or reason; it is generally regarded as an inherent quality of the mind.

❑ Intuition derives from the idea of a self-evident proposition that does not require proof, and is an ability to identify what is right without drawing on any supporting information.

❑ Intuition can be defined as part of an individual's subconscious thinking process, sometimes against judgements made by others. It is therefore referred to as a "**gut feeling**" or "**hunch**". These common terms may be more understandable to businesspeople, when they have a crucial decision to make.

There are quite a number of practical uses of intuition in business and management. To experienced managers, they probably apply this means without even noticing its existence.

❑ Intuition helps to sense the existence of problems. On top of routine work and programmed decisions, a manager gets an extra alert from intuition of incoming trouble or a potential crisis.

❑ Intuition helps to identify signals, clues and directions. Managers have to catch the trend of the market and signals in price, supply and demand, fashion, and upgrading. They are to cope with these difficult tasks with the help of intuition.

❑ Intuition helps to put together information and screens them before getting an integrated picture.

❑ Intuition helps to select alternatives and take actions based on practice and experience. This is particularly acute when more than one alternative presented look attractive. A manager using intuition will tilt to pick one among equals. Such an occasion can be seen in the popular US TV series "The Apprentice", where the boss regularly has to choose between two equally capable candidates. Some from the audience may consider his choices odd.

❑ Intuition helps to check end results against collected data. This lifts the decision maker above loads of numbers and displays a clearer picture of the whole.

What is judgement? Judgement is the evaluation or categorising of a person, object, or event. It can be defined as the cognitive aspect of the decision making process. Decision making reflects both evaluative and predictive judgments.

The principal difference is that a decision requires a commitment to some form of action, while a judgement does not require such a commitment.

Intuition is closely linked with judgement. Judgement and intuition can be very useful when an individual is faced with conditions of uncertainty or if the situation is new.

Cisco and its CEO Mr. Chambers

Mr. Chambers was once in charge of dealing with redundant employees of a company, and he adopted harsh measures to sack many of them. That painful experience had great influence on him, and when he became the CEO of Cisco, he made a public promise that he would never sack a single employee. During the time of economic boom, Cisco achieved both a high growth rate and stable employment. When economic bubbles burst in the early 21st century, Cisco could not avoid sacking large numbers of employees due to bad company performance and losses. Mr. Chambers broke his word and has not made similar promises thereafter. It was when the company business was on the rise, that he could afford to give a certain guarantee to employees of their job security.

Group Decision Making

This section is to introduce group dynamics into the scene. Groups exist in all business organisations, particularly in large corporations where a board or a group of top executives exercises full and tight overall control. Politics and decision making in groups are parts of organisational behaviours. This politics has little to do with political or party power; it refers to politics of power, influence and relations. Various groups exert their influence on the decision making process in many ways. In an organisation, the issues of conformity and obedience are often related to leadership styles and the power structure. In a Confucian cultural environment, for example, people tend to conform to majority opinions and obey orders from an authority.

A group has its common goals for members and is attractive and approachable to the individual. A group also forms a particular group identity, with its own methods and norms.

Members in a group perform their specific roles, such as leaders, task specialists, social-emotional specialists (counseling), decision makers (not necessarily a leader, but one with a tendency to decide for others), experts (computer, communications etc.), powerful members (behind-the-scene shakers, king makers), representatives (spokespersons), followers, and coworkers.

The **assets** of group decision making include a greater sum total of knowledge or information available, a greater number of approaches to a particular problem, a general acceptance of the final decision by members, which gathers more strength for a decision to be carried out, a better comprehension of the decision, stronger organisational commitment, and a practice of division of labour.

On the other hand, **liabilities** of group decision making include apparent social pressure on members to reach a consensus, a tendency to accept earlier solutions (relying on precedents), a domination by certain individuals in the group over others, a likelihood of endorsement of extreme positions due to group pressure, a propensity for consuming time, a tendency of over conformity and a lack of creativity, and finally in a worst case scenario, the existence of groupthink.

Social Loafing

This is a tendency of individuals to exert less effort when they work in a group than when they work alone. Another related occurrence is free-riding, when certain members get a free ride as others work. The main reasons for these two related occurrences are, first, that individual contribution or level of performance in a group is not identifiable or hard to evaluate. This says something about the division of labour and effective supervision and rewards in the group. Second, group members sometimes think their own efforts are unimportant or not needed. Extra effort does not draw the deserved attention.

The Halo Effect

This occurs when a perceiver uses a general impression as the basis for judgements about more specific traits of others. In essence, the perceiver's evaluation is influenced by an overall impression, and some undesirable characteristics of a person may be covered up or ignored, due to this generous tolerance.

The halo effect explains why a subordinate who is liked by a superior can do no wrong in the superior's eyes, while a subordinate who is disliked may have difficulty obtaining a favourable review from the same superior no matter how hard he tries. In a group situation, the leader's views of other members are inevitably influenced by this halo effect, and these members could be divided into favoured and disliked categories.

Group Decision Making Techniques

Unlike individual decision making, groups need to reach consensus or a certain kind of agreement for their final decisions. As information varies and views differ, the process towards a consensus could be complicated and tiring. There are usually three ways for making a sensible group decision.

Brainstorming

There are no pre-determined or fixed ideas, the group is open to criticisms, freewheeling, free association of ideas—even far-fetched ones get attention, quantity of ideas is emphasised, improving on others' ideas and initiatives, and hopefully the final decision comes out with merits of good ideas but without drawbacks of mediocre ideas.

The Delphi Technique

This technique originated from the Rand group. It combines the information and insights of a group of people to reach an accepted conclusion as the final decision. The questions are sent to selected experts and recognised professionals in the related fields. Their opinions go back to the organisation for a preliminary assessment. Contributors then receive opposing views and judgements from others. They are to make comments on those different views and defend their choices convincingly. The organisation examines if these responses result in a narrower gap, and sends these back to contributors for further narrowing of choices. This process goes through a number of rounds of presentation and review, until experts reach a consensus as to the final decision. In this whole process, experts don't get to meet face-to-face, thus there is no group pressure, and opinions are expressed most freely.

Nominal Group Technique

The group accepts various ideas from individual members. Nominated ideas are listed, and members make their presentations one after another to describe the merits of the ideas. The group then engages in discussion and response. The next step is the vote, with the idea of the highest-ranking (most votes) taken as the group decision. This is basically a majority decision, with some members not being totally convinced by and agreeing with the chosen alternative.

Among these techniques of group decision making, brainstorming is a less effective technique than the other two. Unrelated issues may occupy members' attention and cause concentration fatigue. In some cases, it may just be a way of wasting time on endless enquires and debates. The other two techniques have the merits of controlled exchanges and of gaining a consensus after a few rounds of path-searching.

Group Polarisation

This concept comes from James Stoner. A group has its unique inner mechanisms which make unexpected moves at times. Group polarisation refers to a shift of the group's stance, after group discussions, to either of the two extremes, depending on the direction of the initial stance. This polarisation creates two kinds of shift, and each derives from momentum within the group.

Risky Shift

The tendency of groups to endorse a riskier position than its individual members would. The main cause would be that members eagerly display their boldness during discussions and suppress those cautious opinions. An example of this shift could be a war cabinet.

Cautious Shift

The tendency to move in a more conservative direction than individual members would. It may be the situation that the majority of members fear the realisation of an aggressive approach.

In these two kinds of shift, the roles of leaders and deciders are crucial and may have influenced the initiatives of other members towards a direction of shift that the leaders desire.

Groupthink

This is a term coined by Irving Janis after his study of failures in decisions and strategies. Groupthink is a mode of thinking that people delve in and comprises features that characterise **defective** group decisions.

Symptoms of Groupthink

❏ Collective illusion of group invulnerability: Members are fully convinced of their strength and justification of their actions, whatever these are.

❏ Rationalisation of past failures: Members tend to dig out reasons and excuses for their past losses and setbacks, thus justifying their current direction and plans.

❑ Unquestioned belief in the group's morality: Members are highly sensitive of the moral high ground they take and readily deny the moral standards of others.

❑ Stereotypical view of the group's opponent: Members hold consistent views of their opponents outside the group. Opponents belong to unacceptable categories.

❑ High pressure to conform: Members are subject to constant internal pressure to adhere to the set rules, and any wavering is a punishable offense.

❑ Tendency to withhold disagreements and self-censorship: Members engage in self-disciplinary activities to diminish disagreements, and differing opinions are silenced. Apparent unanimity is thus maintained among group members.

❑ Presence of "mind guards" who emerge to protect the apparent unanimity by condemning deviations from the majority and dominant opinion.

❑ Escalation of Commitment: Members tend to be emotionally committed to the decisions made and want them to succeed. There is little possibility to retract that particular decision; on the contrary, more effort and commitment are to be made to support the decision. These kinds of moves are often ego-related. Actions taken under this mentality are ignoring contrary information, holding subjective views and having an inability to accept failures, even if these are obvious facts to others outside the group.

Examples of Groupthink

From the studies by Irving Janis, several cases of early failures by US governments and corporations are cited as examples of groupthink:

❑ The American invasion of Cuba (Bay of Pigs): the responsibility of the Kennedy administration;

❑ The American involvement in the Korean War: the responsibility of the Truman and Eisenhower administrations;

❑ The American mismanagement of the Vietnam War: the responsibility of the Kennedy, Johnson and Nixon administrations;

❑ General Motor's creation of the ill-fated Corvair and Ford's Edsel car models;

❑ NASA's mismanagement leading to the Challenger tragedy in 1986 (and the more recent Columbia tragedy in 2003);

❑ Drug companies and new medication: Making a new medicine involves billions of dollars these days, and pharmaceutical companies are not sure whether their work will succeed. Their typical reaction is an escalation of commitment, continuing to invest money in the designated projects and believing they are getting closer to a new invention and application of medicines.

❑ A more recent example of groupthink is given by a Senate report in 2004 on US intelligence on Iraq, in which the Bush administration is criticised for the existence of "groupthink" in their intelligence gathering, selection and decision making.

Factors Conducive to Groupthink

❑ The group is under threat or stress;

❑ Group cohesion is high;

❑ Leadership is highly directive;

❑ The group is insulated from the outside world and from alternative opinions and facts.

Based on these examples and listed characteristics, one will be able to identify certain existence of groupthink in organisations—commercial or otherwise. There are growing numbers of business cases in recent years involving large or small corporations, which can be put to the groupthink tests.

Leadership Styles

Leadership styles are related closely to the factors of groupthink and group dynamics. There are two extremes of leadership styles—Boss-centred leadership and Subordinates-centred leadership (see Figure 16.1). Varying degrees of leadership styles exist in the middle. Managers deal with employees in different styles. Those with high authority make decisions single handedly, while those more conscious of subordinate contribution consult and take in suggestions.

*Boss-centered leadership   *Subordinates-centered leadership

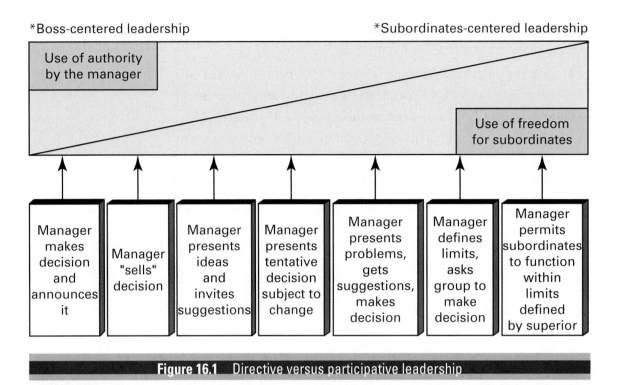

Figure 16.1   Directive versus participative leadership

The former CEO of Enron Corp., Kenneth Lay, used to be seen as an exemplary leader in business. He has the required education background and wide-ranging experience in the energy industry and in dealing with government regulations. He was regarded as highly knowledgeable and extremely self-confident. These qualities are essential for a CEO of a top company. In the 1990s, when Enron grew rapidly, Lay was praised widely for his vision, risk-taking, willingness to transform the company, and his leadership qualities in general. In those heady days, Lay was also praised for his ability to communicate with and motivate employees. Delegation was adopted, and managers given a free run in their operations and encouraged to take initiative. The autonomy within Enron was well known and perhaps unprecedented at that time. Above all, Lay was seen as an energetic man of high integrity. Before 2000, Kenneth Lay and Enron were cited repeatedly as the quintessential examples of leadership and business success.

This scene has been dramatically changed since the high-tech bubble burst in 2001, and Enron entered into bankruptcy. Lay is facing a series of charges of fraud and business misconduct. Through the abuse of the autonomy, those Enron managers had created dummy subsidiaries. That is a central factor which killed Enron. It seems that the leadership qualities many people hold do not guarantee certain desired results, especially long-term steady growth of company business.

Social and Political Aspects of Decision Making

We now turn from groups to organisations and place individual and group decision making in the context of organisations.

Organisational Structures

A Tall Stucture

A tall structure, under which each section with certain ranges of authority is clearly placed from the top to the bottom (see Figure 16.2). It is very similar to a military organisation, with a clear line of command. Each section is responsible to the level right above it, and the gap between the top management and bottom sections is quite significant.

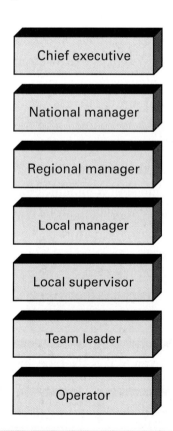

| Chief executive |
| National manager |
| Regional manager |
| Local manager |
| Local supervisor |
| Team leader |
| Operator |

Figure 16.2   Organisation structure - A tall structure

A Flat Stucture

A flat structure, under which the number of layers is reduced, and the distance between the top management and bottom sections is shortened (see Figure 16.3). Each department is responsible for decisions regarding all sections below, and the top management needs only to deal with these rather autonomous departments.

A Matrix Structure

This structure is the most complex of all designs, because it depends upon both vertical and horizontal flows of authority and communication (see Figure 16.4). The structure has dual lines of control, from both functional and product lines, and they both rest on bottom levels employees. These lines both have budget authority, a violation of the unity of command principle, dual sources of reward and punishment, dual reporting channels, and a need for an extensive and effective communication system. A matrix structure can result in higher costs because of more management positions along the two lines of control. For this reason alone, the matrix structure lost its appeal soon after its inception to many companies, and this is primarily an option for multinationals which operate in more than one continent.

Some advantages of this structure are that project objectives are clear, there are many channels of communication, workers can see visible results of their work, and problems can be checked by more than one means. In order for a matrix structure to be effective, organisations need participative planning, training, clear mutual understanding of

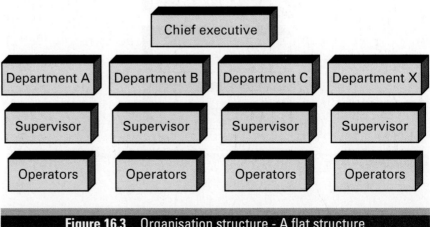

Figure 16.3 Organisation structure - A flat structure

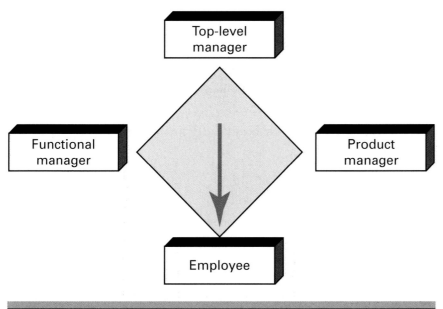

Figure 16.4   Organisation structure - A matrix structure

roles and responsibilities, excellent internal communication, and mutual trust and confidence. The communication within the organisation is now enhanced by new technologies such as Internet and audio/video conferencing.

Conflicts in Organisations

Conflicts come from diversity of views, power positions, command chains, and groups within organisations.

There are many indicators of conflict. Interference into affairs of others, overstatement of one's area of responsibility, withholding of information from relevant departments, creating annoyance, distrust of others, and mutual disrespect are important indicators of internal conflicts in organisations.

Treatment of Conflicts

According to Robert Vecchio, there are five common treatments of conflicts. The appropriate situations for these treatments are also listed.

❑   Competing:
  • When quick decisive action is vital, e.g. emergencies;

- On important issues where unpopular actions need implementing, e.g. cost-cutting, enforcing unpopular rules and discipline;
- On issues vital to company welfare when you know you are right;
- Against people who take advantage of non-competitive behaviour.

❏ Collaborating:
- To find an integrated solution when both sets of concerns are too important to be compromised;
- When your objective is to learn;
- To merge insights from people with different perspectives;
- To gain commitment by incorporating concerns into a consensus;
- To work through feelings that have interfered with a relationship.

❏ Compromising:
- When goals are important but not worth the effort or potential disruption of more assertive modes;
- When opponents with equal power are committed to mutually exclusive goals;
- To achieve temporary settlements to complex issues;
- To arrive at expedient solutions under time pressure;
- As a backup when collaboration or competition is unsuccessful.

❏ Avoiding:
- When an issue is trivial, or more important issues are pressing;
- When you perceive no chance of satisfying your concerns;
- When potential disruption outweighs the benefits of resolution;
- To let people cool down and regain perspective;

❏ Accommodating:
- When you find you are wrong, to allow a better position to be heard, to learn, and to show your reasonableness;
- When issues are more important to others than to you, to satisfy others and maintain co-operation;
- To build social credibility for later issues;

- To minimise losses when you are outmatched and losing;
- When harmony and stability are especially important;
- To allow subordinates to develop by learning from mistakes.

Conflicts can generate both positive and negative effects to organisations. As they are virtually unavoidable in organisations (the Chinese notion of "harmony" primarily points the direction to minimise conflicts), decision makers and top managers are obliged to see both sides of conflicts and work for the best outcomes possible.

Potential Benefits of Conflict

❏ stimulate change and innovation
❏ identify problems and inefficiencies
❏ promote healthy competition
❏ create group cohesion
❏ increase motivation
❏ raise levels of performance
❏ prevent complacency
=>Potential to lead to better decisions

Potential Harms of Conflict

❏ create stress and anxiety
❏ distract from major goals
❏ cause destructive behaviours
❏ impair judgement through emotion
❏ threaten teamwork and cooperation
❏ make coordination of activities difficult
❏ make decisions too "political"
=>Potential to lead to worse decisions

Power Politics in Decision Making

According to Robert Vecchio, bases of power include:

1. Reward power—ability to reward certain members with benefits;
2. Coercive power—fear, consequences, penalty to members in organisations;

3. Legitimate power— authority from positions held;

4. Expert power—knowledge, expertise;

5. Referent power—special qualities, association with influential power sources, identification with the power.

Essentially, power concentration and shift in an organisation shape the form of decisions made. Top management's exclusive authority is shown in access to command posts and information; their actions affect all units of the organisation; and their authorities in rewarding, penalising, intervention and coercion are absolute. Full authority usually makes the decision making process relatively short, and a clear authority to top management is not to be confused with consensus-building or a democratic process. On the other hand, a shift or split of power will render top decision makers vulnerable and indecisive.

Such a full authority still faces constraints at a number of fronts, and one of the drawbacks is enormous burdens on top management to deal with various tasks with this full authority. A right mix in power politics involves sensibly positioning top management and sharing of authority. The following discussions on constraints and delegation illustrate certain balancing forces to power concentration in organisations.

Operating Constraints to Power in Business Organisations

Internal Constraints

❑ Stockholders

❑ Board of directors: a form of corporate governance

❑ Employees

In normal business practice, the top management executes tight control of a company, and challenges from the board and shareholders to managerial decisions are rare. Corporate governance is about the relations between the board which may include some independent members from outside the corporation, and the management which handles everyday operations. Since the management is arranged and supported by the majority shareholders and key members of the board, differing opinions and criticisms rarely matter. For example, Coles Myer, the top retail chain and a listed company in Australia, has run its annual shareholders meeting without trouble. A dedicated small shareholder, who was a lawyer, raised proposals to challenge the CEO and the Board at several meetings but failed to cause any serious consequences. Especially in good economic times, the top management can get away from genuine supervision and scrutiny with remarkable ease. Individual employees, similarly, are unable to exert influence on managerial decisions either.

External Constraints

❑ Legislation and government regulations: These directly affect the ways of doing business and running corporations.

❑ Organised labour—-This is mainly in the form of trade unions, which deal with corporations with industrial actions, negotiated pay packages, collective bargaining etc.

❑ Non-government organisations: These include lobby groups, rights groups, consumer groups, and citizen groups concerned with various issues.

❑ The public, mass media.

In short, these external constraints are more effective than those internal constraints, exerting pressures on different occasions, but their effectiveness on decision making in business organisations is only in relative terms. Even the strictest legislation in a market economy is unable to ultimately alter the power and authority of top management of a business organisation and abruptly change its way of making decisions. A corporation, after all, is not a voting machine, but an entity of business interests. Past studies of corporate governance have shown common practices both accepting and resisting those constraints.

Delegation

Delegation is a process by which tasks and relevant authority are passed on to individuals within an organisation. The aim is to achieve consensus and strong commitment for implementation of decisions.

The delegation process is to have:

❑ Tasks clearly defined;

❑ Levels of performance specified;

❑ Time factors specified;

❑ The scope of authority clarified;

❑ Trust and support rendered.

There are a number of factors to undertaking delegation by top management. These include:

❑ Importance of the decision: More important decisions are made by top management, while less important decision making can be delegated.

❑ Size of the organisation: The number of decisions is crucial. If all the decisions are made by the top management, the business will become less efficient in operation. Delegation is more applicable in large corporations, in order to relieve the top management from routine decision making.

❑ Capability of managers: An organisation is more likely to delegate if lower-level managers are up to the task.

❑ Locations of branches: Delegation is a choice if operations are spread far apart.

❑ Efficiency of control mechanisms: Under effective administrative control and accounting practice, delegation has a higher likelihood to succeed. This is particularly true in the age of Internet and paperless money.

❑ Pace of change in the industry: With the rapid advancement of new technology, as seen in high-tech and dot.com companies, the top management must grasp the trend of change and make decisions by themselves due to the risks in delegation. Lower level managers may not be up to the requirements in a fast changing environment. This point is also related to the process of non-programmed decision making, discussed previously.

There are certain barriers to delegation becoming a common practice in many business organisations. Resistance or opposition to delegation comes from a few fronts, such as:

❑ From managers: There is this acute question about their willingness to give up authority. This unwillingness shows signs of weakness on the part of managers concerned.

❑ From subordinates: They harbour worries about more responsibilities on their shoulders after delegation, and there is the question of whether they have the required experience;

❑ From organisational culture: The entrenched corporate culture may play a somewhat negative role in this process. The prevailing norms and perceptions under a particular organisational culture may run counter to a delegation of responsibility. This point is supported by numerous examples of business operations, such as family businesses.

Organisational Culture

This refers to basic conceptions and beliefs shared by the members of an organisation.

Decision making modes and practices are parts of an organisation's culture.

❑ The power culture: Decisions are made by key persons, with the sole responsibility and judgement from one source.

❑ The role culture: This is a formalised structure with rules, clearly defined roles and tasks for each person.

❑ The task culture: This involves teamwork, and decisions are made collectively. This culture is project-orientated, and sometimes it is a short-term taskforce.

❑ The person culture: This refers to participation of all members, a common goal for members and consensus-building in decision making.

❑ A strong culture: This is a culture with clear definitions of beliefs and accepted practice, reduced or minimal disagreement, motivated members and effective decision making, with members working toward common goals. Such a culture is less flexible and slow to adjust, discourages innovation and creativity, and tends to make collective judgements.

The following are examples of strong corporate cultures in Chinese and Japanese firms.

The Haier Group (Shandong, China)

This Chinese company has many common characteristics of a strong culture within the corporation. Haier has a successful CEO; and a strong Confucianism influence in Shandong province, where Confucius was born and Confucian influence passed on for centuries. The corporation and its employees, as native Shangdong residents, share strong beliefs of human relations, trust, loyalty and honour; and a tendency to follow strong leaders appears well accepted. As a Chinese company, Haier holds long-term views of business, building on trust and cooperation, and focuses on brand names, which also requires lasting effort to be maintained. The company has conducted thorough value education at the training stage for new employees. These activities enhance cohesiveness, collective determination, and a sense of pride towards the company as a big family. An apparent positive result is the low turnover rate, and employees are very proud of working there compared to other local companies, much to the delight of company managers.

The current CEO of Haier has tremendous influence on all employees in the company. He is well known for his moral standards in business, and is regarded as a Confucian scholar type of businessman, a rare honour in China for a company chief. The CEO encourages a pursuit of excellence in work, and is eager to learn, through reading and face-to-face exchanges of views, from all management experts, particularly Western ones. He has a strong Chinese cultural background, being brought up in a locality immersed in Confucian traditions, has a conscious sense of social responsibility and practises profit sharing, a Confucian deed passed on through history.

Haier's mantra is "professionalism at work, contributions to the country". This comes with contributions to their home town as well, since this huge corporation has brought enormous benefits to the city in revenues and employment. This fact gives Haier employees plenty of satisfaction and enhances their willingness to follow the company mantra, which does not seem hollow here.

The Haier group, especially its top management, has been demonstrating cohesive and consistent teamwork, and company performance in the past 18 years has shown a steady upward move, without any major setbacks yet. A question still rings as to whether this company has created a mentality of groupthink. Symptoms of groupthink and that of a strong corporate culture are closely similar.

Matsushita, Japan (Panasonic)

This Japanese multinational was founded by Mr. Matsushita. In July 1933, he set out his business principles, which formed the basis of the Matsushita philosophy and corporate culture. The business principles, or spiritual values as they were called in Japanese, include:

1. Service to the public: to provide high-quality goods and services at reasonable prices, thereby contributing to the well-being and happiness of people throughout the world.

2. Fairness and honesty: to be fair and honest in all business dealings and personal conduct, always making balanced judgements free of preconceptions.

3. Harmony and cooperation: for the common cause, to pool abilities and strength of resolution to accomplish shared objectives, in mutual trust and full recognition of individual autonomy.

4. Untiring effort for improvement: to strive constantly for improvement of corporate and personal performances, even in the worst of adversity, so as to fulfill the firm's mission to realise lasting peace and prosperity.

5. Courtesy and humility: to be always cordial and modest and respect rights and needs of others, thereby helping enrich the environment and maintaining the social order.

6. Adjustment and assimilation: move with time and absorb new things, and benefit from inventions and creativity.

7. Gratitude: This illustrates the satisfaction employees and managers should get from their work and for fulfilling their social obligations listed above.

Matsushita, like other major Japanese corporations, has a strong corporate culture in the context of Japanese national culture. The strength of both these cultures has made Japanese companies appear unique in other people's eyes. Before the decade-old recession in Japan in the 1990s, Japanese employees nearly totally relied on their companies and life-time employment coming with the job. This deep-rooted culture fostered a strong sense of in-group and out-group distinction among employees. As observed by Nigel Holden: "The Japanese discourse perpetuates the Japanese in-group and the non-Japanese out-group, the former speaking the natural language of the company, the language of nearness to the company origins, whilst the latter must make do with potted versions of the essential truths." The obvious drawbacks of this kind of strong culture are blocking of communication channels and inertia in moving forward along with time and change, as shown in Panasonic's less impressive performance since the 1990s. The rules and modes set up by company founders may have to change and modify, in keeping with the trends in the industry and in general business environment.

In the above examples, the benefits and risks of corporate culture are evident. Benefits and positive factors are highlighted in these examples, especially in a relatively stable business environment, as in the examples of Matsushita; and in early business expansion, as in the example of Haier, China. On the other hand, it is harder to put one's finger on risks of cultural values, because setbacks are not apparent; and even if they appear, other factors, some of them purely economic or financial, take the blame. The success of Matsushita (Panasonic) in recent decades perhaps demonstrates the merits of their cultures in generating benefits and in limiting risks at the same time. Significant changes have since occurred. In the Haier example, as shown in a previous chapter on cross-cultural management, its mainstream cultural values have been challenged in its US plant, as an early warning of risks from within a strong corporate culture.

Key Concepts

Programmed and non-programmed decisions
Satisficing behaviour and bounded rationality
Intuition
Group decision making techniques
Groupthink
Treatment of conflicts
Delegation of authority
Organisational culture

Discussion Questions

The following discussion questions can be related to major sections of the contents.

1. What do you understand by the term "bounded rationality"? Provide two or three illustrations from your own experience to demonstrate this.

2. Explain the differences between programmed and non-programmed decisions, and provide illustrations of both from your experience.

3. Describe some applications of intuition in real life business decisions.

4. How do you identify your own role in a group, and what position do you normally hold in a group decision making process?

5. Groups generally make better decisions than individuals. Do you agree or disagree?

6. Identify any symptoms of groupthink in an organisation or during an event, business or political, using the listed symptoms and factors as reference points.

7. How can we distinguish between collective thinking and an extremely strong corporate culture?

8. How did the firm Goldman Sachs maintain its corporate culture? Analyse the relations between the set culture and change, and that between culture and leadership styles, and the influence on decision making.

Related Readings

Beach, L.R., *The Psychology of Decision Making: People in Organisations*, Thousand Oaks, Sage, 1997.

Chow, I., Holbert, N., Kelly, L., & Yu, Julie, *Business Strategy: An Asia-Pacific Focus*, Singapore, Prentice Hall, 1997.

Clemen, R.T., *Making Hard Decisions: An Introduction to Decision Analysis*, 2nd ed., Belmont, Duxbury, 1996.

Cravens, D.W., *Strategic Marketing*, 5th ed., Chicago, Irwin, 1997.

David, Fred, *Concepts of Strategic Management*, 6th ed., New Jersey, Prentice Hall, 1997.

Dearlove, Des, *Key Management Decisions*, London, Pitman Publishing, 1998.

Janis, Irvin L., *Victims of Groupthink*, Boston, Hoghton-Mifflim, 1972.

Hall, W., *Managing Culture: Managing Strategic Relationship Work*, Chichaster, UK, John Wiley and Sons.

Harrison, E.F., *The Managerial Decision Making Process*, 5th ed., Boston, Houghton Mifflin Company, 1999.

Hill, C.W.L. and Jones, G.R., *Strategic Management Theory: An Integrated Approach*, 4th ed., Boston, Houghton Mifflin Company, 1998.

Hogarth, R.M., and Reder, M.W. (eds.), *Rational Choice: the Contrast between Economics and Psychology*, Chicago, University of Chicago Press, 1987.

Holden, Nigel, *Cross-cultural Management: A Knowledge Management Perspective*, London, Pearson Education Limited, 2002.

Lee, David, Philip Newman, and Robert Price, *Decision making in Organisations*, London, Financial Times Management, 1999.

Porter, M.E., *Competitive Strategy: Techniques for Analysing Industries and Competitors*, New York, The Free Press, 1998.

Simon, H.A., *Administrative Behaviour*, New York, The Free Press, 1997.

Stoner, James, R, Edward Freeman, *Management*, Eaglewood Cliffs, NJ, Prentice Hall, 1992

The Essential Drucker, Oxford, Butterworth-Heinemann, 2001.

Vecchio, R.P., *Organisational Behaviour*, 2nd ed., Chicago, the Dryden Press, 1999.

17

Strategies of Market Entry, Expansion and Mergers in China

*T*his chapter discusses issues of strategic decisions and business strategies in the China market. The operations and choices made by some domestic Chinese companies and foreign investing companies will be examined. Evaluations are based on analyses of success or failure of a particular corporation as a result of their strategic decisions. Market entry, expansion, and mergers are the common strategies adopted. As will be seen, the applications of these routine strategies lead to various outcomes under certain circumstances.

Strategic Business Decisions

As discussed before on Chinese management philosophy of *wu wei* and on delegation in organisations, a distinction exists between top management and managers from middle levels down. According to specific tasks, top management of a corporation and managers face different requirements in their work.

Required Skills for Managers

From Figure 17.1, we can see that at the lower level of a corporation, managers are to deal with routine tasks and manage a group of workers. They need to acquire sufficient technical knowledge, basic management

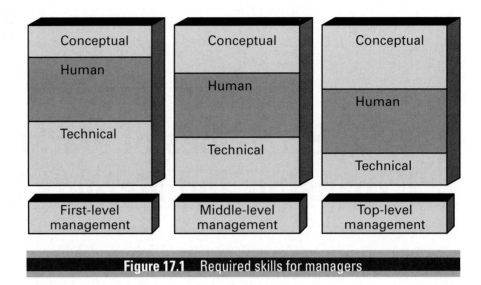

Figure 17.1 Required skills for managers

skills, and some conceptual ability for their work. Emphasis is placed equally on technical and management requirements. At the middle level, managers are to deal with more management and conceptual tasks, and the requirement on their technical capabilities is less significant. Much technical work can be done by their subordinates, thus managing people becomes more important, and they can finish designated tasks without much related technical knowledge. Their closeness with the top management implies that they need to pay more attention to conceptual issues concerning the company as a whole. At the top level, executives must meet requirements mostly in the areas of managing staff and making plans for the company. These two aspects now have equal importance in their work, and technical knowledge in a specific field is minimal. This totally differs from requirements for lower level staff. The roles played by top management are in the fields of strategic decisions.

The Nature of Strategic Decisions

1. They cause a broader span of internal impact:

   A strategic decision made by the top management affects the whole organisation. A business expansion plan will cause a demand for employees, engineers and managers, and control mechanisms will have to double to bear more workload. Shares of business activities will shift, and new projects after expansion could outweigh existing business in importance and in real revenues. It is not uncommon that due to business expansion, a company has to move its headquarters or core business to another location, at the expense of the old establishment.

2. They govern the direction the organisation takes for the future:

    These decisions are mostly in the categories of non-programmed decisions, as opposed to routine operations and programmed decisions. These decisions are crucial for long term development of the business concerned, and may not be fully understood at first. For far-sighted business leaders, their early decision to change direction can only be appreciated at a later stage, and this time gap could win the company precious profits and a position as a pacesetter. Examples of this are Macintosh computer with its departure from the cumbersome DOS format to a mouse and icon format. On the other hand, Kodak is an example of late strategy switching, though its fundamental shift of business from conventional films to digital technology is still to be commended.

3. They are often long-term decisions and extensively involve external conditions:

    Many strategic decisions are made under external pressure. Market competition presents immediate threats to companies and forces them to respond quickly. On top of internal management and sales campaigns, top management must consider long term prospects and market position, in relation to moves of competitors. External factors, such as government regulations or green groups, indicate future paths and opportunities, as well as put constrains on a business. Government bans on cigarette smoking have forced those cigarettes makers to diversify and build up viable business in several lines of production, away from the tobacco industry which is still causing opposition from the public.

The importance of strategic decisions and their distinctiveness from routine management need to be highlighted. Strategic decisions are linked with the very survival of a business, and the high stakes include many people's jobs and lives. They are also very destructive when bad decisions were made. In this case, even smooth running operations and highly efficient management of a company, such as quality control, production capacity, or hard working employees, cannot save a business. It is up to the top management to do the right things and make the best choice with their capabilities. Their job is to draw up plans for the future, so that current routine operations can run with less uncertainty. It is worthwhile to cite a now popular saying from Confucius, "If a man takes no thought about what is distant in future, he will soon find sorrow near at hand".

Typical Examples of Strategic Decisions

Mergers and Acquisitions

These involve takeovers of another company and merging two companies into one. Impacts of such moves on organisations are profound.

Expansion and Retrenchment

A company extends its business scope and increases its size. Management and control would stretch and become less effective. On the other hand, in bad times, a company has to reduce its business scope, shut down running projects, and sack employees. Redundancy causes great pains and headaches, and reduced incomes could further bring down the business. It has been a knotty issue for company executives as to keep good employees during waves of sacking, because at the next economic boom they may find it hard to catch up with the recovery, due to labour and talent shortages.

Re-organisation and Reengineering

These are major internal actions aimed at more effective overall management. Departments and sections are to be re-arranged, and systems revamped. It could involve downsizing as well, and internal conflicts and politics abound. These have to be done for the benefit of future success. A good example is GE's early re-organisation under Jack Welsh, which closed down some profitable departments at the time and was then considered outrageous.

Joint Ventures and Alliances

In business, cooperation is beneficial to partners. The question is how close you want to work with your partners and commit yourself. These moves apparently cause problems in management, since authority and responsibility are often a point for debate. Negative results of the joint venture could impact hard on your own company, and this is why some cooperation cannot go on, as decision makers are under enormous pressure to back down.

Entering (or Exiting) New Markets

Both are considered very brave moves. A market entry involves tremendous investments of time and money, and there is no guarantee of success for an entry. Such an entry faces strong opposing forces from existing players as well. Entering an overseas market presents an even harder choice for business leaders. On the other hand, an exit is not easy either, because it implies the heavy losses of reputation, market shares, loyal employees and clients, and all these are sunk costs. Judging from several examples of exits made by foreign companies from the China market, such strategic decisions were extremely hard to make.

New Product Development

Although technological inventions are lifelines for large corporations, investing on a new product is still risky, demanding a huge amount of funds and political will to support. The example of pharmaceutical companies on development of new medicines has been discussed before.

In market competition, a business decision is also made based on the moves of other competing players. It is here that a competition model (**five forces model**) by Michael Porter is often applied (see Figure 17.2).

Entry of New Competitors

These are potential competitors which are currently outside the industry concerned. Although their entry may be very costly in financial terms, it is a destabilising course of action to existing players and requires a competitive response from the latter.

Rivalry among Existing Competitors

Players in the industry face immediate and direct competition. The tricky question to company chiefs is that even if the situation worsens to a near loss and other players have gained an upper hand, it is still

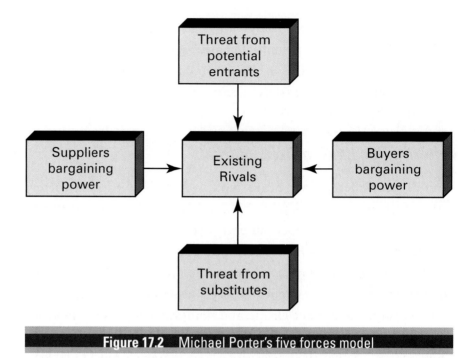

Figure 17.2   Michael Porter's five forces model

hard for them to make an exit decision, because of past investment and costs, as described above.

Threat of Substitutes

Along with technological advancement, product substitutes occur more frequently, and this poses a serious threat to players in the industry, since new products draw customers away and make manufacturers' investments lose real value. A good example is the invention of CD technology which has made VCR production equipment more or less redundant, and makers of VCR player eventually suffered losses.

Bargaining Power of Buyers

This is the ability of customers and users to determine suppliers' profit margins. Buyers could switch to other manufacturers and use bulk purchases to get bigger discounts.

Bargaining Power of Suppliers

Manufacturers need to consider cost and quality factors when making purchases, and it is not an easy matter to switch suppliers, especially long term stable suppliers and when large orders are involved. In specialised industrial areas, such as precision moulds or bearings, there are only a few available suppliers in the whole market and there is thus little pressure from competition.

Fundamental Strategies

These include three levels in regard to strategies, and these cover quite different areas.

Functional-level Strategy

These are usually operational strategies.

❑   The purposes are to achieve efficiency, quality, innovation, and customer responsiveness within the organisation.

❑   The areas of activities are manufacturing, marketing, materials management, research and development, and human resources.

In short, these kinds of strategies involve routine management issues of commercial business, and these are perhaps the responsibilities of middle level managers.

A potentially negative factor to management at functional-level is **subordinate maturity**. It covers job maturity and psychological maturity. The former refers to knowledge and skills required of employees for standard business operations, and the latter refers to the assurance and familiarity employees feel about their work place and environment. These two maturities grow as employees work in a company for a relatively long time.

This process brings certain problems to managers. Subordinates follow instructions from superiors and managers at early stages of operations, and they grow to meet the work requirements. Discipline is not a serious problem at this stage. When they know the jobs very well and are more confident, they feel more content with the work environment and do not see instructions from superiors and rules as that authoritative. Some employees are even more senior in terms of years of service than their young superiors. They stop feeling a need to learn anything from managers. It is then a difficult task for managers to deal with subordinate maturity, to inspire and discipline employees.

Business-level Strategies

These strategies are concerned with the overall competitive theme of a company, how it positions itself and how it gains a competitive edge in the market.

According to Michael Porter, there are three generic strategies at business level. They are **differentiation, cost-based leadership, and focus.**

❑ Differentiation is a strategy aimed at making the products and services be recognised as unique in the industry concerned, and directed at consumers who are relatively price-insensitive. In the end, consumers can pick out the difference between this and other products and are willing to pay for the difference.

❑ Cost leadership emphasises making standardised products at very low per unit cost for consumers who are price-sensitive. This often hurts profit margins.

❑ Focus means producing products and services that fulfill the specific and sometimes exclusive needs of small groups of consumers. It can be seen as niche marketing.

Global Strategies

These refer to strategies of wider application and implications. Global implies strategies covering pan-domestic (nationwide), international, global, and transnational market competition. These are simply differences in scope. Multinationals operate in the last three areas, doing business in international trade and investment, in globalisation of production and service chains, in a number of countries and even continents. In these global operations, strategic alliances and different market entry modes into many countries are often the main themes.

Under global strategies, choices faced by multinational corporations include those between internal development and acquisition, and between joint development and going it alone. Business expansion may adopt one of these options. Market entry into a new economy involves a host of other issues in relation to fixed strategies, such as levels of economic development, political stability, tariffs, and the legal system, culture and communication, and educational and technological levels for business operations.

For global strategies, diversification is an option often considered by business corporations. Diversification serves the following purposes:

❑ Spreading risk (portfolio spread): This is a typical diversification strategy, keeping risks to a minimum by investing in several related or unrelated sectors.

❑ Adding to competitive advantage (synergy):

This is a process gain that occurs when members of a group acting together are able to produce more or better output than would have been produced by the combined efforts of each person acting alone. This also applies to corporations and their subsidiaries. Diversification increases the company's strength as a group of several product lines and thus creates a higher competitiveness, combining gains from a variety of sources.

Factors in Deciding on a Strategy

The SWOT analysis has been thoroughly studied and widely applied in deciding a strategy for a particular project. This analysis covers **strength, weakness, opportunities and threats,** basically taking account of most factors and variables in such an analysis. The first two relate to internal aspects of a company, and the last two refer to the external environment, especially options and competition. Listed points under each category will also influence strategy implementation, such as organisational structure, leadership styles, corporate culture, and personnel selection and development. Decision makers are required to run through the SWOT factors and make estimates of both positive and negative aspects. This analysis is shown in some case studies of this book. The personnel factor is a crucial one in this SWOT assessment. As Peter Drucker put it, "Executives spend more time on managing people and making people decisions than on anything else, and they should. No other decisions are so long lasting in their consequences or so difficult to unmake". This is in the similar vein to the Chinese traditional wisdom of emphasising on managing people and relations.

Strategic Audit

Implementation of strategies needs to be followed by an audit on its outcomes. This will gauge and seek:

- ❑ Acceptance by staff members
- ❑ Acceptance by shareholders
- ❑ Competitors' reactions
- ❑ Customers' reactions
- ❑ Governmental reactions
- ❑ Pressure groups' reactions
- ❑ Effectiveness in terms of growth in market share and profit, and
- ❑ Whether any new opportunities or risks arise.

Ethical and Green Issues in Strategic Decisions

Business ethics is concerned with the impact of actions on the good of the individuals, the firm, the business community, and society as a whole. To be ethical is to conform to principles of human conduct, similar to the terms of **moral, good, right, just,** and **honest**.

Ethics means different things to different people, and managers of business organisations may tend to capitalise on opportunities to be unethical, if such a situation exists. Businesses may focus on goals of purely profit-maximisation that are legal, and they may ignore the impact of their actions on other groups of the society. As Peter Drucker put it rather pessimistically, "There is no such thing as business ethics—a code distinct and unattached from all other ethics. There have always been a number of people who cheat, steal, lie or take bribes." This view has been vindicated by waves of corporate scandals in the US in recent years, and the previous dominant belief of a free market being immune to ethical degradation was severely shaken. These, in return, led to renewed efforts on corporate governance and ethical standards in a money-chasing market.

These are the issues which business leaders need to factor in for their strategic decision.

- ❑ The green factor and environment concerns have become prominent in recent years as a major constraint on business organisations. This derives from people's understanding of and concerns over the long lasting consequences of a project, which may outweigh current and projected gains.
- ❑ The issue of sustainable development of an economy stands opposed to short-term business gains of certain companies, such

as those in timber, natural resources and even in computer industries, since computer makers sell millions of sets, monitors and accessories annually, which cannot be safely disposed of at the current level of technology. As shown in the development of China's economy, the high growth cannot be sustained by careless consumption of available resources.

❑ Inter-generation equity: This is close to the issue of sustainable development and asks the question of how to provide or leave a satisfactory environment and conditions for the next generation and after to enjoy. In many aspects of economic activities, such as financial lending, government debts and consumption of natural resources, the current generation is using available means to maintain an acceptable level of living. Many problems are left to following generations, whether they can cope with them or not. This is of course a macroeconomic issue for the whole society to confront, but business leaders are expected to consider their responsibility and factor in this long term concern in their business plans.

The above considerations of ethical and environment outcomes form a key part of strategic decisions and their following audit. Corporations cannot afford taking these as secondary or negligible factors in their strategic decisions. In fact, the wider the strategic extent and scope they attach to their business projects, the more crucial roles these factors play in final decisions.

Cases of Strategic Decisions

For the purpose of explaining business strategies of expansion, diversification and mergers/acquisitions, several examples are given below of Chinese and foreign companies in their execution of decisions and resulting consequences. It is hard for an analysis to gain conclusive certainty when the outcomes are not yet clear for a particular example of decisions. There is also the possibility of a reversal of fate in business operations, such as a better performance than widely projected. What is possible is an essential understanding of the decision from collected information.

Case 1. Hewlett-Packard and Compaq

In 2001, **Hewlett-Packard(HP)** announced its plan to pay US$25 billion for the purchase of Compaq. This was a strategic move between two computer giants, which occupied the second and third place in the industry. The combined sales of both companies in the previous year was nearly US$90 billion. The deal was described as a merger; it was in fact a takeover initiated by HP, since it offered a price for the target company and thereafter controlled the merging process. Arrangements for new top management were that HP took the position of chairman and CEO, while Compaq took the position of president.

The announcement was received with much disapproval by many investors and analysts, concerned that the merger's costs and hassles could outweigh benefits. The family members of the company founders also challenged the HP top management on feasibility and viability of this merger.

Rationale and Projected Benefits

HP intended to cut costs and improve competitiveness in the stabilising and sometimes shrinking PC market. The initial target was a saving of US$2.5 billion in costs in three years. In previous years, this market grew at an astounding pace and sales moved to a new height in a very short period of time. This trend had been slowed due to market saturation and customers' sluggish response to quick upgrading. Big PC makers like HP and Compaq were thus affected. An option was to merge to consolidate. Duplicated lines and network could be reduced as well as overall costs. Even the number of suppliers could be reduced, as the new company could share combined networks of the two companies.

The strategy intended to cover major areas of business by one company, and enlarged scope of product lines could provide continuing profits. The new company could take up some profitable businesses such as printer, palm PC and peripheries, some of which Compaq had an advantage or even a leading position in the market.

The move was intended to grab No.1 spot in a number of areas of the computer market and create a super company, in competition with the then market leader, namely IBM. It was hard for each of these two companies to challenge IBM for the leading position of PC maker of the world. They then sought to achieve a synergy and lift their ranking.

The merger strategy is devised for long-term gains over short-term hassles. Based on projections and determination of HP top management, they forecast long term gains following the pains caused during the merger. In fact, this was an option they had to consider, since slow growth and competition among top players had been badly affecting them. With willingness, this merger of two of the top players could be a textbook case of brilliant strategy. Bureaucratic obstruction and organisational clash of interests were regarded as acceptable prices to pay for this huge undertaking.

Drawbacks and Risks

Overlapping lines of products

The two companies manufactured and sold similar products; they were direct competitors in many business areas. They had few complementary sections. For this duplicity, the new HP could achieve an overall bigger size but gain little from productivity and synergy.

Extensive restructuring of jobs

Because of the duplicity in business areas, many production lines had to be scraped after the merger, and employees doing similar work will be made redundant. The merging of two colossal organisations meant clashes and headaches of relocating and streamlining. This would hurt the company morale for some time. By the end of 2003, several senior executives left the new HP, including some former Compaq chiefs. The company planned to cut 10,000 jobs by the end of 2002.

Trouble in command chains and cultural shock

The new HP needed to maintain effective running of command chains when two lines of them merged into one and personnel changes disrupted past work patterns. Cultural shock was also severe. Although these two multinationals were from the same country and business environment, their corporate cultures differed significantly. HP has established its rules and styles within the company. With people under Compaq and influence moving in, there would be a long process of getting used to other ways and coping with clashes. As former competitors, past exchanges and impressions of the other have deep roots. The compatibility issue loomed large, combined with cultural diversity.

Gigantic size of corporation and reduced efficiency

This mega corporation will inevitably face obstacles and hassles in the short term deriving from its size and merging process. IBM is also huge, but it has passed the test of transformation in recent years, involving extensive internal restructuring. The new HP consists of two large multinationals, and smooth cooperation of this magnitude is unprecedented. Compaq had also not sorted out its own problems from past rapid expansion and acquisitions of other companies such as Tandem Computers and DEC. With many new business areas brought in, Compaq had a difficult time positioning itself. This further merger with HP could be a delay of previous problems to the future, or it may lead to an eventual explosion and cause serious troubles to the new HP. Consecutive acquisitions are destined to create difficulties in internal realignment and re-organisation. Much of the energy and time would have to be spent on sorting out right orders and patterns, before efficiency moves back to acceptable levels.

Few merger successes in the past

Despite waves of mergers and acquisitions in the last decades of the 20th century, it was estimated in a BusinessWeek study that less than half of such strategies worked, based chiefly on the US information and records. This HP merger may eventually be an exception, but sales and profits dropped sharply in 2002 and only recovered in 2003. Its future remains to be seen.

Assessment

This is a case of strategic decision on business mergers. This merger is conceived with a view of benefits over a longer term and taking accepted risks in business as a price to pay. This is a long-term strategic move, taking account of the situation in the computer industry, with company survival as the top consideration. Cost reduction and synergy were the goals, while restructuring and re-shuffling caused short term pains. In a number of similar situations, a merger of two top giant companies is generally considered a less desirable choice. Surprisingly, the new HP has walked a smooth path without major breakdowns, taking second place in the world PC market with a 15% share.

(Note: The architect of this merger, Carleton Fiorina, was sacked by HP Board on 7 February 2005, for her disappointing overall performance after the merger.)

Case 2: Haier Group, China

In an increasingly competitive China market, business strategies of all kinds now find their places of application and execution. For example, in the one year ended in September 2004, the value of mergers/acquisitions deals involving Chinese companies jumped 185% from the previous year to US$35 billion. Haier is cited here as an example of a Chinese company putting various business strategies on trial. This provincial level state enterprise of Shandong is now an international corporation operating in a number of countries. It holds the position of No. 1 fridge and air conditioner maker in China and has moved up the ladder to become a top household appliances manufacturer in the world. It is worthwhile to trace its major phases and strategies in the process of development.

Development Phases

❑   The first seven years on fridge brand strategy (1984-1991):

The company focused on quality, after-sales services, and designs to meet particular consumer needs. Decisions made at this stage were mostly functional-level or business-level decisions, to establish their own brand name and become an industry leader. Their marketing strategies intended to maintain a positive image in the mind of most consumers, to avoid waging price wars, to dismiss the niche marketing which serves only small groups of people, and to adopt the differentiation approach covering most categories of customers. Haier presents a mix in operations: German technology, Japanese quality control systems, and traditional Chinese thinking on management.

❑   The second seven years on diversification (1992-1998):

After holding secured market shares and enjoying a good business reputation in the fridge industry, Haier's next strategic decision was to enter other markets and compete in new sectors. They made the decision to stay in the household appliances industries and initiated entries to unrelated sectors. In these seven years, the company went through a process of diversification, and achieved expected results, reaching top positions in the new industries they entered. The GE model gave them much aspiration to follow through strategic changes in diversification. Currently, Haier's product lines cover: freezers, fridges, wine cooler, washing machine, computers, TV, hot water system, air conditioner, central air conditioner, mobile phone, furniture, banking, trust, securities, and insurance.

❑ From 1999 on, overseas expansion:

The company realised their goals in being industry leaders and completed the diversification process without serious setbacks or collapse. In view of domestic competition and WTO rules, the company saw the urgent need to make a strategic turn to overseas markets and decided to carry out market expansion in other countries. One side result is that the company entered financial and banking markets with holdings in banks, insurance and securities companies. Such investments involved huge amount of funding from the company and were expected to provide much needed money for overseas projects and expansion. This was also a model learned from GE Capital.

❑ Considerations when planning to go international: dominant position in domestic market; oversupply of products, price wars and narrowing profit margins, less choices for diversification into new markets where demand and profits are high, and increasing competition from foreign multinationals in domestic markets after China's WTO accession.

For overseas markets, exports, as an option, would be monitored and regulated by foreign authorities. They would face trade barriers, anti-dumping laws and local actions to protect domestic markets, high tariffs and restrictions on selling directly to overseas consumers. Setting up local production facilities in those markets may reduce these risks associated with exports. On the other hand, for expansion into foreign markets, Haier's products faced tighter scrutiny and resistance, and the Haier brand was not recognised by foreign consumers, with very limited marketing campaigns.

❑ Haier made a final decision to carry out a 3/3-market strategy: 1/3 sales in domestic market, 1/3 sales overseas (in export), and 1/3 design and manufacturing in overseas plants. Overseas projects include a joint venture with Mitsubishi of Japan, majority shareholding of a Hong Kong listed company, an Italian fridge factory in 2001, and a manufacturing base in Camden, South Carolina, the US. The ultimate objective is to build an international corporation on a par with Japanese electronics giants. By 2003, Haier had manufacturing plants in 13 countries, including the US and EU.

Major Risks in Overseas Expansion

❑ Drawbacks in overseas expansion: high labour costs, unfamiliarity with Western regulations and management styles (a cultural acculturation in reverse), high level requirements on technology used in production process and in products sold on the market, different customer behaviours and responses;

❑ Brand recognition: It takes a longer time for the company to make local customers accept their brands, and despite some success in low-end markets, it is still difficult for new brands from China to be recognised in the mainstream markets and achieve customer loyalty. Haier has to compete with American, European, Japanese and Korean brands for certain shares in the market.

❑ Financial costs: Haier is relying on its own revenues and bank loans to finance overseas projects and expansion, and is bearing a big disadvantage in the foreign exchange rate (RMB/US$), so overseas expansion takes much more financial resources to finalise and make real gains. This overstretch of funds may drag the company down and disrupt cash flows in normal company operations back home.

Potential Troubles

❑ Continuity: Haier's decision making indicates the typical Chinese pattern, with the current CEO, an extremely capable business leader, making all key strategic decisions regarding the direction of the corporation, not dissimilar to the role played by Jack Welsh at GE. There is thus the question of what would happen to Haier under another CEO with different management thinking and decisions.

❑   Financial deals are now causing grave concerns and strains. Haier has so many related subsidiaries within the group that its financial deals are murky and non-transparent. Internal transactions, deals between subsidiaries, including procurement, distribution and sales, reach nearly 100% within the group, being the highest ratio in all listed industrial companies in China. Internal pricing, the numbers game, and financing from the stock markets are regular practices of Haier. Haier keeps its debts and liabilities secretive by not disclosing them to the public and analysts. According to *Fortune*, Haier's finances are a "**black box**". These raise serious concerns of its real financial state and of potential risks to investors.

Haier's Records of Failures

1.   Fans: It entered this market with much fanfare in 1997, but has now effectively disappeared;

2.   Pharmaceuticals: It entered in 1995 to produce health-related products, leading to considerable losses;

3.   Microwave ovens: Even with its leading position in many white goods sectors, Haier lost to Grantz, a domestic company taking dominant market shares;

4.   Noodle shop chains: Haier rushed in with very identifiable CI-VI, in an effort to challenge some foreign fast food giants. It simply disappeared after a short period of time;

5.   Colour TVs: Haier managed to radiate its reputation as a recognisable TV manufacturer, but is well behind market leaders;

6.   Computers: It was a complete failure and production lines were shut down in 2002. There were some new developments in 2004 that Haier would renew its effort in making computers, especially laptops.

It is apparent from the above examples of past failures that Haier is unable to totally avoid making wrong decisions. Many of these came as a result of the urge to enter or desire to take on another seemingly profitable industry. Haier withdrew from several sectors they lost, but remained in others even when losses built up. This is against the CEO's own conviction to follow the GE model that if you are unable to become the number one or number two in an industry, you should leave.

Case 3: Hainan Airlines

This regional airline was set up with the backing of the Hainan provincial government, but its operations were relatively independent from the beginning. It is not a typical state enterprise, but a special type of shareholding company with certain government involvement. The initial investment came from several sources, including the government (10 million yuan as start up funds), banks, founders themselves, and foreign investors; as such the company is effectively a China-foreign joint venture company in the airline business.

The company has adopted flexible business strategies, different from other bigger state run airlines. This is due mainly to its international exposure and investors. The American financier Soros, as the major shareholder, made a vital business investment of US$25 million to hold 100 million B shares, 25% of total company shares. This made him a strategic shareholder, in fact the top shareholder, and provided much needed funds for the company to expand. With tremendous growth of the company, Soros was entitled to sell his shareholding after eight years and receive around US$80 million, an annual return of over 22%. The company has also shown its differences in services, route selection, aircraft selection, staff selection and competition. These have attracted more attention and investment, and analysts have seen the company as a new type of business in the China market and rated it highly.

The company basically adopted a fast growth strategy in the industry, making a series of takeovers of other regional airlines, backed by funds from foreign investors and from the stock markets. Through quick expansion, the company was ranked fourth in assets behind the big three state airline groups (Air China, China Eastern, and China Southern). It has two listings on both A and B stock markets in China and its total assets have grown from the initial 10 million yuan in 1989 to 22 billion yuan in 2003.

The company also uses diversification as its insurance policy. From 2000, it went into related industries, in travel, resort, hotel and airport management (see Figure 17.3). It took over two provincial airlines, took majority shareholding in two regional airports, and re-organised another regional airline. These are not far off from its core airline business. The next stage saw acquisitions by this group company of several financial and securities companies, investing over 2 billion yuan.

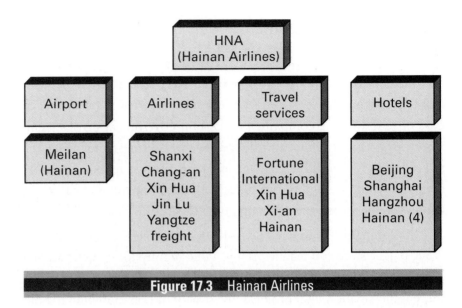

Figure 17.3 Hainan Airlines

These are apparent moves to get a hold on financial resources, in part to mitigate enormous financial pressure on the company.

One of the downsides of this aggressive mergers/acquisitions campaign by a relatively small regional player is a lack of focus in the company's long term plans. This company is now involved in numerous lines of business, pays much more attention to other sectors, and may get bogged down in competition in unfamiliar and unrelated territories. The fact that its CEO is a shrewd financial manager does not guarantee that each and every deal the company makes is immune to financial risks. The peril of diversification into financial sectors is acknowledged by the company, as highlighted in its sudden move in 2004 to halt all further talks of entering financial or securities companies.

The key issue is the company's high ratio of debts, which reached nearly 90% in mid 2004. Since it carried out swift expansion mainly on the basis of loans and money raised from stock markets, the company bears heavy financial burdens, to pay back interests and loans, and to satisfy shareholders by keeping performance and stock prices at satisfactory levels. It has paid interests well over 1 billion yuan to lending banks over these years. To achieve the second objective of high stock price levels, the company may have to get more market shares and take over more small airlines. This cycle can work well for a period of time, but continued financial backing, government or foreign, is not guaranteed. Strategic shareholders like Soros may sell their stocks soon, making a profit in the process, and the only other option is to get more bank loans, leading to even higher debt ratio. The year 2003 saw heavy losses of over 1 billion yuan and net loss of 1.3 yuan per share. Major commercial banks in China have become hesitant to lend more to this company, especially to its ambitious acquisitions, or proposals of that kind.

Fortunately, the airline still received firm financial support from the provincial government, in that over 900 million yuan of aviation construction fees, which the company was supposed to pay, was exempted by the authorities.

The company mostly takes side routes and tourist routes (over 400) for their flight services. It owns 92 airplanes, mostly small-sized Fairchild Dornier jets and medium sized Boeing jets. Due to its controlling share of 70% over side flight routes, it is not competing directly with major carriers on main flight routes. This puts the company in an unfavourable position: while they can earn some profits from the side routes they fly, their market share will not be big in comparison with the big three, and the image and reputation of the company will not be dramatically enhanced.

The company is a model for learning Western ways of management and business strategies. It has attracted loads of praises from foreign analysts on its independent operations from bureaucrats, on efficiency, and on management with a foreign flavour. Praises come also from domestic ones, though the latter often question the financial feasibility of its breakneck pace of expansion. Its decision making style is dominantly autocratic, as shown in the CEO's leadership style of charisma and aggressive decisions made by the top management. Strategic decisions are in the category of market expansion, in the form of high risk acquisitions and takeovers. Evaluation of its early operations would be positive for rapid growth and early profit-making, while its later performance reveals the drawbacks in rash decision making in some cases of expansion and diversification. Heavy debts and aggressive marketing are the two characteristics of this expansion strategy.

This case is a shareholding company taking market expansion decisions, and its future projection is fraught with high uncertainty, which makes it difficult to list this company as a case of business success or a potential failure. Considering airlines around the world, even in the US, which routinely bear heavy financial burdens and follow the rule of "**expand or die**", the ambitious goals and seemingly reckless approach of the Hainan airline group appears understandable.

Case 4: Electrolux (Sweden) in China

Electrolux moved into the China market relatively late, investing in a number of joint ventures from the mid 1990s. Its direct cooperation with a Chinese partner began with the establishment of China-Italy Fridge company in Changsha, the capital of Hunan province. That Chinese company introduced full range fridge assembly lines from an Italian manufacturer in 1984 and at its peak produced 320,000 units in 1993. It then suffered from a following downward spiral. Electrolux, on the other hand, lost an opportunity to join hands with the Snowflake fridge maker in Beijing and therefore picked up a joint venture with this Chinese partner in 1996 to produce fridges and air conditioners. Those years marked a sorry state for foreign fridge brands in the China market, due to the emergence of many domestic competitors, first among them Haier. The joint venture continued to make losses of up to 200 million yuan a year in 1997. These losses were shouldered mostly by the local manufacturer, since the original contract stipulated that Electrolux did not take control of management and thus could take away a fixed percentage of money shares regardless of revenues or losses. Contributions from Electrolux being limited, the joint venture decided to cut the tie and introduced a Japanese partner instead in 2001.

For this foreign multinational, its public image and brand name in China were quite secondary by the end of the 20th century. A new CEO for Electrolux China was a Chinese manager leaving Pepsi. During the restructuring, he implemented a thorough localisation strategy and staged vigorous marketing and brand name promotions. New functions were flashed in commercials, reliable services provided, and customer marketing based on research of local tastes and preferences launched. These opened markets for company products. Electrolux China adopted a low end market strategy and kept prices lower than those of other international brands. Electrolux fridges were sold at about 20%-30% lower than Siemens prices. Electrolux utilised local talents and merged Chinese traditions into promotions, to suit the tastes of Chinese consumers and speak the local language. A prominent innovation was to present the company in advertising as a **"friend by your side"** to customers. Through these efforts, Electrolux achieved profits and became number one foreign fridge brand in 2000, just below the fridge industry leader, Haier, in ranking. This surge gave domestic manufacturers and brands a real scare and surprised many analysts.

Electrolux moved into washing machine and air conditioner markets. A major project is in Hangzhou, a joint venture with a Chinese manufacturer to produce air conditioners. This project was planned to reach the capacity of over 800,000 units annually, while the goal was to reach a top five position in the market.

Unfortunately, this Chinese CEO resigned in early 2003, leaving a huge vacuum for the European multinational. This was due partly to clashes between him and the Swedish company's headquarters. Issues of concern involved authority over personnel, production, and distribution, and the real performance in terms of earnings and losses. His departure sent shocks to the company and its employees. Electrolux appointed another Chinese manager as the CEO of China operations and undertook massive reshuffles of senior executives.

In contrast to previous rising revenue figures, a side effect of localisation strategy is that Electrolux is seen as producing middle level or lower end products which cannot compare with other international brands. This implies a loss of value in the name of Electrolux and a downgrading of its international standing. Analysts often likened Electrolux with domestic maker Haier. For this reason, Electrolux China under new management is re-organising and revamping operations, keeping and developing high end products and dropping lower end products from their catalogues. In May 2004, Electrolux withdrew air conditioner lines from one of the biggest household appliances chain stores, Gome, due to bad sales. Its cooperation with the Hangzhou air conditioner maker also slowed down, with Electrolux contemplating a downsizing or a withdrawal. One new focus is procurement, from which

Electrolux expects to reach over US$1.2 billion. This will be compatible with the company's globalised operations and sales.

Under stiff competition worldwide and slowing down in sales elsewhere, Electrolux closed down a number of factories in countries. There is naturally a question whether Electrolux can maintain its investment drive and even make more efforts in the China market. On strategies, Electrolux faced chiefly two challenges. One is its diversification into other product lines once the fridge business stabilised. Since the company is a maker of a comprehensive range of products, this diversification did not look particularly out of line. The trouble seems to be in the pace of this diversification, which diverted attention and funds from the then profitable fridge business. The other is from the former Chinese CEO, along with his localisation strategies. Electrolux had to make a hard choice between a brand name with fewer sales and more sales with a less valuable brand. This choice becomes more difficult for Electrolux when white goods markets are the battleground of primarily domestic, Japanese and South Korean makers. The taking of the first choice indicates a change of heart of the company's top management on their China strategies.

Diversification has been a hot topic for discussion and a frequently adopted strategy in China since the late 1990s. This is due to the fact that major players in an industry have grown to considerable size, and they have had to formulate certain plans for further and continued development. In a market with evident overcapacity and oversupply in many industries, CEOs jump on any opportunity in a growth market, without giving much thought of the aftermath or real commitment. This rush in decision making has been perfectly demonstrated by a surge in investment on motor car projects. A mobile phone maker, a leading Chinese spirit maker, and a major household appliances maker all made investments on car production lines in the past two years. The first player withdrew after a short sting, seeing little prospect of earnings in a short period of time. The second player recognised the formidable task of producing cars and was satisfied with making car parts moulds instead. The last player has achieved more, since it has deeper pockets and started from making heavy and medium sized trucks. Depending on continued financial commitment, this diversification may work and eventually add a car-making subsidiary to the company.

These are examples of outsiders entering an existing market. Those players generally have little experience and expertise, and their experiences prove that it is not an easy task to transfer successful experience and models into a new industry. These examples also serve as a reminder to potential investing foreign companies that they inevitably will face competition from existing and entering players in this market. Their strategic decisions on diversification and expansion could benefit from past experiences of domestic, as well as foreign, companies.

Key Concepts

Subordinate maturity
Natures and types of strategic decisions
Five forces model
Three levels of strategies
SWOT analysis

Discussion Questions

1. How does functional or operational decision making differ from strategic decision making? Give examples.
2. In your opinion, is the diversification strategy based more on business confidence **or** more out of fear of lagging behind and the risks of being associated with doing business in only one or a small number of sectors? Give examples.
3. With the big three state airline groups in the top market positions, do you see the company's expansion strategy as a right decision to survive? And what suggestions can you make for the company to get out the current situation of expansion and debts?
4. Examine and explain any unwise strategic decisions Haier has made within the above two ranges (entry and expansion), and point out what had gone wrong and what can go wrong.
5. Comment on the cases of strategic decisions presented, with information you read and find from other sources.

Related Readings

David, Fred, *Concepts of Strategic Management*, 6th ed., New Jersey, Prentice Hall, 1997.
Dolven, Ben, "The Best Little Airline in China", *Far Eastern Economic Review*, 17 January 2002.
Henry, David, "Mergers: Why Most Big Deals don't Pay Off", *BusinessWeek*, 14 October 2002.

Luo, Yadong, *Partnering with Chinese firms: Lessons for International Managers*, Aldershot, UK, Ashgate, 2000.

Sprague, Jonathan, "Haier Reaches Higher", *Fortune*, 16 September 2002.

Yi, Jeannie Jinsheng, and Xian, Shawn Ye, *The Haier Way: the Making of a Chinese Business Leader and a Global Brand*, New Jersey, Homa & Sekey Books, 2003.

PART VI

CASE STUDIES OF BUSINESS STRATEGIES IN THE CHINA MARKET

Category I: Case Studies of Business Strategies

his part of the text contains several cases of strategies adopted by Chinese and foreign companies in the China market. It also includes analysis and evaluations of these strategies and outcomes. Case studies have been popular in the West on business and management, which supplement business models and data analysis with live examples of success or setbacks of commercial business in the real world. Models or formulas have been built on sample cases of operating businesses, and the applicability of certain models or generalisations have to be supported by a fair number of real life cases. In the evolving market of China, this practice to combine generalised analysis with case studies is particularly worthwhile, as no guidebooks project clearer images of this market to potential investors than real cases do.

The cases listed below are in two categories. The first is to see business operations of Chinese companies and their approaches in strategic decisions. Chapter 19 covers a number of foreign multinationals which have operated in the China market and gained first hand experience. This category may be more interesting to readers outside China, either in business or academic circles. There are countless cases and stories examined and told by people with experience; fascinating stories influence people's impression, mood, and investment decisions. The cases listed here present a balance of both positive and negative outcomes, and it is essential to note that over a period of time one case deemed to be a success could move towards the opposite direction, or vice versa. In a fast changing market, model corporations of good business practice may one day collapse, likewise the conclusions made on the basis of these past models. This rule applies to mega corporations of the US, such as Enron; and to foreign multinationals in China as well.

Some foreign multinationals listed here as cases are well known top corporations of the world, and reviews or studies of them are aplenty. The focus in this part is on their strategic decisions and outcomes; their chosen strategies in the China market are specifically examined in detail. For this reason of convenience, routine management and operations of the multinationals concerned are not the centre pieces of the texts.

CASE 1 The Expansion and Setback of a Hong Kong Company in the China Market

By and large, Hong Kong companies, as well as many Taiwan companies, represent the right approaches in entering the China market and have produced numerous success stories. They hold close links with Chinese traditions and know the nuts and bolts of the Chinese way of doing business. The quintessential Chinese norm of *guanxi*, which baffles many Westerners and company executives, runs deep in their blood and facilitates their business in many ways. Pioneers in early and low end FDI in mainland China, Hong Kong businesspeople have established widespread networks of operations. As China's economy grows at amazing rates, Hong Kong businesses earn fabulous returns from their mainland investments and hold key positions in many sectors. Their rapport with government authorities provides them with much needed assistance and sometimes crucial favours in business expansion.

Even under these circumstances and with in-depth knowledge of the China market, there are inevitable examples of failures and withdrawals. Hong Kong newspapers tend to report in detail the stories of failures by their fellow businessmen and regularly issue cautions and advice on entering mainland markets.

It is against this backdrop that a case of a Hong Kong company operating in China is worth noting. The following is to trace its process of expansion, strategies adopted, and lessons learned.

Background

This Hong Kong company is in the property management business, a branch of the real estate development industry. Such businesses have been well developed in Hong Kong, and top housing developers retain their own management agencies. Among thousands of agencies, there are large numbers of independent agency companies which are not subsidiaries of giant developers. Their existence and operations are made possible under a Hong Kong government ordinance effective from the late 1970s, which requires property owners to form residents committees to decide on which management agency to run the daily affairs of their shared flat or apartment buildings. Since most Hong Kong residents live in these estate projects, property management can be a very profitable business if the economies of scale are achieved. Under the ordinance, independent agencies are able to market their services to those committees, take part in a public tender process, or talk directly with members of the committee of a particular apartment building or project. Once a contract is signed between the two parties, these agencies receive fees on a basis of each square foot of building area and a management fee total at a certain percentage.

The Hong Kong company in question is one of these independent agencies. From the late 1970s, the founder of this company, known as Mr. X here, started his own business and actively sought contracts from property owners' committees. His energetic campaigning and building of good relationships won approvals in return. By the late 1990s, he managed to establish a wide network of apartment buildings and commercial properties under the management of his company. Annual net profits, from management fees and commissions, came in at over HK$20 million. This company income was so stable that not even the Asian financial crisis in 1997 could disrupt it, even though most large developers in Hong Kong suffered badly and some closed down. Residents, rich or poor, had to pay their management fees for services provided. Mr. X no longer needed to lobby for committees or knock on doors by himself; the company was well established and employed property managers and workers alike to deal with problems and routine tasks. It is probably accurate to say that even if the company did not choose to expand into mainland China, its then stable revenues could sustain the business for a long while.

It was against this backdrop that Mr. X started trials of managing mainland properties and set up a new China department within the company for this specific purpose.

Decision to Enter the China Market

Aims

It is to conduct business expansion into major Chinese cities and set up teams managing local residential and commercial properties.

Entry Mode

This Hong Kong company mostly acted as estate management consultants to mainland developers. This involves negotiations with developers, obtaining contracts and offering consulting services. The company provides training and standard professional consultation to local partners' employees and supervises the establishment of local teams. The contract is normally for a term of one to two years, and the responsibilities of running properties are to be returned to local managers working for developers. The Hong Kong company receives a fixed amount of commission as payment for services rendered.

A second option is to form joint ventures with local developers and run properties as the company did in Hong Kong. This involves investment from both partners, setting up a new company under the control of both parties according to shareholding ratios, and appointment of stationed managers. The term for a joint venture is substantially longer, up to 20 years legally, and it requires considerable commitment from both parties. For reasons that will be discussed, this is an entry mode seldom chosen by Mr. X.

Expansion Techniques

The company relied on early introduction of Hong Kong style property management systems and expertise, and used its established brand image to attract local developers and sell services. It sought business from a wide range of sources, with Mr. X crisscrossing the country, from the far north to south of China near Hong Kong. Mr. X did not restrain his search by geographical boundaries.

Timing

Early contacts and searches by the company began from 1996, but a full throttle drive occurred in 1998, with the establishment of the China department, frequent field trips to many mainland cities, and enlargement of mainland branches. Generally speaking, this decision on the timing of the entry was a correct one. Mr. X later admitted that he considered the year 1998 the time to move in, and that there might not be another chance or another good year for the company to do the same.

There were several reasons for this timing. It was a turning point in real estate development in China, when private home ownerships for average urban residents emerged as the mainstream demand, replacing the urge of the wealthy for luxury homes. Private property ownership also began to be preferred to public housing, which provided cheap but insufficient dwelling for the public. Urban residents thus sought to have their own properties. Along with wage increases, the newly rich and middle classes had more money to spend. As discussed in a previous chapter, new major consumption items now included real estate property.

Chinese home buyers also became more selective and brand-conscious in their buying decisions. At earlier stages, housing projects of dubious quality and unpleasant styles were quickly taken up by buyers who had little choice. They were now faced with a variety of choices and styles, domestic or foreign, offered by developers who would do anything to please potential buyers. In an economy of surplus, such selection was common in almost every industry. A property project helmed by a decent and well known management team has a definite advantage in attracting more customers.

Mainland property developers at this stage began to recognise the extra benefits of a well-managed estate. They had used to concentrate on sales and ignored contributions from management companies. Since many potential buyers made enquires on whether the management company was a responsible one, developers wanted to enlist management companies with good reputations to work for them or to set up their own management companies with a foreign brand name. This change of mind gave many opportunities to top management companies and overseas companies. Those with solid experience in the real estate business received recognition quickly, such as a well known Hong Kong surveyor firm, and First Pacific Davies which developed rapidly in mainland China in about the same period.

Applying a SWOT analysis to this company, the **strength** would be its past experience and established reputation in the business, in Hong Kong as well as in mainland China. Its contacts and rapport with local developers were frequent and cordial. Mr. X was received by them with open arms at each visit. The company used its good image and Hong Kong's reputation to local recruits, with each job ad receiving quick responses. This provided a chance for the company to select well qualified employees. The company set up a main operating office in Guangzhou, where most employees hired were locals. This reduced the number of Hong Kong employees and lowered overall costs, considering wage differences. The company had implemented comprehensive procedures and systems for property management in Hong Kong. Mainland Chinese companies lacked necessary compatible systems for their projects, and the systems this Hong Kong company introduced appealed to many. This was definitely an advantage and a good sales pitch for the company.

There are **weaknesses** in relation to this company. Firstly, it faced a human resources problem. A business expansion must cover wide spaces and large cities far apart. The company had to get teams ready for dispatch swiftly to whatever location of a new business. Secondly, the company, as an independent agency, was relatively smaller than many of its Hong Kong competitors. It had no international profile, and it was not attached to any of the Hong Kong real estate giants, so the company could only claim to potential clients that it was a top player back home. This weakened some of its appeal to mainland Chinese developers who often heard of those big name companies.

Opportunities were obviously present, as described above under the subheading of "timing". In previous years, management companies from outside the country only took on high-end, exclusive properties for foreign expatriates and rich Chinese businessmen. Such business was few and hard to obtain especially for smaller players. As medium sized property projects now opened to professional managers, this Hong Kong company had a good chance. Its own operations in Hong Kong concentrated on residential blocks owned by middle class members. This experience and adaptability proved acceptable to many mainland clients whose projects targeted mostly at average wage earners.

Threats came in several ways. Bigger players moved in as well and competition heated up. They eyed huge projects in major cities, where this company also eagerly scanned. Relationships with developers shift often, and these were not watertight reliable when *guanxi* and other considerations came into play and when government regulations were being constantly modified. As a consulting firm, this company had to train local staff and pass on business knowledge in operations. Local companies in the same industry were learning fast; once they commanded certain required skills and business knowledge, they became confident to work out their own management and expansion. There is always a tricky question of how to keep a safe distance between you and your followers. What is crucial to a consulting firm is that you must meet the demand of transferring techniques and skills to your client company according to agreements, while not passing all of these out so as not to be threatened by these clients in future. Failing to do the former would attract complaints from your clients, and failing to do the latter would bring about more competitors and diminish the chance of getting more business in the future.

These four factors formed this Hong Kong company's basis for considerations of entering the China market. An extra benefit was that Mr. X understood well the Chinese concept of *guanxi* and related etiquettes. As a Hong Konger from the south, he was a fairly good drinker, which drew admiration and favourable comments from his Chinese clients.

Short-term Results

After repeated efforts, the company expanded its property management consulting business with property developers in many major cities, such as Guangzhou, Chongqing, Kunming, Hangzhou, Nanjing, Shanghai, Jinan, Dalian, and Changchun. These are either provincial capitals or key cities in a province. All this was achieved in less than a year. Mr. X signed numerous business contracts with local developers and collected fees for training employees and setting up new management teams. The company hired significant numbers of managers and engineers, and the size of the China department swelled. These new recruits were stationed in cities handling various consulting tasks for their clients. Commission earnings generated from the mainland soon became sufficient for routine operations.

The company made consulting work the basis for cooperation. In very few cases of joint venture projects, Mr. X invested money in property management companies in Shanghai and Hangzhou, those formed jointly with local developers. These joint ventures quickly passed the required procedures for opening a business on the mainland and established footholds in these major cities for further expansion.

Well-managed estates, especially those in Dalian and Shanghai, attracted more interested developers to inspect the sites, and they later expressed an intention to employ the services of this company. These showcases had positive effects on business promotion, and a project ranked by local government as a model boosted the reputation of this Hong Kong company. In following negotiations with potential clients, what had been achieved earlier was used in a sales pitch and taken as an extra reason to persuade developers who emphasise smooth sales and positive feedback from buyers.

Business practice and standardised work procedures became more widely adopted by local authorities, and these became the benchmarks for other players in the field. This company was seen in some regions as a leader with advanced management models, and its suggestions were listened to even by government authorities, such as the government office in charge of urban development and construction. An office in the Dalian municipal government once asked the company to make proposals on new bylaws concerning property management in the region. The company standards were used as unofficial industry standards in several places.

Problems in Expansion

The overall picture seemed pleasing. As a result of this expansion, the Hong Kong company was a recognised agency in the industry and received more enquires and requests for its consulting services. There were, however, undercurrents which became real threats to company business. These threats derived primarily from the management philosophy and rationale of the company, and they caused enormous harm amidst this fast pace expansion.

Major problems were inherent in strategic moves, relationship management and human resources management.

Strategies

The company sought a quick expansion to avoid lagging behind major competitors. It therefore adopted an approach of jumping from one city to another to obtain any contracts possible. Mr. X took frequent flights to places where there was a slim chance of talking with developers and securing a future contract. In this eagerness to get more business, the manpower of the company was overstretched. Mr. X often gathered available hands for a new project to give clients an impression of company strength. When the next project was signed, this group of leaders was on the move again, leaving the previous project with a skeleton force. In a rush to secure more projects, this mobile group ran tight schedules across the country. This was most clearly shown in the transitional phase between the Changchun project and the Nanjing project. An initial group of eight leaders in Changchun quickly shrank to one and remained at this figure for the rest of the contract duration. This shortage of manpower demoralised the personnel stationed there and annoyed clients deeply. As new projects commenced, old projects soon became neglected. In the end, the company was short of model estates as showcases, except the Shanghai and Dalian sites.

Dealing with Local Developers

Often in business cooperation, conflicts are inevitable. In a consulting role, this Hong Kong company faced numerous conflicts with local developers who paid for services and had the right to make requests. Despite the clauses in contracts, developers would not relinquish control over their own management companies. Consultants were left with limited authority and influence. Any quarrel with local managers had to be sorted out at the top level between developers and Mr. X. As training and consultation was under way, local developers would prefer to maintain their own way of operations, taking new models more for display purposes. They also demanded high standards from consultants, penalising consultants for minor mistakes. A Jinan developer gave a 10,000 yuan reduction in commissions to this Hong Kong company for a mistake in morning flag-raising routines, blaming the on-site consultant for failing to prevent the incident from happening. This mixture of tight control and high demands made it extremely hard for consultants to achieve their expected goals.

The Shanghai project was a typical joint venture, which makes it more interesting for analytical purposes. Mr. X and a Shanghai developer invested in a new joint venture company in 50:50 shares, and he took up the CEO position. Mr. X was confident that this project in Shanghai would be an excellent showcase for his company and generate great intangible benefits for future business. He thus opted for a joint venture investment, rather than the usual consulting/commission format. The fact that he saw Shanghai as a good starting ground and made investments there in 1998 testifies to his vision.

This new joint venture recruited staff and employees to manage the real estate project in Pudong, Shanghai, built by the developer concerned. The goals were to establish a model project and win local and national awards. Under the management staff, all tasks, including services provided, maintenance quality and residents' satisfaction, reached high standards.

Conflicts within the joint venture, again, concentrated on control of authority and emerged between the representative of Mr. X and that of the developer. The authority to assign tasks to workers, to deal with resident representatives, to make purchases and sales etc. was not clearly defined between these two persons. Their clashes grew from professional to personal and finally led to the departure of Mr. X's representative. At a higher level, Mr. X lost to the local developer on many accounts. As the CEO, he was supposed to run the joint venture with sole authority. As he often stayed in Hong Kong or inspected sites in other cities, the real authority to run the joint venture fell into the hands of the local manager, and he was left with a nominal title. The local developer made early concessions to allure Mr. X in and waited until the full investment fund went into its bank accounts before taking over control of the joint venture. Although this project was a tiny segment of his total investment portfolio in Shanghai, the local developer succeeded in setting up an operational management company with little investment money. Mr. X failed to have any significant role to play in the joint venture and, despite the contract of 20 years, simply gave it up and made a quiet exit after a few years.

Developers usually clashed with Mr. X on the use of his Hong Kong company brand. It was demanded that this brand could only be used once in one city, and by one developer; otherwise, developers claimed, the value of the brand would depreciate, and their cooperation with this Hong Kong company would be meaningless. They were not happy to see other local competitors flashing the same logo in their ads. A Jinan developer cut short his negotiations with Mr. X because another developer in the same city had used this Hong Kong company's name. Mr. X was in a dilemma. If his company name could be used by only one local developer, he would not be able to secure more business in the locality concerned. On the other hand, he had great difficulties in talking local developers into signing contracts if they knew he had a prior deal there. On average, this Hong Kong company managed to do business with one developer in the cities it entered.

Relationships with local developers proved tough to maintain. It is a key business principle that your company remains on good terms with your partners and clients. Once you withdrew from a locality, whatever the reasons, your business reputation turned bad, and it became near impossible to go back soon after. A reentry would face much cynicism and suspicion. As the memory of past failure lingers, you would find it hard to convince potential clients the second time around.

The Changchun project proves this rule pointedly. It took Mr. X over four years to build up required *guanxi* and get a consulting contract from a local property developer in that city. Due to the difficulties arising from the low quality standards of the project, constant quarrels with managers of the local company and mounting pressures from other projects across the country, Mr. X considered this project a loss. The last consultant left the project after a few months of work, and the company has never been able to return to do business there. With that early retreat, Mr. X in effect lost a regional market in its entirety. Opinions from local developers tended to agree that Mr. X was unable to handle that task. Would they accept Mr. X as consultant for their future projects? Most unlikely. Both credentials and reputation had been seriously damaged. This consensus makes it near impossible for the Hong Kong company to get a new local client. It seems that a company would better test its perseverance and endurance in a tough environment, in order to achieve long term rewards. Unless the company goal has completely shifted to other areas, it should endeavor to pass the first test. This **rule of first attempt** also applies to giant multinationals, as in the case of Whirlpool's withdrawal from and reentry into the China market.

Management of Human Resources on the Mainland

The rapid expansion undertaken by Mr. X created some grave problems he could not foresee. As the number of projects nearly quadrupled in less than a year, there was a severe shortage of qualified managers and engineers to be sent out as on-site consultants across the country. This shortage is listed above as one of the weaknesses inherent in this company. The newly established China department was understaffed and unable to fill vacancies fast enough. The situation became so desperate in some cases that on-site consultants were called away to new posts temporarily, much to the displeasure of their current clients. This imperative issue continued to plague the operations of the company.

Except for the Hong Kong managers of the China department, all managers and engineers were hired locally. The regional company headquarters was located in Guangzhou, close to Hong Kong, and the city was the single source for hiring needed experts. The headquarters ran regular job ads in local newspapers and arranged job interviews as a major part of its work. Large numbers of applicants in Guangzhou who responded to ads came from other parts of the country. This localisation approach caused a side effect, in that developers in other regions doubted if those on-site consultants were genuine experts from Hong Kong. This doubt on credibility undermined Mr. X's persuasive efforts to a certain degree. The applicants were especially attracted by the chance to work for a Hong Kong company. As pressure built up along with business expansion, the recruitment process was rushed. Selection of personnel was randomly decided by two or three executives without careful scrutiny. Several persons were called to form a team for an immediate task in another city, while the suitability of each person for the job was unknown. A related issue is the inadequate training before assignment. There were no standard training programmes to speak of or adequate time for the newly appointed to fit in; they left for a project one or two days after being selected. Some employees, with specific skills not related to property management, did not even understand the tasks and found out the horrors of unfamiliarity after their arrival at the designated projects. Two or more persons abruptly quit the job and fled back to Guangzhou, scared by daunting prospects of dealing with the unknown. These scenarios undoubtedly indicate that the recruitment process was a failure and it could not remotely supply qualified personnel for the expansion.

Apart from this mismanagement in recruitment, the company made a fatal error in pay schemes. Hong Kong companies operating on the mainland are not known for their generous pay packages and fringe benefits, in comparison with Western multinationals. Even by these standards, pay scales offered by this company were seriously inadequate. Mr. X held a strong belief that for relatively low wages he could still find right persons for the job. Early entrants received relatively higher pay, by Guangzhou standards, but this incentive soon disappeared, and later employees had to make do with pay scales similar to the Guangzhou average. In 1998 when the company began recruitment campaigns, 3,000 yuan a month was an acceptable salary level for many managers. Mr. X mistakenly set a level lower than this for the newly hired and offered little incremental pay rises for work after three months, six months, or one year. Such pay scales appeared unattractive to many. People who agreed to work at this company sought for work experience and better resumes with a Hong Kong company name. Mr. X made a miscalculation on wage levels and living costs on the mainland, after two decades of reforms, and he received less work effort from his employees in return.

On management itself, this Hong Kong company suffered from slow response to changing conditions on the mainland. Its own consulting models faced challenges on multiple fronts. During the process of introducing Hong Kong property management models into the mainland, the contents became somewhat confusing after translating English into Chinese, and local residents were often puzzled by unfamiliar wordings. These models and related papers are lifelines for consulting firms; yet the company failed to update and improve on them, even when local companies caught up through learning and adding local contents. Over time, the company found it hard to demonstrate more advanced ways of property management and thus lost a crucial edge over others in business. At a presentation in Nanjing, local workers regarded their own work routines as more detailed and sensible than what Mr. X was strenuously promoting on stage. Due to sluggish actions at invention and systematic upgrading, perhaps due to the time factor, the company's reputation suffered badly. Consulting contracts ended with no renewal, and local companies soon completely took over similar businesses from this company. As a spent force, the company and its expansion lost momentum.

Some Consequences

Lost business in major cities

Despite renewed effort, the company lost its business contracts as fast as it gained them. In two years—a period of time a consulting contract usually lasts—the company withdrew from the major cities listed above and has not entered these places again. With a downgraded business reputation, it was hard for the company to campaign in the same city it lost. The company then made an effort to explore opportunities in second tier cities and towns, for example, a suburban district of Guangzhou. Since it failed to enter Beijing and stayed in Shanghai for only a short period of time, there were doubts in developers' mind about the standards and real strength of this company. Under the weight of many failed projects, to venture again seemed incredibly tough.

Lost to major competitors

There were other players in the field, with similar management models and networks of contacts. A key difference is that those firms enjoyed favourable reputation in real estate industries, some of them being subsidiaries of Hong Kong developers. This strategic threat cast a considerable shadow on the operations of this company. Mr. X clearly felt the heat and was constantly worried about competition from bigger players. His expansion plan was initially designed to move ahead of others, gaining while key players remained stationary. This rush to survive worked for a short while, but the end result was that bigger players took over most property projects as this company retreated.

Loss of work teams

Internally, the company could not escape from the shortage of qualified experts and suffered badly from an exodus. New recruits left the company in droves, once they realised the scale of problems. High turnover rate ensued, as those managers switched jobs after staying the necessary length of time. The personnel problem was so severe that some newly secured projects did not have consultants. Morale was low enough to have company staff frequently making jokes of their boss and their work. The examples of those who left early and found better jobs deeply impacted on those who remained. The top managers of the China department also left one after another for the pursuit of other goals. Inherent defects in human resources management at this company finally brought the whole system down and made it impossible to sustain the initial expansion strategy.

In a nutshell, this is a case of strategic decision on market expansion. The company stayed the course in its own industrial sector, with no diversification or joining up with real estate giants. The company made a correct strategic decision on moving into a potential growth market at a right time. This is shown by early success in gaining market shares and business reputation. On the basis of a combination of SWOT factors, the company eventually lost due to its own weakness in operations and in management. Its reduced role in the industry, after these setbacks, made it miss the opportunities in that emerging market in China, as property management has now become popular and widely accepted on the mainland in the 21st century.

This Hong Kong company has been under liquidation since 2003, for legal and financial reasons beyond the domains of management and strategic decisions. Its Hong Kong clients are actively chasing payments already made to the company.

Discussion Questions

1. What are your views on the strategic decisions this company made, from the angles of background, factors, trends, benefits and potential for this expansion?
2. Considering the quick expansion process and related consequences, give your suggestions on remedies and adjustments.
3. Comment on the right ways of dealing with local Chinese partners, taking reference from this case. Pay attention to issues of authority, investment options and conflict settlement.

CASE 2 **The Zhuhai Airport, a Government Investment Project**

In developed economies, governments normally have little to do with commercial businesses. It is up to the free market to make supply and demand meet at the point of equilibrium. Commercial businesses place costs and profits as the key benchmarks of their business performance and make investments accordingly. For key infrastructure projects such as airports, these are public goods with public funding and thus subject to more strict government regulations and close scrutiny of their financial state. In China, under reforms, responsibilities for major projects rest on the shoulders of governments. For national level projects, they receive state funding or shared funding from both national and local governments. This general rule still leaves great room for local governments to sponsor and push for their own major projects for regional interests. Theoretically, such projects receive funding from and incur debts of local governments alone, but in practice, the central government may have to step in and coordinate for a rescue plan in emergencies. Even under a more or less decentralised political structure, as discussed before, the central government has been dragged down into messy grand plans from growth oriented local governments. The perils which the Zhuhai airport has endured serve here as a reminder of government initiatives in the economy and certain disastrous outcomes.

Background

Zhuhai was nominated as one of the special economic zones in early reform years, along with its bigger rival Shenzhen. This zone went a different direction from Shenzhen's, concentrating on high-tech and tourism and relegating development of manufacturing industries to a secondary place. Zhuhai is so far renowned for its natural beauty and easygoing life style, on par with some famous overseas beach resorts.

The municipality has upheld a steady growth and expansion philosophy which attempted to avoid overcrowding of local population. The city has officially registered residents of over 600,000, yet the total population staying there numbers over 1.2 million when temporary residents are counted. The key point here is that the city acts conservatively and issues limited numbers of residential permits to people coming from other parts of the country. It is still much harder to get a Zhuhai residential permit than a Shenzhen one; hence the huge difference between Zhuhai's population and the much larger population of Shenzhen's. Visitors to Zhuhai comment favourably on its leisurely environment, quiet streets, unhurried traffic, and lack of other urban pollutions common in big Chinese cities. Think of several international events held in Zhuhai, such as the Zhuhai Air Show and Zhuhai Motor Race, and you will get an idea of what this city intends to develop. In more recent years, the Zhuhai government invested heavily on building a university town at the outskirts of the city. Top universities from Beijing, Shanghai and Guangzhou were lured to Zhuhai and set up their new campuses there. Universities see commercial returns in land assets and student fees from this expansion, while the municipal government seeks revenues from business activities and increased consumption brought in by waves of college students. This initiative is also supposed to boost the city's image as an education and high-tech territory, rather than as an industrial base.

One of the drawbacks of this "half-opened door" is that Zhuhai attracts smaller numbers of talents and businesses, many of them moving to Shenzhen where people with employment skills become formal citizens of the city with relative ease. Considering the small size of the economy, many companies cannot attract enough business and customers for their operations. It has in general a slower pace of economic activities, and this has forced many companies to shift to Guangzhou or Shenzhen to service larger groups of consumers. As total numbers of businesses are small, land under the control of city authorities is in low demand, and land prices remain steady. The municipal government therefore has been unable to gain huge financial benefits from land sales, unlike the situation in Hong Kong or Shenzhen where governments receive a big chunk of revenues from such sales and fill their coffers with money from this source. The Zhuhai government has been plagued by financial and budgetary constrains for urban development. The opening of the new university town is but one recent move made by city officials to generate some revenues from unused land in the territory under their administration.

Even under the conservative guiding principle in development and with limited financial capacity, the Zhuhai airport was conceived and constructed on a grand scale. This comes from the ambitious planning by a former city mayor, whose connections with provincial and central government officials boosted his ambition to be seen as a mayor bringing significant progress. Outstanding performance in localities generally facilitates officials' political careers in China. From the outset, this gigantic infrastructure project embodied political motives, and decisions made in relation to this building project then became political strategic ones.

This diversity in development among regions originated from the consistent decentralisation policy of the central government. Regions were left to fend for their own survival and initiated drives to gain advantages over others. A region could lag behind or excel over others as a result of the decisions made by local leaders. The province of Guangdong in southern China was widely seen as a new "wild west" with a tendency to generate a runaway economy and achieve astonishing growth unprecedented in modern Chinese history. This environment of loose control and minimum restrictions prompted many local governments to seek their own goals by whatever means available. The former Zhuhai mayor in question had a deep grasp of the nature of this race and took the initiative to promote his own territory ahead of others. Soon after this airport was completed in the Zhuhai special economic zone, a number of sub-province level cities made loud noises about building their own airports. If that scenario were realised, Guangdong province would have been dotted by a dozen airports. In this regard, the Zhuhai municipal government set a bad precedent in taking advantage of decentralisation and in failing to foresee overcapacity in the long run.

The Zhuhai Airport

The Zhuhai airport was designed and built as an international airport, being designed in 1992 and completed in 1995. The government was the major investor, planning to make a total investment of US$845 million (about 7 billion yuan) for the airport and all attached facilities. Unfortunately, it provided only 3 billion yuan of the 7 billion yuan earmarked for the airport. Funds had to be raised from other sources, such as bank loans and delaying payments to contractors. The original idea was to promote the city and enhance its image. The question then is why the city needed such a big project—building an international airport while being only one of the regional centres in Guangdong province. The answer perhaps lies simply in the fact that the mayor in office insisted on reaching international standards, in effect above any other airport in neighbouring regions. The vanity of the mayor certainly had a place in the whole rationale behind the project. Back in the early 1990s, this great leap forward seemed quite plausible. Guangzhou was stuck with its old Baiyun airport; Hong Kong was building its international standard airport which would only be complete several years later; Macau had an airport of average size; and Shenzhen with its bigger size and busier air traffic had to make do with its own small airport. It seemed fairly reasonable for a city mayor to see out of this status quo that a new airport in Zhuhai would create the impact needed for improving the city's image, as well as improving his own reputation to senior leaders. A simple and basic logic worked here to address local needs and start a course of transformation. Building the airport project was initially calculated as a necessary step, though in reality it went one step further to claim its super status.

This giant airport was designed with forward-looking guidelines, seeking to meet international standards and huge traffic demand in future decades. This decision incurred much more costs than deemed necessary and made the airport the most expensive one at the time. The airport was also one of China's most advanced airports when it was completed. To build it, they imported advanced equipment, set up the largest flight information boards, and installed imported security and luggage delivery systems available on international markets. The airport was designed to handle annual passengers of 12 million, landing and takeoff of 100,000 times, and a total freight and postal handling capacity of 600,000 tons. The airport has a waiting hall of over 90,000 square metres and has to employ 1,200 employees to run it properly.

Current Situation

The airport company owes debts of 1.3 billion yuan to banks, 1.7 billion yuan to contractors, which completed construction work and services for the airport but have yet to get paid. A default on paying a 1.7 billion yuan debt in infrastructure alone took place years ago. This indicates that, despite the sponsorship of the city government, the airport project did not receive the full funding for all construction work when it started. There have been constant claims and rumours of "going broke" or "closing down", which have been fervently denied by airport management and the city government.

The tangible assets of the airport, including land, vehicles, office equipment, even corridors, were confiscated by courts after judgements were handed down. A major contractor from Tianjin city obtained court orders to claim debts of over 70 million yuan but has failed to collect them in full from the airport. Suing project developers is a last resort of many contractors to recoup some of their investment. At this stage of a lawsuit, good business relationships are no longer major concerns, and the plaintiff intends to take money back openly and legally, as well as to damage the image of the defendant.

By court orders, all revenues earned from the airport are paid first to those which lent money to the airport and those who are owed. Although the airport has been in operation with its best efforts, the meagre revenues are diverted to lenders and will not increase the airport's asset value any time soon. This has hampered a successful restructuring of the airport.

Annual revenues were 108 million yuan in 2000 and have not improved dramatically. With the current level of operations, the airport is losing about 20 million yuan per month. The airport handles several dozen flights a day and about 600,000 passengers a year. Significantly different from the original plans, the airport hosts domestic airlines and serves passengers mostly from other regions. The original desires to attract international passengers and make this Zhuhai airport an international air traffic hub have yet to materialise.

The airport management has devised various ways to increase earnings and save costs. So far, benefits have come mostly from the savings side. When most facilities are not used due to few flights inbound and outbound, the lights and some elevators are turned off. Maintenance and cleaning are kept to a minimum, done by low wage employees. On the income side, the airport opens up certain areas of space and even runways to air shows, exhibitions, and driving schools which are having booming business. The airport has been a host of the Zhuhai International Air and Space Expo. After continuing negotiations, this airport is now the pilot training base for Cathay Pacific and Dragon Air of Hong Kong, and for China Southern. As a major government project, the airport also holds rights to massive land areas, with which it could explore further development and sales. These unused lands have been taken into account in the total assets owned by the airport.

In micro management, airport executives perhaps have done their most and see little prospect of further cost cutting.

The airport is closely linked with the state of the Zhuhai economy. Its survival in the long run depends on the pace of urban development. Increases in population and industries are the key. Tourists and business will increase volumes of passengers to the city through the airport, and recent opening of the university town gave a mild but much needed boost for the airport. The ultimate solution to the woes of this airport is a macro one, through actions taken by external players. At early stages of incurring financial losses, the airport management looked to the government for rescue. They made a proposal for a complete government bailout. This has not materialised, partly due to the poor financial state of the municipal government itself. In more recent times, the government gave the direction of finding foreign investors and partners. The Airport Authority of Hong Kong has expressed interest in this airport and may step forward to take over management. It could then be transformed into a hub for express cargo transportation, having links with Hong Kong and other regions of China. An international airport status will be minimised under this plan, and Zhuhai will return to being a regional airport, as it should have been from the outset.

The biggest trouble for new potential partners is the current debts the airport owes. It has been clear that any interested parties, from the Hong Kong airport to the Chinese Aviation Administration in Beijing, show no intention to take on the debts the airport has accumulated, no matter what mode of cooperation in operations. In the end, such cooperation will only improve operational performance and increase revenues. The debt issue will have to be solved by the city government once and for all. Its options include injecting funds from its coffers to the airport to write off all debts, offering substantial concessions to the airport, such as tax exemptions, so that the airport has a shorter time span to pay off debts, or a complete sellout to external investors while taking financial losses.

All these options test the decision making of the city government. Current leaders in office inherited this problem from their predecessors and have no stomach for making rash and dramatic decisions. They now recognise the fatal miscalculation in the original decision to build the airport to this grand scale. Any further investment would face strong opposition. In addition, the Zhuhai government is not in a strong financial position to easily write off huge obligations of this size. If this problem existed in Shenzhen, that municipal government would have the luxury of getting rid of it quickly and sustaining the losses. At the current time, it seems that the Zhuhai government and the airport management intend to await more generous investors or improve their financial state gradually so that the debts would be paid off eventually.

Characteristics of Government Planning and Decision

Since this is a government project, the actions taken clearly reflect the planning and decision making styles of governments and officials. In this case, opportunities and threats are the main considerations, instead of strength and weakness.

In terms of opportunities, the airport was originally designed at a time of early booms in aviation industries. Numbers of people travelling by air grew rapidly and state air carriers began to earn fat profits. Partly on this basis, the Zhuhai government projected higher volumes in air travel and saw unrealistic strong demands for an international airport in its region. Opportunities came also from the fact that the city contains a nice natural environment and is regarded as a well known vacation destination. Combining these twin factors of air traffic boom and tourist inflows, an anticipation of increasing revenues made it look rational to lay out a plan for an airport of its own. In comparison with other major cities in Guangdong province, Zhuhai has neither the urban sprawl of Guangzhou nor the industrial madness of Shenzhen. City planners figured that with this contrast in mind, tourists would prefer Zhuhai. More businesses would follow suit and move in.

In terms of threats, Zhuhai is a minor city in front of the other two giants. No matter what major landmark projects Zhuhai came up with, Guangzhou and Shenzhen almost always performed better and attracted more attention from the media and the public. Even when these two cities lagged behind Zhuhai in building an airport, their overall economic strength and deep pockets allow them to embark on key projects whenever they see the need. The new airport in Shenzhen has served the city well from the late 1990s, and the new Guangzhou airport opened for business in August 2004. These new air traffic centres draw people and tourists to their cities fairly easily. The Zhuhai airport, despite its early start, remains in a sideline position in this provincial contest. These prominent threats just cannot be ignored and should have been in clear sight of Zhuhai city planners when the airport was first conceived. Rivalry with Shenzhen has been frequent; Shenzhen authorities and the media take the Zhuhai airport as a serious miscalculation and mistake by the municipal government, and these are portrayed as an embarrassment simply for the sake of competition.

During the period of building the airport, the projection of future volumes of air traffic was optimistic, but the aviation industries soon ran into trouble. All airlines reported losses, despite increasing numbers of air passengers. The initial hope for more tourists to Zhuhai disappeared due to high fares and costs. Threats to airlines' operations adversely affected the Zhuhai airport.

There are inevitable political motives behind infrastructure projects during the reform years. Local governments love to adopt ambitious plans and favour big government projects that can give an enormous boost to the local economy. They also commonly consider major projects as key incentives for increased FDI. Undoubtedly, local officials also seek career promotions based on completion of these huge projects. Following this reasoning, in design and construction, the Zhuhai government put priority on a bright image of the city and the decisiveness of the government in this project. The profitability of the airport and its operational efficiency were not given sufficient consideration, as shown in the fact that the Zhuhai government provided less than half of the funds for this eagerly promoted project. Designs and technological standards had to be revised up to fit a top international airport. The consequences of overcapacity and huge costs in the airport project are the marked features of this kind of mindset of the government.

Other Factors to be Considered in Relation to Regional Environment

Geographically and historically, business prospects at the western side of the Pearl River have normally been less attractive to investors. Development at the east side of the river overshadows the west. A look at a Guangdong map will reveal the imbalance: along the eastern line, there are Hong Kong, Shenzhen, Dongguan, and Guangzhou; and along the western line are Macau and Zhuhai up to Guangzhou. The aggregate economic power of the east is beyond the reach of the west (see Table 18.1).

Zhuhai has smaller industrial sectors, few national-level large corporations, but possesses a relatively unspoiled natural environment for tourism. This makes the city a place for travel and leisure, not for large investment in manufacturing sectors. Even for tourist industries, Zhuhai faces strong competition from neighbouring cities. It is located very near to the Macau territory, which boasts shinny casinos and attracts large numbers of overseas tourists (as well as gamblers). This disadvantage applies also to the Zhuhai airport which is just a few miles off the Macau airport. If this airport loses to mega airports in other cities of the Pearl River Delta, it in particular suffers further from the proximity to the Macau airport. In market positioning and promotion, Zhuhai lacks the financial prowess and know-how the other major competitors have.

Summary

This is a case of grand government plans and decisions, in disregard of local economic reality, coordination and real costs, resulting primarily from a government's ambitions to be a successful special economic zone like Shenzhen.

In decision making, the airport is the result of an irrational process, without a search for and list of available alternatives. The project also suffers from autocratic leadership styles and typical groupthink. The municipal government followed a strong leader and admired his vision and ambition. Even up to today, government officials have to often defend their past decisions and make themselves free from possible blame. The project symbolises reckless and frenzy development

Table 18.1 Comparisons in operations among the five PRD international airports (2000-2001)			
	Landing/takeoff	Passenger/time	Freight and postal
Guangzhou	130,000	13 million	490,000 tons
Zhuhai	17,000	570,000	9,000 tons
Shenzhen	80,000	8 million	250,000 tons
Macau	20,000	3.23 million	60,000 tons
Hong Kong	N/A	34 million	2.2 million tons

strategies, which have created a **"white elephant"** for a small local economy. In studies of Chinese economy and regional development, this particular case and the five international airports around the Pearl River Delta have been cited as the ultimate examples of failed coordination, bad economic management and great waste of the nation's resources.

As a consequence of this wrong decision, the Zhuhai airport is seeking to cooperate with other regional airports. It has abandoned the original ambition to become a top international airport and has relegated itself to a regional air traffic centre. The massive space in the hands of the airport could serve as a port for cargo and express postal services. One possibility is to receive extra cargo flights from the Hong Kong airport and serve as a port for further logistical operations. Related talks are under way between Hong Kong and Zhuhai authorities. A further prospect on the horizon is that after an energetic drive for a 9+2 cooperation (Hong Kong, Macau and nine mainland southern provinces), the Zhuhai economic zone will integrate deeper into this mega region. This scale of cooperation is expected to provide additional benefits to the city and hopefully to its airport.

This case of strategic decision is a type of government action, which follows rationales different from private commercial business, as well as from the behaviours of government organisations in developed economies. There are considerations more of political directions and leaders' intentions than business estimates and projections. This case in an open market of southern China illustrates the constant influence of government directions on major infrastructure and commercial projects. In special economic zones and across the country, this influence has been deep-rooted and can convincingly explain the fluctuations and overheating in regional businesses and economies.

Discussion Questions

1. Considering opportunities, threats and other factors, what business projections would you make to the city government on the airport project before it started, especially on market positioning?
2. What would you suggest to address the issues of the current situation—continuation of operations, withdrawal, or restructuring?

CASE 3 Hong Ta Group: A Tobacco King to Diversify

Diversification in Perspective

It is not unusual for leading corporations in traditional industrial sectors to seek business opportunities in other related or unrelated sectors. In developed economies, small businesses are able to grow to large corporations and then dominate the industries they are in. Their success may come from certain monopolies or unique methods of production. Under free market competition, these advantages could be copied by followers, and competition will drive up the costs and lower profit margins. Significant changes in the external environment would also lead to new threats to current business, making operations less profitable or creating losses. Saturation in the near future is a clear possibility for these companies. These factors form constant pressure on leading firms to consider long term risks and strive to find sectors for expansion and diversification. This move is often not an option, but a necessity for business survival.

In developed economies, there have been numerous examples of old traditional industrial leaders moving into other sectors for increased revenues and for reduced risks in existing sectors. The famed razor maker **Gillette** has over 100 years of history; yet it recognised that it could not rely on selling razors and shavers as its single source of income. The company considered entering other profitable sectors while holding sufficient financial resources. Gillette acquired appliances maker **Braun** in 1967 and has continued to manufacture kitchen and household appliances. It acquired Oral B in 1984 as an expansion into a related industry. Its acquisition of **Duracell** in 1996, on the other hand, is a move into a quite unrelated area of business. This decision proved to be a wise one, since waves of new products in the 1990s, in particular computers and digital products, require batteries. Gillette, an old time razor maker, caught this trend of new products and has gained large sums of revenues from consumption of batteries.

The example of **Philip Morris**, a top tobacco maker of the world, is closer to the core of this case study below. The cigarettes maker has made astronomical profits from selling top brands to populations around the world. Even as smoking is meeting ever growing restrictions in developed economies, the company and other companies in the industry have succeeded in spreading their smoking business to developing countries, including China. This primary business of the company, however, is becoming more unsecure year by year, and risks needed to be diverted or thinned out. The company has initiated large scale diversification strategies in past decades. Its major move was the acquisition of top foods maker Kraft in 1988 for about US$13 billion. This takeover brought whole new lines of products under the company name and provided increased revenues for the company. Furthermore, the foods business gives the company a better image than the cigarettes business does, and long term business prospects look more secured. The acquisition of Nabisco in 2000 and large shareholding in SAB Miller (a top beer maker) in 2002 cemented the company's pole position in food related industries. Through a series of diversifications, Philip Morris has built up a versatile portfolio and achieved multiple strongholds for its staggering aggregate business results. The company is also less worried now by risks from public criticisms over its cigarettes business.

Hong Ta's Strategies of Diversification

Taking references from the above examples of diversification by foreign multinationals, the Hong Ta case illustrates similar features of strategic decision making by the top management of a Chinese company. Considerations for the decisions included internal and external factors, and the outcomes of strategies are presented here for a close examination.

Background

The Hong Ta Group (literally "red pagoda" in Chinese) is a state enterprise located in Yunnan province of southwestern China. It started from 1979 with a small cigarettes factory of 10 million yuan worth of fixed assets. Its founder Mr. C took over the management of this factory, facing competition from over 1,000 cigarettes factories in the province alone and built it up to a business empire of its own. Yunnan province is renowned for its tobacco leaves and long history of tobacco plantation. Tobacco leaf there has top qualities, benefiting from favourite conditions of fertile soil, rainfall and plentiful sunshine. At that early stage, tobacco and alcohol in China were under state monopoly and distribution. As other goods became subject to market demands and pricing, these two had long been monitored and controlled by state offices throughout the country. Quality tobacco brands had little worry over sales, even if their output jumped many times. There was a deep "**hunger**" among Chinese consumers who had the first taste of purchasing a variety of quality goods.

Basic requirements for a good tobacco business manager or leader were simply quality and quantity. Mr. C managed to establish several national brands, on the basis of technology and quality control. He followed a similar path to success as that of Mr. Zhang of the Haier Group. Cigarettes from Hong Ta became high end and sought after goods on the market. For many consumers, smoking Hong Ta cigarettes projected an image of wealth and status, similar to smoking imported foreign brands such as Marlboro. The company gained enormous profits from sales and grew in size rapidly. It set up numerous subsidiaries across the province and later the country. Each of them operated independently and was filthy rich in cash. In 1995, the Hong Ta Group Company was fully established, and one of its top brands was named "the most valuable brand name" in China, worth an estimated 46 billion yuan. The company has since been one of the top five corporate taxpayers of the country. In that year as well, the company integrated many local cigarettes makers into a dominant business entity of the province. The next step was to expand across the borders and undertake diversification if necessary.

Strategies to Dominate Domestic Markets

Tobacco industries are unique in that the state has not relinquished its control over them. Unlike other industries, such as household appliances and computers, tobacco industries in China are under strict control of state authorities, in the form of the State Tobacco Monopoly Administration. This administration has offices in provinces which produce tobaccos and controls production, distribution, and sales of tobacco and cigarettes across the country. A top tobacco brand will surely enjoy the favours from this administration and will earn profits trouble-free. Since tobacco companies are big taxpayers, the administration holds a proactive attitude towards the interests and losses of those companies. Domestic tobacco makers were threatened in the 1990s by inflows of foreign brands and by smuggling. Facing smaller revenues collected from domestic tobacco makers, the central government tightened rules on smuggling and severely punished officials concerned in waves of public campaigns. This led to a recovery of sales by domestic makers and of increased tobacco revenues to government coffers.

The state administration is also a major backer for market domination by large tobacco makers. The number of tobacco makers increased before 1992 and reached 185 enterprises by that year in the whole country. This trend then turned to a decrease in numbers, with encouragement from the state administration. The economies of scale improved and the industry became more manageable for the administration. Large tobacco enterprises began to take over smaller ones, and the total number of tobacco enterprises is expected to reduce to 40 by 2005. Hong Ta stood to benefit from this merger trend. It is a big player in the field and enjoys numerous favours from the state administration. After merging provincial level tobacco manufacturers, Hong Ta carried out its expansion outside the provincial borders. Hong Ta took over the Changchun Tobacco Company in the northeast in 1999 and formed an alliance with Hainan Tobacco Company in the south. In the meantime, Hong Ta invested on new high end brands to command the most profitable sections of tobacco consumption. With the passing of time, Hong Ta is now a top national brand and a leading enterprise among domestic competitors. Its dominance in the industry is undisputable. Without intended diversifications, Hong Ta might have been in an even more stable position today, at least financially.

The Strategic Decision to Diversify

The company began diversification from the cigarettes industry from the early 1990s on and invested in other unrelated industries. This strategic move was based on assessments of the situation in that period of time and in particular on the weakness within the company and threats outside the company.

Strength

Hong Ta had accumulated enormous amounts of cash from past earnings and profits. Even after paying huge amounts of taxes to the state and being the number one taxpayer for a few years in a row,

Hong Ta never faced a shortage of cash. Even its third tier subsidiaries had plenty of funds to make separate large investments. These cash reserves needed to find places of investment. The solid financial strength would enable Hong Ta to beat many contenders and facilitate smooth business deals.

Weakness

There were downward trends in tobacco sales in the latter half of the 1990s. This heralded slow future growth for the tobacco industry as a whole. Anti-smoking campaigns became worldwide movements, and giant international tobacco companies were dragged to court to face charges on damage to health. Chiefs of Chinese tobacco enterprises began to worry that their secured businesses would not last long and their good days were numbered. The single source of income from tobacco production, no matter how huge now, would dry up soon. If they did not respond quickly and set up new businesses unrelated to tobacco, their future growth and revenues would be in question. This urge to get additional insurances has led to a variety of diversifications, not just by Hong Ta, but by many other players in the industry. The heavy reliance on tobacco incomes must be reduced.

Opportunities

There are various business opportunities in other sectors to be explored. A financially sound Hong Ta would be able to grab new factories and enterprises. Once a diversification strategy was implemented, Hong Ta could move swiftly to enter the sectors it desired. In the industries it entered, Hong Ta could choose to adopt both joint venture and wholly-owned investment approaches.

As the Chinese economy entered a phase of oversupply from the mid 1990s, many domestic enterprises were short of funds and found it much more difficult to do business. The financial resources Hong Ta controlled made it a preferred business partner in many industries. This situation favoured its entry and reduced resistance from existing players there. As it turned out, Hong Ta had the luxury to select the industries to enter.

Threats

In many industries that Hong Ta planned to enter, there were large number of players and even clear leaders. With funding but without commanding advantages in the market, Hong Ta would end up as an average player in the second tier group. It would be extremely hard for Hong Ta to become a top player soon, unlike the position of GE in its diversification drive. This would earn the company some income, but in comparison with the huge investment Hong Ta made, there would be a clear imbalance, and eventually those projects would cost the company dearly.

Threats also came from the shifting of investment to other sectors and leaving the tobacco production and brands in a lesser status. Incomes from this business could drop and damage the total financial soundness of the company.

Additional Considerations

The company reached a peak in tobacco output and in tax payments to provincial and central governments in the mid 1990s. Unfortunately, the then CEO and founder Mr. C committed economic crimes and was sentenced to a jail term (see previous chapter on state enterprises). A new CEO had to be appointed to rein in wild and sometimes chaotic management. In particular, those numerous subsidiaries which conducted tobacco businesses of their own needed to be put under much closer scrutiny. During this internal restructuring, the new CEO, Mr. Z, recognised the urgency to lead the company to become a more versatile entity. External pressure on tobacco sales and internal disorganisation provided a timely warning to the top management, and Mr. Z was forced to initiate a comprehensive diversification strategy. This was perhaps a coincidence of change of leadership and of company direction, combined with a pent-up ambition to walk on the national stage and be treated as a national multi-sector corporation, instead of a mere top tobacco maker.

Steps in Diversifications

Hong Ta purposefully set up Hong Ta Investment Corp. in 1993 under the group company to handle diversification, expansion and investment portfolios. This subsidiary has the full financial backing of the group company and is able to make investment decisions on its own. It has so far made investments of over 17 billion yuan into more than 70 projects in numerous industries. These include energy, transportation, chemicals, pharmaceuticals, finance, tourism, hotels, real estate, paper making, and motor cars. Some analysts believe that the company has overstretched itself in expansion.

Hong Ta formed a joint venture with a Virgin Island registered company and invested 2 billion yuan on a paper making project in the Zhuhai special economic zone. The paper mill set up advanced equipment and production lines imported from the US, Germany, France, and Japan. The mill's lines went into operation from the late 1990s and churned out specialised papers for cigarettes, packaging, paper cups, cupboards etc. Another paper mill was built with a German partner, in a joint investment of US$73 million. That project makes specialised rolling paper for cigarettes and for filter tubes.

Hong Ta entered the hotel business and built several four-star hotels across the country. One of them is located at a prime and spectacularly scenic tourist destination, Huangshan Mountain, in a joint venture with a Hong Kong investment company. Another is located in Pudong, Shanghai, next to Holiday Inn.

Hong Ta spread its operations into pharmaceuticals, chemicals and construction materials, and through share buying became major shareholders of many companies in other industries. It invested in two cement factories, with profits of 18 million yuan in 2002. Its investment on pharmaceuticals was chiefly through a 23% stake in a listed company which produces traditional Chinese medicines. Other investments included timber processing, aluminium, a power station and hydropower station, and tolled freeways in Yunnan province.

In 1996, Hong Ta made significant investment in Huaxia Bank, Everbright Bank, and other insurance and securities companies. Investment in financial sectors ran up to nearly 1 billion yuan. In numbers, these investments appear small in comparison with financial assets top national banks hold; it was expected that Hong Ta would be able to draw financial support from these institutions when it owned some stakes in them.

The most prominent example of this diversification is Hong Ta's entry into the motor car industry. Hong Ta hooked up with the number one motor maker, the First Auto Works (FAW) in Changchun in 1998, with the auspices and official push from the provincial government. The two sides set up a new joint venture named **FAW Hong Ta**, with 51:33 shareholdings and another Yunnan vehicle company taking up the rest of shares. This joint venture invested in a project in Yunnan province to produce light trucks for sale nationwide using the FAW name. That was the first move made by Hong Ta into the car industry, and the company focused on this sector of the industry with intensity and firm financial backing. The total sale of light trucks produced there reached 30,000 units in 2003, a small figure by international standards, but a considerable figure for a local vehicle maker in China.

Hong Ta shifted its attention in later years to passenger cars, spurred by unexpected booms in car sales in the China market. Hong Ta and FAW poured over 400 million yuan in a huge undertaking to build a site of multiple production lines for passenger cars. The complex is expected to be complete by 2007 and produce over 150,000 vehicles, with 50,000 passenger cars among them. For FAW, this is their manufacturing base in the south, along with their headquarters in the northeast. For Hong Ta, to have this "dragonhead" car corporation to lend them a hand certainly reduced the risks in their entry into the car industry. The Hong Ta investment company claimed that this motor car venture and these two projects (truck and sedan) are the most successful in its overall diversifications. Even with a relatively negligible market share in comparison with that of mighty players and some strategic shifts in later years, this commitment to car making remains a centre piece of Hong Ta's diversification strategy.

Hong Ta undoubtedly went full throttle ahead in its diversification campaign from the late 1990s on. Backed by its enormous financial strength, Hong Ta made investments whenever it made a picking, sometimes perhaps too lightly. The total of these investments was so huge that Hong Ta could have created a new viable and leading business in a single industry. Instead, it showered money on numerous choices and, unlike Philip Morris, the big brother in the tobacco industry of the world, Hong Ta took over businesses that were far from being industry leaders themselves. This shortcoming diminished the likelihood of Hong Ta claiming its ascendency in new territories any time soon. Companies Hong Ta took over did not have outstanding performance, except the cooperation partner in the motor car industry, FAW. Even in that particular sector, it is commonplace that huge investments are required before an investing company is even recognised as a real player. The efforts by Hong Ta have not made much difference to the status quo in the motor car industry, and the company must lower its expectations for quick results and returns.

Hong Ta's efforts in diversification are well known as a typical example of the kind, but its performance did not match its original projections. Hong Ta was recognised as a diversified corporation gaining a minimum presence in many industries, yet its growth and prospects showed signs of downward trends. A simple line up of huge investment and returns gives the impression that the strategic decision needed to be re-examined. It is with this background that Hong Ta made a further move.

The Strategy of "Returning to the Core" in 2002

Hong Ta's original plans to spread out risks through diversification may cause more risks. Its main source of incomes—tobacco production—made less contribution to total revenues, while newly invested projects were unable to generate real profits and fill the holes. In 1997, the second year of diversification, Hong Ta reported a combination of profits and taxes of 19.3 billion yuan. In 2001, this figure fell one-third to 12.7 billion yuan. By simple calculations, the diversification strategy failed. It increased the size of the company but was unable to create real growth that mattered. As the owner of this state enterprise, the Yunnan provincial government moved in to make changes. Mr. Z was replaced by Mr. L as the CEO of Hong Ta in 2002. This personnel change also signals the end of a six-year long diversification and a crucial turn in strategies.

It requires an overall review of the situations before making strategic turns. Hong Ta's top management acknowledged that their past assessments of industries proved faulty and inaccurate. A downward trend in tobacco industries was listed as a major cause for igniting diversification into other business sectors. These proved wrong. Tobacco industries had increased sales and returns, and averaged 4% growth in 20 years. The state administration continued to encourage mergers/ acquisitions among domestic tobacco makers, which provided vital opportunities for Hong Ta to grab more market share and secure its leading position in the industry. Competition from foreign cigarettes brands remained fierce, yet top domestic brands received wide recognition among consumers. Hong Ta brands enjoy great popularity. China has 350 million regular cigarettes smokers. This is an attractive figure for domestic and foreign cigarettes makers alike. Despite worldwide anti-smoking campaigns and restrictions on international tobacco makers, tobacco consumption in China has not been affected dramatically, and authorities and the public move slowly in changing their smoking habits. This sluggishness has allowed foreign brands to flourish in the China market and also made domestic cigarettes makers big winners in business. Hong Ta would have to readjust its priority to prevent it from missing out on these opportunities.

In a reorganisation of operations, Hong Ta can certainly count on the backing from the central and provincial governments to be a "**backbone**" enterprise in the industry. Its mergers and acquisitions would get approvals and assistance quite easily. Despite its size and dominance in domestic markets, Hong Ta stands little chance in a full frontal competition with top foreign tobacco makers. It now ranks behind the top four international tobacco companies, and building an international brand requires large investment and long term planning. Furthermore, in 2004, China scraped specially issued tobacco retail licences and allowed millions of Chinese cigarettes sellers with retail licences to sell imported foreign brands freely. In addition, tariffs on imported tobacco leaf went down from 40% to 10%, and those on imported cigarettes from 65% to 25%. This would benefit foreign brands and importers significantly, lead to price wars, and put enormous pressure on domestic tobacco makers. Hong Ta would have to factor this change in and respond proactively, through building up a strong business empire before the crunch time comes.

Based on these considerations, Hong Ta's top management made a strategic decision of "**returning to the core**" in 2002, meaning a refocused strategy and an emphasis on its core business—tobacco production. Hong Ta recognised that the company was overstretched in its investment and a restructuring was inevitable. The shift in strategy also implies a halt to diversification and investment in those related projects. By 2004, the company declared that it made 80% of profits from its traditional tobacco production, and investment in other industries received steady incomes. Investment in sideline industries, such as finance, securities, sports (a soccer team in the national league under the Hong Ta name), and advertising were to be sharply reduced against previous plans. One key investment from previous diversification remains in operation, which is the investment in the motor car industry. Other smaller scale investment projects, such as cement and construction materials, will continue with less enthusiastic financial support.

Hong Ta utilised its financial wealth and accumulated R&D in tobacco production to launch new "platinum" series cigarettes, as a new generation of low tar and nicotine cigarettes with fragrant scent. Other Hong Ta brands were also redesigned and repackaged to meet market demands. These new investments indicate the shift in focus and renewed efforts on boosting sales, enlarging market shares, and winning back customers.

In 2002 when the new top management took over, total sales and profits stopped sliding, and in 2003 the company reported mild increases across the board.

For international exposure and cooperation, Hong Ta has formed alliances with Imperial Tobacco of the UK, the world's fourth largest international tobacco company just ahead Hong Ta. The company received permission from Imperial Tobacco to produce the "West" brand cigarettes for sales in domestic markets. In this 10-year cooperation deal, Imperial Tobacco will be obliged to make an annual investment of US$8.4 million in the project, while it plans to sell 10 million cigarettes in China every year. In return, Imperial Tobacco will market Hong Ta brand cigarettes to the overseas market through its established distribution networks. Hong Ta also takes a cut of 60% in sales income from Imperial Tobacco's "West" brand.

In legal terms, this alliance agreement with a foreign tobacco maker is on questionable grounds. This form of business venture is officially banned, and the WTO promises made by the Chinese government contain no references to opening domestic enterprises to foreign tobacco makers. Imperial Tobacco has been low-key on this agreement. Strictly speaking, this is not a joint venture like those which go through normal procedures and obtain official approvals. The Hong Ta factories which produce the "West" brand cigarettes are not newly set up facilities by joint venture partners. The project, however, is in the general category of foreign investment, in that Imperial Tobacco made real investment in the project run jointly with Hong Ta. Imperial Tobacco took existing facilities as the site of their investment. Together with distribution agreements and rights, this cooperation between Hong Ta and Imperial

Tobacco is in fact a joint venture in nature without the official name. This deliberate ambiguity indicates the eagerness of this international tobacco maker to enter a potential growth market, the leniency of state authorities which looked the other way, and unreserved support from the provincial government.

This shift of strategic goals came along with the background of a more enthusiastic push for consolidation by the state tobacco administration. In China, tobacco makers are scattered all over the country, producing over 2,500 brands of cigarettes, with the top eight makers accounting for only a 26% share of the national market. This dispersed production capacity not only increases the difficulty for the state administration to effectively monitor and regulate the industry, but also makes the overall efficiency in tobacco production unsatifactory. This low level of economies of scale creates an industry-wide vulnerability when facing imminent threats from foreign tobacco giants once open competition is allowed.

The government, and the state administrationin in particular, devised adjustment measures from 2001 onwards. The administration promoted a trend of "bigger market, grand brands, and larger enterprises" and implemented a series of consolidation measures for the fragmented industry. Smaller companies were to be closed down or merged into other groups, while companies owned by provincial governments will be enfolded into a number of national tobacco makers. Local trade barriers and protectionism are to be swept away, and newly restructured leading companies will encounter minimum provincial resistance in their sales and marketing. This general guideline fits Hong Ta extremely well, since it has been the number one tobacco maker of the nation for over a decade and is deemed a favourite in the government's restructuring campaign. The number of competitors and of small players will be drastically reduced, in order to give way to top players, such as Hong Ta, to forge alliances and to command larger market shares. No commercial corporation is to pass over this lucrative business opportunity of securing their leading position and of gaining huge returns. This is the main reason for Hong Ta to reset its priority on tobacco production and make necessary contraction to unrelated subsidiary projects set up under the previous diversification strategy. The urge from the provincial government of Yunnan for rapid increase in tobacco revenues plays a central role as well.

Hong Ta has retained its number one tobacco maker status and has failed miserably in becoming a giant in multiple industries. What will happen to its various sorts of investment projects remains to be seen.

An Assessment of Strategies of Diversification and "Core" Focus

The latter strategy is a decisive shift from an initial strong intention to build a non-tobacco business empire comparable with its traditional businesses. This shift guarantees short-term returns and benefits; it also increases the chance for the company to become a domestic and international heavyweight in the tobacco industry. The long term worries, however, will not disappear after this shift. Even if Hong Ta reached a top three position in the world, it would still have to face the problems those international giants have faced and are still facing. Worldwide anti-smoking campaigns and official bans hang above those tobacco makers, and government lawsuits corner them frequently with large sums of settlement paid out. International tobacco makers have not ceased their business operations thanks largely to marketing campaigns to developing countries where restrictions are lax and smoking populations are huge. Their rush into the China market creates additional challenges to Hong Ta in the domestic market and also indicates the limited prospects for its incomes from overseas markets when it grows into a significant international player.

Hong Ta is particularly vulnerable in a comparison with Philip Morris, in that it lacks outstanding results in diversification and receives negligible incomes from non-tobacco subsidiaries. If Philip Morris effectively controls subsidiaries in food industries as its secured source of income, Hong Ta has yet to establish a similar alternative business for the same purpose, despite its continued investments. This raises a critical question about a future re-entry into non-tobacco industries and of transforming the company into a multi-industry conglomerate. In short, Hong Ta has large gaps between it and Philip Morris, which has achieved goals in both core and diversified businesses. From this angle of observation, Hong Ta may have to review its market positioning and shift focus back to diversification at a later stage, with a more successful implementation.

As some analysts recommended for Hong Ta to hold on to its core businesses, the diversification strategy from the late 1990s on is accordingly regarded as a miscalculation of the trends in the industry and a rushed decision. In fact, that diversification warrants a more positive comment. Considering the factors listed above, domestic and international, a diversification towards non-tobacco industries certainly made sense. There are several reasons for this strategy to halt at Hong Ta. The company took its financial strength as the key in diversification and bought up stakes in other companies with amazing ease. The company did not and does not have the know-how and expertise to run enterprises in industries which require more complicated knowledge and skills than making cigarettes. Through buying and spending money on projects, Hong Ta added up the numbers of companies under its name but was unable to manage them in a professional way, let alone making them industry leaders. This lack of expertise led to the situation where Hong Ta could only approach or acquire minor players in the industries concerned. In the only joint venture with a recognised industry leader, the FAW-Hong Ta project, FAW will continue to focus on producing cars with an engine capacity of 1.8 litres or above and leave mini cars to be made by the joint venture. Even with this relatively better known venture, it will be a long way to go before Hong Ta receives some recognition as a real player in this most expensive and competitive industry.

Hong Ta was also lacking required personnel to set up and run new projects in unfamiliar territories. The company by and large relied on its staff from the Yunnan base to fill positions in far away locations and far-flung projects. It is said that Hong Ta dragged factory workers from its Yunnan tobacco lines to work in other cities. There was not only a problem of staff shortage but a more serious problem of lack of qualified staff. This severely limited Hong Ta's expansion drive and damaged its reputation as a respectable corporation as well. Its diversification projects failed to reach major cities such as Beijing and Shanghai; its subsidiaries in these two cities were mostly for the tobacco business instead of more diversified ones. Judging from Hong Ta's performance in this aspect, it is far from a recognised national conglomerate.

A further handicap to Hong Ta in diversification is its official owner—the Yunnan provincial government. Diversification requires long term planning, commitment and investment. The trouble is, as a state enterprise, Hong Ta is subject to directions from the provincial government. When diversification failed to produce tangible rewards in a few years, the provincial government got nervous. It was not merely a financial matter of losses; it also affected officials' political career in more ways than one. A drop in tax revenues made those officials look bad in the eyes of their superiors. When revenues kept shrinking and returns from new diversification projects remained feeble, the provincial government as the ultimate owner panicked and summarily sacked the CEO who embodied the diversification strategy. Weighing up the alternatives, the government and the company opted to consolidate to receive stable returns rather than risking further losses from expansion. To a great extent, the decision made to halt diversification and return to the core tobacco business was not a purely commercial one.

It is clear that Hong Ta from now on will follow its core businesses and treat diversification with caution. An ultimate fear of Hong Ta and analysts is that the company loses its core tobacco incomes, in addition to achieving little from huge investments on diversification. Its retrenchment and realignment serve as an acknowledgement of previous misjudgement in development direction and strategic planning. In a cyclical way, Hong Ta has returned to the business it knows best and has thrown out of the window some popular models of business strategies, including diversification.

Discussion Questions

1. Review and describe the factors for the diversification strategy and those for the "returning to the core" strategy. Find similarities and discrepancies between the two groups of factors and explain how these were used to devise and support each of the strategic decisions.

2. In regard to anti-smoking trends and difficulties multinational tobacco makers are facing, make an assessment on Hong Ta's future growth after its return to its core tobacco business; analyse the future directions in government policies on tobacco production and sales in China; and make an assessment on potential effects of policy shifts on Hong Ta's reliance on the tobacco business and its future development.

3. Make suggestions on how to enter new businesses under a diversification strategy and manage new projects in other industries; make projections on what will happen to those diversification projects with investment from Hong Ta, selecting one example to explain.

CASE 4   Legend: A Gamble Amid a Dot.Com Craze

Legend Group is a top national computer and IT corporation headquartered in Beijing. In brand name and business status, Legend is on par with the famed Haier Group, and these two leading corporations are universally regarded as pacesetters of Chinese enterprises. Studies and books on this amazing company have been overwhelming and sometimes suffocating. Large numbers of domestic companies watch closely what Legend, as well as Haier, is doing in operations and in strategies. They undoubtedly see Legend as an outstanding representative of new Chinese enterprises on the world stage and hold enormous respect for its achievements. With this background, this case study intends not to trace Legend's achievements in management, marketing, human resources etc. Other published writings have done just that. This case study will focus instead on the hard choices Legend made in recent years and on its strategic decisions, some of which might be judged as ambitious and rash. The two strategies under examination here are Legend's entry into the Internet business and its diversification.

Internet and dot.com Frenzy

Legend achieved market leader status in the computer industry through right pricing, marketing and distribution channels. Opening for business in 1984 under the auspices of the Chinese Academy of Sciences, Legend has grown into a colossal corporation in computer and IT businesses. It is more specifically a computer maker, holding around 30% of national market share in that industry. Its annual revenues in the 21st century average around US$3 billion, and Legend brand computers have commanded the market many years in a row. It also ranked as the fifth world player in computer sales in 2003, with an annual production capacity of 5 million units. As one of the most valuable Chinese brands, Legend was estimated as worth 27 billion yuan.

The company built up its own distribution networks from scratch and now has over 4,000 exclusive agents across the country. This is not matched by any of the players in the industry. The company also managed to transform itself into a shareholding company, with a listing on Hong Kong stock exchanges, founders and senior executives becoming shareholders, and the original investor of the Academy as the majority shareholder. This gave the company a fresh look and a precious chance to operate freely almost like a private enterprise. In 2001, the company founder, Mr. Liu, stepped back from running daily operations and even from setting long term goals. Legend Holding under Mr. Liu controls two companies: Legend Group and Digital China. The former became what is now referred to as Legend, while the latter moved to telecommunication and value-added services. A new and much younger CEO, Mr. Yang, took over the rein of Legend Group and was granted authority by the board to make strategic decisions on his own for this gigantic corporation. It seems that the issues of power transfer and leadership in a typical Chinese enterprise had been resolved. It is, however, in those years from the end of the 1990s that strategic decisions began to matter most to the company and tested the top management on its agility, vision and responsiveness.

Legend at a Crossroad

Strength

Considering Legend's position in the computer market, it seemed that the company did not have to do more. Business competitors were fairly distant threats, and current growth in computer sales was more than satisfactory. Legend could simply sit on this revenue and watch others compete. Its secured market leader position and financial strength granted it a leisured choice of engaging in something else or maintaining the status quo. In the area of strategic decision, Legend had not made serious mistakes, and it had kept that track record by clearing a series of obstacles on its path to being a leading national corporation.

Weakness

The comfortable life of leading the industry, however, caused Legend's top management to worry. Their reliance on a single computer business looked unfit for a large corporation of national standing, and profits extracted from each computer sold were getting smaller. This dropping in average profit level was an acute problem for Legend especially because the company relied on Intel to supply the CPU to fit in the computers it assembled, in the forms of Pentium chips and following upgrades. Legend was in effect subject to demands from Intel, and once Intel raised CPU prices, Legend would have to squeeze its operating costs until it was no longer feasible to do just that. Legend's top management had tried ways to get out of this weakness and find attractive business opportunities in other sectors.

Opportunities

There indeed emerged enticing business opportunities in other industries. Prominent among them, the new IT and Internet businesses were most appealing to Legend. This was a trend flowing in from the US. High-tech firms there were most favoured on stock markets and to investors, and a new dot.com firm fetched larger capitalisation than that for traditional old industrial giants with decades of standing. Even old-fashioned computer makers like IBM could not escape the embarrassment of being rated below new dot.com start-ups. This example in the same industry in particular sounded loud warnings to Legend's top management. In early 2000, the prime Internet company AOL took over Time Warner in a US$184 billion bid. This acquisition sent shockwaves to Chinese business leaders, those at Legend included. It dawned on Legend that immense new opportunities did exist in Internet and dot.com ventures, and new undertakings would realise Legend's ambition of becoming a multi-industry giant corporation and bypass a tedious and painful process of steady growth. Like many other Chinese enterprises, Legend began to look for opportunities more in IT and Internet sectors, rather than in industries they operated in.

Threats

Legend had little knowledge or idea of business models in Internet and dot.com sectors. Not many Chinese managers understood them either. Information on these new types of business came mostly from the US. Legend lacked the required expertise and professionals to set up and run new projects. This shortage would be a big handicap to Legend, as shown in following examples. In newly opened business sectors, Legend had to face competition and even suppression from a few established dot.com companies, which borrowed business models directly from the US and enjoyed first mover advantage in the China market. These companies, such as Sina, Sohu, and Netease, relied on their founders' thorough knowledge of the Internet and unlimited financial resources from overseas venture capitalists. If Legend made a decision to enter this market, it would face enormous pressure from these genuine dot.com companies and an up-hill battle to remain counted. These threats were beyond the imagination of Legend's top management at that time, and they realised the magnitude of these risks only too late.

Legend's founder Mr. Liu, like Mr. Zhang of Haier, is a big fan of Jack Welsh of GE (he went to attend an executive training course at GE's headquarters on management and strategies). The GE model of expansion and diversification, along with its achievements in these two areas, profoundly impacted on Mr. Liu's management thinking. The responsibility of running a large corporation like Legend forced him to seek alternatives for future growth. The stable status at Legend then implied to Mr. Liu more of a coming slowdown or a potential crisis.

Driving forces also came from another corner. Legend Hong Kong is a listed company, and fund managers there, such as Goldman Sachs, made repeated advices to Legend's top management, especially Mr. Liu, on investing in the Internet at an early stage. Their logic was simple: with Legend's outstanding performance in earnings and market share, its stock price would rise much higher if the company inserted new concept businesses such as the Internet in its portfolio. They saw little market value in Legend's computer making and enthusiastically promoted new economy businesses to Legend. Conventional criteria of stock pricing, for instance, the P/E value, lost their relevance, and contrasting examples already existed in the US, where small start-up companies were valued higher on stock markets than ancient industrial mammoths. Mr. Liu was persuaded by this reasoning partly because of his concerns over Legend's stock price on Hong Kong exchanges.

In Mr. Liu's own words, he saw only two paths to the goal of US$10 billion sales by 2005, from a figure of 3 billion in 2000. One was to concentrate on the products his company makes and expand its product sales to most international markets. This way, the company would be a brand name of world scale. The examples of this type are Intel, Cisco and many other single brand multinationals. The other choice was to stay in domestic markets and develop multiple products in various industries. This way, the company diversifies and takes over as many businesses as possible so long as they generate earnings. Expansion in the first case seemed a hard choice to Mr. Liu, as the company lacked financial resources and required expertise in overseas expansion. The mediocre performance of Legend's overseas push testifies to this weakness. The second choice of diversification appealed immensely to Legend's top management, especially Mr. Liu, as they knew this market well, and Legend's past success was primarily built on its strength in domestic markets, including the defeating of foreign brand PC makers since 1994. Legend top management was convinced by their track records and the feasibility of diversification in the coming new century. Eagerness to enter other growth sectors, together with the astonishing boom of dot.com business in the end of the 1990s, led to Legend's collective decision to diversify and enter Internet business.

In many ways, Legend's move mirrors the diversification of Hong Ta, discussed previously, in that current business earnings were taken as insufficient and revenues from other sectors were projected as greater. The difference is that Hong Ta has its stable tobacco revenues well protected, while Legend's revenues from computer sales did seem fragile in the long run. Diversification by Hong Ta was a typical risk aversion, while Legend's drive into Internet business was then regarded as taking up challenges of the new economy and hi-tech revolution, which was more commendable.

Internet Business Projects under Legend

The FM365.com project

Legend was a novice in Internet business when it conceived a diversification strategy at the time of the early dot.com craze in China. At the time this strategy was put into place, Legend's top management found out that they had nearly nothing to be a credible Internet firm, not even a section in the whole group company having similar business lines or capacity. There was definitely an urgent need to find or set up such sections as a showpiece of the company's determination to diversify and catch the bandwagon of Internet revolution.

In late 1999, Legend launched a website specifically serving the users of its Internet ready computers. The website provided Internet access and email services to Legend computer buyers. In April 2000, the business scope of this website was widened and its name changed to FM365.com as a formal Internet contents provider (ICP). This event served as a confirmation of Legend's official entry into Internet businesses and of the establishment of a subsidiary in the sector of information services.

The subsidiary aimed at reaching the status of three top Internet companies (Sina, Sohu and Netease). Normal ranking criteria were the numbers of registered users and page views. As FM365 was unable to draw more users to enter and view its contents, it relied on promotion and publicity campaigns. It attempted to act as a formal news channel and produced some sensational news reporting. It also got involved in reporting the Sydney Olympics and signed Hong Kong stars on to do company promotion. To widen the scope of business related to the Internet, FM365 tried numerous online programmes, including English teaching (in cooperation with a sought after training school of English for overseas education), e-commerce, stock market information and commentary, finance and economy, Chinese chess, school curriculum, entertainment, donations against poverty etc.

As more contents were added onto the FM365 website, budgets and the number of employees increased sharply at the subsidiary. Legend's top management, in particular Mr. Liu and his young CEO, paid extra attention to the project and delivered promises on funding to this subsidiary. To formally launch this FM365 website on 18 April 2000, Legend's top management decided to buy up all signboards along main boulevards of Beijing and nine other major cities and fill them with uniform advertising posters announcing the birth of this website. This unprecedented advertising campaign in China cost Legend over 100 million yuan. It undoubtedly attracted attention from the media and the public, and Mr. Liu was happy that Legend's transformation to an Internet company finally received some recognition. Mr. Liu even declared that the Legend of the future will be a full-fledged Internet company.

As Legend had little talent reserves in Internet fields and lacked real experts, it adopted aggressive recruiting approaches to hire people and fill positions. For this, Legend headquarters had to make concessions to its usually strict employment policies, in order to allow the recruiting process to match unprecedented demands on human resources. At the peak of the dot.com craze, any young engineers who commanded certain Internet knowledge and short work experience would be hired on the spot and paid high salaries. Legend, as a computer company, had apparent disadvantages in hiring, and the offers it made failed to attract key company executives from top Internet websites. On average, however, employees at FM365 received higher pay than those working in other sections of Legend.

Legend also relied on a mergers and acquisitions approach to expand its Internet business. Legend spent 300 million yuan on a top website company in 2000 when the latter was in financial crisis. Legend held 40% of shares and employed many staff from that Internet company to fill up the positions at FM365.

In June 2001, Legend announced that the US company AOL was introduced as a strategic shareholder of FM365 and would provide support services. The two companies invested US$100 million each on an Internet joint venture. In this deal, AOL agreed to pay the bills accumulated from past years on FM365; in return, AOL eyed business licences in telecommunication and news in the hands of FM365 and future computer sales at Legend. After this deal, FM365 remained in business for some time and eventually ceased to exist.

Full retreat from Internet business

The burst of dot.com bubbles and the stock market crash of 2001 made Chinese Internet companies live in constant fear. Those top three Internet providers suffered badly on the US stock markets, while their minor competitors in China collapsed in droves. Legend responded at a relatively fast pace to this upheaval, as fast as it entered the Internet business. As a traditional company essentially focused on returns and profits, Legend top management abandoned those Internet projects which had not made money. FM365 swiftly lost its favour and suffered a massive 30% layoff of its employees, and this was a clear sign of the end of the Internet adventure by Legend. Furthermore, by the end of 2003, Legend announced the termination of its Internet cooperation with partner AOL, which was facing its own mounting problems in the US.

With a deceased FM365 and termination of cooperation with the quintessential Internet company AOL, Legend sharply downgraded its expectations and made a clear departure from Internet related business from 2002. Its huge spending on the Internet, including that on FM365, on acquisitions of other big and small Internet companies in a buying spree (they disappeared), on cooperation with specialised websites such as travel and English learning (some of them survived), on promotion and hardware etc. ran up to several hundreds of million yuan. If the failed joint venture with AOL is counted (US$100 million from Legend), the total figure of spending could be over 1 billion yuan. These spending was a complete waste, producing negligible revenues for Legend. The only compensation for these Internet ventures is perhaps that they indirectly helped Legend raise funds of billions of yuan on Hong Kong stock exchanges. Those investors in Legend stock believed that the company was making a successful transformation and would reap huge benefits from its Internet business. Legend stock price once shot up to over HK$70 at the height of the Internet frenzy. As the bubble burst and Legend halted all investment in related sectors, those investors lost as well, and Legend stock price at Hong Kong exchanges has since hovered between HK$2 and HK$4 in past years.

A more serious matter is that Legend top management suffered a huge credibility loss. Their previous leadership had demonstrated right decision making. This time around, the top management, from the founder Mr. Liu to his young successor and senior executives, was unable to resist the strong temptation from the booming Internet frenzy. Their judgement proved questionable and strategies unsuccessful, and Legend's reputation in the industry, besides its earnings, went down as a result. This leading company suffered its first major setback in its operations in two decades. As a middle level manager of Legend summarises in a book on this gamble, Legend is puffing under its own weight.

Diversification, Core PC Business and New Leadership

The dot.com fiasco at Legend is only one part of its diversification drive. Legend's top management had long set the ultimate goal to become an internationalised IT company, and the model without doubt is the diversified GE in the US. For this purpose, Legend drew up a three-year plan in 2001, which coincided with the transfer of the CEO position and authority to Mr. Yang. The plan contained ambitious goals to be achieved by the end of this period. Legend would focus on service, high-tech and internationalisation. The total revenues of Legend Group had to reach over 60 billion yuan, making Legend a company close to the top 500 world corporations in size. This translated into a 50% growth in revenues every year from 2001. Legend also projected to reach the goals of income from services at 10% in three years and 30% in five years. This target setting apparently took reference from an international giant IMB, which maintains such a ratio. These ambitious plans of the new CEO were laid out to demonstrate both continuity of and divergence from past practices of Legend.

Under the previous leadership of Mr. Liu, Legend had a strict decision making process on major strategies. The top management followed three principal entry criteria: strong demand in the market and from customers, large profits or potentially large profits, and synergy with Legend's current businesses. The top management had to go through lengthy and thorough discussion processes to ensure minimum chance of mistakes in predictions. The bottom line is that an entry decision primarily depends on projected contributions to the company. Judging by these criteria, the entry into Internet business was expected to bring increased revenues at the time of that boom. Legend's top management also approved the three-year plan rolled out in 2001, confirming a full diversification drive in the hope of gaining an advantage on the basis of multiple income sources. The selection decision on which industry to enter was then left to the new CEO.

To achieve this great leap forward, Legend had to find profitable new businesses on top of its still solid foundation on the PC business. Diversification is a choice managers regularly face, out of searching for new sources of income for future growth. Legend's secured market leader position and situation at the time of diversification indicate that this shift was made not out of potential saturation or imminent crisis. A lack of urgency should have given Legend much more room and time to make necessary adjustments. This course of transformation, however, was drastically shortened by the three-year plan approved by the company board. Legend was eager to change its image and direction.

Major Diversification Projects

Apart from the decision to jump on board the Internet bandwagon, Legend made other efforts to diversify. As its Internet ventures ceased to exist, investment in other sectors became more prominent and formed parts of Legend's business empire.

A major diversification drive was to enter the mobile phone business. By Legend's selection criteria, this industry fitted well. It demonstrated amazing growth potential and showed rising figures of users and unit sales. This growth was backed by enlarged phone networks managed by China Telecom and China Unicom, improved quality in phone communication, and dropping price levels. Mobile phones were once the symbol of the wealthy and privileged, thanks to its high prices and limited access, but by the end of 1990s, it increasingly became a common communication device for average wage earners. The market grew sharply in size, and domestic phone makers began to have an upper hand over foreign brand makers. This surge was in line with the new round of consumption of major items during the reform years (as discussed in a previous chapter on consumption). Anticipation of a boom in mobile phone sales became a regular feature in business analyses and surveys. The phone consumption caught the eye of Legend's top management, and the close links between PC and mobile phone provided them with additional confidence, since this business to be entered was undoubtedly in the general category of IT businesses. All in all, the mobile phone business fitted well with Legend's standard criteria, and an entry decision was thus made.

Legend spent 90 million yuan in 2001 to form a joint venture with a major electrical applicances maker in Fujian province. Legend obtained a 60% stake in the joint venture, so that it could obtain an official permit to produce mobile phones legally. Legend manufactures "Legend" brand mobile phones in GSM and CDMA modes and intended to become a top national phone maker in three years. Legend invested over 100 million yuan on R&D to design and improve mobile phones made there. This investment alone dragged down total performance and made a 25 million yuan loss in 2003. Due to Legend's persistence in developing hand-held devices and positive projections of future wireless applications between various kinds of electronic goods, the mobile phone business remains a key part of its development plan and continues to receive investment from Legend. During the financial quarter between April and June in 2004, mobile phone business made a contribution of 11% to the total revenues at Legend, being the only non-PC business which achieved a double digit increase. For 2004, Legend planned to produce 3 million sets of mobile phones annually, up from 1.67 million sets in the previous year. This business finally made a crucial turn and made some profits in 2004.

The company entered a related industry and became one of the digital camera makers in China. It launched several series of low-end cameras to sell to middle level families. This is a fairly new business in China, with major brands sold on the market coming from foreign manufacturers. Legend has followed market and consumption trends and taken this as a new core business under the company's planning. It has developed technology to build and sell a series of small sized cameras with specifications of up to 4 million pixels.

Legend also found partners in other businesses. The company formed a joint venture with a Singaporean corporation to invest in a logistics company in 2002. It joined hands with China Merchants Bank to launch and promote online wireless banking, in which Legend provided wireless palm devices and the bank handled transactions and accounts. In the first case, Legend followed economic trends or fashion at the time for wider application of logistics management, as foreign multinationals relied on massive logistics operations to run their regular business smoothly. This has become more popular in the early 21st century, and many Chinese companies joined in the race. In the second case, Legend was aiming at transplanting the GE diversification model, which receives considerable incomes from financial management on top of its manufacturing complexes. In a quite unrelated sector, Legend entered the real estate business with a bang. Mr. Liu announced that Legend planned to spend 3 billion yuan on real estate projects, managed by a holding company under Legend Group. The company already completed work on a number of industrial projects and Legend's own headquarters building in Beijing, which cost 300 million yuan.

A key part of this three-year plan is internationalisation. Legend has been cautious and relatively unsuccessful in entering overseas markets. Its brands seldom sold to buyers in other countries. This weakness was addressed in the three-year plan, and a target was set at 30% of sales revenues from overseas markets by 2006, a significant jump from less than 5% at the time this plan was announced. Since the brand name Legend had been registered by many enterprises in other countries, Legend (the group company) made the decision to change its name in English to **Lenovo** for overseas promotion campaigns. This word contains meanings of Legend and innovation,

indicating the company's intention to emphasise its technology core in their products. The Chinese name and logo are retained for domestic markets. Some analysts likened this name change to that which happened at the Japanese electronic giant National, which was changed to Panasonic for wider acceptance from foreign customers. Legend has established seven overseas subsidiaries, six of them in Western Europe and one in the US. This illustrates the importance of European markets to Legend.

Moving Back to Core Businesses

By early 2004, it was clear that Legend would not meet its targets stipulated in the plan. Total sales revenues hovered over 20 billion yuan (see Table 18.2). That is far from reaching the 60 billion yuan target and in fact was close to the 2001 level. This stagnation is of course the result of multiple factors, including huge investment on other businesses, collapse of Internet businesses, and little improved PC sales under fierce market competition.

At a shareholders meeting in Hong Kong, after reviewing business results of the past years, Legend CEO Mr. Yang conceded publicly that the company failed to realise the goals set in the three-year plan. He put forth causes to failure as overestimating growth potential in the market, thus setting higher targets; market competition in PC and in other industries becoming more intense after China's WTO accession; and that the company had inadequate knowledge and management capacity for an all-out diversification. With sales of company stakes, Legend announced a meagre growth in profits. Mr. Yang certainly felt the heat and made public his worry over the company's survival.

At another shareholders meeting six months later, the situation had not improved dramatically. PC businesses, including servers and laptops, still held over 85% of revenues Legend generated. This secured business has been under threat from a dropping market share and

Table 18.2 Annual revenues of Legend						
	1999	3/2000	3/2001	3/2002	3/2003	3/2004
Revenues (in billion HK$)	11.6	17.4	27.2	20.8	20.2	23.1

(Adapted from Lenovo's corporate website)

aggressive advances made by Dell in domestic markets. IT businesses, including Internet, managed only to contribute 1% in revenues, despite enormous investment and promotion. Legend's mobile phone sales has gained remarkable growth; the trouble was that it had made consecutive losses, the brand stays in the second tier group, far from catching up with the first tier players, and market saturation in the mobile phone business becomes apparent as the number of players shoots up. In other sectors, Legend remains at a stage of investment and will not see sizable earnings for a long while.

Under these circumstances, Legend made a swift turn in strategy and began to draw up a new three-year plan. The plan is in many aspects similar to Hong Ta's policy reversal of "returning to the core". In the following three years, Legend will return to its core business and concentrate on PC related sales. The company must invest in those businesses which generate earnings. In this regard, the PC business is irreplaceable to Legend. The new mobile phone business seems to fit in well in the restructuring of Legend and has shown certain potential in growth and in earnings. The new three-year plan retains this business as a strategic focus and core, and perhaps a growth sector for the future. Mr. Liu personally named PCs and mobile phones as core businesses, but no other, in his analysts meeting on 11 August 2004. His words firmly backed Mr. Yang's new plan.

Legend will also develop effective sales networks and boost sales of PCs across the country. As the focus shifts back to PCs, Legend will have to pay more attention to retail sales and customer promotion. These will cover two sub-strategies. One is to develop networks in second and third tier cities and towns, to target rural, as well as urban, consumers. Legend made projections that the top tier cities (Beijing, Shanghai, and Guangzhou) and major provincial capitals will see slower growth in PC sales, due to a 70% level of PC household ownership. This forces Legend to move down the ladder and seek sales growth in lower tier cities and towns. The other is a consideration to implement a Dell-like direct sell system. Legend has relied on its own distribution channels through authorised agents for most sales and resisted a direct sell approach. To keep satisfactory market shares and fending off attacks from Dell, Legend gave this approach a serious thought and is going to implement it in the near future.

To further utilise price advantages, according to Michael Porter's competitive edges, Legend launched low price computers with AMD CPU, instead of Intel CPU. The price difference between the two CPU brands provided Legend an additional opportunity to lower their computer prices further, in order to penetrate low-end markets. This switch in CPU supplier has put certain strains on Legend's relationship with Intel. In response, Intel may switch sides and adopt a more positive approach to support Legend's domestic competitors.

Strategies and Leadership

The failure in achieving set goals laid out in the first three-year plan, and for that matter the setting out of those ambitious goals in the first place, seriously undermined the trust and confidence on the leadership of the new CEO from his employees as well as from business analysts. His first three-year plan is now seen as an over ambitious leap forward. Regardless of the Internet fiasco, diversification drives into other sectors are widely questioned. So far, no solid, significant returns or potential has materialised from those various investments, except that from the mobile phone business. Mr. Yang had to defend himself in front of shareholders and devise a second three-year plan as an urgent remedy. In a stark contrast to the first, this plan made full scale retreat and contraction, initiated restructuring, and refocused priorities. Mr. Liu also came out to defend his successor by saying that the decision was a collective one, and that temporary setbacks are acceptable. He mildly raised questions about Mr. Yang's earlier plan. To him, the top management was not ready for a full frontal diversification, and their attention on the core PC business was easily distracted by new ventures, which indicates a lack of capability of handling overall management of a giant corporation.

This lack of capability is shown by a small incident as well. At a shareholders meeting in Hong Kong, the top management was asked the question why while Legend's profits increased in the past year at only 3.5%, payments to board members in salary and bonuses, increased by 25.6%. Mr. Liu, as chairman of the board, was evidently rattled by this enquiry and announced on the spot that all board members would receive a 40% pay cut and Mr. Yang, the CEO, would have his pay reduced by 50%. This impromptu promise was later formally confirmed in a statement from the company's spokesperson. It is a common feature in modern management that executives give themselves pay cuts when business performance or stock prices drop sharply. This is a clever way to demonstrate their responsibility for guarding shareholders' interest and to gain their continued confidence as well. Most management teams of Chinese companies have seldom taken this approach, and Legend seems to have fared no better. The fact that these pay cuts had to be announced first by the company founder does indicate a lack of capability of corporate management among Legend top executives.

On a balance sheet, financial losses of a failed diversification have been minimal, and Legend's core PC business has so far been immune to bad news of sharp drops. In Mr. Liu's comforting words, those failed projects are prices paid for learning the right way of management. Legend's financial state remains sound, though a little disappointing to shareholders. As long as the PC business continues to generate sizeable incomes, Legend is relatively free from the danger of breaking down. This also provides a safe base for the top management to launch further projects and ventures. On the other hand, Legend faces threats on three fronts. Its primary task is to maintain a leading position in domestic market shares and neutralise its most formidable rival in the PC business, Dell. An increasingly threatening competitor is TCL, with firm backing from Intel. On top of dealing with these strong rivals, Legend must find ways to sharply increase its own PC revenues. Sales figures have hovered around 20 billion yuan for years. Even if the 60 billion yuan target in the first three-year plan was over optimistic, a figure well above the 20 billion mark should be achieved soon, in order to secure Legend's leading position in domestic PC market and make it a recognised force on the world stage.

The next threat comes from an age-old question in business: **when and how to diversify?** Chinese companies with relatively large sizes face this question every now and then. Even after the failed diversification on its first attempt, diversifying business investment is inevitable for Legend. The company is currently happy with some of the results from the first diversification, since its mobile phone business is operational and on the rise. This new business, however, will soon be a hotly contested ground with an overcapacity and drop in average profit margins. Since Legend phone brand currently can only squeeze into the second tier group of players, it could be easily victimised by larger players during an industry-wide consolidation. To survive such a crash, Legend has to make continued investment in technology and equipment. Another alternative appears to be in digital camera production. This is a growth business for domestic manufacturers like Legend, and there seems a long way from saturation. With firm financial backing and smart brand promotion, Legend could be able to take up a big market share. Inevitably, major players in this market have to face ultra intense competition from foreign brand names, especially from Japanese brands, which are industry pacesetters. The performance of and contributions to Legend from these two new businesses remain to be seen, and Legend will have to continue its search for more business opportunities outside its PC territory.

As discussed before in this chapter, Legend made the choice of the first diversification partly out of its worries about overseas expansion. It is possible for a company not to diversify and instead concentrate on its core business. This requires, first, advanced technology in the hands of the company concerned, and second, its ability to successfully sell its core products to markets across the world. Legend is not good at either, its CPU coming from Intel or AMD and its overseas sales piecemeal. The company has yet to make the door open to its products in the US. In nature, Legend is a domestic "dragonhead" enterprise. This sits uncomfortably with its declared goal of an "**internationalised Legend**" and with 30% sales revenues from overseas markets by 2010. Legend top management needs to seriously consider the feasibility of this goal. A key consideration is that overseas expansion should not severely damage its domestic market shares and core businesses.

(On 8 December 2004, Legend announced that it paid US$ 1.25 billion to take over the PC business of IBM. After this acquisition, Legend is to become the number three PC maker of the world, after Dell and HP. Its annual sales will reach about 100 billion yuan, and annual output will reach over 11 million PC sets. The acquisition achieved two goals: the recognition of an "internationalised Legend", and the target of sharply lifting annual sales figures from the previous plateau of 20 billion yuan. The tasks ahead are daunting for Legend, which has to solve problems in synergy and face lows in PC markets around the world in coming years. It is not surprising that the boss of Dell saw a pessimistic outlook for this acquisition).

The key question is Legend's positioning. As a declared leading IT company, Legend may choose one of the alternatives to make it happen: diversification or expansion. Based on the company's current financial state, this divergence implies a focus on domestic markets or on overseas markets. After a damaging setback of a magnitude not seen in Legend's development path before 2000, the company now adopts a more conservative approach in its second three-year plan. The focus is on core businesses and on domestic markets. It can be said that this is a temporary retreat and gathering of strength during the time set in the plan. As a saturation of the PC market nears, it is interesting to see what choice, diversification or expansion, will be selected again at the expiry time of this plan. One tangible benefit from this retreat and refocus is that Legend has lowered its target of entering the top 500 world enterprises club, and its real business will immensely benefit from uninflated figures and goals.

Summary

The above four cases represent a variety of operational patterns of Chinese and Hong Kong companies. The central strategy for the two leading companies in their industries, Hong Ta and Legend, is diversification. Similarities abound for both of them. Diversification was a catch phrase among Chinese business executives in the 1990s. This tendency emerged strongly after Western management models were vigorously introduced and Chinese companies grew to certain large sizes. The world's leading diversified corporation, GE, was a favourite model of Chinese managers, and GE practices were enshrined in Chinese MBA and EMBA course textbooks. Many such practices were faithfully followed and influenced industry leaders such as Mr. Liu of Legend. There seemed no reason why a large Chinese company could not make a strategic decision on diversification.

Another main reason for the popularity of diversification is the impatience of Chinese executives over steady growth. They desire to have company sizes multiplied, in order to leave competitors far behind. As most of these large companies lack their core technology and specialised advantages over others, they tend to transfer resources and attention to another unexplored sector when the current market was filled with overcapacity. Higher profit margins in other sectors appeared more attractive, and shifting funds and energy there might result in quick returns. In both Hong Ta and Legend cases, a deep fear of operating in only one sector cast great influence on diversification decisions made by top management teams.

The tide turned from the late 1990s, when a row of large Chinese companies which diversified began to suffer badly from overstretching and even stepping into their own demise. Diversification strategy in general, and its application in China in particular, is under closer scrutiny. Hong Ta and Legend have so far survived their over exposure to many related and unrelated businesses. The logical step next is to return to the core business and improve productivity and competitiveness. A major problem of their diversification was that the huge costs involved affected overall performance. With a focus on core businesses, these companies will be able to grow with higher levels of efficiency.

The case of the Hong Kong company illustrates certain critical requirements for doing business in China. Although this company was fully Chinese in nature, it failed to heed significant changes in the environment and thus could not turn good business opportunities into stable operations. The case of Zhuhai airport demonstrates a wide-ranging government involvement in business operations. Large investment projects often come with significant government backing and control. Considerable shares of economic activities in China are government-related, in projects, in investment, and in management.

These cases of Chinese companies may serve to provide foreign investors with a fuller understanding of the business environment and patterns of operations in this market.

Discussion Questions

1. What are the major factors which led to Legend's entry into Internet businesses? If you are in a decision making position at Legend, would you make the same entry decision or otherwise? How would you cope with a situation of endless spending and little revenues, typical of a dot.com company? Would you make further investments or cut losses and exit?

2. Given the situation of Legend now, make suggestions on a proper balance among businesses that Legend should undertake. What would happen in three years time to the core PC business in China? What would happen to the mobile phone and digital camera businesses? Suppose Legend has unlimited (huge) investment funds for diversification, which one of these two businesses do you think should be the main place for investment?

Category II: Case Studies of Business Strategies

This second category covers foreign multinationals operating in the China market. The four cases listed are world renowned corporations in different industries. Coming in with similar company goals and rich experience of doing global business, they experience varying outcomes from the decisions they made. This is the reason for a review here of their performance and, based on these cases, for dissecting the patterns and trends in FDI related businesses. Similar to the sections in Category I, the focus in these sections is on the particular business strategies of these companies and outcomes, leaving generalised studies on management or marketing untouched.

CASE 1 Guangzhou Peugeot: Failure in Upgrading

Guangzhou Peugeot

Peugeot is part of PSA (Peugeot Société Anonyme), a French car making corporation that is the second biggest in Europe. Unlike its German and US competitors, Peugeot produces mainly medium sized family cars, excluding the types of luxury cars, sports cars or SUVs. At an early time of China's reforms, Peugeot formed a joint venture with a Guangzhou factory which made cars and other types of vehicles. The deal was signed in 1985, with five partners involved: the Guangzhou

Automotive Industry Corp taking 46% of shares, Peugeot with 22%, China Trust and Investment with 20%, a finance company with 8%, and a Paris based bank with 4%.

The joint venture was designed to produce Peugeot F504 and F505 cars. Its capacity was initially set at 30,000 vehicles a year, and later investment by partners aimed at building satellite factories to supply most Peugeot cars with locally made parts. The models introduced were with the standards of the late 1970s, relatively advanced for Chinese car buyers of the 1980s. Foreign cars were still rare on streets, and Peugeot brand cars sold well to work units and government departments. Some private car buyers came from newly rich businesspeople in southern China. There was a widespread demand for sedan cars in China after the open door policy was implemented, and most foreign car models, except Jeep from the US, became extremely popular. Peugeot gained its market share of 16% by 1991 and sold over 85,000 vehicles by the mid 1990s. These are remarkable results considering competition from better known imported German and Japanese car brands. An early advantage was that Peugeot cars were perhaps the only foreign brand available on the market that was made locally on a large scale. The Santana sedan from Shanghai VW, which dominated China's car market for over a decade, had not established its superior status and popularity to the Chinese customer. At best, these two European brands were neck and neck throughout the 1980s.

The following downturn was a little too dramatic. The Guangzhou Peugeot joint venture suffered financial losses in consecutive years and lost market share as well. The number one problem is widely recognised as the aging of Peugeot's car models produced at the joint venture. This would be an exceptional case in the motor car industry these days that mainstream car models provided to customers were unchanged for over a decade. F504 and F505 were the models for the 1970s, so the Guangzhou joint venture in effect produced car models that were 20 years old by the middle of the 1990s. Since these standard models ceased to be produced in Europe, let alone spending on R&D on them, there were no upgrades or modifications to the models at the Guangzhou factory.

In decisions regarding models and upgrading, Peugeot appeared passive, sticking to these models and refusing to add new features and technology to them. This demonstrates a typical pattern of prolonging product life cycle by the company which puts the product on the market. While new car models were launched by Shanghai VW, First Auto Work, and even Peugeot's sister company Citroen in a separate joint venture with Dongfeng Motors, Peugeot continued to make these two models only. F504 and F505 in their standard shapes looked so old on streets that even their owners felt a little embarrassed. Chinese car buyers in the 1990s stopped picking Peugeot cars as one of their first choices. Peugeot cars sold mainly in southern coastal regions of China, where people with new money changed their cars more often than those in inland regions. A 20-year old model could not appeal to them at all, and switching to other models on the market became inevitable. In fact, the Chinese word for the Peugeot brand is quite romantic and attractive, meaning "elegant" or "handsome". Those outdated and increasingly shabby appearances of Peugeot cars certainly could not match these descriptive Chinese words and ruined Peugeot's reputation further.

Deriving from this problem of model upgrading, Peugeot developed wide-ranging frictions with the municipal government throughout the years. The government was not at all happy to see stagnation and a loss of business to other regions. As the most vibrant, free and prosperous region of China, the Guangzhou government could not stand having a second rate car factory in their territory and a public embarrassment to their records of foreign investment. Peugeot's relationship with the government was cordial at best, and their 22% shareholding, with no increase for years, indicated to others their lack of intention to stay in the Guangzhou joint venture for long. This lack of commitment caused quarrels with the government, especially in follow up investments and priority of investment. Peugeot had no plan to enlarge production capacity well above its initial 30,000 vehicles a year. Investment plans on newer models of 405 and 406 did not receive adequate funding and got suspended. This in turn further soured already strained relationships between Peugeot and the municipal government.

From the point of analysis of decision making, Peugeot might not have had the intention to stay in the China market for long after all. Its focus, of course, was firmly on Europe, especially after its failure in the US market. As a minor player worldwide while facing attacks from VW in China, Peugeot grew pessimistic and adopted a very conservative, defensive approach in its operations. It watched the losses in revenues and in market shares with indifference to some degree and held off further investment. The French company had not planned for long-term prospects of the joint venture, and even with those outdated car models, its intention to transfer technology appeared weak. Locally-made components reached over 65%, while key parts and components continued to be imported. Peugeot suffered from losses at the joint venture, but it gained from selling CKD (complete knock down) kits to Guangzhou Peugeot. As the Chinese currency RMB devalued sharply against French francs since the early 1990s, Peugeot received a handy advantage in larger incomes from parts sales, on which the Guangzhou production lines relied. This situation fit Peugeot's conservative strategy and approach fine, and its overall risks remained low. Guangzhou Peugeot shouldered the bulk of losses, where Peugeot was not a majority shareholder.

Due to these passive responses, the Guangzhou Peugeot joint venture stepped into loss-making territory, with losses starting to build up from 1994 and mounting to nearly 3 billion yuan and total assets valued at 2.8 billion yuan. F504 and F505 were nearly completely abandoned by Chinese car buyers. In 1997, Guangzhou Peugeot had a miserable sales figure of just over 1,000 vehicles. It had to make a fire sale to clear the stocks in the following year, selling at an unbelievably low price of 100,000 yuan per vehicle.

In that year, quarrels became irreconcilable, and both partners intended to exit from this relationship. For Peugeot, it was the painful realisation that it could not recoup the losses and compete effectively with much bigger players, especially the German car marker VW, which rose to dominate the market with a tight grip. For the Guangzhou municipal government, they were deeply disappointed with the performance of the Peugeot project and completely lost confidence in this French car maker. The huge losses called for financial subsidies from the government, after initial contributions of a couple of billion yuan. This depleting loss became unbearable as time went by. Furthermore, the government was eager to get rid of this burden and sign of bad reputation, in order to seek an alternative and qualified car manufacturer. Under the prevailing state regulations concerning the motor car industry, a city cannot set up two car joint ventures and build two car plants. The Guangzhou Automotive Industry Corp. was a relatively small player in the industry, considered unfit for the status of Guangzhou, the richest city in China. As Peugeot lost its appeal and convincing capacity for further development, the municipal government decided to end this partnership as soon as possible, so that they could vacate the place for a more suitable car maker. The goal was to form an alliance with a market leader to boost the city's reputation. This would also look good on city officials' resumes.

In 1997, Peugeot and the Guangzhou government signed an agreement which transferred Peugeot's 22% shareholdings to Chinese partners, with a symbolic price of 1 franc paid to Peugeot. The Chinese partners took up the obligation to pay off all remaining debts. This French car maker made a full retreat from the China market. Peugeot promised at the time of retreat to continue to maintain its after-sales services for vehicles it had produced in China. By 2004, there were still around 20,000 Guangzhou Peugeot-made vehicles in use in China. It is possible today that one can occasionally spot an old Peugeot F505 in the traffic.

Peugeot and Honda

The perils of Guangzhou Peugeot gave the French parent company a bad name in the industry, and with the withdrawal of some other foreign multinationals from China in those years, such as Whirlpool, foreign analysts and the media raised serious concerns of whether this was a market worth investing in when even big names got burned. In retrospect, Peugeot adopted some questionable strategies for its China operations. Its mistakes are explicitly exposed in its comparisons with Guangzhou Honda, and with its own re-entry into the China market at a later stage.

Peugeot's overall strategy was conservative and short-term, entering the market without full commitment. This approach was shown in other strategies of Peugeot.

Peugeot adopted a one model product strategy for the market, without improvement or upgrading. This came from its contingency-nature plans for the joint venture and the overall conservative approach. The Guangzhou Peugeot project was taken as a trial, and the company could leave the market at a time it desired. With existing production capacity and sales, the company sought not to aggressively expand its business scale.

In relationships with government authorities, Peugeot failed in nurturing right *guanxi*, in order to conduct meaningful and constructive communication and resolve outstanding issues. In bad times, partnerships were under increasing strains, which could lead to the breaking point. *Guanxi* is particularly important in these occasions to soothe emotions and smooth things out. Due to conflicts of interest and divergence in priorities, Peugeot no longer received backing from the municipal government, and a termination of the joint venture was inevitable.

Peugeot moved slowly to adapt to changing consumption trends in the car market. At its early stage of production, car sales were primarily for work units (state enterprises and government departments). As there were small quantities of cars available on the market, work units needed to obtain quotas to buy cars. On the other hand, money was not a problem, since these work units obtained allocations from their regular budgets submitted to their superiors. The competition was mainly in getting quotas from authorities in charge. Under these circumstances, Guangzhou Peugeot had no problems selling cars they made for customers. This situation changed dramatically in the late 1990s, when private car buyers began to outnumber work unit buyers, and when private car ownerships extended to middle class members. These new customers had their own selection criteria and tastes, and the market was flooded with different car models and types. Customers with new choices would more likely refuse to buy an old model Peugeot. The French company responded to this change too passively, almost showing no sign of concern.

Guangzhou Honda offers a stark contrast to Guangzhou Peugeot, from which we can see more clearly what went wrong with this French car marker (see Table 19.1). Despite Peugeot's endeavours at an early stage of reforms and its rather pleasing business performance, it chose

Table 19.1   Comparisons between Peugeot and Honda in Guangzhou

	Goals	Models	Capacity	*Guanxi*
Peugeot	Short term	Two (504, 505)	30,000 vehicles to 50,000 vehicles suspended	Low marks
	Follower	No upgrades		Nominal
	Trial in China	No replacement		Conflicts
Honda	Long term	One (current model Accord)	30,000 vehicles	High marks
	Market leader	Upgrades	200,000 vehicles	Cooperative
	Base in China	New models	(2004)	Contributions (taxes, jobs)

to halt any further expansion and to stay with its then increasingly insufficient capacity. The misreading of the changes in the market (neglecting market research) and uncertainty of the government's opening policies led to fast aging models and sharp drops in sales. This French car maker, however, made a quick strategic decision on a market exit, based on its considerations of loss-cutting. The decision may be a right choice for the company at the time, when it saw no immediate prospects of recovery and would not provide further funding. Overall, it is unfortunate that a pioneer in the industry first hesitated on expansion and then left the China market in a rush. Its sister company, Citroen, fared much better in the same industry. Even the US car maker in a more desperate situation (Beijing Jeep) staggered along until its rescue by Chrysler and remains in operation today. The exit of Peugeot has been listed as a prime example of how tough the China market was and is; this exit also illustrates certain unwise ways of doing business in this market, as described above. The jumping of ship has made it hard for Peugeot to regain confidence from authorities and the public, especially when it attempted to make a re-entry decision.

Guangzhou Honda took over the plant abandoned by Peugeot in 1998. The Japanese car maker paid US$200 million in exchange for a partnership with the Guangzhou Automotive Industry Corp. in a 50: 50 ratio. For that, Honda obtained a fully operational plant of a production capacity up to 50,000 vehicles a year and a fully functional, experienced workforce and management team. Honda could start production without being bothered by lengthy training and restructuring.

Honda also offered current models of the popular Accord from the beginning (US market 98 model), having them made at the plant as promised. In following years, every upgrading and new generation of Accord models made by Honda in Japan was simultaneously implemented at Guangzhou Honda. The Guangzhou government and car buyers welcomed this swiftness in upgrading with their surging purchase orders. Guangzhou Honda has been used to long waiting lists and minimum stocks. At the height of Accord sales, car buyers made additional payments of up to 70,000 yuan, to jump the queue, to buy a roughly 350,000 yuan new Accord. Guangzhou Honda added more car models like Fit, Odyssey and others in later years. In 2003, this joint venture sold 117,000 vehicles nationwide, ranked fourth in the industry, securing its top position under stiff competition. The number of vehicles sold in 2004 rose to 200,000. Considering that this joint venture was made between a second tier foreign car maker and a regional government, without the full backing and coordination granted to the big three by the central government, this self-made entity is indeed a marvellous achievement.

Guangzhou Honda stunned the car industry in another field: its ability to gain profits from the day the production lines started running. With ready facilities left over by Peugeot, Guangzhou Honda made full use of them and switched production lines to manufacture Honda cars in the minimum time required. In March 1999, the first Accord rolled off the assembly line and was sold right away. This ignited a rolling process, during which the finished cars were sold quickly, and the money came back to finance the rest of the assembly work, in paying for parts and workers' salaries etc. Guangzhou Honda lost no time in between production and sales. With its annual production capacity of 30,000 vehicles, the joint venture earned 1 billion yuan in net profits in its first year of operation. In fact, the total sales by vehicle was 31,000, above its normal capacity, as Guangzhou Honda squeezed in more parts for finished cars to accommodate customer demands. Gaining significant amount of profits in the first year of operation is an exceptional achievement for motor car makers, domestic or foreign.

The success of Guangzhou Honda at the exact site of Peugeot makes interesting points regarding enterprise strategies. Honda made grounds whereas Peugeot lost theirs; this speaks volumes of pitfalls in Peugeot's planning, decisions and operations. Peugeot's worse record may be explained by the deteriorating business environment, as some analysts observed, in terms of unfriendly local government bureaux and demanding partners. As shown above, these seem to be minor obstacles in light of a suspension of model upgrading and of long term commitment by Peugeot. It can be said that the withdrawal by Peugeot is a courageous decision, making a decisive departure when loss making seemed irreversible. This decisiveness, however, could have been more effectively applied in refocusing and restructuring of operations under Peugeot's management at the joint venture. It is hard to tell what Peugeot would make of Honda's spectacular success in Guangzhou, a city Peugeot probably looks back on with painful memories.

Peugeot's Re-entry

Peugeot's predicament in Guangzhou is highlighted by its own decision years later to enter the same market again.

From 2003, Peugeot was undertaking negotiations with Chinese partners on joint ventures in car making plants. The first new model Peugeot 307 rolled off the assembly line in April 2004 at a joint venture between PSA and Dongfeng Motors in Wuhan. Peugeot CEO Frederic Saint-Geours admitted that "we have learned the lesson from the failure of our operation in Guangdong that we have to co-operate with a big Chinese automaker to produce our latest products and build perfect sales and service networks, if we want to be successful in China".

Considerations and Opportunities

Unlike the situation in the early 1990s when Peugeot first encountered financial difficulties and downward sales, China in the early 21st century suddenly became a darling of car makers around the world. The boom in car sales, described by Chinese analysts as a "volcano eruption", made China the world's fastest-growing car market. Its 2 million passenger car production in 2003 exceeded projections of most industry analysts and created heightened expectations of market potential to be realised soon. This optimism was supported by the sign that by now private car ownerships have become commonplace and will generate more sales than that from government purchases. Most multinational car makers have joined the flood of investment, keen to tap into this burgeoning market.

Apart from the success story of Guangzhou Honda, Peugeot's sister company under PSA, Citroen, made a direct point of reference to the question of entry by making remarkable progress of its own in the China market, while Peugeot fell into a mountain of losses. Citroen hooked up with Dongfeng Motors (one of the big three) and produced cars less sophisticated than Peugeot's. Its assembly lines started rolling in the early 1990s, when Peugeot already got into trouble. Citroen's Fukang sedans (ZX series) won popular votes from car drivers and taxi drivers for its agility, interior roominess given its size, and reliable engine. Citroen has made necessary upgrades and revisions, the most well known being a switch from a hatchback shape to a standard sedan shape in response to complaints and demands from customers. Citroen models have established their special places in China's car market and among car buyers. In 2003, Citroen sold over 100,000 vehicles. To Peugeot, a logical reasoning for its strategic decisions would be that it could imitate its sister company's work.

As the parent company PSA holds both Peugeot and Citroen under its umbrella, coordinated planning and concerted strategies are possible. This cooperation proves imperative, since Citroen, with its sizable market shares, urgently needs a car model aiming at a higher level segment than that of Fukang. Citroen's model line-ups have been weakening in the market, and car buyers felt unsatisfied with the cars of generally small engine capacity offered by Citroen. Peugeot, with its new models popular in Europe and solid performance cars, will fill in the gap and improve overall outlook for the French car group company. The full line-up combining both Peugeot and Citroen will cover sedan cars from small to medium sizes and meet most demands from customers. In this dual player structure, Peugeot and Citroen will achieve synergy and complementary effects.

Peugeot's re-entry proposal indicates its strong hope that the second entry may bring better results than the first one. This includes factors that the company has more understanding of the China market, that it may enter at a more promising time than the last time, and that it may benefit from the existing manufacturing bases in Wuhan under Citroen. Although Peugeot faces an embarrassing situation where it cannot move back to Guangzhou, it could move into the structure built up by PSA quite comfortably. Its relationship with the local government will be sheltered by relationships between PSA and the Wuhan government, so that Peugeot will face fewer hassles than it did while operating as a single company years before.

In products, Peugeot is well prepared. The company has developed new models and line-ups. Its strong showing at Auto China 2002 made a good impression on Chinese car buyers, and its series of 307, 407, and 607 performed well in European markets. The successful 307 model was eagerly expected to lead the charge on the consumer market in China. The shabby images of old 504s and 505s have been shrugged off by Peugeot. These new models will convince Chinese buyers that Peugeot is serious about this market and could win back potential customers. Peugeot, in general, has acknowledged that it made a vital mistake in the 1990s in not making upgrades and not offering new models. This time, as promised, Peugeot launched one of its latest models in China for the first time out of France. The reversal in approach and attitude was astonishing.

On the negative side, there were perhaps doubts on the possibility of boosting the total market share. The competition in the car industry is much fiercer than it was when Peugeot exited in 1997. The giant Shanghai and Changchun motor car bases pose constant threats to PSA, with their overwhelming car production capacity and sales figures. Even the previous minor player, Guangzhou Automotive Industry Corp., moved up to the fourth position with close cooperation with Honda. PSA faces a dilemma on whether more investment would improve these situations and its standing. This common concern, however, cannot change the nature of all market competition these days, in that an investment decision has to be made under the premise of "**March or die**". On the basis that a withdrawal from China by PSA is certainly not an option, a decision to add Peugeot to the equation then seems more plausible.

With these considerations of potential and feasibility, Peugeot formally re-entered the China car market in 2004, signing a contract with Dongfeng for a 600 million Euro investment in three years. This deal was to introduce new Peugeot series car models into the existing joint venture between Dongfeng and PSA and to increase the total production capacity to 300,000 vehicles, up from the current 150,000 vehicles. This event announced a formal return of Peugeot to a market it once quit. Peugeot planned not to repeat its early error in judgement and acted positively this time on both investment and products offered.

Summary

Peugeot adopted a positive approach in its first market entry, but stopped short of taking an effectual expansion strategy. The key point in Peugeot's dilemma is its approach in dealing with the issue of upgrading. Despite a good start and satisfactory sales, Peugeot failed in the key area of product upgrading and was thus forced to make a spectacular exit. This may serve as a reminder to foreign companies intending or planning to enter the China market. As this market is still seen by many as a third world market, entering companies perhaps feel alright at bringing in the products they reckon fit the development levels of the country. This perception comes from an underestimate of the pace at which this market matures. With low-end products on the market, they either satisfy a certain group of consumers while neglecting the majority, or they may succeed initially but soon take a beating from other players on the basis of multiple comparisons. In the China market today, entries with low-end products represent a misreading of the market and of overall purchasing power. As discussed in a previous chapter, Chinese consumers have grown choosy and selective, following closely current trends while passing over outdated products.

It is no surprise now that predictions of the China market are hard to be accurate. Take Peugeot's sister company, Citroen, for example. In the early 1990s, when Citroen's Fukang series began to take a hold in the market, the company made projections that national sedan car production could rise to between 1 to 1.5 million vehicles by 2000. Citroen made subsequent plans to meet that target. The Chinese car market, however, stayed at the level of 500,000 vehicles for a number of years. Citroen thus quietly revised downwards their investment plans and production targets. By the end of 1990s, car production rose to new heights so swiftly that Citroen had little time to revise its plans upwards and thus missed the chance to deliver more cars to a market which took in all cars available. Car makers with sufficient capacity in those booming years made fortunes and laughed all the way to the bank, especially in 2003. Citroen's plans to enlarge its own production capacity lagged behind schedules and will be realised at a time when the market may have reached a plateau.

Peugeot has made a U-turn in its product strategy upon its re-entry and brought in new car models to the China market. Other foreign multinationals are doing the same, in some cases launching new models in China and in their home countries simultaneously. The issue of product upgrading to suit growing and varied demands from Chinese consumers remains crucial in production and marketing strategies of any foreign company.

Discussion **Questions**

1. What suggestions would you make on improving the situation Peugeot was in before its 1997 departure? Check other relevant readings and reports, and search for plausible solutions, such as in the areas of products and investments.

2. Why are the performances of Peugeot and that of Honda at the Guangzhou plant so vastly different? Considering that another French car maker Renault succeeded in restructuring the Japanese car maker Nissan and that Honda succeeded in a China project where a French car marker failed, what can you make of these two examples? Do particular cultural characteristics determine end results in business, and are there certain patterns in successfully managing a project or cooperation in another country?

3. What do you think are the major considerations for Peugeot's re-entry decision? What do you think are the prospects of this attempt the second time around? What lessons could Peugeot learn and borrow from its first-time experience?

CASE 2 Whirlpool: Withdrawal and Re-entry

Whirlpool is an international brand name for household appliances (white goods) and was listed as world number one in kitchen appliances production in 2002. This US company has a dominant market position in north America and has also extended its operations to other continents, mostly Europeans countries. On the company's agenda of globalisation, a venture into the China market attracted some interest at quite a late stage, while FDI in China had by then undergone a decade long process. Its China experience testifies to a tendency of rushed strategic decisions and an utter unfamiliarity with the environment, at least during the first half of the venture.

Strategies of Joint Ventures

Whirlpool primarily relied on its solid company strength and brand name in formulating its strategies of market entry into China. Whirlpool is not a pioneer foreign household appliance manufacturer in the China market. It turned around from other matured markets to give some consideration to this new market from the early 1990s. This delay in exploration and lack of attention may have led to its unusual China experience in following years.

In an analysis of its proposed entry into the China market, Whirlpool has obvious internal strengths and weaknesses. Its long experience in white goods manufacturing, expertise and technology for being a market leader, experience in managing overseas operations, and its abundant financial resources, are all essential elements for a multinational to be successful in a new market. The brand name Whirlpool represents quality, advanced technology and trustworthiness to consumers in many countries. For previous market entries, the Whirlpool brand itself proved powerful enough to win a large market share and created satisfactory sales. Especially in European countries, Whirlpool expanded its power bases and sales networks without much hassle. The company therefore reckoned that its comprehensive range of advantages would now make it smooth sailing in just another new market, on the back of cumulated past experiences.

A prominent weakness Whirlpool had was its total lack of knowledge of economic and business environments in China. Whirlpool was quite unfamiliar with state policies and legal frameworks in China and had little understanding of market conditions and trends. The company, in particular, did not obtain full information of the industries it was going to enter, including information regarding market competition or major players. It is doubtful if Whirlpool had undertaken studies in detail of early pioneering foreign companies in this market, especially those from the US. By the early 1990s, examples of successes or troubles foreign companies experienced had become numerous. For one of the main forms of FDI, equity joint venture, there were ready cases for Whirlpool to take reference from. Whirlpool, as a typical American company, has an aggressive and task-oriented management and business style, which contrasts sharply with the Chinese style which focuses on relations and people, in particularly in those non-commercialised state enterprises. A failure in grasping these differences proved to be a key weakness of Whirlpool in its China operations.

Whirlpool was evidently attracted by potential business opportunities in this new market. By the early 1990s, economic reforms had brought sweeping changes to China's economy and consumption. Increased average incomes made it possible for millions of people to become customers of manufacturing enterprises. Household appliances began to sell quickly, as people shifted from the last round of big item purchases to a new round. Fridge and washing machines gradually became popular items and standard features in urban family homes. Foreign brands in China achieved popularity and sold well. Whirlpool reckoned that there were enormous opportunities if it moved in and introduced its full range of products to Chinese consumers. As a widely shared overall observation, the China market in the early 1990s presented a picture of huge unexplored potential to optimistic foreign investors.

Whirlpool thus paid little attention to the question of threats. As this market became profitable, it attracted both foreign and domestic players. Japanese brands had established their image of top end products among Chinese consumers, while domestic manufacturers emerged to upgrade their technology and competitiveness. It was the latter group of players that dealt Whirlpool a fatal blow. Open competition and existing market leaders were major threats to Whirlpool's operations in China, and the company failed to pay sufficient attention to this type of vital information, confident instead in its own brand name and overwhelming financial strength.

In overall considerations, Whirlpool focused on its strength and potential business opportunities to make a strategic entry decision into the China market.

Whirlpool's Partners

Among entry modes, Whirlpool selected equity joint venture. This is largely due to the restrictions from the Chinese government at the time on wholly foreign-owned companies, though those restrictions were gradually relaxed by the middle of the 1990s. Inherent troubles at joint ventures were already on open display at such projects as Beijing Jeep and Guangzhou Peugeot. In fact, Peugeot was in exit mode from the Guangzhou project when Whirlpool contemplated an entry through joint ventures. It would be better if Whirlpool had heeded those typical troubles and improved its own performance later.

In February 1995, Whirlpool formally entered a joint venture with Beijing Snowflakes Electrical Company to produce fridges. Whirlpool took 60% of shares in the venture of a registered capital of US$30 million. With this majority shareholding, Whirlpool demanded, and obtained, the authority to manage and run the joint venture with a free hand.

In 1995 as well, Whirlpool invested in another joint venture with a Shanghai company. The joint venture was called Whirlpool Narcissus and produced washing machines of Narcissus brand. Whirlpool took 55% of shares in this venture of a registered capital of US$75 million.

Whirlpool also bought majority shares in a microwave oven maker in Shunde, Guangdong province. This was a Hong Kong invested company, aiming mainly at exporting microwave ovens to overseas markets. The market leader, a domestic company called Grantz, posed serious threats to this Hong Kong company. Whirlpool decided to join in and took over 100% of company shares in two instalments. The goal was to utilise existing production facilities and Whirlpool's brand name, in order to open the little explored domestic market for microwave ovens at that time. This joint venture, in effect a wholly foreign-owned subsidiary company after Whirlpool's stock purchase, attempted to challenge Grantz and grab that market leader position. It soon suffered heavily from Grantz's lethal price wars and completely lost the domestic market, instead of gaining more shares. From then on, Grantz has never looked back or lost its grip over the market. Whirlpool had to re-focus on export markets for its microwave oven products.

Whirlpool also entered a joint venture with a Shenzhen company to produce air conditioners. Other minor projects include fridge compressor factories.

In a flash, Whirlpool entered the China market in a spectacular fashion, targeting four major sectors of white goods (fridge, washing machine, microwave oven, and air conditioner) and setting up a number of joint ventures in a short period of time. The total initial investment (for registered capital) and follow up investment reached US$500 million.

Strategic Decision on Exit

The Beijing and Shanghai projects, in areas of fridges and washing machines respectively, received most investments from Whirlpool within that total of US$500 million. Yet, these two joint ventures performed less than satisfactorily judging by Whirlpool's initial expectations. There are several agreed factors to these unexpected and undesirable situations.

Based on its past performance and overseas experience, Whirlpool was quite confident that it could get a hold on the China market with its brand name and large investments. A vital factor was ignored in an assessment of this market. Whirlpool totally underestimated the heightened market competition in this economy from the early 1990s. In their calculations, China as a socialist and transitional economy would not be a market economy for many years, and in official documents Western countries did not recognise China's market economy status as such. This generalisation was correct in an overall sense, but Whirlpool omitted a crucial difference. While most sectors of the economy were much less liberalised than those in Eastern European countries and key industries were under vigorous state protection, the white goods industries were already wide open to market competition. Unlike the motor car industry, white goods industries were considered light industries and closely related to people's living conditions. These less strategic industries enjoyed certain lenient government treatments in opening, in order to provide more goods for Chinese families and consumers. Competition thus became fierce and domestic players of various ownership types entered the fray. Adding the number of other foreign players, especially Japanese ones, the playing field was already quite crowded for a giant like Whirlpool at its time of entry.

The implication of this increasingly intense competition to Whirlpool was that it no longer had the luxury of an easy entry and could not afford to introduce less advanced, secondary technology and products to this market. An example in point is Whirlpool's choice of mainstream fridge type made at its Beijing project. Since the Whirlpool side held majority shareholding, it made decisions on selection of models for production and sales. Whirlpool chose to continue to produce the previous models from the Beijing company, despite the objections of its Chinese partners. Although Whirlpool had mastered the technology to produce CFC-free fridges, the company considered it too premature and forward-looking to launch this type of model in the China market. They expected the consumption power and consciousness of environmental protection in China not to reach required levels for some time to come, so that the current models would be sufficient for them. In the meantime, a leading domestic fridge maker, Haier, was going full speed ahead in launching its own CFC-free fridge models. Under this competition, Whirlpool's Beijing project made a loss of nearly 100 million yuan in 1996, one year after Whirlpool became a partner.

In a slow response, Whirlpool finally decided to answer the challenge head on and launch CFC-free fridge models of its own in China. This time Whirlpool went to the other extreme, introducing the most advanced production lines it had to the Beijing project. The complexity and high standards of those complete systems slowed down installation and launching. It took over 18 months for the new facilities to be operational. By that time, Haier had made CFC-free models its standard product for sales, and the CFC-free feature was splashed in advertising of most models on the market. These delays cost Whirlpool dearly in lost time and sales. In those two years, the joint venture incurred 170 million yuan in losses. This Beijing project never recovered from this setback.

Similar troubles in responsiveness in this market happened to Whirlpool's management in its microwave oven project as well. The market leader Grantz waged price wars in order to eliminate competitors and expand market share. Whirlpool had considerable existing market shares and financial backing to cope with price cutting and even beat Grantz in its own game. Instead, Whirlpool hesitated and delayed the releasing of timely responses. Its communication channels passed information from southern Guangdong to Hong Kong and to the US. Decisions made at Whirlpool headquarters were transferred back to the project through the same layers and channels. Whirlpool might have hesitated on an all out offensive in a price war, due to its considerations of company reputation or brand name. For a well known foreign brand and a typical top-end product manufacturer, engaging in a price war with a lightweight domestic player seemed unimaginable. Whirlpool's wavering and slow response gave Grantz sufficient time to eat up market share and it won in sales through offering low prices. In the end, Whirlpool was forced out of domestic markets and largely turned to exporting microwave ovens overseas. Its Guangdong project became an OEM manufacturer exclusively for overseas markets. This was definitely not the purpose in Whirlpool's original plans of large investments in China.

As the number one white goods manufacturer of the world, Whirlpool was overly confident of its brand name and almost neglected the task of brand promotions in the China market. This caused brand confusion in the minds of Chinese consumers. After enduring years of advertising and promotions, Chinese consumers began to be able to quickly identify certain brand names with certain product lines. For fridges and air conditioners, Haier received high marks and wide recognition. Even Siemens and Electrolux had positive responses from Chinese customers. Japanese brands, of course, often occupy high-end positions in many sectors of white goods. For Whirlpool, its consumer awareness was low and corporate image weak. Chinese consumers generally could not tell what this company was producing and which of its products were top brands. This identity crisis troubled Whirlpool all along, from the time its Beijing project churned out products bearing the previous Chinese brand Snowflakes.

In addition, Whirlpool's typical bulky and square fridge designs, which were suitable in North America, matched unfavourably with slick and smart designs of Japanese and European fridges available on market. Whirlpool had not conducted comprehensive surveys on what Chinese consumers desired. Instead, it relied on introduction of its own existing product lines to China, while declining to initiate localisation.

Whirlpool thus failed to meet local demands and varying customers' preferences. Its insistence on producing CFC fridges fell far behind market trends, which indicated, on the part of Whirlpool, a lack of thorough market research and of realistic estimates of consumers' needs. This appears to be a major failure in marketing.

Whirlpool also lost ground at this early stage in handling relationships with its Chinese partners. The Beijing and Shanghai projects were all in partnership with state enterprises, and their operations went on vastly different from Whirlpool's. Since Whirlpool had the full control over management, it implemented its own plans and systems. Unsatisfactory coordination and cooperation created unsatisfactory results. For example, at the Shanghai joint venture, Whirlpool decided to abandon existing sales networks of Narcissus and established its own throughout the country. The original intention was perhaps to rid of possible interference from the Chinese partner. Expatriate personnel were brought in to control key sections of the joint venture, at production, marketing, sales, human resources etc. The end result was a rise in total operating costs and drop in sales, as newly set up channels could not handle the volume flow. These moves also eroded trust between Whirlpool and its Chinese partner, in that the latter felt both threatened and ignored in this joint venture. In the end, the Chinese partner decided to reduce its shareholding in steps and eventually sold the remaining shares of 20% to Whirlpool for US$9 million in 2002. In the meantime, this Whirlpool project in China suffered consecutive years of losses, over several hundred million yuan.

After a few years of operations in this market, Whirlpool could not see clear prospects for its China projects. Despite its large investment, brand name and non-stop efforts, Whirlpool could not gain any significant market share in any of the sectors it entered. Especially in the area of fridges, Whirlpool had a miserable market share of 0.33% in 1997-1998, while the market leader Haier had 29% of the market. The situation became quite hopeless for Whirlpool.

As it was impossible to see any light at the end of tunnel, Whirlpool decided to make a full contraction of its operations and cut losses. In 1997, two years after the beginning of the Beijing project, Whirlpool sold its 60% share back to Beijing Snowflakes for US$2 million, a figure significantly smaller than the initial investment. This signalled a loss in investment and a failure of the joint venture. The Shanghai project was turned from a joint venture to a wholly foreign-owned entity of Whirlpool, with continuing losses incurred. That joint venture was also a kind of failure, as Whirlpool broke the usual regulations laid on top of a joint venture and rushed to gain full ownership. Whirlpool withdrew from the China market in the four sectors it entered: fridge and air conditioner, while the washing machine project bled, and the sector of microwave ovens lost domestic market shares. Whirlpool saw little hope of reviving sales and profits any time soon.

The decision to withdraw was made primarily on considerations of cutting losses and shifting focus. It was clear to Whirlpool that its handling of relationships in China was unsatisfactory. Its relationships with the government, other players in the industries, and Chinese customers deteriorated along with the passing of time, and the Whirlpool brand name did not offer much help. It was perhaps a shocking reality to Whirlpool that its world famous brand name had little appeal in this market. The only powerful means Whirlpool had was its investments in projects. As investments did not achieve the expected goals, the only thing to do was to cut down the size and suspend further investment. The option to withdraw was selected by Whirlpool quite in a decisive way, and the company moved quickly to cut losses, cut ties with Chinese partners, and shift focus to other countries' markets.

This withdrawal was executed as a result of major changes in the company's overall policy. Whirlpool decided to leave the China market at this stage and pursue its goals in other markets. The principal consideration was to give the China market a pass and to arrange for a retreat as soon as possible. Financial and human resources could be more efficiently utilised elsewhere, rather than being spent on this hopeless battle ground. In view of strategic decisions, Whirlpool acted responsibly in the interests of its shareholders. This demonstrates the flexible nature of a multinational, in that the corporation was able to make prompt decisions on entry or exit, and it managed not to get stuck in a quagmire. A multinational has sufficient funds to execute a retreat, regardless of present costs or losses. This swiftness in maneuvering makes it possible for a multinational to seek opportunities worldwide and stage a future return to a market. Under this overall change of direction, despite some remaining projects still in operation, Whirlpool's investments and projects in China were by and large suspended.

Similar to Peugeot, Whirlpool suffered a setback in its reputation in this market. Industry analysts and Chinese consumers alike treat this withdrawal as a clear failure by a big name American corporation and a vindication of the strength of leading domestic companies. Damages to a reputation are hard to mend, and it is doubly difficult to convince the locals of your worthiness in a re-entry. Since Whirlpool was the one that broke the ties in joint ventures, Chinese partners in future would be more cautious towards proposals from Whirlpool. A domestic diversified manufacturer, Hisense, took over what Whirlpool left behind and formed a partnership with the Beijing Snowflakes company. It claimed to have achieved good results in this cooperation, in stark contrast to Whirlpool's spectacular failure. Such publicity is bad for Whirlpool's image in its future sales or operations in China.

Strategic Decision to Re-enter

In 2001, China formally entered the WTO to become a key player in international trade. In the same year, Whirlpool's top management contemplated a re-entry into the China market. The company formally announced its return with a launching of 30 products in 3 series into this market. A new CEO for Whirlpool's China headquarters was also appointed. The target set for Whirlpool China was to reach top three positions in all related industries.

According to Whirlpool, the central rationale of its return is that Whirlpool never left the China market. Its remaining operations in China generated revenues, as well as incurred losses. Whirlpool essentially had these operations producing for overseas markets and avoided direct confrontation with leading domestic players in various industries. In 2000, Whirlpool made revenues of US$300 million mainly from the exports of its microwave ovens and washing machines in the remaining projects. These footholds could be enlarged and transformed for further expansion.

At this turning point, Whirlpool fully recognised the potential in the China market, an observation already proven by many other foreign multinationals. This potential includes both consumption power and consolidation in related industries. The purchasing power of Chinese consumers had been demonstrated by rising sales figures in consecutive years and by growing appetite to buy new large items for their families.

Whirlpool places enormous hopes on this huge purchasing power to be released on buying household appliances and on upgrading when desired. The situation in relevant industries also stabilised, with a number of top players taking hold of majority market shares. Price wars had eliminated many smaller players and cost survivors dearly. Fairer competition, based on brand name, technology and service, had become the mainstream. This shift would benefit those large foreign multinationals like Whirlpool. The company decided its re-entry primarily on catching opportunities that derived from these new conditions. According to Whirlpool's new CEO in China, there was no reason a major manufacturer like Whirlpool could not take certain shares in this growth market. The company's focus will thus shift back from exports to competing in domestic markets.

To move forward, Whirlpool has to carefully review its previous mistakes and strategies (see Figure 19.1). The central point in defending their choices is that the first withdrawal was not a failure, but a temporary exit for strategic realignments. This may sound rational and explain Whirlpool's determination in quitting at that time. For Whirlpool, price wars and non-stop losses would keep them stuck in the quagmire and swallow up their financial strength designated for later revival. It is out of this consideration that they would rather bear temporary losses and leave than making continuous investments. It is important to note that when Whirlpool made its retreat, it had lost its market competitiveness. When it now returns, the question remains as to how Whirlpool will improve its competitiveness this time around.

Under the new plans, Whirlpool will move back to the four sectors it entered. The company will enlarge its microwave oven manufacturing base for more exports. This is the part that earns stable revenues. Whirlpool has to face Grantz again in this sector, but this time both sides will be in talks of cooperation, in that Grantz will produce for overseas markets through Whirlpools' networks. For washing machine production, Whirlpool will rely heavily on its wholly-owned company in Shanghai and attempt to increase sales from there. Whirlpool needs to get breakthroughs in the sectors of fridges and air conditioners, the territories occupied by domestic giants like Haier. A simple, easy alternative is to cooperate with a major fridge manufacturer Kelon in Guangdong, in the form of OEM production for exports. Manufactured goods in these China projects could be merged into the overall globalised

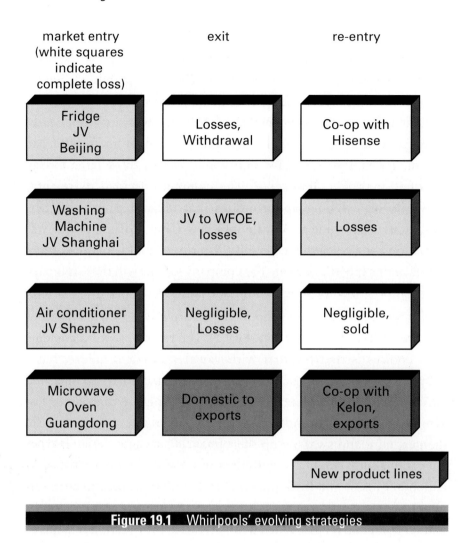

market entry (white squares indicate complete loss)	exit	re-entry
Fridge JV Beijing	Losses, Withdrawal	Co-op with Hisense
Washing Machine JV Shanghai	JV to WFOE, losses	Losses
Air conditioner JV Shenzhen	Negligible, Losses	Negligible, sold
Microwave Oven Guangdong	Domestic to exports	Co-op with Kelon, exports
		New product lines

Figure 19.1 Whirlpools' evolving strategies

production and supply chains of Whirlpool, helping to raise efficiency and cut costs.

For all these four intended sectors, Whirlpool will have to introduce new products and upgrades to appeal to Chinese consumers. What happened years before served as a critical reminder to Whirlpool that it did rush into this market with minimum preparations. Whirlpool has made promises to pay more attention to what Chinese consumers want and to suit their preferences consistently. For their marketing and sales purposes, Whirlpool now emphasises on market research and has conducted numerous surveys covering a large number of Chinese cities. One of their recent efforts has been spent on penetrating inland regions, selling directly to small city residents, in order to avoid the tight grip of leading domestic manufacturers in major cities. This option created certain initial excitement, but seems to have encountered enormous troubles, in that local protectionism, unreliable local distributors, and overstretched supply chains are causing enough headaches to Whirlpool China managers. This kind of localisation in marketing may prove to be another mistaken strategy as time goes by.

In contrast to Whirlpool's twists and turns in its China strategies, Siemens, another major player in household appliances industries, demonstrated consistently improving performance in the China market. Siemens stepped into troubled joint ventures in China as well, similar to the situation of Whirlpool in Beijing. Its two joint ventures suffered losses five years in a row. Instead of sticking to its own plans and quitting in a rush, Siemens increased investment, revamped production lines, introduced new products, researched extensively on Chinese consumer needs, and implemented strict unified quality standards for all its products. It replaced fridge production lines at the joint venture and sold many relatively old equipment as scrap metals. Siemens was the first manufacturer to introduce front loading washing machines to Chinese consumers, targeting high income families. This differentiation strategy set Siemens apart from other manufacturers of standard types of washing machine. Through tireless efforts, Siemens has established its top brand name and considerable market share in China. Currently, Siemens has annual production capacities for fridges and front loading washing machines of 1 million sets each, with an accumulated investment on these two projects at US$300 million. Considering that Siemens is in fact a diversified corporation and is now a leading company in telecommunications, including 3G and operating systems, its achievements in household appliances industries are even more astounding. It is estimated that with an aggregate investment of Euros 655 million in China, Siemens had generated a total of Euros 3.3 billion in revenues by 2003.

It is no secret that German companies display their usual consistency and persistence wherever they enter a market. It is not surprising that major German corporations in the China market have stayed to reap benefits and seldom left. This characteristic illustrates itself in full in a comparison between Whirlpool and Siemens. The American company lost in areas of market research, overestimate of its strength, relationship handling, defective decision making etc., but compensated for these with swift entry and exit plans. As a result, Whirlpool cut certain losses financially, while hurting its reputation badly in the market. Whirlpool's announced moves are often viewed as on shifting ground, and few analysts have the confidence to predict a future success for this giant company in the China market. In contrast, decisions from German companies like Siemens earn deserved confidence, due to their reliability and long term commitment. Their products and brands thus receive wide acceptance among Chinese consumers.

Discussion Questions

1. What did Whirlpool do to cope with problems in its joint ventures? What are the major causes of failures at these early joint ventures? Would wholly foreign-owned investment projects better serve Whirlpool's goals and lead to success?

2. Would you consider Whirlpool's re-entry a rational strategic decision and why? What made Whirlpool try its luck again and not leave this market altogether (considering its satisfactory operations worldwide)? What options would Whirlpool take to make things differently the second time and get desired results?

CASE 3   VW: A Consistent German Player and Market Domination

Volkswagen (VW) is a German car maker less well known worldwide than other German marques like Mercedes, BMW and Porsche, but this company is a major provider of mass produced family cars. In this sense, the car models coming out of VW may just better suit customer demands in a developing country like China. VW grabbed precious business opportunities in a China under reform and through a series of strategic decisions built up a car empire in a new growth market. We will examine briefly the key strategies VW adopted, with which VW has succeeded where other major international players hesitated or tumbled.

Strategic Decision on Market Entry

Reforms in China opened the door for foreign car makers for the first time since 1949. Confronting official enquires of cooperation, world class car makers made their widely varied responses. Top-line car markers in Germany, such as Mercedes and BMW, had no interest at all in an industrial project in a developing country and literally laughed off the invitations from Beijing. Even their sales of luxury cars to China at the time stayed at low numbers. American auto giants were preoccupied with offensives from Japanese car markers. The only respondent, American Motors, moved in and set up a joint venture in Beijing to build Jeep. The company later regretted this due to continued troubles and losses. Japanese car makers, in turn, chose to sell their finished cars to China at premium prices. Their business projections showed an unlikelihood of any major car project in China for at least 20 years. These foreign car makers later paid the price for their initial passive responses in heavy investments on their belated entries.

Among these negative responses, VW stood out. The company made a strategic decision to enter the China market at this early time. Unlike the Japanese, VW's links to this new market is built on concrete investment in manufacturing factories, rather than in sales offices. This commitment was made with considerations of several key factors.

VW saw a potentially vast and rapidly growing market for the future and decided to nurture that market through setting up car making projects there. The window of opportunity would allow VW to take "**first mover**" advantage. This vision and understanding of long term trends led VW to enter, together with a conviction that a company can prosper in a field where others have not come in. As a relatively less known brand, VW was eager to find additional space and ground for development outside existing competitive markets. VW was later able to take advantage of its early entry to the full.

This move also represented a vital stage in the development of VW's own global strategy, which sought to encompass China as well as the Asia-Pacific region. In the 1980s, VW was looking for a way to wage battles with the then flourishing Japanese car manufacturers in their own backyard. Major international car makers focused on the US and European markets for sales and market shares. VW chose to search for markets around the world and practise globalisation at an early time. The company already had many subsidiaries in many countries, including in developing countries, and sales from overseas markets reached 64% of the total in 1983. A potential market the size of China's thus would not be ignored by VW.

VW had a ready car model for the proposed car project in China. The Santana model had been promoted to Brazilian companies but failed to win continuing cooperation from local partners. The standards and performance of this model apparently suit the demands of car buyers of a developing country in the early 1980s. In a venture in China, VW could sell this model again to Chinese companies. It would lose little if the model failed in China after introduction, and costs involved would be relatively small for a multinational like VW. If it succeeded, VW would achieve the aim of prolonging product life cycles and receive double returns for its R&D expenditures. VW, like other foreign multinationals at the time, had little knowledge of this new market, and its decision to undertake a joint venture in China was indeed a gamble. This gamble, however, was considered by VW as an affordable one, judging from the car model it offered.

VW was also very interested in favourable treatments from the Chinese government. It understood that in a socialist country the government could provide many beneficial conditions for certain preferred companies, and that those with these favours face fewer restrictions and obstacles than those under competition in a free market. Since the invitation came from official bureaux and partner companies had to be leaders in the industry in China, VW would receive double insurances in its venture and also government assistance in times of need. This official guarantee gave VW much needed confidence, in compensation for its worries of business failures and losses.

VW also took some precautions before formally stepping into a joint venture. From 1983, VW shipped CKD kits to China and supervised the assembly of the first Santana sedans in Shanghai, China. This is the equivalent of exports to China and would not hurt VW's interests if this experiment failed. As the assembly process proved its applicability and government authorities took Santana as a good car model for Chinese buyers, VW moved into meaningful negotiations with the Chinese side. At this stage, VW finally made the strategic decision to enter the China market.

In 1985, VW signed contracts with Chinese partners to set up a joint venture named Shanghai VW. Negotiations went on between VW and the central government, the Shanghai government, and Shanghai Automotive Industry Corp. The joint venture took a 50:50 ratio and was to last for 25 years. As promised, the Chinese government offered the industry leader and best manufacturing establishment in the industrial centre of Shanghai for this joint venture with a German car maker. In an overall comparison, this Shanghai project fared better than the Beijing and Guangzhou projects, and VW obtained firm backing from the municipal government and valuable service from the cream of management talents of China in Shanghai.

For this strategic decision on market entry, a SWOT analysis will reveal an overwhelming tendency. VW had sufficient strength to carry out this project, based on its established internalisation experience, advanced technology in car making in comparison with its Chinese partners, and solid financial capacity (which VW lacked in the early 1990s). Opportunities were potentially huge, though meagre returns in early years clouded them. VW faced almost no threat in this unexplored market, at least not from other car making multinationals. Domestic players had not emerged to pose any challenges, either. The only threats came from uncertainties in this new market and from VW's internal weakness in that it had little knowledge and experience of coping with operations in China. This weakness soon subsided as VW quickly learnt Chinese ways of doing business, won high praises from the central government, and became an outstanding model corporate citizen in China. From this analysis, we can see that VW put itself on the safe side for its market entry and began a rolling process of successes in a growth market.

Strategies on Products and Localisation

Similar to the other two early foreign entrants into the car market in China, VW had its own problems. These could be put into two categories: choice of products and level of localisation. VW took the alternatives different from those of other players to address these issues.

The Santana model of VW had an even lower percentage of local components than that of Peugeot's car models. In the first three years of operation, Shanghai VW produced over 10,000 units, well short of the 30,000 annual capacities agreed in the contract, and the level of local components was at a miserable 3%. Santana cars rolled off assembly lines basically out of CKD kits shipped in from Germany. These inevitably increased costs of making cars in Shanghai. Although the Chinese currency RMB was dearer at the time, China as a whole was extremely short of foreign currencies, and these purchases made the government spend heavily on imported components. Car prices rose high as a result. The central government could not tolerate this situation and eventually issued an ultimatum to the Shanghai government and Shanghai VW. If locally made components could not reach 40% in three years, the joint venture would have to be shut down.

VW responded swiftly to this threat. If the company had been half-hearted in its commitment to the joint venture, as it received steady revenues from CKD imports, it now went full speed ahead in implementing a localisation strategy. VW set up a special taskforce for coordinating and certifying localisation throughout the group's operations in China. With permission from the central government, Shanghai VW was able to set aside a certain percentage of Santana sales to a special localisation fund. This fund provided over 5 billion yuan for various localisation programmes.

Selected suppliers to Shanghai VW had to pass stringent tests and were ordered to revise their production systems if failing tests. Only those which received certifications from VW could become long term suppliers and secure their stable business. VW helped in setting up hundreds of domestic parts companies across the country, benefited local economies, and built up wide networks during this process. This provided a guarantee for car making at VW's various plants and enhanced its control over the industry. This localisation proceeded for 10 years, and by 1993, CKD production at Shanghai VW was replaced by locally made parts. The level of local components reached 98% for the original Santana model in 1996. For Santana 2000, the level went over 85% in 2000, and for an early model of Audi 100, it reached 70%. After this localisation, Shanghai VW itself needed only to maintain 20% of production facilities at its headquarters in Shanghai. During the same period, car production capacity at Shanghai VW surpassed 100,000 vehicles in 1993 and reached 300,000 vehicles by 2000.

VW's patience, pragmatism, and tremendous effort in localisation paid off and received high marks from government officials and industry leaders alike. This effort made VW a recognised force in the industry, with hundreds of parts suppliers and nationwide beneficiaries. In return for this localisation process, the Shanghai government decided to close down its own auto company which had produced a well known Chinese car brand "Shanghai". Under a policy to list the car industry as the number one "pillar" industry of Shanghai, Shanghai VW became the core of this industry, and all related factories in Shanghai switched to work for Shanghai VW as its suppliers. This signalled a watershed policy shift of the government from developing the domestic car industry to relying on cooperation with foreign multinationals. VW successfully eliminated potential domestic challengers and was from then on able to enjoy dominating market shares for over a decade.

This localisation policy was so successful that other foreign car makers which moved in later could hardly copy it or achieve what VW did. At a time when Beijing and Guangzhou projects ran into serious troubles, the German joint venture in Shanghai went along according to government plans and desires, and its thorough localisation, except for key technology, connected VW's interests tightly in a web with those of local governments and local companies. Rewards for this German persistence and delivered promises were immeasurable. The government now regarded Shanghai VW as almost a domestic car maker and protected its interests in many ways. The official policy on the car industry was issued in 1994, in which the government decided, in principle, not to grant permits for new sedan manufacturers from 1996. New applications would be subject to strict scrutiny on a case-by-case basis. Before this policy shift, the government had welcome foreign car makers with open arms. This new policy apparently placed VW's operations in China on the inside, against other major international car makers as outsiders. Under this definition, VW in China enjoyed little competition and challenge from those bigger players which threatened VW in other markets. VW-made cars in China were also protected from threats posed by imported cars, which were subject to up to 200% tariffs. This unique favourable position made VW a selected leader in the industry of China, not seriously challenged until GM moved in years later.

On product strategy, VW performed a little less satisfactorily. It followed a one model approach, like Peugeot in Guangzhou. The Santana model was the mainstream car from 1983 through to 1995, and is still made and occasionally promoted by Shanghai VW today. The fact that this model lasted over 10 year with no replacement did puzzle many analysts and Chinese consumers as well. The cause to this delay lies with Shanghai VW's parent company, VW in Germany. VW went through a very difficult period of time from the late 1980s. Its market shares in Europe and the US shrank sharply, and financial constrains made VW unable to spend loosely on R&D. VW even had no new models for its own domestic market, let alone models to be made in a small new market. By the early 1990s, VW passed the time of financial difficulties and won some market shares back. Its newly launched models such as the Golf became popular, especially in European markets. Due to this downturn, VW was unable to deliver new car models in the China market for a painfully long time.

This long absence of new generation cars was quite unique and caused mounting troubles to Shanghai VW. In comparison with Guangzhou Peugeot and its old models, the joint venture in Shanghai soldiered on with careful make-overs and diversions. When Shanghai VW had no new models to replace the original Santana, it undertook many modifications and additions to the old model. It changed model series numbers to give consumers an impression that a relatively new car was now on the market, such as a G series to F series. Modifications were also made to lights, control panels, seats, interior design etc., while the car was basically the same as before. This hard work on diversions continued until 1995 when the new Santana 2000 was launched. As VW in Germany recovered from financial troubles, Shanghai VW received more advanced and upgraded car models in shorter periods. VW's Passat was introduced from the late 1990s, not long after its launch in Germany in 1997.

A key factor for the survival of VW in China, in escaping the fate of Guangzhou Peugeot which suffered the same product problem, was that VW relied on government purchases and favourable treatments. In the 1980s and early 1990s, car buyers were mostly work units, being government departments or state enterprises. Their requirements for cars at work were simple and fit well with the Santana made by Shanghai VW. This type of car was bought by work units nationwide for a considerably long time, and from the middle level officials downwards, this was perhaps the only choice they had for their work needs. The simplicity of demands made Santana a hot product on the market. This demand was constant and predicable, so VW could expect sales as long as government (group, fleet) purchases continued. With these biggest clients standing by, VW had little worry about its Santana cars having fewer buyers. As other major international car makers were blocked out, VW was almost the only supplier of passenger cars to officials of various ranks.

The bad situation at VW in China also troubled governments from top levels down. As projects in Beijing and Guangzhou encountered mounting problems, the government expected this joint venture in Shanghai to overcome difficulties and succeed. VW's localisation drive won over the government, which now saw it as a key reliable partner. The government made an effort to assist VW, including instructing bureaux and enterprises to buy Santana, rather than other car models (there were very few for selection, anyway). In Shanghai and some southern regions, Santana was taken as the standard taxi type, which guaranteed some fixed business revenues. With these strong official and semi-official support, Shanghai VW sold over 1 million Santana vehicles by 1998, a remarkable feat in a car market in its infancy.

Strategy of Expansion

With favourable conditions including firm government support, semi-domestic treatment, and smooth car sales, VW in effect had the China market to itself. There, however, emerged a question of its direction of further development. In this regard, VW chose to form another partnership in 1991 with a Chinese car corporation in the northeast. This was an interesting strategic decision made by VW.

Considerations

VW needed to implement a multi-brand strategy to further its hold on the car market. The Santana model was in fact a family car. For government officials, this model suit them well, but their demands did change along with time, and a more luxurious and formal model was needed. In that category, there were only imported German marques of Mercedes and BMW. The whole field was effectively wide open. This created an urge on VW to introduce its luxury line-up. Shanghai VW declined this proposal. The Chinese partner in the Shanghai joint venture paid more attention to the enlargement of production capacity at that complex and to secure more market share for Santana. They apparently had no appetite for another more luxurious model at the same place. VW had to search for other Chinese partners.

The Chinese partner of Shanghai VW, Shanghai Automotive Industry Corp., was commonly regarded as the second player among domestic players, with regular backing from the central government. The "dragonhead player" was the First Auto Work (FAW) in Changchun, a motor complex originally built with aids from the former Soviet Union. When foreign car makers came in the China market, FAW was left out with no foreign partners. The central government initially tried to preserve this complex as the national base of domestic car manufacturing. This aging complex in fact complained to the central government about this lack of attention. When VW began to sell the cooperation plan of a new luxury car model, FAW was selected as a front runner for a future joint venture. A partnership with another heavyweight would enhance VW's leading position in the country, and it was a dream situation for VW to hook up with the number one and number two car makers of China.

VW had the car market in southern China in its hands through Santana sales. It needed to set up another manufacturing base outside Shanghai, especially in the north. As problems prolonged at Beijing Jeep and Dongfeng Motors hooked up with Citroen, among major car bases in China at the time, VW had little choice but to pick FAW. Geographically speaking, this move would give VW a north-south control over China's car market.

VW had had some early contacts with FAW. FAW was essentially a producer of commercial vehicles (trucks), with small numbers of official Chinese limousines, "Red Flag", a model similar to Cadillac. VW offered its Audi 100 model to FAW for assembly. This was a kind of licensed production, and FAW began to make mass produced sedan cars for the first time. On the basis of this early cooperation, VW established a working relationship with FAW, which laid the foundation for their further joint venture.

With no jockeying and competition from other foreign carmakers, VW had the luxury to set up a formal joint venture with FAW with ease. In 1991, the FAW-VW partnership was announced, with a 60:40 ratio, and both sides promised to build a car plant producing 150,000 vehicles a year. VW initially figured that this capacity was over optimistic, but later developments proved that VW was over conservative. With FAW-VW, investments made by VW in China amounted to 3 billion German marks by 2000.

This expansion strategy won VW enormous market shares and, more importantly, established VW as the unchallenged leader in the China market. The launching of the new Audi series there caused a sensation and was a miracle in car sales. In three years after the launch, FAW-VW sold nearly 180,000 Audis. This was well beyond VW's original projections, and its worries about small numbers of buyers due to the exceptionally high price tags for Audi cars vanished. In recent years, Audi was universally recognised in China as the representative of luxury cars and set the standards for this top category. Its hot sales and reputation created strong demands and pushed up prices even higher. On the other front, the family car model Jetta, made at FAW-VW as well, also won popularity in that category and sold extremely well.

VW not only met little resistance from weak domestic car makers, but also received little threats from international car giants. As the partner in two gigantic joint ventures, VW dominated the market all over the country. Its market share once reached 70%, and VW cars became standard vehicles for government officials. It became an unwritten rule that state leaders, ministers, high ranking officials should ride in Audi sedans for their official business. Any other foreign brand cars were not allowed, except for private citizens. Audi cars from FAW-VW are considered domestically made and belong to the non-foreign category. Santana and the later Passat models were for officials at lower ranks. With the surge in private car ownerships in China, the two VW joint ventures offered a comprehensive line-up to meet customers' demands at different levels (see Table 19.2).

With this full line-up unmatched by any other, VW products in effect cover nearly all categories and meet demands from most car buyers in China. VW's government purchases remain strong, while car models at lower family brackets suit private car buyers. VW's hold on the car industry in China further strengthened, as two out of three top domestic car makers are in joint venture with VW. This near total monopoly is unprecedented, in that some exclusive rights were granted to a foreign car maker in this industry. In many ways, this permission

Table 19.2 VW car line-up in China (excluding imported Audi A8)

High bracket:	
Audi A6	FAW-VW
Medium High bracket	
Audi A4	FAW-VW
Passat	Shanghai VW
Golf	FAW VW
Bora	FAW VW
Touran	Shanghai VW
Medium bracket (family)	
Santana	Shanghai VW
Santana 2000	Shanghai VW
Santana 3000	Shanghai VW
Jetta	FAW VW
Polo	Shanghai VW

from the government represents a rare reward for the vision and persistence of this German car maker.

From a point of view of strategic positioning, many questioned the move by VW to cooperate with FAW. Some reckoned that VW should concentrate on Shanghai VW and solve its problems in product upgrading and market shares. A more serious question relates to a possible duplicity or overlapping in VW's products. Its mainstream family car from FAW-VW, Jetta, was a Santana equivalent and directly clashed with the latter in the market. Other later introduced VW car models caused the same problem (see the above line-ups). An expansion to FAW-VW could be trouble for Shanghai VW and lead to brand confusion.

With the set up of FAW-VW, VW placed the coordination of these two huge projects in the hands of VW China. The view from VW on expansion was that the China market would be huge enough for two VW joint ventures to grow together. Based on this belief, an enlarged production capacity at the Shanghai site was then impractical, and VW had to look for another site with a heavyweight domestic player. Production capacities from these two sites certainly fed the needs and proved just enough for booming car sales in later years.

VW also considered product strategy in this expansion. Santana was the heart of Shanghai VW, and a similar model Jetta, though relatively newer, would not interest the Shanghai government at all, which was then preoccupied with the Santana brand and localisation. In introducing a different VW model and enlarged production capacity, VW had to move out of Shanghai for a nationwide search, even if this action implied a sense of detachment from Shanghai VW. VW was also worried that the lack of a luxury car model would hurt its long term relationship with the government. If VW was unable to launch such a model, government bureaux would have to choose imported Mercedes or BMW as their official vehicles. That territory would then remain closed to VW, despite its pride in its own Audi series.

This expansion illustrates VW's vision and flexibility, in that competition from other foreign multinationals in future was factored in. This strategy caused foreign multinationals who were late-comers headaches, since they found little room in a market already occupied by not one but two models of family cars, and they had to differentiate their models from these two models one way or another. In fact, they chose not to directly challenge the fields guarded by VW's twin models. Honda, GM, and Nissan all made their mainstream cars at a more expensive and luxurious level above Santana and Jetta, while others moved down the ladder and focused on mini cars. Only the Sonata model from a South Korean car maker competes in the same category and poses some threat in more recent years. The initial expectations of VW's top management perhaps aimed at grabbing as much market share as possible while other foreign players were blocked out; the end result of this bold expansion provided VW with some solid defence of its turfs when real and open competition began.

The worry over duplicity-induced downward sales did not materialise. Things went the other way. As a later development shows, this dual track marketing of Santana and Jetta under VW did achieve the initial goals of offering customers more choices and filling the market with cars from either of VW's sites. Chinese car buyers have got used to making purchasing choices between these two models. As Santana sold well, Jetta sales rose sharply as well, often at double digit growth. Car buyers are particularly impressed by Jetta's durability and easy-to-replace parts. There have been numerous news reports that some Jetta drivers clocked over one million kilometres on their metres. Jetta is also a favourite among taxi drivers, on par with Citroen's Fukang. Based on this dual track strategy, VW maintained its marker shares consistently and remarkably, with one model's sliding sales compensated by the other's rising sale numbers.

It was abundantly clear by the late 1990s that VW achieved spectacular success in China that no other foreign car companies had achieved. Its market shares routinely went over 50%, its brands remain widely accepted by Chinese customers, its relationships with Chinese government and clients solid, its dominant position in the market unchallenged. In 2003, the two VW joint ventures sold 700,000 vehicles of different models, and by late 2003, these two car projects had sold a total of over 3.3 million vehicles in past years. VW achieved what it could not in its own home market, or in any other markets for that matter. Even the big three in the US could not match this feat of overwhelming dominance by a single player. With further investment in following years, VW has made China its second biggest market after Germany. VW's strategic decisions on market entry, localisation, and expansion demonstrate that their overall merits outweighed shortcomings.

Pricing and Expansion Strategies in Open Market Competition

Into the 21st century, VW in China faces a new round of expansion and consolidation. Fundamental changes occurred in this market, and strategic decisions need to be made to catch new opportunities and fend off emerging threats.

The single most significant change in this environment was the real opening of China's car market. This was part of the efforts by the central government to enter the WTO, through liberalisation of major industries, which were under state protection. The car industry was prominent on the list of issues for negotiations, bearing mounting pressure in particular from giant American car makers. This issue figured highly at official China-US entry negotiations. The central government used to uphold a **"three big, three small"** structure as an ideal format, under which VW took two of the big three. Other entrants to this market were met with outright rejection or passive responses. This situation gradually changed from the mid 1990s, and the biggest car maker of the world, GM, grabbed an opportunity to form a joint venture with Shanghai Automotive Industry Corp. in 1997. This move opened the door for a flood of entrants of major players. Soon the formidable Toyota hooked up with FAW and took hold in Guangzhou as well, Honda was allowed to take over the failed Peugeot site, Nissan under the leadership of Mr. Carlos Ghosn joined hands with Dongfeng Motors, and a long list of international car makers followed suit. Even the once disgraced Peugeot contemplated a return. Behind this rush, previous restrictions were superseded, and the market monopoly enjoyed by VW alone could no longer be viable. VW must devise strategies to counter this tide of intrusion and face those competitors, which unwittingly missed earlier chances.

A second shift of trends came from surging consumption in the country. Santana and Jetta from the two VW projects seemed not enough to satisfy Chinese consumers who now received higher incomes. A sense of dullness in this market caused many consumers to complain, which forced the government to consider more options. This appetite for other choices of cars displayed itself clearly in the unexpected successful sales of Honda Accord in the first year of the project's operation.

This consumption drive further eroded VW's strong hold in the market. Government and fleet purchases made the bulk of VW sales. Even if VW cars made little changes or modifications over the years, these big clients would not break the tie or make loud noises. As private car buyers grew sharply in number, customer preferences played a bigger role in purchasing decisions. Loyalists to VW cars still form the majority, but many began to compare and search for more choices, rather than picking up the same old Santana or Jetta. If VW failed to heed their demands and continued to take government clients as the main source of incomes, it would see further sales decreases and lose emerging new groups of car owners.

One further negative factor is that the government began to be less tolerant towards VW's slow pace of technology transfers and product upgrading. To increase more activity, the government granted a permit for GM to form a joint venture with one of VW's original partners in the same city of Shanghai. GM made a US$1.6 billion investment in brand new factories and facilities and launched its Buick series. These cars would pose serious threats to VW cars such as the Passat and pull customers (including government clients) away from the dated Santana and Jetta. In response, VW evidently quickened its pace of launching more new models and modified old models to the market. The permission given to GM is a clear sign that favours to VW would not be taken for granted and that a total reliance on preferential treatments would be unconceivable in future.

VW has responded to this wave of new entrants with relatively swift actions. In order to offset erosions of market shares under competition, VW opted for a further expansion strategy. This indicates VW's confidence on the potential of this market, which has been proved by booms in car sales during the years of 2002-2003. If VW had doubts over future prospects, it could have adopted a rather conservative approach, holding on to its current revenues and making cautious investment on existing projects. Instead, VW decided to face off new challenges by implementing progressive or even ambitious long term plans.

In new plans rolled out by the VW Group chairman in 2003, the company was to invest Euros 6 billion in five years, in order to raise production capacity from 800,000 vehicles to 1.6 million vehicles a year. This increases total investments from VW in China to around

US$10 billion. As VW projects are currently quite profitable in operations, the company is able to rely on local funding for building up three completely new factories.

VW also revised its priority in strategies. Since the company enjoyed domestic treatments and policy protection, it had focused on profit margins rather than worrying about market share. No matter what prices it set on cars for sale, VW could maintain market share and achieve profit targets at the same time. This is the reason that VW cars, including Audis, sold in China at premium prices, well above regular prices on world markets. Along with the opening of this market, VW lost considerable market share, down from 50% in 2001, 40% in 2002, to 32% in 2003 (Shanghai VW and FAW-VW sales combined). The company continued to exchange market share for profits, not intending to deplete the company's financial resources as a whole.

Under the new expansion strategy, however, VW decided to make a switch of priority from profitability to market share. In a series of announcements made in 2004, VW lowered prices on most of its line-up, from Audi A6 to Bora, the highest being a 15% reduction. The Audi A6 has been a top profit making machine for VW and a symbol of VW luxury cars. A price reduction on Audi had never happened before. VW is not known for its pricing strategies or price cutting wars either. This new pricing strategy sent shock waves to other major car makers, and some of them certainly felt the heat and may have to follow. The aim of VW in this price cutting was to take back lost market shares and put a squeeze on those which pose threats to VW. As a result, profit margins may be lowered, but VW car prices will get more realistic and reasonable. This trade of profit margin for market share would help get back those lost customers. This campaign, along with increased production capacity, will enhance VW's leading position and slow down the pace of those aggressive challengers. Somewhat unfortunately for VW, its first attempt targeting low-end car segments suffered a setback when the two door model Gol, costing less than 100,000 yuan per vehicle, made unimpressive sales. With improvement and adjustments, new VW models in these lower end categories are expected to make more sales and take some hold in the market.

Increased investment and transferred production capacity to China at this stage have come from another immediate concern: the appreciation of the Euro. As the Chinese currency RMB is linked with the US dollar, the Euro has been risen sharply in value against RMB in the past two years. Car components from Europe became dearer for VW operations in China, especially for higher end car models, and these joint ventures suffered heavy losses as a result of this currency appreciation, nearly 2 billion yuan at FAW-VW alone. VW in Germany thus decided that it was a good idea and a way of hedging against foreign exchange risks to shift more production capacity to its China operations as soon as possible.

Now VW China controls four joint ventures in China: Shanghai VW, FAW-VW, VW Shanghai Gearbox Limited, and FAW-VW Components Limited. With the planned Shanghai VW Engine Factory and FAW-VW Engine Factory at Dalian, to be completed soon, VW China has established its full production lines and is able to build car series independently within this market. One obvious advantage is that VW cars can share platforms at each of these four joint ventures, so cost saving and efficiency rises are enormous. Other foreign multinationals so far cannot match the economies of scale and versatility at VW China. The company is also supported by a wide national network of parts suppliers. Measured by this complete structure, VW in China still holds pole position and is able to choose prioritised market strategies on market shares or on profit margins (see Table 19.3).

Table 19.3 Top ten car makers in sales, 2003 (sedan vehicles)	
Shanghai VW:	396,000
FAW VW:	298,000
Shanghai GM:	201,000
Guangzhou Honda:	117,000
Tianjin Auto:	114,000
Chang-an Suzuki:	100,000
Dongfeng Citroen:	99,900
*Chery:	85,000
*Geely:	74,300
Dongfeng Nissan:	61,800

* domestic car makers

Summary

Major strategies of VW in the China market can be divided into categories **of market entry, expansion, localisation and product/pricing.** Each of them dealt with a specific issue at a particular time. The prominent feature of these decisions is that this German car maker has demonstrated their typical persistence and patience in entering a new market. Their ability to cope with slow and unfamiliar environments is quite amazing. In this period of 20 years, VW has mastered the skills of gaining confidence from the government and utilised this goodwill in other business affairs. Despite the slow pace of launching new car models, VW avoided the fate of Peugeot through business expansion and thorough localisation. These efforts won rewards in government preferential treatments and public acceptance. When the time came for open market competition, VW was ready with established networks and complete model line-ups for Chinese consumers. Even top international car giants face a difficult task in dislodging VW from its leading position in this particular market.

The progress made by VW in China demonstrates a crucial fact in this market: the government plays important roles for the foreseeable future. VW received preferential benefits and solid support in the implementation of its various strategies, and few restrictions on its operations.

The case of **BMW** in China may illustrate this point from another angle. BMW insisted on forming a partnership with a non-state car maker which was also not on the list of state assisted major car companies. This intention has been applauded by Western car industry analysts. In the end, BMW decided to join hands with Brilliance China Automotive Holdings in Shenyang of the northeast in 2001. Brilliance is a listed shareholding company, previously making minivans and locally designed "China" brand sedans. The joint venture was a 50:50 ratio, with a 4 billion yuan investment. The joint venture was to build the 3 series BMW and later the 5 series BMW for the China market.

BMW had high confidence in this joint venture, partly because of Brilliance's shareholding structure. The chief of BMW stated that the company was looking for such a Chinese company as its partner, judging not by company size or government support but by management ideals and strength in quality and production. It seems that BMW would not choose any other partner over Brilliance.

In reality, the Brilliance BMW joint venture has not progressed as planned. Brilliance has been in turmoil and faces its own problems in shareholding and government relationships. The company received legal challenges from a previous CEO, who claimed that he in effect owned majority company shares. The municipal government took over the company acting as the original investor and major shareholder, after that CEO fled to the US. This legal wrangling caused enormous confusion and led to sharp downfalls of its stock price at Hong Kong exchanges. The city government is now controlling the company and was the entity which finalised joint venture deals with BMW. Deep-rooted problems surfaced when several senior executives announced their intention to leave and rumours emerged of panic selling of their Brilliance stocks before departure. (The latest reshuffle sacked those executives.) Due to these tangled affairs, the central government has kept clear of any dealings with the company and has let the province deal with this project. Brilliance suffered 30% drop in total net profits in 2004, affecting Brilliance BMW in more ways than one. This drag has forced BMW to halt any expansion plans at Brilliance BMW for the foreseeable future. In a twist of fate, BMW began to bypass Brilliance to talk directly with the provincial government regarding business cooperation outside Brilliance BMW. The German car maker now recognises that, with its small size and the poor standing of the province in the whole economy, Brilliance is a less favoured player in the car market, even if it now wears a BMW hat.

In the market BMW went in to compete, BMW 3 series cars are marked with high price tags and demonstrate no obvious advantages over other luxury cars such as Audi A6. In fact, BMW cars sold well in the China market with or without import tariffs. For example, in 2004 up to October, BMW sold over 5,700 imported vehicles, while locally made BMW 3 series sales reached not much higher than this figure, at about 8,500 vehicles, due to limited production capacity. This was before VW announced its across the board price reductions on Audis. Then in October, sales of Brilliance-made BMWs were merely 312 vehicles. In addition, by 2006 when tariffs on imported cars drop as promised, BMW 5 series cars will have a very small gap between its price tags and those of imported ones, and it is a question whether manufacturing luxury cars locally is a sensible option. BMW China executives are now in effect spending more time on managing car imports. Furthermore, as BMW cars began to be made at Brilliance, the "China" series sedans of that company are getting squeezed and sidelined, and this may cause troubles and potential conflicts within the joint venture. This awkward situation is clearly shown in repeated declination of Brilliance's top management to talk about the future of "China" brand cars.

Back to VW, despite its huge success in expansion and leading the market, the company has yet to overcome its weakness in distribution channels. At the early times of Shanghai VW, VW chose not to bear risks in distribution and sales, as it knew next to nothing of the market. The Chinese partner took the full responsibility for these tasks, utilised their own networks, and earned huge profits as sales soared. VW later realised the value of participating in distribution and managed to build a joint venture subsidiary with Shanghai Automotive Industry Corp. in 2000, which was in charge of all sales of VW products coming out of Shanghai VW. This appears to be an attempt by VW to take back some of the controls in distribution and sales, and VW has yet to obtain full management authority over these networks, especially those involving FAW-VW.

The VW fortunes are expected to continue, and if the GM shares are not doubled miraculously, the likelihood of losing the number one position for VW in China is quite low. As such, the VW experience and its strategic decisions on market entry, expansion and localisation provide relevant and invaluable lessons for those new entrants to the China market.

Discussion Questions

1. Do you think it is quite ambitious and risky for VW's expansion into a second joint venture with FAW? Examine VW's model line-ups from those two joint ventures and list potential benefits and drawbacks in coordination.
2. What are the major causes of VW's overall success in the China market? What are recent changes which have led VW to lose some of its long held advantages? As a less well known international marque, do you think VW will continue to hold its leading market position in China, considering the aggressiveness of bigger international players such as GM and Toyota?

CASE 4 Danone: A Quiet Achiever

At early stages of opening to foreign direct investment, equity joint venture was the preferred format in China for large projects, especially for those in cooperation with state enterprises under government administration. Foreign multinationals were persuaded to form joint ventures with certain selected large state companies, often the leading companies in the existing market. Results varied widely, with outstanding successes such as the case of Shanghai VW and with open disappointment such as the case of Beijing Jeep. When restrictions began to be relaxed in the 1990s, many foreign multinationals chose to set up their own operations (wholly foreign-owned) and leave joint ventures as a secondary option. As situations further evolved, in particularly with China's WTO accession and the nearing of national treatments for all enterprise types, a variety of options are available to new foreign entrants and existing foreign players. One of the new options is to acquire shareholding or majority shareholding of domestic companies and then get a piece of the action. This is not strictly a joint venture format or wholly foreign-owned one, but a simple form of mergers and acquisitions common in developed economies. The following case of Danone is a typical example of this new market strategy in the China market.

From JV and WFOE to Mergers and Acquisitions

Danone is a French multinational in fresh dairy products, beverages and cereal products. Danone Group reached sales of Euros 2 billion in the Asia-Pacific markets in 2003. Its entry into the China market is part of its globalisation strategy which constantly searches for growth markets.

Danone entered the China market in the 1980s. The company followed conventional modes and government policies at the time, and formed a joint venture with Guangzhou Dairy Milk Company to produce and sell Danone brand yogurt. It set up another company in Guangdong province to produce Danone brand biscuits. In 1994, the company set up factories in Shanghai to make Danone brand yogurt and biscuits. The Chinese partner was Shanghai Bright Dairy, and Danone took 75% of shares in these factories.

These continuous efforts in investment did not reward Danone with expected success in market shares and in sales. The Shanghai factories made losses for nearly 10 years, and even Danone's cherished yogurt brand did not help win wide acceptance from Chinese consumers. In the market for biscuits, there were large numbers of small scale biscuit makers in China, and Danone had to move into narrower high-end markets where foreign brands like Nestle engaged in constant fights over limited market shares. Danone has no clear advantages over other international brands, and taking top positions in this market appeared extremely difficult for Danone. These unexpected tough competition frustrated Danone for quite some time.

Even in the two industries Danone dominates worldwide, bottled water and yogurt, Danone faced stiff competition from domestic brands. The market leaders in China were Wahaha in Hangzhou and Robust in Guangdong. The CEOs of these companies of outstanding performance are both self-made entrepreneurs, starting from scratch to build up their business empires. They are extremely experienced in the industries they operate and know the nuts and bolts of doing business. Wahaha rose to be the biggest producer and seller of bottled water and a variety of drinks. Robust contested the number one position fiercely, but lost out on a less extensive distribution network than what Wahaha held. The CEO of Wahaha, Mr. Zong, is well known for his brilliant ideas to penetrate rural Chinese markets down to the village level. His company products, such as bottled water and fruit juice, could reach remote areas through loyal company agents. These two leading companies were able to serve customers across the country. Their local distributors were happy to expand service areas for products from these companies, which made their own trading businesses prosper. Through blanket advertising and extensive networking, these two companies gained clear advantages over other competitors, domestic or foreign. By the middle of the 1990s, Wahaha and Robust became undisputed leaders in markets for bottled water and fruit drinks, and their brands were household names.

Danone, on the other hand, failed to gain the market share it desired. The company even could not get its brand name recognised by most Chinese consumers. In the areas of bottled water and fruit drinks, Danone was a negligible player in comparison with the two leading domestic brands. It would take Danone enormous effort and huge investment to establish parallel networks and boost sales to the levels Wahaha and Robust had reached. The uncertainty of reaching this ambitious goal was understandably high. Taking account of unsatisfactory performance at other Danone invested projects, the full picture was even more pessimistic for Danone.

Under these circumstances, Danone made a critical turn in its strategies. Danone started to contemplate ditching the joint venture form of FDI and taking up the approach of mergers and acquisitions. State policies and regulations at the middle of the 1990s began to relax, and investment modes and ratios became more versatile. This gave Danone precious opportunities to carry out its expansion plans. In the meantime, an executive of Chinese-origin took up the rein of Danone's China operations. This coincidence of strategic and personnel changes paved the way for Danone to reach a turning point and become more successful in the China market.

Danone's expansion plans met with acceptance from Wahaha. The Chinese company had achieved what it could, on the basis of existing advertising and networking. That company urgently needed to acquire more advanced technology and enlarged production capacity, in order to stand as an undisputed pacesetter. Wahaha had engaged in protracted wars with its arch rival Robust and could not completely rule out the possibility of being pushed out some day by the latter. In this precarious situation, Wahaha looked for a strong backer from the outside and was eager to upgrade its own playing skills. The goal was to get to the top of the game and establish secured market dominance. The arrival of Danone with a merger proposal would serve this purpose well and fit in with Wahaha's ambitious plans.

Wahaha made searches and enquires in the market and had been in talks with Danone's rival Nestle. Danone moved in swiftly and succeeded in persuading Wahaha to accept its own offers. Danone promised to make concrete cash investment, leave management to the Wahaha team, retain the Wahaha brand, and provide help in extension of business to overseas markets through Danone's own networks. These offers appeared pretty tempting to Wahaha. The CEO of Wahaha, Mr. Zong, had maintained all along that conditions for a merger or takeover should be self-management under its own brand name. He was extremely worried that a change of brand name would cause a loss of domestic customers and cause sharp downfalls in sales. Offers from

Danone seemed to have met key demands from Wahaha, and risks of being superseded seemed minimal.

In 1996, Danone won a last minute bid, snatching from Nestle the chance to buy majority shares of Wahaha. The deal gave Danone controlling shares in the company, after paying US$71.2 million. With these new investments, Wahaha built a series of factories and purchased state-of-the-art technology and production lines from Western countries. In two years after the merger, sales of bottled water from Wahaha reached 4 billion units from 800 million units. It then appeared quite unlikely that another competitor would threaten Wahaha with similar sales figures.

With the backing of Danone, Wahaha became more confident in entering other profitable sectors and challenging existing players. In carbonated drinks, Wahaha launched "Future cola", in a clear frontal attack on the dominant Coca Cola and Pepsi Cola in China. Wahaha relied on technology borrowed from Danone and the rising nationalism in the country for the sales of "Future cola". This new cola was branded the "only cola from and for Chinese people". "Future cola" is sold through existing networks of Wahaha and reaches lower tiers of cities and towns, those territories by and large ignored by cola giants. With its competitive pricing and popularity in rural regions, "Future cola" now ranks third after Coca Cola and Pepsi Cola, and its sales in 2004 have reached 30% of Coca Cola's and 60% of Pepsi Cola's.

On a whole, Danone's takeover of Wahaha achieved amazing synergy rarely seen in cooperation between foreign and Chinese companies. This early success of mergers and acquisitions brought Danone immeasurable benefits. By making cash investment for Wahaha company shares, Danone not only eliminated a strong business rival, but also gained stable revenues from the operations of that company. The merger also saved Danone enormous amounts of expenditures on production facilities and distribution channels. Existing capacities at Wahaha readily turned to Danone's favour and added to Danone's own total assets. These multiple benefits encouraged Danone to apply the mergers and acquisitions approach as more business opportunities came by. The conventional FDI and joint venture approaches were thus downgraded and seldom applied since.

In March 2000, after careful searches and patient negotiations, Danone made a deal with the other major competitor, Robust. The choice of timing was appropriate, since Robust felt enormous pressure from competition with a Wahaha strengthened by Danone backing, and its market shares in some areas were shrinking. This time again, Danone made an investment of approximately 1 billion yuan for majority shareholding of Robust. Following the same pattern, Danone took the controlling shares and enjoy the benefits coming with this position, but left the management to the Robust team of executives. Danone promised not to interfere. It sent no personnel into Robust, and the latter had the authority to use its own brand name in the market. This deal, again, was a snatched opportunity by Danone from Nestle. The latter had engaged in talks with Robust for a long time, and Robust indicated publicly its interest in and favour towards a deal with Nestle. Danone came in and made offers appealing to Robust executives. After many rounds of bidding, Danone won out and nailed the deal.

After this second major acquisition, Danone had control over two of the leading companies in beverage and dairy products sectors. By applying this new approach, Danone now has no rivals to worry about in the sectors concerned. The two companies themselves are well managed and post excellent annual results. Danone could make full use of existing talented managers, experienced workforce and networks for its own business gains. Danone's involvement, in turn, greatly boosted performance of these two domestic companies. Their brand names were retained, which continue to draw customer loyalty, and their production size and standards increased, so both sides won from these deals. At this stage, Danone became the true market leader in certain sectors, on the basis of its control over two top domestic companies. If Danone had failed to work its own way out in previous FDI endeavours, it achieved its goals in a more creative way, skilfully riding the bandwagon of mergers and acquisitions.

Danone continued to implement its expansion strategy in the China market, primarily following its success model of mergers and acquisitions. There is no more Danone joint venture to speak of, and a financially healthy Danone pours money into projects where they matter. Still in the bottled water market, Danone spent 180 million yuan to acquire over half of the shares of a Shanghai company with a famous local brand. This move opened the way for Danone to enter lucrative markets in Shanghai and the surrounding prosperous coastal regions.

A series of acquisitions by Danone conclusively secured its undisputed hold on this particular market.

In these mergers and acquisitions, Danone takes an enviable favourable position. Danone has transformed its presence in China into a holding company. In its usual fashion, Danone approaches its target companies and makes reasonable offers. It has been well known to industry insiders that Danone is willing to pay higher prices in bidding. This aggressive manner won it major deals a few times in competition with Nestle. The deals made are in acquisition of company shares, so that Danone would have a say in the target company. Danone insists on taking majority shareholding, at levels higher than what the target company holds. With this secured shareholding, Danone does not get involved in running those profit-making companies, even their strategic planning, and stands to enjoy tremendous benefits brought in by those companies. Danone's own total sales in the Asia-Pacific regions are boosted by steadily rising figures from the China market. If things did not proceed along as planned and business targets are not reached, as the majority shareholder, Danone is entitled to make boardroom reshuffles and change top management at those companies, in order to achieve better results. This position fits Danone's company interests extremely well.

Danone's Strategy to Overcome its Last Barrier

In areas of beverage and yogurt, Danone has achieved its original goals. Wahaha is the biggest bottled water and fruit drinks maker in the country, and the two companies under Danone produced most of the yogurt on the market, plus Danone's own high-end products. In Danone's three core businesses, two of them take the top positions in the country, and it seems that Danone is very much near the ultimate goal of having its complete core in the top rankings (see Figure 19.2).

The one core business short of success is the diary business. Major international diary product makers have achieved little in the China market. The central obstacle is the control over dairy farms, which are in the hands of local authorities. Major domestic diary product makers all have firm backing of local land and diary industry authorities. They take hold of large land areas and of large cow herds. This is a type of crucial resource that domestic players would not share with foreign

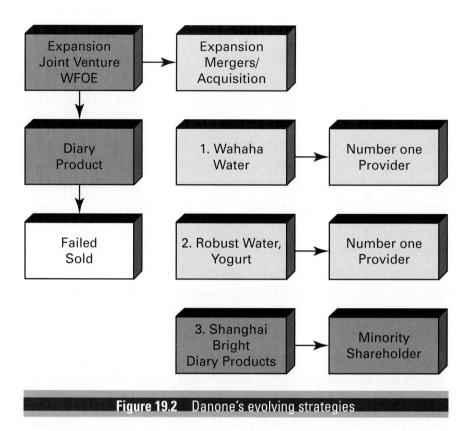

Figure 19.2 Danone's evolving strategies

players. Without a stable source of milk, diary product makers have only limited capacity to supply consumers with a variety of dairy products. For this reason alone, a number of international diary giants, such as Parmalat and Kraft, made their strategic retreats from this particular market, after a period of trial and experiment. The situation was no better for Danone either, being ranked behind a number of domestic players.

Danone is well informed of multiple difficulties in this industry, in sourcing of milk, sales networks, and customers' acceptance. Its own effort in this industry yielded little satisfactory results, after years of investment and operation. When it seemed near impossible to achieve the goal of being at the top within a short period of time, Danone turned to its well tested approach: through purchasing company shares of target local players. Danone was to give up building its own capacity and to invest in selected major diary product makers. This had been a more cost effective way of business expansion than throwing money on one's own bases.

The difference in this plan from previous acquisitions is that Danone had little hope of controlling a major diary product maker, as it did to Wahaha and Robust. Prices paid for taking over these two companies (for Wahaha, Danone's shareholding reached over 90%) were considered low by analysts in later years, and those companies Danone expressed interest in were too huge for a bidding by Danone alone. For example, the Shanghai Bright Dairy, the largest packaged milk producer in China, is a listed company and has the backing of an even more formidable industrial giant Shanghai Industries, a diversified corporation listed on both Shanghai and Hong Kong stock exchanges. In previous encounters, Danone, as a major diary product maker itself, did not gain an edge over its rival Shanghai Bright. It was thus also difficult for Danone to launch an all out bid for majority shares of Shanghai Bright.

Under the guiding mergers and acquisitions strategy, Danone made alternative, incremental moves to reach its final goals. To obtain consent from Shanghai Bright, Danone offered to let Shanghai Bright use its trademark and freely transferred the ownerships of its three established diary factories to the latter. The shareholding structure of Shanghai Bright was 40% each for Shanghai Milk Company and Shanghai Industries, and the remaining 20% was divided among other shareholders. Danone paid 121.03 million yuan (US$14.59 million) in 2003 for 3.58% stake of Shanghai Bright. This made Danone the biggest foreign shareholder and gave it a foothold in this target company. On this basis, Danone could act to acquire more shares when opportunities emerge. In 2004, Danone paid 78.14 million yuan (US$9.44 million) to another Shanghai Bright shareholder, in exchange for 2% of company shares. The total shares in the hands of Danone rose to 5.85%, a relatively large share in the existing structure. By further purchasing shares on stock markets, Danone held nearly 10% of Bright shares by the end of 2004. As the two major shareholders, especially Shanghai Industries which focuses on its own core businesses, later revealed their intention to offload Shanghai Bright shares in the near future, it is expected that Danone is likely to hold more Shanghai Bright shareholdings.

In its last core business, diary products, Danone has yet to achieve its original goals. This is simply the result of a much tougher situation in this sector than in the other two where Danone prevailed. Danone had acted like other international giants, retreating and contracting its operations in diary production. Danone also acted to stage a comeback, in that it invested money on company shares, in order to gain benefits indirectly and avoid being completely excluded in this market. This strategy in principle imitates the one applied before on Wahaha and Robust acquisitions; yet Danone has not been able to wage a full acquisition of a major target diary product maker. It had to lower its expectations and take the process step-by-step. From this respect, it will be a long way for Danone to become a majority shareholder of Shanghai Bright. Even if the shares in the hands of Shanghai Industries are to be placed on the market, the Shanghai municipal government, as the real owner, would likely balk at a big sale of shares to a foreign company. One possible scenario will be for Danone to at best be granted a position of second major shareholder, while another domestic company is introduced as the majority shareholder. Under these circumstances, Danone will receive increasing benefits as Shanghai Bright grows and expands steadily. This is perhaps the most plausible outcome for Danone to get certain desired business results in the diary product sector.

Under the mergers and acquisitions strategy, Danone has achieved excellent results in its expansion and overall business in the China market. In 2002, Danone made sales of over US$1 billion in China. Two-thirds of these sales came from beverages. Its activities and acquisition processes display two prominent features. One is a wide range of concessions made to the target company. This pattern repeated itself several times. Domestic companies like Wahaha retained its brand name and management rights. All products made by these companies are sold in their own brand names, with an added-on Danone logo. This low profile approach proved very effective in softening resistance from domestic companies and from government authorities. Even after Danone acquired Robust, few in China realised that Danone had been the boss of two top Chinese drinks companies. As many Chinese officials, executives and consumers became more sensitive of foreign brands flooding markets from the middle of the 1990s, Danone's modesty and concessions in takeover deals quickly won Chinese negotiators over. In addition, the unusually detached management styles of Danone made it recognised almost as a domestic company. Although many foreign multinationals like Coca-Cola China claim that they are in fact a Chinese company, to many Chinese consumers, Danone's similar claim would be accepted as a true statement.

Another feature of Danone's approach is its reliance on well managed finances to sustain a series of acquisitions. The initial investment seemed quite large even for a multinational like Danone, but considering the target of the takeover, such investment was well spent. The same amount of money on production capacity and distribution would not achieve the same business results in a short period of time. Early acquisitions did put strains on Danone's finances, especially when it had suffered from ongoing losses in its own joint venture projects. This temporary burden was offset by the fact that the asking prices from domestic companies, such as that from Wahaha, appeared small on a balanced assessment. Danone also quickly gained from acquired business operations and from generated profits. This kind of self-financing made later acquisitions less stressful, and Danone could utilise financial resources from one company to acquire the next target company. The question is how Danone could keep financing its series of acquisitions. Higher prices to be paid and larger sizes of target companies have made such acquisitions more costly and difficult. This growing threat has shown itself in the example of Shanghai Bright, which is currently difficult to be acquired by Danone.

The Danone experience in China is quite unique. Danone failed in the conventional form of FDI, namely joint ventures and wholly foreign-owned erterprises, and in gaining noticeable market shares on its own. Its business empire is in fact built on controlling a cluster of Chinese companies which are themselves market leaders. This is an unusual way of localisation. Danone has demonstrated no discernible advantages in management, marketing, and even production technologies over domestic companies. This lack of a clear edge is shown evidently in Danone's giving away of management authority to domestic companies and staying behind the curtains. Remarkable performance and rising sales have been achieved by management teams of domestic companies alone. It is doubtful that if Danone stepped ahead and took over full management responsibilities, these subsidiary companies would have achieved similar excellent results. Danone has no such track records of success in the China market.

When one considers the above inabilities of Danone's, it is even more surprising to see that Danone succeeded after all. The key is its flexible application of mergers and acquisitions in places where its previous FDI schemes failed, and its understanding of intricate relationships and business trends. An acquisition similar to the Wahaha takeover would not be possible in the 1980s, when even FDI was under strict government regulations. With adequate financing, leveraging, and government tolerance, Danone persuaded its Chinese partners to surrender company shares and to continue operations at the same time. Danone's astute business skills and detached management styles are perhaps unmatched by other major foreign companies in China. In a comparison with many foreign multinationals which are viewed as overwhelming threats to domestic enterprises, Danone is a relatively quiet player which has somehow managed to achieve its final goals.

Summary

The above four cases of foreign multinationals in China illustrate varying experience, strategies and outcomes in this market. The central strategy is not diversification, since these international corporations focus on their core businesses with no intention to diversify. This stands vastly different from the strategy taken by many Chinese companies, as discussed in Category I cases. The common central strategies of foreign companies are market entry and expansion. Similarity stops here, and divergence emerges. In the motor car industry, Peugeot and VW displayed their separate lines of strategies. What are the **key factors** for their strategic decisions, and what determined whether an operation succeeded or failed? As described in previous chapters, final results depend in fact on some simple essential elements in original planning. If a new market is seen as an experiment for potential gains, decisions after the entry are likely to be conservative with less commitment. A quick move to cut losses and exit will eventuate. On the other hand, an entry to establish a presence in this market is likely to call for persistence and agility in times of difficulties. More commitment and flexible coping patterns would impact on operations positively and lead to improved performance. Whirlpool took an approach similar to Peugeot's, seeing the opening of the China market as a one time opportunity and stepping back when business operations there did not run smoothly. On the contrary, Danone seems to have opted to integrate the China market operations into its global setting, thus having little contemplation of a withdrawal. On the basis of this conviction, Danone experimented on various approaches and found an effective one after bearing loads of losses.

Outcomes of an entry also depend on an ability to adapt in unfamiliar local environments. A tough task is to deal with local markets, customers, governments and enterprises. Skilful relationship building and comprehensive understanding of these environments are the keys. VW mastered the skills of handling government authorities, mainly in the areas of localisation and government purchases, while Danone scored big points in keeping a low profile and using domestic brand names for its own products. Mismanagement or failure in handling key relationships proves to have hurt some foreign companies dearly in their business operations.

Business strategies taken by these four foreign multinationals vary widely. All of them formed joint ventures with Chinese partners, but only one succeeded. A major difference exists in the partners they hooked up with. Strategic decisions of expansion are often made when there are emerging business opportunities and when competition from other major players arises. These expansions involve continued investment on major projects, enlarged production capacity, and careful selection of market segments. VW applied a dual brand expansion strategy and managed to take hold of most categories with its full product line-ups. Satisfying results of this strategy of course derive from VW's firm commitment and efforts in maintaining key relationships.

Danone's reliance on mergers and acquisitions definitely set it apart from the other three cases. With repeated failures and frustrating setbacks, Danone could have made its departure a long time ago. Its perseverance led to an eventual finding of a format for success. Its unique choice of strategy and experience may provide useful references and models for later foreign companies moving into the China market, as the business environment in China begins to allow more varieties of modes and options of investment.

These cases point to some common features of current market conditions in China. There will be little guarantee that a transplanted business model will prevail. There will be no possibility of success if introduced products are second grade in this increasingly competitive market. Smooth operation and satisfactory business results are possible if the strategies taken closely follow changing trends and momentum.

Discussion Questions

What are the major factors for Danone to carry out a mergers and acquisitions approach and for its success? Why Danone did fail in its own joint ventures but win in takeovers? Do you think the Danone story can be repeated by other foreign companies?

PART VII

FUTURE PROSPECTS

20

China in the 21st Century

*I*n an overall generalisation and from the standpoint of investing foreign companies, future prospects cover **three ranges of variables:**

❑ **First,** changes and future trends in the Chinese economy, which may at times cause severe, violent economic fluctuations.

❑ **Second,** those changes in relation to business environment and foreign investment in particular.

❑ **Third,** various strategies and options for foreign multinationals or companies engaging in market competition.

Prospects of Economic Growth

There are major issues and variables which may have unforeseen and long term impact on future direction and performance of the Chinese economy. Put simply, how do analysts and company heads view this market? What will be the future of this market—a growth market, or a shrinking or stagnant market? Answers from groups of people to these key questions will determine the actions they are going to take and the options selected in their business plans.

It has been a century-old divide in opinions on the potential or risks of the China market. Debates went back to the 19th century, and both optimistic and pessimistic views abound ever since. Expectations ran high when traders reckoned that if Chinese residents all bought clothes just one inch longer than before, there would be endless business orders to Lancaster weaving mills. This view was countered by closer observations that few Chinese could afford buying extra imported clothes and that they wore locally made materials most of the time. For contemporary China under socialism and reforms, expectations and projections from both camps continued to clash. The tide turned a few times as the economy went through high and low phases alternately, apparently corresponding to the twists and turns in perceptions of China by the Americans, as identified by Paul Cohen.

A popular and routinely surfacing theme is that the Chinese economy is bound to tumble and collapse. This recurring theme often emerged when there came more recognition of the strength in the Chinese economy, and when market opportunities triggered more interests in investing there. The theme also increased its appeal when the Chinese economy ran at a slow pace. Looking back, such pessimistic views gained strength after the 1989 political crisis in China, during the high inflation of the mid 1990s, through the turbulent Asian financial crisis of the late 1990s, and most recently at the combination of deflation and overheating of the early 21st century. Descriptions of "disintegration", "crash", and "hard landing" were overwhelming in news reports and business analyses, and many accepted these as rational projections, on the basis of plenty of data and figures provided.

At the current stage, structural problems in China have reached such a precarious state that any single move by the government met resistance from certain interest groups. Sweeping and effective reforms of the 1980s and early 1990s have gone. Many deep-rooted troubles have to be handled urgently, since there is little possibility of further delaying. These pictures of mounting problems have prompted a new tidal wave of pessimistic projections, in that the Chinese economy is described as moving towards a "coming collapse". This has been in stark contrast to the trend of growing foreign investment in China and the rising ranking of the Chinese economy on the world stage. It thus warrants a closer look here.

The crux of the "coming collapse" claim lies in the weaknesses of China's financial systems. It has been described that inflated figures distorted GDP growth rates, and the Chinese economy in reality grew at a much slower pace than officially declared. The trick is to issue more money notes, increase lending, start more large projects, draw more foreign investment, stock more unsold products, and then you get higher GDP figures and growth rates. All of these did not increase the wealth of the nation or raise living standards of the public; on the contrary, they have burdened banks in China with mountains of debts. The whole thing is a scam or mirage. This credit crisis will lead to a serious financial crisis, and when Chinese residents realise the magnitude of risks, their lost confidence in existing financial systems will destroy those insolvent banks and, along with it, cause the collapse of the entire economy. The earliest date of this "coming collapse" is tentatively set between 2005 and 2006. In a similar vein of this view from overseas, some mainland economists made bold but more detailed projections that the high risk period is after 2006 when financial sectors of China are open, and that in the following 20 years China will suffer at least three major large scale financial crises.

Needless to say, such a scenario of "collapse" would scare large numbers of existing and prospective foreign investors to halt and ponder. In its nature, this new pessimism is no different from previous ones in the 1980s and the 1990s. The Chinese economy is bound to collapse because it cannot overcome a certain obstacle by its own effort. A new feature this time around is that it identifies the financial sector as the chief culprit, where entangled problems do exist while short cut solutions do not.

To present a different perspective, we need to start from a principal understanding of the Chinese economy, namely its "**transitional**" nature. The economy is no longer a "single colour" entity; it is more of a mixed economy inclining towards perhaps a Singaporean type. Furthermore, structural problems and inconsistency are exposed more openly for scrutiny and diagnosis. This situation resembles closely a painting job in home improvement. A visitor could instantly make an observation that "you missed a spot there" or "where do you expect me to sit in this mess?" The sweating occupant is at that moment obviously more concerned about finishing the task before dusk than missing one particular spot or the tidiness in the dwelling. The essence of the matter here is to get results.

The variations of observations also stem from the fact that no modern standard economic theories have successfully tackled or explained the course of transition from a socialist/traditional economy to a free market economy of today. Their emphases are, and have been, economic phenomena in Western developed economies. Modern development economics are similarly inadequate for the transitional economy of China, since they cover mostly up to the era of the "Asian tigers". Studies of those NIEs are naturally extended to studies of the Chinese economy, in the hope that they can sufficiently explain the phenomena in another Oriental economy. While they are right on specific occasions and on technical grounds, such as inflation rates, they have witnessed more exceptions to their generalisations. This paucity of standard and recognised theoretical frameworks derives from a shortage of convincing evaluations of recorded practice in the Chinese economy and in turn, not surprisingly, gives rise to all sorts of explanations and projections.

With a huge population and land area, the transition in China has to proceed steadily and progressively. In fact, the real danger is that a rush to transform would make it fall to pieces and fail to rise again. A more sensible mentality is "**handle with care**". Inherent weakness and bottlenecks are easily exposed in this course of transition, and any intended change would create a series of chain reactions and consequences. Applications of Western economic principles have been under way in China and created varying, unexpected results. With a reference to the famous shock therapy in Russia, the feasibility of a similar solution in this transition is quite low.

This "transitional" nature also implies the introduction and insertion of new patterns and trends in the economy. These may replace and supersede existing ones and prove their vitality and efficiency in practice. These changes to institutions and programmes would make incremental improvements possible and minimise destructive effects of rushed plans. Newly established or improved institutions will play key roles in regulating economic and social activities and helping the society to evolve eventually into one with rule of law.

The central idea is that a slower pace does not necessarily indicate a tendency to collapse. There are many ways and means to prevent that from happening, but structural problems can only be dealt with in a gradual, progressive manner.

Regarding the crux of the "collapse" claim—the financial systems—there are several factors for consideration. For China's GPD figures, debates on its reliability have been on for decades. A GDP-orientated policy would surely encourage the government and officials to raise targets higher and inflate figures whenever they can. GDP criteria also boost the value of service industries and make slow-moving manufacturing industries appear to be lagging. Governments and businesses are apparently encouraged to move into tertiary industries for high growth rates and higher earnings. The total national GDP figures are thus affected to a certain degree, and the strength of the economy is likely to be exaggerated. These are the basis for doubts over the real growth and standing of the Chinese economy in recent years, perhaps from the time of Professor Thomas Rawski's paper in 1999.

These doubts have a point. The State Bureau of Statistics is in charge of national figures, and provincial and regional authorities are in charge of their own figures. The national authority only makes regular auditing of figures supplied from provincial level authorities. Discrepancies occur in this process, and there are in fact both inflated and deflated figures of GDP from local authorities, for various reasons on the basis of local interests. For GDP growth in the first half of 2004, the sum of GDP growth statistics from local governments reached 13.5%. The central government made weighted calculations and trimmed the final national growth rate to 9.3%. This time around, however, many overseas analysts believed the lower national figure to be an underestimate.

In these cases of statistical variations, the nature of the Chinese economy needs to be highlighted. It remains very much an economy of manufacturing production. Leaving those GDP figures aside, this economy consumes huge quantities of resources and products. Apart from growth in GDP, growth in all production and consumption has risen as well. In many categories of production and consumption, China is the number one player, such as steel output and mobile phone users. These could be taken as more accurate indicators of economic activities and scales in China.

In more recent years, the new leadership has openly announced its shift from a GDP-oriented economy to one with people as the foundation, a traditional Confucian ideal. Local officials who were promoted through showing higher GDP figures in their regions have been exposed and criticised publicly. Governments at all levels are under pressure to shift attention from raising GDP levels to improving real living conditions. The GDP disguise will get smaller, as well as the discrepancies.

For the financial systems, a heavy burden on the Chinese economy does exist. As discussed in a chapter of Part III on the banking industry, Chinese banks hold large amounts of bad debts and non-performing loans. This is precisely the main reason for a prediction of "coming collapse". Some of the debts include those owed by state enterprises, loans to real estate industries, and more recently loans to car buyers. State assets management agencies have taken over 1.4 trillion yuan of such debts owed by state enterprises in the late 1990s, and with new debts growing every year, the total has reached over 2 trillion yuan. Bank finances also spurred booms in real estate industries, pumping in billions of yuan for any sizeable projects. This is a major cause to overheating in the economy in recent years. Banks also lent out over 180 billion yuan as car loans to car buyers, for financing a new spot of consumption. Bad loans acount for over 50% of the total lending.

There is no denying that Chinese banks incur large sums of bad loans and their irregular operations led to inflated investment and GDP figures. The **question** is: how would this financial predicament lead to a crash in the economy as a whole? The entire banking system relies on people's confidence in the currency they are holding. The typical Chinese thrift behaviour still prevails, with bank deposits rising even in the years of deflation and at extremely low interest rates. Deposit figures routinely went over 10 trillion yuan, equivalent of annual national GDP figures. This usual behaviour also follows a rational pattern, showing in marked reduction of deposits in 2004, in response to more attractive investment options in housing, stocks and motor cars. These huge financial reserves have thus far supported China's financial systems well, and those debt-ridden state banks are the biggest receivers of personal bank deposits. Chinese residents identify these banks with the credibility of the government. As long as there are no dramatic outflows of bank deposits, Chinese residents are **betting** on political stability and an improving economy with their hard earned money.

China's financial systems face extraordinary difficulties, in that banks rely on interest rate differences between deposits and lending as their main source of income. While profitable projects and reliable clients are hard to find, banks receive less revenues while paying deposit interests. This erodes their profit margins and incurs losses. Banks also have worries over future competition from foreign banks, which may be able to grab local customers from these domestic banks and further reduce their total earnings. By and large, these are serious problems requiring intelligent and hard-nosed strategies and management. They remain far off from being crises over entire financial systems. Banks' credibility is guaranteed by the credibility of the government, and as it is in developed economies, the central bank (the People's Bank) is the lender of last resort. There have been no bank runs since the reforms began, and the government is supposed to prevent it from happening under any circumstances. There are also plenty of funds circulating within the economy, providing individuals and companies with needed capital. This more or less mitigates anxiety over cash shortages.

Growing capacity of the central government to collect taxes and make bigger budgets further softens the seriousness of credit issue. This capacity definitely has room to expand along with more efficient tax collecting (minimised corruption and evasions) and widening tax bases. For debt burdens on the government (see Figure 20.1), increasing foreign debts could be offset by huge foreign exchange reserves in the hands of the central government (idling, for most of the time), and domestic debts are mostly for long term investment projects. An additional assurance comes from the big pool of personal bank deposits, at 11.6 trillion yuan in October 2004 and rising. These financial capabilities enable the government to take action when a financial crisis looms. In the past, the government has been able to mobilise funds and

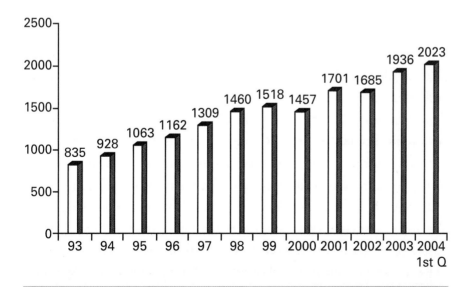

Figure 20.1   China's foreign debts (in 100 million US$)

pump them into selected state banks, in order to increase equity and achieve a more balanced financial state at these banks. With enlarged tax sources and foreign exchange reserves, the government will utilise these formidable resources in any emergency.

Even in a worst case scenario, if Chinese banks cannot hold off demands from depositors and bank runs do occur, these will not make a big difference. Opening to portfolio investments was an essential premise for financial crises to occur in countries such as Mexico, Argentina and some East Asian economies. The financial and stock markets in China will be under the managed control mode for the foreseeable future, and FDI on concrete projects are in the mainstream. QFII and managed foreign currency controls will keep taps on capital inflows and outflows and minimise the chance of a full scale assault by international financiers and speculators. Thanks to these mechanisms and restraints, a repeat of the Asian financial crisis in China is positively unlikely. Taking away this most crucial threat, handling a crisis arising from domestic financial institutions is a relatively lighter task to undertake. The first defence is to prevent banks from collapsing. This requires intervention from the central bank and injection of funds to provide confidence among depositors. The government could in the meantime make personnel reshuffles to replace bank bosses with more capable professionals. If some banks do declare bankruptcy during a financial consolidation, the government needs to draw up plans for compensations to bank depositors. Funds could come from foreign exchange reserves or from special government budgets. This rescue practice has been commonly conducted in developed economies, such as Australia's. With adequate funding and arrangements, depositors of collapsed banks are able to retrieve a certain percentage of their deposited money. The key is to keep the financial systems intact and survive the shocks.

Based on these considerations, the prospect of a coming collapse of the economy due to defective financial systems is to a large extent exaggerated. The real questions to be asked are on the possibility of a slowing economic growth and the tough job of transforming Chinese banks. The first question relates to the real size of this promised huge market and has immense implications for foreign investors. The second refers to financial institutions in China, which has been discussed in previous chapters.

It is now abundantly clear to everyone that the time of breakneck economic growth in China has passed, much to the relief of government officials and business analysts. Growth rates now fall back within a more sensible band of between 7% and 9% annually. With reforms and openings in place, economic cycles are increasingly seen as normal patterns in China, similar to the cycles in developed economies. The government learned from past experience that a sharp surge in growth would lead to some spectacular downfalls afterwards and make investments an eventual waste. The tricky part of the responsibilities is to manage fluctuations and gain reasonable growth. A growth rate lower than 2% or 3% will be undesirable, since population growth in China brings out extra numbers of people every year to consume this level of economic output. A double digit growth, on the other hand, is likely to easily run out of control. Under the new leadership, again, the emphasis is no longer on GDP growth figures, but on efficiency and real living standards. In official papers, high growth is now synonymous to overheating, which heralds bad news down the road and enormous wastes. With such a dramatic turn in mentality, it is likely that economic growth in China will stand at rates well below the double digit threshold in future years.

A pattern of slower growth in future derives also from additional pressure of reduced exports and the still weak domestic consumption. The export-orientated policy has proved costly to the Chinese economy, which traded precious resources for foreign currencies on the back of cheap labour and snail-paced increase in real wages to large numbers of factory workers. Such trade practices brought about worsening terms of trade, and exports from China face numerous non-tariff trade barriers and anti-dumping sanctions. Imports are to be increased, partly for satisfying rising domestic demands and partly for soothing anxiety of those countries with trade deficits with China. In the meantime, low wages, a trump card to attract foreign investment, has been a major cause to slow improvement in average purchasing power and flat consumption in recent years. These caused troubles to manufacturers and service providers. As a response to this awkwardly mixed situation, the central leadership has announced a shift of policy focus from export drives to meeting demands primarily from domestic markets. As this crucial adjustment takes effect, overall trade deficits are to increase sharply and contribute to slower growth in GDP.

A slowing down may create certain side effects and repercussions to people doing business in China. There would be less business orders from China for imported equipment and raw materials, and sales of many products would decrease. Enlarged investment and production capacities of foreign multinationals may exceed actual needs and demands in this market. This trend may noticeably reduce the appeal of this market and impact on strategic decisions of potential and existing foreign investors.

There is a hidden side of this growth story. Economic growth in China has demonstrated its extensive nature in relying heavily on enlarged size and output. Productivity levels in reality are comparatively low by world standards. This indicates that the economy has yet to reach its full growth potential, due to structural and efficiency obstacles. If the economy gradually shifts to a mode of intensive growth, and if Chinese enterprises reach the productivity and efficiency levels of those in Germany or Japan, the real net gains will be enormous. This shift implies that the economy may have plenty of room to grow, and with more productivity gains compensating for reduction in total inputs and investment, future growth rates may be likely to stay at reasonably high levels for many years to come. Business projections on the Chinese economy must factor this scenario into their assessments, evaluating both slower headline growth and real gains in the economy coming from cutting of slack and technological advances.

Another caution about this economy is the occasional emergence of "bubbles". With insufficient skills to manage vibrant markets, the government has in fact battled with economic bubbles ever since the time of early reforms. Rounds of bubbles occurred in several sectors, especially in real estate and related construction industries. Overinvestment led to consumption of all sorts of resources, and speculation loomed for future high returns, which pushed for more input. The economy then appears to stride forwards at a high speed. For example, there are perhaps between 20% and 40% of properties sold in Shanghai which are for investment and resale purposes. Oversupply is supported by speculation and bank financing. These huge bubbles will burst under a financial squeeze and cause losses to investors. This pattern has played its rounds in many economies including Hong Kong's. The Chinese economy under transition is fast taking up this pattern. An overheating mostly leads to correction, slow down and even recession. Considering the recurrence of this pattern, the Chinese economy is likely to grow on average at a slower pace, with occasional deceptive bubbles.

Barring a major full scale confrontation between China and the US, it is very unlikely that the scenario of a "coming collapse" of the Chinese economy will become a reality. This scenario is even less a sensible assumption if it is built on those detected faults in financial systems. We need to observe what will happen in 2005 and afterwards to verify the validity of this assumption. On the other hand, a slower pace of growth, in terms of GDP growth, has become a regular feature of the economy. These prospects of the Chinese economy as a whole form the basis for business prospects in the following two categories.

Prospects of Changing Business Environment and Foreign Investment

For over two decades of reforms, remarkable and even fundamental changes have occurred in the business environment, at increasingly shorter intervals. This implies that even very recent generalisations and summaries of this environment may soon be seen as outdated. This poses serious challenges to researchers and business analysts over the relevance and practicability of their work.

Past studies of Chinese economy and business can be put into two **time zones** of the 1980s and the 1990s. Early experiments provided rare cases of foreign investment in China, and these encounters gave birth to a series of studies as vital guides for late comers. These studies include many accounts of unhappy moments of clashes of two cultures and systems. One example is a case study of Beijing Jeep, a joint venture between AMC and Beijing Auto Works. Another is a detailed study of negotiations with Chinese counterparts, which had since influenced the viewpoints of numerous foreign companies in the following decade.

During this initial process, understanding of the Chinese business environment and operations were rudimental and minimal, while a decision to enter the China market was often driven by a simple assumption of market size based on population figures. This idea among foreign investors was not dissimilar to the expectations of British traders of the 19th century. Many foreign companies went in to test the waters and had no long term plans for their China operations, as shown in the case of Peugeot in Guangzhou. It is then not surprising at all that most investments came from Hong Kong and overseas Chinese.

The 1990s showed a different picture, when foreign investment flooded in as economic booms began. The Asian financial crisis made the China market more attractive and safe to foreign investors, while high growth and manufacturing capacity made it appeal to multinationals coordinating their global operations. Optimism and expectations ran high for potential in this market. Business analyses reflected this high hope in their own ways and routinely presented rosy pictures. China was described as the next economic superpower, and even the 21st century was predicted as a China century. Despite sporadic bad news and warnings, the general mood was high. To counter this optimism, there emerged frequent sayings of crisis or "coming collapse", with different emphases on particular faults in the economy and the society as a whole. Some even resorted to dynastic cycles and communist internal fighting as the guiding clues to prophesy a crumbling economy around the corner. The clashes of opinions and projections between the two sides became intense.

As shown in past records of studies, the key components of business environment, government regulations and policies, have been changing quite slowly in the 1980s, when trials and experiments were cautiously made. The 1990s saw bolder moves and concerted effort on market reforms, and high growth generated wide optimism for lasting prosperity. At the time of deflation and economic bubbles, restructuring and wider opening continued to provide impetus to improve the business environment for foreign investors.

What will be the future prospects of changes in this business environment? The biggest **impact** came from China's WTO accession. That entry basically changed the rules of doing business in China. As thousands of regulations and bylaws are under revision to be compatible with international rules, the environment is moving towards a more standard setting for business activities. New and revised laws also offer more protection to business interests, at least on paper. It is therefore essential for multinationals to keep themselves up to date on China's compliances with WTO rules.

Several recent and coming changes are closely related to foreign investment. **First,** under the signed WTO agreements, foreign companies and banks will enjoy **national treatment** by 2006, the same treatments as those accorded to domestic companies. Their operations in China will meet less rigid barriers. It will be more convenient and take a shorter time to get required paper work and official approvals done for business purposes. So far, Shanghai is perhaps the only place with standard procedures and clear instructions on foreign business-related applications. Most government bureaux operate on *guanxi* or favours in dealing with outsiders. If foreign investors find a local government with work schedules and efficiency which match the standards of Shanghai's, that is likely to be a good place for investment. After 2006 when national treatment rules are applied nationwide, foreign investors may be able to find more Shanghai-style business environments and face less hassles. One benefit of these new rules is that once business interests are at risk, foreign companies have official channels to lodge complaints and sort things out. It is also legally viable to file law suits. With a more transparent government operation promised, foreign companies would save considerably on relationship building and *guanxi*.

Second, controls over foreign enterprises are to be relaxed significantly. Market entry to foreign investors has been simplified and related barriers lowered. Foreign companies are able to enter more industries and form alliances with Chinese partners. A good example is the telecommunications industry, which has opened in steps to foreign companies for cooperation, though the big two state service providers still dominate. Similarly, the banking industry offered wider opening and attracted large number of entries of foreign players, while the wholesales and logistics sectors have opened only recently. Certain government regulations have been revised or scrapped along with time and with pressure from foreign companies. These include the regulations which dictated the level of shareholding foreign companies could have in a joint venture, the percentage of locally made components in finished products, and sales through distribution networks in the hands of local companies. More constraints on foreign companies will be removed by new government regulations, in accordance with WTO rules. These will place foreign players on a more equal footing with domestic players.

Third, national treatment rules apply across the country, thus reducing risks in doing business at certain localities. Regional differences and protectionism have been chronic problems for foreign companies. The new rules will assist them in facing less resistance and opening more local markets. This of course depends on the effective implementation of those rules by the central government; foreign companies benefit most from these rules when the central government is financially strong and has a clear upper hand in the central-local relations. While the selection of regions to enter is a decision to be made by foreign multinationals on many complex considerations, such as income levels and consumption behaviours, an effective implementation of national treatment is to provide a positive factor for such entry decisions.

Fourth, numerous national and local **preferential treatments** to foreign companies will be retracted under new rules of national treatment. In practice, local governments often offered additional attractive treatments to foreign investors, in land use, tax exemption, or labour hire. A future uniform implementation of national treatment will make certain local preferential treatments invalid and null. Some foreign companies may face more constraints than they had before. For example, Wal-Mart is currently resisting pressure from the national union body about setting up a workers' union within the company's branches in China. The company may soon lose the argument that it was granted the exception under agreements with local governments. For its refusal, Wal-Mart has not been successful in entering Shanghai, where the union rule is more strictly observed than in other regions. Previous case-by-case deals have provided some foreign multinationals with enormous opportunities and exclusive benefits. National treatment rules may significantly limit such chances in their future operations.

Prospects of Market Competition

On the basis of prospects of economic growth and business environment, foreign companies need to make their choices in strategy and operation. While there is a more open economy and fewer barriers to market entry, foreign companies will meet more challenges and competition in this market not only from domestic enterprises but also from other foreign multinationals. In many industries and sectors, this has been a common phenomenon. It is thus the time to offer a reminder to foreign companies that market competition may not wane but heat up instead. Their business strategies will have to be adjusted accordingly.

Foreign multinationals need to, **first,** consider whether their China operations fit in with their global operations. This is basically a question on strategic decisions of entry, further investment or withdrawal from this market. Many invested in China for the benefits of selling products, market shares, or outsourcing. The last option is now taken up by growing numbers of foreign companies, as their main targets are home markets. This kind of investment is most likely to continue unabated, having weathered storms including rising protectionism back home. The gaps between costs and earnings are so wide that resisting these business opportunities proves futile. For the other two goals, foreign companies may have based these on their perceptions of the China market and huge numbers of Chinese consumers. This consumption potential will be realised if economic growth continues as desired. When these two goals are set with certainty, foreign companies will then need to make other follow up strategies in their China operations.

Second, they have to be prepared to face stiff market competition. The days when foreign companies could make large sales of foreign brand products have gone. Except in high-end categories, Chinese consumers have become more selective and price-conscious. Domestically made brand products have taken away large market shares from foreign players, and in many sectors, such as white and black goods, domestic brands hold significant shares and sell well. This recent trend has forced many foreign brand names to seek revenues from high-end markets. Foreign companies also cannot avoid meeting old rivals from back home and fighting feuding wars on a new battleground. A good example is China's motor car market, where German, American and Japanese car makers all entered with huge production capacity and brought their competition in global markets into China. With so many car makers in one place, average profit margins are certain to drop and every player will receive fewer revenues as a result. This rule has been true for VW China.

Third, foreign companies need to consider the ratios of returns on their investment. In response to higher living costs, wage levels are on the rise, and labour costs in China tend to increase. This adds to total operating costs of a foreign company. So far, labour costs are apparently low and it is quite profitable to outsource. Migrating rural labourers also provide crucial inputs to curb rises in wages. But this situation will change, since cheap labour in China is against the promise and goal of the new leadership to raise general living standards of the nation. Media coverage of poor salary earners in coastal manufacturing bases has attracted attention from the government and the public, and pressure will be on enterprise owners of all types to raise wage levels with CPI rises and increase real incomes their employees receive. These domestic issues will have certain impact on investing foreign companies and push up average levels of labour costs.

Fourth, foreign companies also face the critical issue of technology and upgrading in this market. They normally have outstanding edges in developing countries, but local competitors' learning process and ability to imitate have made sales of second grade products much harder. For major items of consumer goods, domestically made products show little differences from foreign brand products. These close similarities in function, design and quality hurt sales of foreign brand products dearly. They have to acutely apply a differentiation strategy to distinguish their products from others on the market.

Another alternative is to keep a tight hold on core technology, such as a laser tube or compressor, so that domestic companies have to pay premium prices for these centrepieces, regardless of their sales records. One more advantage foreign companies have is protection of intellectual property rights, which will be more vigorously enforced by the Chinese government in the near future. The negative side is the costs involved in chasing knock outs and uncertainty of winning such cases in court. With so many designs and products available on the market, it is hard to identify a stolen intellectual property or a unique design. For example, GM launched a mini car Spark in 2003, derived from a design by a Korean car maker acquired by GM. Six months before this launch, the Chinese car maker Chery launched its own mini car QQ. With right pricing and engine capacity, QQ beat Spark hands down, with sales of over 70,000 vehicles against Spark's 6,000 vehicles. GM was outraged and accused Chery of stealing Spark designs, especially its cute "big eye" front lights. Due to difficulties in proving the uniqueness of its design and complexity of legal wrangling, GM found it hard to pursue a legal resolution of this dispute. GM turned to cut business ties with Chery, including the ties between Chery and GM's Chinese partner, Shanghai Automotive Industry Corp. This example testifies to the difficulties in defending one's own intellectual property rights and designs; it is, however, extremely crucial for foreign companies to differentiate their products from domestic companies, in order to gain certain advantages in market competition.

A worse mistake made by foreign companies is that they allow local companies to learn and catch up, without always keeping one step ahead. This leads to loss of an edge and respect from local competitors. Early glows on foreign companies may quickly fade in the eyes of local enterprises and consumers. The case of the Hong Kong company in China, in Part VI, illustrates this point perfectly. Gradually, some Western companies even receive less respect from Chinese companies and consumers. This derives from foreign companies sending in less experienced personnel, selling outdated models of products, or from simply failing to pay required attention to this market. The end results are often the losses suffered by foreign companies in many ways. Their sales go down and products disappear from the market. In enterprise management, this is particularly acute, since business models can be learned quickly, and they do not always work in the China market. One failure leads to doubts over the plausibility of introducing foreign models and of paying for services provided. In the case of Start Technologies, these doubts emerged and affected the restructuring schemes initiated by external consultants. Foreign companies have to be alert and retain their competitiveness in the market.

In short, foreign multinationals have multiple choices in their strategies in the China market. A prospect of pressing market competition must be recognised, so that the chance of neglecting business essentials can be minimised and overall performance enhanced.

Central Issues of Concern

With an adequate understanding of the above prospects in general areas of concern, we need to highlight a number of issues for a closer scrutiny. These issues draw our particular attention because evolving events may have unforeseen and unpredictable impact on the direction of the economy and on foreign investment as well.

Macroeconomic Management

This is the most worrying problem in relation to economic growth. Structural problems and traditional bottlenecks have made this management ineffective and precarious on some occasions. This issue can be divided into two sub groups.

The Relations between Central and Local Governments

This issue is politically sensitive and chronically problematic. Contrary to public perceptions in the West of a centralised country of China, except in extreme cases of foreign invasion or political upheaval, the central government today has enormous difficulties in implementing and enforcing its major policies and regulations throughout the country, without deviation or distortion in the process of communication. In economic spheres, a pattern of decentralisation has long set in and a centrifugal tendency has been repeatedly detected by Western observers. Local governments have been driven to seek the most assuring means to serve their own interests. Their intentions often clash with directives from the central government, which in turn causes wild fluctuations in the economy.

This is bad news for the economy and its steady growth. Local initiatives and overinvestment created numerous rounds of chaos in the past. Even though the central leadership has shifted focus away from GDP growth, that benchmark remains the guiding principle of large numbers of local governments. State investment in local projects, exports to overseas markets, and FDI deals all increase GDP in regions and provinces. Any profit making or loss making projects are acceptable, as long as they jack up total output numbers. These intentions often lead to identical and repeated investments in various regions. The worst example is Dongguan in Guangdong province, where you can hardly tell the difference between products of one factory and another. Yet, aggregate GDP figures have always been high in Dongguan among many other counties of Guangdong. Satisfaction to local officials spell trouble for the central government, since such duplicated investments made by local governments cannot be smoothly absorbed by the market and drive up prices of many kinds of raw materials and crude oil. Coordination by the central government often fails to impress, and macroeconomic management often achieves desired goals too late in economic cycles.

In the most recent tug of war between the central and local governments, a detected potential overheating forced the central government to issue warnings in 2003 to halt large investments. Local governments went exactly the other way. No one wanted to be the one left out, so there emerged a race to make investments on hot projects after those warnings went public. When the central government warned of over expansion and capacity in the steel industry, large numbers of steel mills got approvals and started construction work. Contrary to the wishes of the central government, investment in steel making rose over 100% on a yearly basis. In cement and aluminium smelter, the rises were 100% and 40% respectively. Similar patterns of control/response occurred in natural resources, non-ferro metallurgy and real estate industries. With the urging of local interest groups, local governments tended to ignore directives from the central government which may disfavour or suspend particular local development projects. In the example of real estate expansion, industry leaders in the country even succeeded in overruling a central directive which attempted to curb lending to that sector and to cool down the buying fever. When the central government tried to put a leash on heads of state enterprises to minimise the scale of lost state assets, local governments sped up their liquidation schedules and sold state enterprises under their charge like hot cakes, with an overwhelming urgency and at much discounted prices.

All of these **contradictions** indicate a degree of loss of control by the central government. Local governments, interest groups and some business circles found ways to defy unfavourable directives from the central government and pursue their own interests whenever they could. Macroeconomic measures often lose effectiveness in this tug of war, and the credibility of the central government may come into question. This will be very risky for the market and the economy, since there will be no clear indication of direction, and government authority will be diminished. Especially during the periods of overheating and recession, macroeconomic measures will become useless, and most players in the economy and the public will be hurt badly. This uncertainty and ambiguity have proved damaging to normal business and to foreign investment.

The central government must exert authority over local governments and smooth out troubled spots. Revenues for local governments have been proportionally reduced against revenues for the central government since the taxation reform in 1994 (see Figure 20.2). In 2003, the central

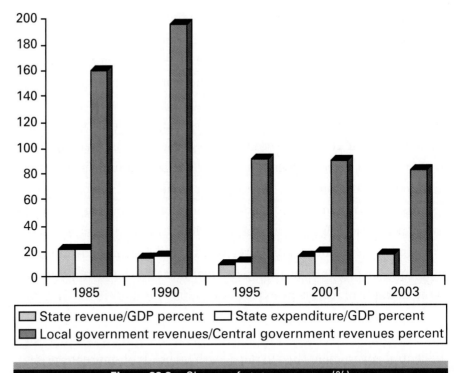

Figure 20.2   Shares of state revenues (%)

government made transfer payments to local governments at a total of over 800 billion yuan, which took 50% of local government spending. The central government could have better used these financial resources to strengthen its control over localities. There should be more coordination in the central-local relations, and improved financial strength in the hands of the central government should be effectively applied, in addition to conventional administrative means and Party disciplines.

The Issues of Corruption and Rule of Law

With the near ubiquitous existence of official corruption and graft, the effectiveness of administration has been persistently on the way down. Corruption tends to weaken people's confidence in the government and established systems. The first issue of central-local relations is also affected by corruption, since local governments find enough motives to defy central instructions, especially those on macroeconomic controls, if they are fed with bribes from special interest groups in their localities. A major cause of official corruption has been the gap between relatively low wages for officials and the immense authority they hold. Rent-seeking became unavoidable.

Corruption has additional implications for foreign investment and the business environment. As a double edged sword, corruption hampers normal business operations in many ways and increases operating costs, but it also greatly facilitates certain business activities, even those against official guidelines, if bribes are involved. Corruption in the second scenario is often reluctantly called by analysts as the "**lubricant**" of doing business in China. For those with right *guanxi* or setting up *guanxi* networks, business deals are so easily done that they achieved results far beyond their initial expectations. A growing number of foreign companies took this approach to sidetrack restrictions and solve problems in their business in China. As some preliminary data show, about 64% of corruption cases in China involve foreign companies and international trade, mostly in obtaining permits, special treatments, or extra favours.

The means to get rid of, or minimise, official corruption are in political, cultural, and institutional spheres. One feasible way is through more transparency. The WTO agreements signed by the Chinese government highlight the need for transparency in government functions, and the imposition of this rule will generate some positive results in later years. Access to information and reduction in rent-seeking opportunities will lead to less bureaucratic bundles and demands for bribes. A rule of law in China will provide legal and independent means for settling business matters and protecting investors' interests in court. This of course requires drastically improved court and legal systems in China. Even if it is unlikely that China will adopt a common law system, a respect by the government and the public of laws and courts will tremendously reduce business risks. For this, the paramount demand is to establish and improve institutions which can guarantee people's rights and protect their interests against draconian rules and unfair treatments.

Issues of Lasting Complexities

With the above discussions on economic prospects and the business environment in China, we should never ignore the existence of threats from the tyranny of conditions. Regardless of differences in political movements, ideological divides, or economic transformation, certain primary conditions of extreme rigidity exist in this economy. There are a number of major challenges which are constant and immune to short term policies. These are cold hard facts and the realities China faces in the foreseeable future.

Unemployment, Poverty and Social Welfare Cover

Job creation has become a top priority of the government, primarily for the purpose of social stability. This task is mind boggling. China now regularly has a migrating population of 140 million roaming in the country, moving from rural regions to urban regions. This is a gigantic pool of labour, yet also an unprecedented shock to existing systems of social controls. The task to provide them with jobs and minimum welfare has never been harder. In the 25 years between 1978 and 2003, 150 million rural residents have moved into cities to work and settle down. This pace is going to get faster, and according to an annual figure of 10 to 15 million rural residents settled in cities, in the following 20 years, Chinese cities will have to supply nearly 300 million jobs for incoming rural migrants. Compared with the figures in the first 25 years, pressures on the economy are doubly intense. Together with natural population growth and a new labour force entering the market annually, the employment situation for China in future years is less than optimistic.

The problem is that the economy is expected to grow at lower rates in future, and along with wider applications of technology, manufacturing industries will create smaller numbers of jobs for new recruits. Even foreign companies operating in China will markedly reduce their labour demand for low quality process workers. The industries which create most jobs in developed economies—service industries—are not well developed in China, taking roughly one-third in total GDP in the past 10 years and having created jobs at 29% of the total in 2002. These industries are to be well utilised to provide jobs for newly arrived rural labourers. Some of them, such as real estate, logistics, restaurants, community services, and travel, usually employ large numbers of people. Since the 1990s, an increase of one percentage point in GDP growth created only 700,000 jobs, down from 2.4 million in the 1980s. It is evident that GDP growth has a reduced positive effect on the employment situation. This has forced the central government under the new leadership to shift focus from "**growth** priority" to "**employment priority**" in the 21ˢᵗ century. The future is somewhat grim considering the trend and pace under which rural labourers are released from land.

As discussed in previous chapters on social disparity, the divide between the rich and the poor has constantly widened. Forbes' annual lists of richest Chinese stand awkwardly by the side of poverty figures issued every year. In official figures, there were 30 million rural residents in poverty and 22 million urban low-income residents in 2003. Adding unemployed labourers and laid-off workers, the figures for people in relative and absolute poverty are bound to be much higher. Unfortunately, large industrial and commercial projects, as well as brute government forces, keep dislodging people from land and throwing them into the quarters of poverty. Social welfare covers for these large groups of people have been inadequate and only gained some priority on government agenda in recent years. Social welfare expenditures have kept a share well below 2% in government budgets.

New schemes of superannuation, pension and other covers have been installed since the late 1990s, including unemployment benefits. They either cover small numbers of residents or provide assistance to those with lower than required living standards. Lack of funds is certainly a constant problem, from government budgets or from other fundraising. An even graver problem is the pension liabilities on the part of the government. When the time comes for retired employees to claim their benefits, the funding for social welfare will see deficits and there may even be a failure to pay. Funds collected in accounts may have been used for other purposes or projects during the years in between. An official study in 2001 by the Ministry of Labour and Social Security predicts a shortage of pension funds of 1.8 trillion yuan in the following 25 years, averaging 71.7 billion yuan per year. Pension payouts are a problem for many developed economies as well, due to the big figures involved and strains on current budgets. Most adopt voluntary contributions or ease pressure out over a longer time span. In China, the time of reckoning is still far off, but funds available at current levels are certainly not sufficient to cope with future claims.

These problems in employment, poverty and social welfare pose threats to social stability and the economy as well. These are internal factors not directly related to foreign investment decisions, but they are related to projections of the Chinese economy as a whole.

Resources Consumption

As discussed before, the Chinese economy is now relying on consumption of crude oil for most economic activities and production. China spent nearly US$20 billion in 2003 to import over 90 million tons of crude oil and US$6 billion to import 30 million tons of oil products. In 2004, China imported a total of over 100 million tons of crude oil. As a result of drastically rising international oil prices in 2004, China is paying much higher in US$ to purchase crude oil to satisfy demands and hunger in domestic markets. Over 100 million tons of annual oil imports and huge deficits in oil trade will be regular features of China's overall trade in international markets. This has provided enormous business opportunities to resource-rich countries such as Australia, which secured a 25-year agreement with China in 2003 to supply liquefied natural gas as a key alternative energy source.

The urgency in securing energy resources is so high on the national agenda that a US-style strategic oil reserve is planned to be set up; this gave sufficient impetus to international oil speculators to hike up oil prices further in 2004 and after. The central government already announced in 2004 that crude oil exports (mainly from Da Qing oilfields in the northeast) would be cut by two-thirds next year. The government also seeks available oil sources across the world, in light of the US occupation of Iraq, a major oil producing country. Efforts in this search have not yielded assuring results. This critical situation will not improve in a short period of time and could add significantly to economic uncertainty and insecurity. To foreign investors, a direct impact will be felt if power shortages cause production and operations to halt, as what happened in many coastal regions in 2004.

Environment and Sustainable Growth

Environment degradation is another worrying prospect in the future. Protecting the environment has not been high on the national agenda, and with toothless national legislation, there is hardly any attention paid by local governments to this issue. Economic growth, in terms of GDP growth, has overwhelmed all other concerns. As long as this figure increases, by way of land reclamation, deforestation to sell timber, polluted waters from chemical downpours and dried rivers due to digging for all sorts of natural resources, serious environmental consequences are ignored or brushed aside by governments at all levels. In 2003 alone, China lost a net 2.53 million hectares of farm land to land reclamation. To a great extent, economic growth in China is achieved by consumption and exhaustion of existing resources, at the expense of the welfare of future generations. New industrial and commercial zones have made large arable areas land of concrete, and pollution problems have become social problems. It will take enormous efforts and funds to clean up the mess in many regions, in order for people to have average living conditions.

The energy and environment issues are essential in any future plans of sustainable economic development. It is only in the new century that the mood and mentality are beginning to change. The State Council under Premier Wen gave a moderate target of 7% growth for 2004, lower than the achieved figure of 9.1% for 2003. This was to acknowledge that previous breakneck growth is both excessive and unsustainable. In policy terms, there is a genuine desire to consider the unbearable costs and consequences of such high growth.

These three issues show degrees of their inelasticity, indicating that no matter what political changes or economic policies are in place, the government and society have to bear with them and even suffer from deterioration in these conditions. A mishandling of these issues would extensively jeopardise economic stability and growth, in turn affecting investments made by millions of domestic and foreign investors.

Issues Related to Foreign Business and Investment

Under the macroeconomic conditions and trends summarised above, foreign companies need to focus on some specific prospects for their business operations in China.

First, they should watch closely China's WTO compliances in future years. These cover many areas including trade barriers, national treatment, transparency, and intellectual property rights. The time for a full compliance is 2006, and judging from the changes since 2001 when the agreements were signed, comments from Chinese and Western observers are mixed. The positive side is that compliances are by and large on schedule with the signed agreements, and the negative side is the occasional resistance towards enforcement. The reason is that the government needs more breathing space before the full opening and that there are problems hindering compliances, such as frictions between the central and local governments. Foreign companies need to make their own judgements and test the case in reality. Regulations and their applicability are to be checked out carefully, so that they can enjoy the full benefits from this opening. It is important for foreign companies to recognise that some regulations are now superseded, and they are no longer subject to certain restrictions in the industries they operate. Examples of this are rules of shareholding and market entry. Foreign banks provide good examples of catching up with the trend and attached opportunities. They made moves in business expansion closely following the steps in relaxation of official restrictions on foreign players in the banking industry.

Second, they should select particular regions and consumer groups to do their businesses. It seems clear now that foreign companies realised the diversity in this market. China is not seen as a big single market, but a market with several dividing lines. A key decision to be made is which region they are going to enter and to expand in. As discussed before, major blocs are the PRD and the YRD, with Beijing-Tianjin as the next circle of economic activities. In terms of human resources, purchasing power, production capacity, and more importantly, government efficiency, the YRD has the advantages over others. With WTO compliances, Shanghai and the YRD regions will demonstrate more consistency and vitality for the operations of foreign multinationals. The PRD remains the most vibrant and free market in China, with its accumulated wealth and willingness for trials. Its large numbers of manufacturing enterprises are able to meet any business orders, so OEM production for exports is prevalent. On the other hand, the problems in environmental protection and industrial relations are chronic.

With near saturation in consumer markets and rising operational costs in coastal regions, especially in the YRD and the PRD, large multinationals will consider expansion into inland regions. A better time to undertake such an expansion is after 2006, when nationwide compliances of the WTO rules take effect. Risks always exist in more regulated local economies, but the implementation of national treatment will provide more assurance and security for business organisations. For small- and medium-sized foreign companies, extra protection in regulations proves vital. Troubles in inland regions are in communication, transportation, and easy access to those regions.

Third, they need to consider the timings of decisions and observe trends and shifts. An old Chinese saying describes **"being born in the wrong time"**, referring to wasted skills and unaccomplished feats in a particular period of time. In regard to entry and expansion decisions by foreign companies, timing proves crucial on many occasions. A beer company may enter the market early to find small numbers of beer drinkers and exit just when the market is getting mature under its previous tireless nurturing. Economic cycles could disrupt operational plans of a company and cause significant waste. A company which keeps a small production capacity may miss a great deal of business opportunities in an economic boom. In the China market, hot selling large items of consumer goods shift positions at shorter intervals, such as an upgrading from VCDs to DVDs, so that a slower response in entry or expansion may cost the company in question dearly. It is thus important for companies to detect trends and make projections far ahead, in order not to implement a market strategy with a wrong timing.

The above brief summary of future prospects is made in a descending order. It is essential to first get certain grasps of the economy and the likely future directions, in order to establish a balanced assessment of risks and opportunities in this economy. Political and economic systems with uncertainties and chaos generate little appeal to profit-orientated business organisations. The next and harder part is to detect and identify market potential in this **transitional** economy. It is here that viewpoints diverge wildly, and investors are easily influenced by certain optimistic or pessimistic claims. Even academic studies and systematic analyses often fail to make right judgements or debunk certain mysteries convincingly. It is then common that the matter is in the hands of the investing company to either weather the storm or call it quits, on the basis of their priorities, intuition and concrete business results.

The business environment in China is going to change dramatically in the following years. This change of game rules requires more vigour and responsiveness from foreign companies operating in China. They are to heed modifications and variations in government policies and regulations, in order to maximise gains and minimise risks and losses. Freer business activities (rising private business sectors) and increased volumes of production and consumption would provide more opportunities in this economy. However, it is important to remind oneself that market competition is going to heat up, not calm down. As such, making right strategic decisions will then be more critical for foreign companies to conduct smooth operations and achieve business goals.

As a rule of thumb, initial entries by foreign investors are usually made on assumption of potential business opportunities for their investments in China, while hassles and troubles at later stages affect or shake their confidence. A further recovery after learning the tricks would complete this "U" curve of experience. In fact, the Chinese term *"wei ji"* (crisis) has two characters, which explain separate meanings of "danger (risks)" and "opportunity". This illustrates perfectly the nature of business prospects, as each strategic decision inevitably involves both elements. This combination is to manifest itself in 2005, as that is a crucial year of WTO rule-implementation before the anticipated full opening in 2006. A smooth process will clear more barriers to fair business and trading, which will deliver increased opportunities to foreign investors. The year 2005 is, on the other hand, the first year speculated as the time for a "coming collapse", which casts a shadow over many prospective investors. Whether they hesitate or forge ahead, their actions, again, incur *"wei ji"*.

This summary aims at dealing with a number of fundamental issues of primary importance. It presents mostly generalised observations and offers preliminary analysis. For dealing with particular issues and future prospects, more detailed contents in various chapters can provide some references to draw from.

Concluding Remarks

This book has proceeded under a framework categorising Environment, Momentum, Strategies, and Prospects ("EMSP"). The framework is adopted to undertake an analysis on essential variables in the field of China business.

Without doubt, the **environment** of an economy and a potential market should be the key background to a business analysis. Knowledge and understanding of this environment are basic requirements of company heads who contemplate a market entry into China. This may not have to be the case, since many foreign companies did enter the China market with minimum knowledge of the environment. Experience, however, shows the value of such knowledge and time spent on acquiring it. Large foreign multinationals remain standing and forge ahead primarily based upon their amazingly huge financial resources to write off incurred losses. They are also fast learners of key elements in this environment and Chinese rules of doing business, as well as being earnest executors of the localisation strategy. The business environment cover central parts of political, economic, and cultural backgrounds, many of them bearing age-old traditions and patterns. A direct application of business models from back home unavoidably leads to a clash with these established "alien" systems and rules, which would in turn generate certain unexpected negative impacts. Adequate knowledge of this environment should be the primary requirement of investing foreign companies and the first test to be passed.

An economy is in constant motion, with countless undertakings of business activities at any one time. A **transitional** economy is even more so. The Chinese economy has undergone several stages of transformation since the beginning of reforms, so that this business environment is not at all static. Tremendous changes have taken place, as described in previous chapters, and improvements in many aspects of business have been steadily made. China's WTO accession can be seen as a fundamental change to this environment and will have significant impact on the way of doing business in China. From another angle, the economy has progressed towards a more market-orientated one, generating huge output, wealth, and purchasing power. Many foreign multinationals have managed to tap into this potential market, with remarkable or even phenomenal successes. It is now a clear and simple requirement for foreign companies to detect trends of change and follow the right **momentum** in the China market.

Within the same environment and economy, foreign companies took a variety of **strategies** and approaches in the China market, and have seen varying outcomes of their consistent efforts. In the above case studies and other examples, the key strategies are expansion and mergers and acquisitions, with the latter coming to be a more preferred option in future as the market is getting less regulated by the day. Right strategic decisions are now central to a company's performance. Adaptation to local conditions and demands has been a common trend simply because foreign companies are facing not a common type of competition, but a specific type of competition in the China market. It is also worth noting that a decision to withdraw is not necessarily a bad choice, considering incurred losses or financial liabilities. On average, persistence or perseverance perhaps better serves foreign companies' purposes.

Future **prospects** cast great influence on foreign companies' operations due to their long term impact. These include economic cycles, coming crisis, political or economic upheavals, and, in extreme situations, a breakdown of normal trade. Foreign investors seek stable growth markets to place their funds, and figuring out future prospects should be a key part of the job for top management of foreign corporations. The task requires skills and vision in handling globalisation, understanding of the first two categories above, environment and momentum, and built up experience in the third category of strategies.

It can be said that a business success in the China market depends on skilful handling of a combination of these four key categories under the framework. Past experience and the case studies presented in previous contents highlight a variety of solutions to problems faced by foreign investors in China. Looking back, a study of China business may very well lend a hand to making sensible investment decisions there through enhancing your understanding and offering useful references.

Discussion Questions

1. Give your opinions on prospects of this economy, based on the examples cited, including financial woes, debts, central-local relations, social divide, or lasting complexities.
2. What will be the major changes to the business environment, and how would those affect strategies of foreign companies?

Related Readings

Chang, Gordon, *The Coming Collapse of China*, New York, Random House, 2001.

Clifford, Mark, "How Fast is China Really Growing?", *Business Week*, 10 March 2003.

Cohen, Paul, *Discovering History in China: American Writing on the Recent Chinese Past*, New York, Columbia University Press, 1984.

Goldstone, Jack A., "The Coming Chinese Collapse", *Foreign Policy*, No. 99, 1995, pp.355–64.

Mann, Jim, *Beijing Jeep: the Short, Unhappy Romance of American Business in China*, New York, Simon & Schuster, 1989.

Powell, Bill, "China Shock: It is All Made in China Now", *Fortune*, 4 March 2002.

Pye, Lucian, *Chinese Commercial Negotiating Style*, Cambridge, Mass., Oelgeschlager, Gunn & Hain, 1982.

Rawski, Thomas, "What is Happening to China's GDP Statistics?", *China Economic Review*, 4 December 2001

Roberts, Dexter, "China's Economy is no 'House of Cards'", *Business Week*, 16 January 2003.

Terrill, Ross, *The New Chinese Empire: Beijing's Political Dilemma and What It Means for the United States*, New York, Basic Books, 2003. Also, Clifford, Mark, "Is China Bound to Explode?", *Business Week*, 5 May 2003.

China Business deals with major aspects of economic development, foreign investment and business operations in the transitional economy of China. To foreign-invested companies and multinationals, the issues being discussed remain highly relevant in any of their business decisions and strategies to be adopted.

In a fast moving and transforming economy such as China's, market conditions and variables could change dramatically within a short period of time. Completed analyses based on gathered data do quickly become outdated. Many data provided in this book will soon need revising as well. For example, in the year 2004, China's total GDP output gained a real growth rate of 9.5%, and the total trade value reached over US$1.15 trillion, which moved China up to be the third trading country of the world after the United States and Germany. In the category of export, however, foreign-invested businesses have indeed played their increasingly crucial roles, making a large contribution of over 60% to the total export from China in 2004. One of the more recent surprises is the increase in the total of national foreign exchange reserve from over US$500 billion in 2004 to US$660 billion by March 2005. These new figures show significant rise above those just one or two years before. It is therefore imperative for an investing company to make timely information updating and fresh estimates for their short term business analyses, after previous economic or trade projections proved less accurate.

There are also more tangible rewards for foreign multinationals and companies operating in China. The corporate income tax these foreign entities paid to the government in 2004 amounted to 93.2 billion yuan. Taking a reference of the average preferential tax rate of 15% for foreign-invested companies and discounting generous tax exemptions and extensive tax avoidance, a conservative estimate would put the total profit earned by these foreign companies for the past year at around 621 billion yuan (US$75.5 billion approximately).

These kinds of remarkable changes to numerous economic and business data are to be carefully probed and promptly factored in short term business plans of corporations. Economic growth rate, import/export figures or retail figures, all provide important information of the economy and of market opportunities. Huge consumption of iron ore and crude oil by Chinese manufacturers, erupted like a volcano just a couple of years ago, have provided lucrative rewards to responsive foreign suppliers.

In the long term, however, a right investment decision or strategy is made ultimately based on an adequate understanding of the market and the overall trends of change, rather than on annual or quarterly figures published. One needs to put a certain new figure in perspective and examine its various implications. For example, roving masses of rural migrant workers of 100 million indicates a pool of comparatively affordable labour for industrial manufacturing in the foreseeable future, even when the recent public urging on raising average wages is taken into consideration. Market opportunities may emerge and grow in sectors of housing and other urban services, in a rush to accommodate the demands from this particular social group. As shown by some of the examples in this book, it is also common that an investing company which weathered the storm of short term financial losses or early uncertainties was able to reap benefits at a later stage of operations. It needs to point out that long term commitments and strategic positioning of a company should not be easily shaken by short term outcomes and constraints.

Into the new millennium, every year passed brought new experiments and readjustments in market opening. A foreign company entering the China market now faces extensively modified official requirements and newly enacted regulations from that of a year earlier. This is particularly true as the year by year timetable of China's WTO promises and opening obligations is observed in an acceptable manner and in straight order. There will be either more appealing opportunities or emerging risks as competition intensifies. Regardless of these short term shocks, the longer term trends toward a market economy and a fair play business environment have been able to maintain the momentum as a result of the two and a half decades of reforms and of the agreed WTO timetable.

There will still be numerous problems arising from the sheer magnitude of transition under way. The leadership has got a taste of nasty economic cycles common in the West. Since a serious setback on the scale of the Asian Financial Crisis has yet occurred in China, the handling of potential economic disasters by the leadership remains to be tested. Under these circumstances, foreign companies need to watch closely the underlying changes in this market, as well as headline economic figures, and devise their strategies and maneuvers accordingly.

Previous chapters of this book provide descriptions of long term trends of the economy, politics and business environment of China, as well as available data and information to date. As discussed in the "Prospects", the focus needs to be on the essentials listed in the chapters, and lessons are to be drawn from case studies and examples of business practices.

Adler, M.J., "Cultural Synergy: The Management of Cross-Cultural Organisations", in Burke, W. and Goodstein, L.D. (eds.), *Trends and Issues in Organisational Dynamics: Current Theory and Practice*, San Diego, California, University Associates, 1980, chapter 8.

Alston, Jon and He Yongxin, *Business Guide to Modern China*, East Lansing, Michigan State University Press, 1997.

Ambler, Tim and Morgen Witzel, *Doing Business in China*, London, Routledge/Curzon, 2nd ed, 2004.

Anderson, Jonathan, "The Coming Slowdown in China", *South China Morning Post*, 22 June 2003.

Barton, Laurence, *Crisis in Organisations*, Ohio, South-western Educational Publishing, 1993.

Beach, L.R., *The Psychology of Decision Making: People in organisations*, Thousand Oaks, Sage, 1997.

Blackman, Carolyn, *China Business: the Rules of the Game*, Sydney, Allen & Unwin, 2000.

Bergere, Marie-Claire, *The Golden Age of the Chinese Bourgeoisie: 1911–1937*, Cambridge, Cambridge University Press, 1989.

Brook, Timothy and Gregory Blue (eds.), *China and Historical Capitalism: Genealogies of Sinological Knowledge*, Cambridge, Cambridge University Press, 1999.

Bucknall, Kevin, *A Cultural Guide to Doing Business in China*, Oxford, Oxford University Press, 1994.

Campbell, Nigel, *China Business Strategies, a Survey of Foreign Business Activity in the PRC*, Oxford, Oxford University Press, 1988.

Cass, Deborah, Brett Williams and George Barker (eds.), *China and the World Trading System: Entering the New Millennium*, Cambridge, Cambridge University Press, 2003.

Chang, Gordon, *The Coming Collapse of China*, New York, Random House, 2001.

"Chasing the Leader: Are Europeans Really So Much Worse Off Than Americans?" *The Economist*, 6 February 2003.

Cheng Li, *The World of Lao Zi, Truth and Nature: Dao De Jing*, with English translation of original texts, Taipei, the World Book Company, Ltd., 2000.

Chow, I., Holbert, N., Kelly, L., and Julie Yu, *Business Strategy: an Asia-Pacific Focus*, Singapore, Prentice Hall, 1997.

Clemen, R.T., *Making Hard Decisions: an Introduction to Decision Analysis*, 2nd ed., Belmont, Duxbury, 1996.

Clifford, Mark, "How Fast Is China Really Growing?", *BusinessWeek*, 10 March 2003.

Clifford, Mark, "Is China Bound to Explode?" *BusinessWeek*, 5 May 2003

Cohen, Paul, *Discovering History in China: American Writing on the Recent Chinese Past*, New York, Columbia University Press, 1984.

Corne, Peter Howard, *Foreign Investment in China: the Administrative Legal System*, Hong Kong, Hong Kong University Press, 1997.

Cravens D.W., *Strategic Marketing*, 5th ed., Chicago, Irwin, 1997.

David, Fred R., *Strategic Management Concepts*, 8th ed. New Jersey, Prentice Hall, 2001.

Davis, Deborah (ed.), *The Consumer Revolution in Urban China*, Berkeley, University of California Press, 2000.

Dearlove, Des, *Key Management Decisions*, London, Pitman Publishing, 1998.

Dixon, John E., *Entering the Chinese Market: the Risks and Discounted Rewards*, Westport, Connecticut, Quorum, 1998.

Dolven, Ben, "The Best Little Airline in China", *Far Eastern Economic Review*, 17 January 2002

Drucker, Peter, *The Essential Drucker*, Oxford, Butterworth-Heinemann, 2001.

Einhorn, Bruce, "Winning in China", BusinessWeek, 27 January 2003.

Enright, M., *The Hong Kong Advantage*, Hong Kong, Oxford University Press, 1997.

Fang, Tony, *Chinese Business Negotiating Style*, London, Sage Publications, 1999.

Fung, K.C., *Trade and Investment: Mainland China, Hong Kong and Taiwan*, Hong Kong, City University of Hong Kong Press, 1997.

Gilley, Bruce, "Provincial Disintegration", *Far Eastern Economic Review*, 22 September 2001.

Goldstone, Jack A., "The Coming Chinese Collapse", *Foreign Policy*, no. 99, 1995, pp. 355–64.

Gold, Thomas, *Social Connections in China: Institutions, Culture and the Changing Nature of Guanxi*, New York, Cambridge University Press, 2002.

Haley, George Chin Tan and Usha Haley, *New Asian Emperors: the Overseas Chinese, their Strategies and Competitive Advantages*, Oxford, Butterworth/Heinemann, 1998.

Hall, W., *Managing Culture: Making Strategic Relationship Work*, Chichester, UK, John Wiley and Sons, 1995.

Hamilton, Gary (ed.) *Business Networks and Economic Development in East and Southeast Asia*, Hong Kong, Centre of Asian Studies, University of Hong Kong Press, 1991.

Harding, Harry, *China's Second Revolution: Reform after Mao*, Sydney, Allen & Unwin, 1987.

Harrison, E.F., *The Managerial Decision Making Process*, 5th ed., Boston, Houghton Mifflin Company, 1999.

Harwit, Eric, *China's Automobile Industry: Policies, Problems and Prospects*, New York, M.E. Sharpe, 1995.

Henry, David, "Mergers: Why Most Big Deals Don't Pay Off", *BusinessWeek*, October 14, 2002.

Hill, C. W. L. and Jones, G. R., *Strategic Management Theory: an Integrated Approach*, 4th ed., Boston, Houghton Mifflin Company, 1998.

Holden, Nigel, *Cross-Cultural Management: a Knowledge Management Perspective*, London, Pearson Education Limited, 2002.

Hofstede, G., *Culture's Consequences: International Differences in Work-Related Values*, Beverly Hills, California, Sage, 1980.

Hofstede, G., "The Cultural Relativity of Organisational Practices and Theories", *Journal of International Business Studies*, Fall 1983, pp. 75–88.

Hofstede, G. and Bond, M.H., "The Confucius Connection: from Cultural Roots to Economic Growth", *Organisational Dynamics*, 1988, no. 16, pp. 4–21

Hogarth, R.M. and Reder, M.W. (eds.), *Rational Choice: the Contrast between Economics and Psychology*, Chicago, University of Chicago Press, 1987.

Hsu, I., *The Rise of Modern China*, New York, Oxford University Press, 1970.

Huang, Yasheng, *Selling China: Foreign Direct Investment during the Reform Era*, New York, Cambridge University Press, 2003.

Janis, Irvin L., *Victims of Groupthink*, Boston, Houghton-Mifflin, 1972.

Jones, Eric, *Coming Full Circle: an Economic History of the Pacific Rim*, Melbourne, Oxford University Press, 1993.

Jones, Stephanie, *Managing in China: an Executive Survival Guide*, Singapore, BH Asia, 1997.

Kelly, Lane and Oled Shenkar (eds.), *International Business in China*, New York, Routledge, 1993.

Kelly, Lane and Luo Yadong (eds.), *China 2000: Emerging Business Issues*, Thousand Oaks, California, Sage Publications, 1999.

Keijzer, Arne J.de. *China: Business Strategies for the 90s*, Berkeley, California, Pacific Review Press, 1995.

Krugman, Paul, "The Myth of Asia's Miracle", *Foreign Affairs*, vol.73, no.6, 1994, pp. 62–78.

Lam, Willy Wo-Lap, *The Era of Jiang Zemin*, Singapore, Prentice Hall, 1999.

Lardy, N.R., *China's Unfinished Economic Revolution*, Washington, D.C., Brookings Institution Press, 1998.

Lardy, N.R., *Integrating China into the Global Economy*, Washington, D.C., Brookings Institution Press, 2002.

Lee, David, Philip Newman and Robert Price, *Decision Making in Organisations*, London, Financial Times Management, 1999.

Li, F. and Li Jing, *Foreign Investment in China*, New York, St. Martin's Press, 1999.

Li, Conghua, *China: the Consumer Revolution*, Singapore, John Wiley & Sons Asia Ltd, 1998.

Lieberthal, Kenneth and Michael Oksenberg, *Policy Making in China, Leaders, Structures and Processes*, Princeton, New Jersey, Princeton University Press, 1991.

Limlingan, V.S., *The Overseas Chinese in ASEAN: Business Strategies and Management Practices*, Manila Vita Development Corp., 1986.

Lu Tong, *Legend Puffing (in Chinese)*, Hangzhou, Zhejiang People's Publishing House, 2003.

Lubman, Stanley, *Bird in a Cage: Legal Reform in China after Mao*, Stanford, Stanford University Press, 1999.

Luo, Yadong, *Partnering with Chinese Firms: Lessons for International Managers*, Aldershot, UK, Ashgate, 2000.

Luo, Yadong, *How to Enter China: Choices and Lessons*, Ann Arbor, University of Michigan Press, 2000.

MacFarquhar, Roderick (ed.), *The Politics of China: 1949–1989*, Cambridge, Cambridge University Press, 1993.

Mann, Jim, *Beijing Jeep: the Short, Unhappy Romance of American Business in China*, New York, Simon & Schuster, 1989.

Macleod, Roderick K., *China Inc.: How to Do Business with the Chinese*, New York, Bantam, 1988.

Moore, Thomas G., *China in the World Market: Chinese Industry and International Sources of Reform in the Post-Mao Era*, Cambridge, Cambridge University Press, 2002.

Murray, G., *Doing Business in China: the Last Great Market*, Sandgate, Kent, China Library, 1994.

Naughton, Barry, *Growing Out of the Plan: Chinese Economic Reform, 1978–1993*, Cambridge, Cambridge University Press, 1995.

Shenkar, Oled, *International Business in China*, London, Routledge, 1993.

Overholt, W., *China: the Next Economic Superpower*, London, Weidenfeld & Nicholson, 1993

Perkins, Dwight, *Market Control and Planning in Communist China*, Cambridge, Massachusetts, Harvard University Press, 1966.

Porter, M.E., *Competitive Strategy: Techniques for Analysing Industries and Competitors*, New York, The Free Press, 1998.

Powell, Bill, "China Shock: It Is All Made in China Now", *Fortune*, 4 March 2002.

Prasad, S.B. and Y.K. Shetty, *An Introduction to Multinational Management*, New Jersey, Prentice Hall, 1976.

Pye, Lucian, *Chinese Commercial Negotiating Style*, Cambridge, Massachusetts, Oelgeschlager, Gunn & Hain, 1982.

Rawski, Thomas, "What is Happening to China's GDP Statistics?", *China Economic Review*, 4 December 2001

Riskin, Carl, *China's Political Economy: the Quest for Development since 1949*, New York, Oxford University Press, 1987.

Riskin, Carl, Zhao Renwei and Li Shi (eds.), *China's Retreat from Equality: Income Distribution and Economic Transition*, New York, M.E. Sharpe, 2001.

Roberts, Dexter, "A Hard Sell for Microsoft", *BusinessWeek*, November 1, 1999, p. 60.

Roberts, Dexter, "China's Economy is No 'House of Cards'", *BusinessWeek*, 16 January 2003.

Rodrigues, Carl, *International Management: a Cultural Approach*, 2nd ed., Ohio, South-western College Publishing, 2001.

Roehrig, Michael F., *Foreign Joint Ventures in Contemporary China*, London, Macmillan, 1994.

Rosen, D.L., *Behind the Open Door: Foreign Enterprises in the Chinese Marketplace*, Washington, D.C., Institute for International Economics, 1999.

Seagrave, Sterling, *Lords of the Rim: the Invisible Empire of the Overseas Chinese*, London, Corgi Books, 1997.

Selden, Mark, *The Political Economy of Chinese Socialism*, New York, M.E. Sharpe, 1988.

Shapiro, James, *et al. Direct Investment and Joint Venture in China: a Handbook for Corporate Negotiators*, New York, Quorum Books, 1991.

Simon, H.A., *Administrative Behaviour*, New York, The Free Press, 1997.

Skinner, G.W. (ed.), *City in Late Imperial China*, Stanford, Stanford University Press, 1977.

Spence, Jonathan, *The Search for Modern China*, London, Hutchinson, 1990.

Sprague, Jonathan, "Haier Reaches Higher", *Fortune*, 16 September 2002.

Stoner, James, R. Edward Freeman, *Management*, Englewood Cliffs, NJ, Prentice Hall, 1992.

Story, Jonathan, *China: the Race to Market–What China's Transformation Means for Business, markets and the New World Order*, London, Prentice Hall, 2003.

Strange, Roger, Jim Slater and Limin Wang (eds.), *Trade and Investment in China: the European Experience*, London, Routledge, 1998.

Strange, Roger, *Management in China: the Experience of Foreign Business*, London, Frank Cass. 1998.

Strasser, Steven, "China: Rules of the Game", *Newsweek*, 21 February 1995, pp. 44–9

Strutton, David and Lou Pelton, "Scaling the Great Wall: the *Yin* and *Yang* of Resolving Business Conflicts in China", *Business Horizons*, September–October 1997, pp. 26–7.

Studwell, Joe, *The China Dream: The Quest for the Last Great Market on Earth*. New York, Atlantic Monthly Press, 2002.

Tang, Jie and Anthony Wade, *The Changing Face of Chinese Management*, London, Routledge, 2002,

Terrill, Ross, *The New Chinese Empire: Beijing's Political Dilemma and What It Means for the United States*, New York, Basic Books, 2003.

Tu, Wei-ming (ed.), *Confucian Traditions in East Asian Modernity*, Cambridge, Massachusetts, Harvard University Press, 1996.

Vecchio, R.P., *Organisational Behaviour*, 2nd ed., Chicago, the Dryden Press, 1991.

Vroom, V. and Yetton, P., *Leadership and Decision Making*, Pittsburgh, University of Pittsburgh Press, 1973.

Walker, Danielle Medina, Thomas Walker and Joerg Schmitz, *Doing Business Internationally: the Guide to Cross-Cultural Success*, 2nd ed., New York, McGraw-Hill, 2003.

Weidenbaum, Murry, *The Bamboo Network*, New York, Free Press, 1996.

Weinshall, Theodore D. (ed.), *Culture and Management: Selected Readings*, Harmonds-worth, Penguin Books, 1977.

Yan, R., "To Reach China's Consumers, Adapt to *guo qing*", *Harvard Business Review*, September-October, 1994.

Yan, Yanni, *International Joint Ventures in China: Ownership, Control and Performance*, London, Macmillan Press, 2000.

Yany, Anne Stevenson, "Protecting the Pepsi Taste", *China Business Review*, January–February 1990, pp. 32–3.

Yau, Oliver H. M., *Consumer Behaviour in China*, New York, Routledge, 1994.

Yau, Oliver H. M.and Henry C. Steele (eds.), *China Business: Challenges in the 21st Century*, Hong Kong, The Chinese University Press, 2000.

Zewig, David, *Internationalising China: Domestic Interests and Global Linkages*, New York, Cornell University Press, 2002.

English journals with regular information and commentaries on China-related business and management topics:

- *BusinessWeek*
- *The Economist*
- *Far Eastern Economic Review*
- *Harvard Business Review*
- *The China Quarterly*

Index